Lecture Notes in Computer Science 16367

The series Lecture Notes in Computer Science (LNCS), including its subseries Lecture Notes in Artificial Intelligence (LNAI) and Lecture Notes in Bioinformatics (LNBI), has established itself as a medium for the publication of new developments in computer science and information technology research, teaching, and education.

LNCS enjoys close cooperation with the computer science R & D community, the series counts many renowned academics among its volume editors and paper authors, and collaborates with prestigious societies. Its mission is to serve this international community by providing an invaluable service, mainly focused on the publication of conference and workshop proceedings and postproceedings. LNCS commenced publication in 1973.

Irfan Awan · Muhammad Younas ·
Yanchun Zhang · Mahmoud Barhamgi ·
Hua Wang
Editors

Web Information Systems Engineering – WISE 2025

26th International Conference
Marrakech, Morocco, December 15–17, 2025
Proceedings, Part I

Editors
Irfan Awan
University of Bradford
Bradford, UK

Muhammad Younas
Oxford Brookes University
Oxford, UK

Yanchun Zhang
Zhejiang Normal University
Zhejiang, China

Mahmoud Barhamgi
Qatar University
Doha, Qatar

Hua Wang
Victoria University
Melbourne, VIC, Australia

ISSN 0302-9743 ISSN 1611-3349 (electronic)
Lecture Notes in Computer Science
ISBN 978-981-95-7393-6 ISBN 978-981-95-7394-3 (eBook)
https://doi.org/10.1007/978-981-95-7394-3

This Springer imprint is published by the registered company Springer Nature Singapore Pte Ltd.
The registered company address is: 152 Beach Road, #21-01/04 Gateway East, Singapore 189721, Singapore

Preface

Welcome to the 26th International Conference on Web Information Systems Engineering (WISE 2025). It is a great privilege to present the proceedings of WISE 2025, which was held in the historic city of Marrakech. Marrakech is a former imperial city and is still one of the economic and intellectual centres in Morocco. Historically, Morocco was one of the most intellectual centres in the world. The University of Al-Qarawiyyin was the first university in the history of humanity and still exists in the city of Fez. It was founded by an Arab lady, Fatima Al-Fihri, between 857 and 859.

WISE has been successfully running for more than two decades, and it has established itself as one of the top-tier conferences in the area of the World Wide Web. Research on the Web is highly dynamic and has continuously evolved since its invention in the late 1990s. Developments in the Web are driven by technological advances in both hardware and software, continuously opening up new directions and opportunities in various domains, including education, business, science, the public sector, and governmental organisations.

The WISE 2025 program committee put together an exciting technical program that brought together effective solutions, methods, and models that contribute to addressing critical research and development problems in the Web. The research papers covered interesting and timely work on state-of-the-art topics such as web applications and services, AI, machine learning, recommender systems, large language models, deep learning, networking, knowledge graphs, sentiment analysis, information retrieval, usability, HCI, and data management. In addition, the papers presented work on practical applications in supply chains, healthcare, finance, education, and social media, among others.

This year, the conference received 140 papers from authors from different countries. The review followed a single-blind review process. Each paper was reviewed by at least three reviewers. Based on the review, a total of 54 regular papers and 22 short papers were accepted for the final technical program. The acceptance rate was 38% for the regular submissions. The papers are presented in two proceedings volumes.

We sincerely appreciate the support of the international and local organising committee members in organising the conference. We extend our gratitude to the technical program committee members for providing constructive feedback to the authors. We are also thankful to all the authors for submitting quality papers to the conference. We truly appreciate the support of the Program Co-Chairs, Publication Co-Chairs, Publicity Co-Chairs, Workshop Co-Chairs, Web Chair, DEI Chair, and Local Organising Co-Chairs for their help and support throughout the conference. We sincerely thank the members of the senior program committee for their continuous support for the WISE conference series.

We are greatly indebted to our distinguished keynote speakers, Jie Lu (University of Technology Sydney), Yannis Ioannidis, (University of Athens), and Mounir Ghogho,

(University Mohammed VI Polytechnic) for delivering engaging and thought-provoking keynote talks.

Alongside the leading conference, WISE 2025 also featured international workshops, special topics, a PhD symposium, and a Demo and Poster track. The workshops included the International Workshop on LLM-Driven Agents (LLMA 2025) and the 7th International Symposium on Advanced Web and Mobile Applications (AWMA 2025). We greatly appreciate the efforts and contributions of the organising and program committee members of the international workshops, special topics, PhD symposium, and the Demo and Poster track. The papers accepted for these events will be published in a separate volume as the WISE 2025 Workshops series.

December 2025

Irfan Awan
Muhammad Younas
Yanchun Zhang
Mahmoud Barhamgi
Hua Wang

The original version of the book has been revised. The title, of this book has been corrected. A correction to this book can be found at https://doi.org/10.1007/978-981-95-7394-3_41

Organization

General Co-chairs

Yanchun Zhang	Zhejiang Normal University, China
Muhammad Younas	Oxford Brookes University, UK
Hua Wang	Victoria University, Australia

Program Co-chairs

Mahmoud Barhamgi	Qatar University, Qatar
Xin Wang	Tianjin University, China
Joe Tekli	Lebanese American University, Lebanon

Senior Program Committee

Qing Li	Hong Kong Polytechnic University, China
Xiaohua Jia	City University of Hong Kong, China
Elisa Bertino	Purdue University, USA
XiaoFang Zhou	Hong Kong University of Science and Technology, China

Local Organizing Co-chairs

Youssef Iraqi	University Mohammed VI Polytechnic, Morocco
Ismail Berrada	University Mohammed VI Polytechnic, Morocco
Loubna Mekouar	University Mohammed VI Polytechnic, Morocco
Jamal Bentahar	Khalifa University, UAE

Finance Co-chairs

Irfan Awan	University of Bradford, UK
Anitta P. Namanya	Broad Institute of MIT & Harvard, USA

Academia/Industry Relationships Chair

Hamad Al-Mohannadi	MoD, Qatar

Publication Chair

Irfan Awan	University of Bradford, UK

Workshops Co-chairs

Salima Benbernou	Université Paris Cité, France
Allel Hadjali	ENSMA, Poitiers, France

DEI Chair

Jinli Cao	La Trobe University, Australia

Publicity Co-chairs

Attila Kertesz	University of Szeged, Hungary
Ji Zhang	University of Southern Queensland, Australia
Meriyem Chergui	Hassan II University Casablanca, Morocco
Bohan Li	Nanjing University of Aeronautics and Astronautics, China

Web Chair

Fatima Zahrah	University of Bradford, UK

Program Committee

Abdelhak Belhi	Joaan Bin Jassim Academy for Defence Studies, Qatar
Abdelhak-Djamel Seriai	University of Montpellier, France
Abyayananda Maiti	Indian Institute of Technology Patna, India

Adam Wójtowicz	Poznań University of Economics and Business, Poland
Afonso Delerue Arriaga	University of Luxembourg, Luxembourg
Alessandro Campi	Politecnico di Milano, Italy
Alessandro Tundo	TU Wien, Austria
Alexander Knapp	Universität Augsburg, Germany
Alexandra Cristea	Durham University, UK
Alfredo Cuzzocrea	University of Calabria, Italy
Allel Hadjali	LIAS/ENSMA, France
Amirhossein Ghaffari	Oulu University, Finland
Andrés Rodríguez	Universidad Nacional de La Plata, Argentina
Aneesh Krishna	Curtin University, Australia
Aniello Castiglione	University of Salerno, Italy
Arash Mahboubi	Charles Sturt University, Australia
Armin Haller	Australian National University, Australia
Ashkan Sami	Edinburgh Napier University, UK
Aydin Abadi	Newcastle University, UK
Ayman El Hajjar	University of Westminster, UK
Azadeh Ghari Neiat	Deakin University, Australia
Barbara Catania	University of Genoa, Italy
Bin Cao	Zhejiang University of Technology, China
Boris Sedlak	TU Wien, Austria
Boualem Benatallah	University of New South Wales, Australia
Bernd Amann	Sorbonne Université, France
Bo Dang	San Francisco Bay University, USA
Bo Tang	Southern University of Science and Technology, China
Catarina Ferreira da Silva	Iscte, University Institute of Lisbon, Portugal
Catuscia Palamidessi	Inria, France
Cédric Eichler	INSA Val de Loire, France
Chaima Ben Rabah	AI Innovation Lab Weill Cornell Medicine, Qatar
Chamikara M. Arachchige	CSIRO, Australia
Chadni Islam	Queensland University of Technology, Australia
Chao Tong	Beihang University, China
Chaogang Tang	China University of Mining and Technology, China
Chen Wang	Huazhong University of Science & Technology, China
Chouki Tibermacine	University of Montpellier, France
Cindy Chen	University of Massachusetts Lowell, USA
Cinzia Cappiello	Politecnico di Milano, Italy
Conggai Li	CSIRO's Data61, Australia

Cynthia Marcelino	TU Wien, Austria
Damiano Distante	University of Rome Unitelma Sapienza, Italy
Dan Lin	Vanderbilt University, USA
Daniela Grigori	Université Paris-Dauphine PSL, France
Dario Colazzo	Université Paris-Dauphine PSL, France
Devis Bianchini	University of Brescia, Italy
Dimitri Theodoratos	New Jersey Institute of Technology, USA
Dimitris Kotzinos	CY Cergy Paris University, France
Dickson K. W. Chiu	University of Hong Kong, China
Dimitris Plexousakis	Institute of Computer Science, FORTH, Greece
Dimitrios Katsaros	University of Thessaly, Greece
Erisa Karafili	University of Southampton, UK
Esma Aïmeur	University of Montreal, Canada
Eleanna Kafeza	Technology Innovation Institute, UAE
Elio Masciari	University of Naples Federico II, Italy
Epaminondas Kapetanios	University of Hertfordshire, UK
Faheem Ullah	University of Adelaide, Australia
Fouzi Harrag	Ferhat Abbas Sétif1 University, Algeria
Flavius Frasincar	Erasmus University Rotterdam, Netherlands
Florence Sèdes	University of Toulouse, France
Francisco Jose D. Mayo	University of Seville, Spain
Francesco Marchiori	University of Padua, Italy
Gang Wang	Northeastern University, China
Garrison Gao	CSIRO's Data61, Australia
Gefei Zhang	Hochschule für Technik und Wirtschaft Berlin, Germany
George Papastefanatos	ATHENA Research Center, Greece
Georgia Kapitsaki	University of Cyprus, Cyprus
Georgios Kambourakis	University of the Aegean, Greece
Gorrab Abir	National School of Computer Science, Tunisia
Guanfeng Liu	Macquarie University, Australia
Guy-Vincent Jourdan	University of Ottawa, Canada
Hajer Baazaoui	CY Cergy Paris University, France
Haobing Liu	Ocean University of China, China
Hanchen Wang	University of Technology Sydney, Australia
Harsha Vasudev	University of Padua, Italy
Hassan Mehmood	Oulu University, Finland
Hayato Yamana	Waseda University, Japan
Heiko Schuldt	University of Basel, Switzerland
Hong-Tri Nguyen	Aalto University, Finland
Hossein Shirazi	San Diego State University, USA
Hongzhi Wang	Harbin Institute of Technology, China

Hong Va Leong	Hong Kong Polytechnic University, China
Huizi Yu	Amazon Science, USA
Imen Megdiche	University of Toulouse, France
Ismail Badache	Aix-Marseille Université, France
Jarogniew Rykowski	Poznań University of Economics, Poland
Jayamine Alupotha	University of Bern, Switzerland
Javier Luis Canovas Izquierdo	Universitat Oberta de Catalunya, Spain
Ji Zhang	University of Southern Queensland, Australia
Jiafan Wang	CSIRO's Data61, Australia
Jiaxin Li	University of Padua, Italy
Jide Edu	University of Strathclyde, UK
Jiefu Song	IRIT – Université Toulouse Capitole, France
Jinli Cao	La Trobe University, Australia
Jiujing Zhang	University of New South Wales, Australia
Joe Tekli	Lebanese American University, Lebanon
Jose Ignacio Panach Navarrete	Universitat de València, Spain
José María de Fuentes	Universidad Carlos III de Madrid, Spain
Junhu Wang	Griffith University, Australia
Julián Grigera	Universidad Nacional de La Plata, Argentina
Jürgen Ziegler	University of Duisburg-Essen, Germany
Kewen Liao	Australian Catholic University, Australia
Khouloud Boukadi	University of Sfax, Tunisia
Ladjel Bellatreche	LIAS/ENSMA, France
Laurent Bobelin	INSA Centre Val de Loire, France
Leong Hou U.	University of Macau, China
Liang Yuan	Swinburne University, Australia
Liu Peng	Singapore Management University, Singapore
Lizhen Wang	Yunnan University, China
Lizhou Fan	Harvard Medical School, USA
Lokesh Jain	Delhi Technological University, India
Lotenna Nwana	University of Arkansas at Little Rock, USA
Lucia Cascone	Università degli Studi di Salerno, Italy
Luciano Baresi	Politecnico di Milano, Italy
Manolis Gergatsoulis	Ionian University, Greece
Malik Khalfallah	Airbus, France
Marco Anisetti	Università degli Studi di Milano, Italy
Marco Winckler	Université Côte d'Azur, France
Marco Minici	University of Pisa, Italy
Marco Aiello	University of Stuttgart, Germany
Maria Malek	CY Cergy Paris University, France
Marinette Savonnet	University of Burgundy, France
Maristella Matera	Politecnico di Milano, Italy

Markel Vigo	University of Manchester, UK
Martin Weise	TU Wien, Austria
Maumita Bhattacharya	Charles Sturt University, Australia
Maurizio Leotta	Università di Genova, Italy
Michael Bewong	Charles Sturt University, Australia
Mingming Li	University of Chinese Academy of Sciences, China
Mitsunori Ogihara	University of Miami, USA
Mohamed Reda Bouadjenek	Deakin University, Australia
Mohamed Sellami	Télécom SudParis, France
Mohamed-Amine Baazizi	Sorbonne Université, France
Mourad Khayati	University of Fribourg, Switzerland
Muhammad Ali	Anglia Ruskin University, UK
Murali Mani	University of Michigan-Flint, USA
Mehmet Dalkilic	Indiana University, USA
Nathalie Moreno	Universidad de Málaga, Spain
Nawal Guermouche	INSA de Toulouse, France
Nicolas Anciaux	Inria, France
Nicola Zannone	Eindhoven University of Technology, Netherlands
Nora Faci	Université Lyon 1, France
Osama Almurshed	Cardiff University, UK
Peiquan Jin	University of Science and Technology of China, China
Peter Rønne	University of Luxembourg, Luxembourg
Qi Luo	University of New South Wales, Australia
Qiang Zhu	University of Michigan – Dearborn, USA
Qiang Ma	Kyoto University, Japan
Rafiqul Islam	Charles Sturt University, Australia
Romain Bourqui	University of Bordeaux, France
Roberto Metere	University of York, UK
Sajib Mistry	Curtin University, Australia
Saeid Hosseini	Sohar University, Oman
Sanjay Chaudhary	Ahmedabad University, India
Santiago Melia	Universidad de Alicante, Spain
Sandeep Kumar	Indian Institute of Technology Roorkee, India
Schahram Dustdar	Vienna University of Technology, Austria
Sebastian Link	University of Auckland, New Zealand
Sergio Ilarri	University of Zaragoza, Spain
Shaoyi Yin	University of Toulouse, France
Sharif Abuadbba	CSIRO's Data61, Australia
Shiting Wen	Zhejiang University, China
Shigang Liu	CSIRO's Data61, Australia

Silviu Maniu	Université Paris-Saclay, France
Slim Kallel	University of Sfax, Tunisia
Stefan Tai	TU Berlin, Germany
Stefano Cirillo	Università degli Studi di Salerno, Italy
Sven Groppe	University of Lübeck, Germany
Stéphane Jean	University of Poitiers, France
Syed Atif Moqurrab	University of Southampton, UK
Tanzima Hashem	Bangladesh University of Engineering & Technology, Bangladesh
Thomas Richter	Rhein-Waal University of Applied Sciences, Germany
Tomas Vitvar	Czech Technical University, Czech Republic
Tommaso Bianchi	University of Padua, Italy
Tooba Aamir	CSIRO's Data61, Australia
Toshiyuki Amagasa	University of Tsukuba, Japan
Tsz Nam-Chan	Shenzhen University, China
Venkata M. V. Gunturi	University of Hull, UK
Verena Kantere	University of Ottawa, Canada
Vianney Perchet	ENSAE & Criteo AI Lab, France
Victor Casamayor Pujol	TU Wien, Austria
Vitaliy Yakovyna	University of Warmia and Mazury in Olsztyn, Poland
Vincent Oria	New Jersey Institute of Technology, USA
Wafa Ben Slama Souei	University of Sousse, Tunisia
Wei Shen	Nankai University, China
Wenjie Zhang	University of New South Wales, Australia
Werner Retschitzegger	Johannes Kepler University Linz, Austria
Wieland Schwinger	Johannes Kepler University Linz, Austria
Xiang Lian	Kent State University, USA
Xiangmin Zhou	RMIT University, Australia
Xiaoyi Liu	Arizona State University, USA
Xiaohui Tao	University of Southern Queensland, Australia
Xiangyang Gou	Peking University, China
Xiaoye Miao	Zhejiang University, China
Xin Cao	University of New South Wales, Australia
Xun Yi	RMIT University, Australia
Xuhong Zhang	Indiana University, USA
Yain-Whar Si	University of Macau, China
Yicheng Feng	Chinese University of Hong Kong, China
Yixiang Fang	Chinese University of Hong Kong, China
Yiyi Tao	Peking University, China
Yijie Weng	University of Maryland, College Park, USA

Yilei Zhao	Zhejiang University, China
Yongfeng Ge	Victoria University, Australia
Yonghong Yu	Nanjing University of Posts and Telecommunications, China
Young-Gab Kim	Sejong University, South Korea
Yuting Wang	University of Michigan, USA
Zhao Li	Zhejiang University, China
Zhigao Zheng	Wuhan University, China
Zhisheng Huang	Vrije Universiteit Amsterdam, Netherlands
Zhizhong Wu	University of California, Berkeley, USA
Zichao Li	University of Waterloo, Canada
Nikolaos Polatidis	University of Brighton, UK

Contents

Web Applications and Services

Security and Privacy

Large Language Models I

Security and Networking

Security and Trust

Sentiment Analysis and Classification

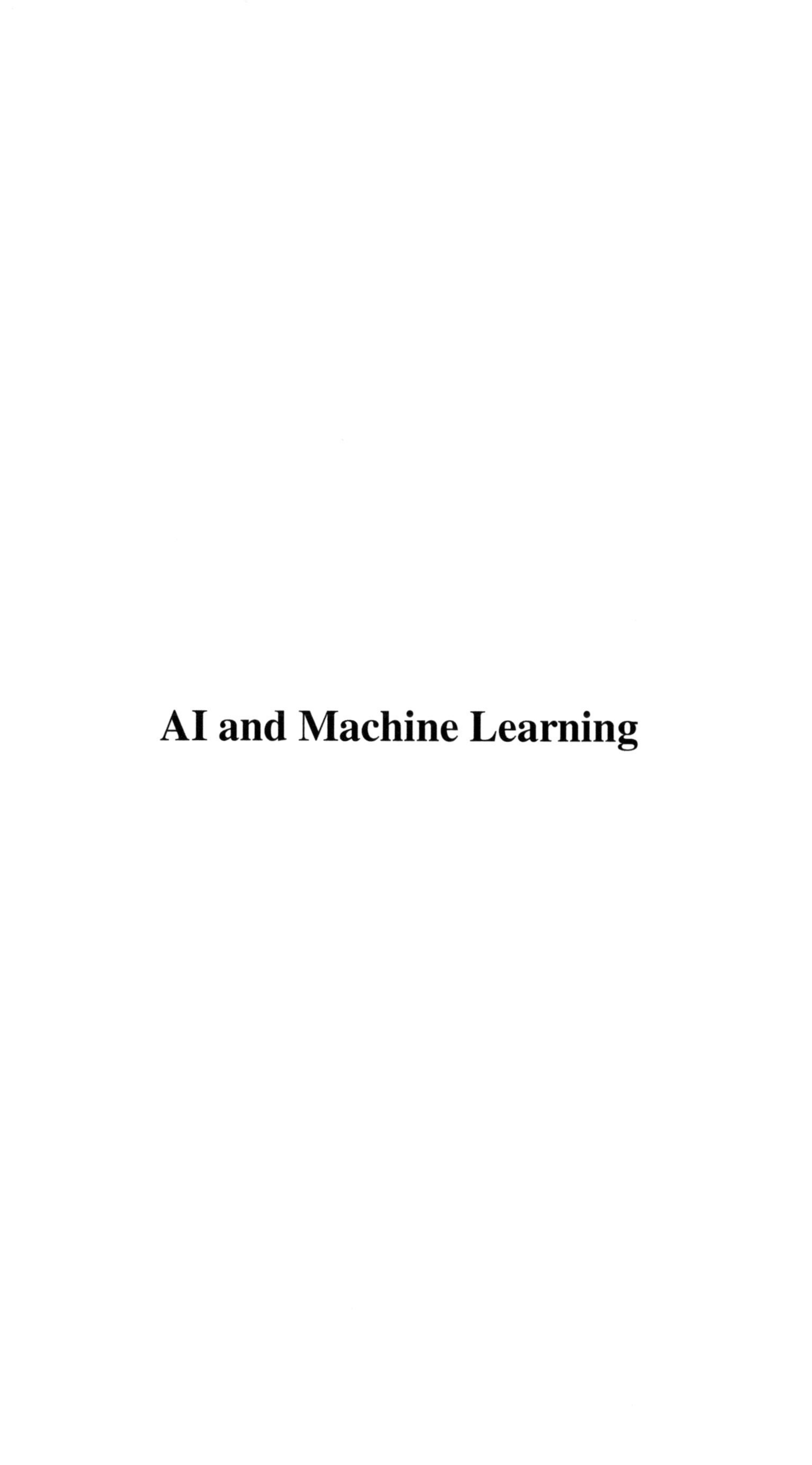

AI and Machine Learning

Towards Cost-Effective Model Update in Online Feature-Incremental Learning

Zirui Tan(✉), Hechuan Wen, Shazia Sadiq, and Tong Chen

The University of Queensland, Brisbane, Australia
{zirui.tan,h.wen,tong.chen}@uq.edu.au, shazia@eecs.uq.edu.au

Abstract. Machine learning models on tabular datasets must adapt efficiently to evolving feature spaces—a common scenario in domains such as healthcare and insurance, where new diagnostic tests or policyholder attributes are introduced over time. Existing solutions either require full retraining, which is computationally expensive, or rely on transformer-based or variational autoencoder (VAE) architectures that incur significant computation overhead. We propose a cost-effective model update framework that incorporates Feature-Incremental G-Shapley (FIGS) to enable fast adaptation to newly added features. FIGS estimates changes in data Shapley values to identify samples whose marginal contributions to model performance shift most after feature expansion. These informative points are selected as a coreset for fine-tuning, enabling accurate model updates using only a small subset of data. Unlike prior Shapley value estimations that assume static feature spaces and require costly recomputation, FIGS efficiently predicts contribution shifts from differences in feature representations. Experiments on medium- and large-scale tabular datasets, across multiple backbone models, show that FIGS consistently outperforms existing coreset selection strategies. Our proposed framework achieves near full-retrain accuracy with significantly reduced update time. The implementation repository is open-sourced at: https://github.com/tzralice/FIGS.

Keywords: Feature-incremental learning · Data Shapley values · Coreset selection · Tabular dataset

1 Introduction

Machine learning models on tabular data lie at the core of many dynamic decision-making applications, such as customer analytics in recommendation systems and predictive diagnostics in healthcare. Consider an insurance company that begins with a risk model trained on $\{\text{Age}, \text{Gender}, \text{Income}\}$, then gradually integrates $\{\text{Credit Score}\}$, and finally appends $\{\text{No. Of Claims}\}$ as claim history becomes available. Figure 1 illustrates this evolving feature space and highlights a key challenge: each time a new feature emerges, the existing model must be updated. Yet full retraining on the entire augmented dataset can demand hours of computation and extensive memory usage.

I. Awan et al. (Eds.): WISE 2025, LNCS 16367, pp. 3–18, 2026.
https://doi.org/10.1007/978-981-95-7394-3_1

Id	Age	Gender	Income
001	28	F	45000
002	45	M	62000
003	31	F	54000
004	36	M	71000
005	29	F	39000

Time t = 0
Initial model trained on
basic demographic data.

Id	Age	Gender	Income	Credit Score
001	28	F	45000	690
002	45	M	62000	710
003	31	F	54000	680
004	36	M	71000	740
005	29	F	39000	660

Time t = 1
Credit scores integrated
As a new feature attribute.

Id	Age	Gender	Income	Credit Score	No. of Claims
001	28	F	45000	690	1
002	45	M	62000	710	3
003	31	F	54000	680	0
004	36	M	71000	740	2
005	29	F	39000	660	1

Time t = 2
Claim history appended
in the latest feature update.

Fig. 1. Feature expansion in an insurance dataset. New attributes are added over time (e.g., credit score, claims), requiring efficient model updates at $t = 0, 1, 2$.

While incremental learning methods have traditionally focused on the continuous addition of new instances or classes [18,22,26,32], the problem of incrementally added features has received comparatively less attention [10]. Recent works such as TransTab [23] and OLD3S [9] address this by using transformers or variational autoencoders to learn shared latent representations across feature subsets. However, these approaches introduce heavy computational costs, particularly for large-scale tabular datasets. In parallel, coreset selection methods have been widely used to reduce training cost by identifying representative data subsets [2,6,16,21,25]. Yet most are developed under the assumption of static feature spaces [4,14,15,24,28,31]. When new features are added over time, these methods cannot account for how new attributes change a data point's impact on model predictions. For instance, new features may reveal previously hidden patterns or shift a sample's position relative to the decision boundary. As a result, they might fail to select the most valuable samples under the newly expanded feature space. Another line of work focuses on data Shapley value, which provides a principled approach to quantify the marginal contribution of individual data points to model performance [2,12,20]. However, current Shapley value estimation methods [17,18,30], including widely used approaches like Truncated Monte Carlo Shapley (TMC-Shapley) and Gradient Shapley (G-Shapley) [2], assume static feature spaces and thus require costly re-estimation whenever the feature space evolves. This makes them computationally impractical for iterative updates within large-scale, real-time applications.

In this work, we address the gap by proposing an efficient **model update framework** tailored for feature-incremental settings in tabular data. Central to our framework is a **coreset selection mechanism based on Shapley values**, specifically designed to identify data points whose contributions to model performance change most meaningfully after feature expansion. To make this process computationally feasible, we introduce the **Feature-Incremental G-Shapley (FIGS)** pipeline, which efficiently approximates data Shapley value shifts. FIGS employs a lightweight regression model trained to predict these shifts from feature representation dissimilarities, substantially reducing computational cost while preserving the effectiveness of the selected coreset.

Specifically, our contributions are: (1) formalizing the problem of feature-incremental learning in tabular data; (2) proposing a Shapley-value-guided coreset selection criterion suited for evolving feature space; (3) developing the efficient FIGS pipeline for scalable Shapley value updates; and (4) empirically validating our approach on two medium-to-large-scale benchmark datasets and two commonly used backbone models, achieving near full-retrain accuracy at significantly reduced computational costs.

2 Related Work

Feature-Incremental Learning. Feature-incremental learning adapts models as new features arrive. TransTab [23] uses transformer-based architectures to align feature spaces for reuse without full retraining, but incurs substantial computational cost. OLD3S [9] learns a shared latent space via deep variational models, requiring retraining at each feature expansion. In contrast, our method enables lightweight model updates without expensive representation alignment.

Coreset Selection. Coreset selection reduces training cost by selecting informative subsets. FDMat [28] matches distributions via optimal transport; Moderate-DS [27] selects points near class centers; CCS [31] balances coverage and importance; and EL2N [15] scores early prediction errors. These methods target static datasets and do not address feature evolution. Iterative methods like Craig [14], GradMatch [7], and Crest [29] align gradients but require repeated retraining, making them unsuitable for online settings. Our approach avoids these costs and dynamically estimates data utility as features evolve.

Data Shapley Value. Data Shapley value quantifies the contribution of individual points to model performance [2]. Exact computation is NP-hard; TMC-Shapley uses early-stopped Monte Carlo sampling, while G-Shapley estimates contribution after each gradient step during training [2]. Dynamic variants [30] handle instance-level updates but assume fixed feature spaces. Applications include sample selection [17], adversarial coreset construction [18], and medical imaging [19], but none address coreset selection under feature-incremental settings. We bridge this gap by approximating Shapley value shifts over evolving features for scalable model updates.

3 Preliminaries and Problem Statement

We study model adaptation under feature-incremental changes in tabular datasets. At time step t, a neural network classifier f_t is trained on an initial dataset $\mathcal{D}_t = \{(\mathbf{x}_i^t, y_i)\}_{i=1}^N$, where $\mathbf{x}_i^t \in \mathbb{R}^{d_t}$. Given the feature extractor $h_t : \mathcal{X}_t \to \mathcal{Z}_t$ and the decoder $g_t : \mathcal{Z}_t \to \mathbb{R}$, the classifier is a composition in the form: $f_t = g_t \circ h_t$, where the raw features are mapped into latent embeddings $\mathbf{z}_i^t = h_t(\mathbf{x}_i^t)$, which are then passed to g_t to generate class predictions.

At next time step, i.e., $t+1$, assume that a new feature set $\widetilde{\mathcal{F}}_{t+1}$ becomes available, ramping up the feature dimension to $d_{t+1} = d_t + |\widetilde{\mathcal{F}}_{t+1}|$, which leads to an updated dataset $\mathcal{D}_{t+1} = \{(\mathbf{x}_i^{t+1}, y_i)\}_{i=1}^N$. We formally conceptualize the update of the dataset as follows:

Definition 1 (Feature-Incremental Dataset). *A feature-incremental dataset at time step t is defined as* $\mathcal{D}_t = \{(\mathbf{x}_i^t, y_i)\}_{i=1}^N$*, where* $\mathbf{x}_i^t \in \mathbb{R}^{d_t}$*. At time* $t+1$*, an additional feature set* $\widetilde{\mathcal{F}}_{t+1}$ *is introduced, expanding the input space to* $\mathbb{R}^{d_{t+1}}$ *where* $d_{t+1} = d_t + |\widetilde{\mathcal{F}}_{t+1}|$*. Let* $\widetilde{\mathcal{D}}_{t+1} = \{\widetilde{\mathbf{x}}_i^{t+1}\}_{i=1}^N$*, with* $\widetilde{\mathbf{x}}_i^{t+1} \in \mathbb{R}^{|\widetilde{\mathcal{F}}_{t+1}|}$ *denoting the newly added features. The updated input is* $\mathbf{x}_i^{t+1} = \mathbf{x}_i^t \oplus \widetilde{\mathbf{x}}_i^{t+1}$ *via the concatenation operation* $\oplus$*, and the updated dataset becomes* $\mathcal{D}_{t+1} = \{(\mathbf{x}_i^{t+1}, y_i)\}_{i=1}^N$*.*

Since f_t is trained only on the initial dataset $\mathcal{D}_t$, it cannot directly leverage the newly added features in $\mathcal{D}_{t+1}$. A straightforward approach is to train a new model f_{t+1} from scratch on the full expanded dataset, but this is often computationally prohibitive. A more efficient alternative is to selectively update the model using a small, representative subset of data—i.e., a coreset $\mathcal{C} \subset \mathcal{D}_{t+1}$. We formalize this objective below:

Definition 2 (Coreset-based Feature-Incremental Learning). *Given a feature-incremental dataset* $\mathcal{D}_{t+1}$ *of size* N*, the goal is to select a coreset* $\mathcal{C} \subset \mathcal{D}_{t+1}$ *with* $|\mathcal{C}| \ll N$*, such that the fine-tuned model* $f_{t+1}^{\mathcal{C}}$*, trained only on* $\mathcal{C}$*, achieves performance comparable to full retraining on* $\mathcal{D}_{t+1}$*. Formally, we aim to find:*

$$\mathcal{C}^* = \arg\max_{\mathcal{C} \subset \mathcal{D}_{t+1}} \mathcal{U}(f_{t+1}^{\mathcal{C}}), \tag{1}$$

where $f_{t+1}^{\mathcal{C}}$ *denotes the model fine-tuned on* $\mathcal{C}$*, and* $\mathcal{U}(\cdot)$ *is a classification performance metric.*

Unlike traditional online learning [18,22], our focus is on incremental features rather than incremental instances, which is a practical yet under-studied research direction. It can be extended to incorporate instance-level changes by integrating conventional online learning techniques to adapt to evolving data distributions.

4 Methodology

4.1 Model Adaptation in Feature-Incremental Learning

To efficiently adapt a previously trained model $f_t = g_t \circ h_t$ to an updated dataset $\mathcal{D}_{t+1} = \{(\mathbf{x}_i^{t+1}, y_i)\}_{i=1}^N$ with newly added features, we propose a two-stage framework that avoids full model retraining: (1) feature extraction and fusion, where new feature representations are integrated while retaining existing knowledge, and (2) selective fine-tuning using a small coreset to enable efficient model updates. An overview is shown in Fig. 2. We now describe each stage in detail.

1. Feature extraction and fusion. To handle the newly added features without retraining the full model, we freeze the original encoder h_t to preserve learned knowledge, and train a lightweight auxiliary encoder $\widetilde{h}_{t+1}$ on the new feature subset $\widetilde{\mathbf{x}}_i^{t+1} \in \mathbb{R}^{|\widetilde{\mathcal{F}}_{t+1}|}$ from $\widetilde{\mathcal{D}}_{t+1}$. These encoders produce latent embeddings

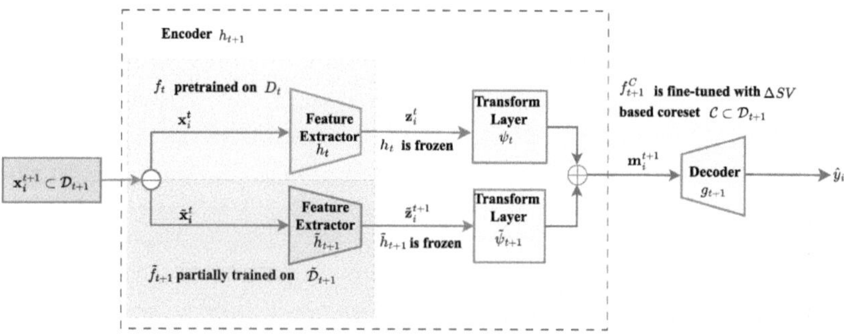

Fig. 2. Overall framework for cost-effective model updates in feature-incremental learning via FIGS coreset selection.

$\mathbf{z}_i^t = h_t(\mathbf{x}_i^t)$ and $\widetilde{\mathbf{z}}_i^{t+1} = \widetilde{h}_{t+1}(\widetilde{\mathbf{x}}_i^{t+1})$, which are passed through learnable transformation layers $(\psi_t, \widetilde{\psi}_{t+1})$ and concatenated into a unified representation:

$$\mathbf{m}_i^{t+1} = \psi_t(\mathbf{z}_i^t) \oplus \widetilde{\psi}_{t+1}(\widetilde{\mathbf{z}}_i^{t+1}), \tag{2}$$

where $\oplus$ denotes the concatenation operation. This modular design avoids costly re-architecting while enabling joint reasoning over both the original and expanded feature space. The combined representation is processed by the final extractor h_{t+1} in the following form:

$$h_{t+1}(\mathbf{x}_i^{t+1}) = \Big((\psi_t \circ h_t(\mathbf{x}_i^t)) \oplus (\widetilde{\psi}_{t+1} \circ \widetilde{h}_{t+1}(\widetilde{\mathbf{x}}_i^{t+1}))\Big). \tag{3}$$

2. Selective fine-tuning with coreset. To further reduce computational cost, we fine-tune only a small subset of parameters—the transformation layers and decoder g_{t+1}—while keeping the encoders frozen. Instead of using the full training set, we construct a coreset $\mathcal{C} \subset \mathcal{D}_{t+1}$ containing the most informative samples, identified via large changes in their estimated data Shapley values. These shifts reflect how much a data point's importance changes due to the expanded feature space. The induced model $f_{t+1}^{\mathcal{C}} = g_{t+1} \circ h_{t+1}$ is trained on this coreset $\mathcal{C}$ using the binary cross-entropy loss function $\ell(\cdot,\cdot)$ [13]:

$$\mathcal{L} = \frac{1}{|\mathcal{C}|} \sum_{i \in \mathcal{C}} \ell\left(g_{t+1}(\mathbf{m}_i^{t+1}),\, y_i\right). \tag{4}$$

This two-stage procedure enables scalable and cost-effective model updates by reusing prior knowledge, limiting retraining, and focusing learning on high-impact samples.

4.2 Shapley-Value-Based Coreset Selection

To support efficient model adaptation in feature-incremental learning, we identify key training examples using data Shapley values. The data Shapley value provides a theoretically grounded estimate of a data point's marginal contribution to model performance [2]. Unlike static settings, the data Shapley value of each data point can shift as new features are introduced in feature-incremental learning. We use the change in data Shapley value, denoted as $\Delta\phi$, to identify data points whose contribution to model performance is most affected by the newly added features. Intuitively, if a data point's contribution to model performance increases or decreases substantially after feature expansion, it likely captures the new predictive patterns. By ranking data points according to the change magnitude $|\Delta\phi|$, we prioritize those that are most affected by the evolving feature space. This enables the construction of a compact, high-impact coreset for fine-tuning. Given a training dataset $\mathcal{D}^{\text{train}}$ of size N, the Shapley value $\phi(p_i)$ of a point $p_i = (\mathbf{x}_i, y_i)$ is defined as [2]:

$$\phi(p_i) = \sum_{S \subseteq \mathcal{D}^{\text{train}} \setminus \{p_i\}} \frac{\Delta V_{D^{\text{dev}}}(S, p_i)}{\binom{N-1}{|S|}}, \tag{5}$$

where the marginal contribution $\Delta V_{D^{\text{dev}}}(S, p_i) = V_{D^{\text{dev}}}(S \cup \{p_i\}) - V_{D^{\text{dev}}}(S)$ is computed on a fixed development set D^{dev}, and the binomial coefficient $\binom{N-1}{|S|}$ normalizes the importance of the contribution. To capture how data utility shifts under feature expansion, the change in Shapley value is defined as:

$$\Delta\phi(p_i) = \phi_{t+1}(p_i) - \phi_t(p_i), \tag{6}$$

where $\phi_t(p_i)$ and $\phi_{t+1}(p_i)$ are the Shapley values of p_i before and after adding new features, respectively. A higher $|\Delta\phi(p_i)|$ indicates a greater shift in marginal contribution, suggesting that the point encodes new or altered information. We then select the top-k samples with the largest $|\Delta\phi(p_i)|$ to construct the coreset:

$$\mathcal{C} = \{p_i \mid |\Delta\phi(p_i)| \text{ is among the top-}k\}. \tag{7}$$

This coreset $\mathcal{C}$ is used to fine-tune the model $f_{t+1}^{\mathcal{C}} = g_{t+1} \circ h_{t+1}$ as described in Sect. 4.1, enabling adaptation to the expanded feature space using a small subset of the training data.

While theoretically sound, exact Shapley computation is NP-hard [2]. Equation (5) requires retraining on all possible subsets of $\mathcal{D}^{\text{train}}$, which becomes intractable on large datasets or deep models. In feature-incremental learning, this cost is even higher because $\Delta\phi(p_i)$ must be recomputed for all points as new features are introduced. To address this, we introduce a scalable approximation method to estimate $\Delta\phi(p_i)$ efficiently in the following section.

4.3 Efficient Feature-Incremental G-Shapley Approximations

Although dynamic extensions are tailored to instance-level updates [30], it does not generalize to the evolving input dimensionality in this work. We address this gap by introducing **Feature-Incremental G-Shapley (FIGS)**, a scalable approximation framework specifically tailored to feature-incremental settings. We base our method on G-Shapley, which estimates Shapley values via stochastic gradient updates over random data permutations. Compared to TMC-Shapley, it is significantly more efficient and well-suited for gradient-based training. However, both G-Shapley and TMC-Shapley involve heavy re-computation under expanded feature space. Notably, our goal is *not* to recover exact $\Delta\phi(p_i)$ values, but to preserve the *ranking* of contribution changes $|\Delta\phi(p_i)|$, which is sufficient for coreset selection. The key to our method is to train a lightweight change estimator by using a small number of computed ground-truth G-Shapley values, without compromising the coreset quality.

We briefly review the G-Shapley approximation [2], which forms the foundation of our method. With a slight abuse of notation, we denote $\phi(p_i)$ as the G-Shapley approximation of the exact Shapley value, which is computed by averaging marginal utility contributions over J random permutations π^j of the training set $\mathcal{D}^{\text{train}}$:

$$\phi(p_i) = \frac{1}{J}\sum_{j=1}^{J}\phi_{\pi^j}(p_i), \tag{8}$$

where $\phi_{\pi^j}(p_i)$ is the contribution of p_i when added to the prefix subset S under permutation π^j. The total number of permutations J is adaptively chosen based on a convergence criterion ϵ, reducing the complexity from $\mathcal{O}(2^N)$ to $\mathcal{O}(JNM)$, where M is the development set size. We refer to the G-Shapley estimation algorithm as Λ in what follows.

When new features are introduced, both data representations and gradient dynamics change, which requires a re-computation by G-Shapley approximation. However, recomputing them from scratch for all training data points remains expensive. To avoid this, we approximate the Shapley value shift $\Delta\phi(p_i) = \phi_{t+1}(p_i) - \phi_t(p_i)$ using a regression model $\mathcal{G}$ that learns its relationship to feature representation shifts $\Delta\Psi(\mathbf{x}_i)$.

We compute $\Delta\Psi(\mathbf{x}_i)$ as the cosine dissimilarity between embeddings induced by pretrained model Ψ at time steps t and $t+1$:

$$\Delta\Psi(\mathbf{x}_i) = 1 - \frac{\Psi(\mathbf{x}_i^t)\cdot\Psi(\mathbf{x}_i^{t+1})}{\|\Psi(\mathbf{x}_i^t)\|\cdot\|\Psi(\mathbf{x}_i^{t+1})\|}, \tag{9}$$

where $\|\cdot\|$ represents the ℓ_2-norm.

To train $\mathcal{G}$, we select a small, representative subset $Q \subset \mathcal{D}_{t+1}^{\text{train}}$ using a distance-based heuristic (e.g., K-Means [11] or Max-Min sampling which maximizes the minimum distance to the current selection) over the embedding space $\Psi(\mathcal{D}_{t+1})$:

$$Q = \text{HeuristicSelect}(\Psi(\mathcal{D}_{t+1}), r), \tag{10}$$

where r controls the subset ratio. We then construct a training set $\widetilde{Q} = \{(\Delta\Psi(\mathbf{x}_i), \Delta\phi(p_i))\}_{i=1}^{|Q|}$ by applying G-Shapley on Q. This further reduces the computational complexity from $\mathcal{O}(JNM)$ to $\mathcal{O}(JQM)$ with $Q \ll N$. The regression model is trained to predict:

$$\Delta\hat{\phi}(p_i) = \mathcal{G}(\Delta\Psi(\mathbf{x}_i)), \tag{11}$$

Algorithm 1: Feature-Incremental G-Shapley Approximation (FIGS)

Input: Datasets $\mathcal{D}_t^{\text{train}}$ and $\mathcal{D}_{t+1}^{\text{train}}$, sampling ratio r, pretrained encoder Ψ, G-Shapley estimator Λ
Output: Approximated Shapley shifts $\Delta\hat{\phi}(p_i)$ for all $p_i \in \mathcal{D}_{t+1}^{\text{train}}$
for $i \in [N]$ **do**
  Compute $\Delta\Psi(\mathbf{x}_i)$ using Eq. (9)
end for
Select $Q = \text{HeuristicSelect}(\Psi(\mathcal{D}_{t+1}), r)$
Compute $\phi_{t+1}(p_i) = \Lambda(\mathcal{D}_{t+1}^{\text{train}}[Q])$
Compute $\phi_t(p_i) = \Lambda(\mathcal{D}_t^{\text{train}}[Q])$
Compute $\Delta\phi(p_i) = \phi_{t+1}(p_i) - \phi_t(p_i)$ for $p_i \in Q$
Construct training set $\widetilde{Q} = \{(\Delta\Psi(\mathbf{x}_i), \Delta\phi(p_i))\}_{i=1}^{|Q|}$
Train regression model $\mathcal{G} \leftarrow \text{TRAIN}(\widetilde{Q})$
for $i \in [N]$ **do**
  Predict $\Delta\hat{\phi}(p_i) = \mathcal{G}(\Delta\Psi(\mathbf{x}_i))$
end for
Return: $\Delta\hat{\phi}(p_i)$ for all $i \in [N]$

where $\mathcal{G}$ is implemented as a general estimator, e.g., linear regressors or non-linear models such as neural networks or random forests, that minimizes the mean squared error (MSE) between predicted and true shifts.

Once trained, the regression model $\mathcal{G}$ is used to estimate $\Delta\phi(p_i)$ for all data points in $\mathcal{D}_{t+1}^{\text{train}}$. We then rank points by $|\Delta\hat{\phi}(p_i)|$ and select the top-k samples to form the coreset $\mathcal{C}$, as defined in Eq. (7). Because coreset selection depends only on the relative ranking of $|\Delta\hat{\phi}(p_i)|$, the approximation remains effective despite minor prediction errors.

5 Experiments

5.1 Experiment Setup

Baselines and Datasets. We compare our approach against several state-of-the-art coreset selection methods and standard training baselines. Our comparison emphasises data-centric methods rather than transformer or VAE-based approaches, as the latter incur substantial computational overhead and focus primarily on feature representation rather than data selection efficiency. Specifically, we consider five representative coreset selection baselines, and for fair comparison, all coreset selection baselines are integrated into the same model update pipeline as FIGS, replacing only the selection strategy while keeping the remaining components identical. The five coreset selection baselines evaluated within our pipeline are: FDMat [28]: uses optimal transport with the Sinkhorn algorithm; CCS [31]: selects coresets based on data coverage and margin-based importance; Moderate-DS [27]: chooses samples near median distance to class centers; EL2N [15]: ranks samples by early-epoch prediction errors. For reference, we also include full fine-tuning and full retraining baselines using the complete dataset. We evaluate our method on two publicly available large-scale tabular datasets: IEEE-CIS Fraud Detection (CIS) [5] with 330,702 samples (187 features, 3.6% positive), and Health Insurance Cross Sell Prediction (Health) [8] with 213,420 samples (11 features, 14% positive). Both datasets have binary targets. To simulate feature-incremental learning, we randomly partition features into multiple groups: CIS initially trains with 25 features and then incrementally adds (25, 50, 75) features at each time step; Health starts with 2 features and then adds (2, 4, 6) features. Data splits are training (65%), validation (10%), and testing (25%), stratified by class distribution. We select 1% from the training set as D^{dev} to calculate G-Shapley in constructing $\tilde{Q}$. **Model structure and implementation details.** We evaluate two common classification models for tabular data: a three-layer feedforward neural network (FFNN) and ResNet [3]. The same model architecture is used across three components: (1) h_t: feature extraction from the initial features, (2) $\tilde{h}_{t+1}$: feature extraction from additional features, and (3) f_{t+1}^C: combined feature model fine-tuned using coreset selected. FIGS and the feature-incremental neural network are implemented in PyTorch, and all experiments are conducted on a CPU (Intel i7-13700K, 16 cores, 24 threads, max clock speed 5.4 GHz). **Training setup and evaluation metrics.** In the model adaptation framework, the additional feature model $\tilde{h}_{t+1}$ is trained for 10 epochs at a learning rate of 1×10^{-3}, and for the initial model f_t and fine-tuning f_{t+1}^C, we train 100 epochs with early stopping based on validation ROC-AUC, using Adam optimizer (learning rate 1×10^{-5}, mini-batch size of 32, and a learning rate scheduler). In the FIGS pipeline, the model architecture mirrors the model used in f_t, employing ROC-AUC as the utility function. Gradients are updated for one epoch using SGD with a mini-batch size of one and a learning rate of 1×10^{-2}, smaller than the main task's learning rate, as recommended by [2]. To balance efficiency and approximation accuracy, we set the convergence rate to 1×10^{-3}. The optimal combination of selection method HeuristicSelect$(\cdot)$, sampling ratio r and regression model $\mathcal{G}$ is determined on a hold-out set. For the regression model $\mathcal{G}$ used in FIGS , we consider three regressors. Linear Regression (LR), Multi-Layer Perceptron (MLP), and Random Forest (RF) regressors are implemented using `scikit-learn`. LR uses ordinary least squares; MLP has two hidden layers (100, 50) with ReLU and Adam, trained for up to 1000 iterations; RF uses 100 trees with default parameters. To evaluate adaptation to online feature increments and handle class imbalance, we primarily use ROC-AUC [1]. To assess training efficiency, we compare the wall-clock runtime. All coreset methods operate under a consistent budget constraint: 1% of the training set is selected once before model fine-tuning. This ensures equal evaluation conditions across methods.

5.2 Main Results

Overall Model Performance. Table 1 reports the ROC-AUC performance using our framework with FIGS or other baseline coreset selection methods in

Table 1. Model adaptation performance with different coreset selection methods (mean ROC-AUC ± std) under feature-incremental for two backbone models.

Dataset	Backbone	Method	+2 Features	+4 Features	+6 Features
Health	FFNN	FIGS	0.7196 ± 0.0940	**0.7772 ± 0.0061**	**0.7829 ± 0.0072**
		CCS	0.7088 ± 0.0701	0.7556 ± 0.0107	0.7117 ± 0.0950
		EL2N	0.4066 ± 0.0661	0.3183 ± 0.0314	0.3182 ± 0.0667
		FDMat	**0.7424 ± 0.0531**	0.7691 ± 0.0024	0.7785 ± 0.0052
		Moderate	0.5988 ± 0.1087	0.6937 ± 0.1047	0.7035 ± 0.0701
		Full Retrain	0.7432 ± 0.0583	0.7814 ± 0.0066	0.7895 ± 0.0034
	ResNet	FIGS	**0.7360 ± 0.0599**	**0.7774 ± 0.0054**	**0.7860 ± 0.0054**
		CCS	0.6496 ± 0.0663	0.6940 ± 0.1124	0.7627 ± 0.0047
		EL2N	0.5016 ± 0.0104	0.4112 ± 0.0716	0.4272 ± 0.0970
		FDMat	0.7356 ± 0.0547	0.7646 ± 0.0055	0.7701 ± 0.0090
		Moderate	0.6452 ± 0.1229	0.6289 ± 0.1235	0.7652 ± 0.0236
		Full Retrain	0.7436 ± 0.0581	0.7815 ± 0.0073	0.7897 ± 0.0035
Dataset	Backbone	Method	+25 Features	+50 Features	+75 Features
CIS	FFNN	FIGS	**0.7460 ± 0.0244**	**0.7656 ± 0.0040**	**0.7778 ± 0.0081**
		CCS	0.6876 ± 0.0620	0.6979 ± 0.0406	0.7114 ± 0.0324
		EL2N	0.4607 ± 0.0361	0.4813 ± 0.0361	0.5172 ± 0.0268
		FDMat	0.7253 ± 0.0244	0.7618 ± 0.0056	0.7769 ± 0.0035
		Moderate	0.6802 ± 0.0615	0.7111 ± 0.0340	0.7337 ± 0.0339
		Full Retrain	0.7549 ± 0.0207	0.7839 ± 0.0068	0.7986 ± 0.0015
	ResNet	FIGS	**0.7429 ± 0.0216**	**0.7478 ± 0.0142**	**0.7679 ± 0.0064**
		CCS	0.7142 ± 0.0374	0.7286 ± 0.0211	0.7527 ± 0.0163
		EL2N	0.4613 ± 0.0816	0.4002 ± 0.0180	0.5026 ± 0.0467
		FDMat	0.7231 ± 0.0187	0.7437 ± 0.0108	0.7557 ± 0.0078
		Moderate	0.6044 ± 0.0849	0.7364 ± 0.0202	0.7602 ± 0.0017
		Full Retrain	0.7569 ± 0.0217	0.7836 ± 0.0079	0.8017 ± 0.0010

the feature-incremental classification task, where f_{t+1}^{C} is fine-tuned using the selected subset at each feature expansion step. Full retraining is included as the upper-bound reference. Across both datasets and backbone architectures, FIGS consistently achieves competitive or superior performance using only 1% of the training data. On the Health dataset, FIGS closely matches full retraining at all feature-incremental stages. On the larger and higher-dimensional CIS dataset, it maintains strong accuracy, demonstrating robustness to scale and complexity. While FDMat remains competitive in the early stages, its effectiveness diminishes later on. In contrast, FIGS increasingly outperforms all baselines as the feature space expands. Heuristic-based methods such as CCS, Moderate-DS, and EL2N perform substantially worse, indicating limited ability to identify representative samples under evolving feature distributions. These results underscore FIGS's advantage in capturing changes in data point importance caused by feature expansion, which is an aspect largely overlooked by existing coreset methods.

Table 2. Model adaptation training time (in seconds, mean ± std) under feature-incremental using two backbone models.

Dataset	Backbone	Method	+2 Features	+4 Features	+6 Features
Health	FFNN	FIGS-based	332.40 ± 112.06	282.73 ± 68.37	396.21 ± 56.03
		Full Retrain	1334.86 ± 410.28	1144.29 ± 182.19	1344.74 ± 247.53
		Full Finetune	1380.24 ± 313.09	1246.11 ± 806.10	1666.58 ± 743.16
	ResNet	FIGS-based	386.42 ± 25.53	402.58 ± 30.99	379.11 ± 26.82
		Full Retrain	1334.86 ± 410.28	1144.29 ± 182.19	1344.74 ± 247.53
		Full Finetune	1380.24 ± 313.09	1246.11 ± 806.10	1666.58 ± 743.16
Dataset	Backbone	Method	+25 Features	+50 Features	+75 Features
CIS	FFNN	FIGS-based	1518.59 ± 212.37	1588.49 ± 137.78	1778.01 ± 291.01
		Full Retrain	2732.50 ± 352.64	2946.44 ± 519.66	3377.78 ± 190.57
		Full Finetune	3804.65 ± 605.94	4101.63 ± 657.52	4265.41 ± 333.91
	ResNet	FIGS-based	1181.92 ± 110.80	1192.76 ± 182.25	1171.28 ± 138.34
		Full Retrain	2401.42 ± 67.72	2443.92 ± 91.91	2395.86 ± 70.02
		Full Finetune	2568.80 ± 613.94	2700.57 ± 749.38	2983.94 ± 291.25

Efficiency Analysis. We evaluate the computational efficiency of our cost-effective model update framework by comparing total training time against full retraining and full fine-tuning. The training time of our framework is equal to the sum of the FIGS coreset selection time, $\tilde{h}_{t+1}$ training time, and f_{t+1}^{C} fine-tuning time. As shown in Table 2, our FIGS-based framework achieves substantial speedup across both datasets and backbone model types. On the Health dataset, our framework is on average 3.8× faster than full retraining and 4.2× faster than full fine-tuning under the FFNN backbone. With ResNet, the speedups are 3.3× and 3.7×, respectively. On the larger and higher-dimensional CIS dataset, our method maintains strong efficiency gains. Under the FFNN backbone, it achieves a 1.9× speedup over full retraining and 2.5× over fine-tuning. With ResNet, the respective speedups are 2.0× and 2.3×. These results highlight the practical efficiency and scalability of our approach in both medium- and large-scale learning scenarios, achieving notable speedup without sacrificing classification accuracy.

5.3 Ablation Studies

Effect of Sampling Ratio and Selection Strategies for Q. The size of Q influences the predictive accuracy of $\mathcal{G}$, which directly affects the quality of the coreset $\mathcal{C}$. We analyze the impact of the sampling ratio r under a fixed selection strategy (K-Means) across both datasets. As shown in Fig. 3, increasing r leads to longer training time, reflecting near-linear growth in computational cost. However, its effect on ROC-AUC is not consistently positive. On the Health dataset, performance improves with larger r in later stages under the FFNN backbone, while ResNet shows only marginal gains. On the CIS dataset, increasing r does not always yield better performance and sometimes results in a plateau or decline, particularly with ResNet. These findings suggest that the trade-off between accuracy and efficiency is model- and dataset-dependent, and tuning r requires empirical validation.

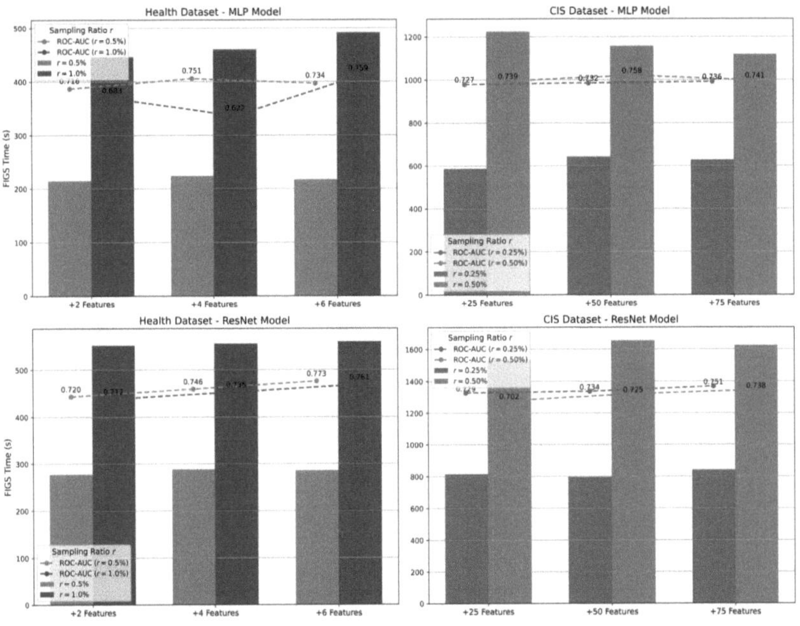

Fig. 3. Effect of sampling ratio r on model performance and FIGS runtime under a fixed K-Means strategy for selecting Q.

We also compare three selection strategies for constructing Q: random sampling, K-Means clustering, and Max-Min (with $r = 0.5\%$ fixed). As shown in Fig. 4, random sampling often performs well in early stages (e.g., Health +2 features, CIS +25 features), while Max-Min shows higher variance across stages. K-Means provides the most consistent performance, especially as feature dimensionality increases, likely due to its ability to capture representative coverage of the data space. These results indicate that no single strategy universally dominates—optimal choices vary with dataset and feature increment stage. In our final evaluations (Table 1, Table 2), we adopt the best-performing combination of selection strategy and sampling ratio for each setting.

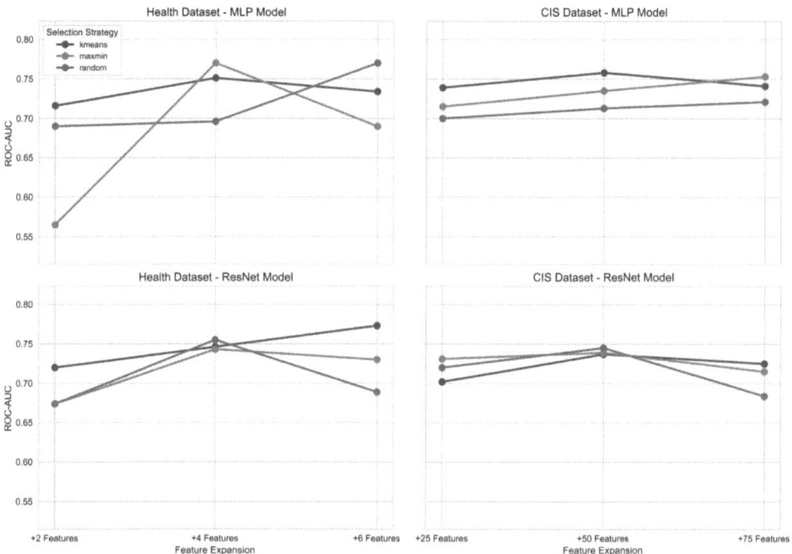

Fig. 4. Effect of different selection strategies for Q on model adaptation performance, under fixed sampling ratio $r = 0.5\%$.

Table 3. Model adaptation performance (mean ROC-AUC ± std) of different regressors used in FIGS across feature-incremental steps on the Health dataset, using FFNN and ResNet backbones.

Dataset	Backbone	Regressor	+2 Features	+4 Features	+6 Features
Health	FFNN	RF	0.7196 ± 0.0940	0.7772 ± 0.0061	0.7829 ± 0.0072
		LR	0.6624 ± 0.0901	0.7691 ± 0.0084	0.7360 ± 0.0437
		MLP	0.6320 ± 0.1145	0.7169 ± 0.0704	0.7425 ± 0.0425
	ResNet	RF	0.7360 ± 0.0599	0.7774 ± 0.0054	0.7860 ± 0.0054
		LR	0.6993 ± 0.1148	0.7007 ± 0.0573	0.7666 ± 0.0065
		MLP	0.6800 ± 0.1107	0.6318 ± 0.1119	0.6956 ± 0.1196

Effect of Regressors for $\mathcal{G}$. We investigate the effect of different regression model $\mathcal{G}$ used in FIGS to predict Shapley value shifts based on feature representation dissimilarities. Table 3 reports the model adaptation ROC-AUC under different regressors on Health dataset: Random Forest (RF), Linear Regression (LR), and a Multi-Layer Perceptron (MLP). RF consistently delivers the highest ROC-AUC across all feature increments and backbones, indicating its strong capacity to model complex relationships between feature embedding shifts and Shapley value changes. LR performs weakly in early stages, but shows strong performance in later stages. This suggests that when embedding shifts are more structured or stable, linear approximations can suffice. MLP yields less stable performance, particularly under ResNet, possibly due to overfitting or insufficient data for training a deeper regressor. These results highlight the importance of selecting an appropriate $\mathcal{G}$, with RF offering a strong trade-off between accuracy and generalization. Despite a slightly higher runtime than LR or MLP, its training overhead remains minimal (within 2 s), making its performance gains practically worthwhile.

6 Conclusion

We introduced a cost-effective model update framework for feature-incremental learning, built around Feature-Incremental G-Shapley (FIGS)—a coreset selection strategy that predicts shifts in data importance based on changes in feature representation. By avoiding costly Shapley recomputation and focusing on the dynamics of evolving feature spaces, FIGS enables accurate and scalable model updates with minimal data. Our framework integrates lightweight representation learning, selective fine-tuning, and Shapley-guided sample selection into a cohesive pipeline. Extensive experiments demonstrate that it achieves near full-retrain accuracy while significantly reducing computational cost across datasets, feature-increment stages, and model architectures. These findings validate the effectiveness of our Shapley approximation approach for guiding coreset selection in feature-incremental settings. More broadly, our work positions FIGS as a practical and generalizable data valuation tool, opening new directions for applying Shapley-based methods to online learning, coreset construction, and other downstream tasks under evolving feature space.

Acknowledgments. This work is supported by the Australian Research Council under the streams of Discovery Project (No. DP240101814), Discovery Early Career Researcher Award (No. DE230101033), Linkage Project (No. LP230200892 and LP240200546), and Industrial Transformation Training Centre (No. IC200100022).

References

1. Fawcett, T.: An introduction to roc analysis. Pattern Recogn. Lett. **27**(8), 861–874 (2006)
2. Ghorbani, A., Zou, J.: Data shapley: equitable valuation of data for machine learning. In: ICML, pp. 2242–2251. PMLR (2019)
3. Gorishniy, Y., Rubachev, I., Khrulkov, V., Babenko, A.: Revisiting deep learning models for tabular data. NeurIPS **34**, 18932–18943 (2021)
4. Hao, J., Ji, K., Liu, M.: Bilevel coreset selection in continual learning: a new formulation and algorithm. NeurIPS **36**, 51026–51049 (2023)
5. Howard, A., Bouchon-Meunier, B., CIS, I., inversion, Lei, J., Lynn@Vesta, Marcus2010, Abbass, P.H.: Ieee-cis fraud detection. https://kaggle.com/competitions/ieee-fraud-detection (2019). kaggle
6. Jiang, W., et al.: Physics-guided active sample reweighting for urban flow prediction. In: CIKM, pp. 1004–1014 (2024)

7. Killamsetty, K., Durga, S., Ramakrishnan, G., De, A., Iyer, R.: Grad-match: gradient matching based data subset selection for efficient deep model training. In: ICML, pp. 5464–5474. PMLR (2021)
8. Kumar, A.: Health insurance cross sell prediction (2020). https://www.kaggle.com/datasets/anmolkumar/health-insurance-cross-sell-prediction, kaggle Dataset
9. Lian, H., Wu, D., Hou, B.J., Wu, J., He, Y.: Online learning from evolving feature spaces with deep variational models. ICDE (2023)
10. Liu, H., Di, S., Chen, L.: Incremental tabular learning on heterogeneous feature space. Proc. ACM Manag. Data **1**(1), 1–18 (2023)
11. Lloyd, S.: Least squares quantization in pcm. IEEE Trans. Inf. Theory **28**(2), 129–137 (1982)
12. Luo, X., Pei, J.: Applications and computation of the shapley value in databases and machine learning. In: ICDM, pp. 630–635 (2024)
13. Mao, A., Mohri, M., Zhong, Y.: Cross-entropy loss functions: theoretical analysis and applications. In: ICML, pp. 23803–23828. PMLR (2023)
14. Mirzasoleiman, B., Bilmes, J., Leskovec, J.: Coresets for data-efficient training of machine learning models. In: ICML, pp. 6950–6960. PMLR (2020)
15. Paul, M., Ganguli, S., Dziugaite, G.K.: Deep learning on a data diet: finding important examples early in training. NeurIPS **34**, 20596–20607 (2021)
16. Qu, Y., Qu, L., Chen, T., Zhao, X., Nguyen, Q.V.H., Yin, H.: Scalable dynamic embedding size search for streaming recommendation. In: CIKM, pp. 1941–1950 (2024)
17. Schoch, S., Xu, H., Ji, Y.: Cs-shapley: class-wise shapley values for data valuation in classification. NeurIPS **35**, 34574–34585 (2022)
18. Shim, D., Mai, Z., Jeong, J., Sanner, S., Kim, H., Jang, J.: Online class-incremental continual learning with adversarial shapley value. In: AAAI, vol. 35, pp. 9630–9638 (2021)
19. Tang, S., et al.: Data valuation for medical imaging using shapley value and application to a large-scale chest x-ray dataset. Sci. Rep. **11**(1), 8366 (2021)
20. Tran, H.V., Chen, T., Ye, G., Nguyen, Q.V.H., Zheng, K., Yin, H.: On-device content-based recommendation with single-shot embedding pruning: a cooperative game perspective. In: WWW 2025, pp. 772–785 (2025)
21. Wang, J., Chai, C., Tang, N., Liu, J., Li, G.: Coresets over multiple tables for feature-rich and data-efficient machine learning. VLDB Endow. **16**(1), 64–76 (2022)
22. Wang, L., Zhang, X., Su, H., Zhu, J.: A comprehensive survey of continual learning: theory, method and application. PAMI (2024)
23. Wang, Z., Sun, J.: Transtab: learning transferable tabular transformers across tables. NeurIPS **35**, 2902–2915 (2022)
24. Wen, H., Chen, T., Gong, M., Chai, L.K., Sadiq, S., Yin, H.: Enhancing treatment effect estimation via active learning: a counterfactual covering perspective. In: ICML. PMLR (2025)
25. Wen, H., Chen, T., Ye, G., Chai, L.K., Sadiq, S., Yin, H.: Progressive generalization risk reduction for data-efficient causal effect estimation. In: KDD, pp. 1575–1586 (2025)
26. Wickramasinghe, B., Saha, G., Roy, K.: Continual learning: a review of techniques, challenges, and future directions. IEEE Trans. Artif. Intell. **5**(6), 2526–2546 (2023)
27. Xia, X., Liu, J., Yu, J., Shen, X., Han, B., Liu, T.: Moderate coreset: a universal method of data selection for real-world data-efficient deep learning. In: ICLR
28. Xiao, W., Chen, Y., Shan, Q., Wang, Y., Su, J.: Feature distribution matching by optimal transport for effective and robust coreset selection. In: AAAI, vol. 38, pp. 9196–9204 (2024)

29. Yang, Y., Kang, H., Mirzasoleiman, B.: Towards sustainable learning: coresets for data-efficient deep learning. In: ICML, pp. 39314–39330. PMLR (2023)
30. Zhang, J., et al.: Dynamic shapley value computation. In: ICDE, pp. 639–652. IEEE (2023)
31. Zheng, H., Liu, R., Lai, F., Prakash, A.: Coverage-centric coreset selection for high pruning rates. ICLR (2022)
32. Zhou, D.W., Wang, Q.W., Qi, Z.H., Ye, H.J., Zhan, D.C., Liu, Z.: Class-incremental learning: a survey. PAMI (2024)

Ilargi: A GPU Compatible Factorized ML Model Training Framework

Wenbo Sun(✉) and Rihan Hai

Delft University of Technology, Delft, The Netherlands
{w.sun-2,r.hai}@tudelft.nl

Abstract. The machine learning (ML) training over disparate data sources traditionally involves materialization, which can impose substantial time and space overhead due to data movement and replication. Factorized learning, which leverages direct computation on disparate sources through linear algebra (LA) rewriting, has emerged as a viable alternative to improve computational efficiency. However, the adaptation of factorized learning to leverage the full capabilities of modern LA-friendly hardware like GPUs has been limited, often requiring manual intervention for algorithm compatibility. This paper introduces *Ilargi*, a novel factorized learning framework that utilizes matrix-represented data integration (DI) metadata to facilitate automatic factorization across CPU and GPU environments without the need for costly relational joins. *Ilargi* incorporates an ML-based cost estimator to intelligently selects between factorization and materialization based on data properties, algorithm complexity, hardware environments, and their interactions. This strategy ensures up to 8.9x speedups on GPUs and achieves over 20% acceleration in batch ML training workloads, thereby enhancing the practicability of ML training across diverse data integration scenarios and hardware platforms. To our knowledge, this work is the very first effort in GPU-compatible factorized learning.

Keywords: Machine Learning · Data Integration · Factorized Learning

1 Introduction

The raw data for machine learning (ML) model training is often dispersed across multiple database tables or physically separate sources [20,26]. These data sources typically undergo a data integration (DI) process, known as materialization, to create a unified view [13] for subsequent machine learning training. Though widely adopted, materialization introduces considerable overhead, both in terms of time and space, due to extensive data movement and replication during data integration.

Factorized learning [5,7,18,19,24,30] offers a strategy to train ML models directly over disparate sources without materialization. Factorized learning can

I. Awan et al. (Eds.): WISE 2025, LNCS 16367, pp. 19–30, 2026.
https://doi.org/10.1007/978-981-95-7394-3_2

improve model training efficiency by pushing operators in ML training down to the data source side. For example, to train a linear regression model using gradient descent to predict transaction amounts (T) based on customer profiles (P) and transaction history (H), traditional approaches first materialize a table by joining P and H on customer ID. This involves substantial data movement and preprocessing time, especially for large datasets. Factorized learning, in contrast, avoids materialization by leveraging additive linear algebra rewriting to decompose the training process. It trains sub-models on P and H separately and combines their outputs using schema and entity mappings [12]. By operating directly on the factorized data, this approach significantly improves the efficiency of model training while maintaining predictive accuracy.

Although linear algebra (LA) representations are central to factorized learning [5,18,24], few studies exploit GPU acceleration for factorized LA operators, despite its proven benefits for deep and statistical ML models [17,27,31]. Existing GPU solutions often require manual LA rewriting [25], missing opportunities for broader speedups. Moreover, factorization does not always outperform materialization: heuristic rules [5,24] based on data characteristics neglect interactions among data, algorithms, and hardware, especially in batch training workloads (e.g., dataset selection [8,11] and hyperparameter tuning). A precise cost estimator is therefore essential for practical factorized learning.

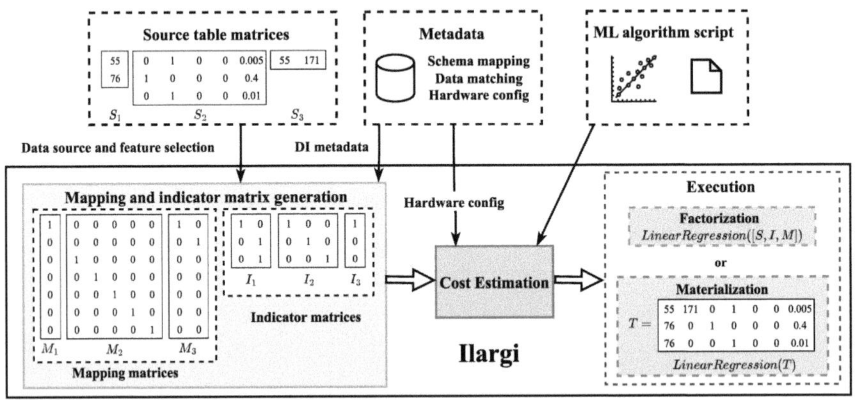

Fig. 1. Ilargi's workflow.

To bridge these research gaps, we present *Ilargi* , an efficient factorized learning framework for training ML models on both CPU and GPU platforms. The novelty of this work lies in its GPU-compatible representation and a learning-based cost estimator. First, we employs a matrix representation of data integration (DI) metadata, which unifies and streamlines both DI and machine learning operations. This unified representation enables highly efficient factorized model training on both CPUs and GPUs. Furthermore, we propose a cost estimator within *Ilargi* that considers memory access behavior to suggest the optimal training strategy and avoid performance degradation due to the misuse of factorized learning. These innovations collectively improve the practical usability of factorized learning. We summarize the contributions of this work as follows:

- *Ilargi* models data integration (DI) and ML training as linear algebra (LA) operations (Sect. 2), enabling automated rewriting into factorized forms. This GPU-compatible approach accelerates diverse ML tasks, achieving up to 8.9× speedups over CPU implementations (Sect. 4.2).
- *Ilargi* includes a learning-based cost estimator (Sect. 3) that predicts whether factorization or materialization is optimal, achieving 97.1% accuracy and over 20% batch training speedup (Sect. 4.3).

2 Ilargi: ML Over Disparate Sources

As shown in Fig. 1, *Ilargi* converts DI metadata and source tables into compressed sparse matrices (Sect. 2.1), enabling GPU-compatible representations of schema mappings and data matching. It rewrites ML training and integration tasks as linear algebra operations (Sect. 2.2), while a cost estimator selects between factorization and materialization based on data, algorithm, and hardware (Sect. 3). The model is then trained with the chosen strategy, enabling efficient factorized training on both CPUs and GPUs.

2.1 DI Metadata as Matrices

Preparing disparate training data for ML models requires understanding and bridging the relationships between the data sources, which is achieved primarily through data integration tasks. The relationships are normally described by following metadata: *i*) mappings between different source schemata [10,29] and *ii*) linkages between data instances [4]. We refer to such vital information derived from data integration process as *data integration metadata* (*DI metadata*).

Schema mappings are traditionally formalized as first-order logic [9], and represented and executed using query languages [10,32]. To accelerate both data integration and machine learning operations using GPUs, it is critical to find a unified representation that is highly compatible with GPU architectures. In Ilargi, we employ a matrix-based representation for schema mappings, which we refer to as *mapping matrices*, denoted as $\mathbf{M}$. Given a source table S_k and target table T, a mapping matrix $M_k \in \mathbf{M}$ has the size of $c_T \times c_k$, and specifies how the columns of S_k are mapped to the columns of T.

Definition 1 (*Mapping matrix*). *Mapping matrices between source tables* $S_1, S_2, ..., S_n$ *and target table* T *are a set of binary matrices* $\mathbf{M} = \{M_1, ..., M_n\}$*.* M_k $(k \in [1, n])$ *is a matrix with the shape* $c_T \times c_k$*, where*

$$M_k[i,j] = \begin{cases} 1, & \textit{if } j\textit{-th column of } S_k \textit{ mapped to } i\textit{-th column of } T \\ 0, & \textit{otherwise} \end{cases}$$

Intuitively, in $M_k[i,j]$ the vertical coordinate i represents the target table column while the horizontal coordinate j represents the mapped source table column. A value of 1 in M_k specifies the existence of column correspondences between S_k and T, while the value 0 shows that the current target table attribute has no corresponding column in S_k. Figure 1 shows the mapping matrices M_1, M_2, M_3 for source tables S_1, S_2, S_3, respectively.

We use the *indicator matrix* [5] to preserve the row matching between each source table S_k and the target table T. An indicator matrix I_k of size $c_T \times c_k$ describes how the rows of source table S_k map to the rows of target table T, as in Fig. 1.

Definition 2 (*Indicator matrix* [5]). *Indicator matrices between source tables $S_1, S_2, ..., S_n$ and target table T are a set of row vectors $\mathbf{I} = \{I_1, ..., I_n\}$. I_k $(k \in [1,n])$ is a row vector of size r_T, where*

$$I_k[i,j] = \begin{cases} 1 & \textit{if}\, j\textit{-th row of}\, S_k\, \textit{mapped to}\, i\textit{-th row of}\, T \\ 0 & \textit{otherwise} \end{cases}$$

(See Table 1).

Table 1. Notations used in the paper.

Symbol	Description
$S_k/I_k/M_k$	The k-th source matrix, indicator matrix, and mapping matrix
T	Target table
j_T	The join type of T (inner/left/outer/union)
r_k/r_T	Number of rows in S_k/T
c_k/c_T	Number of columns in S_k/T
$m_k/m_T/m_X/m_w$	Number of nonzero elements in $S_k/T/X/w$

2.2 Rewriting Rules for Factorization

With data and metadata represented in matrices, we use the example of LA operator *left matrix multiplication (LMM)* to explain how to rewrite an operator over a target schema to source schemas. The full set of rewrite rules based on mapping and indicator matrices is in technical report [1].

Given a matrix X with the size $c_T \times c_X$, LMM of T and X is denoted as TX. The LMM result of our target table matrix T and another matrix X is a matrix of size $r_T \times c_X$. Our rewrite of LMM goes as follows.

$$TX \rightarrow I_1 S_1 M_1^T X + ... + I_n S_n M_n^T X$$

We first compute the local result $I_k S_k M_k^T X$ ($k \in [1, n]$) for each source table, then assemble them for the final results.

In gradient descent for machine learning models such as linear regression, operators like matrix transpose and left matrixâĂŞmatrix multiplication can be rewritten using our strategies. These rewriting rules push operations down to disparate data sources for local computation, and the partial results are assembled at the end. This approach eliminates the need for full data centralization.

3 Cost Estimation in Ilargi

Reducing ML training time through factorization is not always guaranteed: when the target table has low redundancy, factorization may incur more linear algebra operations than materialization [5]. Prior work [5,24] sets sparsity thresholds via empirical models, but thresholds vary with hardware, indicating that sparsity alone does not consistently predict factorization speedups across CPUs and GPUs. This motivates a cost model that accounts for both algorithmic characteristics and hardware properties, beginning with a comparative complexity analysis of materialization and factorization.

3.1 Complexity Analysis of ML Model Training Algorithms

We compare the computational complexity of linear algebra (LA) operations for both materialization and factorization. For materialization, the cost is based on performing LA operations directly on the materialized table. In contrast, factorization considers the operations on each source table individually.

Table 2. Computations complexity comparison of common LA operators.

Operation	Materialization	Factorization
$T \oslash x$, $f(T)$ rowSum(T), colSum(T)	m_T	$\sum_{k=1}^{n} m_k$
TX	$c_X \cdot m_T + r_T \cdot m_X$	$\sum_{k=1}^{n} c_X \cdot m_k + r_k \cdot m_X$
XT	$r_X \cdot m_T + c_T \cdot m_X$	$\sum_{k=1}^{n} r_X \cdot m_k + c_k \cdot m_X$

Table 2 summarizes the comparison. Ilargi stores matrices in sparse format, so the complexity of element-wise operations, rowSum, and colSum depends on the number of non-zero elements.

For sparse matrix multiplication, given two matrices T and X, the complexity of TX is $O(c_X \cdot m_T + r_T \cdot m_X)$, where m_T and m_X are the non-zero elements of

T and X [14]. Since our mapping and indicator matrices are sparse, we calculate matrix operation costs accordingly. With the rewriting rule (Sect. 2.2), the complexity of factorized multiplication is $\sum_{k=1}^{n}(c_X \cdot m_k + r_k \cdot m_X)$. The complexity of ML models depends on the specific LA operators used. We detail linear regression analysis here, with further models discussed in [1].

3.2 ML-Based Cost Estimator

Determining whether to use factorization or materialization is intricate, as it depends on varying dataset characteristics, model structures, and hardware factors. To address this, we introduce a learned cost estimator that makes a binary decision between factorization and materialization. This choice becomes particularly impactful when training multiple models, such as during parameter tuning, where even small speedups can translate into substantial time savings.

Ilargi's Tree Boosting Estimator. Tree boosting is known for its explainability and speed, making it popular in cost estimation tasks [2,6]. We use XGBoost for its ability to capture non-linear relationships, with a focus on identifying key features that influence the choice between materialization and factorization.

Hardware Features. To ensure portability, our estimator emphasizes macro-level hardware features, such as memory bandwidth and parallelism, over micro-level specifics like cache speed. Parallelism, particularly the number of threads used, is included due to its impact on factorized learning speedups. Combined with memory read/write costs, these features enable effective cost estimation for both methods (Sect. 4.3).

Table 3. Data sizes of realistic data integrations scenario based on TPC-DI benchmark. The table shows the number of rows in sources and target table w.r.t varying scale factors.

	Source 1	Source 2	Source 3		Target
Scale factor	Trade	Customer	Stock	Reports	-
3	391.1K	4.7K	2.6K	98.7K	528.8K
7	911.6K	108K	5.8K	297.7K	1.3M

Cost Estimation Pipeline. The cost estimator uses three input groups: `i)` data (source matrices, mapping, and indicator matrices), `ii)` ML algorithm (operators and user-defined hyperparameters), and `iii)` hardware (e.g., parallelism, memory bandwidth). The estimator computes the complexity each operator in learning algorithms (Sect. 3.1) and the theoretical memory I/O for each operator in the ML algorithm. It normalizes these features based on parallelism and memory bandwidth. The output is binary: If True, Ilargi uses factorization; otherwise, it materializes the data before training.

4 Evaluation

We start this section with an overview of our experimental setup, followed by a detailed performance evaluation of machine learning workloads employing both factorization and materialization techniques on CPUs and GPUs. This evaluation also explores the factors that influence the decision-making process between factorization and materialization. Building on these insights, we further evaluate the accuracy of our proposed cost estimator in predicting the optimal strategy.

4.1 Experiment Setup

Synthetic Datasets. We built a data generator to create synthetic datasets with diverse data characteristics. It generates source table pairs that join to form a target table based on specified parameters[1]. We produced 1800 datasets to capture the relationship between data features and training performance. Additionally, the results from these datasets serve as training data for our cost estimator.

Real-World Datasets. To validate the estimator in real scenarios, we used the Hamlet datasets [23], commonly referenced in related works [5,22,24]. The seven datasets in Hamlet simulate ML workflows, originally designed for inner join scenarios but adapted for other join types in this work.

For large-scale evaluation, we used the TPC-DI benchmark [28], involving four datasets across three sources. The fact table, *Trade*, is joined with key attributes to produce a target table with 27 features. Table 3 outlines table cardinalities across various scale factors, highlighting data characteristics in different scenarios.

Hardware and Software. We run experiments with 16, and 32 cores of AMD EPYC 7H12 CPU, and Nvidia A40 GPU. To enable parallelized sparse matrix multiplication on both CPU and GPU, we choose MKL and CuBLAS as LA library respectively. The number of model training iterations is 200.

4.2 Performance Evaluation with Synthetic Data

In this section, we conduct a performance comparison between factorized learning and learning over materialization on both CPUs and GPUs. The purpose of this comparison is to demonstrate the significant acceleration that GPUs can provide for factorized learning, as well as the performance of factorized learning across various data characteristics.

Figure 2 shows the speedups of factorization over materialization ($\frac{T_{materialization}}{T_{factorization}}$) across three hardware setups. Factorized scalar operators achieve greater speedups on GPUs compared to CPUs, while matrix operators show smaller gains. On CPUs, matrix operators outperform scalar operators, but this trend reverses on GPUs. This discrepancy arises because GPU-based matrix

[1] The parameters are elaborated in our technical report [1].

operations are often limited by memory bandwidth. The high parallelism of GPUs generally benefits compute-bound tasks more than memory-bound operators.

For model training, factorization still offers speed improvements, albeit more modestly. This is due to the frequent read/write operations for intermediate results in training algorithms, which diminishes speedups, especially on GPUs where memory bandwidth constraints often dominate.

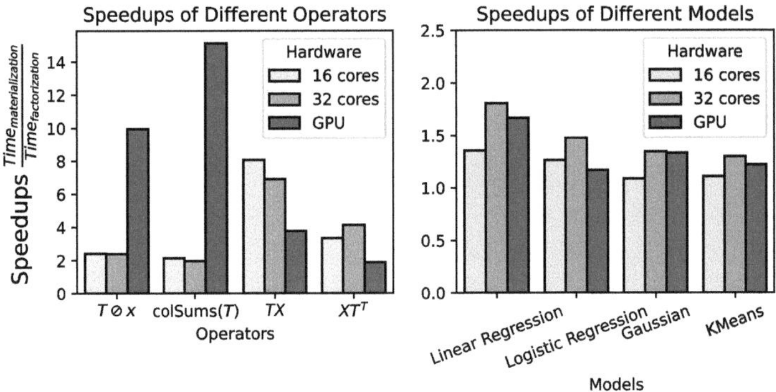

Fig. 2. Speedups ($\frac{\text{Time}_{materialization}}{\text{Time}_{factorization}}$) of LA operators and model training w.r.t varying input parameters. *Here we focus on the cases that factorization performs faster than materialization.*

4.3 Effectiveness of Our Estimator

This section evaluates the tree-boosting cost estimator introduced in Sect. 3.2. Using synthetic data, we generated 7,200 labeled feature pairs to indicate whether factorization or materialization is faster, and split them into training (80%) and test (20%) sets. We assess the estimator by accuracy and F1-score against baseline methods, and further measure its impact on end-to-end batch model training, demonstrating the performance gains from guiding factorization or materialization choices with our estimator.

Four Baselines for Comparison. `i)` To confirm the significance of hardware features, we train another tree boosting model using the same dataset, but *without hardware features.* `ii)` The *tuple ratio and feature ratio* (TR & FR), metrics used in Morpheus [5], quantify the target table's redundancy relative to the joinable tables. Morpheus [5] suggests a threshold of 5 for tuple ratio and 1 for feature ratio. `iii)` Finally, we consider the heuristic rule proposed in [24].

Results on Synthetic Data. Tab. 4 shows that our tree boosting model outperforms others with a 97.1% accuracy and high F1-score, confirming its strong precision-recall balance. Excluding hardware features significantly reduces both accuracy and F1-score, supporting the importance of hardware information in

Table 4. Accuracy, F1-score and Overall Speedups of estimators tested on CPUs (GPUs). Our cost estimator shows superior predictive quality and effectiveness over synthetic test data.

Cost estimators	Accuracy	F1-score	Overall Speedups
Tree Boosting (ours)	**0.971 (0.899)**	**0.936 (0.821)**	**1.24 (1.15)**
Tree Boosting w/o hardware	0.712 (0.535)	0.560 (0.443)	1.19 (1.09)
TR & FR [5]	0.490 (0.244)	0.426 (0.362)	1.16 (0.86)
MorpheousFI	0.864 (0.497)	0.601 (0.477)	1.22 (0.96)

choosing between factorization and materialization. The two threshold-based estimators perform worse in both metrics.

Beyond quality metrics, our estimator achieves a 1.24x speedup over training exclusively with materialization, outperforming all baselines. On GPUs, however, the effectiveness of all estimators declines, with threshold-based models performing worse than default materialization. This highlights the sensitivity of empirical thresholds to hardware variations and demonstrates the limitations of threshold-based methods in cross-platform tasks.

Results on Real-world Data. We further evaluated our estimator using the *Project Hamlet* and *TPC-DI* datasets to test its practical usability in realistic ML tasks, including multiple model training and hyperparameter tuning.

Table 5 shows that the speedups on both CPU and GPU platforms are consistent with those observed on synthetic data, with our tree boosting estimator consistently performing best on unseen data.

Table 5. Average speedups ($\frac{\text{Time}_{materialization}}{\text{Time}_{factorization}}$) of all models across all real-world data. Our tree boosting estimator can consistently accelerate batch model training workload on both CPUs and GPUs.

Cost estimators	Speedups (CPU)	Speedups (GPU)
Tree boosting (ours)	**1.21**	**1.16**
MorpheousFI	1.18	0.88
TR&FR	1.09	0.72

Table 6 provides a breakdown of effectiveness across models and datasets on CPUs. While the estimator generally makes accurate decisions, its performance varies with different datasets. For denser datasets like *flight* and *lastfm*, incorrect decisions led to slower training compared to materialization. Still, when training a single model across various datasets, speedups reached up to 1.29x.

According to the results, we conclude that our tree boosting cost estimator, enhanced with hardware features, outperforms the state-of-the-art estimator, showing consistent effectiveness across diverse hardware platforms.

Table 6. Detailed speedups($\frac{\text{Time}_{materialization}}{\text{Time}_{factorization}}$) w.r.t different models and datasets on CPUs (32 cores). Our tree boosting estimator makes correct prediction in most cases but performs worse on *flight* and *lastfm*.

Datasets \ Models	G.NMF	KMeans	Lin.Reg	Log.Reg	Speedups/dataset
TPC-DI sf=3	1.33	1	1.12	1.33	1.10
TPC-DI sf=7	1.23	1	1.04	1.20	1.09
expedia	1.24	1.56	1	1.07	1.17
flight	0.57	0.7	1	0.49	0.74
lastfm	1	0.9	1	1	0.96
movie	1.8	2.35	2.32	1.88	2.19
yelp	1.10	1.24	1.51	1	1.28
Speedups/model	1.28	1.21	1.29	1.18	#

5 Related Work

Early efforts required *manual* design for factorizing specific ML algorithms, with Orion [19] addressing linear and logistic regression. This was expanded in Santoku [21] to incorporate decision trees, feature ranking, and Naive Bayes. While Orion and Santoku focused on inner joins via PK-FK relationship, F [30] has extended factorization of linear regression to natural joins. Following F, AC/DC [18] adds support to categorical variables, and LMFAO supports more ML algorithms such as decision trees. JoinBoost [15] integrated tree models like LightGBM and XGBoost.

In a more *automated* manner, Morpheus [5] proposed a general factorization framework based on PK-FK and join dependencies. HADAD [3] speeds up the rewriting rules of Morpheus by reordering of multiplication and exploiting precomputed results. Later, Trinity [16] extends Morpheus with compatibility to multiple programming languages and LA tools. MorpheusFI [24] added support to non-linear feature interactions. Non-linear models such as Gaussian Mixture Models and Neural Networks are studied in [7].

Ilargi's main contribution is not on extending ML algorithms. We expand the usability of factorized learning by a GPU-compatible representation. We take a more critical inspection of the speedup of factorization compared to materialization by utilizing DI metadata. We also discovered a third factor, hardware configuration, which has an impact on the decision boundary. We are currently expanding Ilargi to more ML models such as tree models.

6 Conclusion

We proposed *Ilargi*, which leverages matrix-represented DI metadata to enable GPU-compatible factorized model training across disparate data sources. With a unified LA representation, Ilargi supports efficient training on both CPUs and

GPUs, while a tree-boosting estimator guides the choice between materialization and factorization by incorporating data, model, and hardware characteristics. Experiments on synthetic and real data show up to 8.9× speedups from GPU-parallelized factorization and up to 24% faster batch training with our estimator.

References

1. Ilargi: a GPU Compatible Factorized ML Learning Framework - Technical Report (2024), Technical report. https://anonymous.4open.science/r/Ilargi-E1DF/paper/technical_report.pdf
2. Adams, A., Ma, K., Anderson, L., Baghdadi, R., Li, T., Gharbi, M., et al.: Learning to optimize halide with tree search and random programs. ACM Trans. Graph. **38**(4), 121:1–121:12 (2019)
3. Alotaibi, R., Cautis, B., Deutsch, A., Manolescu, I.: HADAD: a lightweight approach for optimizing hybrid complex analytics queries. In: Proceedings of the 2021 International Conference on Management of Data, pp. 23–35. ACM
4. Brizan, D.G., Tansel, A.U.: A. survey of entity resolution and record linkage methodologies. Commun. IIMA **6**(3), 5 (2006)
5. Chen, L., Kumar, A., Naughton, J., Patel, J.M.: Towards linear algebra over normalized data. PVLDB **10**(11) (2017)
6. Chen, T., Moreau, T., Jiang, Z., et al.: TVM: an automated end-to-end optimizing compiler for deep learning. In: Arpaci-Dusseau, A.C., Voelker, G. (eds.) 13th USENIX Symposium on Operating Systems Design and Implementation, 2018, Carlsbad, CA, USA, October 8-10, 2018, pp. 578–594. USENIX Association (2018)
7. Cheng, Z., Koudas, N., Zhang, Z., Yu, X.: Efficient construction of nonlinear models over normalized data. In: 37th IEEE International Conference on Data Engineering, ICDE 2021, Chania, Greece, April 19-22, 2021, pp. 1140–1151. IEEE (2021)
8. Chepurko, N., Marcus, R., Zgraggen, E., Fernandez, R.C., Kraska, T., Karger, D.R.: ARDA: automatic relational data augmentation for machine learning. Proc. VLDB Endow. **13**(9), 1373–1387 (2020)
9. Fagin, R.: Tuple-Generating Dependencies. In: Liu, L., Özsu, M.T. (eds.) Encyclopedia of Database Systems, pp. 3201–3202. Springer, Boston, MA (2009). https://doi.org/10.1007/978-0-387-39940-9_1274
10. Fagin, R., Haas, L.M., Hernández, M., Miller, R.J., Popa, L., Velegrakis, Y.: Clio: schema mapping creation and data exchange. In: Borgida, A.T., Chaudhri, V.K., Giorgini, P., Yu, E.S. (eds.) Conceptual Modeling: Foundations and Applications. LNCS, vol. 5600, pp. 198–236. Springer, Berlin, Heidelberg (2009). https://doi.org/10.1007/978-3-642-02463-4_12
11. Galhotra, S., Gong, Y., Fernandez, R.C.: Metam: goal-oriented data discovery. In: 2023 IEEE 39th International Conference on Data Engineering (ICDE), pp. 2780–2793. IEEE (2023)
12. Hai, R., et al.: Amalur: data integration meets machine learning. In: 2023 IEEE 39th International Conference on Data Engineering (ICDE), pp. 3729–3739 (2023)
13. Halevy, A., Rajaraman, A., Ordille, J.: Data integration: the teenage years. In: Proceedings of the 32nd International Conference on Very Large Data Bases, pp. 9–16. VLDB '06, VLDB Endowment (2006)
14. Horowitz, E., Sahni, S.: Fundamentals of data structures (1982)
15. Huang, Z., Sen, R., Liu, J., Wu, E.: Joinboost: grow trees over normalized data using only sql. Proc. VLDB Endow. **16**(11), 3071–3084 (2023)

16. Justo, D., Yi, S., Stadler, L., Polikarpova, N., Kumar, A.: Towards a polyglot framework for factorized ML **14**(12), 2918–2931
17. Ke, G., et al.: Lightgbm: a highly efficient gradient boosting decision tree. Adv. Neural. Inf. Process. Syst. **30**, 3146–3154 (2017)
18. Khamis, M.A., Ngo, H.Q., Nguyen, X., Olteanu, D., Schleich, M.: AC/DC: in-database learning thunderstruck. In: Proceedings of the Second Workshop on Data Management for End-To-End Machine Learning, pp. 1–10. ACM
19. Kumar, A., Naughton, J., Patel, J.M.: Learning generalized linear models over normalized data. In: SIGMOD, pp. 1969–1984 (2015)
20. Kumar, A., Boehm, M., Yang, J.: Data management in machine learning: challenges, techniques, and systems. In: Proceedings of the 2017 ACM SIGMOD International Conference on Management of Data (SIGMOD), pp. 1717–1722 (2017)
21. Kumar, A., Jalal, M., Yan, B., Naughton, J., Patel, J.M.: Demonstration of Santoku: optimizing machine learning over normalized data. Proc. VLDB Endow. **8**(12), 1864–1867 (2015)
22. Kumar, A., Naughton, J., Patel, J.M.: Learning generalized linear models over normalized data. In: Proceedings of the 2015 ACM SIGMOD International Conference on Management of Data, pp. 1969–1984. SIGMOD '15, Association for Computing Machinery, New York, NY, USA (2015)
23. Kumar, A., Naughton, J.F., Patel, J.M., Zhu, X.: To join or not to join?: thinking twice about joins before feature selection. In: Özcan, F., Koutrika, G., Madden, S. (eds.) Proceedings of the 2016 International Conference on Management of Data, SIGMOD Conference, pp. 19–34 (2016)
24. Li, S., Chen, L., Kumar, A.: Enabling and optimizing non-linear feature interactions in factorized linear algebra. In: Proceedings of the 2019 International Conference on Management of Data, pp. 1571–1588. SIGMOD '19, Association for Computing Machinery, New York, NY, USA (2019)
25. Li, S., Kumar, A.: Towards an optimized group by abstraction for large-scale machine learning. Proc. VLDB Endow. **14**(11), 2327–2340 (2021)
26. Olteanu, D.: The relational data borg is learning. Proc. VLDB Endow. **13**(12), 3502–3515 (2020)
27. Paszke, A., Gross, S., Massa, F., Lerer, A., Bradbury, J., Chanan, G., et al.: Pytorch: an imperative style, high-performance deep learning library. Adv. Neural Inf. Process. Syst. **32**, 8024–8035 (2019)
28. Poess, M., Rabl, T., Jacobsen, H.A., Caufield, B.: Tpc-di: the first industry benchmark for data integration. Proc. VLDB Endow. **7**(13), 1367–1378 (2014)
29. Rahm, E., Bernstein, P.A.: A survey of approaches to automatic schema matching. VLDB J. **10**(4), 334–350 (2001)
30. Schleich, M., Olteanu, D., Ciucanu, R.: Learning linear regression models over factorized joins. In: Proceedings of the 2016 International Conference on Management of Data, pp. 3–18. SIGMOD '16, Association for Computing Machinery
31. Wen, Z., Shi, J., Li, Q., He, B., Chen, J.: ThunderSVM: a fast SVM library on GPUs and CPUs. J. Mach. Learn. Res. **19**, 797–801 (2018)
32. Yan, L.L., Miller, R.J., Haas, L.M., Fagin, R.: Data-driven understanding and refinement of schema mappings. In: Proceedings of the 2001 ACM SIGMOD International Conference on Management of Data, pp. 485–496 (2001)

Multi-Armed Bandit-Based Client Selection for Efficient Federated Learning

Dewei Ning[1], Yong-Feng Ge[1(✉)], Lili Sun[1], and Yunliang Jiang[2]

[1] Institute for Sustainable Industries and Liveable Cities, Victoria University, Melbourne 3011, Australia
dewei.ning@live.vu.edu.au, yongfeng.ge@vu.edu.au, lilisun669@gmail.com
[2] Zhejiang Key Laboratory of Intelligent Education Technology and Application, Zhejiang Normal University, Jinhua, China
jyl@zjhu.edu.cn

Abstract. Federated Learning (FL) traditionally adopts unbiased client selection, which slows error convergence. Existing biased strategies often add communication overhead or fail under Non-Independent and Identically Distributed (Non-IID) data. We propose an efficient FL framework based on Multi-Armed Bandit (MAB) with two scoring methods—Upper Confidence Bound (UCB) and Thompson Sampling (TS)—to evaluate client contributions. In each round, top-ranked clients are trained with local Gradient Descent (GD), while others update with shuffled Stochastic Gradient Descent (SGD). Experiments show our method achieves comparable accuracy to baseline with fewer rounds and reduced time, and remains robust under heterogeneous data, supporting practical deployment.

Keywords: Federated Learning · Client Selection · Multi-Armed Bandits

1 Introduction

Breakthroughs in artificial intelligence (AI) have reshaped people's daily life [6]. The advancement of electronic information technology has led to the miniaturization and integration of electronic devices [2]. With the rapid development of Internet of Things (IoT) devices, advancements in wireless communication networks, and breakthroughs in machine learning, our way of life is being constantly refreshed. Traditional machine learning frameworks require large centralized datasets, which is often impractical for IoT applications due to: (a) privacy concerns, (b) security issues, and (c) high communication costs of transmitting raw data. It impacts the tradeoff between privacy protection and data utility, allowing precise and adjustable control [7,24]. Originally centred around personal connections and content sharing, these platforms have expanded to encompass communication with close friends and the dissemination of official information by large organizations [19]. Google researchers introduced Federated Learning

I. Awan et al. (Eds.): WISE 2025, LNCS 16367, pp. 31–41, 2026.
https://doi.org/10.1007/978-981-95-7394-3_3

(FL) [18] as a promising solution, which has gained attention from both industry and academia. Unlike traditional machine learning, FL is a framework that enables machine learning algorithms to be implemented in a decentralised collaborative learning setting. FL is a distributed optimization framework that enables on-device training while addressing data silo issues caused by privacy regulations and ownership concerns. Each round involves local training, model update transmission, and global aggregation, allowing the server to build a shared model without accessing raw data. Recent advances in FL have focused on challenges such as privacy, communication efficiency, and data heterogeneity [20].

Most FL studies have focused on server-side client selection to enhance training performance, it offers several benefits, including awareness of data collection and usage, improved fairness of algorithms and systems, and enhanced reproducibility of research [8]. While many works [14,17,18] improve efficiency via algorithm design but still rely on unbiased random client selection. This random sampling fails to reflect the global data distribution, especially under Non-Independent and Identically Distributed (Non-IID) settings [15]. Prior research [21,22] shows that excluding adverse local updates can yield better models, highlighting data heterogeneity as a key challenge. In particular, FedAvg [18] suffers from biased updates under Non-IID data, which slows convergence, degrades accuracy, and increases communication costs for resource-constrained clients.

Previous studies [11,16,23,27] have shown that biased client selection in FL towards clients with higher local loss achieves faster convergence compared to unbiased client selection. However, the client selection strategies suggested in previous research either necessitate additional communication between the server and clients to obtain precise local loss values [3] or rely on outdated loss values that were received from the selected clients during earlier communication rounds [5]. Also, it was observed that the existing schemes led to bad local optima [5]. Xia et al. [23] proposed a FL framework based on Upper Confidence Bound (UCB), but it lacks consideration of Thompson Sampling (TS) from Multi-Armed Bandit (MAB) approaches. And also, this method, however, suffers from overfitting to the quickest clients' data when used for scheduling in FL systems. Zhu et al. [27] have used a composite MAB to design a client selection scheme that not only optimizes system energy consumption but also reduces latency. However, it lacks consideration of data heterogeneity across individual clients.

We address the challenge of efficient client selection in FL by proposing a MAB strategy with differential local updates, enabling faster convergence with fewer communication rounds. Two implementations are considered: UCB, which balances exploration and exploitation via confidence bounds, and TS, which selects clients probabilistically using Bayesian inference. To stabilize optimization, high-loss clients use Local Gradient Descent (GD), while others adopt Local Shuffled Stochastic Gradient Descent (SGD) to accelerate training. Experiments under varying data heterogeneity show that our strategy achieves comparable accuracy to standard methods but with lower communication cost and better adaptability to real-world non-IID data. The contributions of this work are summarized as follows:

- We propose a client selection strategy in FL using UCB and TS to prioritize high MAB-score clients, achieving convergence with fewer communication rounds and reduced communication cost.
- Unlike FedAvg, selected clients apply local GD, while unselected clients use shuffled SGD, improving both stability and efficiency.
- Experiments under Non-IID settings show the strategy maintains effectiveness across different data heterogeneity levels.

In this paper, in Sect. 2, we first introduce common FL training methods, followed by our proposed method, which includes the MAB-based client selection strategy and differential updating methods in Sect. 3. Through experiments in Sect. 4, we compare our algorithm with conventional methods and demonstrate that our proposed strategy is more effective and consumes less, especially under varying levels of data heterogeneity.

2 Preliminaries

2.1 Basic FL

FedAVG [18] is the most common aggregation method in FL. The goal of FedAvg is to find the optimal global parameter vector w by minimizing the weighted average loss function of all clients. The contribution of each client is determined by the size of its dataset, which gives a fairer representation of the impact of each client's data volume on the total objective function. Therefore, it is to find the parameter vector w that minimizes the following objective:

$$\min_{w \in \mathbb{R}^d} f(w) \quad \text{where} \quad f(w) \stackrel{\text{def}}{=} \frac{1}{n} \sum_{i=1}^{n} f_i(w) \tag{1}$$

With total K clients, P_k is the dataset for the k-th client; i represents individual data samples within the local dataset P_k; n_k is the number of data samples for the k-th client and n is the total number of data samples across all clients. Therefore, we can re-write (1) to:

$$f(w) = \sum_{k=1}^{K} \frac{n_k}{n} F_k(w) \quad \text{where} \quad F_k(w) = \frac{1}{n_k} \sum_{i \in P_k} f_i(w) \tag{2}$$

The baseline unbiased client selection strategy used in FedAvg [18] chooses clients in proportion p_k which is the proportion of data for the k-th client. So we have:

$$f(w) = \sum_{k=1}^{K} \frac{n_k}{n} F_k(w) = \sum_{k=1}^{K} p_k F_k(w) \tag{3}$$

During each communication round of training, a subset of $m = C \times K$ clients, where $0 < C < 1$, is selected to optimize the model parameter w. Each selected client performs $\tau \geq 0$ iterations and sends its locally updated model back to the server.

3 Proposed Methodology

3.1 Overview of Proposed Methodology

In this section, we reformulate the selection of clients for the training of each round into an MAB problem and propose algorithms to balance the exploration-exploitation trade-off to keep the fairness of biased client selection in FL. The overflow of the proposed strategy is presented in Fig. 1. The training process of FL is an iterative optimization process. Client selection can be viewed as an online decision-making problem [16]. In our strategy, the server computes discounted cumulative losses and selects top clients by MAB scores for the next round. Selected clients update with local GD, while others use shuffled SGD. All clients upload their parameters for aggregation, and this process repeats until convergence.

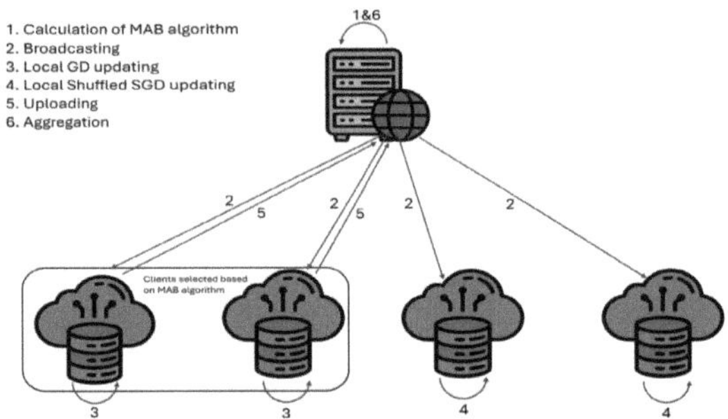

Fig. 1. Overview of MAB Client Selection Strategy

MAB Algorithm. An MAB problem is one of sequential decision problems, where a player should make a decision, in each time slot, about which arms of the bandits are pulled [12]. In [4] consider the clients as arms in the MAB problem and calculate the discounted cumulative local loss values for each client, denoted as $L_t(\gamma, k)$, as well as the discounted count of the number of times each client has been selected, denoted as $N_t(\gamma, k)$, up to communication round t. $L_t(\gamma, k)$ and $N_t(\gamma, k)$ can be represented as below:

$$L_t(\gamma, k) = \sum_{t' \in T} \gamma^{t-t'} \mathbb{1}_{\{k \in S(t'-1)\}} \frac{1}{\tau} \sum_{l=t'-\tau+1}^{t'} \sum_{\xi \in \xi_k^{(l)}} \frac{f(w_k^{(l)}, \xi)}{b} \tag{4}$$

$$N_t(\gamma, k) = \sum_{t' \in T} \gamma^{t-t'} \mathbb{1}_{\{k \in S^{(t'-1)}\}} \tag{5}$$

Here, each client $k \in [K]$ at communication round t calculates $L_t(\gamma, k)$ and $N_t(\gamma, k)$. The hyper-parameter $0 \leq \gamma \leq 1$ determines the weight assigned to outdated values. When $\gamma = 1$, all previous local loss samples are equally considered in the calculation of $L_t(\gamma, k)$. Conversely, when $\gamma = 0$, only the most recent local loss is used for estimating $L_t(\gamma, k)$. In each training round, by computing the estimate for the local loss of clients $(L_t(\gamma, k)/N_t(\gamma, k))$, a fixed number of m clients are selected for training. This leads to faster convergence and represents the exploitation part of the exploration-exploitation trade-off in the MAB problem. The exploration part can be represented as below:

$$U_t(\gamma, k) = \sqrt{2\sigma_t^2 \log T_t(\gamma)/N_t(\gamma, k)}, \quad T_t(\gamma) = \sum_{t' \in \mathcal{T}} \gamma^{t-t'} \tag{6}$$

Here, σ is the maximum standard deviation of local loss from the latest client updates. It enlarges $U_t(\gamma, k)$ for clients not recently selected, prompting the MAB algorithm to explore them. This avoids repeatedly choosing high-loss clients, prevents error floors, and ensures fairer client selection over time. The discounted UCB indices $A_t(\gamma, k)$ can be defined as below:

$$A_t(\gamma, k) = p_k(\underbrace{\frac{L_t(\gamma, k)}{N_t(\gamma, k)}}_{\text{exploitation}} + \underbrace{U_t(\gamma, k)}_{\text{exploration}}) \tag{7}$$

Our strategy for MAB-based client selection for FL is derived into two heuristic algorithms with regard to the framework of representative MAB algorithms including UCB and TS:

Algorithm 1. Pseudo code for UCB

```
Input: m, γ, p_k for k ∈ [K]
Output: S^(t)
Initialize: empty sets S^(t) and list A of length K
Global server do
    Receive (1/τb) Σ_{l=t−τ+1}^{t} Σ_{ξ∈ξ_k^(l)} f(w_k^(l), ξ) from clients k ∈ S^(t−1) and calculate A_t(γ, k)
    Update A[k] = A_t(γ, k)
    Get S(t) = {m clients with largest values in A (break ties randomly)}
    Discount elements in A by A = γA
return S^(t)
```

According to Algorithm 2, all α and β are initialized with (1,1) in TS. During the training, the global server calculates each client's average loss and compares it with the median loss of all the clients to check if the client is passed or not which follows the TS algorithm. The α and β are iteratively updated for each client with a reward. In each round, the clients are sampled based on beta distribution and the m clients with the top largest samples are selected as the set for the next round of training. The α and β are discounted with θ respectively.

In TS, $\theta \in (0, 1)$ controls client selection. A larger θ favors clients with above-median loss, while a smaller θ increases the chance of rarely chosen clients by slowing the decay of α and β, thus retaining more historical information. This reflects the exploration–exploitation trade-off in MAB.

Algorithm 2. Pseudo code for TS

Input: m, α, β, θ
Output: $S^{(t)}$
Initialize: $\alpha = 1$, $\beta = 1$, empty set $S^{(t)}$
Global server do
for each round t **do**
  Receive client losses from clients and update parameters:
  for each client k **do**
    if avg_loss$_k$ < median loss$_K$ **then**
      $\alpha_k = \alpha_k + 1$
    else
      $\beta_k = \beta_k + 1$
  end for
  Sample from Beta distribution: $samples = \mathrm{Beta}(\alpha_k, \beta_k)$
  Select top m clients: $S^{(t)} = \{m$ clients with largest $samples\}$
  Discount parameters: $\alpha = \theta\alpha$, $\beta = (1 - \theta)\beta$
end for
return $S^{(t)}$

3.2 Local GD and Local Shuffled SGD

Clients in the FL process get the global model from sever to perform local training with different types of client local updates. In this section local GD and Local shuffled SGD will be introduced since they are used in our strategy. First, here is how the global model is updated:

$$w^t = w^{t-1} + \Delta^{t-1} \tag{8}$$

Local GD. It calculates the per update step size. By calculating the average gradient on the local data and combining it with the learning rate η to determine the direction and magnitude of the parameter updates, the model parameters are gradually optimized. It can be defined as below:

$$\Delta^{t-1} = -\eta \sum_{k=1}^{K} \frac{n_k}{n} \nabla F_k(w^{(t-1)}) \tag{9}$$

The term $\Delta^{(t-1)}$ represents the parameter update step for the k-th client at step $t-1$. Here, η is the learning rate, which controls the size of the parameter update step. n_k denotes the size of the local dataset for the k-th client. The term $\frac{n_k}{n}$ represents the proportion of data from the k-th client relative to the total data, reflecting the contribution of each client in the global update. The gradient of the local loss function at client k for the global model parameters $w^{(t-1)}$ at round $t-1$ is given by $\nabla F_k(w^{(t-1)})$.

Local Shuffled SGD. It is recently proposed in [25]. With the use of local shuffled SGD, clients partition local data into different disjoint components B. The k-th client local dataset is divided into i disjoint mini-batches. Therefore, the local loss at client k can be expressed as $F_k(\mathbf{w}) = \frac{1}{B_k}\sum_{i=1}^{B_k} F_{k,i}(w)$. In each round, the client performs local updates by reviewing all the components randomly which are $\sigma_t^k \sim \text{Unif}(S_B)$ that S_B is the set of all the permutations of the components B and $b \in B$ in each component. Therefore, Δ^{t-1} for local shuffled SGD can be represented as:

$$\Delta^{t-1} = -\eta \sum_{k=1}^{K} \frac{n_k}{n} \frac{1}{B} \sum_{b=1}^{B} \nabla F_{k,\sigma_t^k(b)}(w_k^{(t-1,b)}) \tag{10}$$

Therefore, $w_k^{(t-1,b)}$ in (10) can be calculated as:

$$w_k^{(t-1,b)} = w_k^{(t-1,b-1)} - \eta \nabla F_{k,\sigma_t^k(b)}(w_k^{(t-1,b-1)}) \tag{11}$$

In our strategy, all clients follow FedAvg in the first round, while from the second round onward the MAB algorithm guides differentiated local updates. High-loss clients use local GD for faster optimization and reduced computational cost, while most non-selected clients adopt shuffled SGD to mitigate order bias and improve convergence. As training proceeds, high-loss clients diminish and new ones emerge dynamically due to the different update rules.

4 Experimental Results

We evaluate the proposed MAB-based client selection with Deep Neural Network (DNN) which is a deep multi-layer perception network with two hidden layers trained on a Non-IID partitioned FMNIST and CIFAR-10 dataset. M is set to 100 which means there are 100 clients in this framework. We set $b = 64$, $T = 100$, and $\eta = 0.005$ where η is decayed with a learning rate decay value of 0.99. The experiment environment is set by [26]. All experiments are conducted with one NVIDIA RTX4060ti GPU. The algorithm is implemented by PyTorch. We use the Dirichlet distribution DirK (α) [9] to partition the data across clients where α determines the degree of the data heterogeneity across clients. A smaller α indicates larger data heterogeneity. For the hyper-parameters γ and θ are fine-tuned for the best performance via grid search (Fig. 2).

4.1 Summary of Experiments

Our experiments demonstrate that our proposed strategy can effectively reduce communication costs because it starts to converge in earlier rounds compared to the commonly used unbiased methods. Additionally, it has lower consumption as it fairly selects a subset of clients to participate in training each round. Moreover, it employs different local update strategies for clients who participate and those who do not, which has also been proven to be both effective and necessary.

4.2 Impact of Parameter Settings

We first evaluate the TS and UCB algorithms from MAB in FL training with a total of 100 clients. By modifying the original TS and UCB algorithms, we

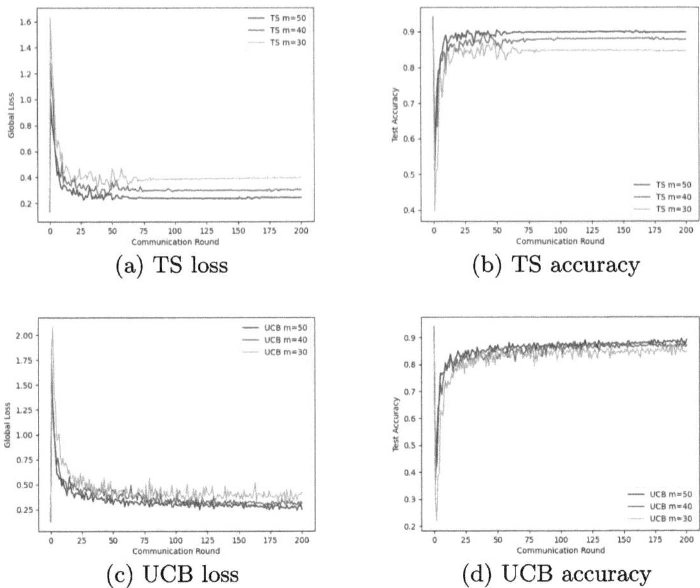

(a) TS loss (b) TS accuracy

(c) UCB loss (d) UCB accuracy

Fig. 2. Global loss and accuracy of TS and UCB with different values of m

achieve a balance between exploration and exploitation. For each round, we select m values of 30, 40, and 50, and plot the global loss and test accuracy. They are presented in Fig. 3.

In Fig. 3, the training loss for image classification on the Non-IID partitioned FMNIST dataset via DNN is presented. The data heterogeneity is set as 0.3 for a quite large value to evaluate the performance of the proposed strategy. With the different amounts of m, the more clients selected for training, the earlier round the global model reaches the convergence. This can be explained by the fact that more clients with the same data volume participate in the training in each round. The diversity and quantity of data involved in the training also increase, enabling the global model to learn more features, thereby reducing the global loss. Apparently, UCB is less affected by the reduction in the number of m and TS can achieve smoother results. TS exhibits better stability and better model performance when the same number of m is set. In fact, TS takes slightly more time per round than that of UCB in the same case.

4.3 Comparison with Unbiased Algorithms

In contrast to random unbiased approach that uses all clients for training such as FedAvg, selecting fewer clients for training in each round will greatly reduce the time required. This is shown in Fig. 3a. We compare the best performance of UCB and TS in $m = 50$ with the common state of arts of unbiased baseline methods to evaluate the difference between biased and unbiased methods. Descriptions of all the methods we compared can be found in Table 1.

Table 1. Overview of Compared Unbiased FL Algorithms

Method	Description
FedAvg [18]	Clients perform several local SGD epochs on their own data, then the server aggregates model updates by simple weighted averaging. Efficient and easy to implement, but may suffer from client drift under heterogeneous data
MOON [13]	Adds a contrastive learning term to each client's local objective, aligning its model with global and previous-round states. Improves representation consistency across clients, especially under Non-IID data
Scaffold [10]	Introduces control variates (variance reduction) on both client and server sides to correct local update bias. Effectively mitigates client drift, but incurs extra storage and communication for the control variates
FedDyn [1]	Augments the local objective with a dynamic regularization term that penalizes deviation from a global "memory" variable. Ensures convergence under heterogeneous data, at the cost of maintaining additional global state on each client

In Fig. 3a, We compare the proposed MAB with the unbiased method FedAvg and other baseline methods in the same data heterogeneity case in FMNIST. Both algorithms' results show that biased client selection strategies achieve higher fairness. The MAB-based client selection method can achieve global model convergence faster or even better with lower communication costs. On the more complex CIFAR-10 dataset, we similarly evaluated against other baseline methods; as shown in Fig. 3b, our algorithm also significantly outperforms the other unbiased methods (Fig. 4).

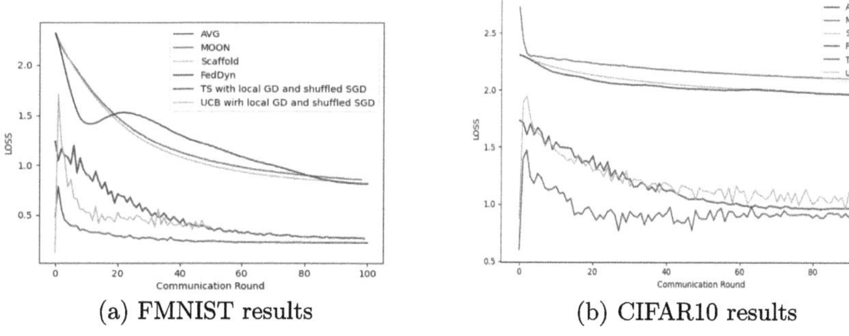

(a) FMNIST results (b) CIFAR10 results

Fig. 3. Comparisons between TS, UCB and other baselines in FMNIST and CIFAR10

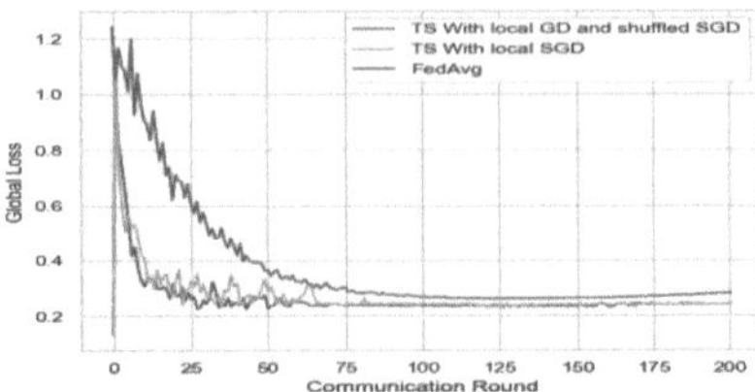

Fig. 4. Comparisons between TS in different updating method with FedAVG in FMNIST

5 Conclusion

We propose an MAB-based client selection strategy in FL, where top-scoring clients update the global model using different local methods. The approach achieves baseline-level accuracy with fewer rounds and lower time cost, and remains robust under heterogeneous data, confirming the feasibility of biased selection to improve fairness and practicality. Future work will extend the strategy to broader scenarios, provide theoretical guarantees, and explore its potential to reduce privacy leakage by lowering communication rounds.

References

1. Acar, D.A.E., Zhao, Y., Matas, R., Mattina, M., Whatmough, P., Saligrama, V.: Federated learning based on dynamic regularization. In: International Conference on Learning Representations (2021). https://openreview.net/forum?id=B7v4QMR6Z9w
2. Chen, G., Wang, M., Han, S., Yin, J., Wang, H., Cao, J.: Deep reinforcement learning-based cloud-edge offloading for wbans. IEEE Trans. Consum. Electron. (2024)
3. Chen, M., Shlezinger, N., Poor, H.V., Eldar, Y.C., Cui, S.: Communication-efficient federated learning. Proc. Natl. Acad. Sci. **118**(17), e2024789118 (2021)
4. Cho, Y.J., Gupta, S., Joshi, G., Yağan, O.: Bandit-based communication-efficient client selection strategies for federated learning. In: 2020 54th Asilomar Conference on Signals, Systems, and Computers, pp. 1066–1069. IEEE (2020)
5. Cho, Y.J., Wang, J., Joshi, G.: Client selection in federated learning: Convergence analysis and power-of-choice selection strategies. arXiv preprint arXiv:2010.01243 (2020)
6. Ge, Y.F., Bertino, E., Wang, H., Cao, J., Zhang, Y.: Distributed cooperative coevolution of data publishing privacy and transparency. ACM Trans. Knowl. Discov. Data **18**(1), 1–23 (2023)
7. Ge, Y.F., Wang, H., Bertino, E., Cao, J., Zhang, Y.: Multiobjective privacy-preserving task assignment in spatial crowdsourcing. IEEE Trans. Cybern. (2025)
8. Ge, Y.F., Wang, H., Bertino, E., Cao, J., Zhang, Y., Zheng, Z.: Distributed bandit-based cooperative coevolution for large-scale multi-objective data publishing. IEEE Trans. Serv. Comput. 1–14 (2025). https://doi.org/10.1109/TSC.2025.3609875
9. Hsu, T.M.H., Qi, H., Brown, M.: Measuring the effects of non-identical data distribution for federated visual classification. arXiv preprint arXiv:1909.06335 (2019)

10. Karimireddy, S.P., Kale, S., Mohri, M., Reddi, S., Stich, S., Suresh, A.T.: Scaffold: stochastic controlled averaging for federated learning. In: International Conference on Machine Learning, pp. 5132–5143. PMLR (2020)
11. Kim, T., Bae, S., Lee, J.w., Yun, S.: Accurate and fast federated learning via combinatorial multi-armed bandits. arXiv preprint arXiv:2012.03270 (2020)
12. Lai, T.L., Robbins, H.: Asymptotically efficient adaptive allocation rules. Adv. Appl. Math. **6**(1), 4–22 (1985)
13. Li, Q., He, B., Song, D.: Model-contrastive federated learning. In: Proceedings of the IEEE/CVF Conference on Computer Vision and Pattern Recognition (CVPR), pp. 10713–10722 (2021)
14. Li, T., Sahu, A.K., Zaheer, M., Sanjabi, M., Talwalkar, A., Smith, V.: Federated optimization in heterogeneous networks. Proc. Mach. Learn. Syst. **2**, 429–450 (2020)
15. Li, X., Huang, K., Yang, W., Wang, S., Zhang, Z.: On the convergence of fedavg on non-iid data. In: International Conference on Learning Representations (2019)
16. Lu, R., et al.: Two-stage client selection for federated learning against free-riding attack: a multi-armed bandits and auction-based approach. IEEE Internet Things J. (2024)
17. Luping, W., Wei, W., Bo, L.: Cmfl: mitigating communication overhead for federated learning. In: 2019 IEEE 39th International Conference on Distributed Computing Systems (ICDCS), pp. 954–964. IEEE (2019)
18. McMahan, B., Moore, E., Ramage, D., Hampson, S., y Arcas, B.A.: Communication-efficient learning of deep networks from decentralized data. In: Artificial Intelligence and Statistics, pp. 1273–1282. PMLR (2017)
19. Ning, D., Ge, Y.F., Wang, H., Zhou, C.: Cadif-osn: detecting cloned accounts with missing profile attributes on online social networks. In: Proceedings of the 33rd ACM International Conference on Information and Knowledge Management, pp. 1795–1803 (2024)
20. Saday, A., Demirel, İ., Yıldırım, Y., Tekin, C.: Federated multi-armed bandits under byzantine attacks. IEEE Trans. Artif. Intell. (2025)
21. Wang, H., Kaplan, Z., Niu, D., Li, B.: Optimizing federated learning on non-iid data with reinforcement learning. In: IEEE INFOCOM 2020-IEEE Conference on Computer Communications, pp. 1698–1707. IEEE (2020)
22. Wu, H., Wang, P.: Node selection toward faster convergence for federated learning on non-iid data. IEEE Trans. Netw. Sci. Eng. **9**(5), 3099–3111 (2022)
23. Xia, W., Quek, T.Q., Guo, K., Wen, W., Yang, H.H., Zhu, H.: Multi-armed bandit-based client scheduling for federated learning. IEEE Trans. Wirel. Commun. **19**(11), 7108–7123 (2020)
24. You, M., Ge, Y.F., Wang, K., Wang, H., Cao, J., Kambourakis, G.: Hierarchical adaptive evolution framework for privacy-preserving data publishing. World Wide Web **27**(4), 49 (2024)
25. Yun, C., Rajput, S., Sra, S.: Minibatch vs local sgd with shuffling: tight convergence bounds and beyond. In: 10th International Conference on Learning Representations, ICLR 2022. International Conference on Learning Representations (ICLR) (2022)
26. Zhang, J., et al.: Pfllib: personalized federated learning algorithm library. CoRR (2023)
27. Zhu, K., Zhang, F., Jiao, L., Xue, B., Zhang, L.: Client selection for federated learning using combinatorial multi-armed bandit under long-term energy constraint. Comput. Netw. **250**, 110512 (2024)

Hybrid Adaptive Resonance Theory Model for Online Noisy Data Classification

Michael Shi[1], Jiao Yin[1(✉)], Hua Wang[1], Chee Peng Lim[2], Jinli Cao[3], and Zhonglong Zheng[4]

[1] Institute for Sustainable Industries & Liveable Cities, Victoria University, Melbourne 3011, Australia
michael.shi@live.vu.edu.au, {jiao.yin,hua.wang}@vu.edu.au
[2] Swinburne University of Technology, Hawthorn 3122, Australia
cplim@swin.edu.au
[3] Department of Computer Science and Information Technology, La Trobe University, Melbourne 3086, Australia
j.cao@latrobe.edu.au
[4] School of Computer Science and Technology, Zhejiang Normal University, Jinhua 321004, China
zhonglong@zjnu.edu.cn

Abstract. In many real-world environments, data samples arrive as continuous streams, and they often contain noise. In this study, we aim to undertake noisy data classification in an online learning setting using a hybrid supervised Adaptive Resonance Theory (ART) neural network model. Specifically, Fuzzy ARTMAP (FAM) is a neural network that is capable of learning new categories incrementally by creating or updating prototype patterns whenever an input is similar enough, subject to a threshold to decide when to form a new category. In view of FAM's ability in tackling the stability-plasticity dilemma, it is utilised as a baseline model for developing a robust classifier with online learning capability for noisy data classification. We equip FAM with pre-processing and post-processing modules to improve its robustness in combating noise in data samples and enhance its online classification performance. On the one hand, the pre-processing feature extraction module exploits the capability of a feedforward neural network to enhance feature representation capabilities. On the other hand, the post-processing module leverages an ensemble structure with majority voting for minimizing classification errors in the presence of noisy data. Evaluated on benchmark noisy datasets, the hybrid FAM model outperforms the base FAM and other variants, offering a robust online learning model for solving noisy classification problems in data streaming environments. The source code can be obtained from https://github.com/Michael-cyber123/eNeuralFAM.

Keywords: Fuzzy ARTMAP · Online Learning · Noisy Data · Ensemble Learning · Feature Extraction

I. Awan et al. (Eds.): WISE 2025, LNCS 16367, pp. 42–60, 2026.
https://doi.org/10.1007/978-981-95-7394-3_4

1 Introduction

In many real-world classification tasks, data streams arrive continuously and often contain substantial noise, posing significant challenges for machine learning models with online or incremental learning capabilities [16,45]. In medical imaging, label noise frequently arises due to inter-observer variability, where different specialists may interpret the same image differently, resulting in inconsistent annotations [16,23]. Real deployments must contend with privacy-utility constraints [10,11], edge computing limits in healthcare wearables [4], and noisy, non-stationary EEG streams [37].

Conventional machine learning models, e.g., back-propagation neural networks, support vector machines, decision trees, and k-nearest neighbours, typically need to revisit the entire dataset whenever new data streams appear, not to mention the challenge of overfitting or catastrophic forgetting [28,34,41].

Despite the impressive performance of modern supervised deep learning algorithms, a number of critical limitations hinder their deployment in real-time, continuously evolving data streaming environments [43]. Fuzzy ARTMAP (FAM) has drawn considerable attention for its inherent capacity for online learning, for example, the work in [36] introduced a voting-based combination of multiple FAM models, where classifiers trained on different sample sequences were aggregated via a sum-rule voting strategy. The ensemble method significantly improved fault diagnosis performance by mitigating the effects of sample order dependency. Extending these ensemble strategies, an FAM ensemble model that fuses classifier outputs through an improved Bayesian belief method [15]. By considering both classifier outputs and historical reliability, their approach achieved notably better classification performance than that of standalone FAM models. While supervised learning typically delivers superior performances, it entails certain challenges:

Offline Learning Paradigm. Most machine/deep-learning models learn in an offline manner, requiring re-training on the entire dataset whenever new data samples arrive, precluding true online learning and adaptation capability akin to the learning characteristics of the human brain [34].

Hyperparameter Complexity. State-of-the-art deep learning architectures often possess thousands to millions of hyperparameter combinations, e.g., learning rates, layer sizes, regularization coefficients, etc., demanding extensive search and/or expert knowledge in hyperparameter tuning. Inappropriate architecture configurations or parameter settings lead to compromised performances, particularly in online, noisy data learning environments [27].

Stability-Plasticity Trade-Off. Online learning models typically suffer from either *catastrophic forgetting* (overwriting past knowledge) or *stagnation* (resisting new information), reflecting the stability-plasticity dilemma [18], i.e., how a learning model could absorb information/knowledge from incoming data streams incrementally (plastic) while preserving already learned information/knowledge from corruption (stable).

Motivated by these challenges, we introduce a hybrid framework that leverages Adaptive Resonance Theory (ART) and its family of incremental learning models to address these gaps. Specifically, ARTMAP (Adaptive Resonance Theory Map) is a neural network designed specifically for incremental learning and supervised classification tasks. In particular, the Fuzzy ARTMAP (FAM) model—grounded in ART and fuzzy logic—provides a foundational architecture for developing data-driven, online learning systems. It learns the incoming data samples in a single pass and dynamically adjusts its learned prototypes captured in the weights. Here, we leverage FAM's ability to handle noisy, sequential data streams both on its own and when paired with two modules: (i) lightweight feature extractors (neural embeddings or random projections) in the pre-processing stage; and (ii) a majority-voting ensemble structure in the post-processing stage. To evaluate the effectiveness of the developed hybrid FAM model, a series of empirical evaluations using benchmark datasets with varying noise levels are conducted. The results are compared with those from the baseline FAM model and its variants, along with statistical measures. The findings demonstrate that the hybrid FAM model consistently enhances robustness and strikes an effective balance between plasticity and stability in handling online noisy data classification tasks. The contributions of our research are summarized as follows:

Incremental Knowledge Acquisition. We propose an innovative hybrid framework that employs an artificial neural network (ANN) for nonlinear feature extraction and FAM to tackle noise in data streaming environments.

Minimal Hyperparameter Overhead. The proposed framework has a parsimonious architecture with only two key parameters, i.e., learning rate (β) and vigilance (ρ) of FAM, dramatically reducing tuning complexity as compared with deep learning networks [3].

Noisy Data Classification Capabilities. The proposed framework works as a robust classifier in the presence of noisy data streams, with pre-processing and post-processing modules for enhancing feature representation and minimizing classification errors [12].

The rest of the paper is organised as follows. Section 2 presents related studies on online learning models and background on ART. Section 3 details our methodology, including the pre-processing feature extractors and the post-processing ensemble voting structure. Section 4 describes datasets, experimental setup, results, and comparisons. Section 5 concludes this study and outlines avenues for future work.

2 Related Studies and Background

2.1 Online Learning

Many classification models, such as deep neural networks, are trained in a batch setting, which requires access to the entire dataset upfront and are unable to learn new samples without full retraining [34]. As dataset sizes continue to grow, this process becomes both time- and memory-intensive. To better reflect humans' perpetual learning characteristics and real-world scenarios in which data streams arrive continuously, online or incremental learning models have been proposed to tackle the challenge. These methods update model parameters with one data sample (or a small stream of data samples) at a time while preserving previously learned knowledge [28].

A "minimal definition" for an online learner stipulates that it must [28]:

1. Learn exclusively from new data streams without reprocessing old data samples.
2. Retain existing knowledge while acquiring new knowledge.
3. Automatically detect and incorporate novel knowledge.
4. Operate without prior access to the full data distribution.

Although many algorithms satisfy the first three requirements, reliably identifying and updating entire knowledge bases within their architectures without suffering from the stability-plasticity dilemma remains a significant challenge in practice.

At its core, online learning seeks to balance stability, the retention of previously learned knowledge, with plasticity, the ability to assimilate novel knowledge. Early efforts in online learning focused on augmenting classical, offline learners. For example, support vector machines were adapted to update only a subset of support vectors or Karush-Kuhn-Tucker constraints when new samples or classes appeared, yielding algorithms such as MSVMIL [31] and VSVM [5]. These models achieve fast, per-sample updates with theoretical convergence guarantees. Beyond the classic Perceptron and Winnow algorithms [22,30], modern online learning frameworks employ update rules that carefully balance stability and plasticity. Specifically, passive-aggressive methods [6] apply margin-based corrections, aggressively updating weights only when errors occur.

Confidence-weighted learning methods [7] maintain a Gaussian distribution over each weight, adjusting both its mean and variance so that new samples meet a prescribed confidence threshold. Truncated gradient learning approaches [6] augment standard gradient steps with a shrinkage operation that drives small weights toward zero, yielding sparse solutions ideal for high-dimensional streams. To capture non-linear boundaries in a data streaming setting, a broad family of kernel-based online learners extends traditional linear updates into the Hilbert Space [8]. These include Kernelized Perceptron [8], which replaces the inner product with a kernel function, and a Kernelized Online Gradient Descent [19] method, which applies stochastic gradient steps in the Hilbert Space under a convex loss. Handling domain shift and temporal adaptation has been studied in vision under open-vocabulary and time-varying conditions [20], reinforcing the need for feature extractors that generalize across evolving data regimes in streaming settings.

While those methods assume a full label is available for every data sample, another core strand of online learning models operates on feedback signals. Bandit learning [39] tackles sequential prediction under partial feedback. At each round, the learner picks one of K "arms" and only observes that arm's reward (or loss), never the others. The core challenge is balancing exploration (trying out uncertain arms) and exploitation (sticking with arms known to perform well). By carefully balancing these forces, bandit algorithms provably bound their cumulative regret—the gap between actual performance and that of the single best action in hindsight [39]. Other early stochastic strategies include ϵ-greedy [35], which occasionally conducts the search at random, and Upper Confidence Bound (UCB) [1], which optimistically picks the arm with the highest confidence bound.

Decision trees have also been adapted for learning data streams via the Hoeffding bound [24]. The Hoeffding Tree [24] grows and splits nodes on the fly with statistical guarantees. Its extensions, such as Online Random Forests [32] and Extremely Fast Decision Trees [25], further enhance accuracy and parallelism [24]. Decision-tree ensemble models like CIRF [13] and hi-RF [42] avoid rebuilding entire forests by inserting or replacing nodes and subtrees incrementally, thereby preserving most of the original model while adapting to new class distributions. Other ensemble schemes, such as online bagging and boosting [26], aggregate multiple weak learners trained on reweighted or resampled data streams to reduce variance and bias.

Building on these traditional learners, the rise of deep neural architectures has enabled hybrid approaches that integrate neural networks with incremental learning strategies [44,46]. Deep learning-based methods tackle catastrophic forgetting by freezing or regularizing parts of the network, e.g., locking the final fully-connected layer or penalizing changes to weights tied to previous tasks [33]. Exemplar-based strategies such as iCaRL [29] maintain a small memory of real samples to rehearse past classes, while balanced fine-tuning methods mitigate class-imbalance when adding new categories. However, these approaches generally still rely on substantial offline training at each update and assume that the old-class distribution remains stable [21].

Among different online learning methodologies, ART has inspired prototype-driven incremental learning paradigms. In rule-based ART clustering [9], each new data sample either resonates with an existing rule or ignites a fresh prototype—an approach to tackle noise and avoid guessing cluster counts (though it can spawn too many rules in high dimensions). Its Bayesian counterpart [40] adds priors over each prototype and performs posterior updates of means and covariances, giving structured, uncertainty-aware clusters but demanding more computation and careful prior choice.

2.2 Fuzzy Theory and Adaptive Resonance Theory

FAM is a neural network architecture designed for stable, incremental supervised learning, capable of adapting to new data without catastrophic forgetting. It is a supervised ART model that combines two unsupervised ART modules, ART_a and ART_b, with a map field for label prediction and match tracking [3]. Figure 1 depicts the overall FAM architecture.

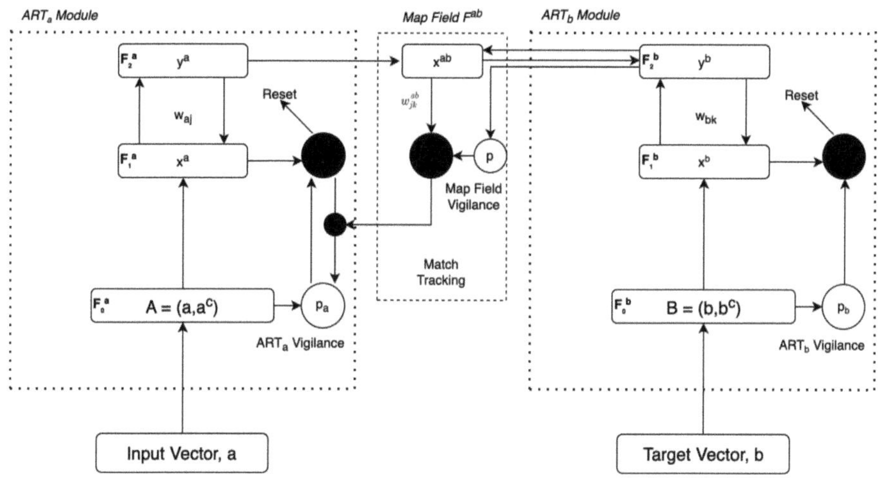

Fig. 1. Overview of the Fuzzy ARTMAP architecture, consisting of two ART modules (ART_a and ART_b) connected through an inter-ART map field for supervised learning and match tracking.

The ART_a module transforms an input vector $\mathbf{a} \in [0,1]^M$ into a $2M$-dimensional complement-coded representation, $\mathbf{A} = (\mathbf{a}, \mathbf{a}^c) = (a_1, a_2, \ldots, a_M, 1 - a_1, 1 - a_2, \ldots, 1 - a_M)$. This ensures that both the presence and absence of features are encoded, preserving constant magnitude, as shown in Eq. (1).

$$|\mathbf{A}| = \sum_{i=1}^{M} a_i + \left(M - \sum_{i=1}^{M} a_i \right) = M \tag{1}$$

Each new category node is initialized with a weight vector of ones, as shown in Eq. (2).

$$\mathbf{w}_j^{(0)} = \mathbf{1} \tag{2}$$

Upon presentation of an input sample, prototype nodes compete based on a category choice function, which measures the fuzzy subsethood degree between the input and each category prototype, as shown in Eq. (3).

$$T_j(\mathbf{A}) = \frac{|\mathbf{A} \wedge \mathbf{w}_j|}{\alpha + |\mathbf{w}_j|}, \tag{3}$$

where $\alpha > 0$ is a small positive constant and $\wedge$ denotes the component-wise fuzzy MIN operator. The best-matched category prototype is declared as a winning node.

The winner then undergoes a vigilance test, as shown in Eq. (4).

$$\frac{|\mathbf{A} \wedge \mathbf{w}_J|}{|\mathbf{A}|} \geq \rho \tag{4}$$

where ρ is the vigilance parameter. If the test is passed, resonance occurs and learning takes place to update the winning prototype, as shown in Eq. (5).

$$\mathbf{w}_j^{\text{new}} = \beta(\mathbf{A} \wedge \mathbf{w}_j^{\text{old}}) + (1 - \beta)\mathbf{w}_j^{\text{old}} \tag{5}$$

If all the prototypes are unable to satisfy the vigilance test, a new node is created. This is the dynamic learning principle of ART that solves the stability-plasticity dilemma. Simultaneously, the ART$_b$ module mirrors the learning process with the target output.

After resonance, the winning category node in ART$_a$ predicts a class label via the map field. If the prediction is incorrect, *match tracking* is triggered, dynamically raising ρ just above the current match level, as shown in Eq. (6).

$$\rho_a = \frac{|\mathbf{A} \wedge \mathbf{w}_j|}{|\mathbf{A}|} + \epsilon \tag{6}$$

where ϵ is a small positive constant. This causes the winning category node to fail the vigilance test, initiating a new search cycle for a more precise category match to improve the prediction. In parallel, explainable modelling grounded in cognitive learning theories has advanced in adjacent domains [14], aligning with ART's cognitive roots and motivating hybrid designs that remain interpretable under drift.

3 Methodology

3.1 Feature Extractor for FAM

To enhance FAM, we devise a pre-processing feature extractor to minimise the effects of noisy input data. Two pre-processing methods for feature representation are developed in this study. The first is to exploit an ANN to learn a compact "feature layer". After training the ANN on a small data stream, we discard its final prediction layer and extract the activations of the hidden layer as the low-dimensional embeddings [27]. The second is to use a Random Projection (RP) scheme, where each input sample is multiplied by a random weight matrix to collapse the original feature space into a small set of dimensions in one shot. Both embeddings are then normalised and fed into FAM for online learning.

3.1.1 ANN as the Feature Extractor

The ANN is first trained on an initial data partition to learn a compact and discriminative feature space. Extracted features are subsequently used as input samples to train FAM incrementally, leading to an ANN+FAM model. As new data samples are introduced, the ANN continues to refine its feature extraction capabilities, while FAM incrementally adapts its categories based on the transformed features from the ANN. By shifting FAM's inputs from raw, noisy high-dimensional vectors into learned, lower-dimensional embeddings, the ANN, as a feature extractor, smooths out variability and suppresses noise-induced fluctuations, mitigating FAM's inherent sensitivity to noisy samples and producing more stable category formation during online learning. The overall hybrid ANN+FAM operation pipeline is depicted in Fig. 2. Our use of compact ANN embeddings is consistent with evidence that temporally adaptive, domain-generalized features can sustain performance under evolving distributions [20].

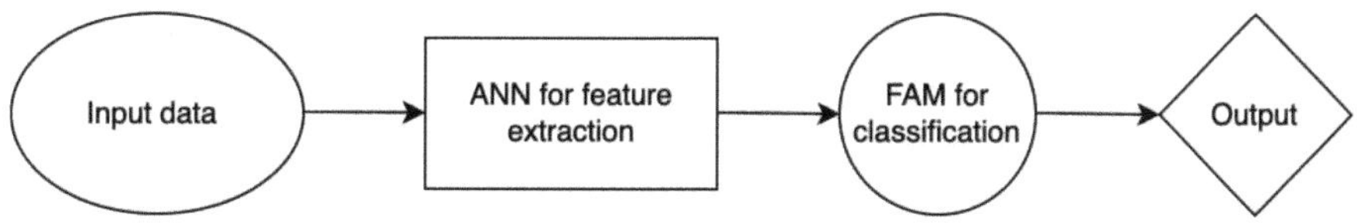

Fig. 2. Features extracted from the ANN hidden layer are fed as inputs to FAM for incremental classification.

3.1.2 Random Projection as the Feature Extractor

RP is used as another feature extractor for FAM, forming an RP+FAM model. RP overcomes issues related to high-dimensional and noisy data. Instead of computing expensive matrix decompositions, a single random matrix is formed, as shown in Eq. (7).

$$\mathbf{R} \in \mathbb{R}^{D\times k}, \quad R_{ij} \sim \mathcal{N}(0, \tfrac{1}{k}), \tag{7}$$

where D is the original feature dimension and $k \ll D$ is the target (reduced) dimension [2]. Each D-dimensional input $\mathbf{x} \in \mathbb{R}^D$ is then mapped to an k-dimensional vector, as shown in Eq. (8).

$$\mathbf{z} = \mathbf{x}\mathbf{R} \quad \in \mathbb{R}^k. \tag{8}$$

Since $\mathbf{R}$ is sampled once (with its Gaussian entries) and then reused, every new data sample is handled with the same transform. As such, no retraining or costly re-computation is required [17].

Besides, the Johnson-Lindenstrauss lemma [2] ensures that, with high probability, the pairwise distances in the original D-dimensional space are preserved within a small relative error after projection into a k-dimensional subspace.

The principle of RP can be explained with Fig. 3. The left panel shows data samples in the original D-dimensional space, with a dashed line indicating the distance d between two samples. The middle arrow denotes multiplication by a fixed random matrix $\mathbf{R} \in \mathbb{R}^{D\times k}$, mapping each D-vector into an k-dimensional subspace. The right panel illustrates the projected data samples lying on a k-dimensional "flat" where the same two data samples have a new distance $d + \Delta$ (a small distortion) [17]. This highlights how RP compresses high-dimensional data while approximately preserving pairwise distances.

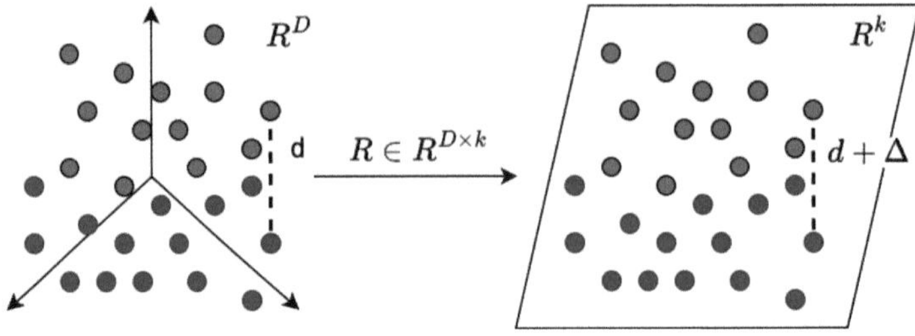

Fig. 3. Schematic of Random Incremental Projection.

3.2 Ensemble Learning

To improve classification performance as well as reduce the risks of overfitting or instability during online updates, an ensemble model with the majority voting strategy is employed. Three independent instances of the hybrid FAM model (i.e., ANN+FAM or RP+FAM) are initialised with identical architectures. Each model independently processes a chunk of data streams with different sequences, learning its own feature transformations and category mappings. During inference, predictions from all three FAM-based models are aggregated using majority voting to produce the final output [26]. This ensemble scheme reduces individual model variance, stabilizes predictions, and offers enhanced robustness against errors that may occur during online learning, particularly in the presence of noisy data. The ensemble ANN+FAM operation pipeline is shown in Fig. 4.

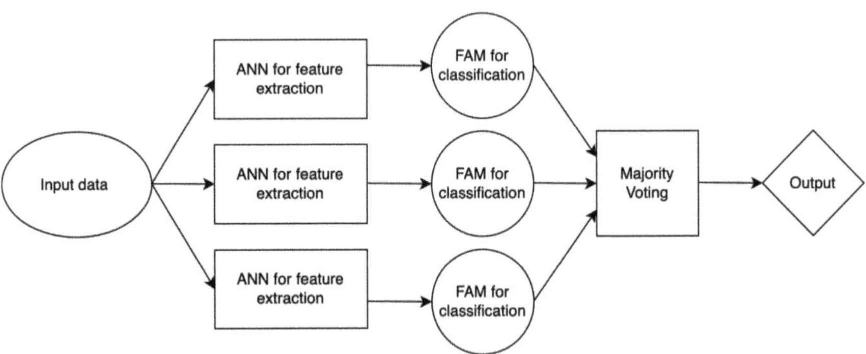

Fig. 4. An ensemble operation pipeline consisting of three hybrid ANN+FAM models that produce independent predictions for aggregation with majority voting.

The overall procedure for the proposed ensemble ANN+FAM model framework is outlined in Algorithm 1. Lines 3–9 perform the initial training of all ANN and FAM models using the first data sample, where feature extractors are established and normalised. Lines 10–24 describe the online learning phase: each new data sample is first used for making predictions (Lines 11–17), and then for incrementally updating the ANN and FAM models (Lines 18–23).

4 Experiments

4.1 Datasets

We evaluated the hybrid FAM-based model on two benchmark noisy binary classification datasets, i.e., Twonorm and Ringnorm. All datasets were sourced from the KEEL repository [38], and more detailed information is presented in Table 1. To assess robustness to corrupted inputs due to noise, we leveraged the KEEL repository's pre-generated noise variants at nominal levels $x \in \{5, 10, 15, 20\}\%$ alongside the original, noise-free data. In each noisy data version (e.g., 10% noise), the corresponding percentages of input features (i.e., 10%) were randomly selected. For each chosen sample and each feature A, it is replaced with an independently drawn value from the uniform distribution on $[\min(A), \max(A)]$ [38].

Table 1. Summary of datasets used in this study

Dataset	Type	Samples	Features	Description
Twonorm	Synthetic	7400	20	Samples drawn from two overlapping Gaussian distributions for binary classification.
Ringnorm	Synthetic	7400	20	Complex ring-shaped distributions requiring non-linear decision boundaries.

Algorithm 1. Pseudocode of the proposed ANN + FAM ensemble model framework

Input: Data stream $\mathcal{D} = \{(X_0, y_0), (X_1, y_1), \ldots, (X_n, y_n)\}$; number of models M
Output: Predicted labels $\{\hat{y}_1, \hat{y}_2, \ldots, \hat{y}_n\}$
Standardize X_0 to obtain X_0^{scaled}
for $m = 1$ to M **do**
  Train ANN$^{(m)}$ using $(X_0^{\text{scaled}}, y_0)$
  Extract features $F_0^{(m)}$ from ANN$^{(m)}$
  Normalize $F_0^{(m)}$
  Train FAM$^{(m)}$ using $(F_0^{(m)}, y_0)$
end for
for $i = 1$ to n **do**
  Standardize X_i to get X_i^{scaled}
  for $m = 1$ to M **do**
    Extract features $F_i^{(m)}$ from ANN$^{(m)}$
    Normalize $F_i^{(m)}$
    $\hat{y}_i^{(m)} \leftarrow$ FAM$^{(m)}$ prediction from $F_i^{(m)}$
  end for
  $\hat{y}_i \leftarrow \text{MajorityVote}(\hat{y}_i^{(1)}, \ldots, \hat{y}_i^{(M)})$
  Evaluate $\hat{y}_i$ with y_i
  for $m = 1$ to M **do**
    Update ANN$^{(m)}$ with $(X_i^{\text{scaled}}, y_i)$
    Re-extract and normalize $F_i^{(m)}$
    Update FAM$^{(m)}$ with $(F_i^{(m)}, y_i)$
  end for
end for

4.2 Parameter Settings

A total of ten independent runs were conducted. All models were instantiated with fixed hyperparameters and architectures, and each experimental run used the same random seeds for data shuffling, weight initialisation, and projection matrix sampling. Reported metrics are aggregated over ten independent runs and expressed as "mean±Std." The ANN accepts the raw feature vectors as its inputs, passes them through two dense hidden layers of 64 and 32 units (ReLU activations), and produces a four-dimensional feature embedding via a ReLU "feature" layer. A final sigmoid output head (unused for feature extraction) is appended for compatibility during initial training. The model is trained for 20 epochs with batch size 32, optimised by Adam (learning rate 10^{-3}, $\beta_1 = 0.9$, $\beta_2 = 0.999$) using binary-cross-entropy loss. All weights were initialised with the Glorot uniform scheme.

Each resulting dataset was stratified, shuffled, and split into ten equal folds to simulate a data stream with ten sequential data folds. The first fold of data samples was reserved for initial model training, while Folds 1–9 were evaluated sequentially in an online fashion, first for testing, then immediately for online model update. Raw features were first standardised to zero mean and unit variance using a `StandardScaler`, ensuring that each feature contributes equally regardless of its original scale. Subsequently, the input features were scaled into the $[0, 1]$ interval with a `MinMaxScaler`, facilitating complement coding and fuzzy-MIN operations in FAM. We reported four performance metrics to evaluate the classifiers: accuracy, precision, recall (sensitivity), and the F_1-score (the harmonic mean of precision and recall).

To match the ANN's embedding dimensionality, the raw features were reduced to four dimensions via an incremental RP technique. The projection matrix was drawn at initialisation from a zero-mean Gaussian distribution with variance 1/output_dim (i.e. $\mathcal{N}(0, 1/4)$). No further training was performed on the projected features. FAM operated in the fast-learning mode with learning rate $\beta = 1.0$ and vigilance parameter $\rho = 0.0$. Inputs to FAM are first min-max scaled to $[0, 1]$ and complement-coded. During online evaluation, FAM is incrementally updated on each new fold following feature extraction with the ANN or RP methods. All experiments were implemented in Python 3.12 and executed on a MacBook Pro equipped with an Apple M3 chip and 8 GB of RAM, running macOS Sonoma 14.0.

4.3 Feature Extraction Performance

In this section, we evaluate the ANN as a feature extractor, comparing it against the baseline FAM and the RP+FAM variant. As shown in Fig. 5, using the ANN to preprocess features consistently boosts FAM performance across both benchmark datasets Twonorm and Ringnorm from 0% to 20% noise. To quantify the impact of feature extraction, we performed a stepwise removal of model components and evaluated performance on Twonorm and Ringnorm benchmark datasets. On Twonorm, ANN+FAM reaches 94.7% ± 3.3 at 0% noise, compared with 78.5% ± 0.6 for FAM (RP+FAM: 67.5% ± 8.1). At 10% noise, ANN+FAM still attains 89.5% ± 3.6, while FAM drops to 63.6% ± 0.9 (RP+FAM: 58.0%

± 6.6). Even at 20% noise, ANN+FAM preserves 81.1% ± 4.2, versus 58.9% ± 0.9 for FAM (RP+FAM: 56.5% ± 3.5). On Ringnorm, ANN+FAM achieves 94.9% ± 1.0 at 0% noise, outperforming FAM at 83.0% ± 1.7 (RP+FAM: 67.1% ± 1.3). At 10% noise, ANN+FAM maintains 69.0% ± 14.3, while FAM falls to 61.2% ± 2.0 (RP+FAM: 56.1% ± 1.2). At 20% noise, ANN+FAM still yields 62.9% ± 3.1 compared with 55.5% ± 1.3 for FAM (RP+FAM: 52.5% ± 0.8). Table 2 summarizes the single-model results, while Table 3 reports the ensemble ANN+FAM model. Overall, ANN-based feature extraction consistently raises the F_1-score across all noise levels on both datasets.

Table 2. F_1-score for single models on Twonorm and Ringnorm at different noise levels (mean ± standard deviation).

Dataset	Model	0% Noise	5% Noise	10% Noise	15% Noise	20% Noise
Twonorm	FAM	0.785 ± 0.006	0.683 ± 0.014	0.636 ± 0.009	0.609 ± 0.013	0.589 ± 0.009
	RP + FAM	0.675 ± 0.081	0.596 ± 0.078	0.580 ± 0.066	0.576 ± 0.043	0.565 ± 0.035
	ANN + FAM	$\mathbf{0.947 \pm 0.033}$	$\mathbf{0.933 \pm 0.026}$	$\mathbf{0.895 \pm 0.036}$	$\mathbf{0.833 \pm 0.117}$	$\mathbf{0.811 \pm 0.042}$
Ringnorm	FAM	0.830 ± 0.017	0.669 ± 0.030	0.612 ± 0.020	0.574 ± 0.014	0.555 ± 0.013
	RP + FAM	0.671 ± 0.013	0.585 ± 0.012	0.561 ± 0.012	0.540 ± 0.007	0.525 ± 0.008
	ANN + FAM	$\mathbf{0.949 \pm 0.010}$	$\mathbf{0.802 \pm 0.023}$	$\mathbf{0.690 \pm 0.143}$	$\mathbf{0.656 \pm 0.048}$	$\mathbf{0.629 \pm 0.031}$

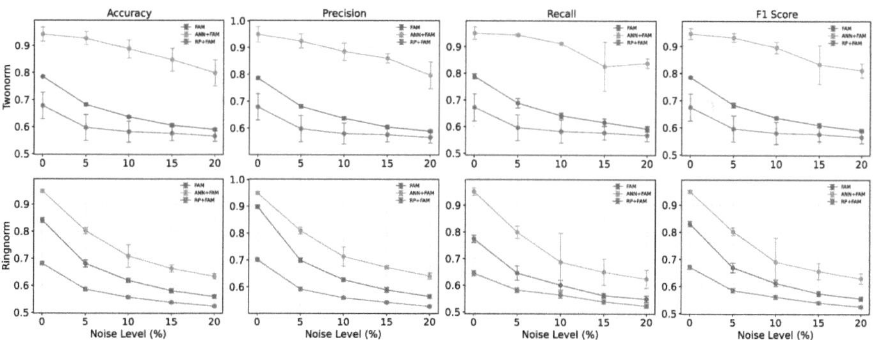

Fig. 5. Performance metrics (Accuracy, Precision, Recall, and F1-score) for single models on Twonorm and Ringnorm datasets across varying noise levels (0%, 5%, 10%, 15%, and 20%).

4.4 Ensemble Learning Performance

In this section, we focus primarily on the relative gains achieved by the ensemble ANN+FAM model over its single-model counterpart. Figure 6 summarizes the online learning results of FAM-based ensemble models with varying noise levels (0%, 5%, 10%, 15%, and 20%). For both benchmark datasets, the ensemble ANN+FAM model not only achieved the highest mean F_1-score but also consistently produced substantially tighter confidence intervals (plotted as error bars) than those from its single-model counterpart, ANN+FAM.

When comparing ensemble models in Table 3 with single models in Table 2, we observe consistent improvements in F_1-score at every noise level. Under no noise, the FAM ensemble model attains 83.4% ± 0.5% on Twonorm and 88.4% ± 0.7% on Ringnorm—each substantially higher than the single FAM model scores of 78.5% ± 0.6% and 83.0% ± 1.7%, respectively. Under moderate noise (10%), the FAM ensemble model achieves 68.3% ± 1.1% and 64.7% ± 1.1% on Twonorm and Ringnorm, compared to single FAM model scores of 63.6% ± 0.9% and 61.2% ± 2.0%, respectively.

At 15% noise, the benefit of ensembling becomes clear on both datasets. On Twonorm, the single ANN+FAM model achieves 83.3% ± 11.7, compared with 60.9% ± 1.3 for the baseline FAM model. By contrast, the ensemble ANN+FAM model reaches 88.0% ± 0.6, while the FAM ensemble attains 64.6% ± 1.1. On Ringnorm, the single ANN+FAM model records 65.6% ± 4.8 against 57.4% ± 1.4 for the baseline FAM model. The ensemble ANN+FAM model improves this to 71.3% ± 0.5, while the FAM ensemble achieves 60.8% ± 1.0. These comparisons show that ensemble voting not only raises mean F_1-scores but also substantially reduces variance relative to the single-model results. At extreme noise (20%), the FAM ensemble model gains become marginal.

On the synthetic Twonorm benchmark, the ensemble ANN+FAM model demonstrated clear superiority under both noise-free and noisy conditions. Without any noise, the ensemble ANN+FAM model achieved accuracy of 97.1 % ± 0.2 % and an F_1-score of 97.0 % ± 0.2 %. By comparison, the single ANN+FAM model reached 94.3 % ± 4.2 % accuracy and 94.7 % ± 3.3 % F_1-score, while the baseline single FAM model and the RP+FAM variant attained only 78.5 % ± 0.6 % versus 67.8 % ± 7.9 % accuracy (78.5 % ± 0.6 % versus 67.5 % ± 8.1 % F_1-score), respectively.

When noise was increased to 10 %, all methods declined predictably, yet the ensemble ANN+FAM model remained remarkably robust at 91.4 % ± 0.23 % accuracy and 91.4 % ± 0.2 % F_1-score. In contrast, the single ANN+FAM model fell to 88.8 % ± 5.5 % accuracy and 89.5 % ± 3.6 % F_1-score. The baseline FAM model dropped to 63.7 % ± 0.8 % accuracy and 63.6 % ± 0.9 % F_1-score, while the RP+FAM model declined to 58.2 % ± 6.4 % accuracy and 58.0 % ± 6.6 % F_1-score.

Even under extreme noise corruption (20 %), the ensemble ANN+FAM model preserved 85.1 % ± 0.4 % accuracy and 85.1 % ± 0.4 % F_1-score, as compared with the single ANN+FAM model, which achieved 79.9 % ± 7.8 % accuracy and 81.1 % ± 4.2 % F_1-score. The baseline FAM model fell further to 59.0 % ± 0.8 % accuracy and 58.9 % ± 0.9 % F_1-score, while the RP+FAM model achieved 56.6 % ± 3.3 % accuracy and 56.5 % ± 3.5 % F_1-score.

Precision and recall metrics exhibited similar trends. In the absence of noise, the ensemble ANN+FAM model delivered 97.1 % ± 0.3 % precision and 97.0 % ± 0.3 % recall, while the single ANN+FAM model achieved 95.0 % ± 4.6 % precision and 95.2 % ± 3.8 % recall. At 20 % noise, the ensemble ANN+FAM model maintained 84.9 % ± 0.5 % precision and 85.3 % ± 0.9 % recall, whereas single ANN+FAM model recorded 79.7 % ± 8.1 % precision and 83.8 % ± 2.9 % recall.

Similarly, on the Ringnorm dataset, in the absence of noise (0%), the ensemble ANN+FAM model achieved 95.8% ± 0.4% accuracy and 95.9% ± 0.4% F_1-score. By contrast, the single ANN+FAM model reached 94.9% ± 1.0% accuracy and 94.9% ± 1.0% F_1-score, while the baseline FAM model recorded 84.1% ± 1.4% accuracy and 83.0% ± 1.7% F_1-score. The RP+FAM variant trailed at 68.2% ± 1.1% accuracy and 67.1% ± 0.8% F_1-score.

Under moderate noise corruption (10%), the ensemble ANN+FAM model maintained 76.1% ± 1.3% accuracy and 75.9% ± 1.8% F_1-score, whereas single ANN+FAM model fell to 70.9% ± 6.8% accuracy and 69.0% ± 14.3% F_1-score. The baseline FAM ensemble model achieved 66.0% ± 1.1% accuracy and 64.7% ± 1.1% F_1-score, as compared with 61.9% ± 1.3% accuracy and 61.2% ± 2.0% F_1-score for the baseline single FAM model and 55.7% ± 0.9% accuracy and 56.1% ± 1.2% F_1-score for the RP+FAM variant.

At the highest noise level (20%), the ensemble ANN+FAM model still led with 66.1% ± 1.1% accuracy and 66.1% ± 1.9% F_1-score. In comparison, single ANN+FAM model declined to 63.4% ± 1.6% accuracy and 62.9% ± 3.1% F_1-score, FAM to 55.9% ± 1.0% accuracy and 55.5% ± 1.3% F_1-score, and the RP+FAM variant to 52.4% ± 0.7% accuracy and 52.5% ± 0.8% F_1-score.

Table 3. F_1-score for ensemble models on Twonorm and Ringnorm at different noise levels (mean ± standard deviation).

Dataset	Model	0% Noise	5% Noise	10% Noise	15% Noise	20% Noise
Twonorm	FAM Ensemble	0.834 ± 0.005	0.740 ± 0.011	0.683 ± 0.011	0.646 ± 0.011	0.610 ± 0.014
	RP + FAM Ensemble	0.727 ± 0.050	0.643 ± 0.033	0.641 ± 0.048	0.587 ± 0.023	0.582 ± 0.017
	ANN + FAM Ensemble	**0.970 ± 0.002**	**0.944 ± 0.002**	**0.914 ± 0.002**	**0.880 ± 0.006**	**0.851 ± 0.004**
Ringnorm	FAM Ensemble	0.884 ± 0.007	0.731 ± 0.012	0.647 ± 0.011	0.608 ± 0.010	0.585 ± 0.010
	RP + FAM Ensemble	0.734 ± 0.008	0.628 ± 0.010	0.582 ± 0.015	0.560 ± 0.012	0.537 ± 0.008
	ANN + FAM Ensemble	**0.959 ± 0.004**	**0.828 ± 0.003**	**0.759 ± 0.018**	**0.713 ± 0.005**	**0.661 ± 0.019**

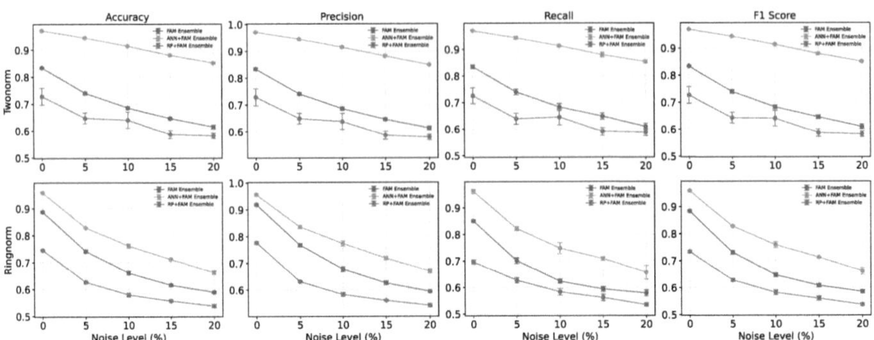

Fig. 6. Performance metrics (Accuracy, Precision, Recall, and F1-score) for ensemble models on Twonorm and Ringnorm datasets across varying noise levels (0%, 5%, 10%, 15%, and 20%).

Precision and recall metrics follow a similar performance trend. At 20% noise, the ensemble ANN+FAM model balanced $67.0\% \pm 1.3\%$ precision with $65.6\% \pm 4.2\%$ recall, whereas single ANN+FAM model exhibited $64.1\% \pm 2.0\%$ precision and $62.4\% \pm 5.5\%$ recall. Both baseline FAM and the RP+FAM model showed lower average values and higher variability, highlighting the stability advantages of the ensemble approach.

Using RP as a feature extractor yields only minimal F_1-score improvements, even with majority voting, although RP remains a fast way to reduce dimensionality. However, an examination of the standard deviations reveals that the ensemble variants exhibit markedly lower variability as compared with those from their single-model counterparts. This reduction in standard deviation indicates that aggregating predictions from independent ANN+FAM models via majority voting not only elevates mean accuracy and F_1-score, but also stabilises performance. In essence, the ensemble method reduces variance by averaging errors of individual models, therefore delivering more consistent performances across different noise levels. This stability makes the ensemble model less susceptible to random fluctuations, yielding more dependable results in real-world, data streaming environments. In practice, privacy-utility constraints [10,11], edge computing limits in health IoT [4], and noisy, patient-specific streams (e.g., EEG) [37] constrain deployment; our online hybrid is designed to remain robust under these conditions.

5 Conclusion and Future Work

In this study, we have developed a hybrid online learning framework integrating a compact ANN feature extractor with FAM and further bolsters robustness through an ensemble majority-voting scheme for undertaking noisy data classification tasks. Using benchmark datasets (Twonorm and Ringnorm) with noise levels up to 20%, the proposed ensemble ANN+FAM model consistently delivers the highest mean F_1-scores and narrows run-to-run data streams variability in its predictions. Even when noise corruption increases, the online learning performance persists to improve, indicating the effectiveness of the ensemble ANN+FAM model to continually learn new data without revisiting past samples. The experiment results verify the usefulness of both feature extractors as pre-processing and ensemble voting as post-processing for noisy data classification with FAM. Firstly, learned ANN embeddings provide informative features that enable FAM to form compact, well-separated prototypes for each category, improving the classification performance from low to moderate noise. Secondly, the ensemble voting scheme acts as a useful variance reduction method. By aggregating a pool of independent ANN+FAM learners, the ensemble voting scheme stabilises predictions that single FAM models alone cannot deliver. For further research, several avenues could enhance the devised ensemble ANN+FAM model. Incorporating advanced denoising or confidence-weighted update rules to help improve the performance, particularly under severe noise levels. Adaptive ensemble weighting for dynamically tuning each member's vote based on recent reliability could better track non-stationary data drifts in noisy environments. In addition, advanced feature extractors, such as lightweight transformer modules or learned kernel mappings, offer more discriminative representations to facilitate online learning with FAM. Future work will integrate formal privacy mechanisms and privacy-utility optimizations [10,11], explore temporally adaptive, domain-generalized feature learning [20], and evaluate edge-deployed pipelines in healthcare/IoT scenarios [4,37], while maintaining interpretability in the spirit of cognitive learning theories [14].

References

1. Auer, P., Cesa-Bianchi, N., Fischer, P.: Finite-time analysis of the multiarmed bandit problem. Mach. Learn. **47**, 235–256 (2002)
2. Bingham, E., Mannila, H.: Random projection in dimensionality reduction: applications to image and text data. In: Proceedings of the Seventh ACM SIGKDD International Conference on Knowledge Discovery and Data Mining, pp. 245–250. KDD '01, Association for Computing Machinery, New York, NY, USA (2001). https://doi.org/10.1145/502512.502546
3. Carpenter, G., Grossberg, S., Markuzon, N., Reynolds, J., Rosen, D.: Fuzzy artmap: a neural network architecture for incremental supervised learning of analog multidimensional maps. IEEE Trans. Neural Netw. **3**(5), 698–713 (1992). https://doi.org/10.1109/72.159059
4. Chen, G., Wang, M., Han, S., Yin, J., Wang, H., Cao, J.: Deep reinforcement learning-based cloud-edge offloading for wbans. IEEE Trans. Consum. Electron. **PP**, 1 (2024). https://doi.org/10.1109/TCE.2024.3504545
5. Chen, Y., Xiong, J., Xu, W., Zuo, J.: A novel online incremental and decremental learning algorithm based on variable support vector machine. Clust. Comput. **22**, 7435–7445 (2019)
6. Crammer, K., Dekel, O., Keshet, J., Shalev-Shwartz, S., Singer, Y.: Online passive-aggressive algorithms. J. Mach. Learn. Res. **7**, 551–585 (2006)
7. Dredze, M., Crammer, K., Pereira, F.: Confidence-weighted linear classification. In: Proceedings of the 25th International Conference on Machine Learning, pp.

264–271. ICML '08, Association for Computing Machinery, New York, NY, USA (2008). https://doi.org/10.1145/1390156.1390190
8. Freund, Y., Schapire, R.E.: Large margin classification using the perceptron algorithm. In: Proceedings of the Eleventh Annual Conference on Computational Learning Theory, pp. 209–217 (1998)
9. Furao, S., Sudo, A., Hasegawa, O.: An online incremental learning pattern-based reasoning system. Neural Netw. **23**(1), 135–143 (2010)
10. Ge, Y.F., Wang, H., Bertino, E., Cao, J., Zhang, Y.: Multiobjective privacy-preserving task assignment in spatial crowdsourcing. IEEE Trans. Cybern. **55**(8), 3584–3597 (2025). https://doi.org/10.1109/TCYB.2025.3573292
11. Ge, Y.F., et al.: Evolutionary dynamic database partitioning optimization for privacy and utility. IEEE Trans. Dependable Secure Comput. **21**(4), 2296–2311 (2024). https://doi.org/10.1109/TDSC.2023.3302284
12. He, J., Mao, R., Shao, Z., Zhu, F.: Incremental learning in online scenario. In: 2020 IEEE/CVF Conference on Computer Vision and Pattern Recognition (CVPR), pp. 13923–13932 (2020). https://doi.org/10.1109/CVPR42600.2020.01394
13. Hu, C., Chen, Y., Hu, L., Peng, X.: A novel random forests based class incremental learning method for activity recognition. Pattern Recogn. **78**, 277–290 (2018)
14. Huang, C.Q., et al.: XKT: toward explainable knowledge tracing model with cognitive learning theories for questions of multiple knowledge concepts. IEEE Trans. Knowl. Data Eng. **36**(11), 7308–7325 (2024). https://doi.org/10.1109/TKDE.2024.3418098
15. Jin, M., Xu, Z., Li, R., Wu, D.: Fuzzy artmap ensemble based decision making and application. Math. Probl. Eng. 124263 (2013). https://doi.org/10.1155/2013/124263
16. Ju, L., et al.: Improving medical images classification with label noise using dual-uncertainty estimation. IEEE Trans. Med. Imaging **41**(6), 1533–1546 (2022). https://doi.org/10.1109/TMI.2022.3141425
17. Kaur, R., Gulia, P., Gill, N., Chatterjee, J.: Big data privacy preservation using principal component analysis and random projection in healthcare. Math. Probl. Eng. **2022**, 1–12 (2022). https://doi.org/10.1155/2022/6402274
18. Kirkpatrick, J., et al.: Overcoming catastrophic forgetting in neural networks. Proc. Natl. Acad. Sci. **114**(13), 3521–3526 (2017)
19. Kivinen, J., Smola, A., Williamson, R.: Online learning with kernels. IEEE Trans. Signal Process. **52**(8), 2165–2176 (2004). https://doi.org/10.1109/TSP.2004.830991
20. Li, R., et al.: Open-vocabulary multi-object tracking with domain generalized and temporally adaptive features. IEEE Trans. Multimed. **27**, 3009–3022 (2025). https://doi.org/10.1109/TMM.2025.3557619
21. Li, Y., Wang, S., Xu, S., Yin, J.: Trustworthy semi-supervised anomaly detection for online-to-offline logistics business in merchant identification. CAAI Trans. Intell. Technol. (2024)
22. Littlestone, N.: Learning quickly when irrelevant attributes abound: a new linear-threshold algorithm. Mach. Learn. **2**, 285–318 (1988)
23. Liu, Y.: Understanding instance-level label noise: Disparate impacts and treatments. In: Meila, M., Zhang, T. (eds.) Proceedings of the 38th International Conference on Machine Learning. Proceedings of Machine Learning Research, vol. 139, pp. 6725–6735. PMLR (2021). https://proceedings.mlr.press/v139/liu21a.html
24. Manapragada, C., Salehi, M., Webb, G.I.: Extremely fast hoeffding adaptive tree. In: 2022 IEEE International Conference on Data Mining (ICDM), pp. 319–328 (2022). https://doi.org/10.1109/ICDM54844.2022.00042

25. Manapragada, C., Webb, G.I., Salehi, M.: Extremely fast decision tree. In: Proceedings of the 24th ACM SIGKDD International Conference on Knowledge Discovery & Data Mining, pp. 1953–1962. KDD '18, Association for Computing Machinery, New York, NY, USA (2018). https://doi.org/10.1145/3219819.3220005, https://doi.org/10.1145/3219819.3220005
26. Mienye, I.D., Sun, Y.: A survey of ensemble learning: concepts, algorithms, applications, and prospects. IEEE Access **10**, 99129–99149 (2022). https://doi.org/10.1109/ACCESS.2022.3207287
27. Pérez-Sánchez, B., Fontenla-Romero, O., Guijarro-Berdiñas, B.: A review of adaptive online learning for artificial neural networks. Artif. Intell. Rev. **49**(2), 281–299 (2018)
28. Polikar, R., Upda, L., Upda, S., Honavar, V.: Learn++: an incremental learning algorithm for supervised neural networks. IEEE Trans. Syst. Man Cybern. Part C (Appl. Rev.) **31**(4), 497–508 (2001). https://doi.org/10.1109/5326.983933
29. Rebuffi, S.A., Kolesnikov, A., Sperl, G., Lampert, C.H.: ICARL: incremental classifier and representation learning. In: Proceedings of the IEEE Conference on Computer Vision and Pattern Recognition (CVPR) (2017)
30. Rosenblatt, F.: The perceptron: a probabilistic model for information storage and organization in the brain. Psychol. Rev. **65**, 386–408 (1958). https://doi.org/10.1037/h0042519
31. Ruping, S.: Incremental learning with support vector machines. In: Proceedings 2001 IEEE International Conference on Data Mining, pp. 641–642 (2001). https://doi.org/10.1109/ICDM.2001.989589
32. Saffari, A., Leistner, C., Santner, J., Godec, M., Bischof, H.: On-line random forests. In: 2009 IEEE 12th International Conference on Computer Vision Workshops, ICCV Workshops, pp. 1393–1400 (2009). https://doi.org/10.1109/ICCVW.2009.5457447
33. Sarwar, S.S., Panda, P., Roy, K.: Gabor filter assisted energy efficient fast learning convolutional neural networks. In: 2017 IEEE/ACM International Symposium on Low Power Electronics and Design (ISLPED), pp. 1–6 (2017). https://doi.org/10.1109/ISLPED.2017.8009202
34. Schmidhuber, J.: Deep learning in neural networks: an overview. Neural Netw. **61**, 85–117 (2015)
35. Sutton, R.S., Barto, A.G., et al.: Reinforcement Learning: An Introduction, vol. 1. MIT Press, Cambridge (1998)
36. Tang, Z., Yan, X.: Voting algorithm of fuzzy artmap and its application to fault diagnosis. In: Fourth International Conference on Fuzzy Systems and Knowledge Discovery (FSKD 2007), vol. 4, pp. 535–538 (2007). https://doi.org/10.1109/FSKD.2007.611
37. Tawhid, M.N.A., Siuly, S., Wang, K., Wang, H.: Genet: a generic neural network for detecting various neurological disorders from EEG. IEEE Trans. Cogn. Dev. Syst. **16**(5), 1829–1842 (2024). https://doi.org/10.1109/TCDS.2024.3386364
38. Triguero, I., et al.: Keel 3.0: an open source software for multi-stage analysis in data mining. Int. J. Comput. Intell. Syst. **10**, 1238–1249 (2017). https://doi.org/10.2991/ijcis.10.1.82
39. Vermorel, J., Mohri, M.: Multi-armed bandit algorithms and empirical evaluation. In: Gama, J., Camacho, R., Brazdil, P.B., Jorge, A.M., Torgo, L. (eds.) Machine Learning: ECML 2005. ECML 2005. LNCS, vol 3720, pp. 437–448. Springer, Berlin, Heidelberg (2005). https://doi.org/10.1007/11564096_42

40. Wang, L., Meng, J.: Incremental clustering algorithm based on bayesian adaptive resonance theory based on local distribution. Control Decision **33**(03), 471–478 (2018)
41. Wang, M., Han, S., Chen, G., Yin, J., Cao, J.: Blockchain-empowered resource allocation and data security for efficient vehicular edge computing. In: Zhang, F., Wang, H., Barhamgi, M., Chen, L., Zhou, R. (eds.) Web Information Systems Engineering – WISE 2023. WISE 2023. LNCS, vol. 14306, pp. 205–219. Springer, Singapore (2023). https://doi.org/10.1007/978-981-99-7254-8_16
42. Xie, T., Peng, Y., Wang, C.: HI-RF: incremental learning random forest for large-scale multi-class data classification (2016). https://arxiv.org/abs/1608.08761
43. Yin, J., Chen, G., Hong, W., Wang, H., Cao, J., Miao, Y.: Empowering vulnerability prioritization: a heterogeneous graph-driven framework for exploitability prediction. In: Zhang, F., Wang, H., Barhamgi, M., Chen, L., Zhou, R. (eds.) Web Information Systems Engineering – WISE 2023. WISE 2023. LNCS, vol. 14306, pp. 289–299. Springer, Singapore (2023). https://doi.org/10.1007/978-981-99-7254-8_23
44. Yin, J., Tang, M., Cao, J., Wang, H., You, M., Lin, Y.: Adaptive online learning for vulnerability exploitation time prediction. In: Huang, Z., Beek, W., Wang, H., Zhou, R., Zhang, Y. (eds.) Web Information Systems Engineering – WISE 2020. WISE 2020. LNCS, vol. 12343, pp. 252–266. Springer, Cham (2020). https://doi.org/10.1007/978-3-030-62008-0_18, http://dx.doi.org/10.1007/978-3-030-62008-0_18
45. You, M., Yin, J., Wang, H., Cao, J., Miao, Y.: A minority class boosted framework for adaptive access control decision-making. In: Zhang, W., Zou, L., Maamar, Z., Chen, L. (eds.) Web Information Systems Engineering – WISE 2021. WISE 2021. LNCS, vol. 13080, pp. 143–157. Springer, Cham (2021). https://doi.org/10.1007/978-3-030-90888-1_12
46. You, M., et al.: A knowledge graph empowered online learning framework for access control decision-making. World Wide Web **26**(2), 827–848 (2022)

Recommender Systems I

Intra-domain Preference Modeling with Cross-Domain Dependency Alignment for Cross-Domain Sequential Recommendation

Tianyu Xiao, Jiwei Qin(✉), Jie Ma, Qiangsheng Feng, Shishen Li, and Ziyang Li

School of Computer Science and Technology, Xinjiang University, Urumqi 830046, Xinjiang, China
jwqin@xju.edu.cn

Abstract. Cross-Domain Sequential Recommendation (CDSR) leverages diverse behavioral data across domains to alleviate the data sparsity issue commonly encountered in single-domain scenarios. However, the potential of intra-domain information remains underexplored in existing CDSR models, despite its importance in modeling domain-specific user preferences. Furthermore, they typically capture the users' preferences independently of each domain, which may neglect the cross-domain sequential dependencies from different domains. To alleviate these issues, we propose **I**ntra-domain preference modeling with **C**ross-domain dependency alignment for **C**ross-**D**omain **S**equential **R**ecommendation(IC-CDSR), which models intra-domain preferences and aligns cross-domain dependencies. Specifically, IC-CDSR consists of two main modules: a cross-domain collaborative modeling module (CDCM) and a cross-domain information alignment module (CDIA). The CDCM module comprises two key components: a selective GRU, which integrates temporal convolution and gating mechanisms to extract fine-grained contextual dependencies and capture users' local preferences within each domain; and a user-anchored cross-attention encoder, which leverages a time-invariant user embedding to attend over behavioral sequences, thereby capturing global preferences and enabling effective cross-domain integration. The CDIA module employs a cross-attention encoder with Rotary Positional Encoding(RoPE), which encodes relative positional information through rotation within the attention mechanism, thereby preserving semantic integrity while aligning cross-domain behaviors and capturing sequential dependencies between source and target domains. Experimental results on the Amazon Book, Movie, and CD dataset validate the effectiveness of IC-CDSR against state-of-the-art(SOTA) baselines.

Keywords: Sequential Recommendation · Cross-domain Sequential Recommendation · Deep Learning

I. Awan et al. (Eds.): WISE 2025, LNCS 16367, pp. 63–78, 2026.
https://doi.org/10.1007/978-981-95-7394-3_5

1 Introduction

Recommender systems aim to predict the next item a user is most likely to interact with based on their historical behavior. Two important approaches in this area are Sequential Recommendation (SR) and Cross-Domain Recommendation (CDR). SR captures users' dynamic preferences by modeling their behavior sequences over time, but often suffers from data sparsity problem. In contrast, CDR alleviates data sparsity in the target domain by incorporating relatively richer behavioral data from source domains. However, most existing CDR models overlook the sequential nature of user behavior, and thus fail to capture users' dynamic preferences. To alleviate these limitations, researchers have introduced a new and emerging paradigm, i.e., cross-domain sequential recommendation(CDSR).

CDSR improves the recommendation performance in the target domain by integrating information from different domains [15], and can simultaneously model cross-domain sequential interactions to capture the dynamic evolution of user interests across multiple domains. π-Net [9] models user behavior sequences with gated recurrent units (GRUs) and transfers knowledge across domains via transfer units. Building on this, PSJNet [13] proposes a split-connect framework to better capture cross-domain representations. DA-GCN [3] leverages graph neural networks (GNNs) to model high-order collaborative signals, while RecGURU [8] uses adversarial learning to unify user representations from different domains. C^2DSR [2] captures collaborative and sequential relationships across domains using contrastive learning, MGCL [17] constructs sequence graphs within and across domains, and DREAM [19] decouples representation extraction from attention and captures inter-sequence relationships via supervised contrastive learning.

Despite progress in cross-domain transfer techniques, one critical challenge faced by existing CDSR models is the neglect of rich, multi-level user preference representations within a single domain. Another key challenge in CDSR is the limited ability of existing models to capture sequential dependencies that span across domains. Most models treat each domain independently, transferring knowledge only after modeling user behavior, which ignores how actions in one domain can influence behaviors in another. For example, a user who reads *Little Women* in the book domain may later be influenced by watching *Thor* in the movie domain, indicating an interest in Marvel-themed content. Similarly, after enjoying *The Sound of Music* in the movie domain, the user might be drawn to related music content in the CDs domain. These examples demonstrate the importance of modeling cross-domain sequential dependencies to enhance recommendation relevance and user satisfaction.

To mitigate the dual challenges of underutilized intra-domain preferences and overlooked cross-domain sequential dependencies, we propose a novel framework for CDSR, referred to as IC-CDSR (Intra-domain preference modeling with Cross-domain dependency alignment). The architecture is composed of two specialized modules designed to complement each other: the Cross-Domain Collaborative Modeling module (CDCM) and the Cross-Domain Information Alignment module (CDIA).

The CDCM module is responsible for modeling user preferences within each individual domain from both local and global perspectives. It incorporates a Selective GRU, which combines temporal convolution with a gating mechanism to capture fine-grained, short-term behavioral patterns, enabling a more nuanced understanding of local context. In parallel, a user-anchored cross-attention encoder utilizes a shared, time-invariant user embedding as the query vector to compute attention over behavioral sequences. This design allows the model to distill global preference signals while maintaining domain specificity, forming a multi-layered user representation that enhances recommendation precision. The CDIA module, in contrast, is dedicated to capturing cross-domain behavioral dependencies. It employs a cross-attention mechanism enriched with rotary positional encoding(RoPE) [12], which introduces relative positional information through rotation matrices embedded within the attention computation. Unlike additive positional embeddings, RoPE maintains the semantic consistency of item embeddings while encoding order-sensitive relationships across domains. This facilitates the alignment of temporally structured behaviors between the source and target domains, thus improving the continuity and coherence of user behavior modeling in a multi-domain context (Fig. 1).

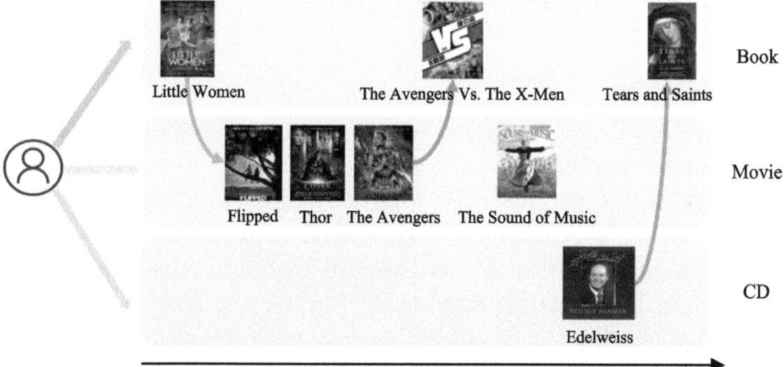

Fig. 1. An example of cross-domain sequential dependencies where user behaviors in one domain (e.g., book) influence subsequent interactions in another domain (e.g., movie or CD).

We summarize our main contributions as follows:

- We propose a CDSR model, IC-CDSR, which addresses data sparsity from two perspectives: intra-domain preference modeling and cross-domain dependency alignment, implemented via two modules—CDCM and CDIA.
- The CDCM module integrates a selective GRU to capture users' local interests by modeling fine-grained sequential dependencies, and a user-anchored cross-attention encoder to extract global preferences through user-specific attention. The CDIA module incorporates a cross-attention encoder with RoPE

to capture dynamic sequential patterns and align behavioral dependencies across domains.

– We conduct extensive experiments on three real-world datasets, demonstrating that IC-CDSR significantly outperforms SOTA baselines and effectively verifies the robustness of the overall model.

2 Proposed Method

2.1 Problem Definition

This subsection formally defines the problem setting that underpins the analysis of our proposed IC-CDSR model. We consider a CDSR scenario involving multiple domains with an overlapping set of users. Reflecting real-world user behavior, where individuals interact across several domains, we illustrate the framework with $n(n \geq 3)$ source domains. Let $U = \{u_1, u_2, \cdots, u_M\}$ denote the set of M overlapping users. For each user $u_i (1 \leq i \leq M)$, their interaction sequences are recorded across the target domain and all source domains. Specifically, the target domain sequence is $S_i^X = \left\{S_1^X, S_2^X, \cdots, S_{|S_i^X|}^X\right\}$, while the sequence in the j-th source domain is $S_i^j = \left\{S_1^j, S_2^j, \cdots, S_{|S_i^j|}^j\right\}$, where $|\cdot|$ denotes sequence length. The objective of CDSR is to predict the next item in the target domain that user u_i is most likely to engage with, leveraging their historical interactions from both the target and multiple source domains.

2.2 Overall Architecture

The aim of IC-CDSR is providing better sequential recommendation performance for a single domain by leveraging useful cross-domain knowledge. The overall structure of our proposed IC-CDSR is illustrated in Fig. 2. IC-CDSR is built upon [18], which serves as the backbone for our proposed model. IC-CDSR consists of two main modules: Cross-Domain Collaborative Modeling (CDCM) and Cross-Domain Information Alignment (CDIA).

In the CDCM module, we explore intra-domain local and global preference features in parallel. Thus, this module has two parts, i.e., local dependency and global interest. In the local dependency part, we apply a selective GRU which is employed to capture the local item-wise dependencies, and selectively learn the sequential information. In the global interest part, we introduce a user-anchored cross-attention encoder which adopts cross-attention mechanism to capture the global interests from target domain to source domains. By combining these two powerful parts, the CDCM performs fine-grained modeling of complex user behaviors.

In the CDIA module, we investigate the cross-domain representation alignment problem from a positional embedding perspective. The alignment consists of two key steps: a) Cross-attention is employed to align source domains representations to the target domain; b) RoPE is utilized to align the target domain representations back to the source domains. The CDIA establishs connection between the target domain and source domains.

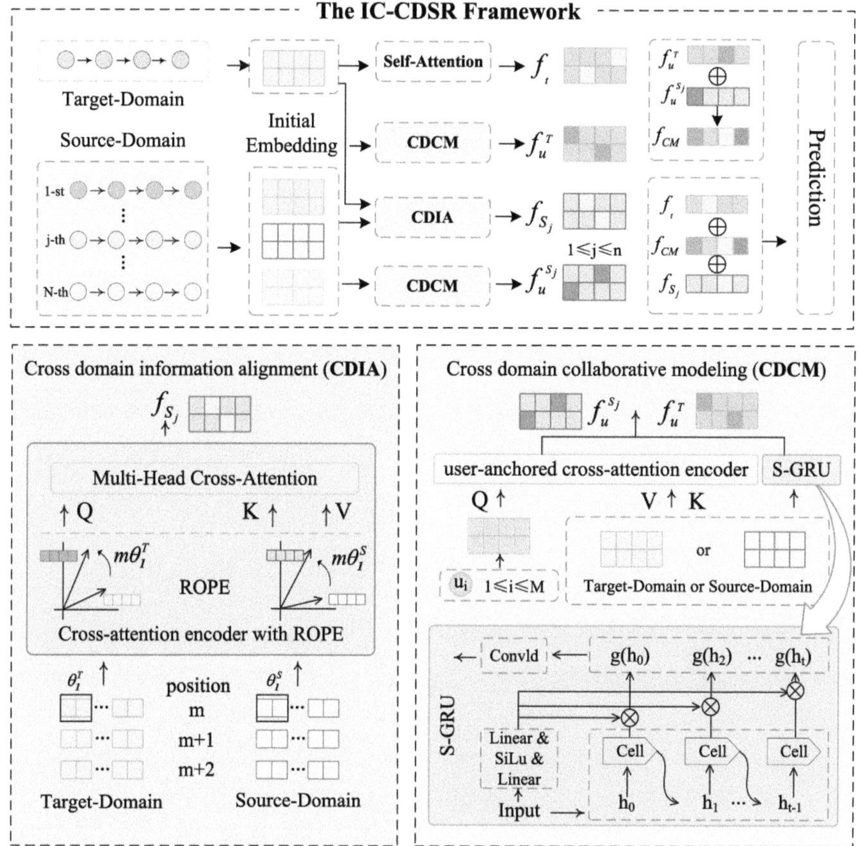

Fig. 2. The overall architecture of IC-CDSR, illustrating the CDCM and CDIA modules. CDCM models collaborative signals within domains, while CDIA aligns cross-domain information using a cross-attention encoder with ROPE to capture sequential dependencies.

2.3 Cross-Domain Collaborative Modeling

To obtain the input for CDCM, we first model the high-order dependency structures within user interaction sequences to obtain tensor representations. Each sequence is truncated or padded to a fixed length t to ensure a consistent embedding structure. As a result, we obtain the user's initial input embeddings in the target domain as $S^X \in \mathbb{R}^{t \times d}$, and in the source domains as $S^Y \in \mathbb{R}^{t \times d}$, where d is the dimension of the latent embedding vectors.

2.3.1 Local Dependency

We introduce a Selective GRU (S-GRU) [20], as shown in Fig. 2, as a core component of CDCM. This module captures local temporal features and uses the

GRU's update mechanisms to generate fine-grained positional representations. Unlike conventional GRUs that propagate information solely from previous time steps, S-GRU also integrates contextual clues from nearby items.

Temporal Convolution. To extract local contextual features, we first apply a temporal convolutional layer to the input embedding matrix $S \in \mathbb{R}^{t \times d}$ from the source domains S^Y. This aggregates adjacent item information before passing it to the GRU:

$$T = TemporalConv1d(SW_0 + b_0) \tag{1}$$

where W_0 and b_0 are learnable parameters, and $T = [t_1, t_2, \cdots, t_t]^T \in \mathbb{R}^{t \times d}$ is the convolved sequence.

Selective GRU. We employ a S-GRU to model fine-grained local dependencies. At each time step n, the GRU cell generates a hidden state h_n as:

$$h_n = (1 - z_t)\tilde{h}_n + \prod_{i=1}^{n} z_i h_0 + \sum_{k=1}^{n-2} \prod_{i=k+1}^{n} z_i (1 - z_k) h_k \tag{2}$$

where z_k is the update gate at time step k, h_0 is the initial hidden state, and the full hidden sequence is $H = [h_1, h_2, \cdots, h_t]^T$. We then project H to a new space using a feature cross layer:

$$\Phi(H) = HW_H + b_H \tag{3}$$

Gating and Final Convolution. To filter and enhance the hidden features, we design a selective gate. It directly combines the linear projection and SiLU activation:

$$\mathcal{G}(H) = (SiLU(TW_\delta^{(1)} + b_\delta^{(1)})W_\Omega^{(1)} + b_\Omega^{(1)}) \otimes \Phi(H) \tag{4}$$

Although the GRU incorporates local context at the input level, each output state mainly depends on previous steps. To further capture temporal dependencies, we apply another temporal convolution over the gated output:

$$Y = TemporalConv1d(G) \tag{5}$$

where $Y = [y_1, y_2, \cdots, y_t]^T$ represents the user's local preference in the current domain. Similarly, we obtain $Y^1, Y^2, \cdots, Y^n$ for source domains. This combination of convolution and GRU enhances temporal information flow and improves modeling of local user behaviors.

2.3.2 Global Interest

We introduce a user-anchored cross-attention encoder [18], as shown in Fig. 2, to model global interests in CDCM. For each domain, a learnable user embedding $u \in \mathbb{R}^d$ derived from the user's ID serves as the query, fixed across time steps to ensure consistent. This enables both information integration across behavioral sources and effective capture of cross-domain commonalities in users' long-term preferences.

Given the input embedding matrix $S \in \mathbb{R}^{t\times d}$, which come from the target domains S^X, we compute attention weights and the global representation as:

$$Z = \sum_{i=1}^{t} \text{softmax}\left(uW_{Q_u}(s_i W_{K_u})^T\right)(s_i W_{V_u}) \quad (6)$$

where s_i is the initial embedding of item i, and $W_{Q_u}, W_{K_u}, W_{V_u} \in \mathbb{R}^{d\times d}$ are trainable linear transformation matrices optimized during training.

The resulting vector $Z \in \mathbb{R}^d$ captures the user's global preference in the target domain. Similarly, we compute $Z^1, Z^2, \cdots, Z^n$ for the source domains, preserving domain-specific characteristics while enabling cross-domain comparison and fusion.

2.4 Cross-Domain Information Alignment

Consistent with the CDCM module, the CDIA module takes as input the target and source domain embeddings $S^X \in \mathbb{R}^{t\times d}$ and $S^Y \in \mathbb{R}^{t\times d}$, respectively. To encode position information in a relative manner, we define the attention mechanism as:

$$q_m k_n^T = \langle F_q(x_m, m), F_k(x_n, n)\rangle = G(x_m, x_n, m-n) \quad (7)$$

where $x_m \in \widehat{S^X}$ and $x_n \in S^Y$ are row vectors, and $F_q(\cdot)$, $F_k(\cdot)$ incorporate relative positional information through rotation matrices. Here, d is typically an even number. As illustrated in Fig. 2, the d-dimensional vectors are split into 2D sub-vectors and combined via linear aggregation of inner products:

$$R^d_{\Theta,m} = \begin{bmatrix} M_1 & & \\ & \ddots & \\ & & M_{d/2} \end{bmatrix} \quad (8)$$

Unlike additive sinusoidal embeddings, RoPE [12] and its inherent long-range decay property enable efficient modeling of sequential patterns and enhance cross-domain feature alignment. The resulting output vectors $f_{S_1}, f_{S_2}, \cdots, f_{S_n}$ represent the aligned preference vectors across domains.

2.5 The Learning Algorithm

Algorithm 1 outlines the training procedure of IC-CDSR. Given sampled sequences S^X, S^{Y_n}, and user embedding e_u, the model first computes the target-domain static preference f_t via self-attention. It then derives the target preference f_u^T and source-domain preferences $f_u^{S_n}$ through collaborative modeling. These are fused into f^{CM}, while cross-domain alignment produces f_{S_n} using cross-attention. All features f_t, f^{CM} and f_{S_n} are concatenated into o_t for prediction $\widehat{y}_t$, and parameters are updated by minimizing the loss $\mathcal{L}$.

Algorithm 1: Learning Procedure of IC-CDSR

Initialize parameters Θ
Repeat for each epoch:
  Sample mini-batch: S^X, $\{S^{Y_n}\}_{n=1}^{N}$, e_u
  Compute target static preference $f_t = \mathrm{SelfAttention}(S^X)$
  Compute target local Y, global Z, $f_u^T = \alpha_1 Y + \alpha_2 Z$
  For each source n: $f_u^{S_n} = \alpha_1 Y^n + \alpha_2 Z^n$
  Fuse: $f^{CM} = \mathrm{MLP}(\mathrm{concat}(f_u^T, \{f_u^{S_n}\}))$
  For each source n: $f_{S_n} = \mathrm{CrossAttention} + ROPE(S^X, S^{Y_n})$
  Compute attention weights across domains
  Aggregate aligned preferences
  Concatenate: $o_t = \mathrm{concat}(f_t, f^{CM}, \{f_{S_n}\})$
  Predict: $\hat{y}_t = \mathrm{MLP}(o_t)^T e_i$
  Compute binary cross-entropy loss $\mathcal{L}$
  Update $\Theta \leftarrow \Theta - \eta \nabla_\Theta \mathcal{L}$
Until convergence or max epochs

3 Experiments

3.1 Experimental Setup

3.1.1 Dataset

We adopt the preprocessed Amazon dataset from [18], which is widely used for cross-domain sequential recommendation (CDSR). It includes three domains: "Movie", "CD", and "Book". The preprocessing follows [18], including user-item filtering, duplicate removal, and a leave-one-out evaluation protocol (Table 1).

Table 1. Statistic details of datasets

Dataset	No. of Overlapped Users	No. of Items	No. of Interactions	Avg. Length	Density
Movie	10929	59513	460226	42.11	0.07%
CD		91169	344221	31.50	0.03%
Book		236049	607657	55.60	0.02%

3.1.2 Compared Baselines

To evaluate the effectiveness of our proposed IC-CDSR model, we compared it with 14 SOTA and competitive baselines from four categories of recommendation models. These include general, sequential, and cross-domain recommendation models.

We first included two traditional baselines:

- BPRMF [10]: a general recommendation model using matrix factorization with pairwise ranking loss.
- CoNet [6]: a neural transfer model for cross-domain recommendation, which introduces cross-connections between MLPs for dual knowledge transfer.

For sequential recommendation, we selected six models:

- FPMC [11]: Combines matrix factorization with first-order Markov chains.
- GRU4Rec [5]: An RNN-based model that uses GRUs to learn sequential behavior.
- GRU4Rec+ [4]: An improved GRU4Rec with advanced loss functions and sampling strategies.
- Caser [14]: A CNN-based model that captures high-order Markov chains using convolutional filters.
- GCSAN [16]: A GNN-based model that encodes session graphs with gated GNNs.
- SASRec [7]: An attention-based model using self-attention to model sequential dependencies. It also serves as the target-domain module in IC-CDSR.

For CDSR, we considered five recent models:

- π-Net [9]: An RNN-based model using cross-domain transfer units.
- DA-GCN [3]: A GNN-based model that builds cross-domain sequence graphs to model complex interactions.
- CD-SASRec [1]: Extends SASRec by incorporating source-domain information into target-domain item embeddings.
- RecGURU [8]: Uses a self-attentive autoencoder and adversarial learning to unify cross-domain user representations.
- C^2DSR [2]: Combines graph and attention encoders with contrastive learning objectives for joint single- and cross-domain modeling.

We also included TJAPL [18], a SASRec-based model that transfers knowledge from multiple source domains by modeling users' global preferences and transition patterns. Most of the baseline models are consistent with those used in [18].

3.1.3 Evaluation Protocol and Settings

We use HR@10 and NDCG@10 to evaluate recommendation performance. HR@10 measures the proportion of true items in the top-10 recommendations, while NDCG@10 accounts for their ranking. To reduce computational cost, we sample 100 popular [7], non-interacted negative items per test case.

We compare with baseline models including GRU4Rec, Caser, SASRec, π-Net, RecGURU, and C^2DSR. We fix $d = 50$, $L = 100$, and use Adam with a learning rate of 0.001 and batch size of 128. For attention-based models, we adopt a single-head attention mechanism with two layers, while for GNN-based models, we utilize two GNN layers. Cross-domain models report the best single-source results, while multi-source models (TJAPL, IC-CDSR) use both sources.

3.2 Overall Performance

Table 2 reports the performance of IC-CDSR and all baselines across three datasets. The best result in each column is marked in bold, and the second-best is underlined. Our IC-CDSR consistently outperforms baselines, achieving an average improvement of 5.91% in NDCG@10 and 4.66% in HR@10, highlighting its effectiveness in modeling sequential behavior with cross-domain data.

Table 2. Overall performance comparison between IC-CDSR and baselines

Model	Movie		CD		Book	
	NDCG@10	HR@10	NDCG@10	HR@10	NDCG@10	HR@10
BPRMF	0.0597	0.1256	0.0492	0.1142	0.0465	0.1088
CoNet	0.0675	0.1489	0.0756	0.1484	0.0764	0.1819
FPMC	0.0723	0.1697	0.0819	0.1785	0.0695	0.1416
GRU4Rec	0.1017	0.1984	0.1210	0.2247	0.1066	0.2162
GRU4Rec+	0.1133	0.2157	0.1440	0.2536	0.1293	0.2407
Caser	0.1231	0.2243	0.1267	0.2473	0.1163	0.2274
GCSAN	0.1576	0.2889	0.1783	0.3206	0.1291	0.2409
SASRec	0.1822	0.3234	0.1978	0.3569	0.1401	0.2607
π-Net	0.1113	0.2080	0.1265	0.2335	0.1042	0.2101
DA-GCN	0.1736	0.3124	0.1897	0.3458	0.1283	0.2375
CD-SASRec	0.1789	0.3173	0.2009	0.3614	0.1481	0.2737
RecGURU	0.1884	0.3433	0.2044	0.3649	0.1373	0.2556
C^2DSR	0.1922	0.3423	0.1978	0.3435	0.1486	0.2752
TJAPL	<u>0.2133</u>	<u>0.3769</u>	<u>0.2199</u>	<u>0.3907</u>	<u>0.1632</u>	<u>0.2984</u>
IC-CDSR	**0.2238**	**0.3971**	**0.2358**	**0.4066**	**0.1727**	**0.3120**
Improve	**4.69%**	**5.36%**	**7.23%**	**4.07%**	**5.82%**	**4.56%**

Sequential recommendation models outperform general ones, emphasizing the value of sequence modeling. Cross-domain sequential models further surpass most traditional sequential models, demonstrating the benefit of leveraging auxiliary domains. The improvement is most significant in the "CD" dataset, likely due to stronger associations between "CD" and other domains, where interactions in "Book" and "Movie" domains influence subsequent "CD" interactions. In contrast, improvements on the "Book" dataset are smaller, possibly due to data sparsity in the source domains ("Movie" or "CD"). Nevertheless, IC-CDSR still performs well on "Book" by effectively leveraging both "Movie" and "CD" as sources, showcasing its multi-domain transfer capability.

For a broader comparison, we also evaluate top-K performance with $K \in 1, 5, 10$, as shown in Table 3. IC-CDSR consistently leads in most cases, and performance trends of different models remain stable across varying K.

3.3 Ablation Study

To evaluate the contribution of each component, we conducted ablation experiments by removing specific modules. The results are illustrated in Table 4 and

Table 3. Top-K recommendation performance comparison for K=1,5,10

Dataset	Metrics	GCSAN	SASRec	CD-SASRec	C^2DSR	TJAPL	IC-CDSR
Movie	NDCG@1	0.0522	0.0694	0.0664	0.0728	0.0868	**0.0954**
	NDCG@5	0.1235	0.1411	0.1375	0.1524	0.1691	**0.1742**
	NDCG@10	0.1576	0.1822	0.1789	0.1922	0.2133	**0.2238**
	HR@5	0.1894	0.2125	0.2061	0.2281	0.2538	**0.2571**
	HR@10	0.2889	0.3234	0.3173	0.3423	0.3769	**0.3971**
CD	NDCG@1	0.0604	0.0737	0.0789	0.0756	0.0896	**0.0963**
	NDCG@5	0.1278	0.1503	0.1587	0.1557	0.1826	**0.1902**
	NDCG@10	0.1783	0.1978	0.2009	0.1978	0.2199	**0.2358**
	HR@5	0.2113	0.2391	0.2441	0.2345	0.2722	**0.2807**
	HR@10	0.3206	0.3569	0.3614	0.3435	0.3907	**0.4066**
Book	NDCG@1	0.0479	0.0506	0.0555	0.0596	**0.0698**	0.0675
	NDCG@5	0.0943	0.1082	0.1184	0.1221	0.1394	**0.1461**
	NDCG@10	0.1291	0.1407	0.1481	0.1486	0.1632	**0.1727**
	HR@5	0.1489	0.1656	0.1792	0.1829	0.2069	**0.2179**
	HR@10	0.2409	0.2607	0.2737	0.2752	0.2984	**0.3120**

Fig. 3. Removing the local user preference network (Model 1) resulted in significant performance degradation, particularly in NDCG@10 and HR@10, highlighting its crucial role in capturing domain-specific preferences within the CDCM module. Next, replacing RoPE positional encoding with traditional positional encoding (Model 2) led to a performance drop, especially in the CD task. This underscores the importance of RoPE in aligning cross-domain preferences effectively, particularly within the CDIA module. Finally, the full IC-CDSR model, combining both components, achieved the best performance, demonstrating their complementary effects. These results clearly show the contribution of each module in enhancing user behavior modeling and cross-domain knowledge transfer.

Table 4. Ablation study results comparing model components

Model	Movie		CD		Book	
	NDCG@10	HR@10	NDCG@10	HR@10	NDCG@10	HR@10
TJAPL	0.2168	0.3773	0.2199	0.3907	0.1632	0.2984
Model1	0.2178	0.3867	0.2281	0.3976	0.1662	0.3050
Model2	0.2169	0.3818	0.2262	0.3955	0.1667	0.3037
IC-CDSR	**0.2238**	**0.3971**	**0.2358**	**0.4066**	**0.1727**	**0.3120**

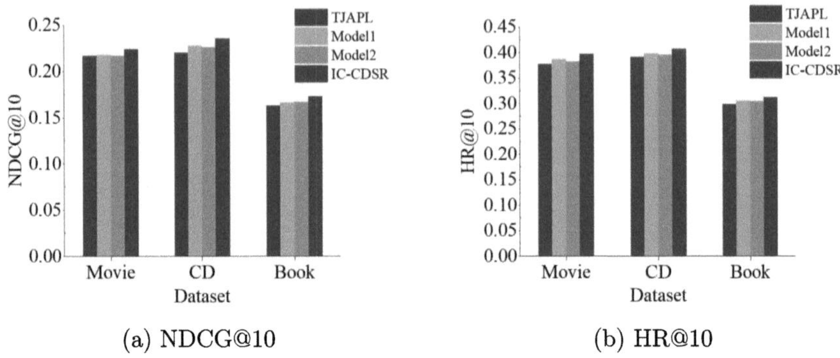

(a) NDCG@10 (b) HR@10

Fig. 3. Results of NDCG@10 and HR@10 on three cross-domain scenarious.

3.4 Hyperparameter Experiments

3.4.1 Number of Attention Blocks (B)

We study the effect of varying the number of attention blocks $B \in 1, 2, 3, 4, 5$, with other settings fixed. Results are shown in Fig. 4. Increasing B from 1 to 2 consistently improves performance on Book and Movie. Beyond $B = 2$, both NDCG@10 and HR@10 decline, likely due to overfitting from excessive model capacity. Thus, $B = 2$ balances complexity and generalization for these datasets. Interestingly, on CD, the best performance occurs at $B = 4$, suggesting that deeper interactions from more attention layers benefit this domain, possibly due

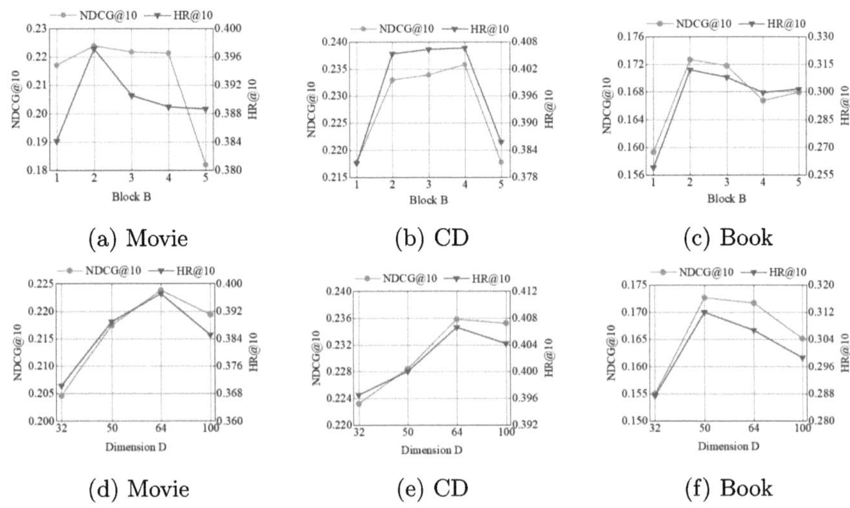

(a) Movie (b) CD (c) Book

(d) Movie (e) CD (f) Book

Fig. 4. Effects of the number of attention blocks (B) and latent embedding dimension (D) on NDCG@10 and HR@10 performance

to greater variability or sparsity in user behavior. This highlights the importance of considering domain-specific characteristics when tuning model depth.

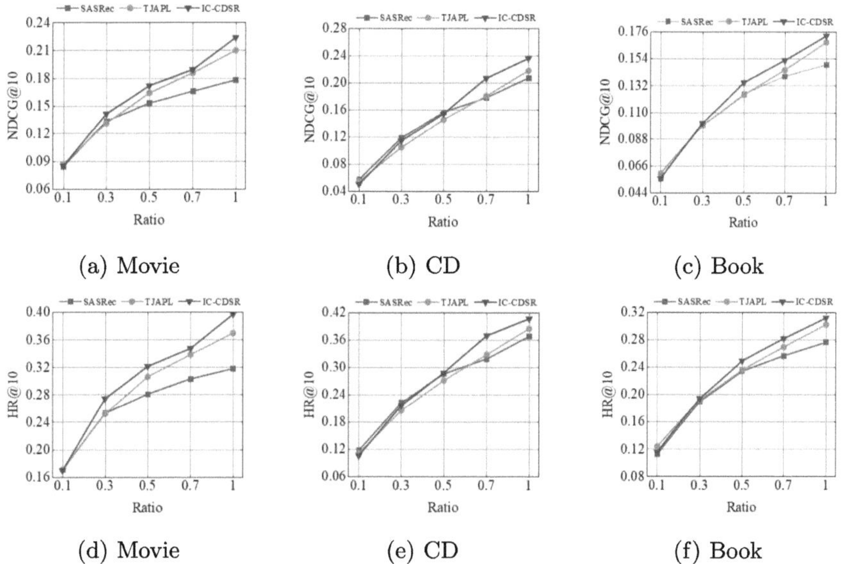

(a) Movie (b) CD (c) Book

(d) Movie (e) CD (f) Book

Fig. 5. Comparison of NDCG@10 and HR@10 under different sparsity ratios across domains

3.4.2 Latent Dimension (D)

We analyze the impact of latent embedding dimension $D \in 32, 50, 64, 100$ on IC-CDSR performance, with other parameters fixed. Results are shown in Fig. 4. Increasing D generally improves performance, but the optimal dimension varies by dataset. On Book, $D = 50$ yields the best result, while on Movie and CD, $D = 64$ achieves the highest NDCG@10 and HR@10. This difference likely stems from data characteristics: Book contains more user sequences, leading to potential overfitting with larger dimensions, while Movie and CD are sparser, benefiting from greater expressiveness with larger embeddings.

3.5 Robustness to Data Sparsity

To evaluate IC-CDSR's robustness to data sparsity, we simulate different sparsity ratios (10%, 30%, 50%, 70%, and 100%) by retaining portions of user interaction sequences. Results are shown in Fig. 5. In the Movie domain, IC-CDSR consistently outperforms TJAPL and SASRec across all sparsity levels, especially under high sparsity (Ratio = 0.1 and 0.3), highlighting its ability to model limited user histories. In the CD domain, IC-CDSR performs best when Ratio

≥ 0.3, while SASRec slightly surpasses it under extreme sparsity (Ratio $= 0.1$), suggesting attention mechanisms may excel with very short sequences. In the Book domain, IC-CDSR maintains an edge over TJAPL and outperforms SASRec at moderate and low sparsity levels (Ratio ≥ 0.5), though SASRec has a slight advantage under extreme sparsity.

These results show that IC-CDSR is generally more robust to data sparsity than TJAPL and SASRec, thanks to its cross-domain integration. While SASRec may perform better under extreme sparsity, IC-CDSR offers more stable and effective performance across varying levels.

4 Conclusion

In this paper, we proposed IC-CDSR, a novel CDSR model that jointly captures intra-domain preferences and aligns cross-domain information. Unlike existing CDSR models that focus mainly on transfer mechanisms, our model emphasizes the importance of multi-level preference modeling within each domain. The proposed CDCM and CDIA modules work together to enhance the expressiveness and alignment of user representations across domains. Extensive experiments on the Amazon Book, Movie, and CD datasets demonstrate that IC-CDSR outperforms strong baselines in most settings, especially under moderate to low sparsity levels. These results confirm the effectiveness of integrating intra-domain preference extraction with cross-domain sequence alignment.

However, we also observe that in extremely sparse scenarios, IC-CDSR may underperform compared to simpler single-domain models like SASRec. This indicates that complex cross-domain architectures may not always be optimal when user history is highly limited. In future work, we plan to explore lightweight hybrid strategies that combine the strength of both single-domain and cross-domain models. This includes integrating simplified sequential encoders, adaptive attention mechanisms, or sparsity-aware fusion modules to maintain performance while reducing model complexity. Such approaches may help improve the robustness of CDSR models under extreme data sparsity.

Acknowledgments. This work was supported by the General Program of the Natural Science Foundation of Xinjiang Uygur Autonomous Region (No. 2022D01C433), the National Natural Science Foundation of China (Grant No. 62467008), and the Xinjiang University Outstanding Graduate Students Innovation Project (Grant Nos. XJDX2025YJS081 and XJDX2025YJS179).

References

1. Alharbi, N., Caragea, D.: Cross-domain self-attentive sequential recommendations. In: Proceedings of International Conference on Data Science and Applications: ICDSA 2021, vol. 2, pp. 601–614. Springer (2022)
2. Cao, J., Cong, X., Sheng, J., Liu, T., Wang, B.: Contrastive cross-domain sequential recommendation. In: Proceedings of the 31st ACM International Conference on Information & Knowledge Management, pp. 138–147 (2022)
3. Guo, L., Tang, L., Chen, T., Zhu, L., Nguyen, Q.V.H., Yin, H.: DA-GCN: a domain-aware attentive graph convolution network for shared-account cross-domain sequential recommendation. In: Proceedings of IJCAI 2021, pp. 2483–2489 (2021). https://doi.org/10.24963/IJCAI.2021/342
4. Hidasi, B., Karatzoglou, A.: Recurrent neural networks with top-k gains for session-based recommendations. In: Proceedings of the 27th ACM International Conference on Information and Knowledge Management, pp. 843–852 (2018)
5. Hidasi, B., Karatzoglou, A., Baltrunas, L., Tikk, D.: Session-based recommendations with recurrent neural networks. In: 4th International Conference on Learning Representations (ICLR) (2016). http://arxiv.org/abs/1511.06939
6. Hu, G., Zhang, Y., Yang, Q.: CoNet: collaborative cross networks for cross-domain recommendation. In: Proceedings of the 27th ACM International Conference on Information and Knowledge Management, pp. 667–676 (2018)
7. Kang, W.C., McAuley, J.: Self-attentive sequential recommendation. In: 2018 IEEE International Conference on Data Mining (ICDM), pp. 197–206. IEEE (2018)
8. Li, C., et al.: RecGURU: adversarial learning of generalized user representations for cross-domain recommendation. In: Proceedings of the Fifteenth ACM International Conference on Web Search and Data Mining, pp. 571–581 (2022)
9. Ma, M., Ren, P., Lin, Y., Chen, Z., Ma, J., Rijke, M.d.: π-net: a parallel information-sharing network for shared-account cross-domain sequential recommendations. In: Proceedings of the 42nd International ACM SIGIR Conference on Research and Development in Information Retrieval, pp. 685–694 (2019)
10. Rendle, S., Freudenthaler, C., Gantner, Z., Schmidt-Thieme, L.: BPR: Bayesian personalized ranking from implicit feedback. In: Proceedings of the Twenty-Fifth Conference on Uncertainty in Artificial Intelligence, pp. 452–461. AUAI Press (2009)
11. Rendle, S., Freudenthaler, C., Schmidt-Thieme, L.: Factorizing personalized Markov chains for next-basket recommendation. In: Proceedings of the 19th International Conference on World Wide Web, pp. 811–820 (2010)
12. Su, J., Ahmed, M., Lu, Y., Pan, S., Bo, W., Liu, Y.: RoFormer: enhanced transformer with rotary position embedding. Neurocomputing **568**, 127063 (2024)
13. Sun, W., et al.: Parallel split-join networks for shared account cross-domain sequential recommendations. IEEE Trans. Knowl. Data Eng. **35**(4), 4106–4123 (2021)
14. Tang, J., Wang, K.: Personalized top-n sequential recommendation via convolutional sequence embedding. In: Proceedings of the Eleventh ACM International Conference on Web Search and Data Mining, pp. 565–573 (2018)
15. Xin, H., Sun, Y., Wang, C., Xiong, H.: LLMCDSR: enhancing cross-domain sequential recommendation with large language models. ACM Trans. Inf. Syst. (2025)
16. Xu, C., et al.: Graph contextualized self-attention network for session-based recommendation. In: IJCAI, vol. 19, pp. 3940–3946 (2019)
17. Xu, Z., Chen, S., Pan, W., Ming, Z.: A multi-view graph contrastive learning framework for cross-domain sequential recommendation. ACM Trans. Recommender Syst. **3**(4), 1–28 (2025)

18. Xu, Z., Pan, W., Ming, Z.: Transfer learning in cross-domain sequential recommendation. Inf. Sci. **669**, 120550 (2024)
19. Ye, X., Li, Y., Yao, L.: DREAM: decoupled representation via extraction attention module and supervised contrastive learning for cross-domain sequential recommender. In: Proceedings of the 17th ACM Conference on Recommender Systems, pp. 479–490 (2023)
20. Zhang, S., et al.: GLINT-RU: gated lightweight intelligent recurrent units for sequential recommender systems. In: Proceedings of the 31st ACM SIGKDD Conference on Knowledge Discovery and Data Mining (KDD), pp. 1948–1959 (2025). https://doi.org/10.1145/3690624.3709304

CLARE: A Category-Aware RAG-Based Framework for Recommending Learning Objects in Education and Professional Training

Ichrak Ennaceur[1,2(✉)], Haytham Elghazel[1], Alexandre Aussem[1], Guillaume Lefebvre[2], and Matthieu Sonnati[2]

[1] Université Claude Bernard Lyon 1, CNRS, INSA Lyon, LIRIS, UMR5205, 69622 Villeurbanne, France
{ichrak.ennaceur,haytham.elghazel,alexandre.aussem}@liris.cnrs.fr
[2] Inokufu, Lyon, France
{guillaume,matt}@inokufu.com

Abstract. The growing diversity of professional training resources and learning objects, from MOOCs and micro-credentials to certified vocational programs, poses significant challenges for learners seeking pedagogically coherent and personalized pathways. In this paper, we introduce CLARE (Category-aware Learning object recommendation with Augmented REtrieval), a hybrid framework that unites sequential category prediction with retrieval-augmented generation (RAG) via large language models (LLMs) to guide learners toward relevant, pedagogically sound opportunities. At its core, CLARE leverages structured learning categories as semantic anchors to align user intent, educational taxonomies, and content retrieval. The framework comprises two key modules: (1) a BERT4Rec-based model that forecasts the next relevant learning categories from a learner's historical interactions and (2) a category-aware prompt engineering strategy enhanced by In-Context Learning (ICL) that supplies the LLM with representative learning patterns to generate highly personalized learning recommendations. We evaluate CLARE on a real-world training dataset under both *full-context* and *cold-start* conditions. Our results demonstrate that integrating category-driven retrieval and ICL-augmented prompt design substantially improves recommendation relevance and coverage. These findings underscore the promise of combining LLM-powered RAG pipelines with domain-structured metadata to deliver adaptive, scalable, and pedagogically coherent learning guidance.

Keywords: Learning object recommendation · Retrieval-Augmented Generation · In-context learning · Learning categories

1 Introduction

The rapid expansion of online educational and training opportunities, ranging from individual courses, structured training programs, MOOCs, and bootcamps,

I. Awan et al. (Eds.): WISE 2025, LNCS 16367, pp. 79–94, 2026.
https://doi.org/10.1007/978-981-95-7394-3_6

has transformed the landscape of lifelong learning. Educational platforms such as Coursera, edX, Udemy, and others now index millions of learning objects, offering unprecedented flexibility for individuals aiming to upskill, reskill, or transition into new career paths. However, this abundance of content brings a critical challenge: how can learners efficiently navigate large, heterogeneous catalogs to identify educational pathways that are not only relevant to their goals and prior knowledge, but also pedagogically coherent?

Traditional search engines rely on keyword matching and often fail to capture the intent behind learners queries, especially when users lack a clear vision of their needs. This limitation becomes even more pronounced with the emergence of new professions, driven by rapid technological change, and the arrival of numerous specialized training programs, which increase the complexity and diversity of available learning options. Conversely, recommender systems based on collaborative filtering or content similarity tend to underperform in educational contexts, particularly when facing cold-start scenarios where historical data on users is unavailable (*user cold-start*) or when new learning objects are recently introduced on training platforms *item cold-start* [2,6,16]. These challenges hinder the construction of meaningful and personalized learning trajectories, an essential requirement in educational platforms.

Recent advances in artificial intelligence, particularly the rise of Large Language Models (LLMs), offer new capabilities for recommendation [15,22]. LLMs can interpret natural language queries, perform few-shot generalization via prompt engineering, and generate human-like recommendations [11]. When paired with Retrieval-Augmented Generation (RAG), they can also ground their outputs in external documents to increase the factual relevance and reduce hallucination [7].

Despite their promising capabilities, LLMs remain notably underutilized in the development of educational recommender systems. Their potential to provide nuanced, goal-oriented guidance and adapt to the evolving landscape of learner needs is still largely untapped. Importantly, LLMs offer a compelling approach to cold-start challenges, both on the user side, by interpreting intent from minimal input, and on the item side, by generating semantically rich representations of newly introduced learning objects, even in the absence of historical interaction data. This makes them particularly well-suited to environments where training content is continuously updated. These advances create an opportunity to rethink educational recommender systems, integrating both structured domain knowledge and generative capabilities.

In line with this vision, recent approaches in educational recommendation using LLMs and RAG frameworks have demonstrated considerable promise [10, 12,14]. However, these approaches frequently overlook the explicit incorporation of structured taxonomies of learning objects, which represent a valuable source of semantic and pedagogical information. The absence of such taxonomical guidance limits the ability of the systems to effectively address cold-start challenges, where newly introduced learning materials lack historical interaction data. Without semantic anchors, the retrieval and recommendation processes risk being less precise and less aligned with educational objectives.

With this motivation in mind, we present a novel hybrid recommendation framework specifically designed for the educational domain, termed Category-aware Learning object recommendation with Augmented REtrieval (CLARE). While inspired by general-purpose hybrid recommenders, CLARE is uniquely tailored to support pedagogical personalization across a variety of learner contexts, including both full-context and cold-start scenarios. The framework operates in two stages. First, a sequential recommendation module based on the BERT4Rec architecture [17] predicts the most relevant next learning categories, drawing on the learner's historical trajectory and structured domain taxonomies. These categories serve as both interpretable semantic anchors that align new content with pedagogical intent, and as guiding signals for the second stage: a RAG-based pipeline that constructs an enriched prompt by integrating the user's query, the predicted categories, and representative learning patterns. These patterns are derived using In-Context Learning (ICL) [4], which selects illustrative examples from users with closely matching learning histories to provide relevant behavioral signals. By conditioning the LLM on semantically aligned user profiles, this mechanism enables the generation of more relevant and personalized learning recommendations. To the best of our knowledge, this is the first attempt to apply ICL in this way within educational recommendation, using examples from similar learners to simulate personalized contexts.

The effectiveness of CLARE for course recommendation is rigorously validated through extensive comparative experiments on a real-world dataset sampled from users training histories within a large-scale educational platform.

The rest of the paper is organized as follow: Sect. 2 reviews recent studies on educational recommender systems. Section 3 details our framework, including sequential category prediction and category-aware prompt engineering with In-Context Learning. Experiments on a real-world training dataset are presented in Sect. 4. We raise several issues for future work and conclude with a summary of our contributions in Sect. 6.

2 Related Work

In this section, we will briefly review several lines of work closely related to ours, including *General recommandation* and *Educational Recommender Systems.*

2.1 General Recommendation

Personalized recommendation has traditionally relied on *Collaborative Filtering* (CF), which captures similarities in user behavior, and content-based approaches that leverage item metadata. Deep learning has advanced this field, notably through sequential models such as BERT4Rec [17], which models ordered user behavior using bidirectional self-attention.

Large Language Models (LLMs) now offer new capabilities for recommendation [3,22]. They can process natural language, perform zero- or few-shot generalization, and generate coherent suggestions. LLMRec [19], for instance, enriches user-item representations and leverages graph augmentation for enhanced performance.

RAG-based approaches [7] augment LLMs with retrieved content, anchoring generation in factual context and reducing hallucination. Prompt engineering techniques like In-context Learning (ICL) [4] guide LLMs through task examples without modifying model weights, enabling adaptation to new tasks efficiently.

Fine-tuning remains an alternative path for aligning LLMs with recommendation tasks. In full-model tuning, GPT4Rec [9] trains a GPT-2 model to generate queries from user histories, which are passed to a retriever. Lightweight methods such as LoRA, as in TALLRec [1], reduce adaptation cost while preserving task specificity.

2.2 Educational Recommender Systems

In education, recommender systems must navigate heterogeneous resources such as MOOCs, certifications, and micro-credentials. LLM-based systems like RAMO [14] integrate RAG with LLMs to produce context-aware course suggestions. However, personalization remains limited due to the absence of user-level benchmarks.

Other works [12] explore fine-tuning GPT or LLaMA models on enrollment histories, showing improved accuracy and diversity. Yet, fine-tuning in education faces challenges such as limited annotated data and domain drift from general pretraining corpora.

A critical gap in both RAG and fine-tuned systems is the lack of explicit integration of structured learning taxonomies. This omission limits semantic alignment and interpretability, particularly in cold-start settings. Addressing this requires approaches that embed pedagogical categories throughout the retrieval and generation process, a key motivation for CLARE.

3 The CLARE Framework for Educational Guidance

3.1 Overview of the Framework

CLARE (Category-aware Learning object recommendation with Augmented REtrieval) supports educational personalization by combining category-level sequence modeling with retrieval-augmented generation (RAG). In Stage 1, a BERT4Rec-based module predicts the next relevant learning categories from a learner's historical trajectory, capturing pedagogical patterns across domains. In Stage 2, a structured prompt is constructed using the user's query, retrieved course descriptions, predicted categories, past history (if available), and few-shot examples from similar users via in-context learning (ICL). The predicted categories act as semantic anchors, while ICL provides behavioral cues to guide generation. This architecture supports both *full-context* and *cold-start* scenarios. Figure 1 illustrates the architecture of CLARE in the standard full-context setting.

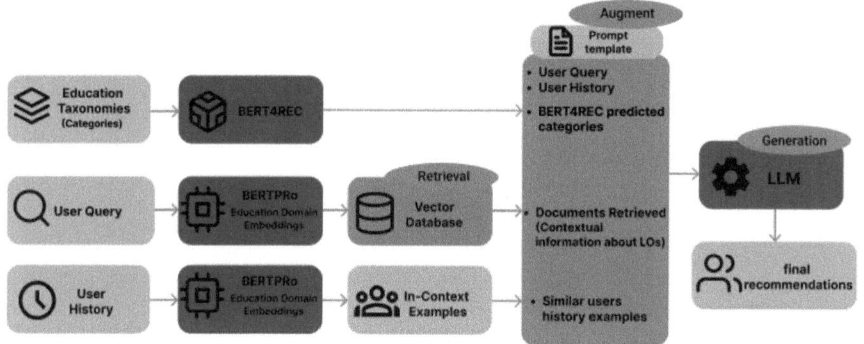

Fig. 1. CLARE in a standard full-context scenario.

3.2 Sequential Prediction of Learning Categories for Structured Guidance

CLARE leverages a sequential recommendation module based on BERT4Rec [17], fine-tuned on chronologically ordered sequences of high-level educational categories (*e.g.*, data analysis, project management). These category-level trajectories capture learners' pedagogical progress over time and help mitigate data sparsity compared to item-level modeling. The model is trained using a masked modeling objective to infer the most probable next steps in a learner's educational pathway. At inference time, it produces a ranked list of predicted categories, which are not used directly for content retrieval, but instead serve as structured semantic signals in the prompt submitted to the LLM. In *user cold-start* scenarios where no historical interaction data is available, this module is bypassed in favor of a query-based category inference mechanism, as described in Sect. 3.5.

3.3 Educationally-Aligned Embedding Representations with BERTEPro

To ensure semantic representations are well-aligned with the education and professional training domain, CLARE integrates BERTEPro [8], a sentence embedding model specialized for educational and professional content. It combines continued pre-training on domain-specific corpora and supervised fine-tuning on Natural Language Inference (NLI) [13] and Semantic Textual Similarity (STS) [18] tasks to produce semantically meaningful embeddings. These representations are used consistently across the pipeline for queries, history, categories, and learning objects ensuring coherent semantic alignment in retrieval and generation.

3.4 Retrieval-Augmented Generation with Learner-Aligned Prompting

In the second stage of CLARE, a retrieval-augmented generation (RAG) pipeline generates personalized learning recommendations using a large language model (LLM). The system builds structured prompts that integrate free-text user input with pedagogically meaningful signals to guide the generation process toward coherent and relevant suggestions.

Each prompt consists of the following elements: the user query, a set of learning categories (either predicted by BERT4Rec or inferred in *user cold-start* scenario), the learner's history (if available), and few-shot examples via in-context learning (ICL). These examples are drawn from semantically similar learners and include a historytarget pair to help the LLM generalize next-step recommendations.

This prompt design balances open-ended input with structured guidance. Learning categories act as semantic anchors, while ICL enhances personalization through behavioral analogy. Together, they enable CLARE to produce recommendations that are both relevant and pedagogically coherent.

3.5 Query-Based Category Inference for Cold-Start Learners

In educational recommendation scenarios, many users arrive without prior interaction history especially on open platforms targeting lifelong learners, job seekers, or career switchers (*i.e. cold-start users*). To address this, we introduce a query-based category inference module that predicts relevant learning categories directly from the user's natural language query. This mechanism allows CLARE to maintain semantic alignment and offer structured guidance even for new or anonymous users.

We use BERTEPro to embed the input query q and compute its cosine similarity with all category embeddings $\mathbf{ec}_1, \ldots, \mathbf{ec}_n$. The top-$k$ most similar categories are selected and incorporated into the LLM prompt as semantic anchors.

Example: Query-Based Category Inference

User Query: *Competitive Business Strategy Course*
Top-5 matched categories (by cosine similarity):

- Business Strategy & Innovation (score: 0.8421)
- Strategic Planning & Policy Making (score: 0.8294)
- Sales & Business Development (score: 0.8012)
- Marketing & Market Strategy (score: 0.7908)
- Business Essentials & Operational Management (score: 0.7743)

These inferred categories are then injected into the prompt presented to the LLM during generation. They act as thematic anchors that steer the model toward pedagogically relevant recommendations, even without prior user history. Figure 2 illustrates the *user cold-start* inference pipeline.

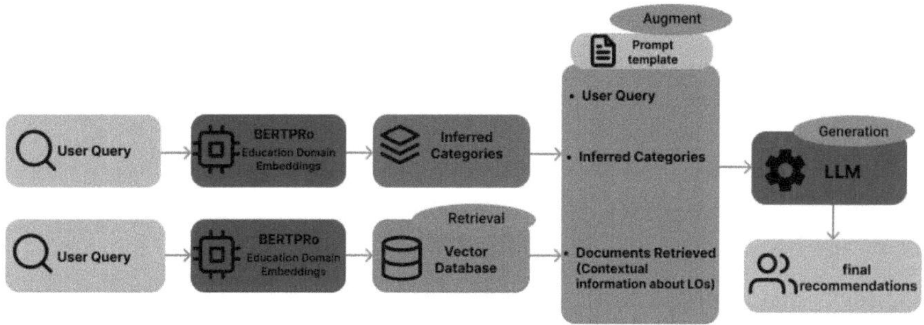

Fig. 2. CLARE in a *user cold-start* scenario.

4 Experiments: Data and Methodology

4.1 Dataset and Preprocessing

We evaluate CLARE using real-world learner interaction data from a large-scale educational platform. A curated subset of Coursera courses and user interactions forms the basis for training and evaluation. The following subsections outline the dataset composition and preprocessing steps for both sequential modeling and retrieval components.

Dataset Description. The raw dataset is extracted from a large-scale educational platform indexing millions of LOs. To ensure metadata consistency and pedagogical alignment, we retain only Coursera courses and their associated user interactions, each annotated with a timestamp and structured metadata (course title, description, and learning categories).

The full dataset contains 45,501 unique learners and 150 unique course categories, with a total of 1,911,954 learnercategory interactions. On average, each user interacted with approximately 42.1 categories, and each category appeared in 12,662 interactions.

To evaluate our framework, we extract a curated subset of 5,594 anonymized learners and 3,416 unique Coursera courses, focusing on sequences with sufficient interaction history and well-annotated metadata. The average sequence length per user is approximately 14.8 course interactions, enabling robust sequential modeling while preserving pedagogical coherence.

Preparation for Sequential Modeling. We represent each learner's trajectory as a sequence of normalized educational categories, selected from a controlled vocabulary of 150 unique labels. Sequences are truncated to 50 tokens and appended with a `[SEP]` token. Users with fewer than five interactions are excluded. The data is prepared in Atomic files format and split chronologically (80/20) for training and evaluation.

4.2 Comparative Analysis

To assess the effectiveness of CLARE across different learner contexts, we design a comparative study structured around three key dimensions: prompt composition, scenario type, and baseline systems.

Prompt Design Variants. We evaluate the impact of different prompt components by testing the following configurations:

- **Query-only:** Includes only the user's raw query. This baseline tests the LLM's ability to generate recommendations from unstructured input without any external grounding or semantic scaffolding.
- **Query + Retrieved Documents:** a RAG-style configuration that augments the prompt with top-ranked learning object descriptions retrieved from the semantic search module using BERTEPro. These documents offer factual and domain-specific grounding, helping to mitigate hallucinations and improve contextual relevance. This setup is comparable to the RAMO approach [14].
- **Query + Retrieved Documents + Categories:** Further enriches the prompt with a set of learning categories titles, either predicted from the learner's history (*full-context*) or inferred from the query (*user cold-start*). These categories serve as semantic scaffolds that guide the LLM's generation toward structured and pedagogically coherent outputs.
- **ICL-enhanced Prompt (Query + Retrieved Documents + Categories + Few-shot Examples):** Adds in-context demonstrations derived from users with similar learning trajectories. Each example includes a historical course sequence and the corresponding next course taken. These examples are added to the prompt to enable in-context learning (ICL), allowing the LLM to generalize via analogical reasoning from behaviorally similar learners.

ICL Prompt Template

Prompt Template:
Your task is to recommend the top 3 courses based on a user's history and similar users' patterns.
User Query: *free-text user query*
User History: *list of previously followed learning items*
Relevant Learning Categories: *list of predicted categories*
Examples from Similar Users:
- User A: followed: *course 1, course 2, ...* → Then: *next course*
- User B: followed: *course 1, course 2, ...* → Then: *next course*
Instruction: Based on these patterns, recommend the top 3 courses for the main user. Provide only course titles.

This experimental setup enables us to isolate and quantify the pedagogical contribution of each prompt component particularly retrieval, category scaffolding, and ICL across both full-context and cold-start scenarios.

Scenarios: Full-Context vs. Cold-Start. We evaluate CLARE under two complementary usage scenarios that reflect realistic learner profiles on educational platforms. In the *full-context scenario*, the learner has a documented interaction history. CLARE leverages this history to predict relevant learning categories using BERT4Rec, which are then incorporated into the prompt along with the learner's past trajectory. Few-shot ICL examples from behaviorally similar users are also included to guide generation, enhancing personalization through implicit modeling of learning paths.

In contrast, the *cold-start scenario* covers both *user-based* and *item-based* variants. In the *user cold-start* setting, where no interaction history is available, the prompt is constructed without ICL examples, and categories are inferred directly from the learner's query to ground the generation. In the *item cold-start* setting, where new courses (LOs) lack interaction data, CLARE naturally supports recommendation through its retrieval-augmented generation pipeline: course descriptions are semantically aligned with predicted categories to enable meaningful retrieval and prompting.

To evaluate performance in the *item cold-start* setting, we follow a targeted evaluation protocol focused on the five most popular courses in the dataset, identified by their high number of enrollments. For each course, we remove it from the interaction histories of users who had previously engaged with it. These courses then serve as target items, and we assess whether CLARE is able to surface them among its top-K recommendations. This setup enables us to test the system's ability to recommend entirely unseen items based solely on their semantic features and alignment with user intent, under various prompt configurations.

Across both cold-start settings, the generated or inferred categories act as interpretable representations of learner interests and serve as semantic anchors to support retrieval and recommendation even in the absence of behavioral data. This evaluation framework allows us to assess CLARE's robustness under varying input conditions.

Compared Systems and Baselines. To contextualize the performance of CLARE, we compare it against representative generative baselines drawn from recent literature on LLM-based recommendation. These baselines reflect two major paradigms: retrieval-augmented generation (RAG) without personalization, and autoregressive fine-tuned language models applied to sequential recommendation.

As discussed above, we implement RAMO [14], referred to as UQ + DR (RAMO). It provides a minimal configuration to assess content-aware generation without personalization or pedagogical alignment.

Second, we evaluate an autoregressive sequence modeling baseline adapted from GPT4Rec [9], where a GPT-2 model is fine-tuned on historical course sequences to generate textual queries, which are subsequently used for retrieval via BM25. This model captures sequential behavioral patterns but lacks semantic scaffolding through structured categories.

Finally, we include fully fine-tuned LLMs (GPT-2 and LLaMA-2) trained on course enrollment sequences as introduced in [12].

4.3 Evaluation Metrics

To provide a comprehensive assessment of CLARE's performance in personalized course recommendation, we adopt standard ranking metrics that are widely used in recommender system research [12]. These metrics evaluate both the accuracy and ranking quality of the generated recommendations, particularly in terms of their ability to correctly predict the course that a learner will enroll in next.

In numerical evaluations, we adopt top-k *Hit Ratio* (HR@K), top-k *Mean Reciprocal Rank* (MRR@K), and top-k *Normalized Discounted Cumulative Gain* (NDCG@K) metrics. HR@K measures whether the ground-truth item appears in the top-K predictions. MRR@K reflects how early the correct item is ranked, rewarding systems that place relevant courses near the top. NDCG@K further assesses ranking quality by applying logarithmic discounting to lower-ranked items, emphasizing both relevance and order. Specifically, we report results on HR@{3,5}, MRR@{3,5} and NDCG@{3,5} for evaluation. All metrics are computed across both *full-context* and *cold-start* settings. This dual setup allows us to measure CLARE's robustness under varying levels of input information.

To assess *item cold-start* performance, we introduce the *Recovery Rate at rank K (RR@K)*, defined as the proportion of users for whom the removed item is successfully retrieved within the top-K recommendations. This evaluation metric quantifies the model's capacity to recommend items with no prior interaction history, relying solely on semantic representations and prompt alignment.

Table 1. LLM token limits and usage cost

Model	Cost	Token Limit
Mistral-Nemo-Instruct-2407	Free	8,000
LLaMA-2-7B-Chat	Free	4,096

4.4 Parameters and Implementation

To support reproducibility and clarify implementation details, we report here the key parameters and resources used across the different components of our system.

BERT4Rec Training. We train BERT4Rec on chronologically ordered learner interaction sequences using the RecBole framework [20,21]. The model is optimized with cross-entropy loss and a 10% masking ratio, using an 80/20 chronological train-test split. Training is conducted on an NVIDIA T4 GPU and takes approximately 9 h to converge.

LLM Inference. As shown in Table 1, we use Mistral-Nemo-Instruct-2407 and LLaMA-2-7B-Chat, two open-source models deployed locally via Hugging Face pipelines. Each prompt generates up to 500 tokens. Generated outputs are parsed to extract top-K course titles. All generations are performed on an NVIDIA A100 GPU.

Retrieval Configuration. Course descriptions are embedded using BERTPRo and indexed with `FAISS` [5] for efficient semantic retrieval. We use the default `IndexFlatIP` configuration, which computes inner product scores between normalized embeddings, effectively approximating cosine similarity. The top-K retrieved documents are injected into prompts alongside the user query, predicted or inferred categories, and, when available, user history and ICL examples.

Table 2. Top-3 and Top-5 recommendation performances across prompt variants and baselines (values shown in %).

Model	Prompt Variant	HR@3	MRR@3	NDCG@3	HR@5	MRR@5	NDCG@5
Mistral	UQ only	0.40	0.21	0.26	0.92	0.33	0.39
	RAMO: UQ + DR	5.82	3.77	4.41	8.40	4.92	5.38
	UQ + DR + INF CATS	7.95	5.51	6.21	10.82	6.08	6.90
	UQ + DR + CATS	9.16	6.24	6.92	11.96	6.72	7.60
	CLARE: UQ + DR + CATS + ICL	**11.75**	**7.42**	**8.12**	**14.28**	**8.06**	**8.93**
LLaMA-2	UQ only	0.12	0.07	0.09	0.33	0.14	0.18
	RAMO: UQ + DR	3.98	2.52	2.91	6.85	3.63	4.21
	UQ + DR + INF CATS	6.94	4.70	5.35	9.90	5.37	6.14
	UQ + DR + CATS	7.55	5.13	5.78	10.41	5.74	6.52
	CLARE: UQ + DR + CATS + ICL	**10.23**	**6.80**	**7.40**	**13.17**	**7.56**	**8.25**
GPT4Rec (1 Query)		4.83	3.08	3.57	6.91	3.94	4.43
GPT4Rec (5 Queries)		6.02	3.96	4.51	8.27	4.71	5.30
GPT-2 Finetuned		5.60	3.93	3.15	6.23	4.76	4.08
LLaMA-2 Finetuned		5.89	4,17	3.74	6.81	4.90	4.26

5 Results and Discussions

This section presents an extensive experimental analysis of the performance of our proposed approach across the different prompt configurations and user scenarios, focusing on the impact of learning categories, prompt design, and cold-start adaptations.

5.1 Full-Context Results

In full-context scenario, CLARE's use of predicted learning categories proves to be a major driver of performance. As seen in Table 2, the inclusion of structured categories in the prompt significantly improves recommendation quality across all metrics compared to both the query-only and RAG-style baselines (RAMO). This confirms that pedagogical categories act as effective semantic scaffolds, aligning user queries with relevant learning trajectories and reducing noise in generation.

Performance further improves when ICL is activated. By injecting examples from behaviorally similar users, the ICL-enhanced variant, corresponding to the full CLARE pipeline (UQ + DR + CATS + ICL), achieves the best overall results. Notably, Mistral reaches 14.28% on HR@5 and 8.93% on NDCG@5, underscoring the synergistic effect of combining structured taxonomies with analogical reasoning through ICL. Experiments confirm the effectiveness of the CLARE strategy, which combines semantic anchoring via predicted categories with in-context learning based on similar users' trajectories. This integrated approach enables the LLM to generate pedagogically coherent and personalized recommendations, significantly outperforming simple query-based retrieval methods.

Compared to GPT4Rec, CLARE offers stronger alignment between user intent and educational structure, while avoiding the ambiguity of free-text generation. Fine-tuned models (*i.e.* GPT-2 and LLaMA-2), though promising in theory, show limited performance in our setup likely due to the small volume of training data and the high cost of full-model adaptation. In contrast, CLARE's prompt-based approach enables efficient, interpretable, and scalable personalization. These findings confirm that combining LLMs with structured educational taxonomies and representative learner patterns enhances recommendation relevance, coherence, and pedagogical value.

To better illustrate the internal dynamics of the CLARE framework, we present in Box titled *LLM Responses for Prompt Design Variants* a concrete qualitative example that highlights the incremental effect of each prompt component. The baseline *Query-only* configuration produces vague and overly generic titles (*e.g.*, "Google Sheets & Excel: The Complete Guide"), which lack alignment with real-world course offerings and provide little actionable value. When *Retrieved Documents* are added, the LLM begins to anchor its output in concrete course descriptions, resulting in more realistic and relevant suggestions (*e.g.*, "Introduction to Data Analysis Using Excel"). However, without pedagogical structure, the output may still lack a clear sense of progression.

Incorporating *Learning Categories* significantly improves thematic coherence. The LLM is now guided not only by content relevance but also by the learner's educational trajectory, enabling the generation of recommendations that fit logically within a broader learning pathway (*e.g.*, "Spreadsheets for Beginners using Google Sheets"). Finally, the inclusion of *ICL Examples* further enhances personalization. By conditioning the model on analogical user behaviors, it learns to suggest next-step courses that reflect empirically observed transitions among similar learners. This culminates in high-quality, context-aware recommendations that are not only relevant but also pedagogically justified.

Overall, the example demonstrates how CLARE transitions from generic, surface-level suggestions to highly targeted recommendations through the cumulative integration of semantic, structural, and behavioral signals.

5.2 Cold-Start Results

Table 3. Recovery Rate at Rank K (RR@K) (%) for $K = 3$ and $K = 5$ on the Top 5 Most Popular Courses under Different Prompt Configurations Using Mistral

Course Title	RR@3		RR@5	
	RAMO: UQ+DR	CLARE	RAMO: UQ+DR	CLARE
Data Visualization With Python	13.3% (2/15)	26.6% (4/15)	20% (3/15)	40% (6/15)
Business Strategy	7.6% (1/13)	15.3% (2/13)	15.3% (2/13)	30.7% (4/13)
Management & Financial Accounting	8.3% (1/12)	25% (3/12)	16.6% (2/12)	25% (3/12)
Data Science Capstone	9.1% (1/11)	18.1% (2/11)	18.1% (2/11)	27.2% (3/11)
Essential Google Cloud Infrastructure	10% (1/10)	30% (3/10)	20% (2/10)	30% (3/10)

CLARE is explicitly designed to handle cold-start scenarios through its use of semantic signals and educational taxonomies. In the *user cold-start* setting, where learners arrive without any interaction history, the system employs query-based category inference to estimate relevant learning domains. As shown in Table 2, this strategy (referred to as (UQ + DR + INF CATS)) significantly outperforms both the **UQ only** and the **RAG-style** (RAMO: UQ + DR) baselines. The inferred categories help the model maintain pedagogical relevance and thematic alignment, even in the absence of behavioral context.

In the *item cold-start* setting, we evaluate the system's ability to recommend previously unseen items by focusing on the five most popular courses removed from users' histories. For each course, the number in parentheses (*e.g.*, 15 for Data Visualization With Python) corresponds to the number of users for whom this course was the next intended item in their target interaction sequence (that is, the "ground truth" next course to recommend). We measure the *Recovery Rate at rank K (RR@K)* as the percentage of these users for whom the removed course appears within the top-K recommendations. As reported in Table 3, the CLARE pipeline CLARE pipeline (UQ + DR + CATS + ICL) consistently outperforms the **RAG-style** baseline (RAMO: UQ + DR) across all courses and ranks. Notably, CLARE nearly doubles the recovery rates in most cases, demonstrating its enhanced ability to retrieve cold-start items by leveraging structured educational taxonomies and representative learner behavior patterns through in-context learning.

LLM Responses for Prompt Design Variants

User Query: *Google Sheets to Excel*
User History:
Excel Basics for Data Analysis, Build a Budget and Analyze Variance using Google Sheets, Create a Home Affordability Worksheet in Google Sheets, Excel Skills for Business: Intermediate I
Predicted Categories:
Statistical Representation,Data & Statistical Analysis, Data Visualization & Tools, Data Management & Warehousing
Retrieved Documents (Top Examples due to space limitations):

- *Create a Financial Statement using Google Sheets*
  Categories: Accounting & Auditing, Cost Management & Corporate Finance, Data & Statistical Analysis
- *Introduction to Business Analysis Using Spreadsheets: Basics*
  Categories: Business Intelligence, Data Management & Warehousing, Operations, Risk Management & Logistics
- *Spreadsheets for Beginners using Google Sheets*
  Categories: Data & Statistical Analysis, Business Essentials & Operational Management, 'Data Visualization &Tools
- *Introduction to Data Analysis Using Excel*
  Categories: Data & Statistical Analysis, Data Visualization &Tools

Model Outputs per Prompt Configuration:

- **Query Only:**
  - Mastering Advanced Google Sheets
  - Google Sheets to Excel Conversion Mastery
  - Google Sheets & Excel: The Complete Guide
- **Query + Retrieved Documents:**
  - Introduction to Business Analysis Using Spreadsheets: Basics
  - Introduction to Data Analysis Using Excel
  - Create a Financial Statement using Google Sheets
- **Query + Retrieved Documents + Categories:**
  - Create a Simple Project Timeline in Google Sheets
  - Create a Financial Statement using Google Sheets
  - Spreadsheets for Beginners using Google Sheets
- **ICL-Enhanced Prompt:**
  - Spreadsheets for Beginners using Google Sheets
  - Introduction to Business Analysis Using Spreadsheets: Basics
  - Introduction to Data Analysis Using Excel

6 Conclusion and Future Work

We introduced CLARE, a category-aware hybrid framework for educational recommendation, which unifies sequential modeling, retrieval-augmented generation, and in-context prompting. By using structured learning categories as semantic anchors, CLARE enhances recommendation coherence, personalization, and relevance even in cold-start scenarios. Experimental results show that CLARE outperforms retrieval-only and fine-tuned generative baselines, particularly by aligning recommendations with pedagogical intent.

As future work, we plan to enrich the framework with a knowledge graph to model user profiles and category hierarchies, and to investigate the grounding of LLM outputs in retrieved documents to better understand hallucination risks. We also aim to evaluate CLARE on larger and more diverse datasets spanning multiple training providers (*e.g.*, edX, Udemy, FUN), in order to assess its effectiveness and robustness in heterogeneous educational ecosystems. These directions will help further validate CLARE's applicability in real-world, multi-source learning environments.

References

1. Bao, K., Zhang, J., Zhang, Y., Wang, W., Feng, F., He, X.: TALLRec: an effective and efficient tuning framework to align large language model with recommendation. In: Proceedings of the 17th ACM Conference on Recommender Systems, RecSys 2023, Singapore, Singapore, 18–22 September 2023, pp. 1007–1014. ACM (2023)
2. Bustos-López, M., Alor-Hernández, G., Sánchez-Cervantes, J.L., Paredes-Valverde, M.A., del Pilar Salas-Zárate, M.: EduRecomSys: an educational resource recommender system based on collaborative filtering and emotion detection. Interact. Comput. **32**(4), 407–432 (2021)
3. Deldjoo, Y., et al.: A review of modern recommender systems using generative models (gen-RecSys). In: Proceedings of the 30th ACM SIGKDD Conference on Knowledge Discovery and Data Mining, KDD 2024, Barcelona, Spain, 25–29 August 2024, pp. 6448–6458. ACM (2024)
4. Dong, Q., et al.: A survey on in-context learning. In: Proceedings of the 2024 Conference on Empirical Methods in Natural Language Processing, EMNLP, Miami, FL, pp. 1107–1128 (2024)
5. Douze, M., et al.: The FAISS library. CoRR abs/2401.08281 (2024)
6. Feixiang, X.: Intelligent personalized recommendation method based on optimized collaborative filtering algorithm in primary and secondary education resource system. IEEE Access **12**, 28860–28872 (2024)
7. Gao, Y., et al.: Retrieval-augmented generation for large language models: a survey. CoRR abs/2312.10997 (2023)
8. Lefebvre, G., Elghazel, H., Guillet, T., Aussem, A., Sonnati, M.: A new sentence embedding framework for the education and professional training domain with application to hierarchical multi-label text classification. Data Knowl. Eng. **150**, 102281 (2024)
9. Li, J., Zhang, W., Wang, T., Xiong, G., Lu, A., Medioni, G.: GPT4rec: a generative framework for personalized recommendation and user interests interpretation. In: Proceedings of the 2023 SIGIR Workshop on eCommerce. CEUR Workshop Proceedings, vol. 3589. CEUR-WS.org (2023)
10. Li, Z., Wang, Z., Wang, W., Hung, K., Xie, H., Wang, F.L.: Retrieval-augmented generation for educational application: a systematic survey. Comput. Educ.: Artif. Intell. **8**, 100417 (2025). https://doi.org/10.1016/j.caeai.2025.100417, https://www.sciencedirect.com/science/article/pii/S2666920X25000578
11. Lyu, H., et al.: LLM-rec: personalized recommendation via prompting large language models. In: Findings of the Association for Computational Linguistics: NAACL, Mexico City, Mexico, pp. 583–612. Association for Computational Linguistics (2024)
12. Ma, B., Khan, M.A.Z., Yang, T., Polyzou, A., Konomi, S.: How good are large language models for course recommendation in MOOCs? CoRR abs/2504.08208 (2025)
13. Nie, Y., Williams, A., Dinan, E., Bansal, M., Weston, J., Kiela, D.: Adversarial NLI: a new benchmark for natural language understanding. CoRR abs/1910.14599 (2019)

14. Rao, J., Lin, J.: RAMO: retrieval-augmented generation for enhancing MOOCs recommendations. CEUR Workshop Proceedings, vol. 3840. CEUR-WS.org (2024)
15. Shehmir, S., Kashef, R.: LLM4rec: a comprehensive survey on the integration of large language models in recommender systems—approaches, applications and challenges. Future Internet **17**(6) (2025). https://doi.org/10.3390/fi17060252, https://www.mdpi.com/1999-5903/17/6/252
16. Song, W., Zhang, Q., Fong, S., Li, T.: Recommendation of learning resources for MOOCs based on historical sequential behaviours. Expert Syst. **42**(5) (2025)
17. Sun, F., et al.: BERT4rec: sequential recommendation with bidirectional encoder representations from transformer. In: Proceedings of the 28th ACM International Conference on Information and Knowledge Management, pp. 1441–1450 (2019)
18. Wang, A., Singh, A., Michael, J., Hill, F., Levy, O., Bowman, S.R.: GLUE: a multi-task benchmark and analysis platform for natural language understanding. arXiv preprint arXiv:1804.07461 (2018)
19. Wei, W., et al.: LLMRec: large language models with graph augmentation for recommendation. In: Proceedings of the 17th ACM International Conference on Web Search and Data Mining, WSDM 2024, Merida, Mexico, pp. 806–815. ACM (2024)
20. Zhao, W.X., et al.: RecBole 2.0: towards a more up-to-date recommendation library. In: Proceedings of the 31st ACM International Conference on Information & Knowledge Management, pp. 4722–4726 (2022)
21. Zhao, W.X., et al.: RecBole: towards a unified, comprehensive and efficient framework for recommendation algorithms. In: proceedings of the 30th ACM International Conference on Information & Knowledge Management, pp. 4653–4664 (2021)
22. Zhao, Z., et al.: Recommender systems in the era of large language models (LLMs). IEEE Trans. Knowl. Data Eng. **36**(11), 6889–6907 (2024)

Recommending the Right Recommender System Software: A Practical Guide

Ayoub Akhadam[1(✉)], Oumayma Kbibchi[2], Loubna Mekouar[3], Youssef Iraqi[3], Bassma Guermah[1], and Mohammed Boulmalf[1]

[1] TICLab, College of Engineering and Architecture, International University of Rabat, 11103 Rabat, Morocco
ayoub.akhadam@uir.ac.ma
[2] ENSIAS, 10000 Rabat, Morocco
[3] School of Computer Science, Mohammed VI Polytechnic University, 43150 Ben Guerir, Morocco

Abstract. Recent advances in Recommender Systems (RSs) have led to the development of numerous software frameworks that facilitate research, evaluation, and deployment. However, these tools vary significantly in their implementations, supported algorithms, evaluation strategies, and usability, making it challenging for researchers to select the most suitable framework for a given task. This paper presents a structured comparative study of RS software frameworks, focusing on their support for recommendation techniques, dataset compatibility, and evaluation metrics. We classify several tools based on different perspectives: the programming languages in which they are implemented, recommendation techniques (e.g., collaborative filtering, content-based, hybrid), dataset compatibility (e.g., MovieLens, Amazon, Netflix), and evaluation metric support (e.g., RMSE, NDCG, Precision). Our analysis serves as a practical guide for researchers and developers in selecting appropriate RS software based on task requirements and evaluation objectives.

Keywords: Recommender Systems · Recommender Systems Software · Open-source Software · Collaborative Filtering · Content-based Filtering

1 Introduction

The adoption of RSs in online services has become increasingly widespread, particularly in movie and video streaming platforms (e.g., Netflix, YouTube) and other digital media applications. Over the years, there has been a surge of interest in RSs within academia, as evidenced by dedicated tracks at leading research venues and an increasing number of scholarly publications on the subject [1–3]. Similarly, the business sector has witnessed a growing emphasis on recommendation algorithms, which have become a fundamental component of modern data science workflows. The academic community has introduced numerous frameworks for RSs [2,4], while others, such as Turicreate and Microsoft

I. Awan et al. (Eds.): WISE 2025, LNCS 16367, pp. 95–107, 2026.
https://doi.org/10.1007/978-981-95-7394-3_7

Recommenders, have emerged from major technology corporations rather than academic institutions [2,4,5]. Although these frameworks generally implement similar recommendation algorithms, they exhibit significant variations in implementation details, data handling strategies, and evaluation methodologies. These differences pose challenges for direct comparisons, particularly when evaluating the same algorithm across multiple frameworks using a standardized dataset.

Given the growing reliance on these systems across various sectors, the ability to assess their effectiveness has become increasingly important. One of the primary challenges in this field is selecting the most suitable recommendation framework for a given application. Effective evaluation requires rigorous scientific testing methodologies to objectively compare different algorithms and frameworks [6,7]. Previous research has conducted a comparative evaluation of RS tools, presenting detailed comparisons of different RS software [8]. Still, there is a need for a structured framework to support the practical selection of RS tools based on project-specific requirements. The present study addresses this gap by developing a practical selection guide that maps core project needs to the capabilities of several RS frameworks, supporting more informed decision-making in RS tool selection. The guide is built on a comparison of actively maintained tools, based on the programming language used, the number of GitHub stars, the type of RS techniques implemented, the datasets supported, and the evaluation metrics available.

The remainder of this paper is organized as follows: Sect. 2 introduces RSs. Section 3 investigates RS software and classifies them based on recommendation techniques, supported datasets, and evaluation metrics. Section 4 suggests recommendations for RS software selection. Section 5 proposes challenges and future directions, while Sect. 6 concludes the paper.

2 Recommender Systems

RSs are specialized systems designed to provide personalized suggestions to users based on various criteria. These systems can identify products or services that users will likely find appealing while also filtering out those that may be of lesser interest [9,10]. Companies like Netflix and Amazon utilize extensive recommender algorithms to help users discover suitable products, movies, or services [9]. RSs have also been investigated in other domains, including peer-to-peer systems [11], and Blockchain [12]. Commonly employed recommender approaches include Collaborative Filtering (CF), Content-Based Filtering (CBF), Demographic-based Filtering (DBF), Knowledge-based Filtering, and Hybrid systems. CF produces recommendations by calculating similarities between user preferences, relying on previous user ratings and user-item interactions, without analyzing item content. However, CF faces challenges like the cold-start problem and potential security issues [9,13]. CBF RSs use user ratings and item attributes to build user profiles, employing similarity metrics like cosine similarity to match user interests with item features [13]. A novel RS architecture with a sharable user profile was developed in [14]. DBF suggests products based on user demographic attributes such as age, gender, or country, assuming similar demographic profiles imply similar preferences; however, it struggles with scalability in handling large datasets [9]. Knowledge-based RSs leverage explicit knowledge about products, user preferences, and recommendation criteria, particularly suitable for complex domains like financial services and tourism [9]. Hybrid RSs combine multiple recommendation methods, typically merging CF with other techniques, such as DBF, to improve accuracy and mitigate individual method limitations [9].

3 Recommender Systems Software

A large and growing body of literature has investigated the development of RS software, with numerous tools emerging in recent years for commercial and open-source use. A summary of some RS tools is presented in this GitHub repository[1], which categorizes software into groups such as Software as a Service (SaaS), open-source platforms, and academically oriented frameworks. This repository, along with this website[2] served as the basis for our Table 1, which we have adapted and extended. This study focuses on open-source software that facilitates transparency, reproducibility, and adaptability for research purposes. This section presents a comprehensive survey of RS software. The goal is to provide a comparative perspective that helps researchers and practitioners select the appropriate tools. Table 1 presents a structured summary of existing RS software frameworks, highlighting the number of Github stars, and the programming languages in which they are implemented. Each row in Table 1 corresponds to an RS software as described in its original paper.

To gain a comprehensive understanding of RS software, we organize our analysis into four key dimensions: the programming languages in which they are implemented, the recommendation techniques they support, the evaluation metrics used to assess model performance, and the datasets provided for benchmarking and experimentation. This classification enables us to highlight the functional and practical differences between software tools, facilitating an informed selection based on specific research goals or deployment requirements.

3.1 Classification of RS Software Based on Techniques

We begin by classifying RS software based on six core techniques: CF, CBF, knowledge-based filtering, hybrid approaches, context-aware recommendation, and sequential recommendation. Among these, CF is the most widely supported technique. Some libraries are specifically designed to support deep learning-based approaches, such as RecStudio, RecBole, DeepRec, Sequeval, Merlin, and Transformers4Rec [1,15–18], reflecting a growing trend in advanced RS research. Although many tools implement the same fundamental algorithms, their implementations vary significantly. Table 2 classifies RS software by the recommendation techniques they support.

[1] https://github.com/grahamjenson/list_of_recommender_systems.

[2] https://recommender-systems.com/resources/software-libraries/.

Table 1. Overview of RS Software Based on Their Published Papers.

Ref	Software	Year	Prog. Lang	Number of Stars	Active	Description
[19]	RePlay	2024	Python	337	Yes	End-to-end pipeline for building RSs, bridging experimentation and production. Allows switching between Pandas, Polars, or Spark at each stage for scalable computation and deployment
[20]	MAB2REC	2024	Python	143	Yes	Modular framework based on higher-order bandit-based recommendation strategies
[21]	RecStudio	2023	Python	189	Yes	Multi-stage recommender with retrieverranker architecture. Implemented +90 algorithms in PyTorch with GPU-accelerated training and web
[22]	RecPack	2022	Python	20	Yes	Toolkit for Top-N recommendation on implicit feedback Prioritizes correct evaluation and ease of reproducibility
[1]	Transformers-4Rec	2021	Python	1180	Yes	Designed for session-based recommendation using Transformer architectures. Enables testing of the latest NLP models for RS tasks
[15]	RecBole	2021	Python	3765	Yes	Built with PyTorch. Includes 73 algorithms. Supports GPU acceleration and scalable model training. Covers various types: basic, context-aware, knowledge-based, and sequential
[23]	Elliot	2021	Python	288	Yes	Modular framework supporting reproducible RS evaluation. Covers the full pipeline from data preparation to model training and evaluation. Allows the integration of custom recommendation models
[24]	Microsoft Re-commenders	2020	Python	20258	Yes	It Provides various recommendation algorithms, utilities, and Jupyter Notebook examples that demonstrate implementation methods. It serves as a centralized resource that reduces development time by offering ready-to-use components for building complete recommendation systems
[3]	LensKit	2020	Python	294	Yes	Focuses on usability and design clarity. Supports metric evaluation and integration of external models
[25]	Cornac	2020	Python	959	Yes	Multimodal RS framework. Supports social networks, product descriptions, images, and other non-traditional data sources. Provides easy access to datasets, modality handling, and evaluation utilities, including k-fold and train/test splitting
[4]	Surprise	2020	Python	6605	Yes	Easy-to-use Python library for RSs. It supports MovieLens and custom datasets via CSV or Pandas data formats. Well-documented, ideal for beginners to prototype custom prediction algorithms
[26]	BETA-Rec	2020	Python	168	Yes	A unified framework that handles dataset preprocessing, model training, monitoring, validation, and testing. Provides nine ready-to-use recommendation models and facilitates consistent experimental pipelines
[16]	Merlin	2020	Python	5241	Yes	GPU-accelerated RS framework capable of handling massive datasets and complex user/item interactions. Built for multi-GPU/multi-node scalability. Includes NVTabular for GPU-based preprocessing, HugeCTR for efficient training, and Triton Inference Server for deployment and performance monitoring
[17]	DeepRec	2019	Python	1101	Yes	Built with TensorFlow and common scientific libraries. Supports rating prediction, item ranking, and sequence-aware recommendation. GPU-enabled and modular with the recommender, backend, and utility components
[27]	SMORe	2019	C++	378	Yes	SMORe introduces a modular graph embedding architecture with sampler, mapper, and optimizer components for the structured comparison of recommendation models. Built-in C++ for fast training and industrial deployment. Supports approximate nearest neighbor search and transfer learning. Ideal for practicing and learning graph embedding in RS
[10]	Case Recommender	2018	Python	496	Yes	Supports both rating prediction and item recommendation. Designed for easy integration and development of new RS algorithms across various domains
[7]	OpenRec	2018	Python	413	Yes	Python-based framework for adaptable RS research. It uses modular components connected via well-defined interfaces. Supports easy customization and integration of new recommendation models
[18]	Sequeval	2018	Python	13	No	Framework for offline evaluation of sequence-based recommenders. Generates recommendations from pre-existing sequences. Composed of five main modules: loader, builder, profiler, splitter, and recommender
[2]	CF4J	2018	Java	59	Yes	Java-based library for CF experiments. Facilitates testing of new CF algorithms. Supports parallel execution to reduce computation time
[28]	TagRec	2017	Java	126	Yes	Open-source toolkit for developing tag-based and hashtag-based RSs. Includes five components: data processing, data modeling and analytics, recommendation algorithms, evaluation, and client-facing result delivery. Supports multiple use cases such as tag/resource/hashtag recommendations and evaluation
[6]	pyRecLab	2017	C++	122	No	C++ backend with Python bindings for ease of use and performance on large datasets. Supports formats like CSV, TSV, and JSON. Includes Item Average, Slope One, UserKNN, ItemKNN, and FunkSVD. Designed for fast prototyping and educational use
[29]	Rrecsys	2016	R	23	No	Rrecsys is an R-package replicating recommenderlab implementations. Implements item-based KNN, Weighted ALS, and Bayesian Personalized Ranking. Suitable for prototyping within R
[30]	Idomaar	2016	Ruby	32	No	Designed for multi-dimensional benchmarking of RS algorithms. Includes modular components: data container, evaluator, orchestrator, and computing environment. Facilitates reuse and dataset standardization. Supports the integration of contextual info and flexible topic/event configuration
[31]	LibRec	2015	Java	3254	No	Easy to install and compatible with Windows, Linux, and Mac OS. Designed to support research on rating prediction and item recommendation. Offers three interfaces for extensibility. Supports both sparse and dense data structures, and organizes algorithms into baseline, core, and advanced categories
[32]	LightFM	2015	Python	4928	Yes	Designed for cold-start recommendation. Combines collaborative and content-based signals. Learns high-quality metadata embeddings. Performs well with limited data and enables related tasks like tag recommendation
[33]	CARSKit	2015	Java	126	Yes	Java-based engine designed for context-aware recommendations. Modular architecture allows easy extension. Supports multidimensional ratings and integrates components for data handling, algorithm configuration, and evaluation
[13]	Mahout	2015	Java	2166	Yes	Uses Big data from reviews, ratings, and feedback to guide personalized recommendations. Employs Machine Learning (ML) algorithms in a distributed Hadoop environment using the Mahout architecture, which enables tracking and optimization of algorithm performance
[34]	RiVal	2014	Java	151	Yes	Offer fine-grained control over the evaluation process. It divides evaluation into four phases: data splitting, item recommendation, candidate item generation, and performance measurement. Property files define the evaluation type, algorithms, and framework used in standalone mode to run the full pipeline
[35]	RecDB	2013	C	367	Yes	A DBMS engine that embeds recommendation capabilities. Consists of input, SQL, and processing layers. Inputs include users, items, and user-item events. Prioritizes extensibility and flexibility within relational database environments
[5]	MyMediaLite	2011	C#	507	Yes	Handles rating prediction and item prediction using implicit feedback. Offers state-of-the-art algorithms, model serialization, and evaluation tools. Designed for both academic experimentation and industrial use

Table 2. Classification of RS Software Based on Techniques

Software	CF	CBF	KBF	Hybrid	Context-aware	Sequential
RePlay	✓			✓		✓
MAB2REC	✓	✓		✓	✓	
RecStudio	✓	✓		✓	✓	✓
RecPack	✓					✓
Transformers4Rec						✓
RecBole	✓	✓	✓		✓	✓
Elliot	✓	✓	✓	✓		
Recommenders	✓	✓		✓		✓
Lenskit	✓	✓				
Cornac	✓	✓		✓		
Surprise	✓	✓				
BETA-Rec	✓	✓			✓	✓
Merlin						✓
DeepRec	✓					✓
SMORe	✓	✓				
Case Recommender	✓	✓		✓		
OpenRec	✓	✓		✓		
Sequeval		✓				✓
CF4J	✓		✓			
TagRec	✓	✓				
pyRecLab	✓	✓			✓	
Rrecsys	✓	✓		✓		
Idomaar	✓					
LibRec	✓	✓				
LightFM	✓	✓		✓		
CARSKit	✓				✓	
Mahout	✓					
RiVal	✓	✓				
RecDB	✓	✓				
MyMediaLite	✓	✓				

3.2 Classification of RS Software Based on Dataset

Datasets play a vital role in evaluating RS software. Through our review of existing tools, we identified a set of 21 datasets frequently used across RS experiments. These datasets span various domains, including movie ratings, music, e-commerce, advertising, scientific articles, etc. Popular datasets such as MovieLens [36], Netflix, and Amazon [37] are widely supported across tools.

For instance, Transformers4Rec and Merlin are designed to handle large-scale datasets, while others like LibRec support specialized datasets such as CiaoDVD [38]. Some tools, such as Cornac, RecBole, and BETA-Rec, support a wide range of datasets, offering flexibility in benchmarking. Table 3 provides a detailed classification of datasets commonly used in RS research, categorized by domain, along with their features and the RS software that offer access to these datasets.

3.3 Classification of RS Software Based on Evaluation Metrics

Evaluation metrics are critical in determining the quality and effectiveness of recommendation models. These metrics fall into three main categories: ranking evaluation metrics (e.g., MRR, MAP, NDCG, AUC), rating prediction metrics (e.g., MAE, RMSE, NMAE), and classification accuracy metrics (e.g., precision, recall, F1-score). Metrics like RMSE and MAE help assess how close the predicted ratings are to the actual ratings while ranking metrics are used when the goal is to recommend items in a particular order. Precision and recall are especially important in classification tasks where the goal is to predict item relevance rather than specific ratings. Less commonly used metrics include Kendall's Tau and Spearman correlation. Tools such as RecStudio, RecBole, Elliot, and Cornac offer extensive support for various evaluation strategies, and in some cases, users can choose their preferred metrics to drive model performance. The formal definitions and formulas of these metrics can be found in [8]. Table 4 summarizes which metrics are supported by each tool.

4 Recommendations for Software Selection

Selecting an RS framework involves aligning software capabilities with the specific needs, goals, and constraints of a project. This section outlines a practical guide for tool selection based on project goals, techniques, datasets, scalability, evaluation needs, and programming ecosystem. Each subsection is framed as a guiding question with suggested tools provided as answers.

4.1 What Is the Primary Goal and Lifespan of Your Project?

For teaching, demonstrations, and prototyping, libraries such as Surprise, LensKit, and pyRecLab are sufficient. For research and experimentation, modular and extensible toolkits like Elliot, RecStudio, or Microsoft Recommenders provide greater flexibility. For long-term or production-oriented projects, scalable frameworks with active maintenance such as RecBole, Merlin, and RePlay are more appropriate.

4.2 Which Recommendation Techniques Must Be Supported?

When collaborative or content-based filtering is required, Cornac, Surprise, and Microsoft Recommenders provide strong implementations. For hybrid and

Table 3. Classification of software based on dataset

Domain	Dataset	Content	Software
Movie Rating	MovieLens[a]	280K users; 27M ratings; 1.1M tags; 58K movies	LensKit, RecBole, Cornac, Implicit, Case Recommender, Elliot, pyRecLab, LightFM, Surprise, DeepRec, Sequeval, CF4J, Mahout, TagRec, LibRec, RiVal, MyMediaLite, Merlin, TagRec, RecStudio, RecPack, Beta-Rec, Recommenders
	Netflix[b]	15K titles; 5B ratings	Cornac, RecBole, CF4J, MyMediaLite, RecPack
	Flixster[c]	2.5M nodes; 7.9M edges	LibRec
	Movie-Tweetings[d]	921,398 ratings; 71,707 users; 38,018 items	Idomaar
	Filmtrust[e]	1,508 users; 2,071 items; 35,497 ratings	Cornac, CF4J, LibRec
	Douban[f]	129,490 users; 58,541 items; 16,830,839 ratings	RecBole, LibRec
	CiaoDVD[g]	72.7K ratings; 40K trust ratings	LibRec
Music Rating	Yahoo! Music[h]	1M users; 600K items; 250M ratings	RecBole
	LastFM[i]	943,347 tracks; 522,366 unique tags	RecBole, Implicit, BETA-Rec, OpenRec, TagRec
E-Commerce	Amazon[j]	48,185,153 items; 54,514,264 users; 571,544,897 intercations	Cornac, RecBole, BETA-Rec, OpenRec, RecStudio, Recommenders
	Retailrocket[k]	2.7M events; 2.6M views; 69K carts; 22K transactions; 1.4M visitors	RecBole, BETA-Rec, RecPack
	Tafeng[l]	119,578 transactions; 24,069 products; 32,266 customers	BETA-Rec
Advertising	Criteo[m]	1M ad; 1TB Click	RecBole, Merlin, OpenRec, Recommenders
Humor	Jester[n]	4.1M ratings; 73,496 users; 100 jokes	RecBole, Surprise, LibRec, CF4J, MyMediaLite
Trust Social Network	Epinions[o]	75,879 nodes; 508,837 edges	RecBole, Cornac, BETA-Rec, LibRec
Business	Yelp[p]	2.1M users; 8.6M reviews; 160K businesses; 200K pictures; 1.1M tips	RecBole BETA-Rec, RecDB, RecStudio
Scientific Papers	CiteULike[q]	5,551 users; 16,980 items; 46,391 tags; 44,709 citations	Cornac, BETA-Rec, OpenRec, TagRec, RecPack
Location-based Social Network	Gowalla[r]	196,591 nodes; 950,327 edges	RecBole, BETA-Rec, RecStudio
Social bookmarking	Delicious[s]	16,105 instances; 500 attributes; 983 labels	TagRec
	BibSonomy[t]	1,326 networks; 5,335 nodes	TagRec
News	MIND[u]	1M users; 160K English news articles	RecBole, Recommenders

[a] https://grouplens.org/datasets/movielens/
[b] https://www.netflix.com/
[c] http://networkrepository.com/soc-flixster.php
[d] https://github.com/sidooms/MovieTweetings
[e] https://guoguibing.github.io/librec/datasets.html
[f] https://www.cse.cuhk.edu.hk/irwin.king.new/pub/data/douban
[g] http://konect.cc/networks/librec-ciaodvd-movie_ratings/
[h] https://webscope.sandbox.yahoo.com/catalog.php?datatype=r
[i] http://millionsongdataset.com/lastfm/
[j] http://jmcauley.ucsd.edu/data/amazon/
[k] https://www.kaggle.com/retailrocket/ecommerce-dataset
[l]https://www.researchgate.net/publication/4182309_A_recommender_for_advertisement_of_unsought_products_in_e-commerce
[m] https://ailab.criteo.com/download-criteo-1tb-click-logs-dataset/
[n] https://grouplens.org/datasets/jester/
[o] https://snap.stanford.edu/data/soc-Epinions1.html
[p] https://www.yelp.com/dataset
[q] https://github.com/js05212/citeulike-a
[r] https://snap.stanford.edu/data/loc-gowalla.html
[s] https://rdrr.io/cran/mldr.datasets/man/delicious.html
[t] http://konect.cc/networks/bibsonomy-2ui/
[u] https://msnews.github.io/

context-aware systems, RecStudio, RecBole, and Elliot offer modular designs and contextual features. If the project involves sequential or session-based modeling, Transformers4Rec, RecStudio, Merlin, and Microsoft Recommenders pro-

Table 4. Classification of RS Software Based on Evaluation Metrics

Software	Ranking Evaluation								Rating Prediction			Accuracy		
	MRR	HR	MAP	NDCG	DCG	Kendall	Spearman	AUC	RMSE	MAE	NMAE	Precision	Recall	F1
RePlay	✓	✓	✓	✓				✓				✓	✓	
MAB2REC			✓	✓	✓							✓	✓	✓
RecStudio	✓		✓	✓				✓	✓	✓		✓	✓	✓
RecPack		✓		✓	✓							✓	✓	
Transformers4Rec			✓	✓								✓	✓	
RecBole	✓	✓	✓	✓				✓	✓	✓		✓	✓	
Elliot	✓	✓	✓	✓				✓	✓	✓		✓	✓	✓
Recommenders			✓	✓				✓	✓	✓		✓	✓	
LensKit		✓							✓	✓		✓	✓	
Cornac	✓	✓	✓	✓	✓			✓	✓	✓		✓	✓	✓
Surprise									✓	✓				
BETA-Rec			✓	✓				✓	✓	✓			✓	✓
Merlin								✓				✓		
DeepRec	✓			✓					✓	✓		✓	✓	
SMORe														
Case Recommender			✓	✓					✓	✓		✓	✓	
OpenRec				✓				✓					✓	
Sequeval												✓		
CF4J				✓					✓	✓		✓	✓	✓
TagRec	✓		✓									✓	✓	✓
pyRecLab			✓	✓				✓	✓	✓		✓		
Rrecsys				✓				✓	✓	✓		✓	✓	✓
Idomaar									✓			✓	✓	
LibRec	✓		✓	✓				✓	✓	✓		✓	✓	
LightFM								✓						
CARSKit			✓	✓					✓	✓			✓	
Mahout														
Rival			✓							✓		✓	✓	
RecDB														
MyMediaLite				✓					✓	✓	✓	✓	✓	✓

vide suitable support. For tag- or graph-based scenarios, TagRec focuses on tag filtering while SMORe specializes in graph embeddings.

4.3 What Type of Data Will You Integrate?

Frameworks differ in how easily they accommodate datasets. RecBole, BETA-Rec, and Cornac simplify the replication of benchmark experiments. TagRec and LibRec are more suited for domain-specific datasets, while RePlay, RecStudio, and Microsoft Recommenders provide flexible pipelines for transforming raw and heterogeneous data into model-ready inputs.

4.4 What Scale and Infrastructure Must Be Supported?

For small to medium workloads, tools such as LightFM and RecBole are sufficient. Projects requiring large-scale processing or distributed environments benefit from frameworks like RePlay and Microsoft Recommenders, which provide Spark or Polars integration. For cloud-based or GPU-accelerated pipelines that require deployment and serving capabilities, Merlin, Microsoft Recommenders, and RecBole offer strong support, including model export to ONNX or TorchScript.

4.5 Which Evaluation Metrics Will You Rely On?

If ranking metrics such as MRR, MAP, NDCG, and HR are central to the evaluation, frameworks like RecBole, Cornac, Elliot, RecStudio, and LibRec are well suited. For rating prediction tasks, Surprise, Microsoft Recommenders, RecDB, RecBole, Elliot, and Cornac are appropriate. For classification-oriented evaluation, Elliot, RecStudio, TagRec, and MyMediaLite provide implementations that support precision, recall, and F1-score.

4.6 What Programming Ecosystem Do You Prefer?

Most RS frameworks are Python-first, including RecBole, Elliot, RecStudio, Cornac, RePlay, Microsoft Recommenders, and Merlin. In Java environments, Mahout and LibRec remain relevant. Others, like SMORe implemented in C++ and MyMediaLite in C#, may offer faster execution or better compatibility with specific enterprise systems.

Several studies demonstrate the practical use and maturity of some of the recommended RS software. RecBole has supported large-scale Top-N evaluations across multiple algorithms and datasets, illustrating its standardized workflow for training and assessment [39], and has continued to evolve with new models, packages, and reproducible configurations since 2022 [40]. Replay has been applied to metric-consistency studies on MovieLens-20M, revealing divergences in ranking metrics under temporal splits [41]. Comparative work has deployed Microsoft Recommenders, LensKit, and Cornac to examine algorithm performance and evaluation practices across common benchmarks [8], while LibRec has recently been extended to support new domains such as group recommendation [42]. In addition, RecPack and Surprise have contributed to reproducible research practices and have been examined through software-quality testing [43].

5 Challenges and Future Directions

Despite the growing ecosystem of RS software, several limitations remain. Many tools lack support for emerging algorithms, such as sequence-aware and reinforcement learning-based models, and offer limited compatibility with diverse datasets. Scalability is also a key issue, with few frameworks that implement parallel processing techniques or optimized training for large-scale datasets. In addition, some tools lack advanced evaluation metrics and have insufficient documentation, making reproducibility difficult. To address these issues, future work on RS software should focus on expanding model coverage, improving scalability, efficiency, evaluation capabilities, usability, and documentation to better support research and development of the next generation of RSs software.

6 Conclusion

Selecting the right Recommender System (RS) software remains a challenging task for researchers and practitioners due to the wide range of available tools and the variability in their capabilities. The main goal of the present study was to provide a practical guide for selecting appropriate RS software. We surveyed widely used frameworks and classified them based on their implemented techniques, supported datasets, and available evaluation metrics. We also suggested some recommendations for software selection as a starting point for informed decision-making. Our analysis also revealed several open issues, such as limited support for advanced algorithms, insufficient documentation, and a lack of unified evaluation practices. Addressing these challenges will support the development of the next generation of RS software that are more robust, scalable, and adaptable to diverse application needs. For future work, the guide can be strengthened by developing a more structured decision framework or rubric to formalize the selection process. We can also incorporate quantitative benchmarking and real-world case studies that illustrate how specific software performs in practice to provide stronger empirical evidence.

References

1. de Souza Pereira Moreira, G., Rabhi, S., Lee, J.M., Ak, R., Oldridge, E.: Transformers4Rec: bridging the gap between NLP and sequential/session-based recommendation, pp. 143–153. Association for Computing Machinery, New York (2021)
2. Ortega, F., Zhu, B., Bobadilla, J., Hernando, A.: CF4J: collaborative filtering for java. Knowl.-Based Syst. **152**, 94–99 (2018)
3. Ekstrand, M.D.: Lenskit for python: next-generation software for recommender systems experiments. In: Proceedings of the 29th ACM International Conference on Information & Knowledge Management, CIKM 2020, pp. 2999–3006. Association for Computing Machinery, New York (2020). https://doi.org/10.1145/3340531.3412778
4. Hug, N.: Surprise: a python library for recommender systems. J. Open Sour. Softw. **5**(52), 2174 (2020)
5. Gantner, Z., Rendle, S., Freudenthaler, C., Schmidt-Thieme, L.: MyMediaLite: a free recommender system library. In: RecSys 2011, pp. 305–308. Association for Computing Machinery, New York (2011). https://doi.org/10.1145/2043932.2043989
6. Sepulveda, G., Dominguez, V., Parra, D.: pyRecLab: a software library for quick prototyping of recommender systems. arXiv preprint arXiv:1706.06291 (2017)
7. Yang, L., Bagdasaryan, E., Gruenstein, J., Hsieh, C.K., Estrin, D.: OpenRec: a modular framework for extensible and adaptable recommendation algorithms. In: Proceedings of the Eleventh ACM International Conference on Web Search and Data Mining, WSDM 2018, pp. 664–672. Association for Computing Machinery, New York (2018). https://doi.org/10.1145/3159652.3159681
8. Akhadam, A., Kbibchi, O., Mekouar, L., Iraqi, Y.: A comparative evaluation of recommender systems tools. IEEE Access **13**, 29493–29522 (2025). https://doi.org/10.1109/ACCESS.2025.3541014

9. Alamdari, P.M., Navimipour, N.J., Hosseinzadeh, M., Safaei, A.A., Darwesh, A.: A systematic study on the recommender systems in the e-commerce. IEEE Access **8**, 115694–115716 (2020). https://doi.org/10.1109/ACCESS.2020.3002803
10. da Costa, A., Fressato, E., Neto, F., Manzato, M., Campello, R.: Case recommender: a flexible and extensible python framework for recommender systems. In: RecSys 2018, pp. 494–495. Association for Computing Machinery, New York (2018). https://doi.org/10.1145/3240323.3241611
11. Mekouar, L., Iraqi, Y., Boutaba, R.: Personalized recommendations in peer-to-peer systems. In: 2008 IEEE 17th Workshop on Enabling Technologies: Infrastructure for Collaborative Enterprises, pp. 99–104. IEEE (2008)
12. Choukry, S., Iraqi, Y., Mekouar, L.: An efficient rating system using blockchain for recommender systems. In: 2023 IEEE International Conference on Artificial Intelligence, Blockchain, and Internet of Things (AIBThings), pp. 1–5. IEEE (2023)
13. Verma, J.P., Patel, B., Patel, A.: Big data analysis: Recommendation system with Hadoop framework. In: 2015 IEEE International Conference on Computational Intelligence Communication Technology, pp. 92–97 (2015). https://doi.org/10.1109/CICT.2015.86
14. Mekouar, L., Iraqi, Y., Damaj, I.: A global user profile framework for effective recommender systems. Multimed. Tools Appl. **83**(17), 50711–50731 (2024)
15. Zhao, W.X., et al.: RecBole: towards a unified, comprehensive and efficient framework for recommendation algorithms. In: Proceedings of the 30th ACM International Conference on Information & Knowledge Management, pp. 4653–4664 (2021)
16. Oldridge, E., et al.: Merlin: a GPU accelerated recommendation framework. In: Proceeding s of IRS (2020)
17. Zhang, S., Tay, Y., Yao, L., Wu, B., Sun, A.: DeepRec: an open-source toolkit for deep learning based recommendation. arXiv preprint arXiv:1905.10536 (2019)
18. Monti, D., Palumbo, E., Rizzo, G., Morisio, M.: SequEval: a framework to assess and benchmark sequence-based recommender systems. arXiv preprint arXiv:1810.04956 (2018)
19. Vasilev, A., Volodkevich, A., Kulandin, D., Bysheva, T., Klenitskiy, A.: RePlay: a recommendation framework for experimentation and production use. In: Proceedings of the 18th ACM Conference on Recommender Systems, pp. 1191–1194 (2024)
20. Kadioglu, S., Kleynhans, B.: Building higher-order abstractions from the components of recommender systems. In: Thirty-Eighth AAAI Conference on Artificial Intelligence, AAAI 2024, Thirty-Sixth Conference on Innovative Applications of Artificial Intelligence, IAAI 2024, Fourteenth Symposium on Educational Advances in Artificial Intelligence, EAAI 2014, 20–27 February 2024, Vancouver, Canada, pp. 22998–23004. AAAI Press (2024). https://doi.org/10.1609/AAAI.V38I21.30341
21. Lian, D., et al.: RecStudio: towards a highly-modularized recommender system. In: Proceedings of the 46th International ACM SIGIR Conference on Research and Development in Information Retrieval, SIGIR 2023, pp. 2890–2900. Association for Computing Machinery, New York (2023). https://doi.org/10.1145/3539618.3591894
22. Michiels, L., Verachtert, R., Goethals, B.: RecPack: an(other) experimentation toolkit for top-n recommendation using implicit feedback data. In: Proceedings of the 16th ACM Conference on Recommender Systems, RecSys 2022, pp. 648–651. Association for Computing Machinery, New York (2022).https://doi.org/10.1145/3523227.3551472

23. Anelli, V.W., et al.: Elliot: a comprehensive and rigorous framework for reproducible recommender systems evaluation. In: Proceedings of the 44th International ACM SIGIR Conference on Research and Development in Information Retrieval, pp. 2405–2414 (2021)
24. Argyriou, A., González-Fierro, M., Zhang, L.: Microsoft recommenders: best practices for production-ready recommendation systems. In: Companion Proceedings of the Web Conference 2020, WWW 2020, pp. 50–51. Association for Computing Machinery, New York (2020). https://doi.org/10.1145/3366424.3382692, https://doi.org/10.1145/3366424.3382692
25. Salah, A., Truong, Q.T., Lauw, H.W.: Cornac: a comparative framework for multimodal recommender systems. J. Mach. Learn. Res. **21**(95), 1–5 (2020)
26. Meng, Z., et al.: BETA-rec: build, evaluate and tune automated recommender systems, pp. 588–590. Association for Computing Machinery, New York (2020)
27. Chen, C.M., Wang, T.H., Wang, C.J., Tsai, M.F.: SMORe: modularize graph embedding for recommendation. In: Proceedings of the 13th ACM Conference on Recommender Systems, pp. 582–583 (2019)
28. Kowald, D., Kopeinik, S., Lex, E.: The TagRec framework as a toolkit for the development of tag-based recommender systems. In: Adjunct Publication of the 25th Conference on User Modeling, Adaptation and Personalization, UMAP 2017, pp. 23–28. Association for Computing Machinery, New York (2017). https://doi.org/10.1145/3099023.3099069
29. Çoba, L., Zanker, M.: rrecsys: an R-package for prototyping recommendation algorithms (2016)
30. Scriminaci, M., et al.: Idomaar: a framework for multi-dimensional benchmarking of recommender algorithms. In: Proceedings of the Poster Track of the 10th ACM Conference on Recommender Systems (RecSys 2016). CEUR Workshop Proceedings (2016)
31. Guo, G., Zhang, J., Sun, Z., Yorke-Smith, N.: LibRec: a java library for recommender systems. In: Umap Workshops, vol. 4. Citeseer (2015)
32. Kula, M.: Metadata embeddings for user and item cold-start recommendations. arXiv preprint arXiv:1507.08439 (2015)
33. Zheng, Y., Mobasher, B., Burke, R.: CARSKit: a java-based context-aware recommendation engine. In: 2015 IEEE International Conference on Data Mining Workshop (ICDMW), pp. 1668–1671 (2015). https://doi.org/10.1109/ICDMW.2015.222
34. Said, A., Bellogín, A.: Rival: a toolkit to foster reproducibility in recommender system evaluation. In: Proceedings of the 8th ACM Conference on Recommender Systems, RecSys 2014, pp. 371–372. Association for Computing Machinery, New York (2014). https://doi.org/10.1145/2645710.2645712
35. Sarwat, M., Avery, J., Mokbel, M.F.: RecDB in action: recommendation made easy in relational databases. Proc. VLDB Endow. **6**(12), 1242–1245 (2013). https://doi.org/10.14778/2536274.2536286
36. Harper, F.M., Konstan, J.A.: The movielens datasets: history and context. ACM Trans. Interact. Intell. Syst. **5**(4) (2015). https://doi.org/10.1145/2827872
37. Hou, Y., Li, J., He, Z., Yan, A., Chen, X., McAuley, J.: Bridging language and items for retrieval and recommendation. arXiv preprint arXiv:2403.03952 (2024)
38. Kunegis, J.: KONECT: the Koblenz network collection. In: Proceedings of the 22nd International Conference on World Wide Web, WWW 2013 Companion, pp. 1343–1350. Association for Computing Machinery, New York (2013). https://doi.org/10.1145/2487788.2488173

39. Zhao, W.X., Lin, Z., Feng, Z., Wang, P., Wen, J.R.: A revisiting study of appropriate offline evaluation for top-n recommendation algorithms. ACM Trans. Inf. Syst. **41**(2), 1–41 (2022)
40. Zhao, W.X., et al.: RecBole 2.0: towards a more up-to-date recommendation library. In: Proceedings of the 31st ACM International Conference on Information & Knowledge Management, CIKM 2022, pp. 4722–4726. Association for Computing Machinery, New York (2022). https://doi.org/10.1145/3511808.3557680
41. Tamm, Y.M., Damdinov, R., Vasilev, A.: Quality metrics in recommender systems: do we calculate metrics consistently? In: Proceedings of the 15th ACM Conference on Recommender Systems, RecSys 2021, pp. 708–713. Association for Computing Machinery, New York (2021). https://doi.org/10.1145/3460231.3478848
42. Silveira, J.D., Salamó, M., Boratto, L.: Enabling reproducibility in group recommender systems. In: Artificial Intelligence Research and Development, pp. 115–124. IOS press (2022)
43. Michiels, L., Verachtert, R., Ferraro, A., Falk, K., Goethals, B.: A framework and toolkit for testing the correctness of recommendation algorithms. ACM Trans. Recomm. Syst. **2**(1) (2024). https://doi.org/10.1145/3591109

Causal Insights for Debiasing Recommender Systems: Future Directions and Challenges

Hui Wang[1,2], Xi Zhou[1,2], Mingming Li[1,2](✉), Hongyue Zhang[1,2], Jiao Dai[1,2], Jizhong Han[1,2], and Tao Guo[1,2]

[1] Institute of Information Engineering, Chinese Academy of Sciences, Beijing, China
{wanghui4042,zhouxi,zhanghongyue,daijiao,hanjizhong,guotao}@iie.ac.cn
[2] School of Cyber Security, University of Chinese Academy of Sciences, Beijing, China
limingming@iie.ac.cn

Abstract. Recommender systems are essential for personalization in digital services but often rely on correlations that introduce spurious biases, impairing quality, robustness, and fairness. Causal inference offers a promising solution, yet a systematic synthesis of debiasing methods–particularly with emerging tools like large language models (LLMs) is still lacking. This paper fills this gap by reviewing three core causal frameworks (potential outcomes, SCM, and counterfactual models) and four debiasing paradigms (propensity score, causal graph, SCM, and counterfactual methods). It highlights current trends and future directions, including LLMs integration, to advance causal debiasing in recommender systems.

Keywords: Recommender Systems · Debias · Causal Inference · Large Language Models · RCM · SCM · Counterfactual

1 Introduction

Recommender systems are widely used in social, e-commerce, and lifestyle services to deliver personalized information filtering, enhancing user convenience. However, their deployment raises critical bias issues that have drawn increasing attention [42]. As illustrated in Fig. 1, biases arise in the "user-data-model" feedback loop, undermining the accuracy of preference representation and distorting recommendation outcomes, thereby challenging fairness and interpretability. Consequently, developing effective bias removal methods has become a pivotal research focus.

Current debiasing approaches in recommender systems fall into two categories: correlation-based and causality-based methods [17]. Correlation-based techniques rely on data balancing and pattern mining but often overlook causal mechanisms, limiting their effectiveness. In contrast, causality-based methods

I. Awan et al. (Eds.): WISE 2025, LNCS 16367, pp. 108–119, 2026.
https://doi.org/10.1007/978-981-95-7394-3_8

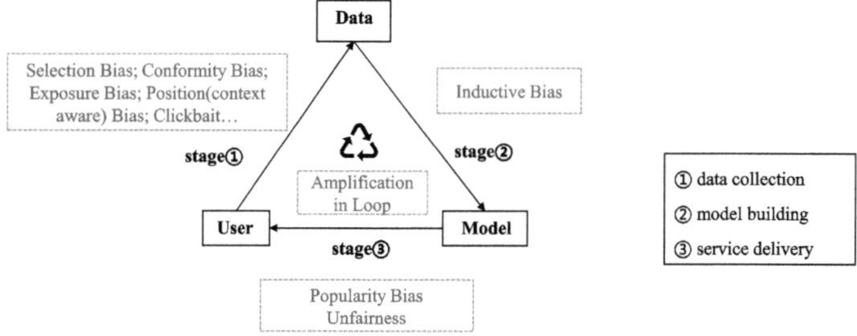

Fig. 1. User-data-model type of biases in feedback loop.

analyze underlying causal relationships, offering more robust solutions to bias mitigation.

Despite their benefits in interpretability and generalization, causal recommender systems remain nascent. Existing surveys highlight causal inference (CI) for improving fairness, robustness, and uplift modeling [47], or addressing data bias and beyond-accuracy optimization [8]. However, a systematic analysis of CI-based debiasing–particularly incorporating recent advances such as large language models (LLMs)–is still lacking.

To bridge this gap, this paper provides a comprehensive review of causality-driven debiasing in recommender systems with integration of LLMs. i) We introduce foundational causal inference theories: potential outcomes, structural causal models, and counterfactual frameworks. ii) We classify four debiasing paradigms–propensity scoring, causal graphs, structural model(SCM), and counterfactuals–and summarize their applications. iii) We offer guidance for future research in causal discovery, general debiasing frameworks, robustness, dynamic adaptation, and LLMs integration.

2 Frameworks for Causal Inference

Causal inference has emerged as a powerful approach for debiasing in recommender systems, facilitating accurate modeling of causal relationships and spurious correlations. The key frameworks are the potential outcomes framework, structural causal model, and counterfactual framework.

2.1 Potential Outcomes Framework

The potential outcomes framework (rubin causal model, RCM) [42], is widely used in observational studies and assumes three key principles: Stable Unit Treatment Value Assumption (SUTVA), positivity and ignorability. In recommender systems, this framework helps estimate the causal effect of treatments, such as user-item interactions, by modeling potential outcomes under different conditions. A formal definition is provided in [23].

2.2 Structural Causal Model

The Structural Causal Model [12] consists of two core components: a causal graph that qualitatively encodes dependencies among variables, and a set of structural equations that quantitatively define each variable as a function of its causal parents and exogenous noise. Causal graphs form the foundation of SCM. As shown in Table 1, they allow the identification of confounding variables and spurious correlations through d-separation–a concept inherited from Bayesian networks–thus clarifying the causal paths affecting recommendations. To estimate causal effects and mitigate biases, interventions are performed using the do-operator, which blocks non-causal paths and enables accurate estimation of unbiased effects for fairer and more robust recommendations.

Table 1. The composition and mechanism of SCM.

Style	Causal Graph	Structural Equations	Illustration
Causal graph of **observation data**	X → T, X → Y, T → Y	$X = f_X(\epsilon^X)$ $T = f_T(X, \epsilon^T)$ $Y = f_Y(X, T, \epsilon^Y)$	the observed associations among variables
Causal graph of **intervention**	X → Y, Do(T=t) → Y	$X = f_X(\epsilon^X)$ $T = t$ $Y = f_Y(X, T, \epsilon^Y)$	an intervention on a specific variable (e.g., T)

2.3 Counterfactual Framework

Counterfactual reasoning extends causal inference by exploring "what-if" scenarios. It is crucial for understanding the effects of unobserved interventions. By fixing most variables and altering select ones, counterfactuals enable the simulation of alternative realities [14]. Formally, given exogenous variables $U = u$, a counterfactual represents the value y of variable Y when X is set to x, denoted as $Y_x(u) = y$. In a structural causal model M with functions G, exogenous variables U, and endogenous variables V, factual and counterfactual scenarios are defined by structural equations. For example, the factual equations $X = aU$, $Y = bX + U$ contrast with counterfactual equations $X = x$, $Y_x = bX + U$. The First Law of Causal Inference proposed by Pearl formalizes counterfactuals as $Y_x(u) = Y_{M_x}(u)$. Counterfactuals hypothesize unobserved scenarios, assuming external variables remain constant except for those under study, distinguishing them from interventions by the role of post hoc judgment.

3 Causal Inference Techniques in Debiasing Recommender Systems

This section first establish a clear taxonomy, categorizing existing work into four major paradigms, then elucidate how these techniques mitigate biases and enhance system performance.

3.1 Classification of Causal Inference Techniques

The "Ladder of Causation" [14] describes three causal levels: association (observing patterns), intervention (altering variables), and counterfactuals (comparing real and hypothetical worlds). This study operates between the intervention and counterfactual levels. RCM and SCM support intervention, while counterfactual reasoning represents the highest level. Their relationships are summarized in Table 2.

3.2 Propensity Score-Based Methods

Propensity scores formalized $P(X = 1|Z)$, representing the probability of receiving treatment $X = 1$ given covariates Z [14], serve as an effective tool for debiasing recommender systems by balancing biased data distributions.

Utilizing Propensity Scores for Data Balancing and Debiasing. Propensity scores methods address biases such as exposure bias [18] and unobserved confounding [2]. For example, ExpoMF [18] integrates user-item exposure as a latent variable for matrix factorization. To tackle unobserved confounders, studies employ proxy confounders. For instance, the Interaction-Oriented Bias Model (IOBM) [2] learns low-dimensional embeddings as proxies for unmeasured confounders.

Inverse Propensity Score (IPS) Methods. Inverse Propensity Score (IPS), or Inverse Propensity Weighting (IPW) methods, such as MF-IPS, are widely applied in recommender systems. Variants like Self-Normalized IPS (SNIPS) [49] and the Clipped IPS (CIPS) [25,26] refine IPS by reducing high-variance estimates. For example, SNIPS improves the stability of IPS estimators by normalizing weights, while CIPS addresses exposure bias through paired propensity scores. Despite their effectiveness, IPS methods face challenges such as high variance in sparse data settings. Recent advancements include doubly robust estimators [9,15,44] and adversarial training techniques (AT-IPS) [50], which further enhance debiasing performance. Researchers have also enhanced IPS through dataset processing [27] and new weighting schemes [35].

Table 2. Causal inference and the expression of causal relationships.

Category	Depiction	Principle	Reference
RCM-based	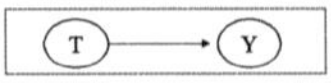 T → Y	observational data; specific assumptions	ExpoMF [18]; AT-IPS [50]
Causal graph-based	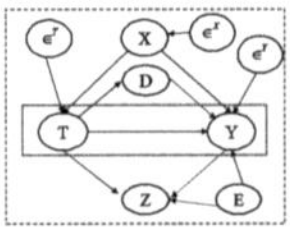	confounders; conditional independencies	match [5]; user-side [39]; item-side [34]
SCM-based	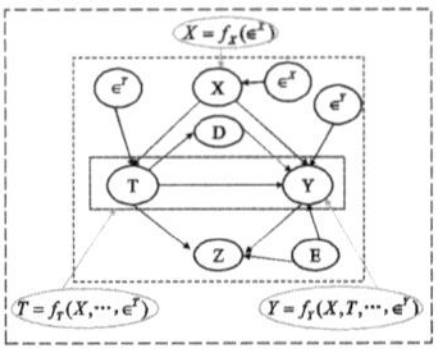 $X = f_X(e^X)$; $T = f_T(X, \cdots, e^T)$; $Y = f_Y(X, T, \cdots, e^Y)$	non-causal paths; interventions; Bayesian networks	DICE [41]; CausalVAE [37]; CDR [38]
Counterfactual-based	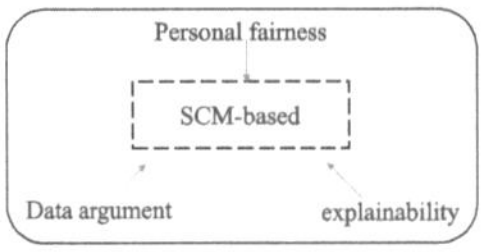 Personal fairness; SCM-based; Data argument; explainability	fairness; interpretability; counterfactual data augmentation	MPCI [11]; TS [13]; CauseRec [48]; LoCal [19]

3.3 Causal Graph-Based Methods

Causal graphs are a cornerstone of modern causal analysis and counterfactual reasoning [10,16]. In the context of recommender system debiasing, Directed Acyclic Graphs (DAGs) compactly encode variable dependencies, independence relations, intervention effects, and bias sources. Causal graph-based methods effectively deconstruct bias generation mechanisms in recommender systems. They prioritize users (U), items (I), and interactions (C/R) as core variables, incorporating popularity (Z/P) [24] as a confounding factor. Refined mediating variables, namely user-item matching features [5], user consistency [39], and item quality [34] uncover complex system dynamics. Path analysis reveals bias co-occurrences, e.g., CauTailReS [45] and DecRS [36].

Moreover, LLMs are emerging as a promising alternative to expert-crafted graphs and purely data-driven causal discovery, especially in contexts with limited data or domain knowledge. By integrating LLMs with data-driven techniques and expert insight, they help uncover latent causal structures in complex systems–such as inferring plausible causal orderings [17] or providing informative priors [33]–and support classical statistical tests with conditional-independence queries [6]. This integration corrects spurious edges from data-only methods, producing sparser and more accurate causal graphs.

3.4 SCM-Based Methods

SCM utilizes Bayesian networks to depict causal and non-causal paths, the latter serving as sources of bias. The do operator, when applied for interventions, effectively blocks non-causal paths influencing a variable, thereby enabling the estimation of causal effects via structural equations. The primary objective of this approach is the rigorous analysis and management of confounding variables, with the methodologies generally categorized into two main types.

Intervention on Confounding Variables. To address the confounding bias identified in the causal graph, researchers employ the backdoor adjustment method. This method provides a formal criterion for selecting a set of covariates to adjust for, enabling the estimation of the causal effect of an intervention from purely observational data. By conditioning on these selected covariates, we can block all non-causal backdoor paths between the treatment and the outcome, thus obtaining an unbiased estimate of the desired causal effect.

To mitigate confounding bias identified in causal graphs, the backdoor adjustment method is employed, which selects a set of covariates to estimate causal effects from observational data. Conditioning on these covariates blocks non-causal backdoor paths, yielding unbiased effect estimates. The effectiveness of this approach depends on confounder observability. For observable confounders, recent studies favor selective blocking of spurious paths rather than all confounding pathways [30,45]. For unobservable confounders, alternative strategies are utilized: proxy variables [47], deep representation learning of confounders in latent space [52], and counterfactual learning robust to hidden confounding via sensitivity analysis or adversarial training [51].

Decoupled Representation Methods for Confounding Factors. Causal decoupled representation methods isolate the latent causal factors from high-dimensional data. Multiple approaches demonstrate this principle: DICE decouples user interest from conformity [41]; certain techniques separate popularity into attribute-driven and popularity-driven components; D2Rec decouples behavior into interest, popularity, and social influence [28]; and some methods leverage network information to approximate unobserved confounders [29]. CausalVAE employs SCMs to learn disentangled causal representations [37], while CDR separates preference shifts from environmental effects [38]. In LLMs-based causal analysis, Causal Prompting [46] uses Chain-of-Thought as mediators to explore debiasing strategies, and CausalEval integrates SCM with instruction tuning to construct a meta-SCM via Structural Instruction Tuning (SIT) [43].

3.5 Counterfactual-Based Methods

Direct Application. Counterfactual methods enhance recommender systems by simulating alternative outcomes to mitigate biases, thereby improving accuracy, robustness, and interpretability. These approaches address various biases through specific strategies: modeling counterfactual clicks to improve CTR prediction [37]; removing item property effects [40] or subtracting bias effects from causal outcomes [11] to counter popularity bias; decoupling sentiment's indirect influence to alleviate sentiment bias [22]; and addressing challenges in Thompson Sampling-based inference [13].

Counterfactual Data Augmentation. This technique generates new training samples by modifying original data to help models identify causal features. For instance, heuristic methods augment user behavior sequences to improve sequential recommendations [3], while CauseRef refines user representations via contrastive learning [48]. Counterfactual data augmentation also adjusts causal features and predictions, as exemplified by Heckman^{rank}, which corrects selection and position bias using a two-stage method to retrain ranking models [21].

Counterfactual Fairness and Explainability. Counterfactual fairness ensures predictions remain invariant to changes in sensitive attributes, emphasizing individual-level fairness while aligning with group fairness considerations [14]. Practical implementations include adversarially decoupling user embeddings from sensitive features [41], balancing fairness-critical attributes [7], and adjusting exposure in two-sided markets [20]. Counterfactual explanation methods such as PRINCE [8], CountER [31], and ACCENT [32] systematically analyze how input variations influence model outputs.

Meanwhile, LLMs have significantly advanced counterfactual causal inference, evolving from data generation to sophisticated reasoning and debiasing. By integrating counterfactual reasoning, LLMs enhance the accuracy, robustness, and interpretability of causal estimates. They are employed to extract counterfactuals [4] and generate bias-mitigating counterfactuals via prompting [1]; they also reason about complex interventions [43] and support fact-checking through counterfactual validation. These capabilities are exemplified by the LoCal agent, which detects contradictions under opposite truth assumptions to improve causal consistency [19].

4 Future Direction

Current methods still face challenges including complex causal graph construction, limited generalizability, insufficient robustness, and poor adaptability. Future work should address these issues.

General Debiasing Frameworks. Future research could develop unified, theory-driven causal inference frameworks that transcend fragmented fixes and jointly establish standard benchmarks and evaluation protocols.

Robustness. Addressing the challenges of noisy confounders, and out-of-distribution (OOD) scenarios, future studies could develop causally aware models that are robust and stable against these changes. This will ensure reliable performance across various real-world recommendation settings.

Dynamic Adaptability. Future work should emphasize the ability of causally aware models to dynamically adapt to environment changes. This can be achieved by effectively modeling temporal changes, feedback loops, and sequential interactions to provide timely and relevant recommendations.

Integration of LLMs. Traditional approaches heavily depend on data quality and quantity, while constructing expert knowledge graphs is labor-intensive. Future research should integrate LLMs with causal inference techniques to address these challenges.

Multi-agent Causal Inference. Recommender systems themselves are interrelated and evolve dynamically. Future research could focus on modeling users and items as interactive agents, enhancing the understanding of how biases are generated, propagated, and evolve in complex dynamic environments.

Computational Efficiency and Scalability. Deploying sophisticated causal methods and LLMs imposes prohibitive training and inference times, heavy resource consumption, and limited scalability. Future work could pursue lightweight causal algorithms, model compression, distributed computation, and incremental learning to enable real-time deployment at web scale.

5 Conclusion

In recent years, causal inference has become a cornerstone topic in recommender systems research. This paper introduces novel analytical frameworks for causal inference methods and demonstrates how mainstream techniques can effectively debias recommender systems, yielding unique insights into their practical application. Moreover, this paper proposes promising directions for future research, notably the integration of LLMs to enhance debiasing strategies. By laying out a clear roadmap, this work aims to guide future efforts toward more effective, bias-aware recommender systems. We hope that this paper will serve as a valuable reference for ongoing research in debiasing and causal inference techniques.

Acknowledgments. This research was funded by the National Key Research and Development Program of China (Grant No. 2024YFC3307400), under the "Social Governance and Smart Society Technology Support" key special project.

References

1. Cai, R., Yu, S., Zhang, J., Chen, W., Xu, B., Zhang, K.: Dr.ECI: infusing large language models with causal knowledge for decomposed reasoning in event causality identification. In: Rambow, O., Wanner, L., Apidianaki, M., Al-Khalifa, H., Eugenio, B.D., Schockaert, S. (eds.) Proceedings of the 31st International Conference on Computational Linguistics, COLING 2025, Abu Dhabi, UAE, 19–24 January 2025, pp. 9346–9375. Association for Computational Linguistics (2025)

2. Chen, M., Liu, C., Sun, J., Hoi, S.C.H.: Adapting interactional observation embedding for counterfactual learning to rank. In: SIGIR 2021: The 44th International ACM SIGIR Conference on Research and Development in Information Retrieval, pp. 285–294. ACM (2021)
3. Chen, X., et al.: Data augmented sequential recommendation based on counterfactual thinking. IEEE Trans. Knowl. Data Eng. **35**(9), 9181–9194 (2023)
4. Chen, Z., Gao, Q., Bosselut, A., Sabharwal, A., Richardson, K.: DISCO: distilling counterfactuals with large language models. In: Rogers, A., Boyd-Graber, J.L., Okazaki, N. (eds.) Proceedings of the 61st Annual Meeting of the Association for Computational Linguistics (Volume 1: Long Papers), ACL 2023, Toronto, Canada, 9–14 July 2023, pp. 5514–5528. Association for Computational Linguistics (2023)
5. Chen, Z., Wu, J., Li, C., Chen, J., Xiao, R., Zhao, B.: Co-training disentangled domain adaptation network for leveraging popularity bias in recommenders. In: SIGIR 2022: The 45th International ACM SIGIR Conference on Research and Development in Information Retrieval, pp. 60–69. ACM (2022)
6. Cohrs, K., Diaz, E., Sitokonstantinou, V., Varando, G., Camps-Valls, G.: Large language models for causal hypothesis generation in science. Mach. Learn. Sci. Technol. **6**(1), 13001 (2025)
7. Ge, Y., et al.: Explainable fairness in recommendation. In: SIGIR 2022: The 45th International ACM SIGIR Conference on Research and Development in Information Retrieval, pp. 681–691. ACM (2022)
8. Ghazimatin, A., Balalau, O., Roy, R.S., Weikum, G.: PRINCE: provider-side interpretability with counterfactual explanations in recommender systems. In: WSDM 2020: The Thirteenth ACM International Conference on Web Search and Data Mining, pp. 196–204. ACM (2020)
9. Guo, S., et al.: Enhanced doubly robust learning for debiasing post-click conversion rate estimation. In: SIGIR 2021: The 44th International ACM SIGIR Conference on Research and Development in Information Retrieval, pp. 275–284. ACM (2021)
10. He, M., Hu, X., Li, C., Chen, X., Wang, J.: Mitigating confounding bias for recommendation via counterfactual inference. In: Machine Learning and Knowledge Discovery in Databases - European Conference, ECML PKDD 2022. Lecture Notes in Computer Science, vol. 13713, pp. 524–540. Springer (2022)
11. He, M., Li, C., Hu, X., Chen, X., Wang, J.: Mitigating popularity bias in recommendation via counterfactual inference. In: Database Systems for Advanced Applications - 27th International Conference, DASFAA 2022. Lecture Notes in Computer Science, vol. 13247, pp. 377–388. Springer (2022)
12. Pearl, J.: Causality. Cambridge University Press (2009)
13. Jeunen, O.: Counterfactual inference under Thompson sampling. CoRR abs/2504.08773 (2025)
14. Jianing, L., Ruibin, X., Yanyan, L., Liang, P., Jiafeng, G., Xueqi, C.: Overview of the frontier progress of causal machine learning. J. Comput. Res. Dev. **60**(01), 59–84 (2023)
15. Kiyohara, H., Saito, Y., Matsuhiro, T., Narita, Y., Shimizu, N., Yamamoto, Y.: Doubly robust off-policy evaluation for ranking policies under the cascade behavior model. In: WSDM 2022: The Fifteenth ACM International Conference on Web Search and Data Mining, pp. 487–497. ACM (2022)
16. Li, H., Zheng, C., Ding, S., Wu, P., Geng, Z., Feng, F., He, X.: Be aware of the neighborhood effect: modeling selection bias under interference. In: The Twelfth International Conference on Learning Representations, ICLR 2024. OpenReview.net (2024)

17. Li, J., et al.: Can large language models help experimental design for causal discovery? CoRR abs/2503.01139 (2025)
18. Liang, D., Charlin, L., McInerney, J., Blei, D.M.: Modeling user exposure in recommendation. In: Proceedings of the 25th International Conference on World Wide Web, WWW 2016, pp. 951–961. ACM (2016)
19. Ma, J., Hu, L., Li, R., Fu, W.: Local: logical and causal fact-checking with LLM-based multi-agents. In: Long, G., Blumestein, M., Chang, Y., Lewin-Eytan, L., Huang, Z.H., Yom-Tov, E. (eds.) Proceedings of the ACM on Web Conference 2025, WWW 2025, Sydney, NSW, Australia, 28 April– 2 May 2025, pp. 1614–1625. ACM (2025). https://doi.org/10.1145/3696410.3714748
20. Mehrotra, R., McInerney, J., Bouchard, H., Lalmas, M., Diaz, F.: Towards a fair marketplace: counterfactual evaluation of the trade-off between relevance, fairness & satisfaction in recommendation systems. In: Proceedings of the 27th ACM International Conference on Information and Knowledge Management, CIKM 2018, pp. 2243–2251. ACM (2018)
21. Ovaisi, Z., Ahsan, R., Zhang, Y., Vasilaky, K., Zheleva, E.: Correcting for selection bias in learning-to-rank systems. In: WWW 2020: The Web Conference 2020, pp. 1863–1873. ACM/IW3C2 (2020)
22. Pan, L., Cao, Y., Huang, C., Zhang, W., Yao, L.: Counterfactual inference for eliminating sentiment bias in recommender systems. CoRR abs/2505.03655 (2025)
23. Ruocheng, G., Lu, C.: Causal Inference and Machine Learning. Publishing House of Electronics Industry, Beijing (2023)
24. Saito, Y.: Doubly robust estimator for ranking metrics with post-click conversions. In: RecSys 2020: Fourteenth ACM Conference on Recommender Systems, pp. 92–100. ACM (2020)
25. Saito, Y., Yaginuma, S., Nishino, Y., Sakata, H., Nakata, K.: Unbiased recommender learning from missing-not-at-random implicit feedback. In: WSDM 2020: The Thirteenth ACM International Conference on Web Search and Data Mining, pp. 501–509. ACM (2020)
26. Sato, M., Takemori, S., Singh, J., Ohkuma, T.: Unbiased learning for the causal effect of recommendation. In: RecSys 2020: Fourteenth ACM Conference on Recommender Systems, pp. 378–387. ACM (2020)
27. Schnabel, T., Bennett, P.N.: Debiasing item-to-item recommendations with small annotated datasets. In: RecSys 2020: Fourteenth ACM Conference on Recommender Systems, pp. 73–81. ACM (2020)
28. Sheth, P., Guo, R., Cheng, L., Liu, H., Candan, K.S.: Causal disentanglement for implicit recommendations with network information. ACM Trans. Knowl. Discov. Data **17**(7), 94:1–94:18 (2023)
29. Sheth, P., Guo, R., Ding, K., Cheng, L., Candan, K.S., Liu, H.: Causal disentanglement with network information for debiased recommendations. In: SISAP. Lecture Notes in Computer Science, vol. 13590, pp. 265–273. Springer (2022)
30. Suhua, W., Hongjie, J., Minghao, Y., Yuling, W.: Enhanced graph learning for recommendation via causal inference. Mathematics **10**(11), 1881 (2022)
31. Tan, J., Xu, S., Ge, Y., Li, Y., Chen, X., Zhang, Y.: Counterfactual explainable recommendation. In: CIKM 2021: The 30th ACM International Conference on Information and Knowledge Management, pp. 1784–1793. ACM (2021)
32. Tran, K.H., Ghazimatin, A., Roy, R.S.: Counterfactual explanations for neural recommenders. In: SIGIR 2021: The 44th International ACM SIGIR Conference on Research and Development in Information Retrieval, pp. 1627–1631. ACM (2021)

33. Vashishtha, A., Reddy, A.G., Kumar, A., Bachu, S., Balasubramanian, V.N., Sharma, A.: Causal order: the key to leveraging imperfect experts in causal inference. In: The Thirteenth International Conference on Learning Representations, ICLR 2025, Singapore, 24–28 April 2025. OpenReview.net (2025)
34. Wang, B., Song, S., Liu, S., Deng, X.: MultiFDF: multi-community clustering for fairness-aware recommendation. IEEE Trans. Comput. Soc. Syst. **10**(6), 2959–2970 (2023)
35. Wang, N., Qin, Z., Wang, X., Wang, H.: Non-clicks mean irrelevant? Propensity ratio scoring as a correction. In: WSDM 2021, The Fourteenth ACM International Conference on Web Search and Data Mining, pp. 481–489. ACM (2021)
36. Wang, W., Feng, F., He, X., Wang, X., Chua, T.: Deconfounded recommendation for alleviating bias amplification. In: KDD 2021: The 27th ACM SIGKDD Conference on Knowledge Discovery and Data Mining, pp. 1717–1725. ACM (2021)
37. Wang, W., Feng, F., He, X., Zhang, H., Chua, T.: Clicks can be cheating: counterfactual recommendation for mitigating clickbait issue. In: SIGIR 2021: The 44th International ACM SIGIR Conference on Research and Development in Information Retrieval, pp. 1288–1297. ACM (2021)
38. Wang, W., Lin, X., Wang, L., Feng, F., Ma, Y., Chua, T.S.: Causal disentangled recommendation against user preference shifts. **42**(1) (2023)
39. Wang, X., Li, Q., Yu, D., Huang, W., Li, Q., Xu, G.: Neural causal graph collaborative filtering. Inf. Sci. **677**, 120872 (2024)
40. Wei, T., Feng, F., Chen, J., Wu, Z., Yi, J., He, X.: Model-agnostic counterfactual reasoning for eliminating popularity bias in recommender system. In: KDD 2021: The 27th ACM SIGKDD Conference on Knowledge Discovery and Data Mining, pp. 1791–1800. ACM (2021)
41. Wei, Y., Wang, X., Nie, L., Li, S., Wang, D., Chua, T.: Causal inference for knowledge graph based recommendation. IEEE Trans. Knowl. Data Eng. **35**(11), 11153–11164 (2023)
42. Xu, S., Ji, J., Li, Y., Ge, Y., Tan, J., Zhang, Y.: Causal inference for recommendation: foundations, methods and applications. CoRR abs/2301.04016 (2023)
43. Yu, L., et al.: CausalEval: towards better causal reasoning in language models. In: Chiruzzo, L., Ritter, A., Wang, L. (eds.) Proceedings of the 2025 Conference of the Nations of the Americas Chapter of the Association for Computational Linguistics: Human Language Technologies, NAACL 2025 - Volume 1: Long Papers, Albuquerque, New Mexico, USA, 29 April–4 May 2025, pp. 12512–12540. Association for Computational Linguistics (2025)
44. Yuan, B., et al.: Improving ad click prediction by considering non-displayed events. In: Proceedings of the 28th ACM International Conference on Information and Knowledge Management, CIKM 2019, pp. 329–338. ACM (2019)
45. Zeyu, H., Yan, L., Feng, W., Wei, Z., Alenezi, F., Tiwari, P.: Causal embedding of user interest and conformity for long-tail session-based recommendations. Inf. Sci. **644**, 119167 (2023)
46. Zhang, C., Zhang, L., Wu, J., He, Y., Zhou, D.: Causal prompting: debiasing large language model prompting based on front-door adjustment. In: Walsh, T., Shah, J., Kolter, Z. (eds.) AAAI-25, Sponsored by the Association for the Advancement of Artificial Intelligence, 25 February–4 March 2025, Philadelphia, PA, USA, pp. 25842–25850. AAAI Press (2025)
47. Zhang, Q., et al.: Debiasing recommendation by learning identifiable latent confounders. In: Proceedings of the 29th ACM SIGKDD Conference on Knowledge Discovery and Data Mining, KDD 2023, pp. 3353–3363. ACM (2023)

48. Zhang, S., Yao, D., Zhao, Z., Chua, T., Wu, F.: CauseRec: counterfactual user sequence synthesis for sequential recommendation. In: SIGIR 2021: The 44th International ACM SIGIR Conference on Research and Development in Information Retrieval, pp. 367–377. ACM (2021)
49. Zhang, Y., et al.: User retention: a causal approach with triple task modeling. In: Proceedings of the Thirtieth International Joint Conference on Artificial Intelligence, IJCAI 2021, pp. 3399–3405. ijcai.org (2021)
50. Zhang, Z., Dai, Q., Chen, X., Dong, Z., Tang, R.: Robust causal inference for recommender system to overcome noisy confounders. In: Proceedings of the 46th International ACM SIGIR Conference on Research and Development in Information Retrieval, SIGIR 2023, pp. 2349–2353. ACM (2023)
51. Zhou, G., et al.: Contrastive counterfactual learning for causality-aware interpretable recommender systems. In: Proceedings of the 32nd ACM International Conference on Information and Knowledge Management, CIKM 2023, pp. 3564–3573. ACM (2023)
52. Zhu, Y., Yi, J., Xie, J., Chen, Z.: Deep causal reasoning for recommendations. ACM Trans. Intell. Syst. Technol. **15**(4), 68:1–68:25 (2024)

Web Applications and Services

Collaborative Multi-agent Anomaly Detection in Web Services Using Machine Learning and Semantic Reasoning

Sihem Tlili[1(✉)] and Mohamed Rahal[2,3,4]

[1] Applied College, University of Tabuk, Tabuk, Saudi Arabia
stlili@ut.edu.sa

[2] Faculty of Sciences of Gafsa, University of Gafsa, Gafsa, Tunisia
rahal.mohamed@fsgf.ugaf.tn

[3] SETIT Laboratory, University of Sfax, Sfax, Tunisia

[4] National Engineering School of Gabes, University of Gabes, Gabes, Tunisia

Abstract. Modern web-based distributed systems are becoming increasingly complex and scaled up, making real-time anomaly detection more challenging. Coordination between components, semantic interpretation and adaptability are often lacking in traditional monitoring approaches. This paper introduces a Distributed Agent-based Intelligent Monitoring System (DAIMS) to address these challenges. It combines machine learning (ML) with semantic reasoning based on ontologies. The intelligent agents monitor service metrics locally and detect anomalies using XGBoost models. By collaborating through a shared knowledge base and message bus, they can infer system-wide problems. SWRL rules enable contextual inference as well as anomaly propagation analysis. Simulations were conducted under diverse workloads and fault injections. Compared to three widely adopted monitoring methods, DAIMS achieved a higher F1-score (0.91), a lower false positive rate (5%) and a higher detection rate (94%), while maintaining low inference latency (85 ms) and moderate overhead. Statistical tests were conducted to confirm the significance of these improvements. DAIMS achieves superior detection accuracy and responsiveness while requiring acceptable computational overhead. It was demonstrated that ML and semantic reasoning enhance fault explainability and robustness in distributed web environments.

Keywords: Anomaly Detection · Distributed Monitoring · Machine Learning · Semantic Web · Web Services

1 Introduction

Microservices and serverless paradigms are increasingly used in cloud-native systems to achieve modularity, elasticity and deployment agility. The complexity of these architectures increases when it comes to observability, fault detection

I. Awan et al. (Eds.): WISE 2025, LNCS 16367, pp. 123–138, 2026.
https://doi.org/10.1007/978-981-95-7394-3_9

and diagnosis. Conventional monitoring solutions, such as Prometheus [9], Datadog [10] or centralized dashboards, suffer from limited contextual awareness, static alert mechanisms and poor adaptability to rapid workload changes as services become more ephemeral and distributed. This paper proposes a decentralized monitoring approach based on cognitive Web agents to address these challenges. These agents can conduct local observations, detect anomalies intelligently and perform reasoning in a collaborative manner. The proposed architecture is inspired by the semantic web and intelligent agent paradigms. Two complementary techniques are incorporated into the proposed framework. First, Machine Learning (ML) models (XGBoost) are trained using execution traces and system metrics collected from Prometheus to detect local anomalies. Second, symbolic reasoning is used to enable contextual understanding through the use of a lightweight Web Ontology Language (OWL) ontology and Semantic Web Rule Language (SWRL) rules. Semantic Web standards (OWL, SWRL) guarantee interoperability, machine understanding and extensibility. Agents exchange insights and collaborate to infer the root causes of anomalies using lightweight Web protocols. By combining ML and symbolic semantic reasoning, fast and local detection is enabled while semantic interpretation and adaptability are preserved. Using an ontology, fine-grained and explainable reasoning can be performed at runtime to capture domain-specific knowledge such as performance degradation, timeout patterns and dependency failures. Thus, the approach can be used both for real-time monitoring and for long-term Web information mining. This study makes the following contributions:

- A multi-agent cognitive model for distributed monitoring in cloud-native, microservice-based environments, combining Web intelligence with agent-based design.
- A lightweight, cloud-specific ontology that represents system states, interactions and fault patterns.
- An AI novel framework that combines XGBoost-based local anomaly detection with collaborative symbolic reasoning.
- An experimental evaluation and a functional prototype under realistic Kubernetes deployments. It includes a comparative study to demonstrate the effectiveness of the proposed approach against state-of-the-art methods in Web-scale distributed environments.

The remainder of this paper is organized as follows: Sect. 2 discusses recent research on microservice monitoring and anomaly detection. Section 3 describes the proposed framework. Section 4 describes the experimental setup and comparative results. Finally, Sect. 5 summarizes the study.

2 Literature Review

Authors in [1] combine asynchronous federated learning with graph neural networks and positive unlabeled learning to detect anomalies in microservice architectures. A Span Causal Graph is used to model intra- and inter-service dependencies, enabling real-time detection without centralized data aggregation. The approach improves F1-score by 4% over state-of-the-art methods like TraceAnomaly [3] and MicroScope [4], while maintaining low detection latency and demonstrating good scalability. Metrics such as recall, precision and detection time were used to confirm the suitability of the method in dynamic and large-scale environments. However, it remains challenging to construct and maintain the Span Causal Graph in highly volatile or complex systems. Further, the approach relies on high-quality trace and log data, which may not always be available in production settings. This potentially limits detection accuracy.

In addition, authors in [2] integrate ML models, specifically Random Forest and Gradient Boosting, to detect anomalies and predict resource usage in microservice-based systems. A microservices architecture is used to build predictive models based on system metrics, enabling early detection of performance issues. Gradient Boosting Regressor achieved an R° score of 0.86, outperforming traditional monitoring approaches in forecasting accuracy and maintaining system responsiveness during peak loads. The observability and scalability of the infrastructure are improved as a result of this approach. However, relying on specific system metrics may limit anomaly coverage and model accuracy may degrade over time as system behavior and data drift evolve.

Furthermore, authors in [5] present MADMM, a multi-modal anomaly detection framework that integrates log and metric data. By combining Graph Convolutional Networks (GCNs), Graph Attention Networks (GATs) and Gated Recurrent Units (GRUs), the approach models spatial and temporal dependencies across data modalities. Based on evaluations using real-world datasets, MADMM outperforms state-of-the-art methods such as OmniAnomaly and SCWarn in terms of precision, recall and F1-score. As compared to single-modal strategies, multi-feature extraction from heterogeneous data sources enhances anomaly detection. Nonetheless, the model may not be applicable to large-scale or real-time deployments, especially in noisy or incomplete environments, due to its complexity and computational requirements.

Additionally, authors in [6] propose a method named ServiceAnomaly. It builds annotated context propagation graphs for anomaly detection in microservice environments by combining distributed tracing data with six system-level profiling metrics. Graph-based modeling and ML are used to identify deviations from normal behavior. The method achieved an F1-score of 0.86 on benchmarks like TeaStore [11] and TrainTicket [12]. It surpasses traditional metric-based techniques and enables early fault detection. In addition to supporting interpretability, annotated graphs facilitate root cause analysis. Nevertheless, the approach requires high-quality trace data and complex graph construction, which may limit scalability and responsiveness. In addition, it does not incorporate semantic reasoning, so ontologies and rule-based logic can be integrated in the future to enhance detection.

Moreover, authors in [7] propose integrating heterogeneous data sources (metrics, logs and traces) into a single Microservice System Twin (MST) graph to detect anomalies in microservice systems. In order to capture intricate dependencies between services and temporal behaviors across modalities, the model is processed using a transformer architecture equipped with spatial and temporal attention mechanisms. The proposed MSTGAD achieved a high F1-score of 0.961 on two real-world datasets, exceeding the compared state-of-the-art baselines by an average margin of 4.85%. However, the framework lacks GPU acceleration, making it less suitable for real-time applications. Moreover, it may be difficult to adapt to new or evolving fault scenarios without explicit semantic reasoning.

The authors of [8] propose using distributed tracing data coupled with natural language processing (NLP) techniques to detect anomalies in microservice environments. LSTM-based deep learning is applied to modeling sequences of span events. This allows the detection of performance anomalies and regressions without requiring prior system knowledge. An experimental study showed that the F-score for this approach was 0.9759, outperforming existing point and collective anomaly detection techniques. Additionally, the Trace Compass integration allows interactive visual root cause analysis and reduces troubleshooting time. However, without contextual metrics such as resource usage and system topology, the framework may have difficulty adapting to complex or volatile cloud-native infrastructures. Additionally, scalability to large-scale dynamic microservices remains an issue.

In summary, previous approaches have demonstrated remarkable advances, but they are limited by high computational costs, lack of semantic context, limited scalability and limited adaptability to dynamic and evolving systems. This paper proposes a novel framework for improving detection accuracy, adaptability and understanding of systems by combining multi-modal learning and lightweight semantic reasoning. The proposed approach bridges the gap between statistical learning and semantic interpretation in order to provide a more scalable and explainable monitoring solution for dynamic microservice architectures.

3 Proposed Framework

We propose a distributed framework for anomaly detection in microservice-based systems, called Distributed Agent-based Intelligent Monitoring with Semantics (DAIMS). It is based on cognitive web agents embedded within microservices. These agents are intelligent and lightweight monitors that detect, contextualize and localize anomalies in a collaborative and adaptive manner.

3.1 System Overview

The proposed architecture (Fig. 1) consists of the following key components:

- Microservices: Serverless cloud-native services. The system consists of N microservices $\mathcal{S} = \{S_1, S_2, \ldots, S_N\}$.
- Cognitive agents: Each agent monitors a specific service. It uses embedded XGBoost models and an embedded ontology for local anomaly detection. Each microservice is monitored by an agent A_i. Each time t, the agent collects a feature vector representing d metrics $\mathbf{x}_i(t) \in \mathbb{R}^d$. For prediction, $\mathcal{M}$ is a

trained ML model. `Anomaly detection` is expressed by Eq. 1. $y_i(t) = 1$ if an anomaly is detected in service S_i at time t.

$$y_i(t) = \mathcal{M}(\mathbf{x}_i(t)) \in \{0, 1\} \tag{1}$$

- Shared ontology: A lightweight OWL model that defines the structure of services, dependencies, events, metrics and anomalies. This shared ontology is used by all agents to interpret their local observations semantically.
- Message bus: Agents can asynchronously share anomaly signals, observations or diagnostic messages via a publish/subscribe layer (Apache Kafka [13]).
- Semantic reasoner: A component that aggregates agent messages and applies SWRL-based inference rules to detect anomalies or global patterns.
- Dashboard/API: A visualization and control layer that provides diagnostics, reasoning traces and anomaly status for automated remediation processes or system administrators.

Figure 1 illustrates the overall architecture of the proposed monitoring framework for microservice environments. Each microservice is monitored by an autonomous cognitive agent that uses ML models and contextual reasoning based on a shared ontology to detect local anomalies. Agents exchange alerts and coordinate distributed inference asynchronously via a message bus. In order to enhance detection precision and support logical consistency, a semantic reasoner applies SWRL rules to the shared ontology. The architecture also includes a dashboard/API interface that allows system operators to visualize monitoring results and interact with the reasoning process in real time.

Running Example: Consider an "Order Processing" service that relies on a "Payment" service. "Payment" service events that experience high latency (anomaly detected by its local agent) are semantically tagged as *LatencyAnomaly* and published to the message bus. After receiving this message and detecting its own rising error rate, the "Order Processing" service agent uses SWRL rules to infer a causal relationship (`triggers`) between the two anomalies. By using collaborative reasoning, the root cause is identified in the "Payment" service rather than the "Order Processing" service.

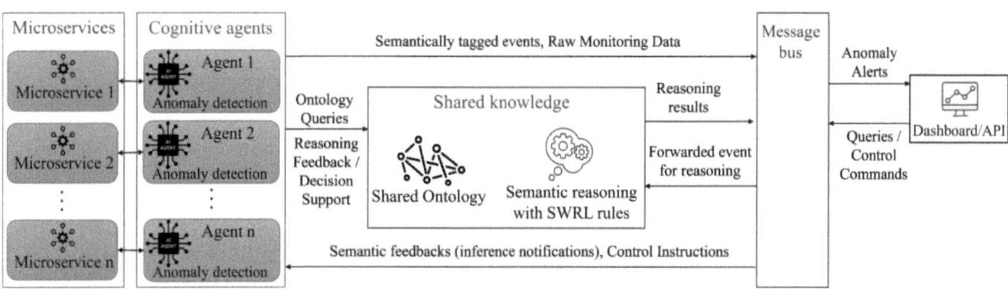

Fig. 1. Overall architecture of the proposed semantic-based framework for intelligent microservice monitoring

3.2 Ontology Design and Semantic Modeling

The proposed framework, DAIMS, formalizes the semantics of anomaly detection and service dependencies in cloud-native systems using a lightweight domain ontology. Five core classes are defined: 'Service', 'Agent', 'AnomalyEvent', 'Metric' and 'Dependency'. Each 'Service' is monitored by a corresponding 'Agent'. The 'hasMetric' relation (object property) can associate a 'Service' with one or more 'Metric' instances. The 'dependsOn' object property enables reasoning about fault propagation by capturing service-level dependencies. Instances of 'AnomalyEvent' are used to represent anomalies. They have temporal attributes (defined by the 'hasTimestamp' data property) and a type (defined by the 'anomalyType' data property). They are related to 'Service' instances and other anomalies of the same class by the 'affects' and 'triggers' object properties to reflect their origin and potential propagation. Figure 2 illustrates the high-level structure of the ontology. It depicts the main concepts and the object/datatype properties that link them, serving as a semantic basis for reasoning.

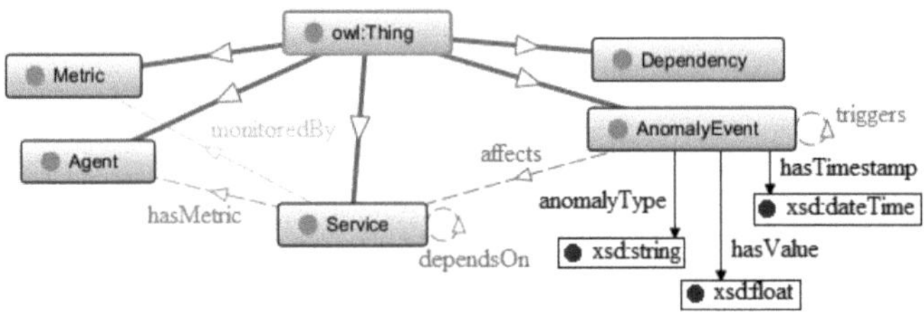

Fig. 2. Main structural composition of the anomaly detection ontology

SWRL rules are defined to enhance reasoning capabilities:

- Rule 1: *Anomaly propagation via service dependency.* If an anomaly affects a service S_1 and another service S_2 depends on S_1, then infer that an anomaly also affects S_2.

$$\texttt{AnomalyEvent}(?a) \wedge \texttt{affects}(?a, ?s_1) \wedge \texttt{dependsOn}(?s_2, ?s_1)$$
$$\rightarrow \texttt{AnomalyEvent}(?a_2) \wedge \texttt{affects}(?a_2, ?s_2)$$

- Rule 2: *Threshold-based anomaly detection.* If a metric M has a value V greater than a predefined threshold (for example, 300), then infer that an anomaly event has been detected.

$$\texttt{Metric}(?m) \wedge \texttt{hasValue}(?m, ?v) \wedge \texttt{swrlb:greaterThan}(?v, 300.0)$$
$$\rightarrow \texttt{AnomalyEvent}(?a)$$

- Rule 3: *Causal triggering between anomalies (or inference of anomaly causality)*: If an anomaly event A_1 affects a service S_1, another service S_2 depends on S_1 and an anomaly event A_2 affects S_2, then infer that A_1 triggers A_2.

$$\texttt{AnomalyEvent}(?a_1) \wedge \texttt{affects}(?a_1, ?s_1) \wedge \texttt{dependsOn}(?s_2, ?s_1) \wedge \texttt{affects}(?a_2, ?s_2) \rightarrow \texttt{triggers}(?a_1, ?a_2)$$

These semantic rules aim to enable consistent, automated anomaly interpretation and cross-agent reasoning. Agents are able to perform contextual inference beyond raw data thresholds using these rules. This enables distributed semantic supervision. The ontology $\mathcal{O}$ and SWRL rule set $\mathcal{W}$ are used to contextualize each detected anomaly using a reasoning function $\mathcal{R}$. A semantic explanation or causal chain linking anomalies across dependent services is produced by the reasoning process.

$$\text{context}_i(t) = \mathcal{R}(y_i(t), \mathcal{O}, \mathcal{W}) \quad (2)$$

For instance, for a dependency $S_j \rightarrow S_i$, the propagation rule is expressed by Eq. 3. δ is the propagation delay.

$$y_j(t) = 1 \wedge S_i \in \text{DependsOn}(S_j) \Rightarrow y_i(t+\delta) = 1 \quad (3)$$

3.3 Communication and Reasoning Flow

This component manages the distributed semantic collaboration between the central reasoning module and cognitive agents. These agents monitor real-time performance metrics (e.g., response time, CPU usage, error rates) alongside microservices. Upon detecting suspicious behavior by the local anomaly detection model, the agent uses ontology-based reasoning to classify and evaluate the event.

Algorithm 1. Semantic reasoning with ontology and SWRL rules

```
Input: OWL instance, collected metrics, SWRL rules
Load ontology and SWRL rules into reasoner
Assert collected metrics as ontology individuals
inferences ← apply_Semantic_Reasoning()
if anomaly confirmed then
    notify_Neighboring_Agents(metrics)
    trigger_Distributed_Reasoning()
else
    Continue local monitoring
end if
Output: Inferred anomalies or reasoning alerts
```

Upon detecting an anomaly with semantic meaning (e.g., "ResourceOverload" or "DownstreamDependencyFailure"), a semantically enriched message is published to the message bus. The semantic reasoner processes these messages in order to apply SWRL rules to the shared ontology. Through this reasoning engine, higher-order situations such as anomaly propagation, dependency failures or correlations can be detected. The insights (e.g., root cause identification or multi-service degradation) are then exposed to the dashboard or sent via APIs to remediation components. Algorithm 1 details how raw metrics are transformed into semantically rich anomaly events by the reasoning loop. It incorporates the monitored metrics into the ontology using SWRL reasoning. Upon confirmation of an anomaly, agents initiate distributed collaboration by sending contextualized alerts to dependent services. Then, anomaly chains and cascading failures not apparent from isolated local observations can be detected.

3.4 Intelligent Supervision and Distributed Inference

This subsection describes the core components of intelligent supervision.

Intelligent Agent Algorithms. Each microservice is monitored by an autonomous cognitive agent able to detect anomalies. Local agents monitor service-specific metrics (e.g., latency, error rate, CPU usage) continuously. The collected data is processed by an embedded ML model that determines whether an anomaly has occurred. Algorithm 2 describes the local reasoning loop of intelligent agents. First, the agent collects metrics over a defined period of time T. A pre-trained ML model uses these metrics to classify service behavior. Upon detecting an anomaly, the agent invokes the ontology-based reasoning process to contextualize and explain it. Otherwise, normal behavior is logged and may be used in retraining or adaptive learning.

Algorithm 2. Continuous monitoring of a microservice

```
Input: ServiceID, Time window T, MLModel
while Service is active do
    metrics ← collect_Metrics(ServiceID, T)
    result ← predict(MLModel, metrics)
    if result = Anomaly then
        call_Ontology_Agent(metrics)
    else
        log_Normal(metrics)
    end if
end while
```

Distributed Coordination and Agent Collaboration. In distributed microservices environments, isolated decisions may result in false positives or misinterpretations. To address this, cognitive agents form a decentralized reasoning network by collaborating with each other. The agent initiates a coordination protocol with neighboring agents monitoring dependent or related services when a local anomaly is detected. In this way, anomalies can be cross-validated and collective decisions can be made. As described in Algorithm 3, if an anomaly is locally inferred, the initiating agent identifies its relevant neighbors first, typically based on dependencies between services. An inference request including the observed metrics is subsequently sent. A validation decision is made by each neighbor based on its own local reasoning engine. Upon confirmation by multiple agents, the event becomes a global anomaly, resulting in coordinated mitigation or alerting actions. This collaborative mechanism aims to enhance robustness, noise reduction and distributed resilience. $\mathcal{N}_i$ is the set of neighbors of the agent A_i. $v_j(t)$ is the binary validation response from neighbor A_j. $D_i(t)$ is the final decision.

$$D_i(t) = \begin{cases} 1, & \text{if } \sum_{A_j \in \mathcal{N}_i} v_j(t) \geq \theta \\ 0, & \text{otherwise} \end{cases} \tag{4}$$

where θ is a consensus threshold: $\theta = \frac{|\mathcal{N}_i|}{2}$).

Algorithm 3. Distributed collaboration among agents

```
Input: Local anomaly alert, serviceID
neighbors ← discover_Neighbor_Agents(serviceID)
for all agent in neighbors do
    send_Inference_Request(metrics)
    response ← wait_For_Response(agent)
    if response = Anomaly Confirmed then
        confirm_Global_Anomaly()
    end if
end for
```

Learning Pipeline: Model Training and Inference. The architecture incorporates a complete ML pipeline that transforms raw data into actionable insights to support proactive anomaly detection (Fig. 3).

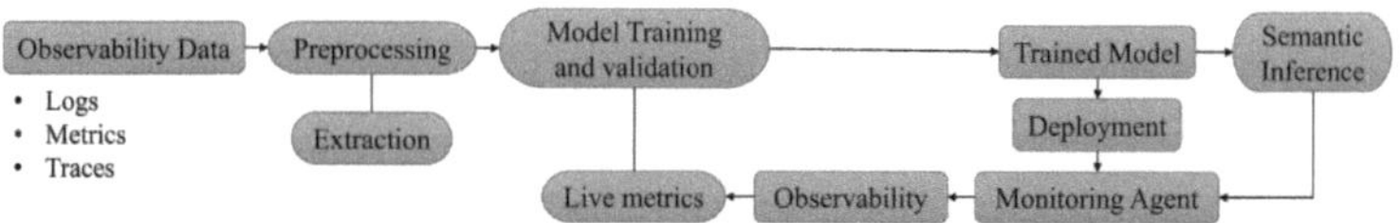

Fig. 3. End-to-End learning pipeline: from data collection to semantic inference

Offline Phase: Model Preparation. Training starts with the collection of data from observability and performance monitoring. The logs and metrics collected include HTTP error rates, latency, throughput, thread count, CPU/memory usage and queue size. Ground truth labels are applied to these data points (e.g., Normal, Overload, Timeout, Crash, NetworkFailure) during supervised learning. The features are extracted after preprocessing (data cleaning, normalization and aggregation). XGBoost models are then trained using cross-validation to avoid overfitting. Trained models are serialized in the ONNX format for deployment.

Deployment Strategies. XGBoost models are deployed as dedicated microservices accessible via REST APIs. This strategy facilitates centralized management, simplified model updates and better scalability.

Online Phase: Inference and Semantic Reasoning. Each agent operates autonomously during runtime. A feature vector is generated by collecting local metrics periodically. ML models classify instances as 'Normal' or 'Anomaly'. When the agent detects a suspicious condition, it engages an ontology-based semantic reasoner. SWRL rules enrich the ontology, helping to contextualize the anomaly by identifying likely causes. The agent initiates distributed validation with its neighbors if uncertainty persists.

3.5 Computational Complexity

The computational complexity of the key components of DAIMS determines its scalability, as shown in Table 1. ML inference and metric collection are local operations with constant or logarithmic costs thanks to the modular agent-based design. The complexity of semantic reasoning increases linearly with the number of rules and concepts, but a well-designed ontology can handle this. Agent collaboration is linear in relation to the number of neighbors per service. This linear scalability makes the framework able to support large-scale deployments.

Table 1. Computational complexity of main components

Component	Description	Complexity
Metric collection	Local Prometheus-based sampling	$\mathcal{O}(1)$ per agent
ML inference (XGBoost)	Prediction over feature vector	$\mathcal{O}(\log n)$ (tree depth)
Semantic reasoning (SWRL)	Rule-based inference on local facts	$\mathcal{O}(r \cdot c)$ (rules $\times$ concepts)
Agent collaboration	Consensus across k agents	$\mathcal{O}(k)$ per anomaly event

4 Evaluation

4.1 Experimental Setup and Evaluation Protocol

Simulations were conducted in a realistic microservices environment.

Simulation Environment. A Kubernetes cluster was used to deploy the open-source TrainTicket benchmark [12,14]. It is a widely used benchmark for microservices research. It emulates a real-world travel booking system composed of several interconnected services (e.g., user, order, payment, search). Prometheus was used for metrics collection. ELK Stack and Jaeger were used for tracing and logging. This setup provides full visibility into the system behavior and allows for the controlled injection of faults (e.g., overload, crash, network failure, timeout). Therefore, it provides a suitable and representative setup for testing anomaly detection solutions in cloud-native environments.

Baseline Methods. DAIMS, is compared with three widely adopted approaches:

- *Rule-based Threshold Monitoring (RBM)*: Frequently used in traditional monitoring systems such as Prometheus AlertManager to measure CPU utilization, error rates and latency.
- *Unsupervised ML Models (UnML)*: Detecting anomalies by using Isolation Forests and Autoencoders trained directly on system metrics.
- *XGBoost-only Model (XGB)*: Detecting anomalies by using a supervised classifier trained on labeled operational data (without integration of agent collaboration or ontological inference).

Baselines chosen reflect various monitoring strategies: RBM represents traditional rule-based monitoring; UnML models detect anomalies without labeled data or semantics; and XGB isolates supervised learning without agent collaboration or ontology use. Due to this diversity, it is possible to evaluate the added value of the proposed DAIMS fairly and comprehensively.

Evaluation Metrics. Those metrics marked with ↑ indicate that higher values are better, while ↓ indicates lower values are better.

- *F1-Score* ↑: Accuracy of anomaly detection (balancing precision and recall).
- *False Positive Rate (FPR)* ↓: The frequency of incorrect anomaly alerts.
- *Inference latency* ↓: Reflects responsiveness by indicating how quickly the system detects and classifies anomalies.
- *Detection rate (Recall)* ↑: Evaluates the proportion of true anomalies identified correctly.
- *Anomaly volume over time* ↑: Highlights the adaptive detection capabilities by indicating the number of anomalies detected over time, regardless of their severity or duration.
- *Agent resource overhead* ↓: Measures CPU costs associated with monitoring agents. It is critical to assess runtime efficiency and scalability.

These metrics measure detection accuracy, responsiveness, adaptability and operational efficiency. They were selected to evaluate the compared methods because their combination provides a balanced and realistic evaluation.

Experimental Protocol. Simulations were conducted under different load profiles and failure scenarios, such as service crashes, request timeouts, CPU exhaustion and network latency. For each run:

- Data was collected over multiple hours of system operation at 30-second intervals.
- Prometheus and logs were used to construct a dataset of 500 labeled observations that included normal and anomalous behavior. With this size of dataset, the XGBoost classifier was trained effectively as it is known for its robustness and high performance even on relatively small datasets.

- Models were trained on 80% of the data and evaluated on 20%.
- To ensure statistical robustness, all experiments were repeated five times with different random seeds.

4.2 Results and Discussion

Comparative Evaluation. Figure 4 presents the F1-Score, FPR, inference latency and detection rate results. The proposed DAIMS framework outperforms other approaches on all metrics except latency, where the XGB model is slightly faster. The variation curves of anomaly volume and agent resource overhead over time are also shown in Fig. 4. While DAIMS consistently maintains the highest anomaly volume, it exhibits moderate but acceptable overhead. These results showed the efficiency and scalability of DAIMS under dynamic conditions. In terms of F1-score, FPR, detection rate and anomaly volume, DAIMS consistently outperforms all other approaches. With an F1-score of 0.91, DAIMS achieved the highest classification performance. Throughout the simulation period, it maintained the highest anomaly volume, demonstrating its effectiveness in timely

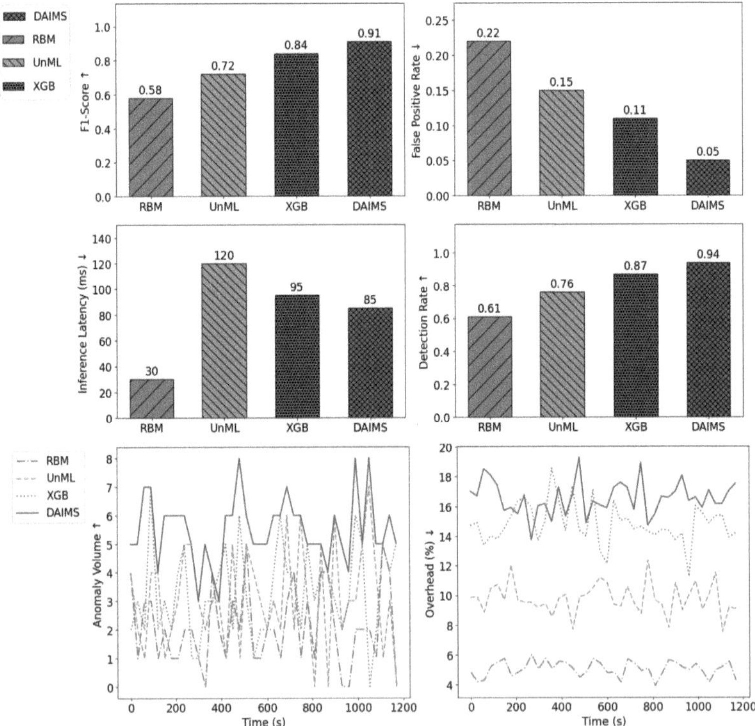

Fig. 4. Comparison of evaluated metrics across methods

Table 2. ANOVA computation details

Metric	F1-score	FPR	Latency (ms)	Detection Rate	Anomaly volume	Overhead
Sum of Squares: Between → Within	0.0747→ 0.0113	0.0475→ 0.0127	3978→ 499	0.0756→ 0.0134	248.519→ 355.475	3247.22→ 179.384
F-statistic	26.37	19.86	42.51	30.23	36.35	941.31
p-value	<0.001	<0.001	<0.001	<0.001	<0.001	<0.001

and accurate anomaly detection. The RBM performed the worst (F1 = 0.58), highlighting the limitations of static thresholding when used in dynamic cloud environments. DAIMS has a lower FPR (5%) compared to UnML (15%) and XGB (11%). This is due to the integration of ontological reasoning and the collaborative verification process between agents. Additionally, DAIMS showed the highest detection rate (94%), demonstrating the advantages of combining ML with knowledge-based reasoning to detect and classify faults.

Although DAIMS incurs modest overhead due to agent coordination and semantic inference, its inference latency remains competitive at 85 ms. It performs significantly faster than UnML (120 ms). In comparison with XGB (95 ms), it is only slightly slower. Moreover, scalability is achieved without compromising system responsiveness by maintaining a moderate resource overhead per agent. While RBM has the lowest latency (30 ms), it underperforms across all other criteria, limiting its suitability for cloud environments. The consistently strong performance of DAIMS confirms its architectural choices. It achieves a balance between efficiency, accuracy and adaptability by distributing learning capabilities among agents and enhancing them with inter-agent collaboration and domain-specific ontological knowledge. Its outperformance of XGB, despite its lower complexity, demonstrates that ML alone is insufficient for resilient and context-aware anomaly detection in dynamic microservices-based systems.

Statistical Analysis. One-way ANOVA [15] and Tukey's HSD [16] statistical tests were applied to determine the significance of performance differences between the compared methods. Table 2 presents the details. The differences between approaches are statistically significant for all evaluation criteria since all p-values are below 0.001. In particular, DAIMS significantly outperforms other approaches in terms of F1-score, FPR, detection rate and anomaly volume. While RBM achieves the lowest inference latency (30 ms), DAIMS maintains a reasonable compromise by being faster than UnML and XGB. In terms of agent resource overhead, DAIMS consumes more resources due to its semantic reasoning component. Tukey's HSD post-hoc analysis confirms the statistical significance of these differences, especially between DAIMS and less accurate or slower approaches, demonstrating its robustness and scalability.

Analysis and Discussion

Discussion and Practical Considerations. The proposed DAIMS is designed to be integrated into real-world cloud-native environments. Monitoring agents can

Table 3. Practical considerations and mitigations

Aspect	Consideration	Mitigation
Model drift	Data distribution may evolve over time	Periodic retraining or online learning
Ontology effort	Manual creation of domain ontologies	Use of templates or semi-automated tools
Reasoning latency	SWRL reasoning may introduce delays	Rule optimization and caching strategies
Scalabilityand trust	Inter-agent communication must remain efficient and secure	Lightweight protocols and authentication

Table 4. Ablation study results

Variant	F1-Score	FPR ↓	Detection Rate
DAIMS (full framework)	0.91	0.05	0.94
Without Semantic reasoning	0.85	0.09	0.88
Without Agent collaboration	0.87	0.07	0.90
ML Only (no reasoning, no collaboration)	0.84	0.11	0.87

be deployed as DaemonSets, interacting with Prometheus for metrics collection. ML models can either be embedded as lightweight services. The consistently high performance of DAIMS confirms the choice of its architectural design. Despite integrating advanced ML and semantic reasoning, the proposed approach remains lightweight and practical for deployment in resource-constrained cloud environments due to its moderate resource overhead. While DAIMS is practically deployable, certain trade-offs must be considered (Table 3). In summary, the architecture is deployable in production settings with minimal adaptation.

Ablation Study. An ablation study is conducted by selectively disabling key modules in order to determine the contribution of each component. Results are presented in Table 4. The removal of semantic reasoning results in a noticeable decrease in precision (↑ FPR), while disabling agent collaboration decreases recall slightly. These results demonstrate that semantic inference as well as distributed validation are critical for improving detection accuracy and robustness.

Limitations and Scalability. The proposed framework performs well in simulations, but certain limitations must be considered. Model retraining, ontology maintenance and reasoning latency at high throughput are the main challenges. Despite this, the architecture is modular and scalable due to decentralized agent-based execution. The modular agent-based design provides linear scalability (Table 1) and limited costs for localized reasoning and inter-agent collaboration. In large deployments, optimizations such as rule pruning and caching may reduce overhead. Overall, the framework remains scalable and suitable for detecting anomalies in distributed environments in real time.

5 Conclusion and Perspectives

This paper presents DAIMS, a Distributed Agent-based Intelligent Monitoring System for enhanced anomaly detection in complex web-based distributed environments. In distributed environments, traditional centralized approaches often have difficulties with responsiveness, fault explainability and scalability. Motivated by these limitations, DAIMS integrates ML (XGBoost) models with ontology-based semantic reasoning for contextualized and collaborative anomaly detection. The system integrates intelligent agents that continuously monitor microservice-level metrics, conduct local inference and collaborate via a message bus. The semantic knowledge is encoded in an OWL ontology with SWRL rules for higher-level reasoning and tracking cascading failure propagation. DAIMS fully supports modern observability pipelines and flexible deployment strategies such as Kubernetes DaemonSets. Simulation experiments showed that DAIMS outperformed three widely used monitoring methods, achieving an F1-score of 0.91, a FPR of 5% and a detection rate of 94%, while maintaining a low inference latency of 85 ms. These results indicate that the proposed approach is well-suited to the dynamic and distributed nature of modern Web applications. Despite its promising results, DAIMS has some limitations. It lacks continuous adaptive learning, uses static rules for reasoning and lacks privacy support in distributed settings. Future work will include online learning to improve adaptability. Secure collaboration will be supported by federated and privacy-preserving learning.

Disclosure of Interests. The authors have no competing interests to declare that are relevant to the content of this article.

References

1. Raeiszadeh, M., Ebrahimzadeh, A., Glitho, R., Eker, J., Mini, R.: Asynchronous real-time federated learning for anomaly detection in microservice cloud applications. IEEE Trans. Mach. Learn. Commun. Network. **3**, 176–194 (2025)
2. Noetzold, D., Rosseto, A., Leithardt, V., Costa, H.: Enhancing infrastructure observability: machine learning for proactive monitoring and anomaly detection. J. Internet Serv. Appl. **15**, 508–522 (2024)
3. Liu, P., et al.: Unsupervised detection of microservice trace anomalies through service-level deep Bayesian networks. In: 2020 IEEE 31st International Symposium on Software Reliability Engineering (ISSRE), pp. 48–58. IEEE (2020)
4. Lin, J., Chen, P., Zheng, Z.: Microscope: pinpoint performance issues with causal graphs in micro-service environments. In: International Conference on Service-Oriented Computing, pp. 3–20. Springer (2018)
5. Wang, P., Zhang, X., Cao, Z., Chen, Z.: MADMM: microservice system anomaly detection via multi-modal data and multi-feature extraction. Neural Comput. Appl. **36**(25), 15739–15757 (2024)

6. Panahandeh, M., Hamou-Lhadj, A., Hamdaqa, M., Miller, J.: Serviceanomaly: an anomaly detection approach in microservices using distributed traces and profiling metrics. J. Syst. Softw. **209**, 111917 (2024)
7. Huang, J., Yang, Y., Yu, H., Li, J., Zheng, X.: Twin graph-based anomaly detection via attentive multi-modal learning for microservice system. In: 2023 38th IEEE/ACM International Conference on Automated Software Engineering (ASE), pp. 66–78. IEEE (2023)
8. Kohyarnejadfard, I., Aloise, D., Azhari, S., Dagenais, M.: Anomaly detection in microservice environments using distributed tracing data analysis and NLP. J. Cloud Comput. **11**(1), 25 (2022)
9. Rabenstein, B., Volz, J.: Prometheus: a next-generation monitoring system (talk). Dublin. USENIX Association (2015)
10. Theakanath, T.: Datadog Cloud Monitoring Quick Start Guide. Packt Publishing (2021)
11. von Kistowski, J., Eismann, S., Schmitt, N., Bauer, A., Grohmann, J., Kounev, S.: Teastore: a micro-service reference application for benchmarking, modeling and resource management research (2018)
12. Zhou, X., et al.: Benchmarking microservice systems for software engineering research, pp. 323–324 (2018)
13. Apache Software Foundation. Apache Kafka (2025). https://kafka.apache.org/. Accessed 14 June 2025
14. FudanSELab. Train-ticket: A benchmark microservices application (2025). https://github.com/FudanSELab/train-ticket. Accessed 19 June 2025
15. Kaufmann, J., Schering, A.G.: Analysis of Variance ANOVA (2014)
16. Nanda, A., Mahapatra, A., Mohapatra, B., Mahapatra, A.: Multiple comparison test by Tukey's honestly significant difference (HSD): do the confident level control type i error. Int. J. Appl. Math. Stat. **6**, 59–65 (2021)

A Web-Based Fauna Taxonomic Rank Identification Application

Qianqian Zhang[1(✉)], Khandakar Ahmed[1], Muhammad Khan[1], and Kate Wang[2]

[1] Victoria University, Melbourne, VIC 3011, Australia
{Qianqian.Zhang,Khandakar.Ahmed,Muhammad.Khan}@vu.edu.au
[2] RMIT University, Melbourne, VIC 3000, Australia
kate.wang@rmit.edu.au

Abstract. The increasing use of automated image capture in ecological and biodiversity studies has created a growing demand for efficient and practical tools for animal image classification. However, most existing methods treat the task as a simple object classification problem, which limits their utility for taxonomists and biologists. This paper presents a web-based application that integrates a hierarchical classification model with an interactive interface to support animal taxonomic research and public engagement. The core contributions are: (1) a multi-rank prediction framework that identifies six taxonomic ranks—species, genus, family, order, class, and phylum—from a single uploaded image, supported by bounding box localisation; (2) an evolutionary relationship comparison feature that determines the closest shared rank when two images are uploaded, enabling users to explore taxonomic proximity; and (3) a privacy-preserving design that automatically deletes user data after processing to ensure confidentiality. By bridging automated classification with taxonomic needs, this application offers a scalable tool for biodiversity conservation, research, and education.

Keywords: Image Recognition · YOLOv9 · Australian Fauna

1 Introduction

Creatures on Earth are facing unprecedented threats. Over the past decades, species abundance has been declining at an alarming rate due to extensive human activities and complex environmental factors [4,33]. Many species have gone extinct before being recorded in scientific literature. Since the advent of automated field-capture devices, researchers have been able to gather extensive datasets on wildlife, including conventional images, thermal imaging, and aerial photography [3,35]. However, identifying the species captured in these datasets remains a significant challenge [30]. Traditional identification approaches rely heavily on manual processes, which are time-consuming, labour-intensive, and prone to errors, especially when performed by non-experts. For instance, one

I. Awan et al. (Eds.): WISE 2025, LNCS 16367, pp. 139–153, 2026.
https://doi.org/10.1007/978-981-95-7394-3_10

study reported that a trained researcher required nine months to manually classify 700,000 images [21].

As a discipline focused on naming, describing, and categorising organisms based on shared characteristics and evolutionary relationships [15], taxonomy has been facing significant challenges due to limited funding and insufficient manpower [9]. The current international classification system is rooted in the principles established by Carl Linnaeus [18]. This system employs a hierarchical structure to classify organisms into progressively narrower categories, reflecting their biological similarities and evolutionary lineage. The classification hierarchy consists of eight major taxonomic ranks, listed in descending order of inclusiveness: domain, kingdom, phylum, class, order, family, genus, and species. Higher taxonomic ranks, such as domain and kingdom, encompass broader categories that describe more general characteristics shared by a large number of organisms. In contrast, lower taxonomic ranks, such as genus and species, are more specific, highlighting precise traits shared by fewer organisms. Figure 1 illustrates the major taxonomic ranks for *Dromaius novaehollandiae.*

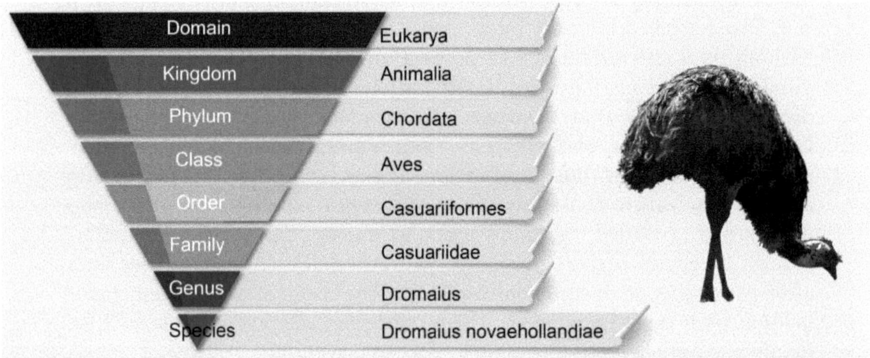

Fig. 1. The Major Taxonomic Ranks of The Emu. The *Dromaius novaehollandiae* (Latham, 1790) is observed in Australia by chloe_14281. This image is background removed and licensed under [CC BY-NC 4.0] (https://creativecommons.org/licenses/by-nc/4.0/)

In recent years, artificial intelligence has spurred significant advancements across a wide array of domains, from medical diagnostics and computer vision [1,5,7,10,17] to optimising complex systems such as traffic networks and wireless communications [1,6]. Furthermore, the latest advancements in computer vision have introduced efficient solutions for species identification, offering automated classification and detection methods [20,22,32]. However, most of these approaches treat the task as a straightforward object classification or detection problem, overlooking the evolutionary relationships between species [2,8,19,29,31]. For example, while existing methods may differentiate between a kangaroo and a koala, biologists prioritise distinguishing Macropus giganteus and Phascolarctos cinereus (the scientific names at the species rank). Such distinctions are crucial for taxonomic studies and conservation efforts.

To address this gap, we collected a dataset containing 50 animal categories comprising a total of 35,000 annotated images. These animals, all observed within Australia, were sourced from an open-source biodiversity database: the Global Biodiversity Information Facility (GBIF). Each image was manually labelled with the corresponding species rank name and bounding box annotations. Building upon this dataset, we proposed a highly efficient framework for species identification, achieving a mean Average Precision (mAP) of 87.5% and a precision value of 98.2% on the testing set [38].

Subsequently, we reorganised the dataset based on the Linnaean taxonomic framework and trained additional models to predict higher taxonomic ranks, including genus, family, order, class, and phylum. These models were integrated into a compound model capable of predicting all six major taxonomic ranks from an input image. Additionally, we introduced a correction mechanism to refine predictions from individual model outputs, ensuring consistency in taxonomic classification.

In this study, we developed a web-based application that integrates the aforementioned research and provides a user-friendly interactive interface for both experts and the general public to perform taxonomic rank predictions and taxonomic relationship comparisons for animal images. The main contributions of this project are as follows:

1. Multi-Rank Taxonomic Prediction: The system enables users to upload a single image and receive predictions across six taxonomic ranks, including species, genus, family, order, class, and phylum. Compared to most animal classification applications, this project provides a precise and comprehensive result rather than a single classification result. Bounding boxes are also provided to precisely localise the animal within the image, improving interpretability and user understanding.
2. Evolutionary Relationship Comparison: Users can upload a pair of images, and the system identifies the closest shared major taxonomic rank between the two animals. This allows users to explore evolutionary linkages and taxonomic proximity in an intuitive and accessible way, with bounding boxes visualising the predictions on both images.
3. Privacy Protection: To ensure user privacy and data security, the system automatically deletes uploaded images and all associated data after a predefined period, minimising storage risks and preserving user confidentiality.

This web-based tool represents a significant step forward in species identification and taxonomic exploration, offering an efficient, non-invasive solution for researchers, educators, and conservationists.

The rest of this chapter is organised as follows: Sect. 2 reviews related work, focusing on recent advancements in web-based applications for species identification and taxonomic classification. Section 3 introduces the design of the application and explains each component. It includes an overview of the compound model, the instruction of system architecture, user interface, and local and cloud deployment. Finally, Sect. 4 discusses the limitations of the current approach and outlines potential future improvements and directions for further research.

2 Related Work

This section discusses the technologies in the animal identification area, including invasive and non-invasive approaches, the development of web-based applications, and the integration of real-time processing frameworks. These studies provide the foundation for addressing challenges in species identification and highlight the need for more comprehensive solutions that incorporate taxonomic classification.

2.1 Species Identification Technology

Invasive devices with real-time monitoring systems are widely used in the livestock industry. As a traditional animal identification technology, these systems remain active in the market due to their low cost and ease of operation [36]. Emanuel et al. proposed an intelligent animal tracking service for zoological gardens utilising Global Positioning System (GPS), Radio Frequency Identification (RFID), and sensors to provide real-time monitoring of animal location, body temperature, and visual data [23]. This system enhances animal management by enabling real-time tracking, including emergency situations such as animal escapes, and a prototype has been developed to demonstrate its functionality.

However, invasive devices often involve altering or implanting equipment into the animal's body, which can lead to physical harm. In contrast, non-invasive technologies have garnered significant attention in recent years, driven by growing awareness of animal welfare concerns and the need for less intrusive monitoring methods. Low-cost and low-maintenance solutions, such as wearable devices (e.g., foot rings and collars) and hair dyeing techniques, are widely employed in wildlife monitoring and livestock management. Moreover, another non-invasive technique that minimises the impact on animals—image recognition—has gained prominence with the advancements in computer vision and high-performance Graphics Processing Units (GPUs). Based on the identification objectives and targets, image identification for animals can be categorised into four main types: static feature recognition (e.g., footprints, patterns, nasal features, irises, ear vein patterns, and wing textures), dynamic feature recognition (e.g., movement patterns and migration trajectories), thermal imaging, and real-time monitoring (e.g., drone-captured aerial imagery and GPS data) [39]. These developments have significantly contributed to both individual and species-rank identification tasks.

For species definition, modern biological taxonomy relies on Deoxyribonucleic Acid (DNA) sequencing. This is primarily because DNA sequencing provides unparalleled accuracy in determining genetic differences, which form the basis for distinguishing between species, even when morphological differences are minimal or absent [28]. Sujeevan et al. utilised DNA-based Operational Taxonomic

Units (OTUs) to automate species-rank identification, significantly advancing biodiversity analysis and taxonomic revision [26]. However, the major limitations of DNA-based methods lie in their time and financial costs, which include DNA sample collection, laboratory processing, and sequencing. These limitations often make such methods impractical for smaller-scale research projects or field-based studies.

2.2 Development of Web-Based Application

The widespread adoption of high-performance GPUs has brought significant advantages to mobile devices, which have increasingly replaced personal computers as essential processing terminals in recent years. Web-based applications, due to their flexibility without requiring installation, real-time processing capabilities, and multi-platform compatibility, have significantly enhanced daily workflows and surpassed traditional software applications in popularity.

A study addresses the conflict between vehicles, humans, and animals on roads. Prema et al. proposed a solution using a DCNN-based classification technique with the ResNet152V2 algorithm to identify animals crossing roads. The system sends notifications via a Wi-Fi-enabled IoT device, which uses the Blynk web application to control an Arduino board through a smartphone [24]. In another study, Jiachi et al. developed a WeChat Mini Program for wheat pest detection, utilising the VGG-16 architecture to identify diseases and pests efficiently from uploaded images [34]. Unlike traditional web applications, mini programs are integrated within social media platforms, utilising the Apache Multipurpose Infrastructure for Network Applications (MINA) framework, which is based on Java technology [12]. This framework supports asynchronous input/output and multithreaded model applications, enabling high-performance, scalable, and lightweight functionalities directly within social media ecosystems. Additionally, more applications move toward online deployment, privacy preservation has become an emerging concern [13,25]. Recent research has proposed adaptive and evolutionary frameworks to safeguard sensitive data in cloud-based and web information systems [11,37]

Mobile applications, constrained by device limitations such as processing speed and operational demands, often require rapid response times. Some frameworks are optimised specifically to meet these requirements. You Only Look Once (YOLO)'s real-time image processing capabilities make it a preferred choice for applications demanding immediate feedback. For example, a study integrated the YOLOv1 algorithm into a K210 chip to enable real-time classification and tracking of wild animals, creating a portable identification device [14]. The recently released YOLOv11 (October 2024) introduces architectural innovations like Cross Stage Partial with kernel size 2 (C3k2), Spatial Pyramid Pooling - Fast (SPPF), and Convolutional block with Parallel Spatial Attention (C2PSA), enhancing feature extraction, computational efficiency, and versatility across various computer vision tasks, including object detection, instance segmentation, and pose estimation [16].

However, despite YOLO's efficiency in object detection tasks, most existing web-based applications struggle to address the complexity of taxonomic classification. These applications are typically limited to identifying individual objects or species within an image and fail to consider broader taxonomic hierarchies or evolutionary relationships. This highlights the necessity for more advanced systems that integrate taxonomic ranks into the identification process, enabling a comprehensive understanding of an animal's placement within the biological classification framework.

3 Methodology

This section outlines the systematic approach employed in developing the proposed animal identification framework. This includes model architecture, system architecture, local and cloud deployment strategies. The following sections provide a detailed explanation of each component, demonstrating the integration of machine learning techniques and cloud-based infrastructure in achieving an efficient and scalable species identification framework.

3.1 Compound Model Overview

The proposed model is an advanced species identification framework built upon the YOLOv9 architecture. It is designed to address classification challenges associated with Australian wildlife, including the high number of species, taxonomic similarities, and intra-species appearance variations observed in natural environments. To enhance classification performance, the model integrates optimised feature extraction techniques and clustering-based refinements, ensuring robust identification across multiple taxonomic ranks.

The model is initially trained and evaluated on a dataset comprising 50 Australian animal species, capturing variations in environmental conditions and species characteristics. Experimental results demonstrate that, compared to the default YOLOv9 model, the proposed approach improves mAP from 73.11% to 87.5%, while the precision value increases from 86.2% to 98.2%. Additionally, when tested on a validation set containing previously unseen images, the model achieves a species identification success rate of 91.29% with an average confidence score of 0.801, indicating strong generalisation capability while maintaining high classification accuracy.

Furthermore, the dataset is reorganised based on the Linnaean taxonomy framework, grouping the 50 species into five higher taxonomic ranks: phylum, class, order, family, and genus. Subsequently, the model is retrained at each of these ranks, resulting in six models optimised for different taxonomic ranks. Each model is designed to capture distinct feature representations relevant to its respective classification task, enabling a hierarchical and structured approach to species identification.

3.2 System Architecture

The architecture of the proposed web-based application is designed to facilitate efficient animal image classification and taxonomic rank comparison. As illustrated in Fig. 2, the system operates in two main phases: single image prediction and two image comparison. The process begins with the initial image upload, where the system validates the input image(s) for format compatibility and applies the necessary preprocessing steps. Once validated, the request is sent to the backend for processing. The decision node, 'Prediction Task', determines whether the application will proceed with single-image species identification or two-image relationship comparison.

In the Single Image Phase, the application uses a compound model to predict taxonomic ranks for a single uploaded image. The prediction process involves running the model, generating results, and returning the annotated output to the user. The final results, including bounding boxes and predicted taxonomic ranks, are displayed through the web interface.

In the Two Image Phase, the system extends its functionality to compare two uploaded images. The compound model is run independently for each image to generate taxonomic rank predictions. Subsequently, these results are compared to determine the closest shared rank between the two animals. The comparison result, along with the annotated images, is displayed to the user, providing insights into the evolutionary relationship between the species in the images.

3.3 User Interface and Local Deployment

The user interface of the developed application is designed to be simple and user-friendly, allowing both professionals and the general public to interact seamlessly with its functionalities. The system offers two primary features—single image prediction and species comparison—which are accessible from the homepage. These features are implemented using Flask, a lightweight and modular web framework, to enable real-time processing and result generation.

Homepage and Navigation. The homepage of the application serves as the primary navigation interface, providing users with a streamlined entry point to its functionalities. Two buttons offer users clear options: "Single Image Prediction" for analysing a single image and "Species Comparison" for comparing taxonomic relationships between two images.

Single Image Prediction. The single image prediction functionality enables users to classify an uploaded image into its major taxonomic ranks. As shown in Fig. 3, users can upload an image, which is processed through the compound model hosted on the backend. The model predicts the taxonomic ranks, including species, genus, family, order, class, and phylum. Alongside the classification, the system generates bounding boxes that highlight the identified animal within the image. The annotated image, along with the predicted taxonomic ranks, is

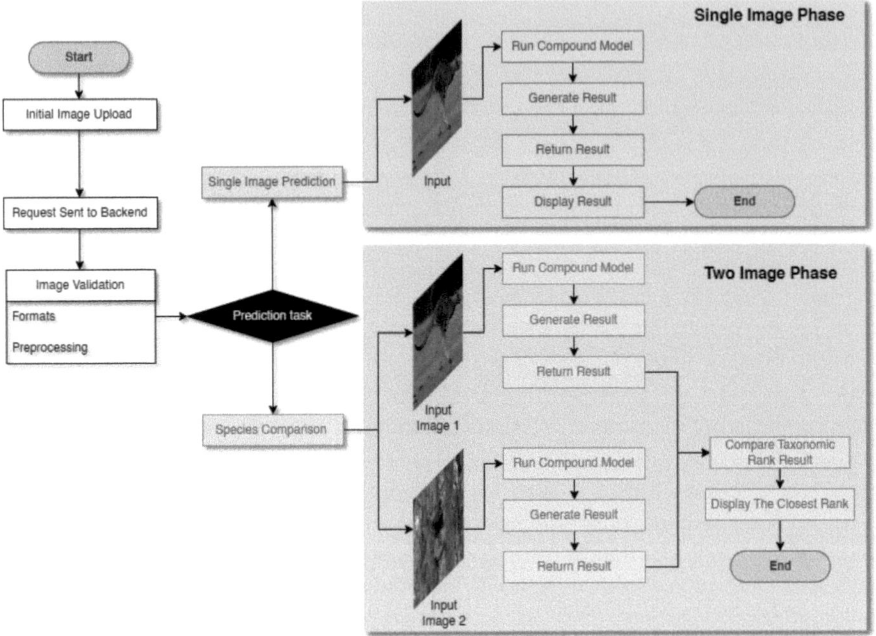

Fig. 2. The Proposed Web-based Application Workflow. Note: The *Macropus giganteus* (Shaw, 1790) image is observed in Australia by Samuel Lee. The *Phascolarctos cinereus* (Goldfuss, 1817) is observed in Australia by Lukas Krug. Those images are cropped and licensed under [CC BY 4.0] (http://creativecommons.org/licenses/by/4.0/)

displayed to the user in a concise result interface. Detailed information, such as the confidence scores for each predicted taxonomic rank, is logged and accessible in the backend system.

Species Comparison. The species comparison feature is designed to identify the closest shared taxonomic rank between two uploaded images. Figure 4 illustrates the comparison result of species *Macropus giganteus* and species *Threskiornis molucca*. The system processes each image independently using the compound model to generate their respective taxonomic classifications. The results are then compared to identify the closest rank, which, in this case, is the phylum Chordata. The final output includes annotated images for both inputs and a comparison summary highlighting the shared rank and the predicted classifications for each image. Similar to the single image phase, additional classification details, such as confidence scores, are recorded in the backend for further analysis. This functionality allows users to explore evolutionary relationships between species visually and interactively, making it a valuable tool for biodiversity studies and ecological research.

Prediction Result

The animal in the picture is Macropus giganteus. Its major ranks are:
Species: Macropus giganteus
Genus: Macropus
Family: Macropodidae
Order: Diprotodontia
Class: Mammalia
Phylum: Chordata

Back to Home

Fig. 3. An Example of Signle Image Prediction Result. Note: The *Macropus giganteus* (Shaw, 1790) image is observed in Australia by Reiner Richteris and is licensed under [CC BY 4.0] (http://creativecommons.org/licenses/by/4.0/)

3.4 Cloud Integration with AWS

The deployment of the proposed animal identification framework on Amazon Web Services (AWS) ensures accessibility, scalability, and efficient computational resource utilisation. AWS provides a cloud-based infrastructure that supports real-time inference, allowing users to upload images for species classification without relying on local computational resources. The integration process involves model deployment, backend API development, and frontend interaction, ensuring seamless communication between system components.

Figure 5 illustrates the workflow of cloud-based deployment.

The model is hosted on an Amazon Elastic Compute Cloud (EC2) instance, leveraging a virtualised environment to execute inference tasks. The instance is configured with Amazon Linux 2023, ensuring compatibility with deep learning frameworks and optimised execution performance. A Flask-based web application is deployed within the instance, serving as the primary interface for handling user requests. The web service processes image uploads, executes the classification model, and returns results to users in a structured format. To enhance request handling efficiency, Gunicorn is employed as the Web Server Gateway Interface (WSGI) Hypertext Transfer Protocol (HTTP) server, enabling concurrent processing of multiple requests.

To ensure secure and controlled access to the EC2 instance, an AWS security group is configured with strict inbound traffic rules. Secure Shell (SSH) access is restricted to the user's specific IP address, preventing unauthorised remote login attempts. Hypertext Transfer Protocol HTTP traffic on port 80 is made

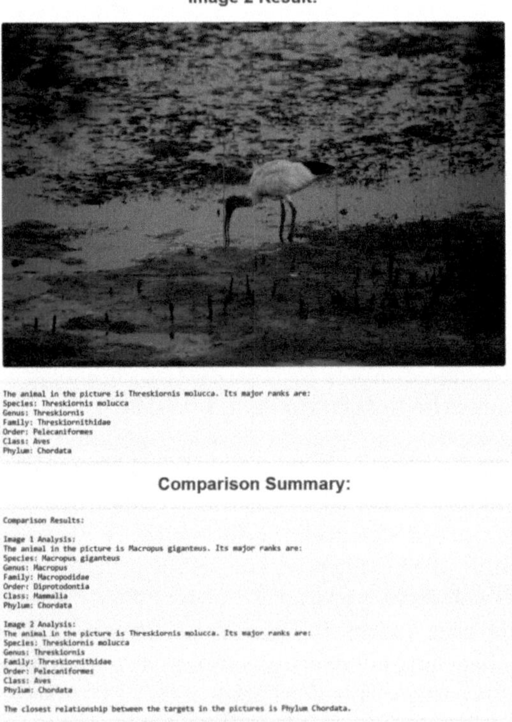

Fig. 4. An Example of Species Comparion Result. Note: The *Threskiornis molucca* (Cuvier, 1829) image on the bottom is observed in Australia by Martin Rady and is licensed under [CC BY 4.0] (http://creativecommons.org/licenses/by/4.0/)

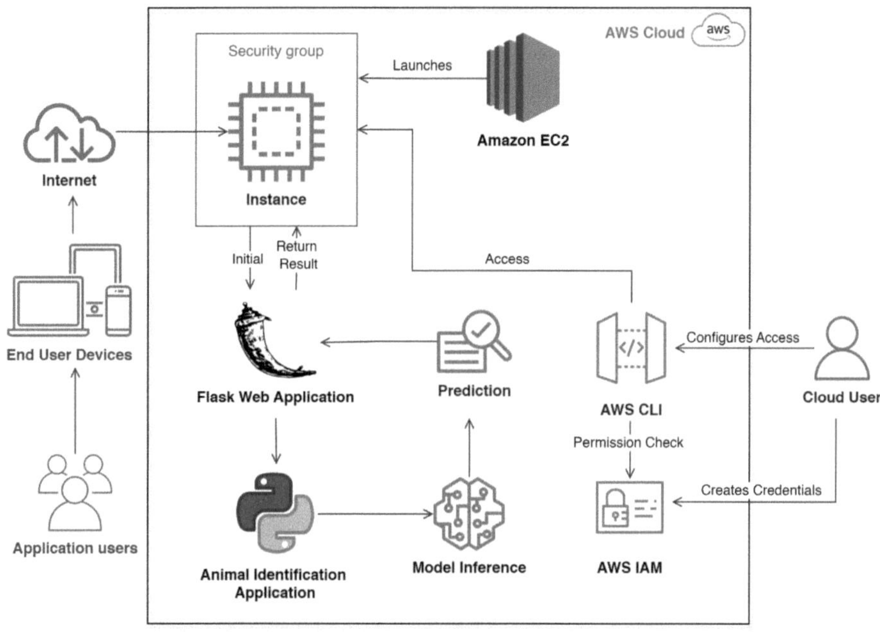

Fig. 5. Cloud-Based Deployment Architecture for Animal Species Identification

accessible to all external sources, facilitating public access to the web-based application. Similarly, Hypertext Transfer Protocol Secure (HTTPS) traffic on port 443 is also permitted for all external connections, ensuring encrypted data transmission between users and the server. The deployed system can be accessed at http://52.62.150.247:5000, which provides a public interface for image submission and result retrieval. Additionally, an automated file-cleaning mechanism is implemented to regularly remove previously submitted images and generated results, maintaining storage efficiency and long-term stability.

Security and Privacy Protection. User privacy is a critical consideration in the deployment of animal image classification systems. Although uploaded images are primarily intended for taxonomic analysis, they may inadvertently contain sensitive information such as identifiable features, geotags, or background objects. To mitigate the risk of privacy leakage, the system enforces strict data-handling policies. All uploaded files are encrypted during transmission via HTTPS, processed exclusively within a secured EC2 environment, and automatically deleted after inference to minimise retention risks. In addition, firewall rules and restricted SSH access prevent unauthorised intrusions. These safeguards ensure that the application not only delivers reliable classification results but also upholds the confidentiality of user data, thereby reinforcing trust among researchers, educators, and the general public.

4 Future Works and Conclusion

Future enhancements to the web-based application will focus on expanding functionality and improving system performance. One potential feature is allowing users to choose whether to retain uploaded images on the server to support future machine learning tasks, offering researchers the option to contribute to model improvement actively. This capability could be complemented by an annotation tool, enabling users to adjust bounding boxes, thereby enriching the training dataset with expert-curated data. As the application evolves to support a broader range of species, additional contextual options, such as incorporating geographic location metadata, could be integrated to enhance prediction accuracy by aligning model outputs with species distribution data.

Moreover, the rapid advancements in Large Language Models (LLMs) in recent years have demonstrated their exceptional reasoning and decision-making capabilities. Future work will explore the integration of image detection models with LLMs to investigate their potential role in improving decision-making processes, such as resolving ambiguities in taxonomic rank predictions or offering contextual explanations for classification results. In our preliminary experiments, several lightweight LLMs were compared to assess their ability to enhance prediction consistency. However, the results were not satisfactory, potentially due to their limited parameter scale, insufficient training on domain-specific taxonomic knowledge, and restricted capability to interpret fine-grained visual features. While larger-scale LLMs may address some of these issues by providing stronger reasoning and contextualisation, their deployment raises additional challenges, including higher computational costs, increased memory demands, and the need for expensive server infrastructures. These practical considerations must be carefully evaluated when designing a scalable system, ensuring that the benefits of integrating LLMs are balanced against resource constraints in real-world applications.

In conclusion, this study presents a web-based application for automated species identification and taxonomic rank comparison. By integrating a compound deep-learning model with an intuitive interface, the system enables both single-image classification and species comparison, supporting biodiversity research, conservation, and education. The framework offers a scalable foundation for extending to more species and refining evolutionary analysis, ensuring continued value for researchers and educators in biological taxonomy.

Usage Permission. This research extensively employs data sourced from the GBIF [27]. The full list of datasets, identified by their DOIs, which have been utilised for the purposes of this research, is accessible at https://cutt.ly/3wBiTeO7. Images from these GBIF datasets are licensed under Creative Commons Attribution-NonCommercial (CC BY-NC), permitting adaptation and sharing for non-commercial purposes with proper attribution. License details can be found at https://creativecommons.org/licenses/by-nc/4.0/.

Disclosure of Interests. The authors have no competing interests to declare that are relevant to the content of this article.

References

1. Alvi, A.M., et al.: XCR-Net: a computer aided framework to detect covid-19. IEEE Trans. Consum. Electron. **70**(4), 7551–7561 (2024). https://doi.org/10.1109/TCE.2024.3446793
2. Binta Islam, S., Valles, D., Hibbitts, T.J., Ryberg, W.A., Walkup, D.K., Forstner, M.R.: Animal species recognition with deep convolutional neural networks from ecological camera trap images. Animals **13**(9), 1526 (2023). https://doi.org/10.3390/ani13091526
3. Boitani, L.: Camera trapping for wildlife research. Pelagic Publishing Ltd (2016)
4. Ceballos, G., Ehrlich, P.R., Barnosky, A.D., García, A., Pringle, R.M., Palmer, T.M.: Accelerated modern human-induced species losses: entering the sixth mass extinction. Sci. Adv. **1**(5), e1400253 (2015)
5. Chen, F., et al.: Supervised graph contrastive learning for cancer subtype identification through multi-omics data integration. Health Inf. Sci. Syst. **12**(1), 12 (2024). https://doi.org/10.1007/s13755-024-00274-x
6. Chen, G., Wang, M., Han, S., Yin, J., Wang, H., Cao, J.: Deep reinforcement learning-based cloud-edge offloading for WBANs. IEEE Trans. Consum. Electron. **71**(2), 4053–4064 (2025). https://doi.org/10.1109/TCE.2024.3504545
7. Chen, L., Liu, W., Wang, H., Jeon, S.W., Jiang, Y., Zheng, Z.: Consistency-guided adaptive alternating training for semi-supervised salient object detection. IEEE Trans. Circuits Syst. Video Technol. **35**(7), 7033–7046 (2025). https://doi.org/10.1109/TCSVT.2025.3539471
8. Deneu, B., Servajean, M., Bonnet, P., Botella, C., Munoz, F., Joly, A.: Convolutional neural networks improve species distribution modelling by capturing the spatial structure of the environment. PLoS Comput. Biol. **17**(4), e1008856 (2021). https://doi.org/10.1371/journal.pcbi.1008856
9. Ereshefsky, M.: Species. In: Zalta, E.N. (ed.) The Stanford Encyclopedia of Philosophy. Metaphysics Research Lab, Stanford University, summer 2022 edition edn. (2022)
10. Fang, Q., et al.: Lcrnet: local cross-channel recalibration network for liver cancer classification based on CT images. Health Inf. Sci. Syst. **12**(1), 5 (2023). https://doi.org/10.1007/s13755-023-00263-6
11. Ge, Y.F., Wang, H., Cao, J., Zhang, Y., Jiang, X.: Privacy-preserving data publishing: an information-driven distributed genetic algorithm. World Wide Web **27**(1), 1 (2024). https://doi.org/10.1007/s11280-024-01241-y
12. Hao, L., Wan, F., Ma, N., Wang, Y.: Analysis of the development of wechat mini program. J. Phys. Conf. Ser. **1087**(6), 062040 (2018). https://doi.org/10.1088/1742-6596/1087/6/062040
13. Jahan, S., Ge, Y.F., Wang, H., Kabir, E.: Dynamic-parameter genetic algorithm for multi-objective privacy-preserving trajectory data publishing. In: Barhamgi, M., Wang, H., Wang, X. (eds.) Web Information Systems Engineering - WISE 2024, pp. 46–57. Springer, Singapore (2025)
14. Ji, P., Zhu, Q.: Research on embedded animal recognition system based on yolo. In: 2022 6th International Conference on Robotics and Automation Sciences (ICRAS), pp. 265–269 (2022). https://doi.org/10.1109/ICRAS55217.2022.9842099

15. Judd, W.S., Campbell, C.S., Kellogg, E.A., Stevens, P.F., Donoghue, M.J.: Plant systematics: a phylogenetic approach. Ecología mediterránea **25**(2), 215 (1999)
16. Khanam, R., Hussain, M.: Yolov11: an overview of the key architectural enhancements (2024). https://arxiv.org/abs/2410.17725
17. Li, R., et al.: Open-vocabulary multi-object tracking with domain generalized and temporally adaptive features. IEEE Trans. Multimedia **27**, 3009–3022 (2025). https://doi.org/10.1109/TMM.2025.3557619
18. Linnaeus, C.: Systema naturae, vol. 1. Stockholm Laurentii Salvii (1758)
19. Marsot, M., et al.: An adaptive pig face recognition approach using convolutional neural networks. Comput. Electron. Agric. **173**, 105386 (2020). https://doi.org/10.1016/j.compag.2020.105386
20. Mitterwallner, V., et al.: Automated visitor and wildlife monitoring with camera traps and machine learning. Remote Sens. Ecol. Conserv. **10**(2), 236–247 (2024). https://doi.org/10.1002/rse2.367. https://zslpublications.onlinelibrary.wiley.com/doi/abs/10.1002/rse2.367
21. Moallem, G., Pathirage, D.D., Reznick, J., Gallagher, J., Sari-Sarraf, H.: An explainable deep vision system for animal classification and detection in trail-camera images with automatic post-deployment retraining. Knowl.-Based Syst. **216**, 106815 (2021)
22. Ou, L., Liu, B., Chen, X., He, Q., Qian, W., Zou, L.: Automated identification of morphological characteristics of three thunnus species based on different machine learning algorithms. Fishes **8**(4), 182 (2023). https://doi.org/10.3390/fishes8040182
23. Pereira, E., et al.: RFID technology for animal tracking: a survey. IEEE J. Radio Freq. Ident. (2023). https://doi.org/10.1109/JRFID.2023.3334952
24. Prema Arokia Mary, G., Nithesh, P.S., Nanthini, V., Thebiksha, G.V.: Wild animal detection system. In: 2023 2nd International Conference on Advancements in Electrical, Electronics, Communication, Computing and Automation (ICAECA), pp. 1–6 (2023). https://doi.org/10.1109/ICAECA56562.2023.10199701
25. Qiao, X., Zhou, X., Zhou, C., Wang, H., Zhang, Y.: EBUD: evolving disaster burst detection over social streams. In: International Conference on Web Information Systems Engineering, pp. 105–115. Springer (2025). https://doi.org/10.1007/978-981-96-0567-5_9
26. Ratnasingham, S., Hebert, P.D.N.: A DNA-based registry for all animal species: the barcode index number (bin) system. PLoS ONE **8**(7), 1–16 (2013). https://doi.org/10.1371/journal.pone.0066213
27. Secretariat, T.G.: What is gbif? (2024). https://www.gbif.org/what-is-gbif
28. Stoeckle, M.: Taxonomy, DNA, and the bar code of life. BioScience **53**(9), 796–797 (2003). https://doi.org/10.1641/0006-3568(2003)053[0796:TDATBC]2.0.CO;2
29. Tang, J., Zhao, Y., Feng, L., Zhao, W.: Contour-based wild animal instance segmentation using a few-shot detector. Animals **12**(15) (2022). https://doi.org/10.3390/ani12151980. https://www.mdpi.com/2076-2615/12/15/1980
30. Van Dyck, L.E., Kwitt, R., Denzler, S.J., Gruber, W.R.: Comparing object recognition in humans and deep convolutional neural networks—an eye tracking study. Front. Neurosci. **15**, 750639 (2021). https://doi.org/10.3389/fnins.2021.750639
31. Vidal, M., Wolf, N., Rosenberg, B., Harris, B.P., Mathis, A.: Perspectives on individual animal identification from biology and computer vision. Integr. Comp. Biol. **61**, 900–916 (2021). https://doi.org/10.1093/icb/icab107
32. Vélez, J., et al.: An evaluation of platforms for processing camera-trap data using artificial intelligence. Methods Ecol. Evol. **14**(2), 459–477 (2023).

https://doi.org/10.1111/2041-210X.14044. https://besjournals.onlinelibrary.wiley.com/doi/abs/10.1111/2041-210X.14044

33. Wagler, R.: The anthropocene mass extinction: an emerging curriculum theme for science educators. Am. Biol. Teach. **73**(2), 78–83 (2011)
34. Wang, J., Fan, Y., Li, H., Yin, S.: Wechat mini program for wheat diseases recognition based on VGG-16 convolutional neural network. Int. J. Appl. Sci. Eng. **20**, 1–9 (2023). https://doi.org/10.6703/IJASE.202309_20(3).008
35. Welbourne, D.J., MacGregor, C., Paull, D., Lindenmayer, D.B.: The effectiveness and cost of camera traps for surveying small reptiles and critical weight range mammals: a comparison with labour-intensive complementary methods. Wildlife Res. **42**(5), 414–425 (2015). https://doi.org/10.1071/WR15054
36. Wolfert, S., Ge, L., Verdouw, C., Bogaardt, M.J.: Big data in smart farming: a review. Agric. Syst. **153**, 69–80 (2017). https://doi.org/10.1016/j.agsy.2017.01.023. https://www.sciencedirect.com/science/article/pii/S0308521X16303754
37. Yin, J., Chen, G., Hong, W., Wang, H., Cao, J., Miao, Y.: Empowering vulnerability prioritization: a heterogeneous graph-driven framework for exploitability prediction. In: Zhang, F., Wang, H., Barhamgi, M., Chen, L., Zhou, R. (eds.) Web Information Systems Engineering - WISE 2023, pp. 289–299. Springer, Singapore (2023)
38. Zhang, Q., Ahmed, K., Khan, M.I., Wang, H., Qu, Y.: Yolo-FCE: a feature and clustering enhanced object detection model for species classification. Pattern Recognit. **171**, 112218 (2026). https://doi.org/10.1016/j.patcog.2025.112218. https://www.sciencedirect.com/science/article/pii/S0031320325008799
39. Zhang, Q., Ahmed, K., Sharda, N., Wang, H.: A comprehensive survey of animal identification: exploring data sources, AI advances, classification obstacles and the role of taxonomy. Int. J. Intell. Syst. **2024**(1), 7033535 (2024). https://doi.org/10.1155/2024/7033535. https://onlinelibrary.wiley.com/doi/abs/10.1155/2024/7033535

Evidence Retrieval for Chinese Tabular Data in the Web Based on Dense Passage Retriever

Xianyu Zha[1,2], Peng Yang[1,2](✉), Xi Lin[3], and Zhenqi Wang[1,2]

[1] School of Computer Science and Engineering, Southeast University, Nanjing, China
pengyang@seu.edu.cn
[2] Future Network Research Center, Southeast University, Nanjing, China
[3] College of Computer and Data Science, Fuzhou University, Fuzhou, China

Abstract. The task of table evidence retrieval of Web Information aims to identify the most relevant Web tables from an extensive corpus for supporting Web information retrieval and text analytics. However, previous methods suffer from low accuracy in scenarios with limited computing resources and incapability of assessing the authenticity of statements with sufficient evidence, posing potential risks to Cybersecurity and spread of false information. To address these challenges, we first restructure three existing table fact verification datasets for evaluating the performance of evidence retrieval of Chinese Web Tabular Data, which accounts for a large proportion in the Web. And then, we propose a novel table evidence retrieval model based on Dense Passage Retriever for enhancing retrieval accuracy in scenarios with limited computational resources. Our experimental results across multiple datasets demonstrate that the proposed model achieves commendable accuracy, validating its effectiveness.

Keywords: Table Evidence Retrieval · Chinese Web Tabular Data · Dense Passage Retriever · Web Information Retrieva

1 Introduction

In the digital age, the rapid advancement of Web technologies and social media has significantly expanded the avenues through which humans access information, with Web tables emerging as a crucial source of structured data in this landscape. However, this progress is concurrently marred by the proliferation of online misinformation, which not only poses a substantial barrier to acquiring authentic information but also entails potential risks to cybersecurity. In this context, when confronted with a complex array of information, it becomes imperative to verify the veracity of statements by leveraging sufficient evidence to discern their truthfulness [1]. Fact-checking rumors and verifying claims from voluminous Web data presents a formidable challenge, thus rendering table evidence retrieval an indispensable task in this process.

I. Awan et al. (Eds.): WISE 2025, LNCS 16367, pp. 154–168, 2026.
https://doi.org/10.1007/978-981-95-7394-3_11

The table-based evidence retrieval task is a fundamental problem in the field of natural language processing, serving as a cornerstone for supporting Web information retrieval and text analytics. It aims to identify the most relevant tables from vast amounts of tabular data based on a given statement, and to assess the authenticity of the statement with such retrieved evidence–thereby ensuring the authenticity of information and safeguarding cybersecurity. Taking the restructured TABFACT [2] dataset as an example, a specific instance of this task is illustrated in Fig. 1: given the Chinese statement "匈牙利的等效每日通货膨胀率是所有国家中最高的 [Hungary's equivalent daily inflation rate is the highest among all countries]", the task involves locating the most relevant Chinese table titled "恶性通货膨胀 [hyperinflation]" from a large corpus of Web tables.

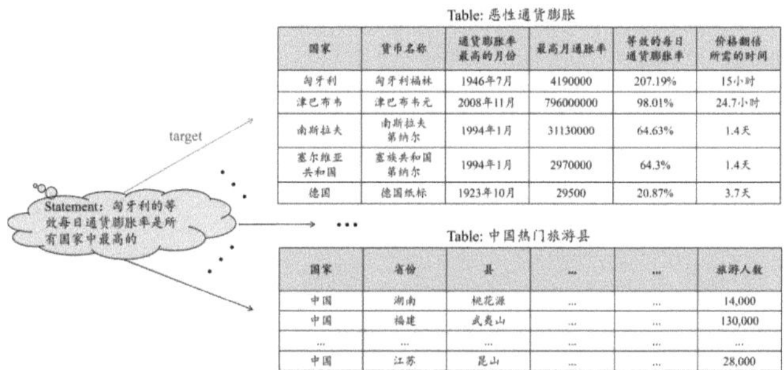

Fig. 1. An Example of Evidence Retrieval for Chinese Tabular Data in the Web

Over the past half century, many scholars at home and abroad have conducted in-depth research on tabular evidence retrieval technology from different disciplinary perspectives to ensure that authentic and reliable information is disseminated on the Internet. Accompanied by the continuous updates and advancements in natural language processing technologies in recent years, table evidence retrieval techniques have likewise achieved further development and optimization. From a historical perspective, the evolution of this research can be broadly divided into three main phases: The initial phase involved methods based on machine learning [3–6], where machine learning models were used to filter relevant table content from a wide pool of candidate corpora, primarily relying on text-matching features between query sentences and table content. Subsequently, the field transitioned to methods based on deep learning [7–9], which, compared to machine learning-based approaches, utilize neural network representations tailored to tables to capture deeper semantic features, thereby significantly enhancing retrieval accuracy. However, these evidence retrieval methods suffered from lower model complexity, often failing to accurately understand the semantics of search texts and evidence tables, resulting in retrieval accuracies not meeting expectations. Recently, with the rise and development of Pre-trained Language Models (PLMs), methods based on PLMs have gradually become the mainstream in research [10,11]. Compared to traditional evidence retrieval methods, the advantage of this approach lies in the powerful representational learning capabilities of PLMs, which can provide a wealth of prior knowledge for the representation of text and table semantics while automatically learning features from input texts. Nevertheless, existing methods based on PLMs [11] often require specific pre-training for tabular data, inevitably leading to excessive resource consumption and prolonged training times. Meanwhile, Chinese, as a language with a rich history and broad application containing rich semantic information, and the prevalence of table-form information in domestic online content, make the retrieval of such information an unavoidable issue. Therefore, research on evidence retrieval for Chinese Web tables is of significant importance. However, studies in this direction are scarcely reported.

Based on the foregoing analysis, we propose a Web table evidence retrieval method based on the Dense Passage Retriever. Addressing the issues of low accuracy in table evidence retrieval models in scenarios with limited computational resources, we employ a combination of existing general PLM, graph neural network, recurrent neural network, templating method, and named entity recognition technology for evidence retrieval from Web tabular data. To fill the research void in the field of Chinese Web table evidence retrieval, we have modified existing Chinese table fact verification datasets, including TABFACT, INFOTABS, and UCLDS [12], to create Chinese table evidence retrieval datasets. The performance of the proposed model was evaluated using these datasets.

To summarize, our contributions are three-fold:

(1) We propose a novel Web table evidence retrieval method based on the Dense Passage Retriever, designed to address the low accuracy of Web table evidence retrieval models in scenarios with limited computational resources. Experimental results validate its effectiveness and architectural validity.
(2) We have developed a method that employs named entity recognition technology to convert statement sentences into graph structures, with the aim of integrating key information from the statement into the graph. Concurrently, we propose a novel Web table serialization method designed to facilitate the processing of tables while maximizing the retention of their structural features.
(3) We have modified existing Chinese Web tabular data fact verification datasets to create Chinese Web tabular data evidence retrieval datasets, intended to support research on Chinese Web tabular data evidence retrieval tasks.

2 Related Work

In the field of Web table-based evidence retrieval, [3,4] were pioneers in introducing groundbreaking work. They developed a method that utilizes keyword-based retrieval techniques to rank Web tables returned by search engines, thereby optimizing Web table retrieval outcomes. This method incorporates a series of increasingly complex ranking functions, including but not limited to naïveRank, filterRank, and featureRank. Notably, the design of the featureRank function does not rely on existing search engine algorithms, representing a novel approach. Following the work of [3–5] proposed a keyword-guided framework to enhance Web-based information retrieval accuracy. They refined the relevance ranking of answers from Web portals by integrating semantic similarity calculation and vector database indexing for Web content, while leveraging keyword extraction to capture core information from Web queries and answers, thereby improving the precision of retrieving relevant web content.

The aforementioned research primarily utilizes machine learning models to filter relevant Web table content from a broad corpus of candidates, fundamentally relying on text-matching features between query sentences and table content. Building on this methodology, [7] pushed the boundaries of technology by proposing an innovative neural network approach that considers not only the textual attributes of elements within Web tables but also incorporates embeddings of vocabulary and entities to enhance the retrieval process. This method, by deeply analyzing the semantic attributes of table elements, provides a richer dimension of information for the retrieval and understanding of Web table content. Further advancing this field, [8,9] made significant contributions by proposing an improved Web table retrieval model. This model not only uses neural network representations tailored to tables to capture their deep semantic features but also ingeniously integrates with the BM25 [13] indexing query mechanism, thereby significantly enhancing retrieval efficiency and accuracy. Specifically, this method begins by extracting structural information from given sentences and then uses this information to execute structure-aware matching between the sentences and Web tables. Through this structured matching approach, it more accurately identifies and retrieves Web table content relevant to the query sentences, thus achieving higher retrieval precision.

With the flourishing development of pre-trained language models (PLMs), they have become an essential tool for researchers in evidence retrieval tasks, significantly enhancing retrieval accuracy with their robust language understanding and representation capabilities. In the domain of text-based evidence retrieval, the Dense Passage Retriever (DPR) framework [10] represents a groundbreaking advancement. Built on the BERT model, this framework is specifically designed to precisely retrieve passages most relevant to a specific query from a vast corpus of articles. For table-based evidence retrieval, [11] further proposed the Dense Table Retriever (DTR) framework based on DPR. This framework conducts specific pre-training for tabular data, uses the resulting model to encode tables, and performs precise retrieval by computing the similarity between question encodings and table encodings. While demonstrating outstanding performance in handling tabular data, it provides an effective solution for table-based evidence retrieval and expands PLMs' application in complex data retrieval tasks. However, as noted in previous analysis, it still faces the limitation of excessive resource consumption due to specialized pre-training for tabular data.

3 Method

We introduce a table-based evidence retrieval model based on Dense Passage Retriever, as depicted in Fig. 2. The model employs a biencoder structure, consisting of a statement feature extractor and a table feature extractor. The statement feature extractor comprises a statement encoder based on the RoBERTa [14] model and a graph encoder based on the Graph Attention Network (GAT) [15]. The table feature extractor is made up of a table encoder also based on the RoBERTa model and a sequential encoder based on Long Short-Term Memory (LSTM) networks.

3.1 Task Definition

Given a dataset instance $(\boldsymbol{S}, \boldsymbol{T_N}, \boldsymbol{L})$, where $\boldsymbol{S} = \{\boldsymbol{s_w} \mid \boldsymbol{1} \leq \boldsymbol{w} \leq \boldsymbol{n}\}$ denotes the set of words in a statement, with n representing the number of words in the statement and $\boldsymbol{s_w}$ representing the w-th word within the statement; $\boldsymbol{T_N} = \{\boldsymbol{t_x} \mid \boldsymbol{1} \leq \boldsymbol{x} \leq \boldsymbol{N}\}$ represents the collection of tables, with N denoting the number of tables in the collection, and $\boldsymbol{t_x} = \{\boldsymbol{t_x^{(i,j)}} \mid \boldsymbol{1} \leq \boldsymbol{i} \leq \boldsymbol{R}, \boldsymbol{1} \leq \boldsymbol{j} \leq \boldsymbol{C}\}$ indicating the x-th table in the collection, which consists of $\boldsymbol{R}$ rows and $\boldsymbol{C}$ columns; $\boldsymbol{L}$ signifies the label, specifically the index of the target table within the collection, which varies in range across different datasets. The objective of this paper is to determine the index $\boldsymbol{L}$ of the most relevant table by sorting and retrieving from $\boldsymbol{T_N}$ given the statement $\boldsymbol{S}$.

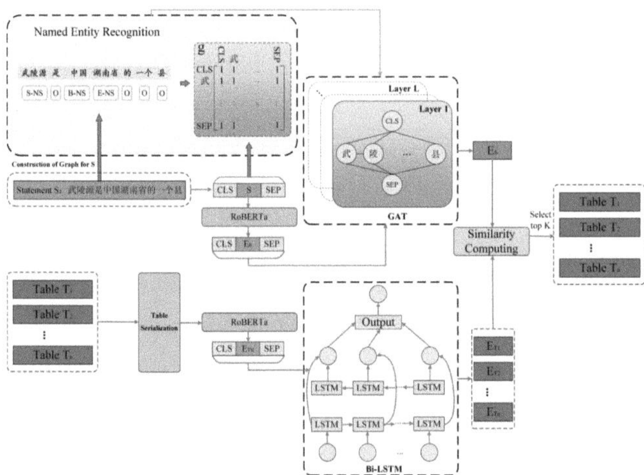

Fig. 2. Table-based Evidence Retrieval Model for Web Tabular Data

3.2 Statement Feature Extraction Module

Construction of Named Entity Connection Graph. Named entities are entities identified by names, such as personal names, organization names, place names, and other entities marked by names. They carry critical information in natural language and hold significant positions within a sentence, representing both a focus and challenge in information processing [16]. Named Entity Recognition (NER) refers to the identification of named entities within text and serves as a crucial foundational tool in application domains.

We employ the Harbin Institute of Technology Language Technology Platform (LTP) [18] for Named Entity Recognition. The construction of a named entity connection graph, which can reflect significant semantic information within statements, is of great importance for evidence retrieval tasks. The steps for constructing the named entity connection graph are as follows:

(1) Utilize the tokenization tool provided by the Pre-trained Language Model RoBERTa to tokenize the statement, resulting in individual word (token) nodes.
(2) Apply the existing named entity recognition tool, LTP, to identify named entities within the statement.
(3) Establish an edge between two word nodes if any of the following relationships exist between them:
   a. Both words belong to the same named entity;
   b. Each word belongs to different named entities;
   c. The word itself.
(4) If there is an edge between two nodes, the edge weight is set to 1; otherwise, it is set to 0.

Given a statement S, from the aforementioned process, we can obtain the adjacency matrix A of the named entity connection graph, represented as $A = Graph(S)$.

Statement Encoder Based on RoBERTa. In order to extract textual features of the statement and to obtain initial features for nodes in the Graph Attention Network, the statement is input into the RoBERTa pre-trained model for feature extraction, thus extracting features while reducing the consumption of computational resources. The process is described as follows:

$$\boldsymbol{E_s} = \boldsymbol{RoBERTa(S)} = [\boldsymbol{h_1}, \boldsymbol{h_2}, \ldots, \boldsymbol{h_n}] \in \mathbb{R}^{n \times d} \tag{1}$$

where $\boldsymbol{E_s}$ represents the textual features of the statement encoded by RoBERTa, d denotes the feature dimension of each word, and $\boldsymbol{h_i}$ represents the textual feature of the i-th word. These features will also serve as the initial features for the i-th word in the Graph Attention Network.

Graph Encoder Based on GAT. After obtaining the named entity connection graph of the statement and the initial features of the nodes within the graph, the graph encoder is utilized to further learn the semantic features of the statement. The specific process is as follows:

$$\boldsymbol{h}_i' = \boldsymbol{GAT}(\boldsymbol{h}_i, \boldsymbol{A}) \tag{2}$$

For a Graph Attention Network with L layers, nodes aggregate information from L-order neighboring nodes, thereby incorporating structural information into the node's feature vector representation.

In summary, this module utilizes the Graph Attention Network to learn and enhance the features of the constructed named entity connection graph of the statement. This enhances the model's ability to capture critical information from the statement. The statement features can be represented as $\boldsymbol{E}_S' = [\boldsymbol{h}_1', \boldsymbol{h}_2', \ldots, \boldsymbol{h}_n'] \in \mathbb{R}^{\boldsymbol{n} \times \boldsymbol{d}}$.

3.3 Table Feature Extraction Module

Table Serialization. We propose a novel template-based method for serializing table data. Specifically, we concatenate the data from each row of the table using a natural language template, which integrates the column names and cell contents into a coherent sentence using common language. For data across different rows, we connect each row using the [SEP] token, and we reset the position counter at the first cell of each row. This counter is used to indicate the precise position of the current word (token) within the row. This serialization method maintains the structural integrity of the table while maximizing the utility of general Pre-trained Language Models. Figure 3 illustrates an example of table serialization using this method.

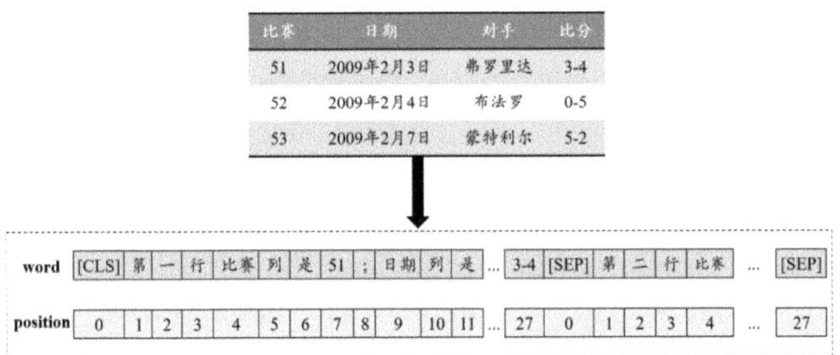

比赛	日期	对手	比分
51	2009年2月3日	弗罗里达	3-4
52	2009年2月4日	布法罗	0-5
53	2009年2月7日	蒙特利尔	5-2

Fig. 3. Table Feature Extraction Module for Chinese Tabular Data

Given a table $\boldsymbol{T} = \{\boldsymbol{t}_{(i,j)} \mid \boldsymbol{1} \le \boldsymbol{i} \le \boldsymbol{R}, \boldsymbol{1} \le \boldsymbol{j} \le \boldsymbol{C}\}$, where $\boldsymbol{t}_{(i,j)}$ denotes the content of the cell at row i and column j, and R and C respectively represent the number of rows and columns. After serialization, the table becomes $\boldsymbol{T}' = \{\boldsymbol{t}_k' \mid \boldsymbol{1} \le \boldsymbol{k} \le \boldsymbol{m}\}$, where $\boldsymbol{t}_k'$ represents the words in the serialized table, and m denotes the length of the serialized table.

Table Encoder Based on RoBERTa. Similar to the statement encoder, in order to obtain the textual features of the table while reducing the consumption of computational resources, the table is input into the general pre-trained language model RoBERTa for feature extraction. The specific operations are as follows:

$$\boldsymbol{E_T} = \boldsymbol{RoBERTa}(\boldsymbol{T'}) = [\boldsymbol{f_1}, \boldsymbol{f_2}, \ldots, \boldsymbol{f_m}] \in \mathbb{R}^{m \times d} \tag{3}$$

where $\boldsymbol{E_T}$ represents the table textual features encoded by RoBERTa, d denotes the feature dimension of each word, and $\boldsymbol{f_i}$ represents the textual feature of the i-th word.

Sequential Encoder Based on LSTM. After obtaining the table features extracted by the table encoder, to fully utilize the characteristics of the serialized table for a deeper understanding of its semantics, we employ a Bi-directional Long Short-Term Memory network (Bi-LSTM) to enhance the features of the table:

$$\boldsymbol{f_t'} = \boldsymbol{BiLSTM}(\boldsymbol{f_t}) \tag{4}$$

Through this process, the model is able to obtain enhanced features of the table, which have undergone sequential processing, extraction, and enhancement by a general pre-trained model and a sequential model. This deeply comprehends the features and semantics of the table, which are represented as $\boldsymbol{E_T'} = [\boldsymbol{f_1'}, \boldsymbol{f_2'}, \ldots, \boldsymbol{f_m'}] \in \mathbb{R}^{m \times d}$.

3.4 Training and Inference Module

Training Module. To accelerate the training speed without compromising the effectiveness of the model, we employ a negative sampling enhancement method based on BM25 to construct several negative samples for the target table, detailed as follows:

We utilize BM25 to select X tables from the table collection $\boldsymbol{T_N}$ that are different from the most relevant table L but most similar to the statement $\boldsymbol{S}$ as the negative sample set $\boldsymbol{T_{neg}}$. The positive sample L and $\boldsymbol{T_{neg}}$ together constitute a training sample $\boldsymbol{T_{train}}$.

During the training phase, the statement $\boldsymbol{S}$ and the table sample set $\boldsymbol{T_{train}}$ are separately input into the statement feature extraction module and the table feature extraction module to obtain the statement encoding $\boldsymbol{E_S'}$ and the encoding of the table sample set $\boldsymbol{E_{Train}'}$. Since both the statement features and table features are concatenations of word features, it is necessary to perform a pooling operation on both to obtain $\boldsymbol{E_S^*}$ and $\boldsymbol{E_{train}^*}$. Subsequently, the similarity between the statement features and each table feature is calculated, and the table with the highest similarity is selected as the target table. The process is as follows:

$$\boldsymbol{L^*} = \boldsymbol{argmax}(\boldsymbol{similarity}(\boldsymbol{E_S^*}, \boldsymbol{E_{\text{Train}}^*})) \tag{5}$$

where $\boldsymbol{L^*}$ represents the predicted target table, $\boldsymbol{argmax}(\cdot)$ denotes the operation of obtaining the index of the maximum value, and $\boldsymbol{similarity}(\cdot)$ represents the similarity measurement function, which can be cosine similarity, dot product, etc.

Inference Module. Due to the vast size of the table collection $\boldsymbol{T_N}$, direct retrieval within this space would be highly time-consuming. To enhance the retrieval efficiency and accuracy of the model during the inference phase, we adopt a "recall + fine-ranking" framework for inferring the target table. Specifically, we first utilize the BM25 algorithm to recall the top K most similar tables $\boldsymbol{T_{sim}}$ from the table collection $\boldsymbol{T_N}$. Subsequently, the model trained in the previous section is used to predict the most relevant table from $\boldsymbol{T_{sim}}$, thereby significantly reducing retrieval time while ensuring the effectiveness of the model.

Loss Function. In the field of deep learning, similarity measurement typically utilizes three metrics: dot product, cosine similarity, and Euclidean distance. Based on these different metrics, we have designed the following three types of loss functions:

(1) Cross-entropy loss. The task of table evidence retrieval can be practically modeled as a text classification task: given a statement $\boldsymbol{S}$, classify the positive sample $\boldsymbol{L}$ from the training sample set $\boldsymbol{T_{train}}$. Consequently, we introduce the following form of cross-entropy loss, utilizing dot product as the similarity metric:

$$\mathcal{L}_{ce} = -\log \frac{\exp(\boldsymbol{E_S^*} \cdot \boldsymbol{E_L^*})}{\exp(\boldsymbol{E_S^*} \cdot \boldsymbol{E_L^*} + \sum \exp(\boldsymbol{E_S^*} \cdot \boldsymbol{E_{neg}^*}))} \tag{6}$$

where $\boldsymbol{E_L^*}$ represents the feature representation of the positive sample (target table), and $\boldsymbol{E_{neg}^*}$ denotes the collection of feature representations for the negative samples.

(2) Contrastive loss. Contrastive loss minimizes the distance between the query text and positive examples while maximizing the distance to negative examples. Using cosine similarity as the metric, the loss is defined as:

$$\mathcal{L}_{cl} = \frac{1}{2}\cos(\boldsymbol{E_S^*}, \boldsymbol{E_L^*})^2 + \frac{1}{2}\sum \max(\text{margin} - \cos(\boldsymbol{E_S^*}, \boldsymbol{E_{neg}^*}), 0)^2 \tag{7}$$

where $\cos(\cdot)$ represents cosine similarity, and margin is a threshold parameter.

(3) Triplet loss. Using Euclidean distance as the similarity metric, triplet loss is defined as:

$$\mathcal{L}_{tl} = \sum \max\left(d(\boldsymbol{E_S^*}, \boldsymbol{E_L^*}) - d(\boldsymbol{E_S^*}, \boldsymbol{E_{neg}^*}) + \text{margin}, 0\right) \tag{8}$$

Where $d(\cdot)$ represents Euclidean distance, and margin is a threshold parameter.

Finally, we combine the three losses via weighted summation to derive the overall loss function:

$$\mathcal{L} = \alpha \boldsymbol{L_{ce}} + \beta \boldsymbol{L_{cl}} + \lambda \boldsymbol{L_{tl}} \tag{9}$$

where α, β, and λ are the balancing coefficients for the three types of loss.

The proposed table evidence retrieval model based on Dense Passage Retriever is shown in Algorithm 1.

4 Experiment

4.1 Datasets and Metrics

The task of table evidence retrieval, as a fundamental task within the field of natural language processing, greatly facilitates numerous downstream tasks. Notably, in the domain of rumor detection, the most impactful is the task of table fact verification. In recent years, with the introduction of English table fact verification datasets such as TABFACT [2] and INFOTABS [18], the fact verification tasks based on English tabular data have developed rapidly. However, fact verification tasks based on Chinese tabular data are rarely reported. Addressing this issue, [12] has introduced Chinese table fact verification datasets including TABFACT, INFOTABS, and UCLDS. The data division and basic information of these datasets are as shown in Table 1.

Algorithm 1. The table evidence retrieval model based on Dense Passage Retriever

Require: Statement $\boldsymbol{S}$, table set $\boldsymbol{T_N} = \{\boldsymbol{t_1}, \boldsymbol{t_2}, \ldots, \boldsymbol{t_n}\}$, target table L
Ensure: Predicted table L^*, loss function $\mathcal{L}$

if Training phase **then**
  $\boldsymbol{T_{neg}} \leftarrow BM25(\boldsymbol{T_N}), \boldsymbol{T_{train}} \leftarrow [L, \boldsymbol{T_{neg}}]$ ▷ Negative sampling of table set
  $\boldsymbol{T'_{train}} \leftarrow serializeTable(\boldsymbol{T_{train}})$
  $\boldsymbol{E_{Train}} \leftarrow RoBERTa(\boldsymbol{T'_{train}})$
  $\boldsymbol{E'_{\mathrm{Train}}} \leftarrow BiLSTM(\boldsymbol{E_{Train}})$
  $\boldsymbol{A} \leftarrow Graph(\boldsymbol{S})$ ▷ Construct Named Entity Connection Graph
  $\boldsymbol{E_S} \leftarrow RoBERTa(\boldsymbol{S})$
  $\boldsymbol{E'_S} \leftarrow GAT(\boldsymbol{E_S}, \boldsymbol{A})$
  $\boldsymbol{E^*_S}, \boldsymbol{E^*_{Train}} \leftarrow meanpooling(\boldsymbol{E'_S}, \boldsymbol{E'_{Train}})$
  $sim \leftarrow similarity(\boldsymbol{E^*_S}, \boldsymbol{E^*_{Train}})$
  $\boldsymbol{\mathcal{L}_{ce}}, \boldsymbol{\mathcal{L}_{cl}}, \boldsymbol{\mathcal{L}_{tl}} \leftarrow CalculateLoss(sim, \boldsymbol{E^*_S}, \boldsymbol{E^*_{Train}})$
  $\boldsymbol{\mathcal{L}} \leftarrow \alpha\boldsymbol{\mathcal{L}_{ce}} + \beta\boldsymbol{\mathcal{L}_{cl}} + \boldsymbol{\lambda L_{tl}}$ ▷ Calculate loss and update parameters
  return $\boldsymbol{\mathcal{L}}$
end if
if Inference phase **then**
  $\boldsymbol{T_{sim}} \leftarrow BM25(\boldsymbol{T_N})$ ▷ Sparse recall of tables
  $\boldsymbol{E^*_S}, \boldsymbol{E^*_{sim}} \leftarrow model(\boldsymbol{S}, \boldsymbol{T_{sim}})$
  $sim \leftarrow similarity(\boldsymbol{E^*_S}, \boldsymbol{E^*_{sim}})$
  $L^* \leftarrow argmax(sim)$
  return L^*
end if

Table 1. Datasets Statistic Data

Dataset			splits		
TABFACT	Train	Val	Test	Simple	Complex
statement	92,283	12,792	12,779	50,244	68,031
table	13,182	1,696	1,695	9,189	7,392
INFOTABS	Train	Val	α_1 Test	α_2 Test	α_3 Test
statement	16,538	1,800	1,800	1,800	1,800
table	1,740	200	200	200	200
UCLDS	Train	Val	α_1 Test	α_2 Test	α_3 Test
statement	13,374	1,500	1,500	1,500	1,500
table	2,229	250	250	250	250

The task of table fact verification involves given a statement and corresponding evidence, determining the correctness of the statement. The essence of the evidence retrieval task is to find the most relevant evidence table from a table library given a statement. Based on this, we modify the aforementioned three datasets to create the Chinese table evidence retrieval datasets TABFACT, INFOTABS, and UCLDS. Specifically, for each statement $\boldsymbol{S}$, we consider all tables as the table collection $\boldsymbol{T_N}$ to be retrieved, and the evidence table paired with the statement in the original dataset is regarded as the target table L. The divisions and basic information of the three datasets obtained through modification are the same as those of the original datasets.

Evaluation metrics gauge the efficacy of a model. In the context of table evidence retrieval model, these metrics assess the model's accuracy in retrieving the target table. We employ the Hit@k metric to evaluate model performance. Hit@k is defined as the success rate of the target table being among the top k tables after sorting a certain number of retrieved table data. A higher Hit@k indicates better retrieval accuracy.

4.2 Experiment Settings

This experiment was conducted using the PyTorch framework, employing the AdamW optimizer [19] with a weight decay of 1e-4 and a warm-up rate of 0.05 to update model's parameters. For the TABFACT dataset, we utilized the RoBERTa-wwm-ext-large-Chinese model [20] with 16 attention heads and 24 layers as both the statement encoder and the table encoder, running 40 epochs with a batch size of 8 and an initial learning rate of 1e-5. For the INFOTABS and UCLDS datasets, the same settings were applied but for 20 epochs. In the experiments, a 2-layer GAT model with 8 attention heads and a dropout rate of 0.6 was used as the graph encoder, alongside a two-layer 512-dimensional Bi-LSTM as the sequential encoder. In the negative sampling enhancement method, the number of sampled negatives X, was set to 49, hence a total of 50 training samples per instance. During the inference phase, a sparse recall strategy was applied, setting the recalled table count K, to 50 to maintain consistency in the retrieval space between the training and inference phases. In the computation of the loss function, the balance coefficients $\boldsymbol{\alpha}$, $\boldsymbol{\beta}$, and $\boldsymbol{\lambda}$ were set to 1, 1, and 0.1, respectively.

4.3 Main Results

The experiments conducted in this study employ the evaluation metrics Hit@1, Hit@3, and Hit@5, and are compared with the following baseline models:

BM25 [13]: A retrieval model constructed using the BM25 algorithm on the collection of table data, employed to retrieve the target table for each statement.

DPR [10]: Evidence retrieval for tables was conducted using the conventional DPR framework, which employs a bi-encoder structure to independently encode statements and tables, subsequently computing similarity to identify the most relevant table.

DTR [11]. Evidence retrieval was carried out using the current state-of-the-art DTR framework, which is pre-trained on table data. The model obtained from this pre-training is subsequently applied to the encoding of tables.

The main experimental results are presented in Table 2. As shown, our proposed model demonstrates improvements across all three datasets in Hit@1, Hit@3, and Hit@5 metrics compared to the baseline models. Specifically, for the TABFACT dataset, which features a large table retrieval space, overall performance tends to be suboptimal. Nevertheless, our model outperforms the computationally intensive DTR model by 0.25% to 9.07% across all three metrics. The BM25 model primarily relies on simple word co-occurrence relationships between statements and tables for rapid retrieval, resulting in lower accuracy due to its simplistic structure. The superiority of our model over DPR validates the effectiveness of the graph encoder and sequence encoder in enhancing retrieval accuracy, while also demonstrating the utility of the named entity connection graph in capturing critical information from statements and the template-based method in comprehending the structural and semantic features of tables. For the INFOTABS dataset, our model exceeds the best-performing DTR baseline by 0.11% to 4.67%. Regarding the UCLDS dataset, due to its relatively straightforward statement content and smaller table retrieval space, the overall performance is generally high. Moreover, as the table collection in the α_2Test set is identical to the training set, its metrics are non-referential and thus not listed in Table 2. Our model surpasses the best-performing DTR model in this simpler dataset by 0.33% to 2.07%. In summary, our model outperforms all baseline models across the three metrics on all datasets, validating the effectiveness of the proposed method in enhancing table evidence retrieval accuracy.

Regarding computational resources, the BM25 model requires only a single Intel Core i5 CPU to meet all computational needs, whereas pre-training the DTR model necessitates the computing power of 32 Cloud TPU v3 units, a requirement that is unattainable for most research teams. In contrast, the proposed model can smoothly complete both training and inference using just a

Table 2. Main Results (%)

Dataset	Metric	Model	Val	Test	Simple	Complex	Small
TABFACT	Hit@1	BM25	39.69	39.98	50.48	36.40	53.51
		DPR	40.48	41.75	51.38	41.65	53.82
		DTR	40.57	43.01	51.45	43.53	55.14
		Ours	42.56	43.74	60.52	46.95	57.94
	Hit@3	BM25	51.21	50.81	72.09	47.48	64.77
		DPR	65.25	65.50	75.04	65.66	74.54
		DTR	65.37	67.13	75.26	67.94	76.12
		Ours	66.28	67.38	75.94	70.77	79.94
	Hit@5	BM25	56.19	55.16	75.85	52.19	70.67
		DPR	75.38	76.26	83.40	76.92	82.94
		DTR	76.41	77.30	84.16	77.70	84.32
		Ours	76.92	77.72	84.52	80.41	87.63
			Val	α_1Test	α_2Test	α_3Test	
INFOTABS	Hit@1	BM25	61.22	58.11	55.78	60.17	-
		DPR	77.72	78.72	74.78	74.61	-
		DTR	78.44	79.89	78.61	77.61	-
		Ours	83.11	82.78	82.56	77.72	-
	Hit@3	BM25	69.89	70.78	67.28	74.28	-
		DPR	87.39	88.78	88.28	85.61	-
		DTR	87.56	90.94	91.17	86.22	-
		Ours	91.61	91.39	93.78	87.33	-
	Hit@5	BM25	73.50	73.33	69.94	78.56	-
		DPR	90.50	91.67	91.94	89.39	-
		DTR	90.89	93.50	93.89	90.11	-
		Ours	93.17	94.28	95.72	91.44	-
			Val	α_1Test	α_2Test	α_3Test	
UCLDS	Hit@1	BM25	89.60	90.40	-	91.00	-
		DPR	90.87	91.00	-	91.20	-
		DTR	91.60	92.40	-	91.60	-
		Ours	91.93	93.93	-	93.67	-
	Hit@3	BM25	95.80	96.60	-	95.27	-
		DPR	96.13	96.67	-	95.07	-
		DTR	96.40	97.13	-	96.53	-
		Ours	97.13	97.53	-	97.40	-
	Hit@5	BM25	96.87	98.33	-	95.87	-
		DPR	96.87	97.20	-	95.87	-
		DTR	97.27	97.93	-	97.33	-
		Ours	98.33	98.33	-	98.67	-

single NVIDIA Tesla V100 32GB GPU under the specified training batch size, thereby demanding significantly lower computational resources.

In conclusion, the proposed model is effective in achieving high retrieval accuracy while maintaining low computational resource requirements.

5 Conclusion

Web evidence retrieval can quickly extract the most relevant information from massive data sources. However, challenges arise due to reduced accuracy in table-based Web evidence retrieval models under resource-constrained conditions and the lack of research in Chinese Web table evidence retrieval, which could potentially lead to the spread of false information. We first reconstruct three existing Chinese Web fact verification datasets to generate datasets suitable for table evidence retrieval, thus filling the research gap in the field of Chinese Web table evidence retrieval. A new table evidence retrieval model based on a Dense Passage Retriever is then proposed. This model initially utilizes a general Pre-trained Language Model RoBERTa to initialize the features of statements and tables, thus efficiently extracting features from both while reducing the consumption of computational resources. Subsequently, it employs named entity recognition technology to build a graph structure for statements and uses GAT to decode deep semantic information in statements. Furthermore, it introduces a novel templated approach to process table data and utilizes the Bi-LSTM model to enhance table features, thereby facilitating a deeper understanding of table structural features and improving the accuracy of table evidence retrieval tasks. Comparative experiments on the TABFACT, INFOTABS, and UCLDS datasets confirm the effectiveness of our model.

Acknowledgments. The authors thank the anonymous reviewers for their valuable comments. This work was supported in part by the National Natural Science Foundation of China under Grant 62272100, the Consulting Project of Chinese Academy of Engineering under Grant 2023-XY-09, and the Academy-Locality Cooperation Project of Chinese Academy of Engineering under Grant JS2021ZT05.

Disclosure of Interests. The authors have no competing interests to declare that are relevant to the content of this article.

References

1. Kuntur, S., Wróblewska, A., Paprzycki, M., et al.: Under the influence: a survey of large language models in fake news detection. IEEE Trans. Artif. Intell. **6**(2), 458–477 (2024)
2. Chen, W., Wang, H., Chen, J., et al.: TabFact: a large-scale dataset for table-based fact verification. In: Proceedings of the International Conference on Learning Representations, pp. 1–13. New Orleans (2019)
3. Cafarella, M.J., Halevy, A., Wang, D.Z., et al.: Webtables: exploring the power of tables on the Web. Proc. VLDB Endow. **1**(1), 538–549 (2008)

4. Cafarella, M.J., Halevy, A., Khoussainova, N.: Data integration for the relational Web. Proc. VLDB Endow. **2**(1), 1090–1101 (2009)
5. Goyal, R., Kumar, P., Singh, V.P.: QFAS-KE: query focused answer summarization using keyword extraction. Inf. Process. Manag. **62**(4), 104104–104120 (2025)
6. Formica, A., Mele, I., Taglino, F.: A template-based approach for question answering over knowledge bases. Knowl. Inf. Syst. **66**(1), 453–479 (2024)
7. Zhang, S., Balog, K.: Auto-completion for data cells in relational tables. In: Proceedings of the 28th ACM International Conference on Information and Knowledge Management, pp. 761–770. ACM, Beijing (2019)
8. Jafarzadeh, P., Ensan, F.: An evidence-based approach for open-domain question answering. Knowl. Inf. Syst. **67**(2), 1969–1991 (2025)
9. Chakrabarti, K., Chen, Z., Shakeri, S., et al.: Tableqna: answering list intent queries with Web tables. arXiv preprint arXiv:2001.04828 (2020)
10. Karpukhin, V., Oğuz, B., Min, S., et al.: Dense passage retrieval for open-domain question answering. In: Proceedings of the 2020 Conference on Empirical Methods in Natural Language Processing (EMNLP), pp. 6769–6781. ACL, Punta Cana (2020)
11. Herzig, J., Müller, T., Krichene, S., et al.: Open domain question answering over tables via dense retrieval. In: Proceedings of the 2021 Conference of the North American Chapter of the Association for Computational Linguistics, pp. 512–519. ACL, Mexico City (2021)
12. Yang, P., Zha, X.Y., Zhao, G.Z., Lin, X.: Fact verification with Chinese tabular data based on capsule heterogeneous graph attention network. J. Softw. **1**(1), 1–22 (2023)
13. Robertson, S., Zaragoza, H.: The probabilistic relevance framework: BM25 and beyond. Found. Trends® Inf. Retrieval **3**(4), 333–389 (2009)
14. Liu, Y., Ott, M., Goyal, N., et al.: Roberta: a robustly optimized bert pretraining approach. arXiv preprint arXiv:1907.11692 (2019)
15. Veličković, P., Cucurull, G., Casanova, A., et al.: Graph attention networks. arXiv preprint arXiv:1710.10903 (2017)
16. Chen, Y.F., Zong, C.Q., Su, K.Y.: Joint Chinese-English named entity recognition and alignment. Chin. J. Comput. **34**(9), 1688–1696 (2011)
17. Che, W., Li, Z., Liu, T.: LTP: a Chinese language technology platform. In: Proceedings of the 23rd International Conference on Computational Linguistics (COLING), pp. 13–16. ICCL, Beijing (2010)
18. Gupta, V., Mehta, M., Nokhiz, P., et al.: INFOTABS: inference on tables as semi-structured data. In: Proceedings of the 58th Annual Meeting of the Association for Computational Linguistics, pp. 2309–2324. ACL, Seattle (2020)
19. Loshchilov, I., Hutter, F.: Decoupled weight decay regularization. arXiv preprint arXiv:1711.05101 (2017)
20. Cui, Y., Che, W., Liu, T., et al.: Pre-training with whole word masking for Chinese BERT. IEEE/ACM Trans. Audio Speech Lang. Process. **29**(1), 3504–3514 (2021)

Multi-layered Framework for Counterfeit-Free Pharmaceutical Chains

Abir Ghannem[1(✉)], Hajer Nabli[1], Raoudha Ben Djemaa[1], and Layth Sliman[2]

[1] Higher Institute of Computer Science and Communication Technologies of Sousse/Miracl Lab, University of Sousse, Sousse, Tunisia
abirghannembapro@gmail.com,
{hajer.nabli,raoudha.benjemaa}@isitc.u-sousse.tn

[2] Efrei Research Lab, Paris Pantheon-Assas University, Villejuif, France
layth.sliman@efrei.fr

Abstract. The proliferation of counterfeit pharmaceuticals represent a significant threat to global public health and the integrity of supply chains. Traditional anti-counterfeiting solutions remain limited by their reliance on manual verification and their deployment mainly at the final stages of the supply chain, often after counterfeit products have already reached patients, thereby undermining the reliability of both medicines and the supply chain system. To address these limitations, this paper proposes ReACT-Pharma (Real-time Anti-Counterfeit Tracking for Pharmaceuticals), an intelligent and modular framework that integrates IoT sensors, Multi-Agent Systems (MAS), Artificial Intelligence (AI) and Blockchain technology. The framework is structured into four functional layers: Real-Time Monitoring Layer, Proactive Agent Layer, Blockchain Layer and Actor Interface Layer. Each layer plays a strategic role in ensuring end-to-end data acquisition, proactive counterfeit detection, autonomous decision-making and tamper-proof event logging. Experimental evaluation demonstrates its effectiveness in real time counterfeit detection and decision reliability, offering a scalable solution for safeguarding drug authenticity.

Keywords: Pharmaceutical Supply Chain · Counterfeit Detection · Multi-Agent System · Blockchain · IoT · AI

1 Introduction

Ensuring integrity, authenticity, and traceability of pharmaceutical products across their supply chains is no longer merely a logistical challenge; it is a global public health imperative. Counterfeit drugs remain widespread, especially in low- and middle-income countries, where around 10% of medical products are subst andard or falsified [1]. These pose serious health risks and contribute to over $200 billion in annual economic losses [2,3].

I. Awan et al. (Eds.): WISE 2025, LNCS 16367, pp. 169–184, 2026.
https://doi.org/10.1007/978-981-95-7394-3_12

Traditional anti-counterfeiting solutions typically operate at the final stages of the pharmaceutical supply chain, relying heavily on manual verification methods, such as serialization, QR code scanning, or barcode authentication conducted by pharmacists, healthcare providers, or end-users [4–6]. While helpful in some contexts, such systems have critical limitations. First, manual scanning requires active participation and vigilance from the human actor, which can introduce delays, inconsistencies, or errors due to fatigue, oversight, or lack of awareness [7]. Second, these checks typically occur too late in the supply chain, by which time a counterfeit or tampered drug may have already reached vulnerable patients, rendering damage control ineffective. Furthermore, counterfeiters are increasingly sophisticated, often replicating packaging, QR codes and serialization data to bypass such checks [6,8]. As a result, reliance on endpoint validation not only exposes patients to severe health risks but also fails to prevent the upstream circulation of falsified medicines, especially in low-resource environments where digital verification infrastructure is limited or inconsistently used. This underscores the need for proactive, automated and real time solutions capable of detecting anomalies during the product's transit, rather than reacting to them after distribution.

To address this urgent challenge, we propose ReACT-Pharma (Real-time Anti-Counterfeit Tracking for Pharmaceuticals), an intelligent, modular framework for proactive, real time counterfeit detection and autonomous decision-making in pharmaceutical supply chains. ReACT-Pharma integrates Internet of Things (IoT) sensors, Artificial Intelligence (AI), Multi-Agent Systems (MAS) and Blockchain technology, aiming to shift counterfeit detection from a reactive, endpoint process to a proactive, in-transit mechanism. Our approach enables multi-dimensional environmental monitoring, such as temperature, humidity and light exposure, through continuous data collection by embedded IoT sensors. This data is analyzed by AI-powered intelligent detection agent capable of identifying anomalies such as threshold violations. Crucially, ReACT-Pharma supports autonomous decision-making. A rule-based decision agent evaluates anomaly severity using contextual data and historical patterns, then automatically triggers mitigation actions, such as alerting stakeholders or excluding affected batches and securely logs the event on the blockchain. This high level of automation significantly enhances both response speed and reliability, reducing delays and eliminating risks associated with manual intervention. The main objectives of ReACT-Pharma are to:

- Ensure real time monitoring of critical multi-dimensional environmental parameters throughout the supply chain
- Detect counterfeit-related anomalies proactively during storage and transport, rather than after distribution
- Automate the decision-making process to enable timely and reliable mitigation of threats
- Provide end-to-end traceability, transparency and tamper-proof auditing through blockchain integration

The remainder of this paper is organized as follows: Sect. 2 reviews related work. Section 3 presents the proposed approach. Section 4 discusses the experimental results. Finally, Sect. 5 concludes the paper.

2 Related Work

The integration of emerging technologies such as IoT, blockchain, and AI in several domains has drawn increasing interest in recent years [9–11]. In the pharmaceutical supply chain, these technologies are being explored particularly for combating drug counterfeiting [12–14]. Several recent studies propose blockchain and IoT-based solutions to improve traceability, transparency and security in the pharmaceutical supply chain. Rizzardi et al. [15] introduced a private blockchain architecture using Hyperledger Fabric and IoT devices to ensure real time monitoring and compliance automation. Similarly, Chinchmalatpure et al. [16] and Nawale et al. [17] combined IoT sensors and blockchain to combat drug counterfeiting, focusing on secure storage condition tracking and immutable data recording.

Other works like those by Alabdulatif et al. [18] advanced the field by integrating AI models within blockchain smart contracts to automate and secure medical decision-making processes. Said et al. [19] and Kambilo et al. [20] emphasized end-to-end drug traceability and proposed decentralized frameworks (e.g., ChainDrugTrac) using smart contracts and Hyperledger Fabric.

Fuyao et al. [21] demonstrated the role of IoT and RFID for anomaly detection and traceability in critical supply chains. Patil et al. [22] presented a decentralized application (DApp) allowing stakeholders to verify drug authenticity via QR codes. Finally, Kumar et al. [23] studied serialization systems integrated with centralized and blockchain-based tracking tools as a regulatory response to counterfeit risks.

While the reviewed approaches demonstrate significant progress in enhancing pharmaceutical supply chain security through the integration of IoT, blockchain and, in some cases, AI, they generally exhibit notable limitations. The majority of reviewed systems monitor only a narrow range of environmental parameters, such as temperature or location and do not support multi-dimensional environmental monitoring, which is essential for preserving the integrity of sensitive pharmaceutical products. Furthermore, most existing works adopt a reactive detection approach, where anomalies or violations are identified only after threshold breaches or scanning events [15–17,19–23]. Decision-making is often manual or entirely absent, with minimal automation in verification and response processes [19–23]. Although some approaches incorporate AI for anomaly detection and prediction [18], they typically lack context-aware reasoning, collaborative intelligence, or integration with real time decision logic. Moreover, while blockchain is commonly used to ensure data immutability and traceability, it often plays a passive role, limited to recording lifecycle events or product information without being directly embedded in detection or decision-making mechanisms [16,17,19,20,22].

In contrast, ReACT-Pharma introduces a proactive, autonomous and intelligent approach that integrates IoT, AI, multi-agent systems (MAS) and blockchain technologies. It enables multi-dimensional environmental monitoring through continuous data collection by embedded IoT sensors, capturing critical parameters. Advanced AI techniques are applied for real time multivariate counterfeit detection, enhancing the system's ability to identify subtle deviations. Decision-making is both automated and traceable, allowing for rapid, data-driven responses and full auditability. The system computes context-aware severity scores by incorporating historical trends, temporal patterns and contextual information to prioritize responses effectively. Blockchain plays a central and active role, not only ensuring data immutability and traceability but also registering detected anomalies, logging AI-generated decisions and securely coordinating stakeholder notifications via smart contracts. By addressing key limitations in detection latency, decision automation and intelligent coordination, ReACT-Pharma provides a comprehensive, proactive and anti-counterfeit solution for the dynamic challenges of pharmaceutical supply chain monitoring.

3 ReACT-Pharma Approach Overview

We developed ReACT-Pharma (Real-time Anti-Counterfeit Tracking for Pharmaceuticals), an intelligent framework that leverages blockchain, IoT, AI, and MAS to enable real time monitoring, automate counterfeit detection, and ensure pharmaceutical supply chain integrity. ReACT-Pharma is structured into four functional layers: the Real-Time Monitoring Layer, the Proactive Agent Layer, the Blockchain Layer and the Actor Interface Layer, as illustrated in Fig. 1. Each layer encapsulates a specific set of responsibilities and technologies, enabling distributed intelligence, traceability and adaptive decision-making throughout the supply chain.

Imagine a pharmaceutical supply chain where a batch of sensitive drugs is transported from the manufacturer to an urban pharmacy. From the start of the journey, smart sensors embedded in the shipment monitor key environmental parameters, such as temperature, humidity, RFID and geolocation, forming the core of the **Real-Time Monitoring Layer**. Collected data is then analyzed by the **Proactive Agent Layer**, where two autonomous agents operate. The *Detection Agent* applies AI algorithms to detect anomalies, such as prolonged temperature deviations or unusual trajectories, that could compromise drug quality or suggest counterfeiting. When an anomaly is detected, the *Decision Agent* evaluates its severity based on contextual and historical data. For non-critical events, it increases monitoring frequency and keeps the product under observation. For critical or persistent anomalies, it triggers a blockchain smart contract that immutably records the event, alerts stakeholders and flags the batch as excluded from circulation. The **Blockchain Layer** ensures the traceability and integrity of recorded events, while the **Actor Interface Layer** enables stakeholders to access alerts, submit updates and track product status in real time. This layered architecture ensures continuous visibility, strengthens drug integrity and provides a proactive response against counterfeiting threats.

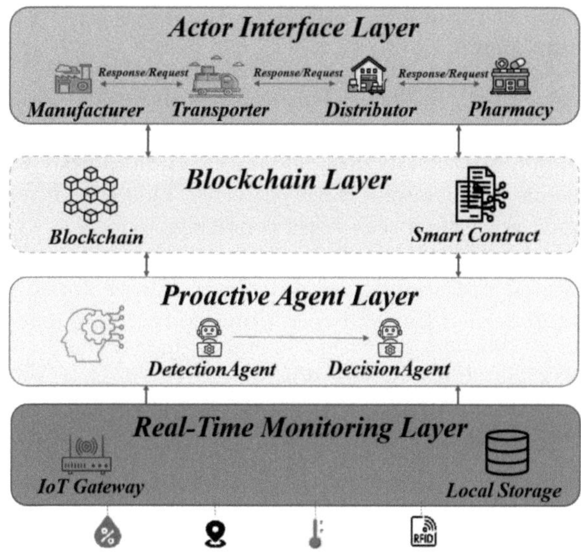

Fig. 1. ReACT-Pharma Architecture.

3.1 Real-Time Monitoring Layer

This layer forms the foundational layer of the ReACT-Pharma architecture. It ensures the continuous collection, intelligent preprocessing and secure storage of environmental data related to pharmaceutical products during transportation and storage. This layer is deployed on an IoT Gateway device (e.g., Raspberry Pi 4) and consists of three key components, as illustrated in Fig. 2.

Sensor Communication. The IoT Gateway first establishes reliable communication with distributed sensors across the pharmaceutical supply chain, which continuously capture key parameters such as temperature, humidity, light intensity, GPS location, and RFID-based batch identification. To ensure lightweight and efficient transmission of this data, the gateway uses the MQTT (Message Queuing Telemetry Transport) protocol, which is particularly suited for low-power and low-b andwidth environments [24]. MQTT follows a publish/subscribe architecture where each sensor publishes its data to a specific topic. The gateway subscribes to these topics and listens in real time for incoming messages. This asynchronous and event-driven communication model enables scalability and rapid reaction to critical environmental changes.

Data Preprocessing Module. Once the raw data is received from the sensors, it is immediately passed to the data preprocessing module within the gateway. This component is vital, as IoT sensor data often includes noise, missing values, or outliers caused by environmental interferences or hardware malfunctions. To ensure the integrity and usability of the data, the preprocessing pipeline applies the following techniques:

- Outlier Detection with Isolation Forest: Each incoming observation is analyzed using the Isolation Forest algorithm [25], an unsupervised machine learning technique specifically designed to detect outliers by isolating anomalous observations from normal data patterns. This step filters out extreme values that may not reflect real-world conditions.
- Data Cleaning: Incomplete, duplicated, or inconsistent records (e.g., missing values, duplicated timestamps, invalid sensor IDs or corrupted values) are identified and discarded to avoid corrupting downstream analytics.

This preprocessing step not only improves the quality of the data but also reduces the computational load on downstream agents by ensuring that only clean and structured data is propagated.

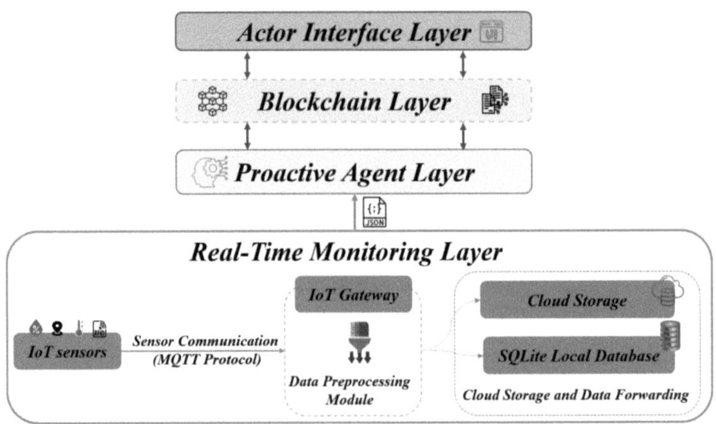

Fig. 2. IoT-Data Acquisition and Preprocessing Workflow.

Cloud Storage and Data Forwarding. After preprocessing, the cleaned sensor data is structured and stored in a cloud-based InfluxDB instance. InfluxDB is an open-source time-series database optimized for h andling high-frequency, timestamped data, ideal for monitoring environmental conditions in pharmaceutical logistics. The decision to store only preprocessed data and not the raw sensor streams, is intentional. It minimizes storage requirements while ensuring that all retained information is valid and actionable.

Each IoT Gateway, uniquely identified by a device_id, represents a physical unit such as a refrigerated transport container or warehouse monitoring station. This identifier enables traceability and source-level diagnostics throughout the supply chain. Measurements are transmitted to InfluxDB via the HTTP API. Each data entry includes:

- a `timestamp` indicating when the data was captured,
- a `device_id` and `batch_id` for source identification,
- location data,
- and a list of structured sensor readings, each with a `sensor_id`, `type`, `value` and `unit`.

Simultaneously, a JSON message is constructed and sent to the next architectural layer, the **Proactive Agent Layer**. This message enables proactive reasoning by supplying real time context (see Listing 1.1).


```
{
  "timestamp": "2025-05-24T13:58:00Z",
  "device_id": "GW001",
  "batch_id": "BATCH456",
  "location": "Warehouse Zone A - Sensor #7",
  "sensors": [
    {
      "sensor_id": "TEMP001",
      "type": "temperature",
      "value": 21.7,
      "unit": "C"
    },
    {
      "sensor_id": "HUM002",
      "type": "humidity",
      "value": 48,
      "unit": "%"
    },
    {
      "sensor_id": "LUX003",
      "type": "light",
      "value": 320,
      "unit": "lux"
    }
  ]
}
```


Listing 1.1. Example JSON Message to Proactive Agent Layer

In the event of a temporary loss of connectivity (e.g., due to mobile network issues), the IoT Gateway continues to operate autonomously by storing the preprocessed data locally on its embedded storage, using an embedded database such as SQLite. Once communication with the cloud storage and upper layers is restored, the gateway automatically synchronizes and transmits the backlog of validated data to the cloud database and forwards the corresponding JSON messages to the **Proactive Agent Layer**. This mechanism guarantees zero data loss, continuous tracking and uninterrupted monitoring even in environments with unstable or limited network connectivity.

3.2 Proactive Agent Layer

The **Proactive Agent Layer** ensures the integrity and authenticity of pharmaceutical products throughout the supply chain. It hosts a Multi-Agent System (MAS) composed of two core agents: the *Detection Agent* and the *Decision Agent*. The *Detection Agent* continuously analyzes incoming sensor data to identify environmental anomalies. Upon detecting an anomaly, the *Decision Agent* evaluates its severity and autonomously decides on appropriate actions such as triggering blockchain-based alerts or isolating compromised batches.

Detection Agent. The *Detection Agent* is a specialized intelligent software component tasked with analyzing environmental data to detect deviations that could jeopardize pharmaceutical product integrity (see Fig. 3). It continuously receives structured messages from the **Real-Time Monitoring Layer**. These messages are encapsulated in unified JSON messages transmitted asynchronously via a RabbitMQ message queue named "env-data-queue", ensuring decoupled, reliable and fault-tolerant communication.

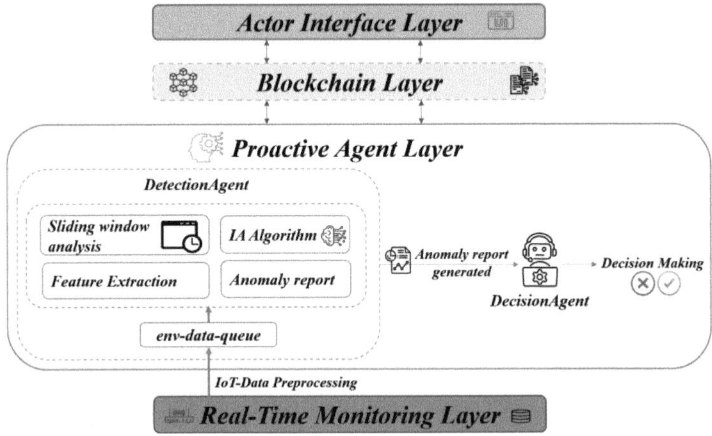

Fig. 3. Detection Agent Workflow.

Upon receipt, the *Detection Agent* queries the blockchain using the batch_id to retrieve product-specific acceptable thresholds (e.g., temperature range, humidity limits) immutably recorded during batch registration by manufacturers or regulatory authorities. For instance, a temperature-sensitive vaccine might have constraints of 2 °C to 9 °C and relative humidity below 65%.

Counterfeit detection in the proposed system is based on a multi-criteria approach that independently monitors environmental variables including temperature, humidity and light exposure. For each criterion, the agent maintains a sliding window of 30 min with 1-min granularity. This approach allows the system to assess short-term environmental fluctuations while maintaining sensitivity to abrupt deviations. Within each sliding window, the system extracts a set of statistical features that characterize the behavior of each criterion over time. These per-criteria feature vectors are merged into a single multivariate vector representing the batch's overall environmental behavior.

The formulation of the structured feature extraction process is presented as follows. Let $C \in \{C_1, C_2, \ldots, C_k\}$ denote an environmental criterion and let C_t represent its value at minute t. At each time step t, a sliding window W_t of 30 consecutive measurements is maintained, sampled at 1-min intervals: $W_t = \{C_{t-29}, C_{t-28}, \ldots, C_t\}$

For each criterion C, we extract a five-dimensional feature vector $\mathbf{f}_C^{(t)} \in \mathbb{R}^5$ characterizing the statistical behavior within the window. The components of this vector are defined as follows:

- **Mean:** Average of all 30 values in the window: $\mu_C^{(t)} = \frac{1}{30}\sum_{i=0}^{29} C_{t-i}$
- **Standard Deviation:** Measures variation/consistency. High std = high fluctuation: $\sigma_C^{(t)} = \sqrt{\frac{1}{30}\sum_{i=0}^{29}\left(C_{t-i} - \mu_C^{(t)}\right)^2}$
- **Number of Threshold Violations:** Count of values that exceed critical thresholds. Let θ_C be a predefined threshold for criterion C. Then: $v_C^{(t)} = \sum_{i=0}^{29} \mathbb{I}(C_{t-i} > \theta_C)$, where $\mathbb{I}(\cdot)$ is the indicator function.
- **Cumulative Duration of Critical Exposure:** Number of minutes that the values were in a critical range. Let CriticalZone_C be the critical value range for criterion C. Then: $d_C^{(t)} = \sum_{i=0}^{29} \mathbb{I}(C_{t-i} \in \text{CriticalZone}_C)$
- **Amplitude:** Difference between the maximum and minimum values within the window: $a_C^{(t)} = \max_{0 \le i \le 29} C_{t-i} - \min_{0 \le i \le 29} C_{t-i}$

The resulting per-criterion feature vector is given by: $\mathbf{f}_C^{(t)} = \left[\mu_C^{(t)}, \sigma_C^{(t)}, v_C^{(t)}, d_C^{(t)}, a_C^{(t)}\right]^\top$

To capture the overall environmental behavior, we concatenate the individual criterion vectors into a single multivariate vector: $\mathbf{F}^{(t)} = \left[\mathbf{f}_{C_1}^{(t)} \parallel \mathbf{f}_{C_2}^{(t)} \parallel \ldots \parallel \mathbf{f}_{C_k}^{(t)}\right] \in \mathbb{R}^{5k}$. Where $C_1, C_2, \ldots, C_k$ denote the monitored criteria and $\parallel$ indicates vector concatenation.

This multivariate feature vector $\mathbf{F}^{(t)}$, which summarizes the environmental conditions over the sliding window, serves as input to the counterfeit detection module based on Deep Support Vector Data Description (Deep SVDD) [26]. Deep SVDD is a neural networkâĂŞbased method designed for unsupervised anomaly detection. It learns a transformation $\phi(\cdot;\theta)$ of the input data into a latent representation space parameterized by network weights θ. The goal of Deep SVDD is to find a network mapping that minimizes the volume of a hypersphere enclosing the representations of normal data samples. Formally, it solves the following optimization problem:

$$\min_{\theta, R} R^2 + \frac{1}{\nu n}\sum_{i=1}^{n} \max\left(0, \|\phi(\mathbf{F}^{(i)};\theta) - \mathbf{c}\|^2 - R^2\right) + \lambda\, \Omega(\theta) \tag{1}$$

where $\mathbf{F}^{(i)}$ is the input feature vector for the i-th training sample, $\mathbf{c} \in \mathbb{R}^d$ is the center of the hypersphere in the latent space, R is the radius of the hypersphere, $\nu \in (0, 1]$ controls the trade-off between the volume of the hypersphere and the number of training samples allowed outside the hypersphere (soft margin), n is the number of training samples and $\Omega(\theta)$ is a regularization term on network parameters weighted by λ.

During training, the network learns to map normal environmental feature vectors close to the center $\mathbf{c}$ in latent space, effectively compacting normal behavior representations. At inference time, the anomaly score for a new observation $\mathbf{F}^{(*)}$ is computed as the squared distance from the center:

$$s(\mathbf{F}^{(*)}) = \|\phi(\mathbf{F}^{(*)}; \theta) - \mathbf{c}\|^2 \tag{2}$$

Higher scores indicate greater deviation from learned normal patterns and thus higher likelihood of anomaly. When a deviation is detected, the *Detection Agent* generates a structured anomaly report that details the detected parameters along with their respective features and thresholds. This report, as illustrated in Listing 1.2, is forwarded to the *Decision Agent*, which evaluates the risk and determines the appropriate mitigation strategy. In critical cases, the affected product may be flagged and excluded from the monitoring pipeline, thereby isolating potentially compromised drugs from the supply chain.


```json
{
  "batch_id": "BATCH456",
  "device_id": "GW001",
  "timestamp": "2025-05-25T14:32:00Z",
  "location": "Warehouse Zone A - Sensor #7",
  "anomalous_parameters": ["Temperature", "Humidity"],
  "feature_vectors": {
    "Temperature": {
      "sensor_id": "TEMP001",
      "mean": 28.7,
      "std_dev": 2.1,
      "threshold_violations": 3,
      "duration_minutes": 5,
      "amplitude": 7.4
    },
    "Humidity": {
      "sensor_id": "HUM002",
      "mean": 85,
      "std_dev": 4.5,
      "threshold_violations": 2,
      "duration_minutes": 4,
      "amplitude": 12
    }
  },
  "regulatory_thresholds": {
    "Temperature": {
      "max_temperature": 25.0
    },
    "Humidity": {
      "max_humidity": 80.0
    }
  }
}
```


Listing 1.2. Example of a structured anomaly report in JSON format

Decision Agent. The *Decision Agent* is the autonomous cognitive unit of the **Proactive Agent Layer** responsible for risk evaluation and responsive decision-making once environmental anomalies are detected (see Fig. 4). Upon receiving a structured anomaly report from the *Detection Agent*, it initiates a comprehensive analysis that considers the severity of the deviation.

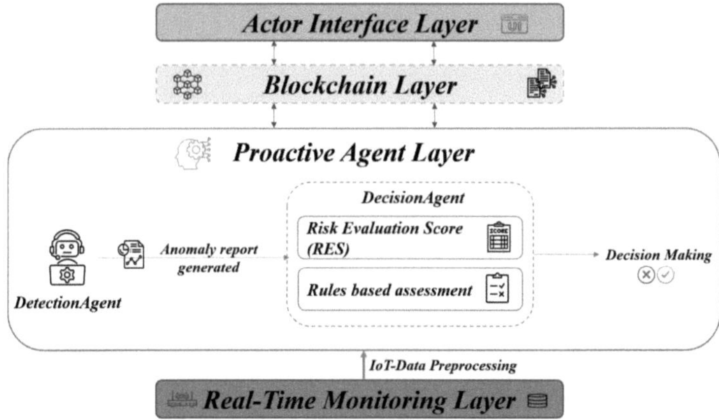

Fig. 4. Decision Agent Workflow.

Severity Scoring Mechanism. To quantify the overall anomaly severity, the *Decision Agent* calculates a composite severity score S based on five key criteria extracted from the structured anomaly report and historical blockchain log. These include:

- the number of threshold violations v_i, from the `threshold_violations` field;
- the cumulative duration d_i (in minutes) during which parameter i exceeded limits, from the `duration_minutes` field;
- the amplitude a_i of deviation, from the `amplitude` field;
- the relative deviation δ_i, defined as: $\delta_i = \frac{\max(0, \mu_i - T_i)}{T_i}$, where μ_i is the mean value from the `mean` field and T_i the threshold from the `regulatory_thresholds`;
- the historical risk factor H_i, calculated per parameter based on prior anomaly trends (more detailed below).

Each component provides a distinct dimension of anomaly assessment. The total severity score S is:

$$S = \sum_{i=1}^{n} (w_1 \cdot v_i + w_2 \cdot d_i + w_3 \cdot a_i + w_4 \cdot \delta_i + w_5 \cdot H_i) \tag{3}$$

where w_1, w_2, w_3, w_4, w_5 are weight coefficients calibrated empirically or through expert knowledge to reflect the relative importance of each component.

Historical Risk Factor H_i. To incorporate temporal context and reinforce risk awareness, the *Decision Agent* computes a parameter-specific historical risk factor H_i that reflects past anomaly recurrence and degradation patterns for parameter i. The historical trace is derived from the blockchain-stored anomaly records and is formulated as:

$$H_i = \sum_{j=1}^{m} \gamma_{ij} \cdot S_{ij} \cdot e^{-\lambda(t-t_j)} \tag{4}$$

where m is the number of previous anomaly events for parameter i, S_{ij} is the severity of the jth past anomaly (retrieved from the blockchain), t_j is the timestamp of that event and t is the current time, λ is a temporal decay rate governing how quickly older events lose influence and $\gamma_{ij} \in [0, 1]$ is a similarity coefficient defined as: $\gamma_{ij} = \alpha \cdot \mathbb{1}_{\text{type}} + \beta \cdot \mathbb{1}_{\text{batch}} + \zeta \cdot \mathbb{1}_{\text{equipment}}$. Here $\mathbb{1}_{\text{type}} = 1$ if anomaly j matches the current anomaly type, 0 otherwise; $\mathbb{1}_{\text{batch}} = 1$ if both anomalies occurred on the same batch; $\mathbb{1}_{\text{equipment}} = 1$ if both occurred on the same equipment or unit; $\alpha + \beta + \zeta = 1$ are adjustable weights reflecting domain priorities.

This formulation enables the agent to encode long-term contextual memory per parameter, emphasizing recent and semantically similar events.

Rule-Based Decision Logic. Based on the computed severity score S and calibrated thresholds, the *Decision Agent* applies rule-based logic:

- If $S < \tau_{\text{low}}$, the anomaly is flagged as *low-risk* and stored.
- If $\tau_{\text{low}} \leq S < \tau_{\text{high}}$, a *supervisor notification* is triggered.
- If $S \geq \tau_{\text{high}}$, the batch is *isolated* and a *blockchain alert* is issued.

Here, τ_{low} and τ_{high} are tuned using historical data or expert knowledge.

Mitigation and Logging. Upon decision, the agent autonomously executes the appropriate mitigation protocol and records all details—severity metrics, historical context, rule thresholds and decisions—into a timestamped audit trail stored on the blockchain. This ensures transparency, traceability and regulatory compliance.

3.3 Blockchain Layer

In our architecture, the Ethereum blockchain plays a central and active role, not only ensuring data immutability and traceability but also registering detected anomalies, logging AI-generated decisions and securely coordinating stakeholder notifications via smart contracts. These contracts encapsulate critical business logic—such as environmental thresholds, risk levels and quarantine rules—enabling automated, consistent and verifiable decision-making. By serving as a decentralized source of truth, the blockchain enables the *Detection* and *Decision* Agents to operate on verifiable, integrity-assured data without relying on centralized entities. Integrated with the IoT and messaging layers, it provides dynamic threshold updates and persistently logs severity scores, contextual data and actions taken. This design strengthens transparency, enhances system resilience and reinforces anti-counterfeit safeguards across the pharmaceutical supply chain.

3.4 Actor Interface Layer

The **Actor Interface Layer** serves as the main point of interaction between human stakeholders and the autonomous system. It provides intuitive dashboards and portals that allow manufacturers, regulators, distributors and healthcare providers to monitor batch statuses, receive alerts and access risk assessments securely and in real time. Role-based access control ensures that users see only data relevant to their responsibilities, maintaining confidentiality and compliance. By presenting blockchain-backed immutable records and clear insights, this layer enables informed decision-making, timely interventions and seamless collaboration across the pharmaceutical supply chain.

4 Experimentation

To validate ReACT-Pharma, we built a real-world hardware testbed simulating pharmaceutical storage and transport conditions. The setup included ESP32 boards equipped with DHT22 (temperature/humidity), TSL2561 (light) and GPS module (NEO-6M) for location tracking. Devices transmitted data via MQTT to a Raspberry Pi 4. Smart contracts deployed on a local Ethereum blockchain (Ganache) recorded anomalies, decisions and triggered alerts.

We evaluated the system across five scenarios, including (1) Gradual temperature rise beyond safe limits (simulating failed refrigeration), (2) Sudden exposure to high light levels (simulating unsealed packaging), (3) Combined humidity and temperature deviation (cross-parameter anomaly), (4) GPS signal loss and location tampering, and (5) Node failure or disconnection (resilience test). As shown in Table 1, ReACT-Pharma consistently detected anomalies in under 2 s and logged decisions to the blockchain within ≈ 4 s. All actions were traceable and smart contracts executed reliably.

Table 1. ReACT-Pharma Testbed Results

Metric	Result
Detection latency	$\approx$ 1.2 seconds per anomaly
Blockchain logging latency	$\approx$ 3.6 seconds per transaction
Severity score accuracy	91% alignment with expert labels
Smart contract reliability	100% successful execution (no rollback/failures)
Energy consumption	$\approx$ 180mA for each ESP32 node during transmission

This testbed confirms the system's ability to provide multi-dimensional monitoring, proactive detection, autonomous decision-making and transparent, tamper-proof coordination, even under constrained and dynamic conditions.

5 Conclusion

This paper presents ReACT-Pharma, a proactive system for real time counterfeit drug detection and autonomous decision-making in the pharmaceutical supply chain, combining IoT, blockchain, AI and MAS. The proposed architecture is based on four layers: (1) a layer to monitor environmental conditions in real time, (2) a proactive agent layer to detect counterfeits based on multiple criteria and assess their contextual severity to automatically trigger decisions, (3) a blockchain layer ensures the traceability and integrity of recorded events and (4) a dedicated actor interface for stakeholders to access alerts, submit updates and track product status in real time. Experiments with this system demonstrate significant improvements in preventing counterfeit drugs, thus strengthening the security and transparency of the pharmaceutical supply chain. For a future work, we plan to adapt a generative AI model to improve the system's ability to automatically propose corrective actions during critical scenarios, in order to enhance the smart contract's real time decision-making capabilities. This approach aims to strengthen the decision-making independence of our system, while ensuring an adaptive and self-healing supply chain.

References

1. World Health Organization: Substandard and falsified medical products. https://www.who.int/en/news-room/fact-sheets/detail/substandard-and-falsified-medical-products. Accessed 6 May 2023
2. Pathak, R., Gaur, V., Sankrityayan, H., Gogtay, J.: Tackling counterfeit drugs: the challenges and possibilities. Pharm. Med. **37**(4), 281–290 (2023). https://doi.org/10.1007/s40290-023-00453-5
3. Ben Abdelghani, S., Nabli, H., Ben Djemaa, R., Sliman, L.: Blockchain-integrated technologies to address counterfeit drugs in the pharmaceutical supply chain. In: International Conference on Hybrid Intelligent Systems, pp. 292–301. Springer, Cham (2023)
4. Muzafar, M.A., Bhargava, A., Jha, A., Nand, P.: Securing the supply chain: a comprehensive solution with blockchain technology and QR-based anti-counterfeit mechanism. Int. J. Performability Eng. **19**(5), 312 (2023)
5. Parvathi, K.G., Krupalini, S., Harshitha, J.P., Tiwari, S., Hanisha, V., Ishrath, S.: Blockchain-enabled product tokenization and CNN-based counterfeit detection for secure supply chain verification. Macaw Int. J. Adv. Res. Comput. Sci. Eng. **11**(1), 46–57 (2025)
6. Picard, J., Landry, P., Bolay, M.: Counterfeit detection with QR codes. In: Proceedings of 21st ACM Symposium Document Engineering, pp. 1–4 (2021)
7. Shaik, C.: Preventing counterfeit products using cryptography, QR code and webservice. Comput. Sci. Eng. Int. J. **11**(1) (2021)
8. Wu, R., Liu, N., Peng, G., Bhattarai, A., Peng, D.: An innovative method for securing QR codes against counterfeits in supply chain management. In: 2024 IEEE 14th Annual Computing and Communication Workshop and Conference (CCWC), pp. 589–596. IEEE (2024). https://doi.org/10.1109/CCWC.2024.1234567

9. Nabli, H., Ben Djemaa, R., Amous Ben Amor, I.: Improved clustering-based hybrid recommendation system to offer personalized cloud services. Cluster Comput. **27**(3), 2845–2874 (2024). https://doi.org/10.1007/s10586-023-04119-2
10. Souki, O., Ben Djemaa, R., Amous, I., Sèdes, F.: An hybridization of LSTM and random forest model to predict road situation. In: 2023 IEEE International Conference on Enabling Technologies: Infrastructure for Collaborative Enterprises (WETICE), pp. 1–7. IEEE (2023)
11. Ghannem, A., Francis, E., Nabli, H., Sliman, L., Djemaa, R.B.: Fuzzy FCA-based elderly activity recognition. In: 2023 International Conference on Computer and Applications (ICCA), pp. 1–6. IEEE (2023)
12. Abdelhamid, M.M., Sliman, L., Ben Djemaa, R.: AI-enhanced blockchain for scalable IoT-based supply chain. Logistics **8**(4), 109 (2024). https://doi.org/10.3390/logistics8040109
13. Nabli, H., Ghannem, A., Ben Djemaa, R., Sliman, L.: How innovative technologies shape the future of pharmaceutical supply chains. Comput. Ind. Eng. **199**, Article 110745 (2025). https://doi.org/10.1016/j.cie.2024.110745
14. Yekeen, A.O., Sam-Bulya, N.J., Ewim, C.P.M.: Enhancing supply chain security and transparency with AI and blockchain integration for future-proof solutions. Int. J. Front. Res. Sci. Technol. **4**(1), Article 0052 (2024). https://doi.org/10.56355/ijfrst.2024.4.1.0052
15. Rizzardi, A., Sicari, S., Coen-Porisini, A.: IoT-driven blockchain to manage the healthcare supply chain and protect medical records. Future Gener. Comput. Syst. **161**, 415–431 (2024)
16. Chinchmalatpure, S., Pala, A., Waghmare, A., Lokhande, A., Goyal, D., Diwnale, T.: IoT-based secure medicine supply chain using blockchain technology. In: Proceedings of 8th International Conference on Computing, Communication, Control and Automation (ICCUBEA 2024), pp. 1–5. IEEE, New York (2024). https://doi.org/10.1109/ICCUBEA.2024.1234567
17. Nawale, S.D., Konapure, R.R.: Blockchain and IoT based drugs traceability for pharma industry. In: Proceedings of IEEE International Conference on Engineering, Technology and Innovation (ICE/ITMC 2021), pp. 1–4. IEEE, New York (2021). https://doi.org/10.1109/ICE/ITMC.2021.1234567
18. Alabdulatif, A., Al Asqah, M., Moulahi, T., Zidi, S.: Leveraging artificial intelligence in blockchain-based e-health for safer decision making framework. Appl. Sci. **13**(2), 1035 (2023). https://doi.org/10.3390/app13021035
19. Said, A.G., Gawali, T., Chavan, M., Bendgude, S., H ande, R.: Fake drug detection using blockchain technology. Int. J. Res. Appl. Sci. Eng. Technol. **11**(5), 4303–4307 (2023)
20. Kambilo, E.K., Zghal, H.B., Guegan, C.G., Stankovski, V., Kochovski, P., Vodislav, D.: A blockchain-based framework for drug traceability: ChainDrugTrac. In: Proceedings of 37th ACM/SIGAPP Symposium On Applied Computing (SAC 2022), pp. 1–7. ACM, New York (2022). https://doi.org/10.1145/3477314.3507118
21. Fuyao, J.: The application of IoT technology in product traceability and anti-counterfeiting. J. Electron. Inf. Sci. **8**(5), Article 080503 (2023). https://doi.org/10.23977/jeis.2023.080503
22. Patil, S., Sawant, V., Kanaji, A., Kadukar, V., Patade, I.: Counterfeit pharmaceutical product detection using blockchain technology. In: Proceedings of International Conference on Computing Communication and Networking Technologies (ICCCNT 2024), pp. 1–6. IEEE, New York (2024). https://doi.org/10.1109/icccnt61001.2024.10725331

23. Kumar, M.: Pharmaceutical serialization dynamics to restrain illicit trade and counterfeiting of drugs. World J. Adv. Res. Rev. **22**(2), Article 1461 (2024). https://doi.org/10.30574/wjarr.2024.22.2.1461
24. Masdani, M.V., Darlis, D.: A comprehensive study on MQTT as a low power protocol for internet of things application. IOP Conf. Ser. Mater. Sci. Eng. **434**, 012274 (2018). https://doi.org/10.1088/1757-899X/434/1/012274
25. Nabli, H., Regaig, I., Ben Djemaa, R., Sliman, L.: Never alone: a quality of context-aware monitoring system for aging in place smart home. In: 2022 IEEE 21st International Symposium on Network Computing and Applications (NCA), pp. 209–215. IEEE (2022). https://doi.org/10.1109/NCA57778.2022.10013515
26. Ruff, L., et al.: Deep one-class classification. In: International Conference on Machine Learning (ICML), pp. 4393–4402. PMLR (2018)

Security and Privacy

Verifying Security Requirements of Fog Services Communication with Event-B

Samia Ben Ismail[1(✉)], Imed Abbassi[2], Marwa Aloui[2], Zied Jaoua[2], Mohamed Graiet[2], and Walid Gaaloul[3]

[1] University of Sousse, ISITCom, 4011 Hammam Sousse, Sousse, Tunisia
samia_benismail@yahoo.fr

[2] University of Monastir, Higher Institute of Informatics and Mathematics of Monastir, Monastir, Tunisia
abbassi.imed@gmail.com, {marwa.aloui,mohamed.graiet}@isimm.u-monastir.tn

[3] SAMOVAR, Télécom SudParis, Institut Polytechnique de Paris, 91120 Palaiseau, France
walid.gaaloul@telecom-sudparis.eu

Abstract. Fog computing is an extension of cloud computing that brings processing power closer to the source of data, thereby enhancing Internet of Things (IoT) applications by reducing latency and improving efficiency. However, this distributed paradigm introduces significant security and privacy challenges due to the limited computing resources and physical accessibility of edge devices. Ensuring the secure development and deployment of fog services requires comprehensive frameworks that consistently integrate robust security mechanisms across various platforms.

This paper addresses these challenges by proposing the Security Policies Model for the Fog (SPM4FOG), a novel solution that uses the Event-B formal method. The $SPM4FOG$ model enables industrial designers to formally validate security requirements during the design phase, promoting the secure development of IoT applications by design. Leveraging mathematical foundations and formal logic, the $SPM4FOG$ model rigorously verifies security policies, mitigates vulnerabilities, and enhances the security of fog computing environments.

Keywords: Fog service · Security policies · Event-B Verification · Secure-by-design

1 Introduction

Fog computing extends cloud capabilities to the edge, bringing computation closer to data sources and users. This paradigm is especially beneficial for IoT applications, reducing latency and improving responsiveness. However, its distributed nature and the limited resources of edge devices pose security challenges, including protocol inconsistencies and increased exposure to physical attacks [3, 15].

This paper addresses the secure development of Fog services, an area still lacking comprehensive integration frameworks [20]. Formal methods like Petri nets [12] and

I. Awan et al. (Eds.): WISE 2025, LNCS 16367, pp. 187–202, 2026.
https://doi.org/10.1007/978-981-95-7394-3_13

Event-B [1] offer rigorous tools for specifying and verifying system properties, particularly in security-critical IoT contexts.

We propose SPM4FOG, a formal Event-BâĂŞbased framework for modeling and validating Fog service security policies. It comprises three abstraction levels: (1) basic Fog service communication, (2) secure session establishment inspired by real-world platforms (e.g., WhatsApp, Signal, Zoom) [17, 18, 24], and (3) session key management with encryption to ensure confidentiality and integrity [21].

The remainder of this paper is organized as follows: Sect. 2 presents the security requirements for IoT services and an overview of the verification methodology. Section 3 provides a detailed description of the proposed $SPM4FOG$ model. Section 4 addresses the model's correctness verification and empirical validation. Section 5 discusses related work. Finally, Sect. 6 concludes the paper and outlines directions for future research.

2 Background and Motivation

In this section, we start by presenting the basics of the Event-B modeling language. Next, we define the security policies for Fog services. Finally, we provide an overview of our methodology for verifying these policies.

2.1 Event-B Basics

Event-B [1] is a formal method grounded in set theory and first-order logic. It offers a correct-by-construction design approach and encompasses the entire software life cycle. In Event-B modeling, two types of entities are used to describe a system: *machines* and *contexts*. A machine represents the dynamic part of a model, which can include variables, invariants, and events. In contrast, a context represents the static part of a model, including carrier/enumerated sets, constants, and axioms. A machine can refer to one or more contexts to access their elements.

An Event-B model is composed of two main components: *machines* and *contexts*. Machines capture the dynamic behavior of the system, containing variables, invariants, and events. Contexts, on the other hand, define the static structure, including carrier/enumerated sets, constants, and axioms. Machines can reference one or more contexts to utilize their defined elements.

A machine is structured into several clauses: the `VARIABLES` clause defines the model's variables; the `INVARIANTS` clause specifies properties that must always be satisfied by the system (including at least the typing of the variables); and the `EVENTS` clause lists the events. Each event is represented as $(G \mid Act)$, where G is the guard and Act is the action. An event is enabled when its guard condition holds true.

A context is similarly organized into the following clauses: the `SETS` clause defines abstract and enumerated types; the `CONSTANTS` clause lists the constants used in the model; and the `AXIOMS` clause states properties about the constants, including their types.

As mentioned earlier, refinement is a central concept in the Event-B method. It enables systems to be developed incrementally by introducing more detail at successive levels of specification. Both *context* and *machine* components can be refined. A context can be extended by defining new sets and/or constants, along with new axioms. A machine can be refined by adding new variables and/or replacing existing ones with new variables that are linked by an additional invariant Inv_r, known as the gluing invariant. New events may also be introduced to implicitly refine a **skip** event.

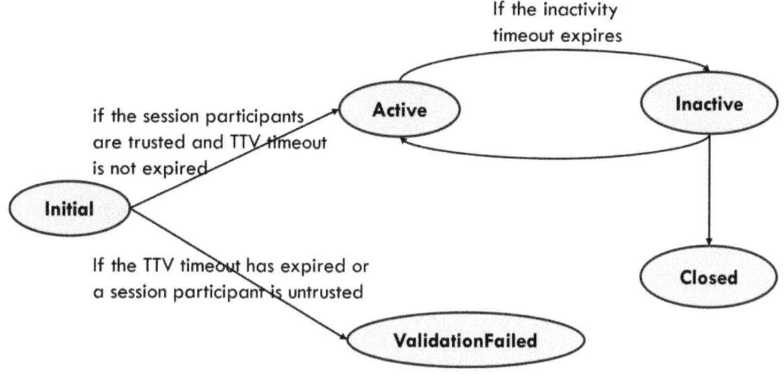

Fig. 1. The state transition diagram of the Fog services communication sessions.

2.2 Fog Services Security Policies

The development of Fog services introduces significant security challenges [11,20]. Developers must address several critical security requirements, including confidentiality, privacy, availability, and integrity. Due to space limitations, this paper focuses on two main categories of security policies:

- **Communication session rules**: These define the conditions and rules governing interactions between communicating entities [7].
  - **Req-1:** Fog services communicate through sessions. A session must be created and validated before two services can interact.
  - **Req-2:** A session is established between two distinct services, referred to as participants, where one acts as the initiator.
  - **Req-3:** Messages can only be exchanged within an active session.
  - **Req-4:** Only a trusted entity is authorized to receive and process session validation requests.
  - **Req-5:** The session lifecycle is modeled as a state diagram, as shown in Fig. 1.
  - **Req-6:** The trusted entity may only validate a session if both the initiator and participant are trusted (i.e., registered in the system).
  - **Req-7:** After a period of inactivity, an active session becomes inactive. It can either be closed or reactivated. Figure 1 illustrates the session lifecycle.
- **Confidentiality and integrity rules**: These ensure the protection of information during transmission [7]. They include constraints on the encryption/decryption keys and algorithms.

- **Req-8:** The session validation request is sent in a message encrypted with the trusted entity's public key. It is decrypted using the corresponding private key.
- **Req-9:** Upon session validation, the initiator generates a secret session key and transmits it to the participant, encrypted with the participant's public key.
- **Req-10:** The participant decrypts the received message using its private key and stores the session key.
- **Req-11:** The session key is used to encrypt and decrypt messages within the associated active session.
- **Req-12:** The session key must be retained by both participants for a predefined duration. After expiration, the initiator must regenerate a new key according to the steps described in Req-9 and Req-10.

These security policies aim to protect the confidentiality and integrity of data transmitted over a Fog network. Without such protection, sensitive data could be intercepted, altered, or compromised by malicious entities. The use of a session-specific encryption key ensures temporal validity, meaning that even if a key is compromised, it cannot be used to access future sessions.

2.3 Verification Methodology of Security Policies

The objective of this work is to verify the correctness of security policies governing Fog service interactions. This verification is performed using the Event-B $SPM4FOG$ model, which is structured across three levels of abstraction, each consisting of a machine and a context:

- **Abstract level (SPM_c0, SPM_m0)**: Introduces the foundational concepts of communication between Fog services.
- **First refinement (SPM_c1, SPM_m1)**: Introduces the concept of communication sessions. This level formally encodes requirements [Req-1 $\Rightarrow$ Req-7]. The remaining instructions are covered in the next refinement.
- **Second refinement (SPM_c2, SPM_m2)**: Incorporates the concepts of message encryption and models security constraints related to confidentiality and integrity, specifically requirements [Req-8 $\Rightarrow$ Req-12].

The $SPM4FOG$ model empowers system designers to formally validate security requirements during the design phase, thereby promoting secure-by-design IoT development. Leveraging mathematical logic and formal methods, the model ensures rigorous verification of security policies, reducing vulnerabilities and strengthening the overall security posture of Fog computing environments.

3 Modeling Security Policies of Fog Services with Event-B

As claimed above, the proposed $SPM4FOG$ model facilitates secure-by-design development of IoT applications, ensuring that security policies are rigorously verified and adhered to throughout the development process. In this section, we explore the three aspects of this model.

3.1 Level 1: Modeling Communication Requirements of Fog Services

To define the $SPM4FOG$ model, the first step is to model the fundamental concepts of Fog service communication. For that purpose, we define the following static elements (sets and constants) in SPM_c0:

- **FOGNodes**: A non-empty finite set of Fog nodes. A node can be a Fog server, a cloud virtual machine, or any IoT device.
- **FOGServices**: A finite set of Fog services.
- **Data**: A finite set of data items.
- **locatedOn** $\in FOGServices \rightarrow FOGNodes$: A total function that indicates the location of each Fog service.
- **storedOn** $\in Data \rightarrow FOGNodes$: A total function that specifies the Fog node on which each data item is stored.

Considering these sets and constants, we define the following variables in SPM_m0:

- $messages \in \mathbb{P}(1 \ldots counter)$: A variable that defines the messages exchanged. Each message is represented by an integer. The variable $counter$ is a message counter that is incremented by 1 after each message is sent.
- $messageContent \in messages \nrightarrow \mathbb{P}(Data)$: A variable that defines the content (data) of each message.
- $sentMessages, receivedMessages \in \mathbb{P}(messages)$: Variables that define the sent and received messages. A message can either be sent or received. Lost messages are automatically removed.
- $messageSource, messageDestination$: Variables that define the source and destination of each message. We define these variables as follows:

$$messageSource \in messages \rightarrow FOGServices$$
$$messageDestination \in messages \rightarrow \mathbb{P}(FOGServices)$$

- $sendingTime, receptionTime \in messages \nrightarrow \mathbb{N}$: Variables that represent the time at which a message was sent and received.
- $messageTTL \in messages \rightarrow \mathbb{N}$: A variable representing the Time-To-Live (TTL) deadline for receiving messages. Upon the expiry of such a deadline, a sent message is considered lost.

The machine SPM_m0 includes the variables mentioned above and three events to manage the processes of sending, receiving, and losing messages. The Figs. 2 and 3 describe the events of sending and receiving messages.

Event $sendMessage$ ensures that messages to be sent are properly initialized with attributes such as content, source, destination, and time-to-live (TTL) set accordingly. Guard conditions validate that the sender and receiver are valid Fog services, that the content is not empty and conforms to the data format, and that there is a network connection between them. Upon execution, the event increments a counter, records message details, and updates relevant variables to track the message's lifecycle within the system.

```
Event sendMessage
ANY service recipient content
WHERE
grd1:service ∈ FOGServices
grd2:recipient ∈ FOGServices \ {service}
grd3:content ∈ ℙ1 (Data)
grd4:locatedOn(service) ↦ locatedOn(recipient) ∈ nodesLink
THEN
act1:counter := counter + 1
act2:messageContent(counter + 1) := content
act3:sentMessages := sentMessages ∪ {counter + 1}
act4:messageSource(counter + 1) := service
act5:messageDestination(counter + 1) := recipient
act6:messages := messages ∪ {counter + 1}
act7:sendingTime(counter + 1) := time
act8:messageTTL(counter + 1) := default_ttl
END
```

Fig. 2. Event of sending messages.

```
Event receiveMessage
ANY source recipient message
WHERE
grd1: message ∈ sentMessages
grd2: recipient = messageDestination(message)
    ∧source = messageSource(message)
grd3: locatedOn(recipient) ↦ locatedOn(source) ∈ nodesLink
grd4: time > sendingTime(message)
grd5: messageTTL(message) > 0
THEN
act1: receivedMessages := receivedMessages ∪ {message}
act2: receptionTime(message) := time
act3: sentMessages := sentMessages \ {message}
END
```

Fig. 3. Event of receiving message.

The $receiveMessage$ event (see Fig. 3) indicates that a service ($recipient$) has received a message sent by another Fog service ($source$). This event verifies crucial conditions, such as the existence of a correct network connection between the recipient and source Fog services, and ensures that the message's TTL (time-to-live) has not expired. These conditions are defined as the conjunction of guards $grd4$ and $grd5$.

3.2 Level 2: Modeling Communication Session Rules of Fog Services

In the second step of the $SPM4FOG$ model, we define the communication session rules (Req-1 $\Rightarrow$ Req-7). As mentioned earlier, communication between Fog services is strictly conducted through sessions. These sessions include authentication and authorization granted by a Trusted Entity (TE). TE ensures that only authorized services can initiate and maintain communication sessions. This approach not only secures the communication channels, but also ensures that all interactions between Fog services are authenticated and authorized, thereby maintaining the integrity and security of the Fog computing environment.

To model these concepts, we first create the context SPM_c1 by extending SPM_c0. This context introduces the following new constants:

- $privacyData \subseteq Data$: Represents a subset of data that encapsulates information intended for private or restricted access within the Fog computing environment.
- $publicData \subseteq Data$: Denotes a subset of Data containing information that is intended for public access or dissemination within the Fog computing environment.
- $Sessions \subseteq privacyData$: Refers to a set containing elements from privacyData, indicating that sessions established for communication or data exchange are based on data categorized under privacyData.
- $STATUS$: Refers an enumerated set containing the different possible states for a session ($Initial$, $Active$, $ValidationFailed$, $Inactive$ and $closed$).
- $trustedFOGServices \in \mathbb{P}(FOGServices))$: Represents a set of trusted Fog services. The services not included in this set are considered untrusted and are not allowed to use network links.
- $trustedEntity \in trustedFOGServices$: Represents a Fog service that holds a special status of trust or authority, often involved in authentication and authorization processes within the Fog computing network. This entity must be deployed on a separate Fog node for security purposes.

$$\mathrm{dom}(locatedOn \rhd \{locatedOn(trustedEntity)\}) = \{trustedEntity\}$$

- $idle\_timeout$: Represents the maximum allowed period of inactivity for a session. Sending and receiving messages are the possible activities within a session.

```
Event openSession REFINES sendMessage
ANY
service session participants ttv
WHERE
grd1:service ∈ FOGServices ∧ trustedEntity ≠ service
grd2:session ∈ Sessions ∧ session ∉ sessions ∧ ttv ∈ ℕ ∧ ttv > 0
grd3:locatedOn(service) ↦ locatedOn(trustedEntity) ∈ nodesLink
grd4:participants ⊆ FOGServices ∧ service ∉ participants
WITH
content:content = {session}
recipient:recipient = trustedEntity
THEN
...
act9:sessionStatus(session) := Initial
act10:sessionInitiator(session) := service
act11:sessionParticipants(session) := {service} ∪ participants
act12:sessions := sessions ∪ {session}
act13:inactivityTimeout(session) := 0
act14:sessionTTV(session) := ttv
END
```

Fig. 4. OpenSession Event.

To model the $createSession$ procedure introduced above and the corresponding rules, we refine the SPM_m0 machine into a new SPM_m1 machine that sees the SPM_c1 context. This refinement is a four-step process. In the first step, we introduce the following new variables:

- $sessions \subseteq Sessions$: Represents the set of sessions. Each session can be active (valid), inactive, closed, invalid or awaiting validation.
- $sessionStatus \in sessions \rightarrow STATUS$: Defines the current status of each session.
- $sessionInitiator$ and $sessionParticipants$: Define the initiator and the participants Fog services of each session.
- $inactivityTimeout \in sessions \rightarrow \mathbb{N}$: Represents the expiry time of each validated session.
- $sessionTTV \in sessions \rightarrow \mathbb{N}$: refers to the Time-to-Validation (TTV) period associated with each session. This variable is crucial for managing the validation process of sessions between Fog services.

The second step is to refine the $sendMessage$ and $receiveMessage$ events. The SPM_m1 machine contains two refined versions of each of these events. This is justified by the fact that the procedure not only initiates the creation of a session but also sends a validation request to the Trusted Entity (TE). Similarly, the process of verifying session validity, performed by the TE, is formally defined as a refinement of the $receiveMessage$ event. This means that the verification process can only begin once the validation request sent by the session initiator has been detected.

Figure 4 describes the openSession event. This event initializes a new session by setting up the necessary parameters and sending a validation request to a trusted entity. It requires a service, a unique session identifier, participants, and a positive time-to-validation (TTV). The event sets the session status to Initial, designates the service as the session initiator, adds the service and participants to the session, adds the session to the session list, sets the inactivity timeout to 0, and assigns the TTV to the session.

The `checkSessionValidation` event captures the validation request sent by the initiator of the corresponding session. It checks if the session fulfills the validity condition:

$$(sessionTTV(session) > 0) \land$$
$$\forall p \cdot p \in sessionParticipants(session) \Rightarrow p \in trustedFOGServices)$$

If the session satisfies this condition, it becomes `Active`; otherwise, it is considered `Invalid` (i.e., $sessionStatus(session) = ValidationFailed$).

The second refinement of the $sendMessage$ (or $receiveMessage$) event introduces a new session parameter, which represents an active session between Fog services. This refinement enhances the event by adding additional guards, ensuring that specific conditions are met before message transmission or reception occurs.

$$session \in sessions \land sessionStatus(session) = Active$$
$$sessionParticipants(session) = \{source, recipient\}$$

These conditions ensure that sending or receiving is only possible if the source and destination of the messages are participants in an active session. This means that the actions of sending or receiving messages can only occur if both the sender and receiver are designated participants in the same active session. This effectively ensures that all interactions are valid and secure within the defined session context.

The SPM_m1 machine includes a series of additional invariants that play a crucial role in defining its behavior. These invariants define constraints on the communication sessions of the Fog services. For instance, the initiator of a session must always be a participant in that session. This is formally defined by the following invariant:

inv7:$\forall s \cdot s \in sessions \Rightarrow sessionInitiator(s) \in sessionParticipants(s)$

The inactivity timeout of a session must be within the range of 0 to the maximum allowed value, defined by **idle_timeout**. This is expressed by the following invariant:

inv8:$\forall s \cdot s \in sessions \Rightarrow inactivityTimeout(s) \in 0 \mathrel{..} idle\_timeout$

If a session is marked as inactive, its inactivity timeout must be equal to 0.

inv9:$\forall s \cdot s \in sessions \land sessionStatus(s) = Inactive \Rightarrow inactivityTimeout(s) = 0$

If the validation time (**TTV**) of a session expires (i.e., reaches 0) and the session is no longer in the initial state, its status must be set to **ValidationFailed**. This is formalized by the following invariant:

inv10:$\forall s \cdot s \in sessions \land sessionTTV(s) = 0 \land sessionStatus(s) \neq Initial$
$\Rightarrow sessionStatus(s) = ValidationFailed$

3.3 Level 3: Modeling Data Integrity and Confidentiality Rules

The main purpose of encryption is to protect the confidentiality and integrity of data in transit over a network. Without this protection, sensitive information could be intercepted, compromised, or even altered by malicious services. In our approach, we use the following encryption process: data is encrypted using a session key within a valid session. When a session is established between two Fog services (e.g. a user and a server), a session key is generated by the initiator in a temporary and session-specific manner. This key is then used to encrypt and decrypt data exchanged during the session. The advantage of using a session key is that it is temporary. This means that the key is only valid for the duration of the current session. Therefore, even if a key is compromised, it cannot be used to decrypt future sessions.

To model the data integrity and confidentiality rules, we start by defining the new context SPM_c2. This context extends SPM_c1 with the following new constants and sets:

- $KEYS$: Represents a set of data used for various key purposes within the session management system. It is defined as $KEYS \in \mathbb{P}(Data)$.
- $publicKEYS$: Represents public keys used for authentication and secure communication within the Fog network. It is defined as $publicKEYS \in \mathbb{P}(KEYS)$ and a subset of $publicData$, indicating the publicly accessible keys.

- $sessionKEYS$: Refers to session keys used to secure communication sessions between Fog services. It is defined as $sessionKEYS \in \mathbb{P}(KEYS)$ and specified as a subset of $privacyData$, indicating the data intended for restricted access.
- $privateKEYS$: Represents an injective function in $publicKEYS \rightarrowtail KEYS$ that maps private keys to corresponding public keys in the system. It ensures that each private key is associated with a unique public key.
- $hasPublicKEYS$: Represents a partial function mapping each Fog service to its respective public key. This function is specified as an element of $FOGServices \nrightarrow publicKEYS$, ensuring that each Fog service has a public key for authentication and secure communication. Some services don't have public keys, especially untrusted ones.
- $key\_expiry\_period \in \mathbb{N}$: Refers to the default expiry period of the session keys.

The refined machine SPM_m2 sees the context SPM_c2 and introduces new variables/invariants while refining some abstract events. Five variables are added, described as follows:

- $sessionKey \in sessions \rightarrowtail\!\!\!\!\!\nrightarrow sessionKEYS$: Represents the secret keys used to secure the communication sessions between Fog services. Two sessions cannot have the same key.
- $sessionkeyValidity \in sessionKey \rightarrow \mathbb{N}$: Represents the current remaining validity period of each session key. When a session key is generated, it is initialized to the default value (key_expiry_period) and then updated (decremented) by the $checkClock$ event until it expires:

$$sessionkeyValidity := sessionkeyValidity \lhd\!\!\!- \\ \{k \mapsto (p-1) \mid k \mapsto p \in sessionkeyValidity \wedge p > 0\}$$

- $keyRetention \in sessions \rightarrow \mathbb{P}(FOGServices)$: Indicates which Fog services retain which session keys.
- $isEncryptedWith/isDecryptedWith$: Represents partial functions defining the key used for the encryption/decryption of messages.

The final step in modeling the session creation procedure is to generate, send and retrieve the session key. To achieve this, the SPM_m2 machine includes two new events: $generateSessionKey$ and $retrieveKey$. The $generateSessionKey$ event refines $sendMessage$ and models the process of generating and sending the key for an active session. The generated session key is sent in a message encrypted with the recipient's public key. The $retrieveKey$ event refines $receiveMessage$ and models the process of retrieving the key for an active session. We define such an event by strengthening guards of $receiveMessage$ event with the following preconditions:

grd9: $recipient = sessionInitiator(session)$
grd10: $\{session\} \lhd sessionKey \neq \varnothing$
$\wedge messageContent(message) = \{session, sessionKey(session)\}$
grd11: $recipient \notin keyRetention(session) \wedge \lhd isEncryptedWith \neq \varnothing$
grd12: $isEncryptedWith(message) = hasPublicKEYS(recipient)$

Second, we update the $retrieveKey$ event by adding the following actions:

act5: $keyRetention(session) := keyRetention(session) \cup \{recipient\}$
act6: $isDecryptedWith(message) := privateKEYS(hasPublicKEYS(recipient))$

The $retrieveKey$ event retrieves the message containing the key and decrypts it with the corresponding private key (Fig. 5); The events described above are the first refinements of the send and receive message events. The second refinement of $sendMessage$ introduces a new action $(isEncryptedWith(counter + 1) := sessionKey(session))$ and the following new conditions, which are closely related to message encryption:

$$\{session\} \lhd sessionKey \neq \varnothing \wedge$$
$$service \in keyRetention(session) \wedge$$
$$sessionkeyValidity(session \mapsto sessionKey(session)) > 0$$

Similarly, the second refinement of $receiveMessage$ introduces a new action and guards to ensure the correct decryption of received messages.

event generateSessionKey **REFINES** sendMessage
any service recipient session key
where
...
grd7: $key \in sessionKEYS$
grd8: $sessionKey \rhd \{key\} = \varnothing \wedge \{recipient\} \lhd hasPublicKEYS \neq \varnothing$
Witness content: content={session,key}
then
...
act10:$sessionKey(session) := key$
act11:$keyRetention(session) := \{service\}$
act12:$isEncryptedWith(counter + 1) := hasPublicKEYS(recipient)$
act13:$sessionkeyValidity(session \mapsto key) := key\_expiry\_period$
end

Fig. 5. The $generateSessionKey$ event.

4 Correctness Verification of the *SPM4FOG* Model

The process of validating the correctness of the proposed $SPM4FOG$ is a critical step prior to its practical use. Such a process is done hand in hand with the modeling phase. It consists of discharging proof obligations (PO) generated by the Rodin platform [2] using proof rules such as Invariant Preservation (INV), Well-Definiteness (WD), Guard Strengthening (GRD), Action SIMulation (SIM) and feasibility (FIS) of the refined event.

WD rule states that each predicate (invariant, axiom, guard, action, function, etc.) in a machine/context must be well defined. For instance, $sendMessage/grd4/WD/$ ensures that $grd4$ guard of the abstract $sendMessage$ event of SD_m0 machine is well defined. It is automatically discharged. For the INV rule, it allows ensuring that:

- The invariant is valid after the initialization of a machine.
- Every enabled event from a state where the invariants are valid leads to a state where the invariants are still preserved.

The proof $activateSession/inv10/INV$ ensures that after activating a session, the $inv10$ invariant of the SPM_m1 machine must be preserved. To demonstrate this PO, we need to prove the following sequent:

$$
\begin{array}{l}
\text{Guards\_activateSession} \\
\vdash \\
\forall S \cdot s \in sessions \wedge sessionTTV(s) = 0 \wedge \\
(sessionStatus \lhd\!\!\!- \{session \mapsto Active\})(s) \neq Initial \\
\Rightarrow \\
(sessionStatus \lhd\!\!\!- session \mapsto Active)(s) = ValidationFailed
\end{array}
$$

This sequent is automatically discharged by the Rodin autoprovers. The SIM rule is applied when an action of an abstract event is modified in the refinement. For instance, the $openSession/act5/SIM$ proof expresses that the $act5$ of $openSession$ must be consistent with the $openSession$ action of the machine SPM_m1. If so, the new action simulates the abstract one. To demonstrate the above PO, we need to prove the following sequent:

$$
\begin{array}{l}
Guard\_openSession \\
\vdash \\
messageDestination \lhd\!\!\!- \{counter + 1 \mapsto trustedEntity\} \\
= \\
messageDestination \lhd\!\!\!- \{counter + 1 \mapsto trustedEntity\}
\end{array}
$$

This sequent is easy to prove with Rodin autoprovers. The last type of refinement proof rule in our model relates to guard strengthening (GRD).

Element Name	Tot.	Aut.	Man.	Rev.	Und.
SPM4FOG	**189**	**142**	**47**	**0**	**0**
SPM_c0	0	0	0	0	0
SPM_c1	1	1	0	0	0
SPM_c2	0	0	0	0	0
SPM_m0	60	56	4	0	0
SPM_m1	79	55	24	0	0
SPM_m2	49	30	19	0	0

Fig. 6. Statistics on the results of the proof phase of $SPM4FOG$ model.

Figure 6 shows that all the proof obligations generated during model construction are discharged by the provers. There are 194 obligations, 153 of which are automatically proved. The remaining 41 obligations are discharged interactively. It should be pointed out that the failure of the proof activity on the remaining POs is due to the many steps required to prove them due to their difficulty. To offload these proofs, we used interactive provers and guided them to find the right tactics and rules to apply. In addition, we made slight modifications to the model to facilitate the demonstration of certain complex proofs.

5 Related Work

The security problem of IoT systems has received particular attention in the last decade [13]. Many interesting approaches have been proposed to address this problem. In the following, we present a synthetic review of these approaches, highlighting their main limitations compared to ours.

The authors of [23] develop a correct-by-construction approach with Event-B for designing IoT architectures that integrate formal verification into the development process. Omri et al. [19] propose a formal Event-B-based method for verifying IoT components and their requirements, specifically adapted to the use of LoRaWAN technology. While these approaches ensure correctness by design, they do not focus on verifying security policies specific to fog environments or on defining concepts such as sessions and encryption.

The work proposed in [22] introduces a hybrid mechanism that combines real-time monitoring with testing techniques (in particular, fuzzy logic) to ensure the security of IoT applications. This approach relies on online monitoring and testing mechanisms, which can introduce significant operational overhead. In contrast, our $SPM4FOG$ model is based on formal modeling through incremental levels of abstraction and refinement, ensuring rigorous validation of security requirements at design time.

The authors of [9] propose a security analysis framework using model checking to identify vulnerabilities and verify security properties in IoT systems. Model checking is often limited by the state explosion problem and does not always address the complexity of interactions. Our Event B model, structured in several levels of refinement, provides a modular approach suitable for verifying security policies in complex fog environments.

In [16], the authors propose a model-checking-based method for verifying the security of protocols used by IoT devices and for detecting potential vulnerabilities. Like other similar approaches, it suffers from the state space explosion problem and is not directly applicable to the global verification of security policies in a fog environment with multiple levels of refinement.

The authors of [14] combine model checking and deep learning techniques to analyze and detect malware in IoT applications, providing a hybrid security approach. While innovative, this hybrid approach focuses on malware detection, while the $SPM4FOG$ model exhaustively verifies security policies and interactions between fog services.

In [10], a rewriting logic-based approach is proposed to formally verify IoT applications by translating their specifications into rewriting rules, thus facilitating the simulation of system behavior. It does not specifically target security policies for fog services, which have special requirements in terms of communication, session management, and encryption mechanisms.

In [6], the authors formally verify a reputation-based multi-factor authentication mechanism using temporal logic to ensure integrity and non-repudiation. This verification is limited to a specific authentication mechanism. Our work takes a more global view, covering several aspects of communication and security (session establishment and encryption) in fog services through a progressive structuring in levels.

Bae et al. [5] addressed security issues in medical IoT communication by proposing a security protocol validated with Casper/FDR, a formal process verification tool. The protocol employs cross-authentication and inter-device encryption to prevent various attacks, ensuring secure wireless connections between medical devices.

Boussada et al. [7] presented an innovative privacy-based solution for IoT in electronic health (e-health) that meets contextual and content privacy requirements. This solution is based on a specific communication scenario and a new identity-based encryption (IBE) scheme, considering the resource-limited nature of connected objects. The proposal is validated through formal analysis using BAN logic [8] and the AVISPA tool [4].

To sum up, the aforementioned studies provide a variety of approaches for verifying the security of IoT protocols and architectures, but none of them deals exhaustively with the security policies of Fog services using a formal refinement approach. Our $SPM4FOG$ model enables rigorous validation of the security requirements of Fog services while ensuring their gradual integration into complex IoT environments. It introduces specific concepts such as session management and message encryption, allowing the security requirements of Fog services to be formally validated at the design stage (secure-by-design).

6 Conclusion and Perspective

In this paper, we addressed the critical security challenges of developing IoT applications in Fog computing environments. The decentralized nature of Fog computing, while beneficial for reducing latency and improving efficiency, introduces significant vulnerabilities and security risks. To tackle these challenges, we proposed the correct Security Policy Model for Fog-based applications ($SPM4FOG$) using the Event-B formal method. Our model provides a comprehensive framework for industrial designers to validate security requirements during the design phase, enabling secure-by-design development of IoT applications.

We are currently working on extending the proposed $SPM4FOG$ model to include additional privacy requirements for Fog services. These requirements refer to the rules for granting access rights to the services' private data.

Acknowledgments. This work was supported by a French government grant managed by the Agence Nationale de la Recherche under the France 2030 program, reference ANR-23-PECL-0006.

References

1. Abrial, J.: Modeling in Event-B: System and Software Engineering. Cambridge edn. Cambridge University Press (2010)

2. Abrial J.-R., Butler M., H.S.: An open extensible tool environment for event-B. In: Liu, Z., He, J. (eds.) ICFEM 2006. LNCS, vol. 4260, pp. 588–605. Springer, Heidelberg (2006). https://doi.org/10.1007/11901433_32
3. Ali, A., Ahmed, M., Imran, M., Khattak, H.A.: Security and privacy issues in fog computing. Fog Comput. Theory Pract. 105–137 (2020)
4. Armando, A., et al.: The AVISPA tool for the automated validation of internet security protocols and applications. In: Etessami, K., Rajamani, S.K. (eds.) CAV 2005. LNCS, vol. 3576, pp. 281–285. Springer, Heidelberg (2002). https://doi.org/10.1007/11513988_27
5. Bae, W.S.: Verifying a secure authentication protocol for IoT medical devices. Clust. Comput. **22**, 1985–1990 (2019)
6. Bezerra, W.R., Martina, J.E., Westphall, C.B.: Formal verification of a reputation multi-factor authentication mechanism using temporal logic. Sensors **23**(15), 6933 (2023). https://doi.org/10.3390/s23156933
7. Boussada, Z., Challal, Y., Bouabdallah, A.: Privacy preserving IoT electronic health records using identity-based encryption. J. Netw. Comput. Appl. **141**, 79–88 (2019)
8. Burrows, M., Abadi, M., Needham, R.: A logic of authentication. ACM Trans. Comput. Syst. (TOCS) **8**(1), 18–36 (1989)
9. Fang, Z., et al.: A model checking-based security analysis framework for IoT systems. High-Confidence Comput. **1**, 100004 (2021). https://doi.org/10.1016/j.hcc.2021.100004
10. Fortas, A., Kerkouche, E., Chaoui, A.: Formal verification of IoT applications using rewriting logic. Sci. Comput. Program. **222**, 102859 (2022). https://doi.org/10.1016/j.scico.2022.102859
11. Gebremichael, T., et al.: Security and privacy in the industrial internet of things: current standards and future challenges. IEEE Access **8**, 152351–152366 (2020). https://doi.org/10.1109/ACCESS.2020.3016937
12. Girault, C., Valk, R.: Petri nets for Systems Engineering: A Guide to Modeling, Verification, and Applications. Springer, Heidelberg (2013). https://doi.org/10.1007/978-3-662-05324-9
13. Haddou-Oumouloud, I., Kriouile, A., Hamida, S., Ettalbi, A.: Towards secure and reliable IoT systems: a comprehensive review of formal methods applications. IEEE Access (2024)
14. Hamza, A.A., Abdel Halim, I.T., Sobh, M.A., Bahaa-Eldin, A.M.: HSAS-MD analyzer: a hybrid security analysis system using model checking technique and deep learning for malware detection in IoT apps. Sensors **22**(3), 1079 (2022). https://doi.org/10.3390/s22031079
15. Kaur, J., Agrawal, A., Khan, R.A.: Security issues in fog environment: a systematic literature review. Int. J. Wireless Inf. Networks **27**, 467–483 (2020)
16. Liu, Y., Zhang, W., Wang, H.: Security verification of IoT device protocols using model checking. IEEE Trans. Reliab. **69**(3), 1054–1070 (2020). https://doi.org/10.1109/TR.2020.2987423
17. Marlinspike, M., Perrin, T.: The Signal Protocol: Advanced Encryption for Mobile Messaging. Technical report, Signal Foundation (2016). https://signal.org/docs/
18. Meta Platforms, Inc.: WhatsApp Security Whitepaper (2022). https://www.whatsapp.com/security
19. Omri, R., Toman, Z.H., Hamel, L.: A formal verification model for iot based applications using event-b. In: Bădică, C., Treur, J., Benslimane, D., Hnatkowska, B., Krótkiewicz, M. (eds.) ICCCI 2022. CCIS, vol. 1653, pp. 528–541. Springer, Cham (2022). https://doi.org/10.1007/978-3-031-16210-7_43
20. Rezapour, R., Asghari, P., Javadi, H.H.S., Ghanbari, S.: Security in fog computing: a systematic review on issues, challenges and solutions. Comput. Sci. Rev. **41**, 100421 (2021)
21. Schneier, B.: Applied cryptography protocols. Algorithms and Source Code in C (1995)
22. Shieh, M.Z., Lin, Y.B., Hsu, Y.J.: Verificationtalk: a verification and security mechanism for IoT applications. Sensors **21**(22), 7449 (2021). https://doi.org/10.3390/s21227449

23. Toman, Z.H., Hamel, L., Toman, S.H., Graiet, M.: Correct-by-construction approach for formal verification of IoT architecture. Procedia Comput. Sci. **207**, 2598–2609 (2022). https://doi.org/10.1016/j.procs.2022.09.320
24. Zoom Video Communications: Zoom Encryption Whitepaper (2023). https://zoom.com/security

Convergence and Variability Assessment and Analysis of QGANs and GANs for Advanced Cybersecurity Applications: An Empirical Study

Md Abdur Rahman[1], Alfredo Cuzzocrea[2(✉)], and Hossain Shahriar[3]

[1] Department of Intelligent Systems and Robotics, University of West Florida, Pensacola, FL, USA
mr252@students.uwf.edu

[2] iDEA Lab, University of Calabria, Rende, Italy
alfredo.cuzzocrea@unical.it

[3] Center for Cybersecurity, University of West Florida, Pensacola, FL, USA
hshahriar@uwf.edu

Abstract. In this paper, we present a comprehensive empirical study on the convergence and variability of *Quantum Generative Adversarial Networks* (QGANs) compared to classical *Generative Adversarial Networks* (GANs) for advanced cybersecurity applications. Our methodology leverages both *real-life* and *GAN-generated synthetic* datasets to systematically assess loss function stability across extensive training epochs. By integrating *Quantum-inspired architectures* with classical discriminators, our proposed framework enables a fine-grained investigation of *Generator–Discriminator dynamics* and *entropy-based stability* metrics. Experimental findings highlight that QGANs consistently achieve lower and more stable generator loss values than traditional GANs, demonstrating enhanced robustness and reliability for cybersecurity tasks.

Keywords: Generative Adversarial Networks · Quantum Computing · Loss Functions · Entropy

1 Introduction

In today's digitally connected world, *Cybersecurity* has become a critical concern for governments, enterprises, and individuals alike (e.g., [4–6]). With the rapid proliferation of networked systems, Cloud platforms (e.g., [7]), and IoT infrastructures, the volume and complexity of cyber threats are increasing at an unprecedented pace. To combat these evolving challenges, *Machine Learning* (ML) and, more recently, *Deep Learning* (DL) techniques have been widely adopted for *intrusion detection*, *anomaly detection*, and *threat prediction* (e.g., [8,9]). Among these, *Generative Adversarial Networks* (GANs) have emerged as powerful generative models, capable of synthesizing realistic data samples and

I. Awan et al. (Eds.): WISE 2025, LNCS 16367, pp. 203–215, 2026.
https://doi.org/10.1007/978-981-95-7394-3_14

enhancing detection systems by addressing issues such as *class imbalance* and *limited data* (e.g., [28]).

However, despite their promising applications, traditional GANs face fundamental challenges during training. Among these drawbacks are *instability*, *mode collapse*, and *fluctuating loss behaviors*, which hinder their ability to consistently generate reliable synthetic datasets for cybersecurity tasks (e.g., [11–14]). As the complexity of cyber datasets increases, ranging from classical benchmark datasets to more sophisticated modern benchmarks, the convergence behavior of GANs becomes increasingly difficult to manage. This instability not only limits their applicability in real-life scenarios but also raises concerns about the robustness of *GAN-enhanced cybersecurity models* [9].

To address these limitations, researchers have begun exploring *Quantum Generative Adversarial Networks* (QGANs), which combine the representational power of classical GANs with the computational advantages of *Quantum Computing*. QGANs leverage quantum properties such as superposition and entanglement, enabling richer feature representations and potentially faster convergence in high-dimensional data environments [19–22]. Early studies have shown that QGANs can mitigate some of the instability issues found in classical GANs, while producing synthetic data with improved fidelity [2,18]. Nevertheless, the convergence patterns and variability of QGAN loss functions remain underexplored, especially in the context of cybersecurity datasets where stability is paramount.

Recent research also highlights the growing role of *Quantum Machine Learning* (QML) in strengthening cybersecurity. In the study by Masum *et al.* [15], software supply chain attacks were detected using QML techniques, demonstrating that approaches such as *Quantum Support Vector Machines* (QSVM) and *Quantum Neural Networks* (QNN) can accelerate quantum computing performance and enhance resilience against cyber threats. Similarly, Faruk *et al.* [16] provide a comprehensive review of relevant quantum computing applications, emphasizing its potential in addressing software security, cybersecurity, and cryptographic challenges. At the same time, this research affirms that quantum computing may also be misused by adversaries to target software infrastructures, thus introducing new risks to cybersecurity.

Furthermore, several research efforts have investigated the integration of GANs and *Quantum-inspired approaches* for enhancing security analytics. For instance, *conditional GANs* (cGANs) [10] and *Wasserstein GANs* (WGANs) (e.g., [13,14]) have introduced improved stability mechanisms, while quantum neural networks and variational quantum circuits have been applied to security tasks such as malware detection and supply chain risk assessment [15,16]. Yet, comparative empirical studies examining QGANs and GANs side by side, particularly from the perspective of convergence and loss variability, are still limited. This gap motivates the need for a deeper investigation into how QGANs beh.

Following these considerations, in this paper, we present a systematic empirical study of GANs and QGANs applied to two prominent cybersecurity datasets, UNSW and NSL-KDD. Our methodology employs both real and GAN-generated synthetic datasets to examine convergence dynamics across extensive training epochs. By conducting a rigorous comparison between QGANs and GANs, our study provides fresh insights into their effectiveness for advanced cybersecurity applications. Moreover, this paper extends the previous short paper [30].

2 Datasets Descriptions

UNSW and *NSL-KDD* datasets are well-regarded in the field of cybersecurity, serving as vital resources for evaluating intrusion detection systems and propelling research in network security.

2.1 UNSW Dataset

The *UNSW dataset* contains a diverse set of features, each contributing to the task of cybersecurity, such as intrusion detection and anomaly classification. Among the important features in the dataset are: (*i*) *Protocol Type*: This feature characterizes the network protocols utilized in the communication, including TCP, UDP, ICMP, etc. It plays a crucial role in identifying different types of attacks targeting specific protocols; (*ii*) *Service*: The service feature indicates the specific network services used, such as HTTP, FTP, SMTP, etc. Analyzing this feature helps in understanding network activities and detecting abnormal behavior; (*iii*) *Source and Destination IP Addresses*: These features identify the source and destination IP addresses involved in network communication. Analyzing these addresses helps detect suspicious patterns or connections from potential malicious sources; (*iv*) *Source and Destination Ports*: These features represent the application ports used for network communication. Anomalies or uncommon port numbers can indicate potential attacks; (*v*) *Duration*: The duration feature indicates the time span of network connections. Long-duration connections may raise suspicions of malicious activities; (*vi*) *Bytes*: The number of bytes transferred during network connections is recorded. Large data transfers can be indicative of suspicious or malicious activities; (*vii*) *Packets*: The number of packets exchanged during network connections is recorded. Unusual packet patterns could be indicative of attacks; (*viii*) *Lags*: The flags feature represents the TCP control flags used in network connections. Unusual flag combinations may suggest attempts to exploit vulnerabilities; (*ix*) *Labels*: The dataset contains labels that categorize network connections as either normal or malicious, identifying different attack types. This feature is essential for supervised learning tasks and evaluating intrusion detection models.

2.2 NSL-KDD Dataset

In *NSL-KDD dataset*, the training subset comprises 125,973 records; however, there are 22,544 records in the test subset. To enhance our understanding the attacks from the dataset's attributes, several protocol types as opposed to attack types are defined. For this work, we extracted the features for this supervised model: `protocol\_type`, `service`, `src\_bytes`, `dst\_bytes`, `dst\_host\_srv\_count`, `dst\_host\_same\_srv\_rate`, `dst\_host\_diff\_srv\_rate`, and `dst\_host\_same\_src\_port\_rate`. The attribute *attack* is chosen for target variables. These attacks fall into four primary categories, as described below: (*i*) *Denial-of-Service* (DoS): This category includes attacks like syn flood, aiming to overwhelm and disrupt services, making them inaccessible to legitimate users; (*ii*) *Unauthorized Remote Access* (R2L): Attacks in this category involve unauthorized access attempts from remote machines, often employing techniques like password guessing to breach security barriers; (*iii*) *Unauthorized Local Access* (U2R): This category entails attacks seeking unauthorized access to local superuser (root) privileges, using techniques like "buffer overflow" attacks to exploit vulnerabilities and elevate privileges; (*iv*) *Probing*: Attacks in this category involve surveillance and probing activities, such as port scanning, where attackers try to gather information about potential system vulnerabilities.

3 Quantum Computing: Fundamentals and Loss Functions

Quantum computing utilizes qubits, the building blocks of information, to perform intricate computations based on quantum mechanics. A quantum bit (qubit) exhibits unique characteristics distinct from a classical bit. Classical bits have binary states, 0 and 1, while qubits can occupy a continuous range of states between $|0\rangle$ and $|1\rangle$, represented in Dirac notation.

It is observed that the sophisticated software programs allow researchers and developers to execute and thoroughly test quantum algorithms on classical computers, which replicates the behavior of quantum computers. This enables exploration of quantum computing intricacies without physical quantum hardware. These ongoing advancements in quantum technology will make commercial quantum computers accessible, which empowers users to directly run applications on these cutting-edge machines. This future holds immense potential to solve complex problems swiftly and efficiently, which revolutionizes cryptography, optimization, drug discovery, and more. The widespread use of quantum computers is offering profound opportunities for cybersecurity.

Loss functions are fundamental components in the training of GANs and QGans. In GANs, binary cross-entropy is employed to optimize the discriminator and generator, while QGANs utilize diverse loss functions, such as Jensen-Shannon divergence, to quantify the disparity between real and generated quantum distributions. The selection of effective loss functions is vital for ensuring stable convergence and generating superior synthetic data in both GANs and QGANs.

The origin of GANs can be attributed to the groundbreaking research conducted by Goodfellow *et al.* in 2014 [8]. GANs feature a unique architectural framework, comprising two key components: a generative network denoted as G and a discriminative network referred to as D. The generative network G serves as a creator by taking a random noise vector, z, as input, adhering to either a

Gaussian or uniform distribution. Employing a sophisticated mapping mechanism, the generator G transforms z into a novel probability distribution, generating synthetic samples represented as $G(z)$. Inspired by game theory, GANs operate as a competitive interplay between the generator and the discriminator. The primary objective of the generator is to produce synthetic samples that closely resemble real data, effectively deceiving the discriminator D. Conversely, the discriminator strives to discern between fake and authentic samples.

QGANs have emerged as algorithmic frameworks that integrate classical and quantum elements, amalgamating GANs and Quantum Machine Learning. In 2018, the QGAL protocol was proposed by Lloyd *et al.* [20], which explored potential scenarios for adversarial learning and speculated on the possibility of QGANs achieving quantum supremacy and unlocking unprecedented computational capacities. To address the limitations of classical GANs in generating discrete data, Situ *et al.* [29] proposed an innovative solution in October 2018. They integrated quantum Born rules into QGANs, complementing classical GAN theory and enhancing the efficacy of discrete data generation. In January 2019, Hu *et al.* [X] successfully implemented QGANs within a superconducting quantum circuit, achieving an impressive fidelity of 98.8% between the generated quantum state and the actual quantum state. This groundbreaking achievement highlighted the exponential advantage QGANs hold over their classical counterparts.

4 A Methodology for Assessing and Analyzing Convergence and Variability of QGANs and GANs in Cybersecurity

Our research successfully employed two neural networks, specifically a quantum generator and a classical discriminator, to accomplish our goal. The quantum generator utilized a quantum neural network, while the classical discriminator was implemented using PyTorch. To optimize hardware efficiency, we adopted a *hardware-efficient ansatz* with six repetitions for the quantum generator. This analysis involved parameterized quantum circuits with R_Y and R_Z rotations, as well as C_X gates, which is built upon the dataset observations as input states.

We were very careful in selection of generator parameters, considering circuit depth, which enables the incorporation of more intricate structures. This deeper circuit depth plays a pivotal role in accurately capturing and representing the observations, which helps comprehensive analysis. The quantum generator with chosen ansatz and its corresponding parameters collaborated with the classical discriminator implemented in PyTorch. Both models were trained using a manual implementation of the binary cross-entropy loss function to assess gradients.

We proposed the integrated framework (see Fig. 1) in which high-quality synthetic data is successfully generated from existing datasets using GANs. The process involved in the strengths of GANs to create synthetic data that closely mirrors the characteristics of the original datasets. This synthetic dataset, along with the existing dataset, was then fed separately into typical QGANs to examine the convergence behaviors of their respective loss functions with the convergence behaviors by GANs. By comparing the performance of QGANs when trained on both synthetic and original datasets, we aimed to gain deeper insights into their learning dynamics and effectiveness. The results highlighted the potential of synthetic data in enhancing the training process and provided valuable information on how QGANs can adapt to different data sources. This integrated approach underscores the importance of combining classical and quantum machine learning techniques to address complex data challenges in cybersecurity.

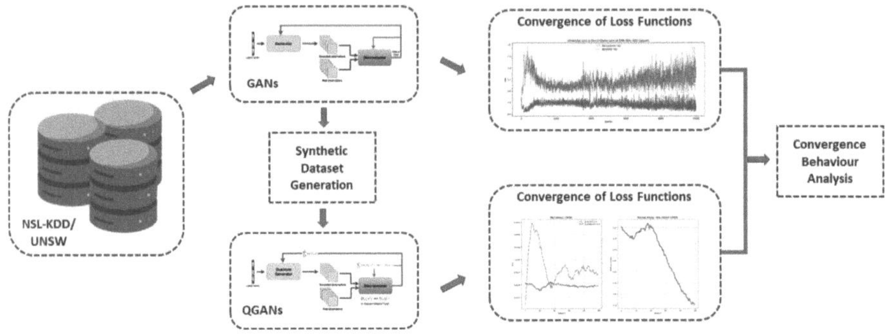

Fig. 1. Proposed Methodology: Logical Scheme.

5 Empirical Evaluation and Results

In our research, we utilized Google Colab as a powerful computing platform to perform quantum computations and implement classical ML as well as Quantum ML. Google Colab provides a cloud-based environment with access to quantum computing resources which enables us to leverage quantum capabilities for our experiments. With the aid of user-friendly interface and integration with QGAN libraries, we efficiently executed the QGAN algorithms and conducted quantum simulations in Colab. This enabled us to explore the potential of QGANs and quantum computing in generating synthetic data and advancing research in the field of quantum machine learning. Access to quantum processors is typically provided through the Google Quantum Computing service through the Quantum Computing API which allows users to submit quantum circuits and execute them. We trained classical ML with cyber dataset, and then QML will be trained to observe the stability as well as convergence.

Firstly, classical ML has consistently higher losses for UNSW dataset than the NSL-KDD dataset. While training the generator and the discriminator of GANs, we observed that ML encounters greater challenges and difficulties in generating synthetic data than QML. It is also noted that the higher loss values suggest a higher degree of fluctuations and potentially slower convergence during training, which may be attributed to the complexity and variability of the UNSW dataset. In contrast, the NSL-KDD dataset appears to be more stable to the GANs model.

Figure 2 shows how loss values were fluctuating for Generator and Discriminator in GANs with two datasets for different epochs: 100, 1000, and 10000. Also, Table 1 provides a summary of the GANs training results for both the datasets. The table includes information on the dataset, the type of network (generator or discriminator), epochs and the minimum and maximum loss values recorded during training.

Table 1. GAN Losses (Epoch 10000 - Real Datasets)

Dataset	Network	Min. loss	Max. loss
UNSW	Generator	0.33	14.45
	Discriminator	0.12	2.6
NSL-KDD	Generator	0.32	2.9
	Discriminator	0.1	1.2

For the UNSW dataset, the generator got a minimum loss of 0.33 and a maximum loss is 14.45, while the discriminator has a minimum loss and a maximum loss which are 0.12 and 2.6. On the other hand, for the NSL-KDD dataset, a minimum loss is 0.32 for the generator and a maximum loss is 2.9 for the discriminator, while a minimum loss and maximum losses are 0.1 and 1.2, respectively. These outcomes suggest that the GAN model faced higher losses for the UNSW dataset compared to the NSL-KDD dataset, both in terms of generator and discriminator losses. This could indicate that the GANs model struggled more with the complexity and variability of the UNSW dataset, which results in higher fluctuations and potentially slower convergence during training.

During QGANs training, the loss function progress of the generator and the discriminator (left column) is illustrated for real and synthetic datasets (UNSW), and the right column displays the convergence of the relative entropy for real and synthetic datasets for various epochs in Fig. 3. Table 2 presents the loss functions during the training of two networks, namely the Generator and Discriminator, for the UNSW dataset. The loss values are recorded as the minimum (Min. loss) and maximum (Max. loss) achieved during the training process. Additionally, the stability of each network is indicated by the Stable column. For the Generator network trained on real data, the minimum loss achieved is 0.602, while the maximum loss is 0.730, with a stable value of 0.693. The Discriminator network trained on real data exhibits a minimum loss of 0.688, a maximum loss of 0.698, and a stable value of 0.692.

On the other hand, when the Generator network is trained on synthetic data, the minimum loss obtained is 0.666, while the maximum loss reaches 0.806. The stable value for the Generator network with synthetic data is 0.694. The

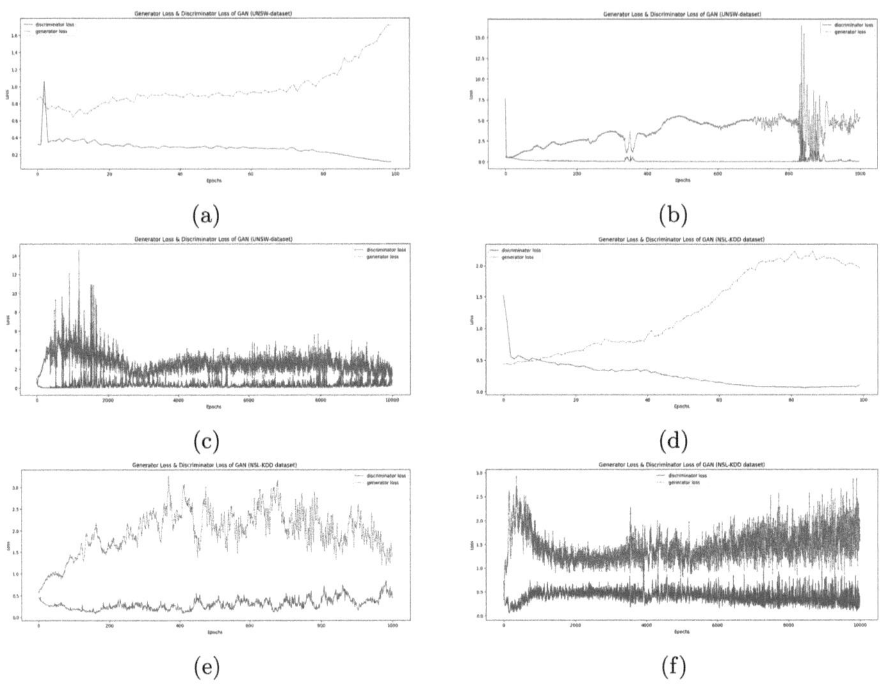

Fig. 2. Loss Functions while Dataset Training by GANs: (a) UNSW - 100 Ep. (b) UNSW - 1000 Ep. (c) UNSW - 10000 Ep. (d) NSL-KDD - 100 Ep. (e) NSL-KDD - 1000 Ep. (f) NSL-KDD - 10000 Ep.

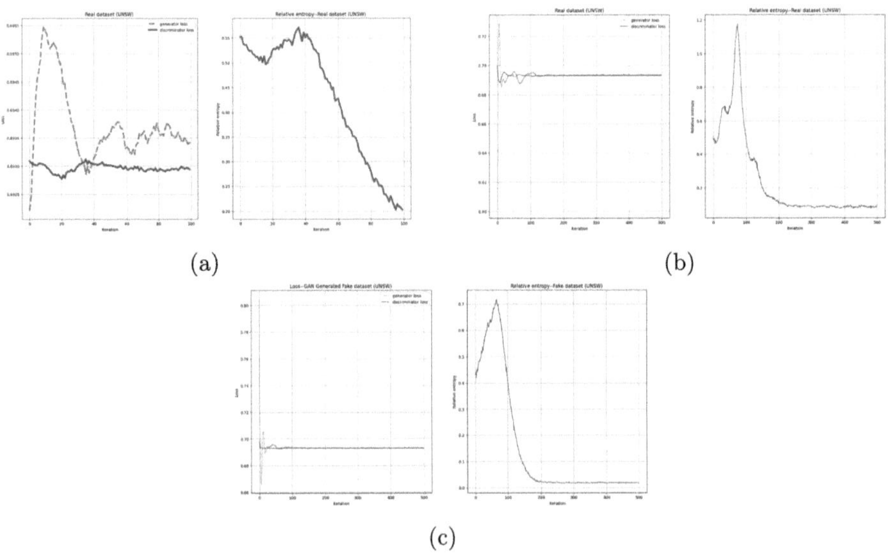

Fig. 3. Loss and Entropy Functions while Dataset Training by QGANs: (a) UNSW - 100 Ep. (b) UNSW - 500 Ep. (c) Synthetic Dataset - 500 Ep.

Table 2. QGAN Losses (UNSW Dataset)

Networks	Dataset	Min. loss	Max. loss	Stable
Generator	Real	0.602	0.730	0.693
Discriminator	Real	0.688	0.698	0.692
Generator	Synthetic	0.666	0.806	0.694
Discriminator	Synthetic	0.692	0.697	0.694

Discriminator network, when trained on synthetic data, has a minimum loss of 0.692, a maximum loss of 0.697, and a stable value of 0.694. Overall, the presented table provides valuable information about the loss functions and stability of the Generator and Discriminator networks during the training process on the UNSW dataset.

In the case of QGANs training, the loss function progress of the generator and the discriminator (left column) is illustrated for real and synthetic datasets (NSL-KDD), and the right column displays the convergence of the relative entropy for real and synthetic datasets for various epochs in Fig. 4. Table 3 displays the loss functions observed during the training of two networks, the Generator and Discriminator, on the NSL-KDD dataset. It includes the minimum (Min. loss) and maximum (Max. loss) loss values achieved during the training process, along with the stability (Stable) of each network.

Table 3. QGAN Losses (KDD Dataset)

Networks	Dataset	Min. loss	Max. loss	Stable
Generator	Real	0.675	0.753	0.693
Discriminator	Real	0.691	0.696	0.693
Generator	Synthetic	0.678	0.802	0.694
Discriminator	Synthetic	0.692	0.696	0.694

For the Generator network trained on real data from the NSL-KDD dataset, the minimum loss recorded is 0.675, while the maximum loss is 0.753. The stable value for the Generator network with real data is 0.693. The Discriminator network, when trained on real data, exhibits a minimum loss of 0.691, a maximum loss of 0.696, and a stable value of 0.693. Similarly, when the Generator network is trained on synthetic data from the NSL-KDD dataset, the minimum loss attained is 0.678, and the maximum loss is 0.802. The stable value for the Generator network with synthetic data is 0.694. On the other hand, the Discriminator network, when trained on synthetic data, demonstrates a minimum loss of 0.692, a maximum loss of 0.696, and a stable value of 0.694. In summary, the table provides a concise overview of the loss functions and the stability of the

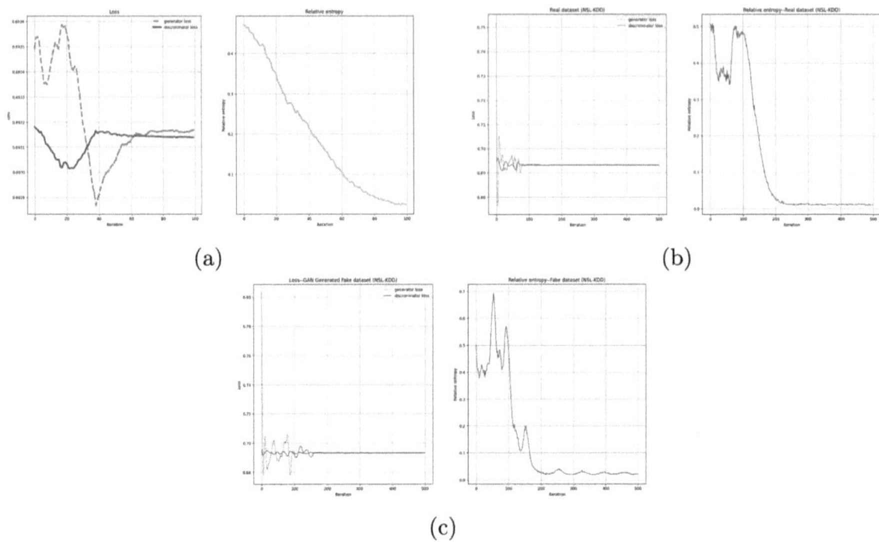

Fig. 4. Loss and Entropy Functions while Dataset Training by QGANs: (*a*) NSL-KDD - 100 Ep. (*b*) NSL-KDD - 500 Ep. (*c*) Synthetic Dataset - 500 Ep.

Generator and Discriminator networks during their training on the NSL-KDD dataset.

Table 4 presents a comparative analysis of entropy values across different datasets, data types, and epochs, providing insights into the level of uncertainty and randomness in the generated data and the discriminator's classification decisions during the training of the QGAN. In the case of UNSW dataset and epochs 500, the generator gets a minimum and maximum values of relative entropy were 0.07 and 1.19 and these values are 0.04 and 0.72 for the synthetic dataset. On the other hand, for the NSL-KDD dataset, a minimum and maximum relative entropy are 0.02 and 0.52, respectively. For the synthetic dataset, 0.03 and 0.69 are the values of minimum and maximum relative entropy, respectively.

Table 4. QGAN Entropy

Dataset-Name	Type	Epochs	Max. diff.	Min. diff.
UNSW	Real	100	0.56	0.21
	Real	500	1.19	0.07
	Synthetic	500	0.72	0.04
NSL-KDD	Real	100	0.48	0.21
	Real	500	0.52	0.02
	Synthetic	500	0.69	0.03

Based on the presented results, it can be concluded that QGANs demonstrate greater stability in generating synthetic datasets compared to traditional GANs when applied to cyber datasets. These research findings have significant implications in the realm of cybersecurity, as QGANs improved stability aids in preventing adversarial attacks by producing more reliable and robust synthetic data.

6 Conclusions

This paper presented a comparative analysis of the stability of loss functions in GANs and QGANs for two prominent cybersecurity datasets. We investigated the convergence behavior and variability of loss functions during the training process. Experimental results indicate that the instability of the loss function is more pronounced in the UNSW dataset compared to the NSL-KDD dataset. The observed discrepancy in loss function behavior highlights the challenges associated with achieving stable convergence during training. The wider range of generator loss values in GANs indicates increased fluctuation and potentially slower convergence. Conversely, QGAN demonstrates superior stability, maintaining consistently lower generator loss values and exhibiting smaller variations for both datasets.

Acknowledgments. This work was partially supported by the National Science Foundation (NSF) Award#2433800, #1946442, and SERICS project (PE00000014) under the MUR National Recovery and Resilience Plan funded by the European Union - NextGenerationEU.

References

1. Arute, F., et al.: Quantum supremacy using a programmable superconducting processor. Nature **574**(7779), 505–510 (2019)
2. Rahman, M.A., Shahriar, H., Clincy, V., Hossain, M.F., Rahman, M.: A Quantum Generative Adversarial Network-based Intrusion Detection System. In: IEEE COMPSAC 2023, pp. 1810–1815 (2023)
3. Rahman, M.A., Akter, M.S., Miller, E., Timofti, B., et al.: Fine-tuned variational quantum classifiers for cyber attacks detection based on parameterized quantum circuits and optimizers. In: IEEE COMPSAC 2024, pp. 1810–1815 (2024)
4. Rahman, M.A.: Detection of distributed denial of service attacks based on machine learning algorithms. Int. J. Smart Home **14**(2), 15–24 (2020)
5. Azad, M.A.K., Khatun, A., Rahman, M.A.: A slotted-sense streaming MAC for real-time multimedia data transmission in industrial wireless sensor networks. Int. J. Adv. Eng. Res. Sci. **4**(3), 237103 (2017)
6. Akter, M.S., Shahriar, H., Rahman, M.A., Rahman, M., Cuzzocrea, A.: Early prediction of cryptocurrency price decline: a deep learning approach. In: IEEE ICCIT 2023, pp. 1–6 (2023)

7. Rahman, M.A., Shahriar, H.: Clustering enabled robust intrusion detection system for big data using Hadoop–PySpark. In: IEEE HONET 2023, pp. 249–254 (2023)
8. Goodfellow, I.J., et al.: Generative adversarial nets. In: Advances in Neural Information Processing Systems, vol. 27 (2014)
9. Rahman, M.A., Shahrier, H.: Towards developing generative adversarial networks based robust intrusion detection systems for imbalanced dataset using Hadoop-PySpark. In: ICR 2024, pp. 449–463 (2024)
10. Mirza, M., Osindero, S.: Conditional generative adversarial nets. CoRR abs/1411.1784 (2014)
11. Radford, A., Metz, L., Chintala, S.: Unsupervised representation learning with deep convolutional generative adversarial networks. In: ICLR 2016 (2016)
12. Mao, X., Li, Q., Xie, H., Lau, R.Y.K., Wang, Z., Smolley, S.P.: Least squares generative adversarial networks. In: IEEE ICCV 2017, pp. 2813–2821 (2017)
13. Arjovsky, M., Bottou, L.: Towards principled methods for training generative adversarial networks. In: ICLR 2017 (2017)
14. Arjovsky, M., Chintala, S., Bottou, L.: Wasserstein GAN. CoRR abs/1701.07875 (2017)
15. Masum, M., et al.: Quantum machine learning for software supply chain attacks: how far can we go? In: IEEE COMPSAC 2022, pp. 530–538 (2022)
16. Faruk, M.J.H., Tahora, S., Tasnim, M., Shahriar, H., Sakib, N.: A review of quantum cybersecurity: threats, risks and opportunities. In: IEEE ICAIC 2022, pp. 1–8 (2022)
17. Akter, M.S., Shahriar, H., Bhuiya, Z.A.: Automated vulnerability detection in source code using quantum natural language processing. In: UbiSec 2022, pp. 83–102 (2022)
18. Akter, M.S., Shahriar, H., Iqbal, I., et al.: Exploring the vulnerabilities of machine learning and quantum machine learning to adversarial attacks using a malware dataset: a comparative analysis. In: IEEE SSE 2023, pp. 222–231 (2023)
19. Mitarai, K., Negoro, M., Kitagawa, M., Fujii, K.: Quantum circuit learning. Phys. Rev. A **98**(3), 032309 (2018)
20. Lloyd, S., Mohseni, M., Rebentrost, P.: Quantum principal component analysis. Nat. Phys. **10**(9), 631–633 (2014)
21. Stein, S.A., et al.: QuGAN: a quantum state fidelity based generative adversarial network. In: IEEE QCE 2021, pp. 71–81 (2021)
22. Huang, H., et al.: Experimental quantum generative adversarial networks for image generation. Phys. Rev. Appl. **16**(2), 024051 (2021)
23. Cuzzocrea, A., Chakravarthy, S.: Event-based lossy compression for effective and efficient OLAP over data streams. Data Knowl. Eng. **69**(7), 678–708 (2010)
24. Cuzzocrea, A., Furfaro, F., Greco, S., Masciari, E., Mazzeo, G.M., Sacca, D.: A distributed system for answering range queries on sensor network data. In: IEEE PerComW 2005, pp. 369–373 (2005)
25. Cuzzocrea, A., Russo, V., Sacca, D.: A robust sampling-based framework for privacy preserving OLAP. In: DaWaK 2008, pp. 97–114 (2008)
26. Cuzzocrea, A., Sacca, D., Serafino, P.: A hierarchy-driven compression technique for advanced OLAP visualization of multidimensional data cubes. In: DaWaK 2006, pp. 106–119 (2006)
27. Cannataro, M., Cuzzocrea, A., Mastroianni, C., Ortale, R., Pugliese, A.: Modeling adaptive hypermedia with an object-oriented approach and XML. In: WebDyn@WWW 2002, pp. 35–44 (2002)

28. Masum, M., et al.: Bayesian hyperparameter optimization for deep neural network-based network intrusion detection. In: IEEE BigData 2021, pp. 5413–5419 (2021)
29. Situ, H., He, Z., Wang, Y., Li, L., Zheng, S.: Quantum generative adversarial network for generating discrete distribution. Inf. Sci. **538**, 193–208 (2020)
30. Rahman, M.A., Cuzzocrea, A., Shahriar, H.: Convergence behaviors and variabilities of loss functions in quantum GANs and GANs. In: IEEE ICDCS 2025 (2025)

MOMA-DPK: A Multi-Objective Memetic Algorithm for Privacy-Utility Trade-Offs in Differentially Private K-Means Clustering

Samsad Jahan[1], Wei Hong[1], Yong-Feng Ge[1(✉)], Hua Wang[1], Enamul Kabir[2], and Changjun Zhou[3]

[1] Institute for Sustainable Industries and Liveable Cities, Victoria University, Melbourne 3011, Australia
{samsad.jahan,wei.hong2}@live.vu.edu.au, {yongfeng.ge,hua.wang}@vu.edu.au
[2] School of Mathematics, Physics and Computing, University of Southern Queensland, Toowoomba, Australia
enamul.kabir@usq.edu.au
[3] School of Computer Science and Technology, Zhejiang Normal University, Jinhua, China
zhouchangjun@zjnu.edu.cn

Abstract. In today's contexts, protecting sensitive information while maintaining usability necessitates privacy-preserving data mining. The Differential Privacy (DP)-based K-means algorithm can achieve this balance by tuning the privacy budget allocation. However, optimizing the privacy budget allocation is a complex task, as it involves striking a balance between privacy protection, data mining performance, and computational efficiency. Motivated by the fact that Evolutionary Algorithms (EAs) can efficiently produce near-optimal solutions, this paper proposes MOMA-DPK, a multi-objective memetic algorithm designed to optimize the allocation of privacy budgets in DP-based K-means clustering. The method balances two competing objectives: maximizing privacy protection by minimizing the total privacy budget spent and preserving clustering utility by minimizing error through the Normalized Intra-Cluster Variance (NICV) metric. By integrating Multi-Objective Optimization (MOO) with an imbalanced local search strategy, MOMA-DPK efficiently explores the privacy-utility trade-off and produces a Pareto front of optimal solutions. Experiments on real-world datasets (heart disease and diabetes) demonstrate that MOMA-DPK consistently outperforms baseline methods—including Naive-DPK, GA-DPK, and NSGA-II-DPK—achieving superior privacy-utility trade-offs and higher hypervolume scores. The source code used in this study is publicly available at https://github.com/Wayne-on-the-road/MOMA-DPK.

Keywords: Differential privacy · Clustering · Memetic algorithm · Privacy and utility · Multi-objective optimization

I. Awan et al. (Eds.): WISE 2025, LNCS 16367, pp. 216–230, 2026.
https://doi.org/10.1007/978-981-95-7394-3_15

1 Introduction

The rapid expansion of data collection and digitization across various industries, including banking, healthcare, and e-business, has increased both the complexity and volume of sensitive data being collected and processed in this age of big data. The significant growth in data is resulting in heightened vulnerabilities, which, in turn, are contributing to a rise in data breaches and global privacy concerns [8,18,25]. Traditional data privacy-preserving measures, such as k-anonymity [22], l-diversity [17], and their variants usually conceal data by generalizing quasi-identifiers; however, these models depend on the attacker's prior knowledge and do not make any valid assumptions about the attack models. On the other hand, Differential Privacy (DP) [3] has shown some advantages in privacy-preserving fields, as its well-defined attack model helps mitigate background knowledge attacks and provides a measurable representation of privacy leakage.

For this reason, researchers adopted DP in the data mining field to preserve the privacy of data or algorithms. The K-means clustering algorithm within the context of DP serves as a notable example of DP's application in the domain of data privacy [14,28]. Previous studies on DP K-means algorithm primarily focus on improving the process of selecting initial centroids [14,20,24]. However, their iterative process also leads to convergence issues and reduces utility due to excessive noise addition. Moreover, the total privacy budget ε is the parameter that controls the level of protection in DP K-means algorithm. Researchers have focused on this parameter by investigating various strategies for allocating it throughout different iterative rounds of the DP K-means clustering algorithm [4]. Current methods for allocating privacy budgets in DP K-means algorithm primarily rely on empirical or heuristic strategies, such as using arithmetic or geometric sequences to distribute the budget in each iteration [4]. These approaches do not always result in optimal allocation nor effectively balance the trade-off between privacy and utility.

At the same time, Evolutionary Algorithms (EAs) have demonstrated their efficiency in solving complex optimization problems as well as finding near-optimal solutions for privacy and data utility [7,9–13,26]. However, existing EA-based DP K-means algorithms generally adopt single-objective optimization approaches, which fail to lay out the privacy-utility trade-off dynamically for institutions to assume specific options based on their privacy leakage tolerance [14,19,23].

To overcome the above limitations and motivated by the fact that the local search strategy in the Memetic Algorithm (MA) can refine the solution with better quality, in this article, we propose a Multi-Objective Optimization (MOO) method with MA to find out the trade-off between privacy and utility in the DP K-means algorithm, where minimizing the spent privacy budget and maximizing the clustering utility is formulated as an MOO problem. Therefore, our contributions are listed as follows:

1. We propose a multi-objective definition for the privacy-preserving clustering problem to find a better trade-off between privacy and clustering utility.

2. We propose a novel Multi-Objective Memetic Algorithm for Differentially Private K-means Clustering (MOMA-DPK), which utilizes an imbalanced local search strategy to achieve better solution refinement than the standard MOO method.
3. Extensive experiments on real-life datasets demonstrate the superiority of our proposed algorithm over baseline DP K-means algorithms, providing a trade-off overview for institutions to tailor their privacy protection strategies.

The rest of the sections are organized as follows: Sect. 2 describes the theoretical overview, Sect. 3 presents the details of the proposed algorithm, Sect. 4 showcases the experimental outcome, and finally Sect. 5 concludes the whole paper.

2 Theoretical Overview

This section presents an in-depth overview of the application scenario, the K-means algorithm, the DP K-means algorithm and the MA.

2.1 Scenario

The entire workflow of publishing health data is shown in Fig. 1. Suppose a hospital wants to publish its patient records for research purposes, to identify the patterns of chronic diseases like diabetes or heart disease. The hospital's primary objective is to share information by clustering the patients into equivalent groups based on the clinical data, such as age, blood pressure, cholesterol levels, etc., to ensure improved diagnosis and treatment facilities. However, the recipients may not be considered reliable, and by leveraging background information, they may attempt to infer the original data. Integrating machine learning techniques with the DP strategy, like the DP K-means algorithm, could mitigate potential privacy breaches.

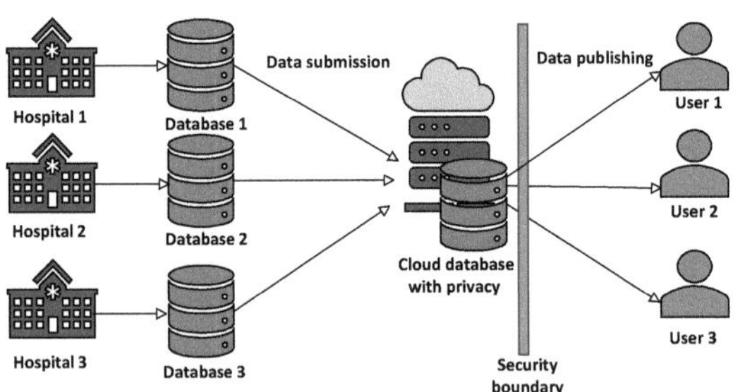

Fig. 1. An entire process of publishing health data with privacy-preserving measures.

2.2 DP K-Means Algorithm

The K-means algorithm is a common unsupervised machine learning technique that divides the dataset into k distinct groups. Let $D = p_1, p_2, ..., p_n$ be a dataset, where each data point p_j represents a vector within a d-dimensional space. The K-means algorithm aims to identify a set of cluster centroids $\{c_i\}_{i=1}^{k}$ that minimize the objective function known as the Sum of Squared Errors (SSE).

$$SSE = \sum_{i=1}^{k} \sum_{p_j \in C_i} \|p_j - c_i\|^2 \tag{1}$$

where k is the number of clusters, C_i is the set of points in cluster i, p_j is a data point in cluster C_i, c_i is the centroid of the ith cluster, and $\|p_j - c_i\|^2$ represents the Euclidean Distance (ED) between the data point p_j and the centroid c_i.

Safeguarding privacy is crucial in certain sensitive scenarios, such as clustering for detection or creating customer profiles in business research involving confidential data. Therefore, DP is implemented in the K-means algorithm to ensure the privacy of the cluster centroid. This approach explicitly incorporates a minimum quantity of noise into the sum p_j of data points inside the cluster and the count $|C_i|$ of elements in the cluster during the update of the centroid stage of the K-means algorithm, therefore ensuring the protection of privacy for the centroid. The mathematical definition of DP is as follows [3]:

Definition 1 (Differential Privacy). *For any two adjacent datasets D_1 and D_2 that vary by a single record, and for a given privacy mechanism, M is said to follow ε-DP if for all S subsets of M it satisfies the following condition:*

$$P[M(D_1) \in S] \leq e^{\varepsilon} \times P[M(D_2) \in S] \tag{2}$$

where the parameter ε is an adjustable privacy budget parameter that specifies the degree of privacy protection. A lower value of ε indicates better privacy protection for the dataset. We have used the Laplace mechanism in designing our algorithm. This mechanism ensures the ε-DP by including random noise that follows the Laplace distribution into the query result. The Laplace mechanism is defined as follows:

Definition 2 (Laplace Mechanism). *Let D represent a dataset and q be a query function with global sensitivity Δq. The randomized method ensures ε-DP protection with a response output $M(D)$ of:*

$$M(D) = q(D) + Lap\left(\frac{\Delta q}{\varepsilon}\right) \tag{3}$$

where Lap $\left(\frac{\Delta q}{\varepsilon}\right)$ represents random noise that follows the Laplace distribution with a scale value $a = \frac{\Delta q}{\varepsilon}$ and Δq is expressed as follows:

$$\Delta q = \max_{D_1, D_2} \|q(D_1) - q(D_2)\|_1 \tag{4}$$

Now, the centroid of the DP K-means algorithm using Laplace noise can be updated as follows [14,15]:

$$c_i^* = \frac{P_i^*}{|C_i^*|} = \frac{\sum_{p_j \in C_i} p_j + \text{Lap}\left(\frac{\Delta q}{\varepsilon_p}\right)}{|C_i| + \text{Lap}\left(\frac{\Delta q}{\varepsilon_c}\right)} \tag{5}$$

where c_i^* denotes the centroid of cluster i with noise, $|C_i^*|$ represents the count of data points within the cluster after adding the DP mechanism, P_i is the sum of all data points post noise incorporation, ε_p signifies the allocated privacy budget during the addition of all data points, and ε_c is the assigned budget during the counting of data points $|C_i|$.The global sensitivity Δq is determined as $d + 1$, with d representing the number of dimensions.

2.3 Privacy Budget Allocation in DP K-Means

In a standard DP K-Means framework, one specifies a total privacy budget $\varepsilon_{\text{total}}$ that governs the overall strength of privacy guarantees. This budget must be divided across the T iterative centroid-update steps as shown by Eq. (5). The choice of how to split $\varepsilon_{\text{total}}$ into nonnegative portions eps $= \left(\varepsilon^{(1)}, \varepsilon^{(2)}, \ldots, \varepsilon^{(T)}\right)$ directly affects the level of noise at each iteration: a larger $\varepsilon^{(t)}$ yields less noise and a more accurate centroid update, while a smaller $\varepsilon^{(t)}$ increases privacy at the cost of accuracy. Commonly, one might allocate $\varepsilon^{(t)} = \varepsilon_{\text{total}}/T$ uniformly. However, uniform splitting is often suboptimal because the clustering error at later iterations depends on both the accumulated noise in previous updates and the remaining budget. In particular, early iterations shape cluster assignments in a coarse manner, whereas later iterations refine the centroids. Allocating too much budget too early (or too little) can degrade the final clustering quality. In subsequent sections, we propose and analyze MOMA-DPK, a multi-objective MA designed to efficiently search the space of feasible allocations, thereby generating a high-quality Pareto front of privacy-accuracy trade-offs.

2.4 Memetic Algorithm

The MA is a sophisticated process in optimization that includes both EA, such as GA, and local search heuristics. The primary objective of the MA is to enhance the global search capability of EAs by incorporating local search techniques. This can find an effective balance between exploration (global search) and exploitation (local search). The main structure of the MA involves initialization, crossover, mutation, local search, fitness evaluation, selection, and finally, the optimal solution [6,13].

3 The Proposed MOMA-DPK

3.1 Optimization Objectives

When noise is added to the cluster centroid using the DP technique, it affects both convergence and the effectiveness of clustering. The MOMA-DPK aims to ensure that modifications to the data do not compromise the privacy of the centroid for each cluster while maintaining the algorithm's convergence and utility. This means that our proposed approach optimizes two key aspects simultaneously: privacy and utility.

Definition 3 (Objective 1: Privacy Aspect). *For a specified dataset D, the goal is to generate a centroid-anonymized clustering result $\{C_i^*\}_{i=1}^k$ while maximizing privacy degree (PD) by minimizing the privacy budget ε spent in the clustering process.*

Definition 4 (Objective 2: Utility Aspect). *For the anonymized clustering result $\{C_i^*\}_{i=1}^k$, the aim is to optimize the utility degree (UD) by minimizing the NICV values among all acceptable utility solutions.*

Definition 5 (Pareto Dominance). *Let A_i and A_j represent two privacy budget allocation solutions for DP k-means clustering. Then A_i is said to have Pareto dominance over A_j, denoted by $A_i \succ A_j$, if and only if:*

$$\begin{cases} \forall m \in \{1,2\}, & f_m(A_i) \geq f_m(A_j), \\ \exists m \in \{1,2\}, & f_m(A_i) > f_m(A_j), \end{cases}$$

where f_1 corresponds to the Privacy Degree (PD) defined in Objective 1, and f_2 corresponds to the Utility Degree (UD) defined in Objective 2.

3.2 Overall Process

In many practical scenarios, DP K-means requires users to decide not only on the total privacy budget ε_{total}, but also on how that budget is divided across the T iterative updates of K-means. A uniform split is simple but rarely optimal in terms of final cluster quality. To measure the cluster quality, the Normalized Intra-Cluster Variance (NICV) is used, which is the average distance between each data point in the clustering outcome and its closest cluster centroid. To address the "budget-allocation" problem, our MOMA-DPK jointly optimizes clustering quality (NICV) and privacy expenditure (ε_{total}) by evolving a population of budget-allocation vector eps $= (\varepsilon^{(1)}, \ldots, \varepsilon^{(T)})$, repeatedly applying selection, crossover, mutation, and a specialized "imbalanced" local search strategy.

The overall process of MOMA-DPK is described in Algorithm 1. The algorithm commences by initializing a population of prospective privacy budget sequences, each explaining how a set of total privacy budget ε_{total} is divided over T iterations while making sure that every iteration gets at least a minimum budget ε_m. Each sequence undergoes an evaluation via a fitness function that quantitatively assesses the balance between cluster utility, as represented by the NICV, and the expenditure of the privacy budget. Subsequently, the algorithm initiates an evolutionary loop spanning G generations, aimed at iteratively refining the population via genetic operations such as crossover and mutation, alongside the imbalanced local search characteristics intrinsic to MA. To preserve genetic diversity, a non-dominated sorting process followed by a crowding distance calculation is employed to identify the Pareto-optimal fronts. The best individual is chosen for the next iteration based on dominance rank and diversity. Finally, the algorithms create a Pareto front of solutions, showing the optimal balance between the privacy budget and clustering utility, as well as the associated privacy budget sequence.

Algorithm 1. MOMA-DPK: Multi-objective Memetic Algorithm in DP K-Means.

Require: Dataset $D \in \mathbb{R}^{N \times d}$, number of clusters k, total privacy budget $\varepsilon_{\text{total}}$, minimum per-iteration budget ε_m, number of iterations T, population size N_m, generations G, crossover probability P_c, mutation probability P_m, imbalanced factor $f >= 1$, step fraction $\tau \in (0, 1)$, max local steps L.

Ensure: Pareto front F (NICV, $\varepsilon_{\text{spent}}$) and allocation series eps $= \{\varepsilon^{(t)}\}_{t=1}^{T}$, where $\sum_{t=1}^{T} \varepsilon^{(t)} = \varepsilon_{\text{spent}} \leq \varepsilon_{\text{total}}$ and $\varepsilon^{(t)} \geq \varepsilon_m$ for all t

$\mathcal{P} \leftarrow \varnothing$
for $i = 1, \ldots, N_m$ **do**
  $\texttt{eps}^{(i)} \leftarrow$ `generate_individual`$(\varepsilon_m, \varepsilon_{\text{total}}, T)$
  $\texttt{fitness}^{(i)} \leftarrow$ `evaluate`$(\texttt{eps}^{(i)}, D, k)$ ▷ returns (NICV, $\sum_t \varepsilon^{(t)}$)
  $\mathcal{P} \leftarrow \mathcal{P} \cup \{\texttt{eps}^{(i)}\}$
end for
for $g = 1, \ldots, G$ **do**
  $\mathcal{C} \leftarrow \varnothing$ ▷ Offspring set
  for $j = 1, \ldots, \lfloor N_m/2 \rfloor$ **do**
    select parents p_1, p_2 by tournament on `fitness`
    $(c_1, c_2) \leftarrow$ `mate_eps`$(p_1, p_2, \varepsilon_m, \varepsilon_{\text{total}}, T, P_c)$
    $c_1 \leftarrow$ `mutate_eps`$(c_1, \varepsilon_m, \varepsilon_{\text{total}}, T, P_m)$
    $c_2 \leftarrow$ `mutate_eps`$(c_2, \varepsilon_m, \varepsilon_{\text{total}}, T, P_m)$
    $c_1 \leftarrow$ `local_search_on_eps`$(c_1, D, k, \varepsilon_m, \varepsilon_{\text{total}}, T, f, \tau, L)$
    $c_2 \leftarrow$ `local_search_on_eps`$(c_2, D, k, \varepsilon_m, \varepsilon_{\text{total}}, T, f, \tau, L)$
    $\mathcal{C} \leftarrow \mathcal{C} \cup \{c_1, c_2\}$
  end for
  for each $c \in \mathcal{C}$ **do**
    `fitness`$(c) \leftarrow$ `evaluate`(c, D, k)
  end for
  $\mathcal{P} \leftarrow \mathcal{P} \cup \mathcal{C}$
  $\{F_1, F_2, \ldots\} \leftarrow$ `non_dominated_sort`$(\mathcal{P})$
  compute crowding distances within each F_i
  select top N_m by (rank, then crowding) to form new $\mathcal{P}$
end for
return Pareto front F_1 and associated `eps` sequences

3.3 Imbalanced Local Search Strategy

The Imbalanced Local Search (ILS) is the key "memetic" component of MOMA-DPK. It starts immediately after each child's crossover and mutation and before that child is evaluated. The goal of ILS is to quickly discover whether a more "skewed" allocation of ε_{total} can reduce NICV while maintaining the constraints. ILS will adjust L elements in the current child budget sequence denoted as $\text{eps}_{\text{curr}} = (\varepsilon^{(1)}_{\text{curr}}, \ldots, \varepsilon^{(T)}_{\text{curr}})$, using an *imbalanced factor* $f > 1$ and a small *step fraction* $\tau \in (0, 1)$.

We first compute the base transfer amount $\Delta_0 = \left(\frac{\varepsilon_{\text{total}}}{T}\right)\tau$. Then, for $h = 1, 2, \ldots, L$, ILS proceeds as follows:

1. **Index Selection.** Randomly choose a single iteration index $i \in \{1, \ldots, T\}$.
2. **Imbalanced Adjustment.** Depending on the Boolean parameter `increase`:
   - If `increase` = true, form
   $$\varepsilon'^{(i)} = \varepsilon^{(i)}_{\text{curr}} + f\,\Delta_0, \quad \varepsilon'^{(t)} = \varepsilon^{(t)}_{\text{curr}} \quad (t \neq i).$$
   - If `increase` = false, form
   $$\varepsilon'^{(i)} = \varepsilon^{(i)}_{\text{curr}} - \Delta_0, \quad \varepsilon'^{(t)} = \varepsilon^{(t)}_{\text{curr}} \quad (t \neq i).$$
3. **Update.** Set $\text{eps}_{\text{curr}} \leftarrow \left(\varepsilon'^{(1)}, \ldots, \varepsilon'^{(T)}\right)$.

After at most L such adjustments, ILS returns the final eps_{curr}. When implementing this local search strategy, we let one child adjust the per-iteration budget in the increase direction and the other in the decrease direction. Because each "increase" adjustment adds a large quantity $f\,\Delta_0$ to one element (and "decrease" subtracts only Δ_0 from one element), the ILS method will encourage a more aggressive spending of budget to produce lower NICV.

4 Experimental Outcome

We have verified the effectiveness of our proposed MOMA-DPK on two real datasets: Heart disease data and Diabetes data. The brief introduction of the basic information is shown in Table 1.

Table 1. Summary of datasets used in this study.

Dataset	Samples	Dimensions	Clusters
Heart Disease[a]	1,025	13	2
Diabetes[b]	5,132	9	2

[a] https://archive.ics.uci.edu/dataset/45/heart+disease.
[b] https://www.kaggle.com/datasets/simaanjali/diabetes-classification-dataset.

We have compared the MOMA-DPK with different baseline methods, which are:

1. **K-means algorithm** [16]**:** This is the fundamental K-means clustering technique devoid of any DP mechanism.
2. **Naive-DPK** [21]**:** This is the K-means method with DP strategy applied to each clustering iteration. It has an equal split of the privacy budget for each iteration.
3. **GA-DPK** [14]**:** For this algorithm, a single-objective GA is used in the DP K-means method to optimize the privacy budget allocation for each iteration. In this algorithm, the total privacy budget is allocated unequally at each iteration in order to gain the best fitness value (i.e. minimal NICV value for K-means clustering).
4. **NSGA-II-DPK:** This algorithm is a general NSGA-II [2], integrated with DP K-means clustering to minimize the total privacy budget spent and NICV at the same time. As an MOO method, it is capable of exploring various trade-offs to approximate the optimal Pareto front.

At the same time, we list the key parameter settings for our MOMA-DPK method in Table 2. In our experiment, the ε_m is computed following the approach in [14] using statistics from the tested datasets. To ensure a fair comparison, we set the total privacy budget range based on ε_m of each dataset, rather than using the same fixed ε value across all datasets.

Table 2. Parameter settings for the MOMA-DPK algorithm.

Parameter	Symbol	Value	Parameter	Symbol	Value
Number of clusters	k	2	Population size	N_m	20
Number of generations	G	50	Crossover probability	P_c	0.9
Mutation probability	P_m	0.1	Local search iterations	L	3
Local search step fraction	τ	0.1	Imbalanced search factor	f	1, 5, 10
Minimum per-iteration budget	ε_m	computed	Total privacy budget range	$\varepsilon_{\text{total}}$	$[3\varepsilon_m, 10\varepsilon_m]$
Trials	–	20			

4.1 Comparison with the Baseline in Terms of Pareto Front

As mentioned earlier, to facilitate cross-dataset comparison, we conducted experiments on both datasets, varying the total privacy budget from $3\varepsilon_m$ to $10\varepsilon_m$ in steps of $1\varepsilon_m$. Note that the computed ε_m value differs across datasets; for example, ε_m for the heart disease dataset is 2.019, whereas for the diabetes dataset it is only 0.240. In Fig. 2, we present the Pareto fronts for four representative budget settings: $4\varepsilon_m$, $6\varepsilon_m$, $8\varepsilon_m$, and $10\varepsilon_m$. Furthermore, to enable comparison across different ε values, both NICV and the spent ε were normalized using Min-Max normalization for each ε_{total} setting.

As we can see, for both datasets, the K-means method without any DP strategy always sits in the bottom-right corner as a single point, which means that without adding any noise, the plain K-means method generates the best

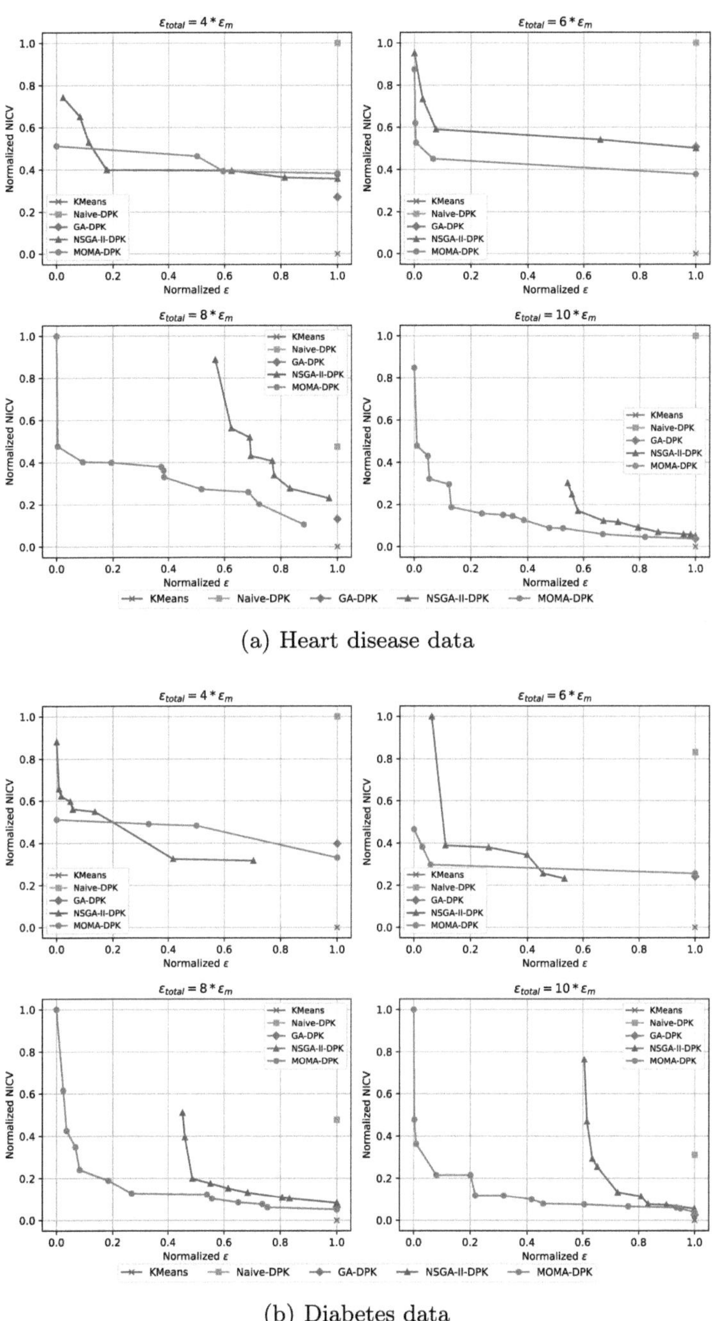

Fig. 2. Comparisons of Pareto front for different methods.

clustering result, measured by NICV. In contrast, applying the DP strategy to the K-means clustering process with a naive equal split of the total budget into each iteration (Naive-DPK) results in the worst clustering performance, characterized by the highest NICV value, when all the budget is spent. For the optimized budget allocation strategy driven by GA, GA-DPK attempts to find the lower NICV while utilizing all the privacy budget, which naturally also displays a single green dot on spent ε=1, but with a significantly lower NICV value.

For the two MOO methods, we can follow the Pareto front line to observe the trade-off between privacy protection (the spent ε) and utility (the NICV). For the heart disease data, for smaller ε_{total}, the Pareto front shows a similar pattern. But as the ε_{total} increases, MOMA-DPK consistently generates smoother and lower NICV curves than NSGA-II-DPK. Overall, MOMA-DPK exhibits greater diversity and offers a more balanced trade-off solution for a higher privacy budget. For the diabetes dataset, for lower ε_{total}, MOMA-DPK shows slightly better improvements than NSGA-II-DPK; however, as ε_{total} increases, it significantly outperforms NSGA-II-DPK in both objectives. For NSGA-II-DPK, when generating the Pareto front, it often fails to explore solutions with a high privacy budget due to its smaller search area.

4.2 Hypervolume Comparison

The hypervolume (HV) is a commonly used quality indicator metric in MOO problems, which evaluates the volume in the objective space that is dominated by a set of non-dominated solutions bounded with respect to a reference point [27]. This measure assesses the quality of solutions from MOO problems based on the Pareto front, including all non-dominated solutions that are not surpassed by any other solution across all goals [5,9,12]. Greater HV values indicate enhanced convergence and increased diversity of solutions, reflecting the algorithm's better performance [1].

In this experiment part, we calculated the HV for NSGA-II-DPK and MOMA-DPK to evaluate the efficacy of our method. Figure 3 demonstrates the average HV for MOMA-DPK and NSGA-II-DPK on the heart disease and diabetes datasets after 20 trials. These values are based on a range of total privacy budget ($\varepsilon_{total} = 3, 4, 5, 6, 7, 8, 9, 10 \times \varepsilon_m$, where ε_m is a dataset-specific value). The HV measure displays both the diversity and convergence of the Pareto front, with a larger value indicating greater coverage of the objective space and a better balance between privacy loss and clustering utility.

On both datasets, the MOMA-DPK consistently achieves superior average HV values in comparison to NSGA-II-DPK across all levels of ε. In the case of the heart disease dataset, while both algorithms perform similarly at lower ε values ($3\varepsilon_m, 6\varepsilon_m$), MOMA-DPK exhibits significant advantages as ε increases. One thing worth noticing is that since HV is a normalized value based on each trial, the declining trend for NSGA-II-DPK does not necessarily mean its absolute performance goes down as ε_{total} increases. However, the trend indeed shows that the performance gap between MOMA-DPK and NSGA-II-DPK enlarged,

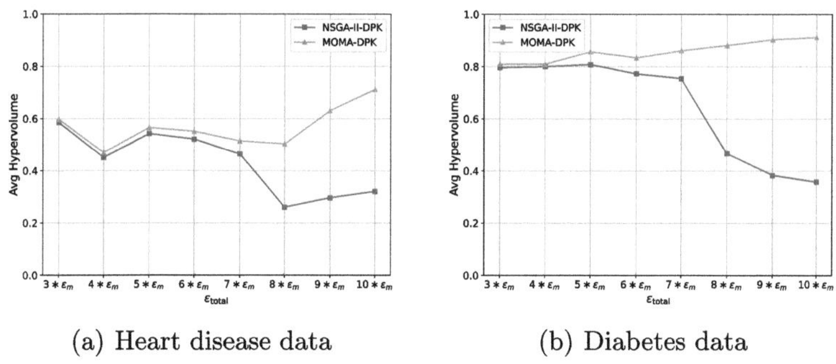

(a) Heart disease data (b) Diabetes data

Fig. 3. Comparisons of hypervolume (HV) for different methods.

indicating our method is capable of maintaining solution diversity or quality under larger privacy budgets, which is also cross-proofed by Fig. 2. Our method works even better with the diabetes dataset, as seen in Fig. 3 (b), where the MOMA-DPK always gets a higher HV for all budgets, and the gap in performance keeps increasing. This improvement occurs because the diabetes dataset has fewer dimensions than the heart disease dataset, which allows our method to explore a larger search space and obtain better solutions compared to the baseline methods, as MOMA-DPK is more effective at finding solutions when a larger budget is available.

We also conducted a Wilcoxon signed-rank test on the 20 trials to verify the significance of the comparison. The results show that for small budget values, such as $\varepsilon_{total} = 3, 4 \times \varepsilon_m$, our method does not demonstrate a significant advantage, which is consistent with Fig. 2. However, for the other ε_{total} values, all results are significant.

4.3 Impact of the Imbalanced Factor

For our MOMA-DPK, the imbalanced factor decides how the local search will be biased to search in the direction of increasing per-iteration budget. The high the value is, the greater step local search will take in the increasing direction.

The impact of different imbalanced factors on the performance of MOMA-DPK is investigated as shown in Fig. 4. The imbalanced factor for the comparison is considered as 1, 5, 10 over a range of total privacy budgets $[3\varepsilon_m, 10\varepsilon_m]$. Generally, for both datasets, high imbalanced factor values exhibit better HV values when the privacy budget is higher ($\varepsilon_{total} \geq 8\varepsilon_m$). This indicates that the higher imbalanced factor provides a more aggressive local strategy, which is beneficial when the privacy budget allows for greater flexibility. Notably, for the diabetes dataset, the performance gap is higher, mainly because a more affluent privacy budget is available for each dimension. This confirms the efficiency of the imbalanced local search strategy in providing marginal improvement in the quality of the Pareto front for high-budget cases under DP constraints.

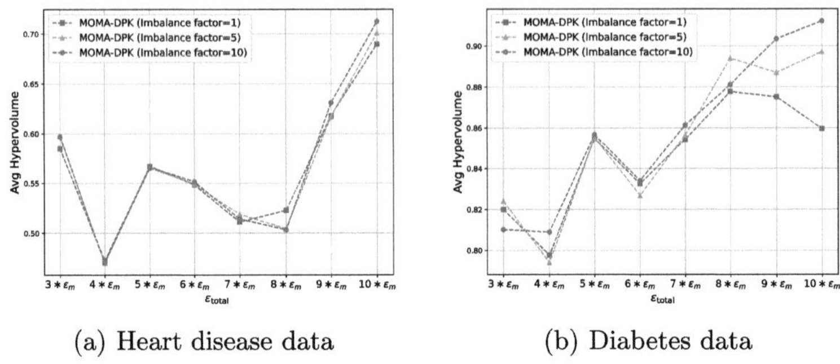

(a) Heart disease data (b) Diabetes data

Fig. 4. Average HV for MOMA-DPK for different imbalanced factor.

5 Conclusion

This article introduced MOMA-DPK, a multi-objective memetic algorithm designed to find an optimal balance between privacy protection and clustering utility in DP K-means clustering. The effectiveness of the proposed algorithm has been verified on two real-world datasets against various baseline methods. Compared to a single-objective optimization method, our multi-objective method can present trade-off options for an institution to choose from based on its privacy protection strategy. The Pareto front comparison with the NSGA-II-DPK method shows that MOMA-DPK constantly generates a high level of clustering utility (low NICV) while utilizing less consumed privacy budget, and this benefit is especially apparent for higher privacy budget $\varepsilon_{total} \geq 8\varepsilon_m$. The HV analysis further validates the superiority, where MOMA-DPK shows higher HV, which indicates better convergence and solution front across the majority of the budget range. Moreover, we conducted an ablation study on the imbalanced local search strategy by varying the factors to demonstrate that with a higher imbalanced search factor, our method yields more improvements for cases with higher privacy budgets. Overall, the results indicate that the proposed MOMA-DPK is efficient in providing a broader view of trade-offs for institutions to position their privacy protection strategy. Future research directions may include adaptive ε-tuning mechanisms to dynamically adjust the privacy budget in accordance with dataset attributes and utility requirements. Additionally, incorporating dynamic privacy constraints and evaluating the cross-dataset transferability would also help enhance applicability and generalization.

References

1. Chen, H., Wu, G., Pedrycz, W., Suganthan, P.N., Xing, L., Zhu, X.: An adaptive resource allocation strategy for objective space partition-based multiobjective optimization. IEEE Trans. Syst. Man Cybern. Syst. **51**(3), 1507–1522 (2019)
2. Deb, K., Pratap, A., Agarwal, S., Meyarivan, T.: A fast and elitist multiobjective genetic algorithm: NSGA-II. IEEE Trans. Evol. Comput. **6**(2), 182–197 (2002)

3. Dwork, C.: Differential privacy. In: Bugliesi, M., Preneel, B., Sassone, V., Wegener, I. (eds) Automata, Languages and Programming. ICALP 2006. Lecture Notes in Computer Science, vol. 4052, pp. 1–12. Springer, Heidelberg (2006). https://doi.org/10.1007/11787006_1
4. Fan, Z., Xu, X.: APDPK-means: a new differential privacy clustering algorithm based on arithmetic progression privacy budget allocation. In: 2019 IEEE 21st International Conference on High Performance Computing and Communications; IEEE 17th International Conference on Smart City; IEEE 5th International Conference on Data Science and Systems (HPCC/SmartCity/DSS), pp. 1737–1742. IEEE (2019)
5. Ge, Y.F., Bertino, E., Wang, H., Cao, J., Zhang, Y.: Distributed cooperative coevolution of data publishing privacy and transparency. ACM Trans. Knowl. Discov. Data **18**(1), 1–23 (2023)
6. Ge, Y.F., Cao, J., Wang, H., Zhang, Y., Chen, Z.: Distributed differential evolution for anonymity-driven vertical fragmentation in outsourced data storage. In: Web Information Systems Engineering – WISE 2020, pp. 213–226. Springer, Cham (2020). https://doi.org/10.1007/978-3-030-62008-0_15
7. Ge, Y.F., Orlowska, M., Cao, J., Wang, H., Zhang, Y.: MDDE: multitasking distributed differential evolution for privacy-preserving database fragmentation. VLDB J. **31**(5), 957–975 (2022)
8. Ge, Y.F., Wang, H., Bertino, E., Cao, J., Zhang, Y.: Multiobjective privacy-preserving task assignment in spatial crowdsourcing. IEEE Trans. Cybern. (2025)
9. Ge, Y.F., et al.: Evolutionary dynamic database partitioning optimization for privacy and utility. IEEE Trans. Dependable Secure Comput. (2023)
10. Ge, Y.F., Wang, H., Cao, J., Zhang, Y., Jiang, X.: Privacy-preserving data publishing: an information-driven distributed genetic algorithm. World Wide Web **27**(1), 1 (2024)
11. Ge, Y.F., et al.: Distributed memetic algorithm for outsourced database fragmentation. IEEE Trans. Cybern. **51**(10), 4808–4821 (2021). https://doi.org/10.1109/tcyb.2020.3027962
12. Jahan, S., Ge, Y.F., Wang, H., Kabir, E.: Dynamic-parameter genetic algorithm for multi-objective privacy-preserving trajectory data publishing. In: Barhamgi, M., Wang, H., Wang, X. (eds.) WISE 2024. LNCS, vol. 15440, pp. 46–57. Springer, Cham (2024). https://doi.org/10.1007/978-981-96-0576-7_4
13. Jahan, S., Ge, Y.F., Wang, H., Kabir, E.: Adaptive-parameter memetic algorithm for privacy-preserving trajectory data publishing: a multi-objective optimization approach: S. Jahan et al. Computing **107**(7), 151 (2025)
14. Li, Y., Song, X., Tu, Y., Liu, M.: Gapbas: genetic algorithm-based privacy budget allocation strategy in differential privacy k-means clustering algorithm. Comput. Secur. **139**, 103697 (2024)
15. Liu, S., Liu, J.: A differential privacy k-means algorithm for improving privacy budget allocation. In: Proceedings of the 2022 5th International Conference on Artificial Intelligence and Pattern Recognition, pp. 96–101 (2022)
16. Lloyd, S.: Least squares quantization in PCM. IEEE Trans. Inf. Theory **28**(2), 129–137 (1982)
17. Machanavajjhala, A., Kifer, D., Gehrke, J., Venkitasubramaniam, M.: l-diversity: Privacy beyond k-anonymity. ACM Transactions on Knowledge Discovery from Data (TKDD) **1**(1), 3–es (2007)
18. Nelson, B., Olovsson, T.: Security and privacy for big data: a systematic literature review. In: 2016 IEEE International Conference on Big Data (Big Data), pp. 3693–3702. IEEE (2016)

19. Ni, T., Qiao, M., Chen, Z., Zhang, S., Zhong, H.: Utility-efficient differentially private k-means clustering based on cluster merging. Neurocomputing **424**, 205–214 (2021)
20. Ren, J., Xiong, J., Yao, Z., Ma, R., Lin, M.: DPLK-means: a novel differential privacy k-means mechanism. In: 2017 IEEE Second International Conference on Data Science in Cyberspace (DSC), pp. 133–139. IEEE (2017)
21. Su, D., Cao, J., Li, N., Bertino, E., Jin, H.: Differentially private k-means clustering. In: Proceedings of the Sixth ACM Conference on Data and Application Security and Privacy, pp. 26–37 (2016)
22. Sweeney, L.: k-anonymity: a model for protecting privacy. Internat. J. Uncertain. Fuzziness Knowl.-Based Syst. **10**(05), 557–570 (2002)
23. Yaling, Z., Lingyu, Q.: Differential privacy protection k-means algorithm based on BWP index. J. Comput. Eng. Appl. **58**(10) (2022)
24. Yao, S.: An improved differential privacy k-means algorithm based on mapreduce. In: 2018 11th International Symposium on Computational Intelligence and Design (ISCID), vol. 2, pp. 141–145. IEEE (2018)
25. Yin, J., Tang, M., Cao, J., You, M., Wang, H., Alazab, M.: Knowledge-driven cybersecurity intelligence: software vulnerability coexploitation behavior discovery. IEEE Trans. Industr. Inf. **19**(4), 5593–5601 (2022)
26. You, M., Ge, Y.F., Wang, K., Wang, H., Cao, J., Kambourakis, G.: Hierarchical adaptive evolution framework for privacy-preserving data publishing. World Wide Web **27**(4), 49 (2024)
27. Zhang, X., Tian, Y., Jin, Y.: A knee point-driven evolutionary algorithm for many-objective optimization. IEEE Trans. Evol. Comput. **19**(6), 761–776 (2014)
28. Zhang, Y., Liu, N., Wang, S.: A differential privacy protecting k-means clustering algorithm based on contour coefficients. PLoS ONE **13**(11), e0206832 (2018)

FP-BSS: Full Privacy Blockchain-Based Self-tallying Score Voting Protocol

Zongrui Tang, Xiaomei Dong(✉), Wenpeng Chen, Hanyu Mao, Shuai Hao, Zeshun Peng, Xiaohua Li, and Ge Yu

School of Computer Science and Engineering, Northeast University, Shenyang, China
xmdong@mail.neu.edu.cn

Abstract. Electronic voting has a wide range of applications in modern society. Self-tallying voting, which allows all voters to calculate the results themselves, is gaining popularity as it eliminates the need for a centralized authority. However, existing self-tallying voting schemes face challenges, such as the lack of a score voting mechanism and inadequate privacy protection. To address these issues, we propose FP-BSS, a full privacy, blockchain-based self-tallying score voting protocol. We extend the traditional binary voting paradigm to support score voting, enabling voters to rate each candidate within a specified range. Candidates with broad acceptability tend to win, while extreme candidates favored by a minority but opposed by the majority are less likely to win. Simultaneously, to guarantee ballot privacy both during and after the election, we design a full privacy ballot encryption scheme leveraging blinding factors to ensure complete voter anonymity, and propose a new zero-knowledge proof to verify ballot legitimacy. We prove that FP-BSS achieves full voter privacy and meets all necessary security requirements. Performance results demonstrate that FP-BSS provides enhanced security while maintaining reasonable practicality.

Keywords: Blockchain · score voting · self-tallying · zero-knowledge proof · homomorphic encryption[

1 Introduction

With the development of science and technology, electronic voting is gradually gaining attention. Electronic voting systems offer many advantages over traditional paper-based voting. For example, they eliminate geographical constraints, and the processes of tallying and verifying results are highly efficient.

However, traditional electronic voting systems also face security challenges. Systems that rely on a centralized authority to manage the voting process prevent voters from verifying whether their ballots are accurately recorded and counted, thereby undermining trust in the credibility of the system. Blockchain technology addresses the shortcomings of traditional electronic voting protocols. It is a distributed, decentralized ledger that records digital transactions securely

I. Awan et al. (Eds.): WISE 2025, LNCS 16367, pp. 231–242, 2026.
https://doi.org/10.1007/978-981-95-7394-3_16

and transparently [1,2], eliminating the need for a centralized authority. Permissioned blockchains enable multiple organizations to securely share data in a decentralized yet controlled environment. They offer greater openness than private chains while providing stronger governance than public ones. This combination of features makes permissioned blockchains an ideal foundation for electronic voting systems. In recent years, a series of blockchain-based voting schemes have been proposed, enhancing security throughout the voting process [3].

However, existing blockchain-based electronic voting protocols suffer from various security limitations:

First, most existing systems focus only on binary voting, with limited exploration of more flexible voting paradigms. Lu et al. proposed a blockchain-based self-tallying protocol using a traceable ring signature [4]. Their approach only supports single binary voting rather than allowing voters to evaluate each candidate within a predefined range. This limitation can lead to situations where extreme candidates, those favored by a minority but strongly opposed by the majority win elections.

Second, existing voting schemes may compromise voter privacy. Miao et al. proposed a blockchain-based publicly traceable self-tallying voting protocol that uses time-lock puzzles to ensure time-limited privacy [5]. In this scheme, election results can only be computed after a fixed period elapses. However, ballot contents are revealed after the election, exposing the choices of the voters.

After investigating existing schemes, we propose FP-BSS, a full privacy, blockchain-based self-tallying score voting protocol that addresses the aforementioned problems. The contributions of this paper are summarized below:

(1) We design a new full privacy ballot encryption scheme based on blinding factors, which ensures voter privacy both during and after the voting process. Specifically, we employ homomorphic encryption to encrypt ballots and then blind the ciphertext using blinding factors. This approach ensures ballot privacy while enabling self-tallying. We extend the traditional binary voting scheme to enable voters to evaluate candidates within a predefined range.
(2) We propose a new zero-knowledge proof for verifying the legitimacy of encrypted ballots. This proof ensures that: the correct blinding factor was used to encrypt the ballot, each score on a ballot lies within a predefined range, and the total sum of points sums to a predefined constant while preserving the complete confidentiality of the encrypted ballot.
(3) We implement FP-BSS, analyze its security, and compare it with existing self-tallying voting schemes. The results demonstrate that our protocol satisfies all requisite security requirements while providing comprehensive security guarantees. Performance evaluation confirms that our protocol maintains practical efficiency.

2 Background

In this section, we introduce background related to protecting privacy and security in electronic voting systems.

With the advancement of information technologies, electronic voting systems have achieved significant gains in efficiency, but their security enhancements remain comparatively limited [7]. Traditional electronic voting systems usually rely on a centralized election authority to manage the voting process, which undermines trust in their credibility. Self-tallying voting eliminates the need for a centralized authority. All voters can collect all legitimate ballots and count the results themselves. In 2002, Kiayias et al. first proposed the concept of self-tallying [8]. However, if malicious voters refuse to participate, the final result cannot be computed. Self-tallying voting also faces the problem that last voter could calculate the vote result in advance. This can be resolve by Homomorphic Time-Lock Puzzle (HTLP) [9]. In essence, HTLP is an enhanced version of the time-lock puzzle that enables computations on multiple encrypted puzzles without requiring access to the hidden values within them. The final result of these computations is itself another puzzle.

Although self-tallying protocols address centralization risks, their practical implementation faces challenges in ensuring universal verifiability. The emergence of blockchain has offered solutions to this problem. McCorry et al. proposed the first self-tallying voting protocol implemented on Ethereum [10]. However, this protocol did not support for score voting. Score voting is a simple yet expressive decision making method where voters assign each candidate a score within a predefined range. Rather than merely choosing yes or no, voters can express their level of support for each candidate, and the candidate with the highest total score wins. For example: In a score voting election with three candidates (Alice, Bob, Mary) and three voters, the first voter scores Alice 10, Bob 6, Mary 0; the second scores Alice 0, Bob 6, Mary 10; and the third scores Alice 6, Bob 6, Mary 4. While Alice and Mary each receive both perfect support and strong rejection from different voters, Bob wins with 18 total points because he is broadly acceptable to all voters. Later, Khader et al. added a commitment round and a recovery round to address the problem of the last voter potentially calculating the result in advance [11]. Then, Lin et al. proposed a complete self-tallying protocol using Schnorr signatures [12], but it incurred additional overhead. In 2020, Yang et al. proposed PriScore using a dual zero-knowledge proof [13]. However, it requires all voters to vote. Otherwise, the final result cannot be computed. To our knowledge, none of the existing protocols address all of the above problems simultaneously.

3 System Architecture

The FP-BSS defines four core entities: **Election Authority**, **Voters**, **Observers**, and **Blockchain**. The system architecture is shown in Fig. 1.

Election Authority (EA): The EA is responsible for election setup and publishes public voting parameters on the Blockchain. It handles voter registration and distributes blinding factors to legitimate voters.

Voters: A voter V_i registers with the EA to obtain a blinding factor, then shares their public key and corresponding proof on the Blockchain. During voting, V_i

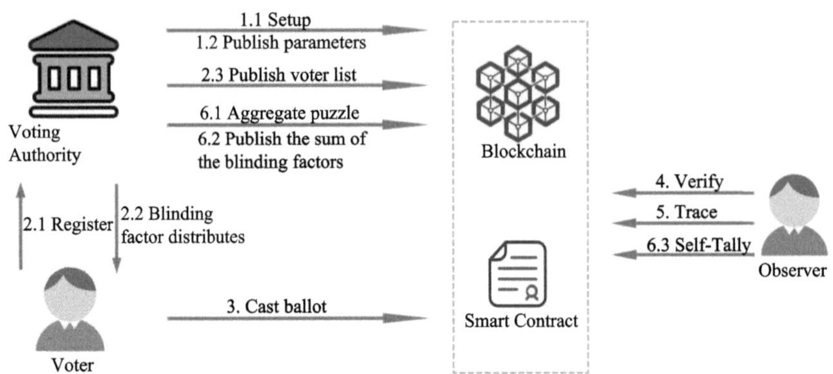

Fig. 1. System architecture.

publishes the encrypted ballot and associated proof to the Blockchain to demonstrate ballot legitimacy.

Observers: An observer can authenticate voter identities, verify encrypted ballot legitimacy, trace malicious voters attempting double voting, and independently compute final election results.

Blockchain: The Blockchain serves as an immutable ledger that permanently records: public keys of voters with corresponding proofs, and encrypted ballots paired with their validation proofs.

The notations used in this paper are summarized in Table 1.

Table 1. Notations and Description

Notation	Description	Notation	Description
n	Number of voters	m	Number of candidates
N	RSA integer	R	Predefined total points
t	Time hardness parameter	$eventID$	Event Identifier
f_i	The blinding factor of V_i	α_i	The verification value of f_i
VL	Voter list	p_{ij}	The point allocate to C_j
$Ballot_{ij}$	Encrypted ballot for C_j	$Ballot_i$	Encrypted ballot of V_i
$NIZK_{ij}$	NIZK range proof	$NIZK_i$	NIZK total proof
σ_i	Signature for $Ballot_i$	p_j	Total point of C_j

Setup$(\lambda, \mathit{eventID}, t, m, R) \rightarrow (PP, \{C_j\}_{j=1}^{m})$**:** Suppose there are m candidates. The EA selects security parameters λ, an event identifier $\mathit{eventID} \in \{0,1\}^*$, a time hardness parameter t, and a predefined total point R. It chooses a cyclic group G of prime order p with generator g. Let $N = \tilde{j} \times \tilde{k}$ be an RSA modulus where $\tilde{j}$ and $\tilde{k}$ are strong primes. Define hash functions $H : \{0,1\}^* \to G$ and $H_1 : \{0,1\}^* \to \mathbb{Z}_p^*$. The EA randomly selects $u \in \mathbb{Z}_N^*$, computes $T = u^{2^t}$, and publishes $PP = \{p, G, g, H, H_1, N, T, u, t, eventID\}$ and candidate list $\{C_j\}_{j=1}^m$ on the Blockchain.

Registration$(PP, VID_i) \to (pk_i, sk_i, b_i, n, VL)$**:** Each voter V_i registers with the EA by selecting random $x_i \in \mathbb{Z}_p^*$ as their private key sk_i, computing public key $pk_i = g^{x_i}$, and sending (pk_i, π_i, VID_i) to the EA, where π_i is a proof of pk_i. The EA verifies proof π_i; if valid, it assigns blinding factor f_i, selects random $s_i \in \mathbb{Z}_p^*$, computes $Y_i = g^{s_i}$ and $\alpha_i = Y_i^{f_i}$, then adds (pk_i, π_i, α_i) to voter list VL. After all registrations, VL is published on the Blockchain.

V_i		Verifier
V_i select random $\rho_i \in \mathbb{Z}_p^*$		
For all $j \neq i$, V_i select random $C_j, K_j \in \mathbb{Z}_p^*$		
$q = H(\text{eventID} \parallel \text{PK}_N)$ $\quad \eta_i = q^{x_i}$		
$D_0 = H(\text{eventID} \parallel \text{Ballot}_i)$ $D_1 = (\eta_i / D_0)^{1/i}$		
$r_i = g^{\rho_i}, \quad t_i = q^{\rho_i}$		
$\eta_j = D_0 \cdot D_1^j \quad \forall j \neq i$		
$r_j = g^{K_j} \cdot y_j^{C_j} \quad \forall j \neq i$		
$t_j = q^{K_j} \cdot \eta_j^{C_j} \quad \forall j \neq i$	$\sigma_i = (D_1, C_N, K_N) \longrightarrow$	
$C = H(\text{eventID} \parallel \text{Ballot}_i \parallel D_0 \parallel D_1 \parallel r_N \parallel t_N)$		the verifier computes the following equations
$C_i = C - \sum_{j \neq i} C_j$		$q = H(\text{eventID} \parallel \text{PK}_N)$ $D_0 = H(\text{eventID} \parallel \text{Ballot}_i)$
$K_i = \rho_i - C_i \cdot x_i$		$\eta_j = D_0 \cdot D_1^j$
		$r_j = g^{K_j} \cdot y_j^{C_j}$
		$t_j = q^{K_j} \cdot \eta_j^{C_j}$
		the verifier checks whether the equation hold
		$\sum_{j=1}^{n} C_j = H(\text{eventID} \parallel \text{Ballot}_i \parallel D_0 \parallel D_1 \parallel r_N \parallel t_N)$

Fig. 2. Sign the encrypted ballot $Ballot_i$.

BallotCast$(PP, PK_N, sk_i, \{p_{ij}\}_{j=1}^m) \to (Ballot_i, NIZK_{Ballot_i}, \sigma_i)$**:** V_i encrypts their ballot to obtain $Ballot_i$, generates zero-knowledge range proof $NIZK_{ij}$ and total proof $NIZK_i$ (see Sect. 4), then signs $Ballot_i$ as shown in Fig. 2 to produce signature σ_i. Finally, $(Ballot_i, NIZK_{ij}, NIZK_i, \sigma_i)$ is published on the Blockchain, which allows public verifiability of the ballot.

BallotVerification$(PP,\ (Ballot_i,\ NIZK_{Ballot_i})) \to \{0,1\}$**:** Any party verifies $Ballot_i$ by checking $NIZK_{ij}$ and $NIZK_i$ (see Sect. 4). For $\sigma_i = (D_1, C_N, K_N)$, validate whether $H(eventID \parallel Ballot_i \parallel D_0 \parallel D_1 \parallel r_N \parallel t_N) = \sum_{i=1}^n C_i$ holds. If any check fails, reject the ballot.

Trace$(PP, PK_N,\ (Ballot_i,\ \sigma_i),\ (Ballot_i',\ \sigma_i')) \to \{pk_i\}$**:** Given two valid ballot-signature pairs, any party can determine if they come from the same voter. For σ_i, compute $q = H(eventID \parallel PK_N)$, $D_0 = H(eventID \parallel Ballot_i)$, $\eta_i = D_0 \cdot D_1^i$.

Compute η_i' similarly for σ_i'. For $i \in \{1, 2, ..., n\}$, if only one of $\eta_i = \eta_i'$ is true, the public key of the malicious voter is pk_i.

Self-Tally$(PP, \{Ballot_i\}_{i=1}^n) \rightarrow (p_1, \ldots, p_m)$**:** The EA runs Trace to identify malicious voters. Let ν be the set of legitimate voters. Aggregate valid ballots:

$$(a_j, b_j) = \left(\prod_{i \in \nu} a_{ij}, \prod_{i \in \nu} b_{ij}\right) \tag{1}$$

Then publish aggregate result (a_j, b_j) and $F_\nu = \sum_{i \in \nu} f_i$ on the Blockchain. After time t, any party computes:

$$c_j = (a_j / u^{F_\nu})^{2^t} \tag{2}$$

$$p_j = \left(\left(b_j / c_j^N \mod N^2\right) - 1\right) / N \tag{3}$$

The candidate scores are $(p_1, \ldots, p_m)$.

4 Full Privacy Blockchain-Based Self-Tallying Score Voting Protocol

In this section, we present our new full privacy ballot encryption scheme and new zero-knowledge proof of encrypted ballot legitimacy.

Prover

Randomly select $\omega, \rho, e_k, d_k, r_k \in \mathbb{Z}_N^*$ where $k \in \{0, 1, \ldots, R\}$ and $k \neq l$

$a_k = (T^N)^{e_k} \cdot \left(b_{ij}/(1+N)^k\right)^{d_k}$

$b_k = u^{e_k} \cdot u^{r_k} \cdot a_{ij}^{d_k}$

$c_k = Y_i^{r_k} \cdot \alpha_i^{d_k}$

$a_l = (T^N)^\rho$

$b_l = u^\rho \cdot u^\omega$

$c_l = Y_i^\omega$

$c = H_1\left(\{a_r, b_r, c_r\}_{r \in [0,R]} || a_{ij} || b_{ij} || h_{ij}\right)$

$d_l = c - \sum_{k \neq l} d_k$

$e_l = \rho - d_l \cdot h_{ij}$

$r_l = \omega - d_l \cdot f_i$

Prover → Verifier: $\{a_k, b_k, c_k, d_k, e_k, r_k\}_{k \in [0,R]}, a_{ij}, b_{ij}, c$

Verifier

For all $k \in \{1, 2, ..., R\}$, check whether the following equations hold simultaneously

$c = \sum_{k=0}^{R} d_k$

$a_k = (T^N)^{e_k} \cdot \left(b_{ij}/(1+N)^k\right)^{d_k}$

$b_k = u^{e_k} \cdot u^{r_k} \cdot a_{ij}^{d_k}$

$c_k = Y_i^{r_k} \cdot \alpha_i^{d_k}$

Fig. 3. Zero-knowledge range proof of the ballot $Ballot_i$.

V_i allocates a point p_{ij} to candidate C_j according to the voting rules. To protect the privacy of the ballot, V_i encrypts the ballot with time-lock puzzles and blinding factors. The specific definitions are provided below:

$$a_{ij} = u^{h_{ij}} \cdot u^{f_i} \tag{4}$$

$$b_{ij} = T^{h_{ij} \cdot N} \cdot (1+N)^{p_{ij}} \tag{5}$$

The point of V_i for the candidate C_j is $Ballot_{ij} = (a_{ij}, b_{ij})$.

A New Range Zero-Knowledge Proof. V_i generates a NIZK range proof to prove that point p_{ij} belongs to $[0, R]$ and the correct blinding factor is used without revealing p_{ij} or the blinding factor h_{ij}. The details of range zero-knowledge proof are shown in Fig. 3. The specific definitions are provided below: $NIZK_{ij}\{(h_{ij}, p_{ij}, f_i) : a_{ij} = u^{h_{ij}} \cdot u^{f_i} \wedge \alpha_i = Y_i^{f_i} \wedge (b_{ij} = T^{h_{ij} \cdot N} \vee b_{ij} = T^{h_{ij}} \cdot (1+N) \vee b_{ij} = T^{h_{ij}} \cdot (1+N)^2 \vee ... \vee b_{ij} = T^{h_{ij}} \cdot (1+N)^R)\}$

For $NIZK_{ij}$, the correctness of the following equations should be checked. $c = \sum_{k=0}^{R} d_k, a_k = (T^N)^{e_k} \cdot (b_{ij}/(1+N)^k)^{d_k}, b_k = u^{e_k} \cdot u^{r_k} \cdot a_{ij}^{d_k}, c_k = Y_i^{r_k} \cdot \alpha_i^{d_k}$. If one of these equations is not true, the verifier aborts.

A New Total Zero-Knowledge Proof. V_i also generates a NIZK total proof to prove that the total of the point p_{ij} equals R and the correct blinding factor is used without revealing p_{ij} or the blinding factor h_{ij}. The details of totol zero-knowledge proof are shown in Fig. 4. The specific definitions are provided below: $NIZK_i\{((h_{i1}, h_{i2}, ..., h_{im}), (p_{i1}, p_{i2}, ..., p_{im}), f_i) : \prod_{j=1}^{m} a_{ij} = u^{\sum_{j=1}^{m} h_{ij}} \cdot u^{\sum_{j=1}^{m} s_i} \wedge \prod_{j=1}^{m} b_{ij} + (T^N)^{\sum_{j=1}^{m} h_{ij}} \cdot (1+N)^R \wedge \sum_{j=1}^{m} p_{ij} = R \wedge \alpha_i = Y_i^{f_i}\}$

For $NIZK_i$, the following equations should be checked. $c = H_1(\tilde{a}||\tilde{b}||\tilde{\alpha}||\prod_{j=1}^{m} a_{ij}||\prod_{j=1}^{m} b_{ij}||\alpha_i), \tilde{a} = (\prod_{j=1}^{m} a_{ij})^c \cdot u^{(\tilde{x_i} + \sum_{j=1}^{m} \alpha)}, \tilde{b} = (\prod_{j=1}^{m} b_{ij}/(1+N)^R)^c \cdot (T^N)^{\tilde{x_i}}, \tilde{\alpha} = \alpha_i^c \cdot Y_i^{\alpha}$. If one of these equations is not true, the verifier aborts.

Prover		Verifier
Randomly select $\{x_{i1}, x_{i2}, \ldots, x_{im}\}$, where $r \in \mathbb{Z}^*$.		
$\tilde{a} = (u)^{\sum_{j=1}^{m} x_{ij}} \cdot (u)^{\sum_{j=1}^{m} r}$		
$\tilde{b} = (T^N)^{\sum_{j=1}^{m} x_{ij}}$		
$\tilde{\alpha} = Y_i^r$		
$c = \mathrm{H}_1\left(\tilde{a} \parallel \tilde{b} \parallel \tilde{\alpha} \parallel \prod_{j=1}^{m} a_{ij} \parallel \prod_{j=1}^{m} b_{ij} \parallel \alpha_i\right)$		
$\tilde{x} = \sum_{j=1}^{m} x_{ij} - c\sum_{j=1}^{m} h_{ij}$		
$\alpha = r - c \cdot f_i$	$\xrightarrow{\tilde{a}, \tilde{b}, \tilde{\alpha}, \prod_{j=1}^{m} a_{ij}, \prod_{j=1}^{m} b_{ij}, \tilde{x}, \alpha, c}$	
		the verifier checks whether the following equations hold simultaneously
		$c = \mathrm{H}_1\left(\tilde{a} \parallel \tilde{b} \parallel \tilde{\alpha_i} \parallel \prod_{j=1}^{m} a_{ij} \parallel \prod_{j=1}^{m} b_{ij} \parallel \alpha_i\right)$
		$\tilde{a} = \left(\prod_{j=1}^{m} a_{ij}\right)^c \cdot (u)^{(\tilde{x} + \sum_{j=1}^{m} \alpha_j)}$
		$\tilde{b} = \left(\prod_{j=1}^{m} b_{ij}/(1+N)^R\right)^c \cdot (T^N)^{\tilde{x}}$
		$\tilde{\alpha} = \alpha_i^c \cdot Y_i^{\alpha}$

Fig. 4. Zero-knowledge total proof of the ballot $Ballot_i$.

5 Security Analysis

5.1 Security Properties

FP-BSS meets the following security properties.

Full Privacy. Voter anonymity is preserved throughout the election lifecycle, under the condition that no voter submits multiple ballots.

Time-Limited Privacy. Within a certain period of time, ballots remain completely confidential against adversaries with arbitrary computational power.

Linkability. In a same voting event, two ballots cast by a same voter will be linked. Legitimate single ballots remain computationally unlinkable even under coalition attacks.

Universal Verifiability. Any observer can independently authenticate voter identities, validate encrypted ballots, and verify that all ballots are accurately included in the final tally.

Self-tallying. After the time-lock expiration. Any observer can independently compute the final voting results. No trusted authority is required.

Robustness. The final election results cannot be manipulated by any party, including EA itself. Valid results remain computable and verifiable even if voters abstain or act maliciously.

5.2 Security Analysis

Now, we conduct an analysis of essential security requirements in FP-BSS.

Full Privacy: In the protocol, each ballot is encrypted with a time hardness parameter t and then blinded with a voter-specific blinding factor f_i, which ensures persistent privacy of ballot contents. Crucially, even after the predefined time t elapses, the specific content of individual ballots remains protected due to the blinding operation. This guarantees end-to-end confidentiality of votes, preserving voter privacy throughout the process.

Time-Limited Privacy: Ballot encryption incorporates $T = u^{2^t}$, which requires at least t sequential squaring operations. This computation cannot be parallelized because each step depends on the previous result. When t is sufficiently large, real-time computation of T becomes computationally infeasible, thereby enforcing time-limited privacy.

Linkability: Each voter generates a signature and corresponding proof using their unique private key. This cryptographic binding ensures that ballots from distinct voters are computationally unlinkable, while simultaneously enabling detection of duplicate votes.

Universal Verifiability: Voters publish encrypted ballots, range proofs $NIZK_{ij}$, total proofs $NIZK_i$, and signatures with proofs to the blockchain, enabling any observer to: verify ballot validity via $NIZK_{ij}$ and $NIZK_i$, authenticate signatures, and optionally recompute final results during self-tallying. This enables universal verification of both individual ballots and aggregated results.

Self-tallying: After the voting phase, any party can collect all ballots (a_{ij}, b_{ij}) and the aggregated blinding factor $F_\nu = \sum_{i\in\nu} f_i$, compute the aggregated values $(a_j, b_j) = \left(\prod_{i\in\nu} a_{ij}, \prod_{i\in\nu} b_{ij}\right)$, decrypt the tally through $c_j = (a_j/u^{F_\nu})^{2^t}$ and $p_j = ((b_j/c_j^N \mod N^2) - 1)/N$, eliminating the need for trusted third parties.

Robustness: Blockchain persistence ensures the immutability of cast ballots. Although EA publishes the final sum of blinding factors F_ν, it also includes all auxiliary verification values α_i in the VL. This design enables: Voters to cryptographically verify blinding factor consistency during ballot encryption by checking α_i against values published by the EA; Independent validation of the authenticity of F_ν during tallying through α_i using zero-knowledge principles. This design enhances protocol robustness against potential EA misbehavior.

6 Performance Evaluation

We compare FP-BSS with existing self-tallying voting schemes. Our protocol robustly achieves comprehensive coverage of all essential security properties. Detailed comparisons are presented in Table 2.

Table 2. Comparison of Self-Tallying Voting Schemes

	[5]	[6]	[7]	[12]	[14]	Ours
Full privacy	●	×	●	×	×	●
Time-limited privacy	●	●	×	●	×	●
Linkability	●	●	×	●	×	●
Universal verifiability	●	●	●	○	●	●
Robustness	×	●	●	●	○	●
Voting type	Binary	Score Voting	Binary	Choose-One	Choose-One	Score Voting

●: completely satisfy; ○: partly satisfy; ×: not satisfy

We implement FP-BSS and conduct a comprehensive performance evaluation. Our experiments included both off-chain and on-chain parts. Each experiment is repeated 10 times with averaged results. The hardware environment we used is a PC with Intel(R) Core(TM) i7-8565U CPU @ 1.80GHz 1.99 GHz, 8 GB RAM and Ubuntu 20.04 system.

Off-chain Performance: We implement FP-BSS in Go and compile it using GoLand 2024. Each experiment is repeated 10 times with averaged results. We configure the system with $n = 3$ voters, $m = 3$ candidates, and time hardness parameter $t = 30,000,000$. This time hardness parameter is adjustable, a larger

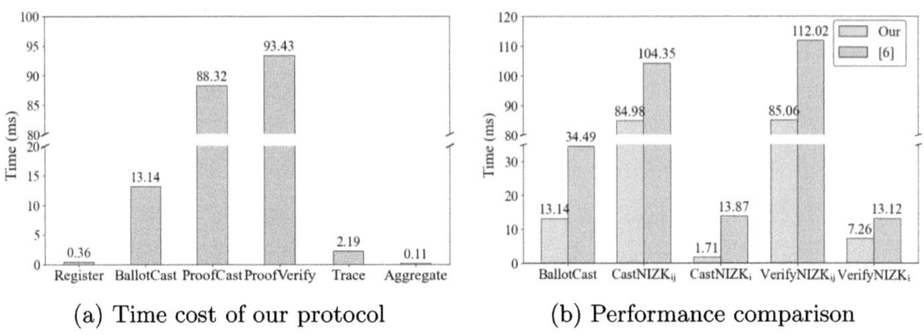

(a) Time cost of our protocol (b) Performance comparison

Fig. 5. Performance evaluation.

value increases the time required to solve the time-lock puzzle. The protocol's time cost is shown in Fig. 5(a). Voters must register with the EA to obtain legal voting status, requiring 0.36 ms per registration. To cast a ballot, voters perform encryption requiring 13.14 ms. Additionally, voters generate range proofs, total proofs, and ballot signatures, with respective times of 84.98 ms, 1.71 ms, and 1.63 ms. Range proof generation constitutes the most computationally intensive operation and therefore consumes the most time. For ballot verification, a verifier must validate the corresponding proofs and signature, requiring 85.06 ms, 7.26 ms, and 1.11 ms respectively. Ballot tracing and aggregation require 2.19 ms and 0.11 ms respectively.

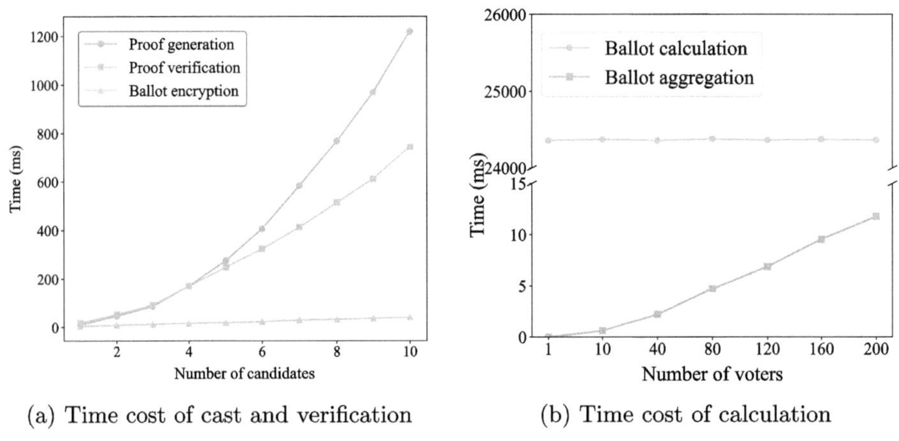

(a) Time cost of cast and verification (b) Time cost of calculation

Fig. 6. Effects of different voters and candidates.

We present a performance comparison with [5], with results shown in Fig. 5(b). It can be observed that the scheme in [5] requires more time for ballot casting and verification. This efficiency improvement in our protocol arises from linking the random number used for ballot encryption to the order of the elliptic curve, which reduces computational costs for modular operations.

We evaluate the time costs of ballot encryption, proof generation, and verification with different numbers of candidates. Based on actual voting application scenarios, we configure the system with up to 10 candidates and 200 voters to simulate realistic voting environments. As shown in Fig. 6(a), we set the number of candidates from 1 to 10, and as the number of candidates increases, the time required for these three steps also increases. We also evaluate the time costs of ballot aggregation and calculation with different numbers of voters. As shown in Fig. 6(b), we set the number of voters up to 200, and as the number of voters increases, the time required for aggregation also increases. When the number of voters is 200, the time required for ballot aggregation is 11.78 ms, and the time required for the calculation remains stable. This enables our system to maintain robust scalability even with progressively increasing voter populations.

Table 3. Time Cost of Operations

Operation	Time Cost	Operation	Time Cost
BallotCast	0.143 s	Trace	0.026 s
Generate range proof	0.556 s	Verify range proof	0.455 s
Generate sum proof	0.053 s	Verify sum proof	0.100 s
Generate signature	0.029 s	Verify signature	0.026 s

On-Chain Performance: We deploy FP-BSS on a Hyperledger Fabric 2.2-based permissioned blockchain network, configured with two organizations and a single ordering node to evaluate its performance. Each experiment is repeated 10 times with averaged results. To better evaluate performance, we conduct comprehensive benchmarking of the smart contract using the Caliper framework under controlled experimental conditions. We use fixed load rate control at 5 transactions per second. We maintain consistency by following the off-chain settings mentioned above. As shown in Table 3, the BallotCast operation requires 0.143 s, while range proof generation, sum proof generation, and signature generation require 0.556 s, 0.053 s, and 0.029 s respectively. Range proof generation constitutes the most computationally intensive operation, consistent with prior analysis. The Trace operation completes in 0.026 s, while range proof verification, sum proof verification, and signature verification require 0.455 s, 0.100 s, and 0.026 s respectively.

7 Conclusion

In this paper, we propose FP-BSS, a full privacy blockchain-based self-tallying score voting protocol. The protocol provides enhanced security. Specifically, we extend voting scheme to support score voting. We design a novel full privacy ballot encryption scheme. Also, we propose a new zero-knowledge proof system for encrypted ballot legitimacy verification. Our protocol satisfies the properties of full privacy, time-limited privacy, linkability, universal verifiability, and robustness. Experimental results from both on-chain and off-chain implementations demonstrate that our scheme maintains practical efficiency.

Acknowledgments. This work is supported by the National Natural Science Foundation of China (62372097) and the Fundamental Research Funds for the Central Universities (N2416003).

References

1. Xiangjuan, J., Xinwei, F., Yijie, Z., et al.: Integration and innovation of blockchain in Web3.0: current status and standardization prospects. World Wide Web **28**, 7 (2025)
2. Ma, Y., Sun, Y., Lei, Y., et al.: A survey of blockchain technology on security, privacy, and trust in crowdsourcing services. World Wide Web **23**, 393–419 (2020)
3. Kshetri, N., Voas, J.: Blockchain-enabled e-voting. IEEE Softw. **35**(4), 95–99 (2018)
4. Yichao, L., Li, H., Gao, L., Jiaxin, Yu., Yong, Yu., Hexing, S.: Self-tallying e-voting with public traceability based on blockchain. Comput. Stand. Interfaces **88**, 103795 (2024). ISSN 0920-5489
5. Miao, M., Tang, L., Li, J., Zhang, X.: New blockchain-based publicly traceable self-tallying voting protocol. IEEE Trans. Network Sci. Eng. **11**(2), 2034–2046 (2024)
6. Huang, J., He, D., Chen, Y., Khan, M.K., Luo, M.: A blockchain-based self-tallying voting protocol with maximum voter privacy. IEEE Trans. Network Sci. Eng. **9**(5), 3808–3820 (2022)
7. Kohno, T., Stubblefield, A., Rubin, A.D., Wallach, D.S.: Analysis of an electronic voting system. In: Proceedings of the IEEE Symposium Security Privacy, pp. 27–40 (2004)
8. Kiayias, A., Yung, M.:: Self-tallying elections and perfect ballot secrecy. In: Proceedings of the International Workshop Public Key Cryptogr., pp. 141–158 (2002)
9. Malavolta, G., Thyagarajan, S.A.K.: Homomorphic time-lock puzzles and applications. In: Proceedings of the Annual International Cryptology Conference, pp. 620–649 (2019)
10. McCorry, P., Shahandashti, S.F., Hao, F.: A smart contract for boardroom voting with maximum voter privacy. In: Kiayias, A. (ed.) Financial Cryptography and Data Security. LNCS, vol. 10322, pp. 357–375. Springer, Cham, Switzerland (2017). https://doi.org/10.1007/978-3-319-70972-7_20
11. Khader, D., Smyth, B., Ryan, P., Hao, F.: A fair and robust voting system by broadcast. Lect. Note. Inform. 285–299 (2012)
12. Lin, Y., Zhang, P.: Blockchain-based complete self-tallying E-voting protocol. In: 2019 Asia-Pacific Signal and Information Processing Association Annual Summit and Conference, pp. 47–52 (2019)
13. Yang, Y., Guan, Z., Wan, Z., Weng, J., Pang, H.H., Deng, R.H.: PriScore: blockchain-based self-tallying election system supporting score voting. IEEE Trans. Inf. Forensics Secur. **16**, 4705–4720 (2021)
14. Li, Y., et al.: A blockchain-based self-tallying voting protocol in decentralized IoT. IEEE Trans. Dependable Secure Comput. **19**(1), 119–130 (2022)

Large Language Models I

FORA: An Efficient One-for-All Cross-Task Reasoning Framework for Financial Domain via LLMs

Zhichao Duan[1], Tengyu Pan[1], Zhenyu Li[1], Bowen Dong[1], Xiuxing Li[2], and Jianyong Wang[1(✉)]

[1] Tsinghua University, Beijing, China
jianyong@tsinghua.edu.cn
[2] Beijing Institute of Technology, Beijing, China

Abstract. In the field of finance, understanding the abundant information encapsulated in comprehensive financial materials is fundamental for analysts to make well-informed decisions and optimize strategies. However, it demands a profound understanding of the financial intricacies. In this study, we introduce ***FORA***, an efficient Financial One-foR-All cross-task reasoning framework via large language models (LLMs). To optimize information processing, ***FORA*** begins by refining raw data, generating a clarified and context-rich analysis via an information refinement module. Subsequently, ***FORA*** utilizes an inference enhancement module to seamlessly integrate information from various sources, including the refined signals, facilitating the accurate mapping from input to output. By leveraging the powerful capabilities of LLMs, these modules can efficiently adapt to diverse task types with minimal data requirements and zero training costs. ***FORA*** is tested across four representative tasks, demonstrating an average performance increase of **6.33%**. In light of this and our subsequent analysis, we argue that ***FORA*** represents a significant stride forward in the exploration of advanced cross-task financial reasoning frameworks.

Keywords: Financial Reasoning · Cross-Task Reasoning · Large Language Models

1 Introduction

In the realm of finance, a vast amount of valuable information is embedded within financial materials, encompassing text documents [17], images [37], etc. Analyzing financial materials is the foundation of making informed investment decisions, understanding market trends, predicting future outcomes, and mitigating risks in the ever-evolving finance landscape. Yet, deciphering these materials requires more than just surface-level analysis. It demands a deep understanding of financial principles, industry dynamics, and advanced analytical tools to extract meaningful insights and draw accurate conclusions. In response to

I. Awan et al. (Eds.): WISE 2025, LNCS 16367, pp. 245–259, 2026.
https://doi.org/10.1007/978-981-95-7394-3_17

these challenges, recent works have leveraged advanced technologies, such as deep learning algorithms [2,15,32] and language models [18,28], to enhance the analysis of financial information. However, a significant portion of the research is focused on specific tasks, such as question answering [10,16,30]. Such methods often overlook the broader, interconnected context that is intrinsic to the financial domain. Conversely, several studies encompass the entire financial domain but tend to prioritize the infusion of domain-specific knowledge into language models [18,28,33], whether it occurs during pre-training or fine-tuning processes. Integrating financial knowledge into the underlying language models proves instrumental in addressing complexities like intricate terminology and resolving ambiguity [28,33]. However, there exist other essential elements to consider in crafting an advanced financial reasoning model.

Firstly, the financial domain encompasses various tasks of different types, each with its distinctive input and output specifications, as well as unique mechanisms to map inputs to outputs [5,26,31]. Secondly, acquiring a sufficient amount of well-labeled training data is crucial. Tailoring the model to each task requires substantial training data, especially when adhering to the pretraining-finetuning paradigm to adjust the model. Furthermore, despite the varying forms of input data across different tasks, they all encounter a shared obstacle: essential information is often dispersed within the raw input data. The challenges mentioned above underscore the crucial importance of adaptability across diverse task types, efficient retrieval of relevant information, and effective execution of reasoning processes to enhance financial domain reasoning.

In response, we introduce FORA, an efficient Financial One-foR-All cross-task reasoning framework via large language models (LLMs). FORA first reduces the heavy reliance on a large amount of training data by leveraging LLMs [9,22] as its core operators. This inclusion equips FORA not only with extensive financial domain knowledge, enabling it to comprehend complex terminology, but also empowers it to swiftly adapt to new tasks with just a few examples for in-context learning [4], bypassing the heavy fine-tuning process. Inside FORA, there are two main components, namely information refinement and inference enhancement modules. The information refinement process encompasses reviewing raw input data, recognizing pertinent information, and crafting a clarified context-rich analysis. This pivotal step serves to distill intricate financial data into concise, manageable units that streamline subsequent reasoning processes. The inference enhancement module, on the other hand, focuses on improving the reasoning capabilities of the model. It integrates various pieces of information, including the refined signals obtained in the previous step. Subsequently, it employs abductive reasoning to generate results that are semantically rich and accompanied by a plausible explanation. In this way, FORA not only provides accurate answers but also offers insights into the underlying rationale, enhancing its transparency and interpretability, which are crucial in the financial domain. The final stage of this module involves grounding the results with task output requirements and completing the reasoning processes. Experiments on four diverse datasets [5,20,21,26] covering essential financial tasks—classification, regression, named entity recognition, and question answering—validate FORA's effectiveness.

This study offers the following primary contributions to the field of financial reasoning:

- We introduce FORA, a highly efficient cross-task reasoning framework explicitly tailored for the financial domain. FORA mitigates the heavy data reliance by wrapping LLMs as it core operators.
- To streamline reasoning processes, FORA includes an information refinement module to distill raw input data and generate a clarified and context-rich analysis.
- To improve the reasoning capabilities, FORA contains another inference enhancement module that integrates various information and performs abductive reasoning to generate the results.
- We showcase the remarkable effectiveness of FORA on four challenging benchmarks covering major financial reasoning task types.

2 Related Work

By examining how others calibrate their model parameters, we can classify them into two primary groups: fine-tuning based methods and fine-tuning free methods.

2.1 Fine-tuning Based Methods

Fine-tuning based financial reasoning algorithms conventionally commence with versatile pre-trained language models (PLMs) [8,13,19,25], followed by fine-tuning on financial task datasets [7,12,29–31] to improve their task-specific comprehension and reasoning capabilities [1,5,6,16]. For example, both [1,36] employ similar approaches. They first conduct extra pre-training on financial corpora to augment their models' competence in the financial domain. Subsequently, they fine-tune the models on sentiment analysis training data, improving their capacity for accurate task inference. On a different trajectory, [28] direct their efforts towards comprehensive financial domain reasoning. Instead of relying on masked language modeling (MLM) [8] as the primary pre-training objective, as seen in the works of [1,36], they integrate preferential token masking and phrase prediction [11] to infuse their model with a deeper understanding of financial concepts.

In the era of large language models (LLMs), considerable efforts have been dedicated to improving financial domain reasoning by fine-tuning these models. Innovations like FinMa [34], FinGPT [18], and InvestLM [35] highlight this trend. Unlike methods based on PLMs, which require retraining on task-specific datasets for each new task, these approaches integrate a diverse set of task datasets. By leveraging the strengths of LLMs in multitasking and training them on this combined dataset, these models are empowered to reason across a wide range of tasks. For instance, FinMa, FinGPT, and InvestLM have all utilized

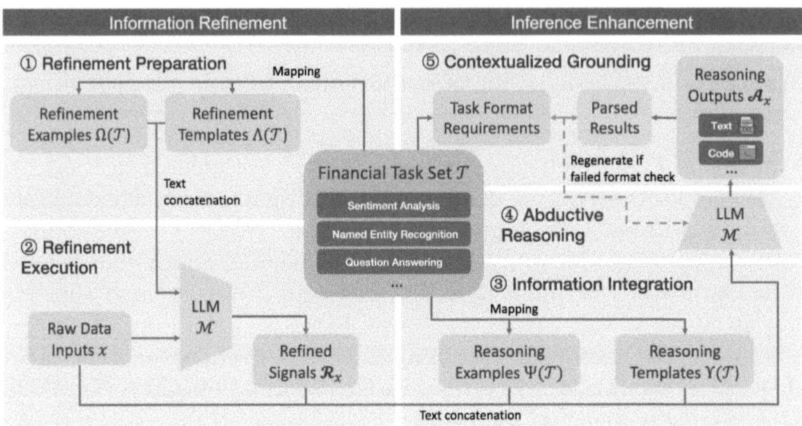

Fig. 1. The overall architecture of FORA.

extensive instruction datasets to fine-tune open-source LLMs. However, this fine-tuning approach not only increases the demand for computational resources but also raises concerns about the models' ability to generalize, as it often relies on training data that is typically from the same source as the test data. Therefore, alternative methods that do not rely on fine-tuning often have broader application potential.

2.2 Fine-tuning Free Methods

While fine-tuning based methods involve adapting PLMs or LLMs to the financial tasks through additional training, fine-tuning free methods harness the remarkable capabilities of LLMs [3,27,33,38] to process, understand, and reason over financial materials without the need for extensive task-specific adaptation. A significant leap in this domain was made by [33], who engineered BloombergGPT, a 50 billion parameter language model that is trained on a wide range of financial data. This model demonstrates exceptional performance on financial benchmarks and maintains a competitive edge compared to general-purpose language models. Later on, the study of LLMs in the context of financial domain reasoning has been further advanced by [14]. Their work has delved into examining of ChatGPT [23] and GPT-4 [24], two influential language models, specifically evaluating their performance across a diverse array of financial tasks. The outcomes of their comprehensive analysis showcase a remarkable level of performance, thereby establishing a robust baseline for subsequent research endeavors.

3 FORA

In this section, we introduce FORA, our one-for-all reasoning framework for the financial domain. We begin by presenting the foundational aspects of FORA, followed by an exposition of its information refinement module. At last, we conclude by explaining how FORA leverages the inference enhancement module to generate reasoning outcomes. The comprehensive structure of FORA is visually depicted in Fig. 1.

3.1 Preliminaries

In the financial domain, tasks in the task set $\mathcal{T}$ exhibit significant variation in both input and output formats. We conceptualize each task as a generation task. This perspective implies that irrespective of the output format—whether it comprises entity spans, numerical data, or class labels—the primary objective remains consistent: to generate the ideal match for the target output. We assume the availability of a generative LLM that has been optimized mainly through maximizing the following likelihood:

$$L(\mathcal{S}) = \sum_{i=1} log\, \mathrm{P}(u^i | u^{i-k}, ..., u^{i-1}; \Theta) \tag{1}$$

where $\mathcal{S}$ is the token sequence, k represents the size of the context window, and the conditional probability P is modeled using a neural network with parameters Θ. We posit that the LLM in question not only demonstrates exceptional natural language understanding capabilities but also excels in generating text of high quality and contextual relevance spanning a diverse array of topics and styles.

3.2 Information Refinement

Raw data in the financial domain typically contains abundant content but often lacks clarity and contextualization regarding the specific task objectives. To address this challenge, the information refinement module employs a two-step process: refinement preparation and refinement execution.

Refinement Preparation. To enhance the effectiveness of our approach and mitigate the need for extensive training data, we integrate a LLM as the cornerstone of the module. Given that LLMs predominantly operate based on the prompts they receive, constructing them is of paramount importance. The process of refining raw data is intricately linked to the specific objective of a task. To cater to the unique requirements of each task, we initially curate task-specific templates. These templates clarify the meaning of the input data, expose task objectives, and serve as guides for the LLM to generate clarified and context-rich analysis. Moreover, to enhance the stability of the refined results, we incorporate several refinement demonstration examples. These examples demonstrate the execution of the provided refinement instructions in the template, thereby reinforcing the connection between raw data and task objectives. We represent the template for the i-th task as R^i:

$$\mathrm{R}^i = Concatenate(\Lambda(\mathcal{T}^i), \Omega(\mathcal{T}^i)) \tag{2}$$

where Λ denotes the mapping from the task type $\mathcal{T}^i$ to its corresponding predefined refinement template, which includes both the refinement instructions and the task objective information. Ω maps the task type to its associated refinement demonstration examples, which are pre-selected for each task. The provided demonstration examples offer explicit guidance to LLMs, illustrating precisely how to implement refinement instructions on the given input data.

Refinement Execution. With a proficient LLM $\mathcal{M}$ and a crafted template R^i, we initiate the refinement execution:

$$\mathcal{R}_{x^i} = \mathcal{M}(Concatenate(\mathrm{R}^i, x^i)) \tag{3}$$

where x^i represents the input of the i-th task. Before feeding the raw data x^i into the LLM $\mathcal{M}$, the template R^i is finalized by concatenating x^i into it. During refinement, the LLM contextualizes the raw financial data within the merged text sequence. It reviews the raw data, recognizes pertinent information, or identifies key patterns and trends, aligning them with the task objectives specified in the template. This contextualization paves the way for the next stage, inference enhancement.

3.3 Inference Enhancement

After obtaining the refined analysis, we advance to the inference enhancement phase, which is also built upon LLMs and divided into three pivotal steps: information integration, abductive reasoning, and contextualized grounding.

Information Integration. In this phase, our objective is to streamline the reasoning process by assembling templates that integrate diverse sets of information. Specifically, we integrate the refined signals $\mathcal{R}_{x^i}$ derived from the previous module, task-specific objective information, abductive reasoning directives, and illustrative examples:

$$\mathrm{U}^i = Concatenate(\Upsilon(\mathcal{T}^i), \Psi(\mathcal{T}^i), \mathcal{R}_{x^i}) \tag{4}$$

where Υ denotes the mapping from the task type $\mathcal{T}^i$ to the corresponding predefined abductive reasoning template, encapsulating both the task's objective information and abductive reasoning guidelines. Additionally, Ψ maps the task type $\mathcal{T}^i$ to a curated set of demonstration examples. These examples illustrate to LLMs how to utilize the combined information in conjunction with pre-selected data instances to engage in abductive reasoning, while also detailing the expected output formats. It's crucial to note that the demonstration examples don't directly correlate the data instance and the combined information with the desired output results across different tasks. Instead, they convert the combined signals and data instance into outcomes that are pertinent to the task, infused with semantic richness, and accompanied by explanations of the results.

Abductive Reasoning. Upon acquiring the merged text sequence U^i, we harness the in-context learning capacity of LLMs to emulate the reasoning process outlined in the template:

$$\mathcal{A}_{x^i} = \mathcal{M}(Concatenate(\mathrm{U}^i, x^i)). \tag{5}$$

As previously mentioned, these demonstration examples guide LLMs to produce semantically rich and pertinent textual responses along with explanations. Such abductive reasoning setting can greatly enhance the model's ability to understand and respond to complex tasks. By capitalizing on the contextual comprehension provided by refined analysis and task-specific instructions, the LLM can engage in sophisticated reasoning, deducing logical connections, and drawing insightful conclusions. The generated explanations can provide insight into the LLM's decision-making process, offering transparency and interpretability to its outputs. This not only builds trust in the model's responses but also enables users to understand the rationale behind its conclusions. Given that the outcomes of abductive reasoning yield text sequences that may not align with the task's desired output space, an additional transformation becomes necessary.

Contextualized Grounding. In the final phase of inference enhancement, the contextualized grounding process fortifies the model's reasoning by aligning the reasoning outcomes with the specific format required for each task. To achieve this, we leverage the results of abductive reasoning $\mathcal{A}_{x^i}$. Initially, we assess the compliance of these outcomes with the predetermined format tailored for each task. Should the initial outcomes fail to meet the format requirements, we continuously conduct the abductive reasoning process until the generated text sequence aligns with the desired format. Following this, we utilize rule-based methods to convert these semantically rich results into the specified output format, thereby concluding the reasoning process. By adhering to task-specific formats and aligning the reasoning outputs accordingly, the model's results become readily interpretable and actionable. Overall, the contextualized grounding process represents a critical component of the inference enhancement module.

4 Applications of FORA

In this section, we explore a range of distinct financial tasks, demonstrating how FORA can adapt to address various challenges and requirements.

4.1 Sentiment Analysis

Financial sentiment analysis is a critical process that entails discerning the market or financial trend based on information gleaned from financial texts, often expressed either in categorical [21] or continuous values [20]. In the initial stage, FORA utilizes the information refinement module to produce a thorough analysis, uncovering latent inclinations towards the specified aspect and scrutinizing contextual cues that may indicate sentiment. Following that, the inference enhancement module merges various information and engages in abductive reasoning, identifying patterns within the input to generate textual responses that potentially explain the outcomes. Finally, the textual responses are aligned with task labels to conclude the reasoning process.

4.2 Named Entity Recognition

Financial named entity recognition stands as a pivotal task within the financial domain, necessitating the precise identification and extraction of financial entities from a given input context. In this task, the objective of the information refinement module in FORA is to process the raw input and extract all potential entities within the context, regardless of their entity types. Subsequently, the inference enhancement module processes the extracted entities and assigns textual entity labels to each one. These predicted entity labels serve as both the responses and explanations. The entity recognition process concludes with aligning the labels with the task's target labels.

4.3 Question Answering

Financial question answer often necessitates the analysis of both textual content and tabular data. This process entails sophisticated reasoning, as well as the execution of intricate mathematical and tabular computations to generate the correct answer. FORA also tackles this task through the two modules. The information refinement module scrutinizes the pertinent data to be retrieved and offers comprehensive, step-by-step guides for arriving at the answers. Following this, the inference enhancement module engages in the task of mapping the refined results, along with other information, to Python programs, which also serve as explanations of the results. Finally, the Python programs are verified and executed to obtain the predictions.

5 Experiments

5.1 Datasets

To comprehensively assess the performance and effectiveness of FORA, we conduct extensive evaluations on four well-established datasets: Financial PhraseBank [21], FiQA SA [20], NER [26], and FinQA [5]. These evaluation datasets cover highly representative financial domain task types, such as classification, regression, NER, and generative QA. It is important to emphasize that the Financial PhraseBank dataset [21] used for evaluating classification performance includes two different splits: the 50% agreement split and the 100% agreement split. The 50% split means at least half the annotators concurred on the labeling results, while the 100% split signifies unanimous agreement among all annotators.

5.2 Implementation Details

Our framework, FORA, is implemented in two variations. The first variation, FORA (ChatGPT), leverages ChatGPT as the core operators within the two modules. In the second variation, FORA (GPT-4), GPT-4 serves as the core operators in the same role. For repeatability, the parameter temperature is initially set to 0. It increases by 0.1 each time the generated results from the inference enhancement module fail the format check.

5.3 Experimental Settings

In light of the diverse evaluation methodologies employed in various studies, we strive to maintain the integrity and comparability of our experimental analyses by utilizing a set of widely recognized and thoroughly documented experimental protocols across four distinct tasks. For the Financial PhraseBank, we follow [14]'s setting and set aside 20% of all sentences for testing. In contrast to the approaches taken by [18,34,35], which converted the regression task into a classification task, our method for FiQA SA follows the framework set forth by [28]. We assess sentiment scores associated with particular targets on a continuous scale from -1 to 1, with 1 indicating a highly positive sentiment and -1 indicating a highly negative sentiment. For Named Entity Recognition (NER), we follow the protocol set by [33] in BloombergGPT, excluding entities labeled as MISC due to their vague categorization, as well as sentences devoid of any entities. For the FinQA dataset, we utilize the provided test set to evaluate our model's performance and report the results in terms of accuracy. To comprehensively evaluate and highlight FORA's performance, we conducted comparisons with several influential and state-of-the-art methods that adhere to the same experimental settings.

5.4 Benchmark Results

The evaluation results of FORA (ChatGPT) and FORA (GPT-4), alongside other established methods, are presented in the subsequent sections. In each result table, the best results are highlighted in **bold**, while the second-best results are underlined. Fine-tuning based methods are denoted by the symbol "♣", while fine-tuning free methods are not assigned any specific label. "/" indicates that the corresponding result for a particular method has not been reported.

Financial PhraseBank. The evaluation results of FORA on the Financial PhraseBank dataset along with other well-established baselines are presented in Table 1. In the 50% agreement setting, FORA (ChatGPT) achieves an accuracy and F1 score of 77%, while FORA (GPT-4) achieves an accuracy and F1 score of 81%. Notably, the results of FORA (GPT-4) outperform all other fine-tuning free methods and remain competitive when compared to the fine-tuning based method FinBERT. However, the test data under the 50% agreement setting exhibits significantly lower quality compared to data with 100% agreement.

Table 1. Results on the Financial PhraseBank dataset [21].

Split	50% Agreement		100% Agreement	
Model	*Accuracy*	*F1 score*	*Accuracy*	*F1 score*
FinBERT♣	**0.86**	**0.84**	**0.97**	0.95
GPT-NeoX	/	0.45	/	/
OPT66B	/	0.49	/	/
BLOOM176B	/	0.50	/	/
BloombergGPT	/	0.51	/	/
GPT-4	0.76	0.78	0.89	0.90
ChatGPT	0.78	0.78	0.90	0.90
FORA(ChatGPT)	0.77	0.77	0.92	0.92
FORA(GPT-4)	0.81	0.81	**0.97**	**0.97**

Achieving excessively high accuracy would indicate overfitting to the chaotic distribution of the data rather than learning the true underlying distribution. Results under this setting highlights the adaptability as well as robustness of FORA. Under the 100% agreement setting, FORA (ChatGPT) achieves an accuracy and F1 score of 92%, while FORA (GPT-4) achieves an accuracy and F1 score of 97%. Among the listed methods, FORA (GPT-4) attains the highest accuracy and F1 score, demonstrating its effectiveness. The discrepancy in performance between FORA (ChatGPT) and FORA (GPT-4) is likely due to the fact that when GPT-4 is used as the underlying operators for FORA, it possesses superior comprehension and reasoning abilities compared to ChatGPT. Furthermore, FORA achieves even better performance than the fine-tuning based model FinBERT, despite requiring significantly less data. This strongly underscores the efficiency and low data requirement of FORA.

Table 2. Results on the NER dataset [26].

Model	*Entity F1*
ChatGPT	51.27
BLOOM176B	55.56
GPT-4	56.71
OPT66B	57.49
BloombergGPT	60.82
GPT-NeoX	60.98
FORA(GPT-4)	66.67
FORA(ChatGPT)	**68.10**

Named Entity Recognition. We report entity-level F1 scores of FORA and other well-established methods in Table 2. In this task, FORA (GPT-4) and FORA (ChatGPT) exhibit a substantial performance advantage over all other methods. In particular, FORA (ChatGPT) achieves a remarkable performance gain of 32.83% compared to ChatGPT, while FORA (GPT-4) exhibits a notable performance gain of 17.56% compared to GPT-4. The fact that the baseline model GPT-4 outperforms ChatGPT while FORA (ChatGPT) outperforms FORA (GPT-4) may be due to FORA's one-for-all design, which indicates there is still room for improvement in the NER task. Specifically, the potential of wrapping GPT-4 as the core operators inside information refinement module and the inference enhancement module can still be further developed. Nonetheless, this does not diminish FORA's overall efficacy, as it continues to demonstrate an average relative improvement of 25.20% on the task.

Table 3. Results on FiQA SA [20].

Model	*MSE*	*R2*
RCNN♣	0.090	0.41
ChatGPT	0.087	/
GPT-4	0.082	/
SC-V♣	0.080	0.40
BERT♣	0.074	0.59
FinBERT♣	0.070	0.57
FLANG-BERT♣	0.052	0.67
ELECTRA♣	0.046	0.72
FLANG-ELECTRA♣	**0.039**	**0.77**
FORA(ChatGPT)	0.078	0.53
FORA(GPT-4)	0.055	0.67

FiQA SA. The results on FiQA SA [20] are presented in Table 3. Considering MSE, FORA (ChatGPT) and FORA (GPT-4) exhibit a reduction of 10% and 33%, respectively, when compared to the baseline methods ChatGPT and GPT-4. Significantly, FORA (GPT-4) achieves performance comparable to fine-tuning based models that inherently possess advantages over fine-tuning free methods. Fine-tuning based models adapt to training data distributions for accurate predictions on test data. In contrast, FORA, a fine-tuning free framework, doesn't require extensive training data yet still matches performance, highlighting its versatility and efficacy. The performance gap between FORA (GPT-4) and FORA (ChatGPT) likely also stems from GPT-4's enhanced capabilities, further emphasizing the significant role of the underlying operators in both modules. It is worth mentioning again that we did not follow the settings introduced by [35], which converts this regression task into a classification task that LLMs can generally handle more effectively. In classification tasks, category labels often carry rich semantic information, making label generation more aligned with the pretraining objectives of LLMs. However, predicting a continuous number as a label lacks an intuitive semantic correspondence, which may lead to poorer performance for LLM-based approaches on such tasks. This explains why Table 1 indicates that employing GPT-4 and ChatGPT alone can lead to favorable outcomes, yet in the context of this experiment, their performance is notably inferior. Nonetheless, this approach provides a more comprehensive evaluation of FORA's effectiveness and generalization capabilities.

Table 4. Results on the FinQA dataset [5].

Model	*Accuracy*
`FinMA`	15.00
`InvestLM`	29.00
`ChatGPT`	57.50
`FinQANet`♣	61.24
`GPT-4`	<u>62.87</u>
`FORA(ChatGPT)`	58.46
`FORA(GPT-4)`	**74.72**
General Crowd	50.68
Human Expert	91.16

FinQA. The evaluation results of FORA on the FinQA dataset [5] are presented in Table 4. This task is the most complex among the four evaluated tasks, involving both unstructured textual data and structured tabular data, requiring integrated reasoning to arrive at the correct answers. As shown in the table, although FORA (ChatGPT) does not surpass the fine-tuning based method FinQANet, it still outperforms ChatGPT by nearly 2%. FORA (GPT-4), on the other hand, demonstrates exceptional performance, surpassing the second-best method, GPT-4, by over 18%. Wth the remarkable performance achieved by FORA, strongly validates the effectiveness of its design, particularly the synergy between the information refinement and inference enhancement modules.

6 Conclusions

In this work, we introduce FORA, an efficient one-for-all framework meticulously designed to enhance financial domain reasoning. FORA operates through an integration of its information refinement and inference enhancement modules, strategically engineered to address the complexities arising from scattered relevant information and diverse task specifications. By leveraging these components in a sequential manner, FORA has shown remarkable performance across various financial tasks, as evidenced by its impressive results on four representative datasets. These compelling outcomes firmly establish FORA as a potent and versatile tool poised to significantly augment the process of financial reasoning.

Acknowledgments. This work was supported in part by National Natural Science Foundation of China under Grant No. 62272264 and No. 62306300.

Disclosure of Interests. The authors have no competing interests to declare that are relevant to the content of this article.

References

1. Araci, D.: FinBERT: financial sentiment analysis with pre-trained language models. arXiv preprint arXiv:1908.10063 (2019)
2. Avramelou, L., Nousi, P., Passalis, N., Tefas, A.: Deep reinforcement learning for financial trading using multi-modal features. Expert Syst. Appl. **238**, 121849 (2024)
3. Black, S., et al.: GPT-NeoX-20B: an open-source autoregressive language model. In: Proceedings of BigScience Episode #5 – Workshop on Challenges & Perspectives in Creating Large Language Models, pp. 95–136. Association for Computational Linguistics, virtual+Dublin (2022). https://doi.org/10.18653/v1/2022.bigscience-1.9, https://aclanthology.org/2022.bigscience-1.9
4. Brown, T., et al.: Language models are few-shot learners. Adv. Neural. Inf. Process. Syst. **33**, 1877–1901 (2020)
5. Chen, Z., et al.: FinQA: a dataset of numerical reasoning over financial data. In: Proceedings of the 2021 Conference on Empirical Methods in Natural Language Processing, pp. 3697–3711. Association for Computational Linguistics, Online and Punta Cana, Dominican Republic (2021). https://doi.org/10.18653/v1/2021.emnlp-main.300, https://aclanthology.org/2021.emnlp-main.300
6. Chen, Z., Li, S., Smiley, C., Ma, Z., Shah, S., Wang, W.Y.: CONVFINQA: exploring the chain of numerical reasoning in conversational finance question answering. arXiv preprint arXiv:2210.03849 (2022)
7. Deußer, T., et al.: KPI-EDGAR: a novel dataset and accompanying metric for relation extraction from financial documents. arXiv preprint arXiv:2210.09163 (2022)
8. Devlin, J., Chang, M.W., Lee, K., Toutanova, K.: BERT: pre-training of deep bidirectional transformers for language understanding. arXiv preprint arXiv:1810.04805 (2018)
9. Du, Z., et al.: GLM: general language model pretraining with autoregressive blank infilling. arXiv preprint arXiv:2103.10360 (2021)
10. Fatouros, G., Soldatos, J., Kouroumali, K., Makridis, G., Kyriazis, D.: Transforming sentiment analysis in the financial domain with ChatGPT. arXiv preprint arXiv:2308.07935 (2023)
11. Glass, M., et al.: Span selection pre-training for question answering. In: Proceedings of the 58th Annual Meeting of the Association for Computational Linguistics, pp. 2773–2782 (2020)

12. Huang, X., et al.: DGRAPH: a large-scale financial dataset for graph anomaly detection. In: Thirty-sixth Conference on Neural Information Processing Systems Datasets and Benchmarks Track (2022)
13. Lewis, M., et al.: BART: denoising sequence-to-sequence pre-training for natural language generation, translation, and comprehension. In: Proceedings of the 58th Annual Meeting of the Association for Computational Linguistics, pp. 7871–7880 (2020)
14. Li, X., Zhu, X., Ma, Z., Liu, X., Shah, S.: Are ChatGPT and GPT-4 general-purpose solvers for financial text analytics? An examination on several typical tasks. arXiv preprint arXiv:2305.05862 (2023)
15. Liang, R., Zhang, W., Ye, H.: Interpretable deep learning based text regression for financial prediction. Expert. Syst. **40**(9), e13368 (2023)
16. Liao, V., Murtaza, S.S., Nie, Y., Lin, J.: Regex-augmented domain transfer topic classification based on a pre-trained language model: an application in financial domain. arXiv preprint arXiv:2305.18324 (2023)
17. Liu, S., Cao, J., Yang, R., Wen, Z.: Long text and multi-table summarization: dataset and method. arXiv preprint arXiv:2302.03815 (2023)
18. Liu, X.Y., Wang, G., Yang, H., Zha, D.: FinGPT: democratizing internet-scale data for financial large language models. arXiv preprint arXiv:2307.10485 (2023)
19. Liu, Y., Ott, M., Goyal, N., Du, J., Joshi, M., Chen, D., Levy, O., Lewis, M., Zettlemoyer, L., Stoyanov, V.: RoBERTa: a robustly optimized BERT pretraining approach. arXiv preprint arXiv:1907.11692 (2019)
20. Maia, M., et al.: WWW'18 open challenge: financial opinion mining and question answering. In: Companion Proceedings of the The Web Conference 2018, pp. 1941–1942. WWW 2018, International World Wide Web Conferences Steering Committee, Republic and Canton of Geneva, CHE (2018). https://doi.org/10.1145/3184558.3192301
21. Malo, P., Sinha, A., Korhonen, P., Wallenius, J., Takala, P.: Good debt or bad debt: detecting semantic orientations in economic texts. J. Am. Soc. Inf. Sci. **65**(4), 782–796 (2014)
22. Meta, A.: Introducing llama: a foundational, 65-billion-parameter large language model. Meta AI (2023). https://ai.meta.com/blog/large-language-model-llama-meta-ai/
23. OpenAI: ChatGPT (2023). https://openai.com/product/chatgpt
24. OpenAI: GPT-4 (2023). https://openai.com/product/gpt-4
25. Peters, M.E., et al.: Deep contextualized word representations. In: Proceedings of the 2018 Conference of the North American Chapter of the Association for Computational Linguistics: Human Language Technologies, Volume 1 (Long Papers), pp. 2227–2237. Association for Computational Linguistics, New Orleans, Louisiana (2018). https://doi.org/10.18653/v1/N18-1202, https://aclanthology.org/N18-1202
26. Salinas Alvarado, J.C., Verspoor, K., Baldwin, T.: Domain adaption of named entity recognition to support credit risk assessment. In: Proceedings of the Australasian Language Technology Association Workshop 2015, pp. 84–90. Parramatta, Australia (2015). https://aclanthology.org/U15-1010
27. Scao, T.L., et al.: Bloom: a 176B-parameter open-access multilingual language model. arXiv preprint arXiv:2211.05100 (2022)

28. Shah, R., et al.: When FLUE meets FLANG: benchmarks and large pretrained language model for financial domain. In: Proceedings of the 2022 Conference on Empirical Methods in Natural Language Processing, pp. 2322–2335. Association for Computational Linguistics, Abu Dhabi, United Arab Emirates (2022). https://aclanthology.org/2022.emnlp-main.148
29. Sharma, S., Khatuya, S., Hegde, M., Dasgupta, A.S., Goyal, P., Ganguly, N., et al.: Financial numeric extreme labelling: a dataset and benchmarking for XBRL tagging. arXiv preprint arXiv:2306.03723 (2023)
30. Sharma, S., et al.: FinRed: a dataset for relation extraction in financial domain. In: Companion Proceedings of the Web Conference 2022, pp. 595–597 (2022)
31. Sinha, A., Khandait, T.: Impact of news on the commodity market: dataset and results. In: Advances in Information and Communication: Proceedings of the 2021 Future of Information and Communication Conference (FICC), Volume 2, pp. 589–601. Springer (2021). https://doi.org/10.1007/978-3-030-73103-8_41
32. Sun, Q., Wei, X., Yang, X.: GraphSage with deep reinforcement learning for financial portfolio optimization. Expert Syst. Appl. **238**, 122027 (2024)
33. Wu, S., et al.: BloomberGGPT: a large language model for finance. arXiv preprint arXiv:2303.17564 (2023)
34. Xie, Q., et al.: PIXIU: a large language model, instruction data and evaluation benchmark for finance. In: Proceedings of the 37th International Conference on Neural Information Processing Systems, pp. 33469–33484 (2023)
35. Yang, Y., Tang, Y., Tam, K.Y.: InvestLM: a large language model for investment using financial domain instruction tuning. arXiv preprint arXiv:2309.13064 (2023)
36. Yang, Y., Uy, M.C.S., Huang, A.: FinBert: a pretrained language model for financial communications. arXiv preprint arXiv:2006.08097 (2020)
37. Zhang, H., Zheng, Q., Dong, B., Feng, B.: A financial ticket image intelligent recognition system based on deep learning. Knowl. Based Syst. **222**, 106955 (2021)
38. Zhang, S., et al.: OPT: open pre-trained transformer language models. arXiv preprint arXiv:2205.01068 (2022)

A Comparative Study of ASRs, LLMs, and Few-Shot Learning for Emotion Recognition in Tunisian Dialect

Latifa Iben Nasr[1(✉)], Ismail Badache[2], Abir Masmoudi[1], and Lamia Hadrich Belguith[1]

[1] MIRACL Laboratory, University of Sfax, Sfax, Tunisia
{latifa.ibennasr,lamia.belguith}@fsegs.usf.tn
[2] Aix Marseille Université, CNRS, LIS, Marseille, France
Ismail.Badache@lis-lab.fr

Abstract. Large Language Models (LLMs) have demonstrated strong performance in Natural Language Processing (NLP), yet their evaluation in Arabic—particularly low-resource varieties like the Tunisian Dialect (TD)—remains a pressing need. This study investigates data augmentation using GPT-4o, Arabic-pretrained models, and LLMs with few-shot learning for spontaneous Speech Emotion Recognition (SER). We employ both open-source and proprietary Automatic Speech Recognition (ASR) systems to generate transcriptions of TD speech, which are then used as input features for SER models. Our findings show that the best performance was achieved with AraBERT, reaching an accuracy of 77% and outperforming all alternatives. These results highlight the critical role of ASR quality in downstream SER tasks, as well as the importance of selecting appropriate models for underrepresented languages, with implications for human-computer interaction and mental health applications.

Keywords: NLP · Emotion recognition · Transcription · Tunisian Dialect · LLMs

1 Introduction

Speech Emotion Recognition (SER) improves human-computer interaction by enabling systems to detect emotions, which shape reasoning, decision-making, and communication [16]. Emotions enrich meaning in speech and text [5], but SER is challenging due to complex expression and spontaneous disfluencies [6].

Speech carries acoustic and linguistic cues [7]: acoustic features reveal how something is said, while linguistic features reflect what is said. Though early work focused on acoustics, transcribed speech from ASR is now crucial for emotion detection [16].

SER has advanced in German, English, and Chinese [8,29], but Arabic remains underexplored due to scarce resources and limited spontaneous data

I. Awan et al. (Eds.): WISE 2025, LNCS 16367, pp. 260–271, 2026.
https://doi.org/10.1007/978-981-95-7394-3_18

[10,29]. The Tunisian Dialect (TD), spoken by 12 million and influenced by Algerian and Libyan Arabic [15], suffers from small datasets and an acoustic bias [9,11,12], while transcription-based SER in Arabic is still unexplored [29].

This study addresses these gaps by focusing on TD spontaneous emotional data and transcription-based approaches with pretrained models and LLMs for augmentation and classification.

The paper is structured as follows: Sect. 2 presents the background and challenges; Sect. 3 reviews SER, focusing on transcription and Arabic studies; Sect. 4 outlines the methodology; Sect. 5 reports experiments and results; Sect. 6 discusses findings; Sect. 7 concludes and suggests future directions.

2 TD Background and Characteristics

Unlike Modern Standard Arabic (MSA), TD is shaped by Latin, Berber, Turkish, and Romance influences, featuring frequent code-switching with French and English [9], reduced gender marking, loss of indicative prefixes, a unique progressive aspect, Subject–Verb–Object order, Turkish-influenced agglutination, and a hybrid lexicon [27].

A major challenge in diglossic code-switching arises from shared vocabulary between MSA and TD, causing ambiguity through cognates or faux amis [28]. For instance, [قلبه/ qlbh] is [his heart] in MSA but [قلبة/ qlbp/ cheating] in TD; [معاناتها/ mEAnAthA / her suffering] in MSA becomes [معناتها/ mEnAthA / that's to say] in TD; and [حكى فيه/ HkY fiyh] implies [he said bad things about him]. These semantic divergences can directly affect emotion recognition, as the same surface forms may convey neutral, positive, or negative sentiments depending on the dialectal context. Misinterpreting TD expressions using MSA-based models may therefore lead to incorrect emotion labels, which underscores the importance of approaches that account for TD-specific lexical and semantic features.

TD also forms a dialectal continuum with significant internal variation [27]. Despite its richness, MSA-based transcription often fails to capture its specificities [27], and scarce TD transcript data [3] hinder encoding spontaneous speech with disfluencies and noise [30], highlighting the need for tailored linguistic resources.

3 Related Work

This section reviews existing studies on SER, providing an overview of approaches, research using transcriptions, and studies on Arabic dialects.

3.1 SER Overview

Initial SER systems relied on acoustic features—prosodic, spectral, and voice quality—combined with conventional classifiers like SVM and KNN [31]. Deep Learning (DL) models, such as RNNs, CNNs, and Transformers, improved SER by learning emotional cues from raw speech, but they require large labeled datasets, often scarce for low-resource languages [32].

Although audio records capture direct emotional cues, transcriptions offer valuable complementary information, especially in noisy or low-resource settings, underlining the potential of text-based SER methods [32,33].

3.2 SER With Transcriptions

Transcriptions are vital in SER, capturing key linguistic and prosodic cues like pauses and hesitations [6]. Multimodal models that combine transcriptions with acoustic features—such as BERT and SpeechCueLLM [34], Wav2Vec, and CamemBERT [35]—show strong promise, with BERT excelling in low-resource settings [36].

LLMs have advanced SER: Zhang et al. [37] reached state-of-the-art with LLaMA 3, Automatic Speech Recognition (ASR) ensembles, and gambler prompts; Santoso et al. [38] used GPT-3.5-turbo for low-cost, accurate results; Gong et al. [24] pre-trained GPT-2 and BERT with Whisper weak labels in LanSER; Bellver et al. [14] and Xu et al. [13] combined Whisper, HuBERT, and LLaMA to separate emotional from linguistic cues. Still, SER research is biased toward high-resource languages [29].

3.3 SER Arabic Dialects

Arabic, spoken by 420 million people, is underrepresented in SER due to scarce datasets [39], while English dominates [7]. Arabic dialect faces a shortage of annotated corpora [10]; only 4.76% of SER datasets (2000–2021) were Arabic, mostly non-spontaneous [29], underscoring the need for natural, Arabic dialect-specific resources.

Non-spontaneous Arabic SER shows high accuracy with features like MFCCs and Mel spectrograms—e.g., SVM (77.14% [8]), Transformers (95.2% [40]), and ASERS-LSTM (96.81% [41]). However, performance drops sharply on spontaneous TD data, with F-scores below 58% even using DL and machine learning methods [9]. Work on TD and non-spontaneous data remains promising [11,12], but highlights the need for deeper linguistic analysis.

4 LLMs for Transcription Emotion Classification

This section provides an overview of the proposed model, as illustrated in Fig. 1, outlining the process from transcription preparation to the classification phase.

4.1 Data Preparation

In this phase, we describe the steps of data preparation, including transcription, data augmentation, and stop-word removal.

4.1.1 Transcription

This research relies on the SERTUS dataset [15], comprising 23.85 h of spontaneous TD speech (3,793 segments) covering politics, economics, culture, and sports. Emotions are distributed as anger (26.04%), satisfaction (22.96%), sadness (21.96%), disgust (18.16%), neutral (7.7%), and joy.

SER transcription combines manual, ASR benchmark, and automatic methods [7]. We used LinTO ASR [42], Voiser[1] and Transkriptor[2], chosen for TD and code-switching support. Voiser suits semi-structured interviews [46], while Transkriptor is praised for efficiency[3]. Whisper[4] and Sonix[5] lack TD support. Free TD systems exist [25] but remain limited. Outputs were benchmarked against manual transcriptions of emotional TD speech.

4.1.2 Data Augmentation

To address model underperformance from data imbalance [17], we used GPT-4o for data augmentation, improving synthesis and passage relevance. Its zero-shot speech synthesis captures emotional nuances and disfluencies [23], with emotional intensity closely matching human ratings (3.43 vs. 3.44) [4], and generates natural dialectal Arabic text [2]. Native-speaking experts validated the synthetic data to ensure quality.

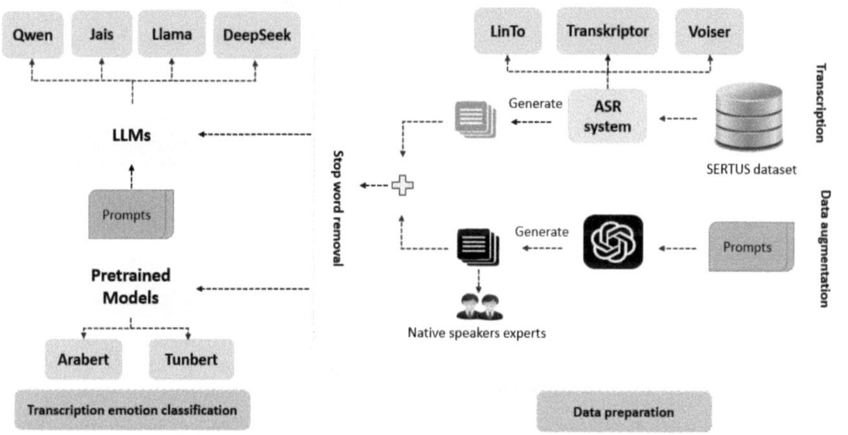

Fig. 1. Workflow for SER in TD through transcription

[1] https://voiser.net/synthese-vocale.
[2] https://transkriptor.com/fr/.
[3] https://www.capterra.fr/software/1030033/transkriptor.
[4] https://openai.com/index/whisper/.
[5] https://sonix.ai.

4.1.3 Stop Word Removal

Stop-word removal, a standard preprocessing step, removes high-frequency words like conjunctions, prepositions, and pronouns, which don't have an impact on sentiment analysis, especially in TD [3].

4.2 Transcription Emotion Classification

For emotion classification, we use pre-trained models TunBERT [18] and AraBERT, which enhance performance by capturing Arabic linguistic features [19]. Additionally, LLMs such as Jais, LLaMA, Qwen, and DeepSeek—recognized for their strong results in Arabic sentiment analysis [1] [43]—are employed to explore strengths in emotion analysis.

5 Experiments

Having established the workflow of this research, we now proceed with the experiment, detailing the setup and presenting the results.

5.1 Experimental Setup

In the setup step, we perform data preparation and proceed with model training.

5.1.1 Data Preparation

The experimentation involved transcriptions generated by three ASR systems: LinTO, with audio processed locally; Voiser, which handled files on its own platform; and Transkriptor, which provided an API-based transcription service.

Data imbalance was mitigated via augmentation. Early methods—word noise, TunBERT fine-tuning, backtranslation—produced errors, while oversampling risked overfitting. GPT-4o (zero-shot) generated 1,083 samples (634 neutrality, 449 joy), with disfluencies across sports, politics, culture, and society. Actif Prompt[6] managed LLM prompts. Following [44], we used GPT-4o's 512-token sequence length. The GPT-4o system role is defined as:

> You are a highly advanced artificial intelligence model trained to generate spontaneous speech in Tunisian dialect. Your task is to create formal, informal, unplanned conversations with natural disfluencies such as hesitations and colloquialisms. Generated text should reflect themes of sports, politics, culture, and society, ensuring linguistic coherence and relevance to the Tunisian context. Examples should be distributed proportionally among emotional tones: neutrality and joy. For neutrality, you generate 634 examples evenly across the four themes. The remaining examples should focus on joy, distributed equally across the themes.

[6] https://actif.numedu.org/.

The user role provides specific instructions:

> Please generate [number] examples of spontaneous speech in Tunisian dialect for the theme of [theme]. Examples should include hesitations, formal, informal expressions, and colloquialisms, while maintaining coherence. Focus on the emotional tone of [neutrality or joy].

Subsequently, stop-word removal such as [و/and/w, هاك/that/hAk, اللي/who/Alỹ] was implemented using a manually curated list of 179 stop words, based on MSA and Arabic corpora: Matar [20], Tarc [21], and TSAC [22].

5.1.2 Model Training

After data configuration, TD was performed using two pre-trained models, TunBERT and AraBERTv0.2, optimized with the Adam optimizer (learning rate 0.002, batch size 16) for 200 epochs. The dataset was split into 70% training, 15% validation, and 15% testing sets.

We also experimented with several LLMs. Despite using English and Arabic prompts for AraGPT2 [26], ArabianGPT-08-V2[7] , and Labess-7B-Chat-16bit[8] , hallucinations persisted.

Building on this, jais-13b-chat, LLaMA-3-8B-Instruct Arabic-DeepSeek-R1-Distill-8B, and Qwen2.5-7B-Instruct were integrated with a 512-token sequence length, and we evaluated zero-, one-, two-, and three-shot learning strategies. The following is the zero-shot prompt:

> You are an artificial intelligence model trained to carefully analyze the text in Tunisian dialect and accurately classify it into one of the following six emotions only: neutrality, joy, anger, satisfaction, sadness, or disgust.
> Instructions:
> The text may contain multiple languages (Arabic, French, English).
> Focus on the overall emotion of the text, rather than isolated expressions or partial statements. Analysis text: [text]
> Answer:

With different few-shot learning strategies—excluding zero-shot—we provided examples for each emotion included in the prompt.

The performance of the models was evaluated using accuracy, precision, recall, and F1-score, within a Kaggle notebook environment equipped with a GPU and 20GB of storage.

5.2 Experimental Results

After the setup, the results can be presented in terms of both data efficiency and model classification performance.

[7] https://huggingface.co/riotu-lab/ArabianGPT-08B-V2.
[8] https://huggingface.co/linagora/Labess-7b-chat-16bit.

5.2.1 Data Efficiency

The performance of LinTO, Voiser, and Transkriptor was evaluated against a reference transcription prepared by two native speakers. The evaluation used standard metrics for ASR transcription accuracy—Word Error Rate (WER) and Character Error Rate (CER) [45]. The results are summarized in Table 1.

As depicted in the table, Transkriptor outperformed Voiser and LinTO in both metrics. Analysis of transcription errors demonstrated specific challenges faced by LinTO ASR. For example, the expression [مزاجي/ mzAjy/ my mood] was mistranscribed as [ميساجي/ mYsAjy/ my message], which has the same tone of pronunciation. Additionally, a common inability to distinguish between certain Arabic letters was handled poorly by Voiser and LinTO. For example, it failed to differentiate between [س/ s] and [ص/ S], producing [السلاح/ AlslAH/ weapon] instead of [الصلاح/ AlSlAH/ righteousness]—an erroneous generation that shifted the emotion from positive to negative. The three transcription systems shared errors in distinguishing [ط/ T] and [ت/ t]—for example, [طابع/ TAbE/ stamp] was incorrectly transcribed as [تابع/ tAbE]. However, Transkriptor successfully captured many words, such as [مغروم/ mgrwm/ infatuated], which was mistranscribed by Voiser and LinTO as [مضروب/ mDruwb/ beaten].

Table 1. Transcription Performance Comparison

Metrics	Voiser	Transkriptor	LinTO
WER	0.31	0.11	0.35
CER	0.14	0.07	0.19

Data augmentation was performed after transcription using GPT-4o to enhance the dataset by generating examples reflecting the spontaneous and emotional nature of TD speech. The augmented data cover various themes and two emotional tones: joy and neutrality. The synthetic dataset thus contains 1,083 sentences and 8,572 words, in addition to the original 9,608 sentences and 430,757 words. Two examples are presented below:

- Joy: شيخة vraiment أأأأ مهرجان قرطاج ديما هكة يهزنا لعالم آخر شيخة/ $yxp vraiment »» mhrjAn qrTAj dymA hk p yhznA lEAlm Axr $yxp / Happiness, truly. The Carthage Festival is always like this—it takes us to another world. Happiness!
- Neutral: المبارة ت تتلعب غدوة إن شاء الله في في ملعب رادس/ AlmubArAp t ttlllEab gduwp >n $A' All h fy fy mlEab rAds /The match will be played tomorrow, God willing, at the Rades stadium.

Two native Tunisian speakers with experience in sentiment annotation independently assessed the synthetic data. The inter-annotator agreement (Cohen's

Kappa) was 0.97, indicating near-perfect consistency. Disagreements—mainly joy samples misgenerated as satisfaction—were removed and regenerated to ensure accurate emotion representation.

The augmentation led to a more balanced dataset: angry 20.30%, satisfied 17.86%, sad 17.10%, disgust 14.07%, joy 15.22%, and neutral 15.42%.

The next step in the data preparation phase, as previously mentioned, is removing stop-words that do not contribute to the semantic meaning or emotional content of the sentences, which did not affect the analysis.

5.2.2 Model Efficiency

Table 2 shows model performance across ASRs. Transkriptor achieved the highest accuracy: 77% with AraBERT after 167 epochs, and 68% with LLaMA (3-shot). Voiser peaked at 71.6% with AraBERT, while LinTO had the lowest, 64% with AraBERT. Qwen and Jais performed similarly but below LLaMA. LLaMA3 improves with more shots but stays below AraBERT. Arabic DeepSeek had the weakest performance, and TunBERT never exceeded 53%, even with Transkriptor.

These results show AraBERT consistently achieving the highest scores among all LLM-based classifiers across the three ASRs. With the best combination, AraBERT with Transkriptor, the recall per class is: angry 61.7%, sad 67.5%, joy 63.2%, disgust 79.4%, satisfied 94.6%, and neutral 95.1%. Angry, sad, and joy are clearly harder to classify. These findings will be explored in the next section.

6 Discussion

This study advances SER for TD using transcribed spontaneous Arabic speech, including disfluencies and code-switching. GPT-4o generated synthetic speech to address class imbalance, validated by humans. Transkriptor was the most effective transcription tool, significantly improving SER accuracy. However, automatic transcription remains challenging—character-level errors (Sect. 5.1.1) can alter meaning and cause misclassifications, e.g., confusing satisfaction with disgust. AraBERT achieved the best results using Arabic-specific embeddings, while TunBERT underperformed due to its Arabizi base. Across LLMs and few-shot settings, none surpassed AraBERT. As noted in Sect. 5.2.2, angry, joy, and sad remain difficult to distinguish due to tonal cues. For example, [توا هما كيف كيف/ kyf kyf tww HmA/ They're the same now] may sound angry but appears neutral in transcription; [Bravo عليك!/ brAwo Elyk/ Well done !] can convey sarcasm or anger, yet its transcription indicated satisfaction.

Building on prior work, [9] used acoustic features on a small TD spontaneous dataset, achieving 58% F-measure with LSTM and random forest. We extend this to a larger, more diverse corpus. Previous results vary: [11] reached 90% accuracy with prosodic features and SVM but on non-spontaneous data, while [12] achieved 60.6% with multilingual wav2vec. No Arabic SER study has leveraged transcriptions, though a multimodal corpus exists [39]. In other languages, transcription-based SER shows progress: [32] obtained 79.89% WA and 77.68%

Table 2. Performance Across Models. Bold values indicate the best performance in each ASR.

Model		ASR											
		Voiser				Transkriptor				LinTo			
		Accuracy	Precision	Recal	F1-Score	Accuracy	Precision	Recal	F1-Score	Accuracy	Precision	Recal	F1-Score
LLaMA-3-8B-Instruct	0-shot	37.5%	40.2%	36.6%	38.3%	42.5%	47%	41.4%	44%	34.5%	37.6%	32.7%	35%
	1-shot	43.6%	48.1%	41.7%	44.7%	56.4%	58.2%	55.7%	56.9%	41.4%	46.3%	40.6%	43.2%
	2-shot	57.4%	60.6%	55.8%	58%	63.1%	65.3%	62.8%	64%	53.4%	56%	51.9%	53.9%
	3-shot	**61%**	64.2%	59.7%	61.9%	**68.5%**	73.2%	66.4%	69.6%	**59.1%**	62.7%	57.4%	59.85%
jais-13b-chat	0-shot	36.1%	38.7%	36.4%	37.5%	37.9%	41.7%	38.2%	39.8%	35.8%	37%	36.3%	36.6%
	1-shot	37,5%	40,2%	37,3%	38.6%	42.5%	49.2%	41.3%	44.9%	36.1%	38.4%	36.7%	37.5%
	2-shot	40.6%	44.2%	41.1%	42.6%	45.8%	57.2%	44.5%	50%	37.4%	42.3%	36.9%	39.4%
	3-shot	43.2%	46.7%	42.9%	44.5%	52.3%	59.7%	52.4%	55.8%	41.3%	45.1%	41.8%	43.4%
Arabic-DeepSeek-R1-Distill-8B	0-shot	32.5%	34.1%	30.3%	32.1%	35.1%	32.5%	34.2%	33.3%	30.7%	32.3%	30.5%	31.4%
	1-shot	35.1%	36.8%	32.2%	34.3%	36.7%	38.4%	35.8%	37%	31.2%	33%	31.6%	32.3%
	2-shot	37.4%	38.9%	35.8%	34.3%	39.3%	40.7%	38.5%	39.6%	33.5%	35.2%	32.7%	33.9%
	3-shot	39,7%	40,1%	37,5%	38,8%	41.9%	42.7%	40.1%	41.4%	36.8%	37.4%	36.3%	36.8%
Qwen2.5-7B-Instruct	0-shot	36.4%	39%	40.7%	39.8%	39.8%	41.2%	45.6%	43.3%	35.2%	38.5%	34.1%	36.2%
	1-shot	38.6%	43.4%	39.7%	41.4%	43.5%	54.8%	43%	48.1%	37.3%	39.6%	36.1%	37.8%
	2-shot	42.1%	45.6%	41.4%	43.4%	47.1%	58.2%	46.8%	51.9%	40.2%	44.6%	41.3%	42.9%
	3-shot	46.8%	49%	47.2%	48.1%	53.6%	61.1%	54.3%	57.5%	45.7%	48.6%	46.2%	47.4%
Tunbert		48.7%	50.2%	48.4%	49.3%	53.7%	57.2%	51.5%	54.1%	47.8%	51.1%	47.9%	49.5%
Arabert		**71.6%**	72.1%	71.4	71.7%	**77.2%**	79.4%	76.4%	77.9%	**64.8%**	69.6%	64.1%	66.7%

UA on English speech using Whisper and BERT, and in French, [35] achieved 92.4% using transcription alone.

Unlike sentiment analysis, which often focuses on Arabizi, we use transcriptions of spontaneous speech with disfluencies to obtain texts in Arabic script, for the low-resource TD variety. Despite limitations—such as tone-dependent misclassifications, character-level errors, and overlapping emotions in the same expression—this approach paves the way for future SER research in TD.

7 Conclusion and Future Work

This study highlights the potential of transcription-based approaches, comparing ASRs and LLMs with few-shot strategies for SER in low-resource TD. Results show that transcription quality and a suitable classifier are crucial, especially given TD's spontaneous speech.

Future work should integrate linguistic and acoustic features, refine LLMs to reduce errors, and add another annotation dimension to address overlapping emotions. Although focused on TD, the dataset's dialectal continuum with Algerian and Libyan Arabic ensures broader applicability.

References

1. Sallam, M., et al.: Chinese generative AI models (DeepSeek and Qwen) rival ChatGPT-4 in ophthalmology queries with excellent performance in Arabic and English. Narra J. **5**(1), e2371 (2025)
2. Wang, Y., et al.: Is human-like text liked by humans? Multilingual human detection and preference against AI. arXiv preprint arXiv:2502.11614 (2025)
3. Fsih, E., Boujelbane, R., Belguith, L.H.: Resources building for sentiment analysis of content disseminated by Tunisian medias in social networks. Lang. Resour. Eval., 1–26 (2023)
4. Bojic, L., et al.: Evaluating large language models against human annotators in latent content analysis: sentiment, political leaning, emotional intensity, and sarcasm. arXiv preprint arXiv:2501.02532 (2025)
5. Duret, J., Rouvier, M., Estève, Y.: MSP-podcast SER challenge 2024: L'antenne du Ventoux multimodal self-supervised learning for speech emotion recognition. arXiv preprint arXiv:2407.05746 (2024)
6. Boughariou, E., Bahou, Y., Belguith, L.H.: Detecting speech disorders using a machine-learning guided method in spontaneous Tunisian dialect speech. SN Comput. Sci. **5**(5), 440 (2024)
7. Atmaja, B.T., Sasou, A., Akagi, M.: Survey on bimodal speech emotion recognition from acoustic and linguistic information fusion. Speech Commun. **140**, 11–28 (2022)
8. Aljuhani, R.H., Alshutayri, A., Alahdal, S.: Arabic speech emotion recognition from Saudi dialect corpus. IEEE Access **9**, 127081–127085 (2021)
9. Ibn Nasr, L., Masmoudi, A., Hadrich Belguith, L.: Emotion recognition from spontaneous Tunisian dialect speech. ACM Trans. Asian Low-Resour. Lang. Inf. Process. **24**(2), 1–16 (2025)

10. Besdouri, F.Z., Zribi, I., Belguith, L.H.: Challenges and progress in developing speech recognition systems for dialectal Arabic. Speech Commun., 103110 (2024)
11. Meddeb, M., Karray, H., Alimi, A.M.: Automated extraction of features from Arabic emotional speech corpus. Int. J. Comput. Inf. Syst. Ind. Manage. Appl. **8**, 11 (2016)
12. Messaoudi, A., Haddad, H., Hmida, M.B., Graiet, M.: TuniSER: toward a Tunisian Speech Emotion Recognition System. In: Proceedings of the 5th International Conference on Natural Language and Speech Processing (ICNLSP 2022), pp. 234–241 (2022)
13. Xu, Y., Zhou, Y., Cai, Y., Xie, J., Ye, R., Wu, Z.: Multimodal emotion captioning using large language model with prompt engineering. In: Proceedings of the 2nd International Workshop on Multimodal and Responsible Affective Computing, pp. 104–109 (2024)
14. Bellver, J., et al.: Multimodal audio-language model for speech emotion recognition. Proc. Odyssey 2024 (2024)
15. Nasr, L. I., Masmoudi, A., Belguith, L.H.: Tunisian dialect speech corpus: construction and emotion annotation
16. Guanxiong, P., et al.: Affective computing: recent advances, challenges, and future trends. Intell. Comput. **3**, 0076 (2024)
17. Bayer, M., Kaufhold, M.A., Reuter, C.: A survey on data augmentation for text classification. ACM Comput. Surv. **55**(7), 1–39 (2022)
18. Haddad, H., et al.: TunBERT: pretraining BERT for Tunisian dialect understanding. SN Comput. Sci. **4**(2), 194 (2023)
19. Alosaimi, W., et al.: ArabBert-LSTM: improving Arabic sentiment analysis based on transformer model and long short-term memory. Front. Artif. Intell. **7**, 1408845 (2024)
20. Zaraket, F.A., Jaber, A.: MATAR: morphology-based tagger for Arabic. In: 2013 ACS International Conference on Computer Systems and Applications (AICCSA), pp. 1–4. IEEE (2013)
21. Gugliotta, E., Dinarelli, M.: TARC: Tunisian Arabish corpus first complete release. arXiv preprint arXiv:2207.04796 (2022)
22. Mdhaffar, S., Bougares, F., Esteve, Y., Hadrich-Belguith, L.: Sentiment analysis of tunisian dialects: Linguistic ressources and experiments. In: Third Arabic natural language processing workshop (WANLP), pp. 55–61 (2017)
23. Chaudhury, R., Godbole, M., Garg, A., Seo, J.H.: Humane speech synthesis through zero-shot emotion and disfluency generation. arXiv preprint arXiv:2404.01339 (2024)
24. Gong, T., Belanich, J., Somandepalli, K., Nagrani, A., Eoff, B., Jou, B.: Lanser: language-model supported speech emotion recognition. arXiv preprint arXiv:2309.03978 (2023)
25. Masmoudi, A., Bougares, F., Ellouze, M., Estève, Y., Belguith, L.: Automatic speech recognition system for Tunisian dialect. Lang. Resour. Eval. **52**, 249–267 (2018)
26. Antoun, W., Baly, F., Hajj, H.: AraGPT2: pre-trained transformer for Arabic language generation. arXiv preprint arXiv:2012.15520 (2020)
27. Turki, H., et al.: Normalized orthography for Tunisian Arabic. In: International Conference on Language Processing and Knowledge Management, pp. 133–142. Springer Nature Switzerland, Cham. https://doi.org/10.1007/978-3-031-85067-7_13

28. Hamed, I., Sabty, C., Abdennadher, S., Vu, N.T., Solorio, T., Habash, N.: A survey of code-switched Arabic NLP: progress, challenges, and future directions. arXiv preprint arXiv:2501.13419 (2025)
29. Iben Nasr, L., Masmoudi, A., Hadrich Belguith, L.: Survey on Arabic speech emotion recognition. Int. J. Speech Technol. **27**(1), 53–68 (2024)
30. Zribi, I., Ellouze, M., Belguith, L.H., Blache, P.: Spoken Tunisian Arabic corpus "STAC": transcription and annotation. Res. Comput. Sci. **90**, 123–135 (2015)
31. de Lope, J., Graña, M.: An ongoing review of speech emotion recognition. Neurocomputing **528**, 1–11 (2023)
32. Sharma, V.: Speech and text-based emotion recognizer. arXiv preprint arXiv:2312.11503 (2023)
33. Padi, S., Sadjadi, S.O., Manocha, D., Sriram, R.D.: Multimodal emotion recognition using transfer learning from speaker recognition and BERT-based models. arXiv preprint arXiv:2202.08974 (2022)
34. Lee, S., Han, D.K., Ko, H.: Multimodal emotion recognition fusion analysis adapting BERT with heterogeneous feature unification. IEEE Access **9**, 94557–94572 (2021)
35. Macary, M., Tahon, M., Estève, Y., Luzzati, D.: Acoustic and linguistic representations for speech continuous emotion recognition in call center conversations. arXiv preprint arXiv:2310.04481 (2023)
36. Rybak, P.: Transferring BERT capabilities from high-resource to low-resource languages using vocabulary matching. arXiv preprint arXiv:2402.14408 (2024)
37. Zhang, E., Poellabauer, C.: Contextual speech emotion recognition with large language models and ASR-based transcriptions. In: Audio Imagination: NeurIPS 2024 Workshop AI-Driven Speech, Music, and Sound Generation
38. Santoso, J., Ishizuka, K., Hashimoto, T.: Large language model-based emotional speech annotation using context and acoustic feature for speech emotion recognition. In ICASSP 2024-2024 IEEE International Conference on Acoustics, Speech and Signal Processing (ICASSP), pp. 11026–11030. IEEE (2024)
39. Al Roken, N., Barlas, G.: Multimodal Arabic emotion recognition using deep learning. Speech Commun. **155**, 103005 (2023)
40. Al-onazi, B.B., Nauman, M.A., Jahangir, R., Malik, M.M., Alkhammash, E.H., Elshewey, A.M.: Transformer-based multilingual speech emotion recognition using data augmentation and feature fusion. Appl. Sci. **12**(18), 9188 (2022)
41. Tajalsir, M., Hernandez, S.M., Mohammed, F.A.: ASERS-LSTM: Arabic speech emotion recognition system based on LSTM model. Int. J. Sig. Image Process. (2022)
42. Naouara, H., Lorré, J.P., Louradour, J.: LinTO audio and textual datasets to train and evaluate automatic speech recognition in Tunisian Arabic dialect. arXiv preprint arXiv:2504.02604 (2025)
43. Zouidine, M., Khalil, M.: Large language models for Arabic sentiment analysis and machine translation. Eng. Technol. Appl. Sci. Res. **15**(2), 20737–20742 (2025)
44. Peng, B., Li, C., He, P., Galley, M., Gao, J.: Instruction tuning with GPT-4. arXiv preprint arXiv:2304.03277 (2023)
45. James, J., Gopinath, D.P.: Advocating character error rate for multilingual ASR evaluation. arXiv preprint arXiv:2410.07400 (2024)
46. Chebotarova, I.: Intelligent text recognition when creating audio books for blind people (2024)

CMANet:Sarcasm Detection with LLMs and Cross-Modal Adaptive Attention Networks

Nan Zhao[1,3], Degang Sun[2,3(✉)], Chen Meng[1], Ning Li[1], Yan Wang[1,3], and Haitian Yang[1,3]

[1] Institute of Information Engineering, Chinese Academy of Sciences, Beijing, China
zhaonan@iie.ac.cn

[2] Computer Network Information Center, Chinese Academy of Sciences, Beijing, China
sundegang@iie.ac.cn

[3] School of Cyber Security, University of Chinese Academy of Sciences, Beijing, China

Abstract. With the widespread popularity of social media, sarcastic expressions have become increasingly common in online communication. Accurately detecting such expressions is crucial for understanding user intentions, conducting sentiment analysis, and maintaining a healthy online environment. However, sarcasm detection faces numerous challenges, such as the subtlety of text semantics and the complexity of multi-modal information fusion. To effectively address these issues, this paper proposes a sarcasm detection method that integrates Large Language Models (LLMs) with a cross-modal adaptive attention network. In terms of text processing, the powerful language capabilities of large language models are utilized to perform in-depth semantic representation of the input text, capturing rich language patterns, contextual relationships, and implied semantic information, thereby providing high-quality textual features. Meanwhile, considering the close association between multi-modal information and text, a cross-modal adaptive attention network is constructed to achieve effective fusion of text and multi-modal data. This network dynamically focuses on key information through an adaptive attention mechanism, automatically adjusting the weights of each modality to fully leverage the complementarity between modalities. In experiments, multiple representative social media datasets are selected for validation, and the results demonstrate that, compared with traditional methods, the proposed method significantly improves evaluation metrics such as accuracy and recall.

Keywords: sarcasm detection · multi-modality · social media · cross-modal adaptive attention · feature fusion

I. Awan et al. (Eds.): WISE 2025, LNCS 16367, pp. 272–287, 2026.
https://doi.org/10.1007/978-981-95-7394-3_19

1 Introduction

More and more social media platforms allow users to post multi-modal information, consisting of text, picture, etc. Inspired by different social media platforms, sarcasm is gradually changing from a pure linguistic behavior to various resources. For example, users can achieve sarcasm by posting a picture that implies the opposite meaning of its counterpart, and vice versa. Undoubtedly, the negligence of information beyond text-only could lead to deterioration of detection performance. Therefore, detecting sarcasm on social media should fully inspect the fusion of multi-modal sources.

In the past few years, there are many multi-modal tasks, from image captioning [1] to visual question answering [2], etc. However, most of the existing sarcasm detection methods that mainly focus on pure texts cannot adequately detect sarcastic tweets, because visual information and textual information are weakly aligned or even completely semantically-irrelevant on Twitter.

Here, we list some recently introduced text-based works on sarcasm detection [3]. It is worth noting that Cai et al. [4] propose a hierarchical model on sarcasm detection. Inspired by previous related works, the method we propose aims to explore more features that are conducive to sarcasm detection. Specifically, we leverage image captioning technology to obtain textual descriptions of images. Then, we fuse these image descriptions with the original text in the dataset (i.e., text attributes) to construct more informative text features. Additionally, we employ a large language model to extract global semantic representations for both the text modality and the image caption modality, while utilizing the ResNet101 model to acquire semantic feature representations for the image modality. Through this approach, we are able to deeply mine the deep-seated semantic information hidden within different modality data.

In this paper, we innovatively propose a cross-modal adaptive attention network model specifically designed for sarcasm detection on social media. The core advantage of this model lies in its ability to collaboratively learn three key types of information: text features, image features, and image caption features, thereby accurately identifying sarcastic content on social media. During the model implementation process, we first extract text attributes, image features, and image caption information separately. Subsequently, we concatenate the text attributes with the image descriptions and input them into the large language model to extract more expressive text features. Meanwhile, we delve into the intrinsic correlations and unique interactions between text features and image features. We introduce a cross-modal adaptive attention mechanism and utilize cross-modal embedding techniques to precisely learn and identify discriminative features. Finally, we reconstruct and fuse the feature information from the text, image, and image caption modalities into a unified feature vector, providing strong support for subsequent predictive analysis of sarcastic content.

The main contributions of this paper can be summarized as follows:

(1) We have conducted in-depth research on the potential of the cross-modal adaptive attention mechanism in mining heterogeneous information from

multimodal data. Experimental results demonstrate that this mechanism can effectively capture the correlations and differences between different modalities, thus achieving significant application effects in the field of sarcasm detection on social media.

(2) To verify the impact of different large language models on the performance of multimodal sarcasm detection, we selected a variety of representative large language models (such as ChatGLM2-6B, Qwen3-8B, LLaMA2-7B, DeepSeekR1-6B) for experiments. During the experimental process, we set up diverse experimental schemes and conducted comprehensive and detailed evaluations of the performance of different large language models in the multimodal sarcasm detection task.

(3) We have thoroughly validated our proposed model on a real-world English tweet dataset. The experimental results show that, compared with the current state-of-the-art benchmark models, our model performs excellently across various performance metrics, significantly surpassing all baseline models. This fully proves the effectiveness and superiority of our method in the task of sarcasm detection on social media.

2 Related Work

2.1 Sarcasm Detection in Text

Early text sarcasm detection primarily relied on feature engineering or contextual information to capture semantic incongruity in emotional expressions. Riloff et al. [5] improved recall rates by learning positive phrases and negative situations in sarcastic tweets. Joshi et al. [6] proposed a system based on contextual semantic incongruity to determine sarcasm at the sentence level. Ashwitha et al. [7] implemented sarcasm detection by collecting target words for emotional shifts and using distributional semantics. Current research has evolved to adopt neural networks, such as Zhang et al. [8] finding higher accuracy with neural network-extracted features than manual ones. Pretrained models on large-scale corpora have proven superior, leading to their widespread use in sarcasm detection, e.g., [9] proposed BERT-LSTM, combining BERT with LSTM, significantly improving sarcasm detection. Traditional sarcasm detection focused on text, but with multimodal content on social media, text-only methods are inadequate [4]. Thus, this work focuses on multimodal sarcasm detection.

2.2 Multimodal Sarcasm Detection

Early multimodal sarcasm detection methods mainly used basic neural networks to extract features or combined contextual information to enhance raw features. Sangwan et al. [10] predicted based on RNN interactions between different modes, Yin et al. [11] fused additional emoji features from text sequences, and like Wang et al. [12] concatenating BERT and ResNet vectors and proposing a 2D attention mechanism. However, people perceive cross-modal incongruity by aligning and fusing visual and text content, then alternately focusing on text and images [13]. Wu et al. [14] detected sarcasm by scoring image-text incongruity, Fu et al. [15] proposed a hierarchical framework integrating emotion dictionaries, vectors, and cross-modal fusion, and Liu et al. [16] combined atomic-level consistency based on multi-head cross-attention and composition-level consistency based on GNNs. Yue et al. [17] utilized conceptual knowledge bases for better collaborative understanding. Xu et al. [18] built decomposition and relation networks to simulate cross-modal contrast and semantic associations, enhancing the interpretability of final decisions.

3 The Proposed Model

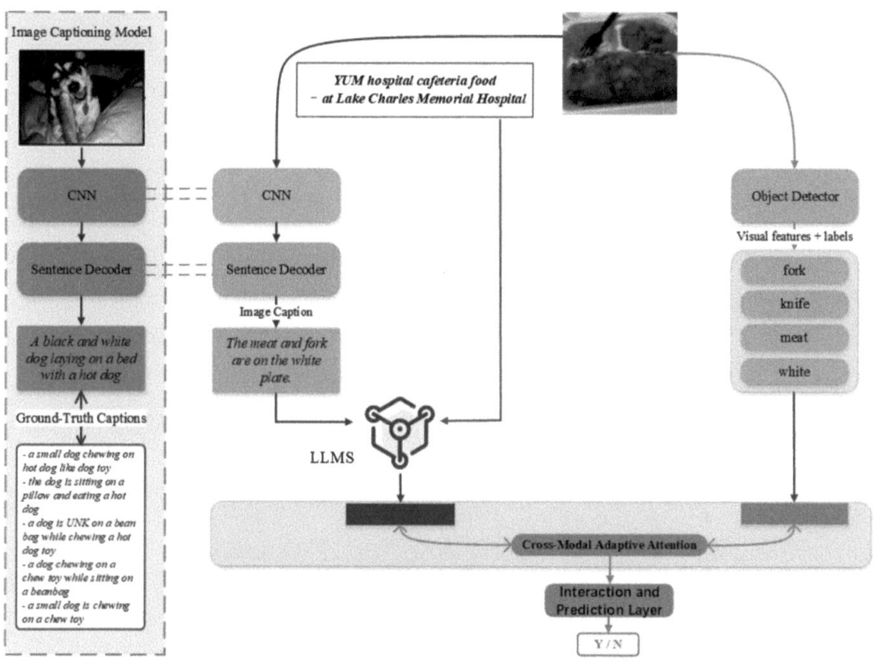

Fig. 1. Overview of our proposed model.

The overall framework consists of two training paths: image captioning and multi-modal learning, as illustrated in Fig. 1. The first path (left part) maps the image into sentences. The second path (right part) detects the label from generated captions, original sarcastic texts, and detected objects, and further fuses them.

3.1 Generation of Image Captioning

First, we introduce details of the image captioning process. Given an image I, our image captioning training aims to generate a sentence S^c to describe the picture vividly. This process mines the deep and rich semantic information of an image. The entire image captioning process can be described in an Encoder-Decoder framework. We train the image captioning encoder on the MSCOCO dataset, then use the trained encoder to encode any given image into sentences.

Specifically, we first use the image encoder $P(F_I|I)$ to extract the image feature F_I, and then use the decoder $P(S^c|F_I)$ to convert the image feature into a textual description. Thus, the image captioning model $P(S^c|I)$ is denoted as $P(F_I|I)P(S^c|F_I)$. During inference, the decoding process is denoted as:

$$\hat{S^c} = argmax_{S^c} P(S^c|F_I)P(F_I|I) \tag{1}$$

where S^c is the generated image description.

3.2 Input Representation

Text Representation: We adopt the dataset presented in [4]. This dataset contains both the image modal and its corresponding text content, however, as shown in the following example (Fig. 2), it is difficult to recognize the irony from either the text content or the image content solely. Therefore, it is crucial to effectively integrate the semantic information of an image with its corresponding text. For each image sample in the dataset, the textual representations consist of two parts: the generated image caption and the original paired text, denoted as image caption S^c (image caption) and S^o (original sarcasm text).

Fig. 2. An image sample in the dataset, whose corresponding text is ['819295937487142912', 'look out ! mega sale !', 1, 1].

We use WordPiece tokenizer [19] to divide $\hat{S^c}$ into word set $\{\hat{w}_1^c, \cdots, \hat{w}_{N_C}^c\}$, where N_c is the number of words in the word set. Inspired by the vision-language pre-training models [20,21], we construct our textual feature based on word embedding, segment embedding, and position embedding:

$$\hat{\mathbf{w}}_i^c = \mathbf{LN}(f_{WordEmb}(\hat{w}_i^c) + f_{SegEmb}(\hat{w}_i^c) + f_{PosEmb}(i)) \tag{2}$$

where $\hat{w}_i^c \in \mathbb{R}^{d_w}$ is the word-level feature, $\mathbf{LN}$ represents the layer normalization, and $f_{WordEmb}(\cdot)$, $f_{SegEmb}(\cdot)$, $f_{PosEmb}(\cdot)$ are the embedding functions.

Next, we apply the same operation to S^o. We divide S^o into word set, denoted as $S^o = \{w_1^o, \cdots, w_{N_O}^o\}$, where N_o is the number of words. The feature for each token is denoted as:

$$\mathbf{w}_i^o = \mathbf{LN}(f_{WordEmb}(w_i^o) + f_{SegEmb}(w_i^o) + f_{PosEmb}(i)) \tag{3}$$

where $\mathbf{w}_i^o \in \mathbb{R}^{d_w}$ is the word-level feature for original sarcasm text token.

We insert the special token [SEP] between and after each sentence. In our framework, we concatenate the embeddings of the image caption along with original sarcasm text $S = \{\mathbf{w}_{1:N_O}^o, \mathbf{w}_{[SEP]}, \hat{\mathbf{w}}_{1:N_C}^c, \mathbf{w}_{[SEP]}\}$, where $\mathbf{w}_{[SEP]}$ is the word-level embedding for special token.

In the final crucial stage of the algorithm workflow, to fully mine the deep - seated semantic information hidden in the text data, we precisely feed the meticulously processed text sequence S as input into a pre - trained Large Language Model (LLM). This step is the core of the entire text semantic analysis process. With its powerful language understanding capabilities and a vast amount of pre - training knowledge, the LLM can extract rich semantic features from the input text. The specific formulas are as follows:

$$\mathbf{Text\_encoding} = \mathbf{LLMs(S)} \tag{4}$$

Image Representation: Firstly, rather than employing the global representation for each image, we use the visual features of detected objects to represent the image. Secondly, we extract and retain a fixed number of semantic region proposals from the pre-trained Faster R-CNN [22]. Specifically, an image I consists of N_v objects, where each object o_i is represented by its region-of-interest (RoI) feature $v_i \in R^{d_o}$, and its positional feature $p_i^o \in R^4$ (normalized top-left and bottom-right coordinates). The calculation of each region embedding is demonstrated as follows:

$$\mathbf{v}_i^o = \mathbf{LN}(f_{VisualEmb}(\mathbf{v}_i) + f_{VisualPosEmb}(\mathbf{p}_i^o)) \tag{5}$$

where $v_i^0 \in R^{d_v}$ is the position-aware feature for each proposal and **LN** represents the layer normalization. $f_{VisualEmb}(\cdot)$ and $f_{VisualPosEmb}(\cdot)$ are the embedding functions.

3.3 Cross-Modal Adaptive Attention Mechanism

In the adaptive attention mechanism, we no longer directly compute the similarity matrix between text and image, but instead introduce learnable parameters to dynamically adjust the attention weights. These parameters can be optimized through the training process to maximize the model's performance on specific tasks.

Computation of Adaptive Attention Weights: Suppose we have a text feature matrix $\boldsymbol{A}^{\text{Text}} \in \mathbb{R}^{m \times d_{\text{text}}}$ and an image feature matrix $\boldsymbol{A}^{\text{Image}} \in \mathbb{R}^{n \times d_{\text{image}}}$, where m and n are the numbers of text and image features, respectively, and d_{text} and d_{image} are the dimensions of text and image features, respectively.

We can introduce two learnable parameter matrices $\boldsymbol{W}_{\text{text}} \in \mathbb{R}^{d_{\text{text}} \times d_{\text{proj}}}$ and $\boldsymbol{W}_{\text{image}} \in \mathbb{R}^{d_{\text{image}} \times d_{\text{proj}}}$ to project the text and image features onto the same dimension d_{proj}. Then, we compute the adaptive attention weights.

Formulas:

$$\begin{aligned} \boldsymbol{Q}_{\text{text}} &= \boldsymbol{A}^{\text{Text}} \boldsymbol{W}_{\text{text}}, \\ \boldsymbol{K}_{\text{image}} &= \boldsymbol{A}^{\text{Image}} \boldsymbol{W}_{\text{image}}, \\ \boldsymbol{S}_{\text{adaptive}} &= \operatorname{softmax}\left(\frac{\boldsymbol{Q}_{\text{text}} \boldsymbol{K}_{\text{image}}^{T}}{\sqrt{d_{\text{proj}}}} \right). \end{aligned}$$

where $\boldsymbol{Q}_{\text{text}}$ is the query matrix of text features, $\boldsymbol{K}_{\text{image}}$ is the key matrix of image features, and $\boldsymbol{S}_{\text{adaptive}} \in \mathbb{R}^{m \times n}$ is the adaptive attention weight matrix.

Computation of Adaptive Attention Matrices: Using the adaptive attention weight matrix $\boldsymbol{S}_{\text{adaptive}}$, we can compute the text-to-image adaptive attention matrix $\boldsymbol{A}_{\text{Text2Image}}$ and the image-to-text adaptive attention matrix $\boldsymbol{A}_{\text{Image2Text}}$.

$$\begin{aligned} \boldsymbol{A}_{\text{Text2Image}} &= \boldsymbol{S}_{\text{adaptive}} \cdot (\boldsymbol{A}^{\text{Image}} \boldsymbol{W}_{\text{value}}), \\ \boldsymbol{A}_{\text{Image2Text}} &= (\boldsymbol{S}_{\text{adaptive}}^{T} \cdot \boldsymbol{W}_{\text{image\_to\_text}}) \cdot \boldsymbol{A}^{\text{Text}} \end{aligned}$$

where $\boldsymbol{W}_{\text{value}} \in \mathbb{R}^{d_{\text{image}} \times d_{\text{output}}}$ is another learnable parameter matrix that maps image features to the output dimension d_{output}. For the image-to-text adaptive attention matrix $\boldsymbol{A}_{\text{Image2Text}}$, the simplified version introduces an additional learnable parameter matrix $\boldsymbol{W}_{\text{image\_to\_text}} \in \mathbb{R}^{n \times n}$. However, in practice, it is more common to use the transpose of $\boldsymbol{S}_{\text{adaptive}}$ directly without introducing additional parameter matrices, as shown in the common version. Here, $\boldsymbol{A}^{\text{Text\_proj}} = \boldsymbol{A}^{\text{Text}} \boldsymbol{W}_{\text{text\_proj}}$, and $\boldsymbol{W}_{\text{text\_proj}} \in \mathbb{R}^{d_{\text{text}} \times d_{\text{proj\_out}}}$ is a learnable parameter matrix that projects text features onto a dimension similar or identical to that of image features.

3.4 Interaction and Prediction Layer

Inspired by previous works [23], we combine the $\mathbf{A}_{Text2Image}$ and $\mathbf{A}^{Text}$ to enhance both global and local semantic information. In the same way, we calculate $\mathbf{A}_{Image2Text}$ and $\mathbf{A}^{Image}$, denoted as:

$$\textbf{Text}_i^m = [\mathbf{A}_i^{Text2Image}; \mathbf{A}_i^{Text}; \mathbf{A}_i^{Text2Image} \odot \mathbf{A}_i^{Text}] \tag{6}$$

$$\textbf{Visual}_j^n = [\mathbf{A}_j^{Image2Text}; \mathbf{A}_i^{Image}; \mathbf{A}_i^{Image2Text} \odot \mathbf{A}_i^{Image}] \tag{7}$$

where $[\cdot; \cdot; \cdot]$ is the concatenation operation of vectors, and $\odot$ indicates element-wise product.

Next, we train our model with bidirectional GRU (Bi-GRU) to acquire context information between original sarcasm text and its corresponding image. The detailed acquisition methods are shown as follows:

$$\mathbf{Text}_i^v = \mathbf{BiGRU}(Text_i^m, Text_{i-1}^v, Text_{i+1}^v) \tag{8}$$

$$\mathbf{Visual}_j^v = \mathbf{BiGRU}(Visual_j^n, Visual_{j-1}^v, Visual_{j+1}^v) \tag{9}$$

After that, we use max pooling and mean pooling of $\mathbf{Text}^v = (\mathbf{Text}_1^v, \mathbf{Text}_2^v, \cdots, \mathbf{Text}_m^v)$ and $\mathbf{Visual}^v = (\mathbf{Visual}_1^v, \mathbf{Visual}_2^v, \cdots, \mathbf{Visual}_n^v)$ to acquire fixed-length vectors. Specifically, we compute max pooling vectors $\mathbf{r}_{Text}^{max}$ and $\mathbf{r}_{Visual}^{max}$, as well as mean pooling vectors $\mathbf{r}_{Text}^{mean}$ and $\mathbf{r}_{Visual}^{mean}$. Then, we concatenate these vectors to get the global representation $\mathbf{r}$. The details are indicated as follows:

$$\mathbf{r}_{Text}^{mean} = \sum_{i=1}^{m} \frac{Text_i^v}{m} \tag{10}$$

$$\mathbf{r}_{Text}^{max} = max_{i=1}^{m} Text_i^v \tag{11}$$

$$\mathbf{r}_{Visual}^{mean} = \sum_{j=1}^{n} \frac{Visual_j^v}{n} \tag{12}$$

$$\mathbf{r}_{Visual}^{max} = max_{j=1}^{n} Viusal_j^v \tag{13}$$

$$\mathbf{r} = [\mathbf{r}_{Text}^{mean}; \mathbf{r}_{Text}^{max}; \mathbf{r}_{Visual}^{mean}; r_{Visual}^{max}] \tag{14}$$

Finally, we feed the global representation $\mathbf{r}$ to the prediction layer, composed of a multi-layer perceptron (MLP) classifier, to determine whether the semantic meaning of the give text-image pair is sarcastic or not. This prediction process can be denoted as:

$$\mathbf{v} = tanh(W_r \cdot \mathbf{r} + b_r) \tag{15}$$

$$\hat{y} = softmax(W_v \cdot \mathbf{v} + b_v) \tag{16}$$

where W_r, b_r, W_v, and b_v are trainable parameters. The entire model is trained end-to-end.

4 Experimental Setup

4.1 Dataset

In our experiments, we adopt datasets: (1) MSCOCO [24] and (2) sarcasm detection dataset [4]. The former is a classic dataset, which has been widely used in tasks such as image captioning [25] and text data augmentation [26]. This dataset consists of 123,000 images and each image has five reference captions. Following the setting of [27], we use 113,287 images for training, 5,000 images for validation, and 5,000 images for testing. For each image, the best image caption is selected based on the highest CIDEr (Consensus-based Image Description Evaluation) score. The second dataset is built by Cai et al. [4] for sarcasm detection on Twitter. This dataset is collected from English tweets, containing positive examples (i.e., sarcastic) composed of images and special hashtags like sarcasm, irony, etc., and negative examples with images but no such hashtags (i.e., not sarcastic). The dataset is divided into training set, development set and test set, based on a ratio of 8:1:1. Table 1 shows the statistics of this dataset.

Table 1. Statistics of sarcasm detection dataset

	Training	Development	Testing
sentences	19816	2410	2409
positive	8642	959	959
negative	11174	1451	1450

4.2 Settings and Parameters

In visual feature preprocessing, we apply the pre-trained Faster R-CNN object detector [22] to extract the RoI features. Specifically, for each image, we fix the number of region proposals, then get the corresponding RoI feature, bounding box, and predicted labels. During image captioning training, the mini-batch size is set to 100. The learning rate is initialized as 1e−4 and gradually decreases to 4e−5. Adam [28] is used as the optimizer. The pre-trained ResNet101 [29] is used as the image encoder, then the weights for the sentence decoder are randomly initialized. During sarcasm detection training, we set the dimension of the hidden state of the transformer to 768. We initialize the transformer in this work with the BERT model pertained in MMF (a modular framework for vision and language multi-modal research from Facebook AI Research). Again, we use Adam optimizer with an initial learning rate of 5e-5, then train for 10,000 steps.

5 Experimental Results

5.1 Comparison Results

Table 2 presents the performance comparison of various methods under different modalities in the multimodal sarcasm detection task. The evaluation metrics include accuracy (Acc), precision (Pre), recall (Rec), and macro-average F1 score (Macro - average F1).

(1)Single-modal Methods

Single-modal methods only utilize either visual or textual information for sarcasm detection, and their performance is limited. For image-based methods, the accuracy is merely 64.76%, and the macro-average F1 score is 65.97%. This is because sarcasm cues in images are often subtle and difficult to capture.

Table 2. Performance comparison of different modalities and methods

MODALITY	METHOD	Acc (%)	F1-score			Macro-average		
			Pre (%)	Rec (%)	F1 (%)	Pre (%)	Rec (%)	F1 (%)
single-modal	Image (Cai et al. 2019[4])	64.76	54.41	70.80	61.53	60.12	73.08	65.97
	ViT (Dosovitskiy et al. 2021[30])	73.72	65.56	71.64	68.46	72.78	73.37	72.97
	TextCNN (Kim 2014[31])	80.03	74.29	76.39	75.32	78.03	78.28	78.15
	SIARN (Tay et al. 2018[32])	80.57	75.55	75.70	75.63	80.34	78.81	79.57
	SMSD (Xiong et al. 2019[33])	80.90	76.46	75.18	75.82	80.87	78.20	79.51
	BERT (Devlin et al. 2019[34])	83.85	78.72	82.27	80.22	81.31	80.87	81.09
	RoBERTa (Liu et al. 2019[35])	85.51	78.24	88.11	82.88	84.83	85.95	85.16
multi-modal	HFM (Cai, Cai, and Wan 2019[4])	83.44	76.57	84.15	80.18	79.40	82.45	80.90
	D&R Net (Xu, Zeng, and Mao 2020[18])	84.02	77.97	83.42	80.60	-	-	-
	Res-BERT (Pan et al. 2020[36])	84.80	77.80	84.15	80.85	78.87	84.46	81.57
	Att-BERT (Pan et al. 2020[36])	86.05	78.63	83.31	80.90	80.87	85.08	82.92
	InCrossMGs (Liang et al. 2021[37])	86.10	81.38	84.36	82.84	85.39	85.80	85.60
	CMGCN (Liang et al. 2022[38])	87.55	83.63	84.69	84.16	87.02	86.97	87.00
	MILNet (Yang et al. 2023[39])	89.50	85.16	89.16	87.11	88.88	89.44	89.12
	G^ 2SAM (Wei et al. 2024[40])	90.48	87.95	89.02	88.48	89.44	89.79	89.65
	CMANet(Our)	**91.32**	**91.87**	**92.25**	**92.06**	**92.07**	**92.83**	**92.45**

ViT achieves an accuracy of 73.72% and a macro-average F1 score of 72.97%. Although it performs better than image-based methods, it still has limitations when handling tasks that require semantic understanding, as it solely relies on visual information. Text-based methods (such as TextCNN, Bi - LSTM, etc.) outperform image-based methods. RoBERTa performs the best, with an accuracy of 85.51% and a macro-average F1 score of 85.16%. BERT also shows decent performance, with an accuracy of 83.85% and a macro-average F1 score of 81.09%. However, single-modal methods encounter performance bottlenecks because they only utilize information from a single modality, making it difficult to capture the complex features that may exist simultaneously in both visual and textual modalities.

(2) Multimodal Methods

Multimodal methods simultaneously leverage visual and textual information, and their performance significantly exceeds that of single-modal methods. The lowest accuracy among multimodal methods is 83.44% for HFM, while the highest is 89.50% for CMANet. The lowest macro-average F1 score is 80.90% for HFM, and the highest is 89.12% for CMANet. The fusion strategy of HFM may not be effective enough. D&R Net shows some improvements but still has room for enhancement. Res - BERT and Att - BERT combine different architectures, and Att - BERT, which introduces an attention mechanism, performs better. InCross - MGs focuses on global information processing and performs well but is inferior to MILNet. CMGCN emphasizes local semantic guidance and outperforms InCross - MGs and other methods but is still not as good as CMANet. CMANet significantly outperforms other methods in all metrics.

(3)Advantages of CMANet

From the comparative experiments, it is clear that CMANet exhibits significant advantages in the multimodal sarcasm detection task. Its performance not only surpasses that of other multimodal methods but also outperforms InCross - MGs, which focuses on global information processing, and CMGCN, which concentrates on local semantic guidance. The outstanding performance of CMANet is attributed to its clever fusion of large language models and cross-modal adaptive attention mechanisms, achieving complementary advantages. Large language models, with their large parameter scales and extensive pre-training data, possess strong semantic understanding capabilities. They can accurately grasp the overall semantic structure of multimodal information from a macro perspective, providing a comprehensive semantic framework. The cross-modal adaptive attention mechanism acts like a keen "detector". It can dynamically allocate attention weights based on the characteristics and importance of different modal information, digging into local details and capturing key cues that are easy to overlook. The combination of these two methods enables CMANet to have both a macro semantic perspective and micro detail insights, allowing it to understand multimodal information more comprehensively and deeply. This all-round understanding ability greatly enhances CMANet's accuracy in identifying sarcasm content, offering an efficient and reliable solution for the multimodal sarcasm detection task.

5.2 Ablation Study

We conducted an ablation study to thoroughly investigate the impact of different input modalities on model performance. The experimental results are presented in Table 3. In this study, "IC" stands for image caption, and "OST" represents original sarcasm text. The base large model used in the experiments is Qwen3-8B.

Table 3. Ablation study

Input	Model	F1-score	Precision	Recall
IC	Qwen3-8B + FC	0.7387	0.7238	0.7543
OST	Qwen3-8B + FC	0.7889	0.7564	0.8245
IC + OST	Qwen3-8B + FC	0.8248	0.7865	0.8672
IC + OST + image	Qwen3-8B + CMANet(Our model)	**0.9187**	**0.9225**	**0.9206**

(Analysis of Row 1 Results) When only the image caption (IC) is input into the Qwen3-8B + FC model, it achieves an F1-score of 0.7387, precision of 0.7238, and recall of 0.7543. This shows that image caption text can provide effective features, indicating it contains valuable task-related information.

(Comparative Analysis: Row 2 vs. Row 1) Switching from IC to original sarcasm text (OST) significantly improves the model's performance, with F1-score rising to 0.7889, precision to 0.7564, and recall to 0.8245. OST offers richer, more accurate semantic information, likely due to its direct derivation from the task scenario, closer to the task's essence, and containing more sarcasm-related details. This enables the model to better capture key information, optimizing detection results.

(Comparative Analysis: Row 3 vs. Row 2) Combining IC and OST further enhances the model's performance, with F1-score reaching 0.8248, precision 0.7865, and recall 0.8672. This demonstrates the effectiveness of combining image description and text modalities. IC provides visual-related text, while OST contains rich semantics, complementing each other to improve the model's sarcasm detection performance.

(Comparative Analysis: Row 4 vs. Previous Rows) Adopting the complete model architecture, including IC, OST, and the image itself, with our proposed model (Qwen3-8B + CMANet and other modules), leads to a qualitative leap in performance. The F1-score reaches 0.9187, precision 0.9225, and recall 0.9206. This significant improvement indicates that visual features in the image are crucial. The image modality provides intuitive visual info, which, when combined with text through the model's adaptive fusion mechanism, captures task-related features more comprehensively, achieving effective cross-modal fusion and greatly improving the model's accuracy and robustness in sarcasm detection.

In conclusion, this ablation study's comparative analysis clearly shows the impact of different input modalities and model architectures on performance. IC text, OST, and the image itself each contain unique info. Combining them reasonably leverages modal advantages, providing richer, more comprehensive features and significantly improving sarcasm detection performance.

5.3 Analysis of Vanilla LLMs

To comprehensively and in-depthly explore the effectiveness of various large language models in the multi-modal sarcasm detection task, a series of rigorous analytical experiments were conducted on four representative large language models using the multi-modal sarcasm detection dataset employed in this paper. In the fusion layer, the cross-modal adaptive attention network (Cross - Modal Adaptive Attention Networks, CMANet) proposed in this paper was adopted to integrate information from different modalities. The experimental results are shown in Fig. 3.

Model (1) ChatGLM2-6B + CMANet: We employed the ChatGLM2-6B model in the text encoding layer. Though a powerful large language model pre-trained on large-scale text data with good language understanding and generation capabilities, its performance in multimodal sarcasm detection is limited. This is because it mainly focuses on text semantics and lacks the ability to capture complex image-text correlations and sarcastic intent, which often lie in subtle text-image interactions. It struggles to mine deep cross-modal associations, resulting in subpar performance.

Model (2) DeepSeekR1-6B + CMANet: We used the DeepSeekR1-6B model. It outperforms ChatGLM2-6B in multimodal sarcasm detection, likely due to more emphasis on modeling complex semantic relationships during pre-training,

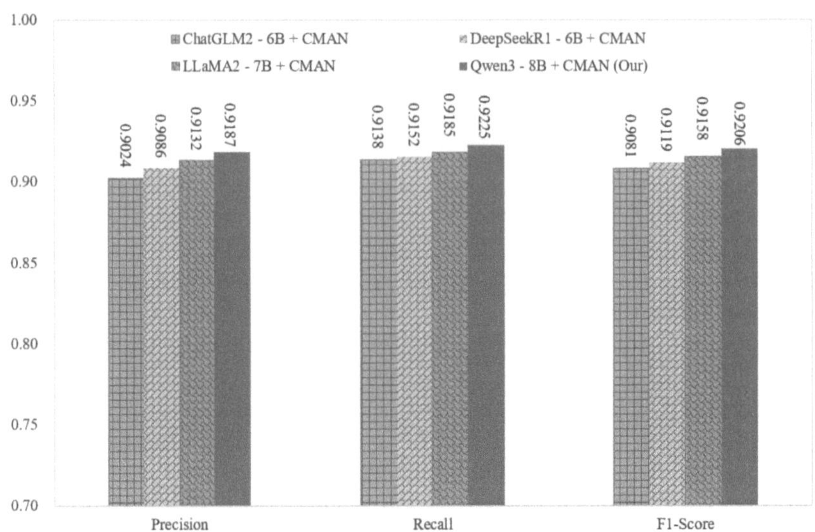

Fig. 3. Vanilla LLMs on Multi-modal Sarcasm Detection Dataset

enabling better capture of subtle semantic clues in text. It may also have been exposed to more sarcasm-related text data, giving it sensitivity to sarcastic expressions. However, it doesn't fully utilize image features or perfectly fuse key visual information with textual sarcastic clues, restricting further performance improvement.

Model (3) LLaMA2-7B + CMANet: We adopted the LLaMA2-7B model. It surpasses DeepSeekR1-6B in multimodal sarcasm detection. With a larger model size and richer parameters, it can learn more complex language patterns and semantic relationships, better understanding sarcastic implications in rhetorical devices. It may also have stronger multimodal fusion capabilities, more effectively associating image visual features with text semantic features. Yet, it still has shortcomings, such as misjudging highly complex and subtle sarcastic expressions due to insufficient contextual understanding.

Model (4) Qwen3-8B + CMANet: We used the Qwen3-8B model, which exhibits the best performance among the four. It not only has powerful text understanding and generation abilities but also has undergone targeted multimodal learning optimization. It can accurately capture semantic associations between images and text, especially recognizing common image-text contradictions in sarcastic content. It may adopt a more advanced cross-modal fusion strategy, fully integrating information from both modalities to accurately judge sarcasm. Additionally, it may have been exposed to more diverse multimodal sarcasm data during training, giving it good generalization ability for various sarcastic expressions.

In conclusion, analyzing and comparing these four large language models in multimodal sarcasm detection, we observe performance differences mainly depending on their abilities in text semantic understanding, cross-modal information fusion, and learning and generalization of sarcastic expressions. Qwen3-8B is the preferred model for this task due to its outstanding performance and is mainly adopted in this paper.

6 Conclusion

Addressing the challenging task of sarcasm detection on social media, this study proposes an innovative detection method based on a cross-modal adaptive attention network. The model adopts a multi-modal feature extraction strategy, independently obtaining information representations from three dimensions: text attributes, visual features, and image captions. In terms of text feature extraction, we innovatively incorporate a large language model to conduct joint deep semantic analysis on text attributes and image captions, effectively enhancing the expressive power of text features. To further optimize the fusion of multimodal information, we have designed a cross-modal adaptive attention mechanism that can dynamically adjust the weight distribution of different modal features, achieving intelligent integration of information embeddings. To validate the model's performance, we conducted systematic experimental evaluations on a real-world dataset of English tweets. The experimental results demonstrate that, compared to the current state-of-the-art benchmark models, our model achieves significant improvements in key metrics such as detection accuracy and F1 score, fully proving the superiority and practical value of the proposed method in the task of sarcasm detection on social media.

References

1. Yang, X., Wu, Y., et al.: Exploring diverse in-context configurations for image captioning. In: NIPS (2024)
2. Qian, T., Chen, J., et al.: Nuscenes-QA: a multi-modal visual question answering benchmark for autonomous driving scenario. In: AAAI (2024)
3. Yue, T., Shi, X., et al.: SARCNET: a multilingual multimodal sarcasm detection dataset. In: COLING (2024)
4. Cai, Y., Cai, H., et al.: Multi-modal sarcasm detection in twitter with hierarchical fusion model. In: ACL (2019)
5. Riloff, E., Qadir, A., et al.: Sarcasm as contrast between a positive sentiment and negative situation. In: EMNLP (2013)
6. Joshi, A., Sharma, V., et al.: Harnessing context incongruity for sarcasm detection. In: ACL (2015)
7. Ashwitha, A., Shruthi, G., et al.: Sarcasm detection in natural language processing. Mater. Today Proc. (2021)
8. Zhang, M., Zhang, Y., et al.: Tweet sarcasm detection using deep neural network. In: COLING (2016)
9. Pandey, R., Singh, J.P.: BERT-LSTM model for sarcasm detection in code-mixed social media post. J. Intell. Inf. Syst. (2023). https://doi.org/10.1007/s10844-022-00755-z

10. Sangwan, S., Akhtar, M.S., et al.: I didn't mean what i wrote! exploring multimodality for sarcasm detection. In: IJCNN (2020)
11. Yin, Z., You, F.: Multi-modal sarcasm detection in Weibo. In: ISCIPT (2021)
12. Wang, X., Sun, X., et al. :Building a bridge: a method for image-text sarcasm detection without pretraining on image-text data. In: ACL (2020)
13. Schifanella, R., De Juan, P., Tetreault, J., Cao, L., et al.: Detecting sarcasm in multimodal social platforms. In: IEEE Multimedia (2016)
14. Wu, Y., Zhao, Y., et al.: Modeling incongruity between modalities for multimodal sarcasm detection. IEEE MultiMedia (2021)
15. Fu, H., Liu, H., et al.: Multi-modal sarcasm detection with sentiment word embedding. Electronics (2024)
16. Liu, H., Wang, W., Li, H.: Towards multi-modal sarcasm detection via hierarchical congruity modeling with knowledge enhancement. In: EMNLP (2022)
17. Yue, T., Mao, R., et al. :KnowleNet: knowledge fusion network for multimodal sarcasm detection. Inf. Fus. (2023)
18. Xu, N., Zeng, Z., et al.: Reasoning with multimodal sarcastic tweets via modeling cross-modality contrast and semantic association. In: ACL (2020)
19. Wu, Y., Schuster, M., et al.: Google's neural machine translation system: bridging the gap between human and machine translation. arXiv preprint arXiv:1609.08144 (2016)
20. Lu, J., Batra, D., et al.: VilBERT: pretraining task-agnostic visiolinguistic representations for vision-and-language tasks. arXiv preprint arXiv:1908.02265 (2019)
21. Li, L.H., Yatskar, M., et al.: VisualBERT: a simple and performant baseline for vision and language. arXiv preprint arXiv:1908.03557 (2019)
22. Ren, S., He, K., et al.: Faster R-CNN: towards real-time object detection with region proposal networks. TPAMI (2016)
23. Mou, L., Men, R., et al.: Natural language inference by tree-based convolution and heuristic matching. In: ACL (2016)
24. Lin, T.-Y., Maire, M., et al.: Microsoft coco: common objects in context. In: ECCV (2014)
25. Gu, J., Zhao, H., et al.: Scene graph generation with external knowledge and image reconstruction. In: CVPR (2019)
26. Wang, S., Gupta, R., et al.: A task in a suit and a tie: paraphrase generation with semantic augmentation. In: AAAI (2019)
27. Karpathy, A., Fei-Fei, L.: Deep visual-semantic alignments for generating image descriptions. In: CVPR (2015)
28. Diederik, P., Kingma, J.B.: A method for stochastic optimization. CoRR, Adam (2015)
29. He, K., Zhang, X., et al.: Deep residual learning for image recognition. In: CVPR (2016)
30. Dosovitskiy, A., Beyer, L., et al.: An image is worth 16x16 words: transformers for image recognition at scale. In: ICLR (2021)
31. Yoon Kim: Convolutional neural networks for sentence classification. In: EMNLP (2014)
32. Tay, Y., Luu, A.T., et al.: Reasoning with sarcasm by reading in-between. In: ACL (2018)
33. Xiong, T., Zhang, P., et al.: Sarcasm detection with self-matching networks and low-rank bilinear pooling. In: WWW (2019)
34. Devlin, J., Chang, , M.-W., et al.: BERT: pre-training of deep bidirectional transformers for language understanding. In: NAACL (2019)

35. Liu, Y., Ott, M., et al.: RoBERTa: a robustly optimized BERT pretraining approach. CoRR, abs/1907.11692 (2019)
36. Pan, H., Lin, Z., et al.: Modeling intra and inter-modality incongruity for multi-modal sarcasm detection. In: EMNLP (2020)
37. Liang, B., Lou, C., et al.: Multi-modal sarcasm detection with interactive in-modal and cross-modal graphs. In: ACM MM (2021)
38. Liang, B., Lou, C., et al. :Multi-modal sarcasm detection via cross-modal graph convolutional network. In: ACL (2022)
39. Qiao, Y., Jing, L., et al.: Mutual-enhanced incongruity learning network for multi-modal sarcasm detection. In: AAAI (2023)
40. Wei, Y., Yuan, S., et al.: Gˆ 2sam: graph-based global semantic awareness method for multimodal sarcasm detection. In: AAAI (2024)

Small Scale, Strategic Advantage: Enhancing LLMs with Domain Knowledge Graphs

Peixin Zhou, Penglin Ge, and Xin Wang(✉)

College of Intelligence and Computing, Tianjin University, Tianjin, China
{zpx_384158,gpl,wangx}@tju.edu.cn

Abstract. Large language models (LLMs) offer a new paradigm for decision making in real-time strategy games. However, closed-source LLMs rely on costly remote APIs, while open-source LLMs require tens of gigabytes of GPU memory and several hours of inference, creating a severe resource bottleneck. To address this issue, we introduce KADR (Knowledge-Augmented Decision Refinement), which augments a fine-tuned small-parameter Qwen model with a Liquipedia-derived domain knowledge graph and tactical texts. Unlike conventional Retrieval-Augmented Generation (RAG) pipelines that start with broad queries, KADR first lets the LLM produce a preliminary action set, then retrieves knowledge based on the actions, and finally outputs refined decisions. We realize this approach on the platform of StarCraft II. Compared with the baseline method, KADR increases the fine-tuned small model LV5 win rate from 0% to 60%, significantly improving resource and population efficiency, which achieves the competitive performance as good as baseline LLMs, while reducing the per-game inference time from more than 7 h on average to just 1.5 h on a single 8 GB GPU.

Keywords: Large Language Model · Knowledge Graph · Retrieval-Augmented Generation · TextStarCraft II · Resource-Efficient Decision Making

1 Introduction

The rapid growth of large language models (LLMs) enhances their reasoning capabilities and enables them to function as multi-task decision makers, even without training in specific domains. Compared with reinforcement learning–based decision-making agents, LLMs have obvious advantages in context understanding, knowledge utilization, and human–AI interaction, which enable their application in broader domains such as Real-Time Strategy (RTS) games like StarCraft II. The release of ChatGPT [16] in November 2022 and GPT-4 [17] in April 2023 demonstrate that computers can perform complex textual reasoning. Motivated by this progress, many studies explore the use of LLMs in strategic decision making and RTS gameplay, achieving significant results. For

I. Awan et al. (Eds.): WISE 2025, LNCS 16367, pp. 288–302, 2026.
https://doi.org/10.1007/978-981-95-7394-3_20

example, TextStarCraft II [14] converts visual observations into structured text and introduces the Chain of Summary (CoS) framework as a benchmark for LLM-based decision making, which enables models to analyze game states and make decisions without additional training, showing strong potential for LLM-based agents.

However, all of their experiments are conducted on closed-source LLMs such as GPT and Gemini, which show strong performance in gameplay tasks. Nevertheless, these models remain proprietary and depend on remote API calls. This dependency results in significant costs, especially in complex scenarios where a single game may involve large amounts of textual interaction. In contrast, open-source LLMs such as DeepSeek-R1 (70B) offer the advantage of local deployment and deliver performance comparable to commercial models. However, these models require tens of gigabytes of GPU memory and still suffer from slow inference, often taking more than ten hours for a single match. When using lightweight LLMs such as Qwen2.5-1.5B and Qwen2.5-7B [4], deployment becomes easier, but their limited parameters reduce their ability to understand game mechanics, unit attributes, and strategic patterns. As a result, both cloud-based proprietary services and locally hosted LLMs face serious resource and cost limitations.

To alleviate these constraints, we propose a novel framework called Knowledge-Augmented Decision Refinement (KADR). Our core insight is that the strategic depth of a large model can be externalized into a structured knowledge base and dynamically injected into a small, efficient LLM at inference time. We validate our approach on the StarCraft II platform. Specifically, we introduce a domain-specific knowledge graph that encodes StarCraft II concepts in a structured form [23]. After fine-tuning the LLMs, we further augment their knowledge base through KADR, which differs from conventional Retrieval-Augmented Generation (RAG) that simply employs a domain-specific knowledge graph [3]. This framework enables lightweight LLMs to achieve reasoning and decision-making performance comparable to that of large LLMs in StarCraft II, while avoiding the high costs of API usage and large GPU memory requirements.

During inference, KADR dynamically retrieves the most relevant knowledge from the knowledge graphs and vector databases based on the current state of the game, covering unit matches and tactical patterns, and integrates it into the input context of the LLMs. This "small model + external knowledge" model systematically fills the gap of the lightweight LLMs, providing the model with a deeper awareness of contextual dynamics.

The main contributions of this paper can be summarized as follows:

1. **A refined RAG paradigm: KADR.** We present KADR, an enhanced retrieval-augmented generation paradigm that inverts the traditional RAG process, which first generates preliminary actions to form precise queries and then retrieves relevant knowledge for verification and refinement, leading to more effective and strategic decisions.
2. **Validation on the platform of StarCraft II.** We show that this "small model + external knowledge" paradigm provides a practical and efficient route to high-performance decision-making agents. Our results on StarCraft II sug-

gest that this approach generalizes to other complex domains where structured knowledge is available, such as logistics, robotics, and other strategic simulations.
3. **Large-model performance under tiny memory budgets.** With only 8–10 GB of GPU memory, the fine-tuned Qwen2.5-1.5B + KADR achieves a 60% win rate against LV5 AI - matching GPT4-Turbo in resource efficiency metrics. These results show that targeted external knowledge can compensate for parameter count, enabling high-performance agents on commodity hardware.

2 Related Work

2.1 StarCraft II Decision Environments

The strategic complexity of StarCraft II—with its vast state–action space, multi-agent coordination, and real-time constraints—makes it a standard testbed for decision-making research [19]. The StarCraft Multi-Agent Challenge introduced in 2019 [20] provides widely used interfaces for reinforcement learning studies. However, neither framework offers a text-based, real-time observation and command channel [7], which restricts their direct compatibility with LLMs.

To address this limitation, TextStarCraft II separates high-level strategic planning from low-level micro-control by delegating the latter to scripted modules, which represents the game state through summaries and accepts natural-language commands, creating an LLM-friendly environment that emphasizes strategic reasoning while abstracting away mechanical execution [6].

2.2 Large Language Models

LLMs with billions of parameters achieve strong results across a wide range of tasks. The releases of ChatGPT and GPT-4 are soon followed by the Claude-2/3 series [1,2] and the Llama-2/3 families [15,21]. In decision-making domains, LLMs can handle complex task descriptions and dynamic environments, enabling more precise actions. However, advanced commercial models such as GPT-4 and Claude depend on remote API calls, which can be prohibitively costly—especially in gaming scenarios where each match involves thousands of textual interactions. Although open-source models which are locally deployed such as DeepSeek-R1 (70B) [8] reduce dependence on proprietary services, their heavy GPU memory needs and high inference latency make them impractical for real-time use.

2.3 Knowledge-Graph-Enhanced Retrieval-Augmented Generation

Knowledge graphs (KGs) [9] are graph-structured systems that organize knowledge through entities and relations, forming a semantic network [10]. KGs become a foundation for intelligent search, question answering, and reasoning [11]. In the StarCraft II decision environment, a KG helps an agent capture key factors such as resource allocation, tactical deployment, and force balance [18,22].

Retrieval-augmented generation (RAG) [13] is a framework designed to improve factual accuracy and knowledge consistency in open-domain tasks. In real-time strategy games, RAG can construct a task-specific knowledge module: given the current battle state, the agent first retrieves historical encounters, tactical templates, and operational principles, and then the language model generates concrete commands [5].

Combining RAG with a structured KG further enhances reasoning in complex tasks [12]. By constructing a domain-specific KG and using a modified RAG to retrieve information aligned with the current game state, we provide LLMs with essential background knowledge. This approach significantly improves decision making in complex games and offers a practical solution for building low-resource systems.

3 Methodology

3.1 Construction of the Knowledge Engineering System

In order to enhance the decision-making ability of LLMs through knowledge graphs, we first need to build a knowledge graph. We use StarCraft II as our verification platform, so we first build a knowledge graph related to StarCraft II. In other fields, the corresponding domain knowledge graphs should be constructed. To build a domain-specific KG for StarCraft II, we first collect diverse information from Liquipedia. Relevant fields such as units/buildings, attributes, and strategies are collected. The raw data comprises unstructured texts—unit statistics, tactical notes, battle details and tabular descriptions of units and buildings. After noise removal and de-duplication, only structured textual fragments are retained.

The cleaned material is separated into (a) **basic facts** (unit/building attributes, descriptions, dependencies) and (b) **strategic facts** (resource allocation, tech research priorities, production plan combat tactics). For downstream retrieval, strategic facts are further categorized into four classes:

- **Resource**: mining and allocation of minerals, vespene gas, ...
- **Building**: timing and ordering of production, research, and defensive structures
- **Research**: tech priorities, costs, and their impact on friendly or hostile entities
- **Army**: micro-control, counter relationships, and concrete battle manoeuvres

As shown in Fig. 1, we adopt the Entity–Descriptor–Context workflow:
Step 1: Information extraction. A LLM is prompted to extract relation triples [entity, relation, entity]. Because extraction is ruleless, entities and relations may be ambiguous or redundant.

Step 2: Entity definition. The extracted items are supplied to the LLM again to obtain precise natural-language definitions, providing normalized tactic.
Step 3: Entity standardization. Entities are embedded and matched against pre-defined targets via cosine similarity; semantically equivalent terms are unified, preventing over-generalization.

After the preceding steps, we obtain a set of knowledge-graph triples that are both structurally normalized and semantically consistent. However, strategy texts usually carry deeper layers of meaning and come in many different language styles. We therefore adopt a hybrid workflow that combines manual curation with targeted annotation. Specifically, strategy texts are first manually screened to extract key timing directives that are directly linked to entities in the graph (e.g., "build a Cybernetics Core before the fourth minute"). Each directive is paired with its executable action sequence and stored as a strategy property of the corresponding entity node, enabling rapid queries and path reasoning. These steps yield the final domain-specific knowledge graph.

A large body of remaining combat strategies—such as recommendations for how Unit A should engage Unit B—are highly detailed, involve complex conditions, and do not map clearly to a triple structure. Representing them as triples would enlarge the graph and reduce both query efficiency and semantic accuracy. We therefore store this unstructured content in the vector database ChromaDB. Before embedding, a sliding-window semantic-chunking algorithm separates the raw text into context-preserving units. Each chunk is then converted into a dense vector using the bce-embedding-base_v1 model, and the resulting embeddings are inserted into ChromaDB to support subsequent semantic retrieval.

3.2 Multi-source Knowledge Retrieval Design

Normally, knowledge within a given field is both broad and complex. Relying only on knowledge graphs or vector libraries for retrieval is often insufficient. For instance, strategy texts in RTS games usually contain underlying logical structures, with important facts spread across the narrative. If these texts are embedded without proper segmentation, the resulting vectors may blur key meanings and reduce the accuracy of retrieving complex tactical information. Conversely, a KG is well suited for representing structured rule-based domain knowledge, allowing explicit encoding of dependencies such as "Stalker strong against Void Ray" or "Void Ray built from Stargate".

In the example of StarCraft II, to take advantage of the strengths of both representations, we integrate a KG with a vector database. The KG supplies structured information and key timing strategies, whereas the vector database contributes combat tactics, together enhancing the understanding of agent and use of complex strategy knowledge. As shown in Fig. 1, retrieval is primarily composed of the following two parts:

Vector-Database Retrieval. Keyword search based on inverted indices often fails to capture deeper semantics and contextual meaning. This limitation is addressed by semantic retrieval using dense vector representations, where each text segment is embedded and queried via K-nearest-neighbour (kNN) search with cosine similarity. A similarity threshold τ (e.g. 0.75) is applied to retain only text chunks with $\cos(v, v_e) \geq \tau$.

Knowledge-Graph Retrieval. At time step t, the observation o_t comprises current resources (minerals, vespene gas), existing units and buildings, tech upgrades, and enemy race. These elements form an entity set that serves as the starting point for multi-hop Cypher queries. For each critical entity, the system retrieves all prerequisite chains and associated strategy attributes. For example, the query "Stalker" returns its full dependency chain and yields the rule "To warp in a Stalker before 4:00, a Cybernetics Core must be completed early, and the Gateway must be transformed into a Warp Gate in time." Such queries supply necessary condition chains and improve the abilities of grasp of temporal order and dependency constraints of models.

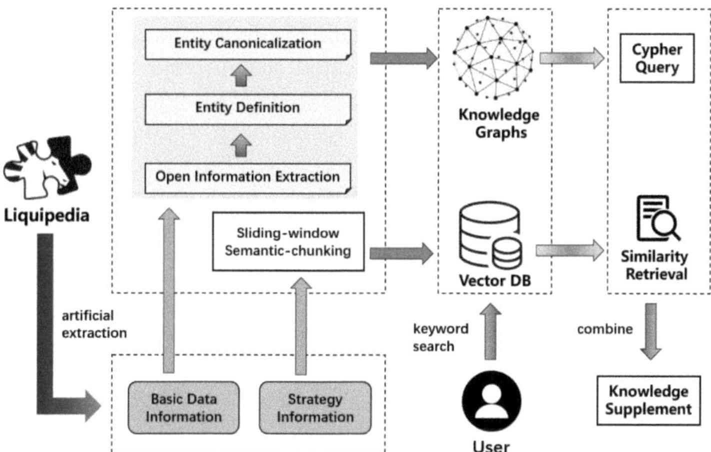

Fig. 1. Construction of the knowledge engineering system and Knowledge Retrieval Design

3.3 Knowledge-Augmented Decision Refinement

In conventional RAG pipelines, a query is first formulated based on the input or question, which is then used to retrieve relevant knowledge. This approach, however, struggles in complex, fast-changing environments like StarCraft II. The fundamental challenge is that a raw game state observation (e.g., "We have 400 minerals, 200 gas, 1 Gateway, and 5 Zealots") does not contain discriminative keywords for effective retrieval. Formulating a broad query like "What should I do next?" would return a vast amount of irrelevant tactical fragments from the knowledge base, most of which would be useless for the current specific situation.

To overcome this limitation, we propose a feedback-driven augmentation framework named KADR. Unlike traditional RAG, KADR first lets the LLM produce a preliminary plan based on its internal knowledge, then uses the proposed actions as queries to retrieve the most relevant knowledge, and finally refines the decision. This approach ensures that the retrieved knowledge is contextually relevant. The KADR pipeline operates over a sliding window of the most recent k frames and consists of the following four stages (as shown in Fig. 2):

Step 1: Preliminary Decision. The sliding window of sequential frame summaries (from frame 1 to frame k) is provided to the LLM. Using the original CoS prompts and format from [14], the model is tasked with generating a preliminary list of m candidate actions. At this stage, the model relies on its parametric knowledge acquired during pre-training. Consequently, these actions may be strategically suboptimal or even infeasible due to a lack of deep domain knowledge (e.g., missing prerequisite buildings or incorrect unit counters).

Step 2: Action Extraction. Since small LLMs may not always adhere to a strict output schema, we employ a dedicated chat prompt to explicitly extract the action list from the preliminary decision. This prompt instructs the model to reread its previous output and list all intended actions in a clear, structured bullet-point format. This method is more robust than relying on regular expressions to parse the initial free-text output. The result of this step is a well-structured list of m action strings, such as ["BUILD NEXUS", "TRAIN PROBE", "CHRONOBOOST NEXUS"].

Step 3: Knowledge Retrieval Augmentation. This is the core step where external knowledge is injected. For each extracted action a_i in the list, we use it as a query to retrieve relevant knowledge:

- **Vector Database Retrieval:** The action string a_i is embedded, and a semantic search is performed over the ChromaDB vector store to retrieve the top-n most relevant text chunks detailing tactical advice, unit counters, or build order tips related to this action.
- **Knowledge Graph Retrieval:** The action string a_i is analyzed to identify key entities (e.g., "Stalkers", "Warp Gate"). For each entity, a Cypher query is executed on the Neo4j graph database to retrieve its dependency chain (e.g., Stalker requires Cybernetics Core) and any associated strategic rules or timing constraints (e.g., "Warp Gate should be researched before 4:00").

The retrieved knowledge snippets from both sources are formatted into a structured text block. This block is then prefixed to the original model context as a system prompt, effectively equipping the LLM with the crucial domain knowledge.

Step 4: Refined Decision. The LLM is executed again, but now with the augmented context that includes the original state summaries of the game and the retrieved knowledge. The LLM is then prompted to reassess the situation and output a final, refined list of actions. The retrieved knowledge grounds the reasoning of model, helping it to produce strategies that are both feasible and sound. These refined actions are extracted (as in Step 2) and appended to the execution queue.

The pseudocode is as shown in Algorithm 1, the time complexity of extracting candidate actions from the plan is $O(m)$, knowledge graph retrieval requires $O(mn)$, and constructing the knowledge-enhanced prompt takes $O(|o| + mn)$. Therefore, the total time complexity is $O(mn + m + 2C_{\text{LLM}})$.

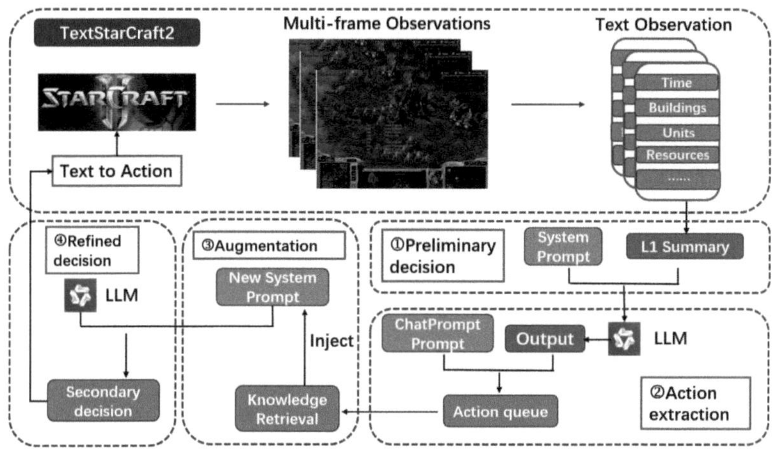

Fig. 2. Interact with LLM: KADR framework in TextStarCraft II.

4 Experiments

All experiments were conducted in the TextStarCraft II environment. To ensure comparability with the baseline in ref [14], we kept the same settings. LLMs were deployed through the Ollama platform, and fine-tuning was carried out with LLaMA Factory. We focused on small and medium-sized open-source models, including DeepSeek-R1-70B, LLaMA3.3-70B, Qwen2.5-1.5B, and Qwen2.5-7B.

We defined six difficulty levels (LV1–LV6). A horizontal comparison was performed across models, evaluating both their decision speed and effectiveness. We designed a set of metrics to measure macro-level decision quality and to analyze how each agent allocates population and resources. An ablation study was also conducted. The results indicate that: (1) fine-tuning significantly improves decision quality and game understanding in small models; (2) adding knowledge-based retrieval further strengthens background knowledge and macro strategies.

4.1 Evaluation Metrics

Following prior studies, we adopted the standard win rate and introduced four additional macro-management metrics to gain deeper insight into the strategic capabilities:

Algorithm 1. KADR(Env, k, m, n, o_0, a_0)

Input: Environment Env; large language model LLM; frame window k; candidate-action count m; knowledge expansion count n; default observation o_0; default action a_0; Extracted Knowledge from KG $Know_{KG}$; Extracted Knowledge from Vector Database $Know_{VD}$; Extracted action A_0

Output: Refined action sequence until episode termination

```
o ← o_0;   a ← a_0;   t ← 0
Env.reset()
while not Env.is_terminated() do
    if t mod k = 0 then
        o ← Env.get_obs()                                         ▷ current textual observation
        msg_1 ← ComposePrePrompt(o)
        rawPlan ← LLM.query(msg_1)
        A_0 ← ExtractTopM(rawPlan, m)
        (Know_KG, Know_VD) ← KGRetrieve(A_0, n)
        msg_2 ← ComposeKnowledgePrompt(o, Know_KG, Know_VD)
        a ← LLM.query(msg_2)                                      ▷ refined decision
    else
        a ← a_0                                                   ▷ fallback action
    end if
    Env.step(a)
    t ← t + 1
end while
return refined action sequence
```

Win Rate (WR): The primary indicator, defined as the percentage of games won by the agent. Although primary, WR alone does not capture the quality of in-game strategy.

Population Block Ratio (PBR): PBR measures macro-management efficiency in population planning:

$$\text{PBR} = \frac{\text{Time at population cap}}{\text{Game duration up to first reach of 200/200}} \tag{1}$$

A lower PBR is desirable, indicating that the agent maintains continuous unit production.

Resource Utilisation Ratio (RUR): RUR evaluates resource management:

$$\text{RUR} = \frac{\text{Total minerals used} + \text{Total gas used}}{\text{Game duration up to first population cap}} \tag{2}$$

A lower RUR reflects stronger management, since the agent uses resources efficiently rather than accumulating them.

Average Population Utilisation (APU): APU captures how efficiently the agent uses its supply:

$$\text{APU} = \frac{1}{N}\sum_{i=1}^{N} \frac{\text{Used population at step } i}{\text{Population cap at step } i} \tag{3}$$

where N is the number of steps before first reaching 200/200. A value closer to 1.0 indicates proactive production.

Technology Rate (TR): TR reflects progress along the technology tree:

$$\text{TR} = \frac{\text{Completed technologies}}{\text{Total technologies available}} \tag{4}$$

A higher TR suggests a more advanced strategy, though it does not guarantee victory if the tech path is suboptimal.

Because sc2reader has limitations when parsing AI-generated replays, we analyzed detailed game logs instead, ensuring comprehensive and precise evaluation under the custom metrics.

4.2 Fine-Tuned Model Comparison

We first evaluated the effect of fine-tuning on Qwen2.5 models. Using the full interaction logs produced by DeepSeek-R1 in the TextStarCraft-II environment, we fine-tuned the open-source Qwen2.5-1.5B. Because of the hardware constraints, chain-of-thought traces are removed; only the input–output pairs are retained. Due to the small parameter size of the model, the fine-tuning process required significantly less time and GPU memory compared to larger models.

Table 1 reports win counts at six difficulty levels. Without fine-tuning, both Qwen2.5-1.5B and Qwen2.5-7B show sharp performance drops from LV4 to LV6, where the win rate approaches zero—revealing limited reasoning and decision ability. Fine-tuning significantly improves decision quality, suggesting better knowledge generalisation.

Table 1. Win rate of baseline and fine-tuned models at each level.

Model	LV1	LV2	LV3	LV4	LV5	LV6
Qwen2.5-1.5B (baseline)	7/8	6/8	1/8	0/8	0/8	0/8
Fine-tuned Qwen2.5-1.5B	8/8	8/8	8/8	**5/8**	**1/8**	0/8
Qwen2.5-7B (baseline)	8/8	7/8	2/8	0/8	0/8	0/8
Fine-tuned Qwen2.5-7B	8/8	8/8	8/8	**7/8**	**2/8**	0/8

4.3 Ablation Study on KADR

To assess the impact of external knowledge, we conduct an ablation study comparing models with and without the KADR pipeline. All matches are played at difficulty level LV5. Table 2 reports five macro-management metrics defined in Sect. 4.1.

Table 2. Performance at LV5 with and without KADR. WR, PBR, RUR, APU, and TR are defined in Sect. 4.1.

Model	Method	WR	PBR	RUR	APU	TR
GPT3.5-Turbo-16k	w/o KADR	5/10(0.5)	0.0781	7 875	0.7608	0.4476
GPT4-Turbo	w/o KADR	3/6(0.5)	0.0337	8 306	0.7194	0.3452
LLaMA3.3-70B	w/o KADR	2/8(0.25)	0.0998	12 577	0.6744	0.1205
DeepSeek-R1-70B	w/o KADR	6/10(0.6)	0.0431	7 301	0.6805	0.2167
Qwen2.5-1.5B	w/o KADR	0/8(0)	0.0878	14 955	0.6781	0.0941
Fine-tuned Qwen2.5-1.5B	w/o KADR	1/8(0.125)	0.0452	7 850	0.6924	0.2448
Qwen2.5-7B	w/o KADR	0/8(0)	0.0723	12 312	0.6871	0.1513
Fine-tuned Qwen2.5-7B	w/o KADR	2/8(0.25)	0.0342	5 892	0.7085	0.3367
Qwen2.5-1.5B	KADR	3/10(0.3)	0.0728	12 516	0.6842	0.2142
Fine-tuned Qwen2.5-1.5B	KADR	**9/15(0.6)**	0.0321	3 558	0.8058	0.4048
Qwen2.5-7B	KADR	4/10(0.4)	0.0612	10 245	0.7129	0.2527
Fine-tuned Qwen2.5-7B	KADR	**10/15(0.67)**	0.0236	2 314	0.7381	0.4673

Without the KADR module, models must interpret the game state purely through raw textual descriptions. While larger language models exhibit relatively stronger performance, they still suffer from shallow strategic understanding. GPT-3.5-Turbo and GPT-4-Turbo achieve modest win rates but display low RUR and TR, suggesting suboptimal resource control. LLaMA3.3-70B secures only two victories out of eight games, highlighting the importance of embedded domain knowledge. DeepSeek-R1-70B achieves better performance (6/10), but its high PBR indicates remaining supply issues. In contrast, the Qwen models record almost no wins and low TR scores, confirming their weak macro-level planning.

After enabling KADR, all models show improvement. The fine-tuned Qwen2.5-1.5B increases from 3/10 to 9/15 wins, with its APU rising to 0.806 and TR to 0.405. The fine-tuned Qwen2.5-7B reaches 10/15 wins, the highest TR, and the lowest RUR, showing efficient resource use. Even without fine-tuning, the Qwen models improve, suggesting that knowledge retrieval helps compensate for their smaller size.

Table 3 summarizes the win counts for the two fine-tuned Qwen models with KADR in all six difficulty settings.

Table 3. Win counts (out of eight for LV1–LV3 and out of fifteen for LV4–LV6) with KADR.

Model	LV1	LV2	LV3	LV4	LV5	LV6
Fine-tuned Qwen2.5-1.5B	8/8	8/8	8/8	14/15	9/15	4/15
Fine-tuned Qwen2.5-7B	8/8	8/8	7/8	15/15	10/15	4/15

As shown in Fig. 3, smaller LLMs reason faster than DeepSeek-R1-70B, whose use of chain-of-thought prompting leads to slower inference. The *small-model + fine-tuning* strategy substantially reduces inference overhead while preserving high decision quality. Coupling this with retrieval-augmented generation compensated for limited knowledge breadth and depth, enabling small models to achieve strong performance even in fast-changing environments.

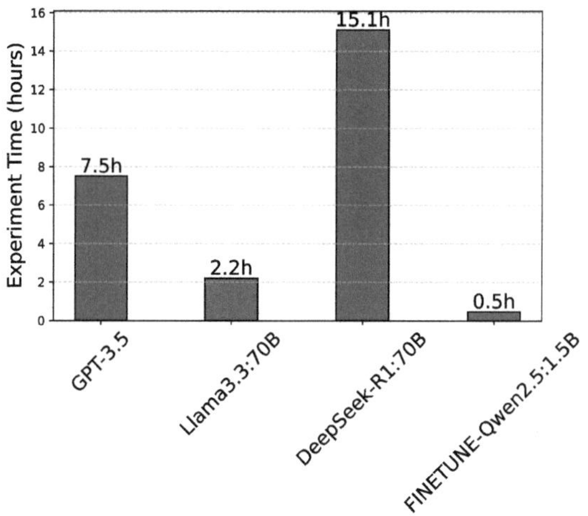

Fig. 3. The average duration of game.

4.4 Details Analysis

To understand how KADR contributes to victory, we tracked four supply-related metrics over time for fine-tuned Qwen2.5-1.5B: Supply Used, Army Supply, Supply Cap, and Supply Left. Figure 4 contrasts the KADR variant (blue) with its non-KADR baseline (red); solid curves denote the mean, and shaded regions indicate variance.

(a) Supply Used. The KADR agent converts available supply into workers and combat units more efficiently, reaching values close to the 200 cap in the late game.

(b) Army Supply. Between 10 and 20 min, the KADR curve rises continuously and remains substantially above the baseline, indicating stronger battlefield presence and adaptive force growth.

(c) Supply Cap. Both variants expand supply at a similar pace early on; mid-to-late game, the KADR agent maintains a slight edge, confirming timely construction of capacity buildings.

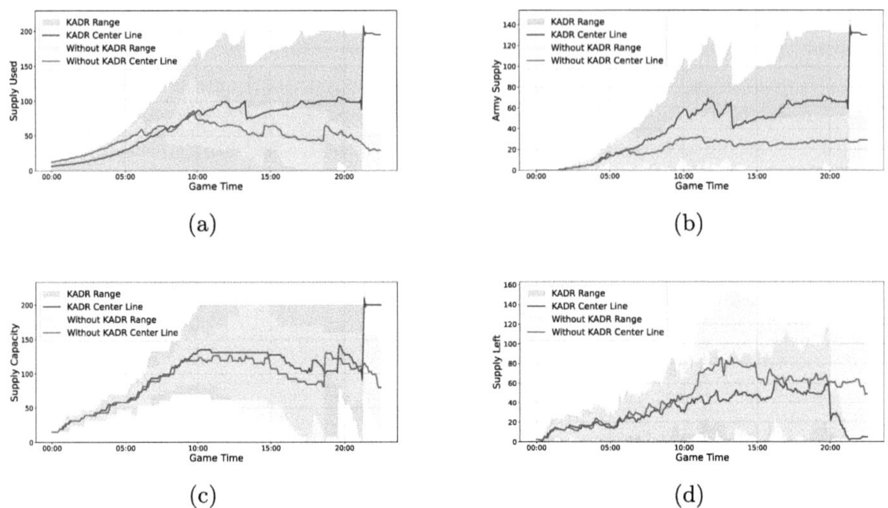

Fig. 4. Comparison between using and not using KADR across four supply-related metrics during the game: (a) Supply Used, (b) Army Supply, (c) Supply Capacity, and (d) Supply Left.

(d) Supply Left. The KADR agent keeps unused supply low, whereas the baseline accumulates surplus in the late game, revealing delayed production decisions.

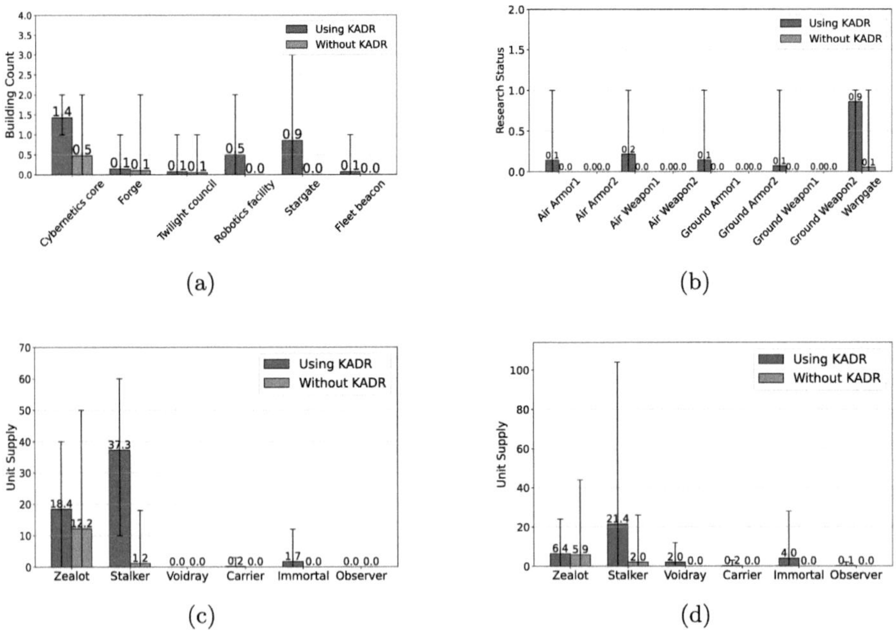

Fig. 5. Comparison between using and not using KADR: (a) Building count, (b) research progress at 10 min, and (c)(d) unit supply at two different time.

Figure 5 (a) and (b) shows that KADR enables the agent to complete key buildings (e.g., Cybernetics Core) and critical upgrades (such as Warpgate) significantly earlier.

Finally, Fig. 5 (c) and (d) highlights more efficient unit production and composition. At the ten-minute mark, the KADR agent fields a markedly larger number of Stalkers, demonstrating its ability to allocate resources towards counter units in response to the evolving battlefield, thereby boosting win rates.

5 Conclusion

This paper proposes the KADR framework, which can improve the decision-making ability of the lightweight LLMs. We realize it on the platform of StarCraft II. We augment a fine-tuned Qwen model with a domain-specific knowledge graph and semantic vector retrieval. Experiments show that KADR significantly improves win rate against high-level AI, enhances resource and population efficiency, and accelerates technology progression. With KADR, a small fine-tuned LLM achieves the competitive performance as good as the baseline LLMs while reducing inference time by a wide margin. These results demonstrate that targeted retrieval of domain knowledge, together with expert strategies, can endow lightweight LLMs with high-quality macro-decision capabilities, providing a practical route to deploy high-performance game agents under low-cost, low-memory constraints.

References

1. Anthropic Claude-2 team: Claude-2 (2023). https://www.anthropic.com/news/claude-2
2. Anthropic Claude-3 team: Claude-3 family. https://www.anthropic.com/news/claude-3-family (2024)
3. Bahr, L., Wehner, C., Wewerka, J., Bittencourt, J., Schmid, U., Daub, R.: Knowledge graph enhanced retrieval-augmented generation for failure mode and effects analysis. J. Ind. Inf. Integr. **45**, 100807 (2025)
4. Bai, S., et al.: Qwen2. 5-VL technical report. arXiv preprint arXiv:2502.13923 (2025)
5. Borgeaud, S., et al.: Improving language models by retrieving from trillions of tokens. In: International Conference on Machine Learning, pp. 2206–2240. PMLR (2022)
6. Chevalier-Boisvert, M., et al.: BABYAI: first steps towards grounded language learning with a human in the loop. In: International Conference on Learning Representations, vol. 105. New Orleans, LA (2019)
7. Côté, M.A., et al.: TextWorld: a learning environment for text-based games. In: Computer Games: 7th Workshop, CGW 2018, Held in Conjunction with the 27th International Conference on Artificial Intelligence, IJCAI 2018, Stockholm, Sweden, July 13, 2018, Revised Selected Papers 7, pp. 41–75. Springer (2019). https://doi.org/10.1007/978-3-030-24337-1_3
8. Deepseek team: DeepSeek-r1 (2025). https://github.com/deepseek-ai/DeepSeek-R1

9. Fensel, D., et al.: Knowledge graphs. Springer (2020). https://doi.org/10.1007/978-3-031-01918-0
10. Guo, W., Wang, X., Chen, J., Li, Z., Chen, Z.: Ontology-enhanced knowledge graph completion using large language models. arXiv preprint arXiv:2507.20643 (2025)
11. Hogan, A., et al.: Knowledge graphs. ACM Comput. Surv. (CSUR) **54**(4), 1–37 (2021)
12. Izacard, G., Grave, E.: Distilling knowledge from reader to retriever for question answering. arXiv preprint arXiv:2012.04584 (2020)
13. Lewis, P., et al.: Retrieval-augmented generation for knowledge-intensive NLP tasks. Adv. Neural. Inf. Process. Syst. **33**, 9459–9474 (2020)
14. Ma, W., et al.: Large language models play starcraft II: benchmarks and a chain of summarization approach. Adv. Neural. Inf. Process. Syst. **37**, 133386–133442 (2024)
15. Meta Llama team: Llama 3 (2024). https://github.com/meta-llama/llama3
16. OpenAI ChatGPT team: ChatGPT. https://openai.com/chatgpt/ (2022)
17. OpenAI GPT-4 team: GPT-4. https://openai.com/index/gpt-4/ (2023)
18. Pan, S., Luo, L., Wang, Y., Chen, C., Wang, J., Wu, X.: Unifying large language models and knowledge graphs: a roadmap. IEEE Trans. Knowl. Data Eng. **36**(7), 3580–3599 (2024)
19. Rashid, T., Samvelyan, M., De Witt, C.S., Farquhar, G., Foerster, J., Whiteson, S.: Monotonic value function factorisation for deep multi-agent reinforcement learning. J. Mach. Learn. Res. **21**(178), 1–51 (2020)
20. Samvelyan, M., et al.: The starcraft multi-agent challenge. arXiv preprint arXiv:1902.04043 (2019)
21. Touvron, H., et al.: Llama 2: open foundation and fine-tuned chat models. arXiv preprint arXiv:2307.09288 (2023)
22. Wang, L., Zhao, W., Wei, Z., Liu, J.: SIMKGC: simple contrastive knowledge graph completion with pre-trained language models. arXiv preprint arXiv:2203.02167 (2022)
23. Xu, J., Wang, H., Niu, Z., Wu, H., Che, W.: Knowledge graph grounded goal planning for open-domain conversation generation. In: Proceedings of the AAAI Conference on Artificial Intelligence, vol. 34, pp. 9338–9345 (2020)

Deep Learning and Networks

Interpretable Tree-Structured Deep Learning Model for Extracting Cognitive Pathways from Social Media

Hanfei Liu[1], Yijing Yu[2], Meng Jiang[1], Qing Zhao[1], Jianqiang Li[1], Hongzhi Qi[1], Wei Zhai[1], Bing Xiang Yang[2], Xiaoqin Wang[2], and Guanghui Fu[3](✉)

[1] School of Software Engineering, Beijing University of Technology, Beijing, China
liuhanfei@emails.bjut.edu.cn
[2] School of Nursing, Wuhan University, Wuhan, China
[3] Sorbonne Université, ICM, CNRS, Inria, Inserm, AP-HP, Hôpital de la Pitié-Salpêtrière, Paris, France
guanghui.fu@inria.fr

Abstract. Cognitive Behavioral Therapy (CBT) serves as a powerful tool in addressing and resolving irrational thoughts, especially when related to mental illness. Therefore, accurate identification of cognitive pathways is essential for its successful application in providing psychological support. Today, people's negative emotional expressions on social media about certain topics (such as "depression") often contain cognitive distortions and follow incorrect cognitive paths. However, there is a distinct lack of data to analyze cognitive pathways, as well as tools to help psychotherapists identify them effectively. In this study, we defined the cognitive path extraction task as a hierarchical text classification task based on cognitive behavioral therapy, which contains four parent categories and nineteen subcategories. We collected a total of 5,282 sentences from social media and then annotated the data to create a cognitive path extraction dataset. We proposed an interpretable tree structure model and explored three different hierarchical classification strategies. It was verified that our model outperformed five other encoder-based models and far outperformed four decoder-based models while maintaining interpretability. On another public comparison dataset, it also achieved better performance than the other seven models. We have released the code publicly: https://github.com/liuhanfei0426/Hierarchical-Text-Classification-wise2025.

Keywords: Deep learning · Hierarchical text classification · Interpretability · Cognitive behavioral therapy · Natural language processing

1 Introduction

Mental health issues, including depression and suicide, pose significant global challenges. The World Health Organization estimates that 3.8% of the global

I. Awan et al. (Eds.): WISE 2025, LNCS 16367, pp. 305–320, 2026.
https://doi.org/10.1007/978-981-95-7394-3_21

population suffers from depression, with nearly 1 billion people affected by mental health disorders and approximately 700,000 suicides annually [16]. These statistics underscore the urgent need for effective interventions. Cognitive behavioral therapy (CBT), as one of the most widely studied psychological interventions, may be an effective solution. CBT, originating from Beck [2], was later expanded by Ellis [10] into a structured ABCD framework, dividing cognitive pathways into four main categories and multiple subcategories. They believed that emotional and behavioral issues arise from cognitive distortions and negative automatic thinking. This focus on altering thought patterns makes CBT an effective long-term treatment for psychological problems. In order to carry out cognitive behavioral therapy (CBT) effectively, it is first necessary to identify the cognitive pathways of patients with psychological problems [10], which will help psychologists quickly analyze and locate specific problems [8]. However, individuals with mental health issues often adopt passive coping strategies and face barriers such as social stigma and limited access to professional help, leading many to express their struggles on social media platforms like Twitter and Sina Weibo [17]. Therefore, implementing CBT by identifying cognitive pathways in social media data has become a promising solution [14].

Advancements in natural language processing (NLP), particularly with models like BERT [7] and large language models (LLMs) such as ChatGPT [1], have enhanced text processing for mental health applications [26]. Qi et al. [18] verified the performance of supervised learning models and LLMs in the field of psychology for cognitive distortion and suicide risk classification tasks using social media data. Among them, AI is also used in CBT in psychology. Dino et al. [9] developed chatbots to provide CBT services to users with various psychological problems. In addition to using AI to directly provide CBT, Jiang et al. [13] used a variety of deep learning models and LLMs to explore the effect of AI in cognitive path extraction tasks. However, to the best of our knowledge, there are no relevant open-source datasets or tools available for cognitive path extraction, particularly in the Chinese context [14].

Based on Ellis' ABCD framework theory in CBT [10], we collected social media data and defined the cognitive path extraction task as a hierarchical classification task (HTC), which is an important natural language processing (NLP) task. To the best of our knowledge, there is only one study that has attempted to extract cognitive pathways from social media [13]. However, the proposed method not only achieved better performance, but also has interpretability. There are already some studies that model the text classification problem in the news field as a hierarchical classification task [27]. However, the models they proposed lack interpretability, which is crucial in the medical field.

In this study, we collected dataset from various social media platforms for the cognitive pathway extraction task, and modeled this task as a hierarchical text classification problem. We propose an interpretable tree-based hierarchical classification model and explore three distinct strategies to address this task. Experimental results on benchmark models and datasets demonstrate the superior performance of the proposed model.

2 Background and Task Definition

Cognitive behavioral therapy, influenced by Rational Emotive Behavior Therapy (REBT), posits that emotional and behavioral problems stem from cognitive distortions and negative automatic thoughts. The core of CBT is the ABCD framework, which asserts that external events (A: Activating event) do not directly cause emotional and behavioral reactions (C: Consequence); rather, it is the beliefs (B: Belief), particularly irrational ones, that lead to these reactions. By challenging and disputing (D: Disputation) irrational beliefs, psychotherapists help patients develop effective coping mechanisms, thereby improving emotions and behaviors in a more targeted manner [8,20].

- (A) Activating event, 5 subcategories: An external event or situation that triggers emotional and behavioral reactions, influenced by individual beliefs. For example, different people may react differently to the same event due to their beliefs or the way of thinking.
- (B) Belief, 10 sub-categories: An individual's interpretation of the activating event, which can be rational or irrational. Irrational beliefs often lead to negative emotions and behaviors.
- (C) Consequence, 2 sub-categories: The emotional and behavioral outcomes of beliefs, including both emotional and behavioral effects.
- (D) Disputation, 2 sub-categories: The process of challenging irrational beliefs, either habitually or effectively. Effective disputation involves rational thinking and evidence.

Therefore, according to the ABCD framework of CBT theory, we can define the cognitive path extraction task as a Hierarchical Text Classification task (HTC) with four parent classes and 19 child classes. Each piece of data may have label classification results of multiple cognitive paths, so it belongs to the task category of Hierarchical Multi-label Text Classification (HMTC). Detailed subclass labels are shown in Table 1.

3 Method

3.1 Model Architecture

Although large-scale pre-trained language models have been used in psychology, their black-box nature limits interpretability. This paper proposes a tree-structured deep learning model for hierarchical classification to extract cognitive pathways. Our model consists of a feature extraction module, a tree classification module, and contrastive learning enhancement. Both the feature encoder and the decision path can be visualized for explanation or interpretation. The model architecture can be seen in Fig. 1.

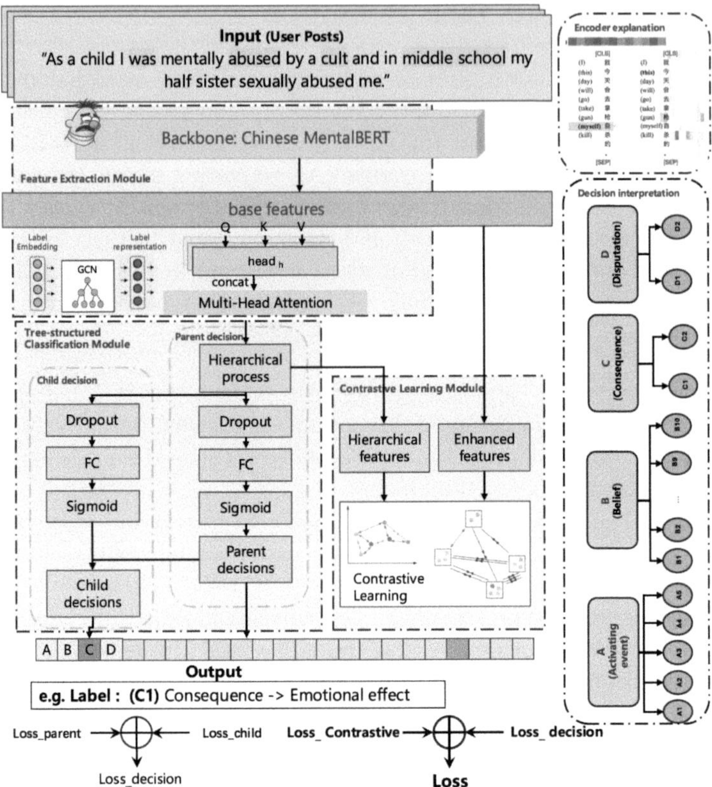

Fig. 1. Processing flow of our proposed interpretable tree-structured model. The backbone network uses Chinese MentalBERT, and the template is defined according to the cognitive path structure.

Feature Extraction Module

Backbone Feature Encoder. The backbone feature encoder is a pre-trained language model M_e, which processes the input text and converts it into feature embedding X_x:

$$X = M_e(x) \tag{1}$$

These token embeddings X are subsequently used as the keys and values in the multi-head attention mechanism Our proposed method is not restricted to a specific encoder; it is flexible and can accommodate various model architectures. We used Chinese MentalBERT [26] to serve as the feature extractor in our experiment.

Label-Aware Multi-head Attention. To enable each label to attend to semantically relevant parts of the input text, we introduce a label-aware multi-head attention mechanism. This component allows each label embedding to serve as a *query* vector, attending over the token representations (used as *keys and values*) produced by a pretrained encoder.

Let $X = [x_1, x_2, \ldots, x_T] \in \mathbf{R}^{T\times d}$ be the sequence of contextualized token embeddings obtained from backbone feature encoder, where T is the number of tokens and d is the hidden dimension. Let $L = [l_1, l_2, \ldots, l_C] \in \mathbf{R}^{C\times d}$ denote the initial trainable label embeddings, where C is the number of labels. These embeddings are further refined via a Graph Convolutional Network (GCN) to incorporate hierarchical label dependencies.

For each label l_k, we use it as the query Q, and use the token sequence X as both the keys K and the values V, to compute a label-specific semantic representation $v_k \in \mathbf{R}^d$ via standard multi-head attention:

$$v_k = \text{MultiHead}(l_k, X) = \text{Concat}(\text{head}_1, \ldots, \text{head}_H)W^O \tag{2}$$

$$\text{head}_h = \text{Attention}(Q_h, K_h, V_h) = \text{softmax}\left(\frac{Q_h K_h^\top}{\sqrt{d_h}}\right)V_h \tag{3}$$

where: $Q_h = l_k W_h^Q$ (label embedding as query), $K_h = XW_h^K$, $V_h = XW_h^V$ (token embeddings from the backbone encoder as keys and values), $W_h^Q, W_h^K, W_h^V \in \mathbf{R}^{d\times d_h}$ are trainable projection matrices for the h-th head, H is the number of heads, and $d_h = d/H$ is the dimension of each head.

The output v_k serves as a label-aware representation of the input text, aggregating semantic information from multiple attention heads. These representations are then passed to the hierarchical decision modules described in Sect. 3.3.

Tree-Structured Classification Module

Parent Node Processing. At the parent level, each parent node p_i applies a transformation function $M_p^{(i)}$ to its corresponding label-aware feature vector $v_p^{(i)}$ derived from the multi-head attention output X, producing an intermediate representation $f_p^{(i)}$:

$$f_p^{(i)} = M_p^{(i)}(v_p^{(i)}), \quad v_p^{(i)} \in X \tag{4}$$

A sigmoid activation function σ_p^s is then used to obtain the classification probability at the parent level:

$$P_p^{(i)} = \sigma_p^s(f_p^{(i)}) \tag{5}$$

These probabilities determine which parent categories are active, influencing the subsequent child-level decisions.

Child Node Processing. Each child node c_{ij} under parent p_i receives the transformed parent feature representation $f_p^{(i)}$ and applies its own transformation function $M_c^{(ij)}$:

$$f_c^{(ij)} = M_c^{(ij)}(f_p^{(i)}) \tag{6}$$

The child node then computes its classification probability, which is dependent on both its own feature processing and its parent's decision:

$$P_c^{(ij)} = P_p^{(i)} \times \sigma_c^s(f_c^{(ij)}) \tag{7}$$

This ensures that a child category can only be activated if its parent category is also active, enforcing hierarchical consistency in classification.

Final Decision. The final classification probability set consists of decisions at both parent and child levels:

$$P = \{P_p^{(1)}, \ldots, P_p^{(m)}, P_c^{(11)}, P_c^{(12)}, \ldots, P_c^{(mn)}\} \tag{8}$$

where each $P_c^{(ij)}$ is constrained by its respective parent node $P_p^{(i)}$. This hierarchical structure allows the model to refine predictions using top-down decision dependencies while maintaining classification flexibility. The selection of loss function is also flexible, and the loss functions at the parent-child level are not required to be necessarily the same.

In our classification module, the model can flexibly employ the most suitable loss functions to compute the loss for both child and parent nodes separately. The total decision loss $L_{decision}$ can be derived as a weighted combination of L_{parent} and L_{child}:

$$L_{decision} = \alpha_c L_{child} + (1 - \alpha_c) L_{parent} \tag{9}$$

where α_c (e.g., 0.7) is a weighting factor that balances the contributions of child and parent losses.

Contrastive Learning Module. To enhance the hierarchical representation, we introduce a contrastive learning module. The contrastive features F_c are derived by concatenating the enhanced features from the label-aware multi-head attention and the hierarchical features from the tree-structured classification module. This module employs a custom supervised binary contrastive loss, inspired by the InfoNCE loss, to pull together semantically similar samples and push apart dissimilar ones. Positive samples are defined using Jaccard similarity, including strong positives (same parent class, same subclass) and weak positives (same parent class, different subclass), while negative samples include weak negatives (different parent classes) and strong negatives (semantically confusing samples). The final loss is derived by weighting the contrastive loss function and the decision loss, ensuring a balanced optimization of feature representation and classification accuracy.

$$L_{contrastive} = L_{con-parent} + L_{con-child} + \beta L_{con-hier} \tag{10}$$

where: $L_{con-parent}$ is the parent node contrastive loss, based on the similarity of projected parent features. $L_{con-child}$ is the child node contrastive loss, based on the similarity of enhanced features. $\beta L_{con-hier}$ is the weighted hierarchical consistency loss, measuring the difference between child and parent node features, with β as the weighting factor.

The formula for the total loss is given by:

$$L_{total} = L_{decision} + \lambda L_{contrastive} \tag{11}$$

3.2 Encoder Explanation and Decision Interpretation

As noted earlier, interpretability is a key strength of our proposed model. According to [19], explanation refers to methods designed to elucidate black-box models, whereas interpretation denotes inherently interpretable models by design. From the explanation perspective, we visualized the attention weights of the feature encoder to assess the transformer-based model's ability to link keywords critical for the downstream task. The encoder's attention mechanism comprises word-level attention weights, indicating focus on each word during encoding, and the role of each attention head, which captures diverse word relationships through varying weights. We employed BertViz [22][1] for head attention visualization, with details shown in Fig. 2. From the decision-making perspective, our model is inherently interpretable, with decisions driven by top-down reliance on parent nodes and probabilities. Interpretation is readily derived by analyzing probabilities at each node, as depicted in Fig. 3.

4 Experiments

4.1 Data Collection and Annotation

The cognitive pathways extraction dataset was collected from user comments on the "ZouFan treehole" on Weibo[2], a platform for emotional venting with significant psychological research value, now inaccessible due to its negative societal impact. The dataset includes 5,282 sentences, split into training (3,135), validation (1,072), and test (1,075) sets in a 3:1:1 ratio at the post level to prevent data leakage. Detailed distribution is shown in Table 1.

The dataset was annotated by 12 psychologists: 10 junior (with master's degrees in psychology and clinical internship experience) and 2 senior (with Ph.D.s and over 10 years of clinical experience). Using the doccano platform[3], junior psychologists independently labeled categories based on psychological constructs. Inter-rater reliability was assessed with Cronbach's Alpha (0.83, high reliability) [5] and Cohen's Kappa (0.76, substantial agreement) [4]. Senior psychologists refined annotations via consensus discussions, ensuring accuracy and robustness.

4.2 Experiment Design

In this research, we aim to answer two questions: 1) What is the best model for the proposed cognitive pathways extraction task under the basic HTC strategy? 2) Using the best model, what is the optimal modeling strategy for model training? To answer these questions, we set the HTC task as a multi-label classification task and validated four decoder-based models and four high-level encoder-based models under the flattening strategy. We selected the best-performing

[1] https://github.com/jessevig/bertviz.
[2] https://www.weibo.com/xiaofan116.
[3] https://github.com/doccano/doccano.

Table 1. Distribution of experimental data for hierarchical text classification. The parent nodes representing the cognitive pathways framework ABCD, and the child nodes corresponding to its sub-categories.

Parent nodes	Child nodes	Train set	Val set	Test set	Sum
(A) Activating Event	Disease symptom	196	66	69	331
	Social relation	200	69	70	339
	Life	214	72	68	354
	Study and work	184	69	60	313
	Emotional	154	47	52	253
(B) Belief	All-or-nothing thinking	151	54	56	261
	Over-generalization	101	39	35	175
	Mental filter	84	39	36	159
	Disqualifying the positive	120	46	39	205
	Jumping to conclusions	230	75	77	382
	Magnification and minimization	95	34	30	159
	Emotional reasoning	206	64	74	344
	Should statements	99	36	35	170
	Labeling and mislabeling	171	59	64	294
	Blaming oneself/others	80	20	24	124
(C) Consequence	Emotional effect	361	118	123	602
	Behavioral effect	276	94	99	469
(D) Disputation	Habitual disputation	109	38	33	180
	Effective disputation	104	33	31	168

model and used it to test other modeling strategies: the ensemble strategy and the proposed tree-structured model. We used precision, recall, and F1-score as evaluation metrics. Considering the problem of class imbalance in the dataset, we used micro-average to calculate these metrics.

4.3 Modeling Training Strategies

HTC employs various training strategies that leverage the label hierarchy differently [25]. These can be broadly categorized into three approaches: the Flat approach, which treats all labels as independent, ignoring hierarchical relationships; the ensemble approach, which trains multiple models for different levels or parts of the hierarchy, combining their outputs for improved accuracy; and the tree-based approach, which models the label hierarchy explicitly, making classification decisions in a structured, hierarchical manner. We conducted experiments employing all these strategies.

Flat Strategy. The flat strategy treats all labels as being on the same level, disregarding the hierarchical relationships between them. This method simplifies the problem to a traditional multi-class or multi-label classification task. While this approach is straightforward to implement, it often fails to utilize the hierarchical information.

Ensemble Strategy. The ensemble strategy involves training multiple models, and trained deep learning models at the parent level, allowing each model to focus solely on predicting its sub-categories. The final predictions are derived by combining the outputs of all these models. This approach can capture various aspects of the hierarchical structure, leading to improved performance in complex classification tasks. However, it also increases computational complexity.

4.4 Ablation Experiments

To assess the impact of various components on our proposed method, we conducted ablation studies. Specifically, we evaluate the effects of the best backbone, frozen backbone, and contrastive learning modules, as well as the choice of loss function. The optimal backbone was selected based on the performance under the flat training strategy. After the model trained under the flat strategy, we can use the trained model as a feature extractor to evaluate the impact of freezing the backbone's layers. This allows us to assess the effect of the frozen mechanisms. In addition, we also added an exploration of the effect of the contrastive learning module.

4.5 Benchmarking on WOS-46985

To evaluate the effectiveness of our approach, we benchmark our proposed model against state-of-the-art hierarchical text classification (HTC) models using the publicly available WOS-46985 dataset [15]. This dataset, comprising English abstracts from published papers in the Web of Science, features a two-layer hierarchy with 7 parent categories and 134 subcategories, covering a broad range of scientific topics. The dataset includes 46,985 samples, stratified into 30,070 for training, 7,518 for validation, and 9,397 for testing, ensuring a balanced distribution across categories. For our experiments, we adopt DeBERTa-v3 [12] as the backbone network, which demonstrates its strong potential for extension to other languages. Detailed results of model evaluation are provided in Sect. 5.

4.6 Implementation Details

For Encoder-based models, We implemented our models in PyTorch and fine-tuned them for 100 epochs with early stopping (patience = 20) using an NVIDIA GeForce RTX 4090 24GB GPU. The best validation model was selected for test evaluation. For flat and ensemble strategies, we used a learning rate of 1e-5, batch size of 16, and BCE loss. For tree-structured models, we set the learning rate to 2e-5, batch size to 32, and used BCE loss. The random seed was set to 42. We have made the detailed code public. For Decoder-based models, We did not perform fine-tuning for the LLMs experiments; instead, we used zero-shot prompts to drive the models.

5 Results

The first step of our experiment is to select the model that performs the best under the flat strategy. The performance of four decoder-based models and four encoder-based models under this strategy is shown in Table 2. We can find that there is still a large gap between decoder-based models and encoder-based models. Although we included zero-shot LLM baselines, we acknowledge that such

Table 2. This table reports the performance at the parent, child, and overall levels for both decoder-based models and encoder-based pretrained models.

Type	Models	Level	Precision	Recall	F1
Encoder-based	BERT [7]	Parent nodes	76.68	78.13	77.01
		Child nodes	51.84	41.85	44.66
		Overall	65.56	59.71	62.50
	XLNet [24]	Parent nodes	69.18	76.36	74.39
		Child nodes	34.54	40.21	43.98
		Overall	58.59	57.58	62.85
	ERNIE 3.0 [21]	Parent nodes	74.92	77.29	76.64
		Child nodes	40.21	41.33	46.70
		Overall	66.30	58.83	62.34
	Chinese MentalBERT [26]	Parent nodes	79.68	78.76	79.22
		Child nodes	50.70	44.82	47.58
		Overall	65.82	61.58	**63.63**
Decoder-based	GPT-3.5	Parent nodes	28.61	36.50	32.08
		Child nodes	12.19	14.92	13.42
		Overall	20.27	25.31	22.51
	GPT-4 [1]	Parent nodes	31.69	41.47	35.93
		Child nodes	15.44	19.45	17.22
		Overall	23.43	30.07	26.34
	GLM-4 [11]	Parent nodes	32.99	43.62	37.57
		Child nodes	15.68	20.08	17.61
		Overall	24.16	31.43	27.32
	ERNIE Bot [23]	Parent nodes	34.23	43.16	38.18
		Child nodes	14.76	17.75	16.12
		Overall	24.37	29.99	26.89

settings may not fully reflect their potential. More advanced configurations (e.g., few-shot prompting or fine-tuning) could yield stronger performance but are left for future work due to resource constraints. The best-performing decoder-based model is GLM-4, which achieved an F1-score of only 27.32% at overall level, making it 36.31% points lower than the ChineseMentalBERT. The performance of different decoder-based models is similar, typically around 26% F1-score at overall level. Among encoder-based models, the performance are similar which are around 62 % F1-score at overall level. Chinese MentalBERT outperforms other encoder-based models, which achieve 63.63% F1-score at the overall level. Therefore we select Chinese MentalBERT for the next step experiment. The performance of different modeling strategies at various levels, including detailed performance at the parent node level, can be seen in Table 3.

Table 3. This table reports the performance of different modeling strategies for the cognitive pathway extraction task, including detailed performance at each parent node.

Modeling strategy	Level	Precision	Recall	F1
Flat	Parent nodes	79.68	78.76	79.22
	Child nodes	50.70	44.82	47.58
	Overall	65.82	61.58	63.63
	(A) Activating Event	83.96	79.10	81.46
	(B) Belief	77.17	80.00	78.56
	(C) Consequence	79.04	81.53	80.27
	(D) Disputation	40.35	36.51	38.33
Ensemble	Parent nodes	76.56	80.11	78.29
	Child nodes	41.65	57.08	48.16
	Overall	56.55	68.45	61.93
	(A) Activating Event	81.35	84.05	82.68
	(B) Belief	82.82	74.81	78.61
	(C) Consequence	84.23	77.27	80.60
	(D) Disputation	44.44	47.46	45.90
Tree (Proposed model)	Parent nodes	76.90	83.80	**80.23**
	Child nodes	65.20	41.00	**50.63**
	Overall	71.50	63.10	**66.82**
	(A) Activating Event	88.20	78.40	**82.97**
	(B) Belief	71.80	91.00	**80.30**
	(C) Consequence	81.90	82.00	**81.95**
	(D) Disputation	65.50	55.30	**59.94**

Continuing our analysis of different modeling strategies, we found that compared with the simpler flat strategy, the ensemble strategy—training a separate model for each parent node—did not yield an overall performance gain. Although it improved the F1-score of child nodes by 0.58%, it decreased the overall F1-score by 1.7% points. In contrast, the proposed tree-structured model achieved the best performance. When examining performance across different parent nodes, the proposed model consistently outperforms both the flat and ensemble strategies, with particularly notable improvements at level (D). The relatively lower performance on the (D) Disputation category is likely due to class imbalance, the abstract linguistic nature of disputation expressions, and annotation inconsistencies. Addressing these issues through targeted data augmentation or refined annotation guidelines represents an important avenue for future improvement. At the overall level, the proposed model surpasses the flat and ensemble strategies by 3.19 and 4.89% points, respectively, highlighting the strengths of our approach.

Table 4. This table reports the performance (average in micro) of our proposed model in the ablation experiments for the cognitive pathway extraction task.

Experiment setting					F1-score		
Training	Frozen	Loss-child	Loss-parent	Contrastive Learning	Parent	Child	Overall
From scratch	F	MLSM	MLSM	F	50.63	44.80	47.97
	T	MLSM	MLSM	F	13.14	13.42	13.28
	F	MLSM	MLSM	T	53.12	46.45	49.39
	F	BCE	MLSM	F	77.99	48.14	64.51
	F	MLSM	BCE	F	76.23	44.37	62.22
	F	BCE	BCE	F	79.59	46.23	64.85
	T	BCE	BCE	F	76.44	40.26	60.87
	F	BCE	BCE	T	79.89	50.12	66.18
Fine-tuning	F	MLSM	MLSM	F	50.63	44.80	47.97
	T	MLSM	MLSM	F	46.71	18.98	36.60
	F	BCE	BCE	F	78.96	49.37	65.38
	T	BCE	BCE	F	76.62	41.39	61.42
	F	BCE	BCE	T	**80.23**	**50.63**	**66.82**

We conducted ablation experiments to investigate the impact of training strategies, loss functions, freezing of backbone layers, and contrastive learning (Table 4). Using a pre-trained model fine-tuned under the flat strategy generally outperformed training from scratch, with less than 1% gain in F1-score. Configurations using BCE loss at both child and parent levels consistently achieved better performance, especially when combined with contrastive learning, reaching the highest overall F1-score of 66.82%. Freezing the backbone did not lead to performance improvements. These findings highlight the effectiveness and flexibility of our model design.

Table 5. Comparison of the proposed model with SOTA hierarchical text classification models on the WOS-46985 dataset [15].

Type	Models	Precision	Recall	F1
Pretrained	BERT [7]	85.20	76.95	80.87
HTC	HiAGM [27]	82.77	78.12	85.95
	HTCInfoMax [6]	80.90	77.27	84.65
	HiMatch [3]	83.26	77.94	86.04
HTC+Pretrained	HiAGM+BERT	81.81	78.86	85.83
	HTCInfoMax+BERT	79.95	79.59	85.18
	HiMatch+BERT	82.29	80.00	86.46
	The proposed model	**87.60**	**85.65**	**86.61**

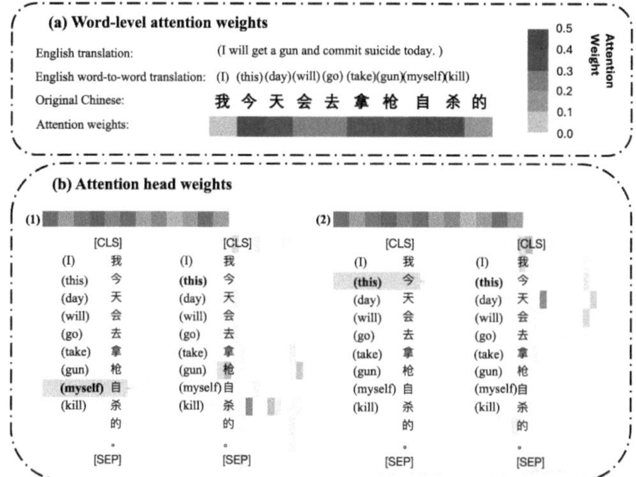

Fig. 2. The visualization of the attention weights in the encoder module is presented as follows: (a) illustrates the weight of each word in a sentence as extracted by the feature extraction module. (b) displays the attention head weights. Each color block represents an attention head, with lines indicating attention weights between words. Thicker lines signify stronger relationships. To account for language differences, the right side shows English words corresponding to each Chinese word.

In the comparative experiment detailed in Sect. 4.5, our proposed model achieves the highest F1-score (86.61%) on the WOS public dataset, as shown in Table 5, outperforming seven strong baselines including both flat and hierarchical models, thereby confirming the effectiveness and generalizability of our framework.

The encoder's behavior is elucidated through visualizations of word-level attention weights and attention head weights, presented in Fig. 2 (a) and (b), respectively. Figure 2(a) highlights the highest attention weights on "this" and

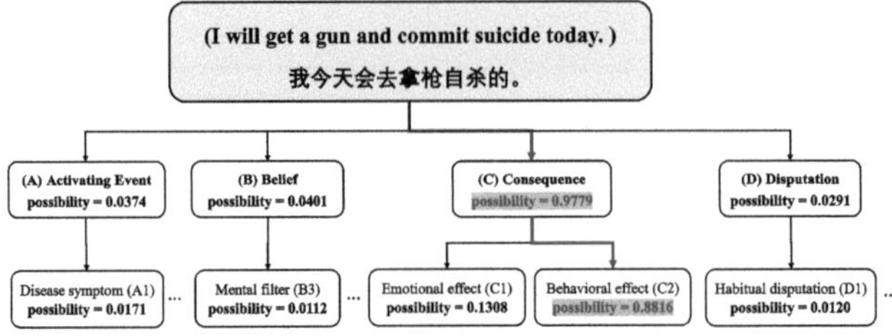

Fig. 3. An example of a decision path visualization of our model. The figure shows the decision path for sentences belonging to Behavioral effect (C2) in Consequence (C).

"day" (forming "today") and the second-highest on "kill" and "myself" (indicating "suicide"), reflecting the timing and method of suicidal ideation, which are the key indicators of serious mental health issues. This demonstrates the encoder's effectiveness in identifying context-relevant keywords. Figure 2(b) further clarifies these relationships: in (b)(1), "myself" strongly correlates with "kill" and "gun", and with "[CLS]" for sequence semantics, while in (b)(2), "this" and "day" combine to form "today". The decision path interpretation is visualized in Fig. 3, underscoring the model's inherent interpretability.

6 Conclusion

In this paper, we explore cognitive pathway extraction by collecting social media data, expert-annotating it, and releasing an open-source dataset. We model this task as a hierarchical classification problem and propose an interpretable tree-structured model. The proposed model achieved an F1-score of 65.38%, outperforming other comparison methods, including four decoder-based models and four encoder-based models. We are the first to provide an open-source dataset, aiming to support and advance research within the community. We plan to extend this tool for large-scale social media analysis and adapt it for clinical data applications.

Acknowledgments. This study was funded by the Beijing Natural Science Foundation (No. 7254302).

Disclosure of Interests. The authors have no competing interests to declare that are relevant to the content of this article.

References

1. Achiam, J., et al.: GPT-4 technical report. arXiv preprint arXiv:2303.08774 (2023)
2. Beck, A.T.: Cognitive therapy: nature and relation to behavior therapy. Behav. Ther. **1**(2), 184–200 (1970)

3. Chen, H., Ma, Q., Lin, Z., Yan, J.: Hierarchy-aware label semantics matching network for hierarchical text classification. In: Proceedings of the 59th Annual Meeting of the Association for Computational Linguistics and the 11th International Joint Conference on Natural Language Processing (Volume 1: Long Papers), pp. 4370–4379 (2021)
4. Cohen, J.: A coefficient of agreement for nominal scales. Educ. Psychol. Measur. **20**(1), 37–46 (1960)
5. Cronbach, L.J.: Coefficient alpha and the internal structure of tests. Psychometrika **16**(3), 297–334 (1951)
6. Deng, Z., Peng, H., He, D., Li, J., Yu, P.S.: Htcinfomax: a global model for hierarchical text classification via information maximization. arXiv preprint arXiv:2104.05220 (2021)
7. Devlin, J., Chang, M.W., Lee, K., Toutanova, K.: BERT: pre-training of deep bidirectional transformers for language understanding. arXiv preprint arXiv:1810.04805 (2018)
8. DiGiuseppe, R., Leaf, R., Linscott, J.: The therapeutic relationship in rational-emotive therapy: some preliminary data. J. Rational-Emot. Cognitive-Behav. Ther. **11**(4), 223–233 (1993)
9. Dino, F., Zandie, R., Abdollahi, H., Schoeder, S., Mahoor, M.H.: Delivering cognitive behavioral therapy using a conversational social robot. In: 2019 IEEE/RSJ International Conference on Intelligent Robots and Systems (IROS), pp. 2089–2095. IEEE (2019)
10. Ellis, A., Dryden, W.: The Practice of Rational Emotive Behavior Therapy. Springer, Cham (2007)
11. GLM, T., Zeng, A., et al.: ChatGLM: a family of large language models from GLM-130b to GLM-4 all tools. arXiv preprint arXiv:2406.12793 (2024)
12. He, P., Gao, J., Chen, W.: Debertav3: improving deberta using electra-style pre-training with gradient-disentangled embedding sharing. arXiv preprint arXiv:2111.09543 (2021)
13. Jiang, M., et al.: AI-enhanced cognitive behavioral therapy: Deep learning and large language models for extracting cognitive pathways from social media texts. arXiv preprint arXiv:2404.11449 (2024)
14. Jiang, M., et al.: A generic review of integrating artificial intelligence in cognitive behavioral therapy. arXiv preprint arXiv:2407.19422 (2024)
15. Kowsari, K., Brown, D.E., Heidarysafa, M., Meimandi, K.J., Gerber, M.S., Barnes, L.E.: Hdltex: hierarchical deep learning for text classification. In: 2017 16th IEEE International Conference on Machine Learning and Applications (ICMLA), pp. 364–371. IEEE (2017)
16. World Health Organization et al.: Depressive disorder (depression). 2023. Retrieved from Depressive disorder (depression)(who. int) (2023)
17. Primack, B.A., et al.: Social media use and perceived social isolation among young adults in the US. Am. J. Prev. Med. **53**(1), 1–8 (2017)
18. Qi, H., et al.: Evaluating the efficacy of supervised learning vs large language models for identifying cognitive distortions and suicidal risks in Chinese social media. arXiv preprint arXiv:2309.03564 (2023)
19. Rudin, C.: Stop explaining black box machine learning models for high stakes decisions and use interpretable models instead. Nat. Mach. Intell. **1**(5), 206–215 (2019)
20. Sarracino, D., Dimaggio, G., Ibrahim, R., Popolo, R., Sassaroli, S., Ruggiero, G.M.: When REBT goes difficult: applying ABC-def to personality disorders. J. Rational-Emotive Cogn.-Behav. Ther. **35**, 278–295 (2017)

21. Sun, Y., et al.: ERNIE 3.0: large-scale knowledge enhanced pre-training for language understanding and generation. arXiv preprint arXiv:2107.02137 (2021)
22. Vig, J.: A multiscale visualization of attention in the transformer model. In: Proceedings of the 57th Annual Meeting of the Association for Computational Linguistics: System Demonstrations, pp. 37–42. Association for Computational Linguistics, Florence, Italy (2019). https://doi.org/10.18653/v1/P19-3007. https://www.aclweb.org/anthology/P19-3007
23. Wang, S., et al.: Ernie 3.0 titan: exploring larger-scale knowledge enhanced pre-training for language understanding and generation. arXiv preprint arXiv:2112.12731 (2021)
24. Yang, Z., Dai, Z., Yang, Y., Carbonell, J., Salakhutdinov, R.R., Le, Q.V.: XLNet: generalized autoregressive pretraining for language understanding. In: Advances in Neural Information Processing Systems, vol. 32 (2019)
25. Zangari, A., Marcuzzo, M., Rizzo, M., Giudice, L., Albarelli, A., Gasparetto, A.: Hierarchical text classification and its foundations: a review of current research. Electronics **13**(7), 1199 (2024)
26. Zhai, W., et al.: Chinese mentalbert: domain-adaptive pre-training on social media for Chinese mental health text analysis. arXiv preprint arXiv:2402.09151 (2024)
27. Zhou, J., et al.: Hierarchy-aware global model for hierarchical text classification. In: Proceedings of the 58th Annual Meeting of the Association for Computational Linguistics, pp. 1106–1117 (2020)

Adaptive Online Index Selection with a Noisy Dueling Deep Q-Network

Md. Rakibul Hasan[1], Xiaoying Wu[2], and Dimitri Theodoratos[1](✉)

[1] New Jersey Institute of Technology, Newark, NJ, USA
{mh629,dth}@njit.edu

[2] School of Computer Science, Wuhan University, Wuhan, China
xiaoying.wu@whu.edu.cn

Abstract. Efficient query performance is critical for modern web information systems, where dynamic and unpredictable workloads demand adaptive indexing strategies. Traditional heuristic-based and static tuning approaches often fail to respond effectively to evolving query patterns, leading to suboptimal database performance. To address these challenges, we propose a Dueling NoisyNet framework that leverages deep Q-networks for adaptive online index selection. Our approach integrates a dueling architecture to separately estimate state values and action advantages, enhancing learning stability, while NoisyNet-based exploration enables adaptive, state-dependent indexing decisions. By dynamically adjusting indexing strategies in real time, our method significantly improves query execution efficiency without requiring explicit workload predictions. Extensive experiments on benchmark datasets demonstrate that our model achieves faster convergence, superior adaptability, and reduced query execution times compared to state-of-the-art indexing solutions.

Keywords: Online Index Selection · Deep Reinforcement Learning · Dueling NoisyNet-DQN · Adaptive Database Tuning · Workload-Aware Indexing

1 Introduction

The exponential growth and pervasive deployment of web-based applications have dramatically increased the volume, variety, and velocity of data handled by modern information systems. Web-scale applications such as e-commerce platforms, online social networks, and cloud-based services routinely handle dynamic workloads and large-scale data operations. Efficient data retrieval and query optimization have therefore become critically important for ensuring seamless user experiences and timely information delivery across these web platforms. Adaptive index selection, a key aspect of database performance tuning, directly impacts query execution efficiency, significantly influencing the responsiveness and scalability of web information systems.

Online index selection (OIS), which dynamically tunes indexing strategies based on changing workloads, is particularly relevant in web environments

I. Awan et al. (Eds.): WISE 2025, LNCS 16367, pp. 321–336, 2026.
https://doi.org/10.1007/978-981-95-7394-3_22

characterized by highly volatile and unpredictable query patterns. Traditional heuristic-based methods [1,4] for online indexing often fail to adapt quickly to rapidly shifting user behaviors and web traffic patterns, leading to suboptimal indexing decisions and degraded application performance. Recent research has proposed leveraging reinforcement learning (RL) techniques to address these limitations, demonstrating the potential of RL-based methods in dynamically adjusting database indexes to fluctuating web workloads [10]. However, standard RL methods often face significant challenges, such as inefficient exploration and unstable convergence, limiting their practical deployment for online index tuning tasks.

Motivated by these challenges, we propose a novel approach leveraging recent advances in reinforcement learning, specifically a Dueling Deep Q-Network architecture enhanced with NoisyNet layers (Dueling NoisyNet-DQN). By combining the explicit separation of state-value and action-advantage estimation in the Dueling architecture [16] with the adaptive exploration capability introduced by NoisyNet [6], our approach significantly enhances exploration efficiency and training stability. The major challenges addressed by this work include effectively balancing exploration and exploitation, stabilizing convergence, and adapting robustly to highly dynamic query workloads. Unlike previous methods relying heavily on heuristic or simple epsilon-greedy exploration, our Dueling NoisyNet-DQN model provides structured and learnable exploration through noise-injected neural network parameters, significantly enhancing indexing decisions' adaptability and efficiency. The key contributions of this paper can be summarized as follows:

- We propose a novel Dueling NoisyNet-DQN architecture explicitly designed for online index selection for changing query workloads. This architecture efficiently captures workload dynamics and adapts indexing decisions in real time without requiring explicit workload predictions or heuristic interventions.
- Our method effectively combines the state-value and action-advantage streams in a dueling architecture, enhancing the neural network's ability to learn robust value representations and improving overall decision-making in index selection tasks.
- We introduce adaptive exploration in online index selection by employing NoisyNet parameter sampling, which allows the reinforcement learning agent to efficiently explore the indexing configuration space, significantly outperforming traditional epsilon-greedy and heuristic-based exploration methods.
- We conduct extensive experiments on benchmark datasets to demonstrate our approach's effectiveness. Experimental results indicate that our Dueling NoisyNet-DQN method consistently achieves superior performance, faster convergence, and robust adaptability compared to state-of-the-art traditional online learning-based indexing solutions.

2 Related Work

Traditional index selection strategies have predominantly relied on heuristic and cost-based optimization methods to recommend indexing configurations based on historical query workloads [1,4]. Some methods rely on exhaustive search methods combined with cost estimation models provided by the query optimizer. For instance, studies like [2] introduced an automated solution that leverages workload analysis and optimizer feedback to select beneficial indexes. While effective, such methods generally assume a relatively static workload and struggle to adapt quickly to dynamic query patterns. To overcome the limitations of traditional methods, recent studies have turned to learning-based techniques that leverage historical query workload information to adapt indexing dynamically. For example, A self-driving database system concept was proposed in [12], employing machine learning techniques for index and configuration management; however, the initial approaches primarily relied on supervised methods with limited adaptability. Reinforcement learning has emerged as particularly promising due to its ability to adaptively optimize decisions based on direct interactions with the environment. Q-learning-based approaches for index tuning have been investigated in [9,15], showing dynamic adaptability to changing workloads. Similarly, reinforcement learning techniques have been applied for adaptive index recommendations [3,8], demonstrating effectiveness in handling evolving query patterns.

Recently, deep reinforcement learning (DRL), particularly Deep Q-Network (DQN), has gained significant attention for addressing complex decision-making problems due to its ability to handle large state-action spaces efficiently. Deep reinforcement learning (DRL) has been applied to database configuration tuning [10], showing advantages over some methods. Its use for online index selection has also been studied [14], with neural networks enabling adaptation to complex query patterns. Despite advancements, standard DQN-based methods still face challenges related to exploration inefficiencies and unstable convergence when applied to database tuning scenarios. To address exploration challenges in RL, NoisyNet [6] was proposed, demonstrating effective exploration in DRL by introducing learnable parameterized noise directly into the neural network parameters. While NoisyNet has been successfully applied to various RL tasks [7], its application specifically to OIS problems remains underexplored. Our work addresses these critical research gaps by proposing a Dueling NoisyNet-DQN framework tailored explicitly for OIS, combining the robust state-action value separation of Dueling Networks [16] and the adaptive exploration capabilities of NoisyNet [6]. This approach not only enhances exploration efficiency but also stabilizes convergence, significantly improving over traditional heuristic-driven and standard DRL-based methodologies.

3 Preliminaries

3.1 Markov Decision Process Formulation of Online Index Selection

The online index selection problem in database management systems can be effectively modeled as a Markov Decision Process (MDP), defined by a tuple $(\mathcal{S}, \mathcal{A}, \mathcal{P}, \mathcal{R}, \gamma)$, where $\mathcal{S}$ denotes the state space, $\mathcal{A}$ is the set of possible actions, $\mathcal{P}$ represents the transition probabilities, $\mathcal{R}$ defines the reward function, and $\gamma \in [0, 1]$ is the discount factor.

State Space $\mathcal{S}$: In the context of online index selection, the state $s_t \in \mathcal{S}$ at timestep t encapsulates the current indexing configuration of the database and recent workload characteristics. Formally, the state at timestep t can be represented as:

$$s_t = (\mathbf{I}_t, \mathbf{W}_t) \tag{1}$$

where:

- $\mathbf{I}_t \in \{0, 1\}^{|\mathcal{C}|}$ is a binary vector indicating the presence (1) or absence (0) of indexes on each column $c \in \mathcal{C}$, where $\mathcal{C}$ is the set of all candidate columns.
- $\mathbf{W}_t \in \mathbb{R}^{|\mathcal{C}|}$ represents the workload vector summarizing recent query column usage frequencies, reflecting how queries interact with individual database columns.

Action Space $\mathcal{A}$: The action set $\mathcal{A}$ defines the operations of creating or dropping indexes on specific columns, as well as the option to perform no operation. Formally, the action at timestep t, denoted by a_t, is represented as:

$$a_t \in \text{Create}_c, \text{Drop}_c, \text{NoOp}_{c \in \mathcal{C}} \tag{2}$$

where Create_c and Drop_c denote creating and dropping an index on column c, respectively, and NoOp indicates no changes in the indexing configuration.

State Transition Dynamics $\mathcal{P}$: Given a current state s_t and action a_t, the state transitions deterministically to a new state s_{t+1}. Specifically, the indexing configuration updates according to the selected action:

$$\mathbf{I}_{t+1}(c) = \begin{cases} 1 & \text{if } a_t = \text{Create}_c \\ 0 & \text{if } a_t = \text{Drop}_c \\ \mathbf{I}_t(c) & \text{otherwise} \end{cases} \tag{3}$$

The workload vector $\mathbf{W}_{t+1}$ updates based on recent query interactions and is typically computed using a sliding window of queries executed after taking action a_t.

Reward Function $\mathcal{R}$: The reward function $r_t = \mathcal{R}(s_t, a_t)$ at timestep t measures the immediate impact of taking action a_t in state s_t, typically formulated based on query execution costs. Formally, the reward is defined as the improvement in query execution cost due to the index operation:

$$r_t = \frac{1}{|\mathcal{Q}|} \sum_{q \in \mathcal{Q}} (\text{Cost}(q|s_t) - \text{Cost}(q|s_{t+1})) \tag{4}$$

where $\mathcal{Q}$ represents the set of queries in the recent workload window, and $\text{Cost}(q|s)$ denotes the execution cost of query q given indexing configuration s.

The objective of this MDP-based formulation for online index selection is to learn an optimal policy π^* that maximizes the expected cumulative discounted reward:

$$\pi^* = \arg\max_{\pi} \mathbb{E}_{\pi} \left[\sum_{t=0}^{\infty} \gamma^t r_t \right] \tag{5}$$

where $\gamma \in [0, 1]$ is the discount factor determining the importance of future rewards. By maximizing this expectation, the RL agent learns to select indexing operations that minimize long-term database query execution costs, effectively optimizing database performance.

3.2 Deep Q-Network (DQN)

Deep Q-Network (DQN) is a reinforcement learning algorithm designed to handle high-dimensional state spaces by utilizing deep neural networks to approximate the Q-value function. Q-values represent the expected cumulative discounted reward when following a policy π after performing an action a in state s. Formally, given a policy π, the Q-value function $Q^{\pi}(s, a)$ is defined as:

$$Q^{\pi}(s, a) = \mathbb{E}_{\pi} \left[\sum_{t=0}^{\infty} \gamma^t r_t \mid s_0 = s, a_0 = a \right] \tag{6}$$

where $\gamma \in [0, 1]$ is a discount factor determining the importance of future rewards.

The optimal Q-value function $Q^*(s, a)$ satisfies the Bellman optimality equation:

$$Q^*(s, a) = \mathbb{E} \left[r + \gamma \max_{a'} Q^*(s', a') \mid s, a \right] \tag{7}$$

where s' is the next state after taking action a in state s.

In DQN, a neural network parameterized by θ approximates the Q-function as $Q(s, a; \theta)$. The network is trained by minimizing the mean-squared error (MSE) between predicted Q-values and target values y_t, which are computed as:

$$y_t = r_t + \gamma \max_{a'} Q(s_{t+1}, a'; \theta^-) \tag{8}$$

Here, θ^- denotes the parameters of a separate target network periodically updated from the primary network parameters θ. Thus, the loss function for the DQN update at timestep t is given by:

$$L(\theta) = \mathbb{E}_{(s_t, a_t, r_t, s_{t+1}) \sim \mathcal{D}} \left[(y_t - Q(s_t, a_t; \theta))^2 \right] \tag{9}$$

where $\mathcal{D}$ represents a replay buffer storing past experiences (s_t, a_t, r_t, s_{t+1}). This replay buffer breaks correlation among sequential samples, improving training stability.

3.3 NoisyNet for Exploration in Online Index Selection

Efficient exploration is particularly challenging in online index selection due to the large and dynamic indexing action space and delayed rewards associated with indexing decisions. Traditional methods, such as epsilon-greedy strategies, rely on uniform randomness, which fails to capture the complexities and state-specific nuances inherent in dynamic workloads. We adopt NoisyNet to tackle this problem by introducing learnable parameterized noise directly into the neural network weights, enabling adaptive, state-dependent exploration without per-step hyperparameter tuning. This approach dynamically guides exploration towards promising indexing configurations based on workload characteristics, significantly enhancing the model's ability to efficiently identify effective indexing strategies in complex and changing database environments. In NoisyNet, each linear layer (termed *NoisyLinear*) injects stochastic perturbations into its weights and biases. Specifically, each parameter within a NoisyLinear layer consists of a deterministic component and a stochastic component. Given input x, the output y of a NoisyLinear layer is computed as:

$$y = (\mu^w + \sigma^w \odot \varepsilon^w)x + (\mu^b + \sigma^b \odot \varepsilon^b) \tag{10}$$

where μ^w, σ^w represent learnable parameters for weights, and μ^b, σ^b represent learnable parameters for biases. The terms ε^w and ε^b represent noise variables sampled independently from factorized Gaussian distributions at each forward pass, significantly reducing computational complexity compared to fully correlated noise models. Detailed mathematical formulations and factorized noise derivations are provided in [6].

4 Dueling NoisyNet-DQN Algorithm for OIS

4.1 System Overview

Our Dueling NoisyNet–DQN framework for online index selection comprises several integrated components that collectively facilitate efficient index tuning in dynamic database environments. Figure 1 provides an overview of the complete system pipeline.

The pipeline begins with a sliding *workload window* capturing recent query activity. These workload statistics are fed into a *state encoder*, which translates raw workload information and current index configurations into a structured state representation suitable for the reinforcement learning agent. The *Dueling NoisyNet–DQN agent* uses this encoded state to determine the optimal indexing action–creating, dropping, or maintaining existing indexes. Index actions proposed by the agent are immediately evaluated by a What-if [5] *cost Model*, which estimates the associated query execution costs. These cost estimations are used to compute rewards, guiding the reinforcement learning agent to refine its indexing policy through iterative training. Selected indexing actions are then executed in the database environment, directly influencing subsequent workload interactions and closing the feedback loop by updating the workload window.

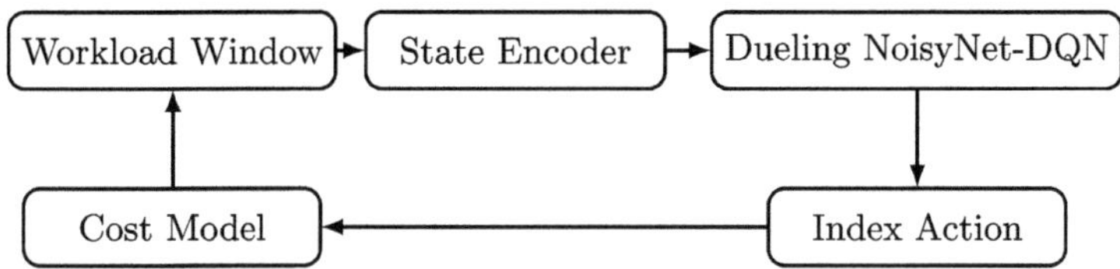

Fig. 1. System overview pipeline for Dueling NoisyNet–DQN-based online index selection.

4.2 Dueling Network Architecture

To effectively handle the complexity inherent in the online index selection problem, we employ a Dueling Network architecture enhanced with NoisyNet layers, combining the advantages of robust state-value estimation and efficient exploration. Our Dueling Network architecture explicitly separates the representation of state-value and action-advantage within the neural network, enabling more nuanced estimations of Q-values. Given a state representation s, the Dueling architecture decomposes the Q-value into two separate streams: a state-value stream $V(s;\theta,\beta)$ and an action-advantage stream $A(s,a;\theta,\alpha)$, parameterized by θ, α, and β.

The overall Q-value for each state-action pair is then computed as:

$$Q(s,a;\theta,\alpha,\beta) = V(s;\theta,\beta) + \left(A(s,a;\theta,\alpha) - \frac{1}{|\mathcal{A}|}\sum_{a'} A(s,a';\theta,\alpha) \right) \tag{11}$$

where $\mathcal{A}$ is the set of possible actions. This formulation improves learning stability by decoupling the estimation of the state's inherent value from the comparative advantage of specific actions. In our proposed implementation, the shared feature extraction part of the Dueling network employs a NoisyLinear layer, which integrates parameterized noise to promote effective exploration:

$$h = \text{ReLU}(\text{LayerNorm}(\text{NoisyLinear}(s, 256))) \tag{12}$$

where h is the hidden state representation generated from input state s.

Value Stream: The state-value function $V(s;\theta,\beta)$ predicts the scalar expected cumulative reward of state s independent of actions. The value stream is defined by:

$$V(s;\theta,\beta) = \text{NoisyLinear}(\text{ReLU}(\text{LayerNorm}(\text{NoisyLinear}(h, 128))), 1) \tag{13}$$

Advantage Stream: The advantage function $A(s, a; \theta, \alpha)$ estimates the relative advantage of each action in state s. It is formulated as:

$$A(s, a; \theta, \alpha) = \text{NoisyLinear}(\text{ReLU}(\text{LayerNorm}(\text{NoisyLinear}(h, 128))), |\mathcal{A}|) \quad (14)$$

By utilizing Layer Normalization (LayerNorm) and rectified linear units (ReLU), the network stabilizes training and facilitates convergence. Each NoisyLinear layer comprises learnable parameters μ^w, σ^w for weights and μ^b, σ^b for biases, with noise sampled at each forward pass, as previously detailed in Eq. (10). The final output of the Dueling NoisyNet-DQN network, given input state s, aggregates the state-value and advantage streams to produce robust Q-value estimates from Eq. (11), guiding the selection of indexing actions that maximize long-term database performance.

4.3 Noise-Driven Index Tuning via Weight-Space Perturbation

NoisyNet's strategy of injecting learnable, parameterized noise into network weights directly addresses the unique exploration challenges inherent in online index selection.

Delayed Reward: Index creation and dropping actions pay off only after several future queries, so one–shot methods like ε-greedy waste effort on uncoordinated, per-step probes. NoisyNet injects learnable, state-dependent weight noise, tying successive decisions together. This yields coherent multi-step exploration that tracks workload drift and captures the delayed reward of creating or dropping an index more efficiently.

State-Aware Exploration: The noise parameters (σ) in NoisyNet are learned and dynamically adapt based on observed states. Initially, high uncertainty leads to aggressive exploration of the indexing action space. Over time, as workload familiarity increases and the model converges, σ decreases, naturally reducing unnecessary exploration. This adaptive behavior allows the agent to promptly react when novel or unexpected workload patterns emerge, providing efficient, targeted exploration without manual tuning.

Action-Space Coupling: Database indexing involves interdependent actions, such as creating composite indexes like "idx(c1, c2)" versus "idx(c2, c1)", which share closely related characteristics. NoisyNet's factorized noise structure induces correlated noise among related actions, implicitly linking their exploration. This effectively reduces redundant exploration of similar indexing decisions and accelerates convergence toward optimal index configurations.

Together, NoisyNet's temporally coherent, state-adaptive, and correlated exploration lets the agent traverse the dynamic index-selection space far more efficiently. To enhance clarity, we briefly summarize the parameter update steps for the NoisyLinear layer in the context of training:

- At each forward pass during training, new noise samples $\varepsilon^w, \varepsilon^b$ are generated, and the parameters are perturbed accordingly, as discussed in Sect. 3.3.

- The perturbed parameters are then used to compute the network outputs, leading to varied Q-value estimates and thus promoting exploration.
- During backpropagation, gradients are calculated with respect to $\mu^w, \sigma^w, \mu^b, \sigma^b$ enabling the noise distribution parameters to be learned and optimized in an end-to-end fashion.

4.4 Replay Buffer Mechanism

The replay buffer, a crucial component in our model training process, significantly enhances learning stability and sample efficiency. Our model leverages this mechanism effectively to manage experience reuse and break correlations among sequential data, facilitating a more robust gradient estimation and stable learning. In our proposed methodology, the replay buffer $\mathcal{D}$ is implemented as a finite-sized memory storing historical interactions between the agent and environment in the form of transitions. A transition is formally represented as a tuple $(s_t, a_t, r_t, s_{t+1}, d_t)$ where s_t is the state at timestep t, a_t is the action taken, r_t is the reward received, s_{t+1} is the subsequent state, and d_t indicates whether s_{t+1} is terminal. When the replay buffer reaches its maximum capacity N, the oldest stored transitions are discarded to accommodate new transitions, maintaining a diverse set of experiences for training. During the training phase, transitions are sampled randomly and uniformly from the replay buffer $\mathcal{D}$ in mini-batches to approximate the expectation in the gradient computation effectively:

$$\mathcal{B} = (s_j, a_j, r_j, s_{j+1}, d_j) \sim \text{Uniform}(\mathcal{D})_{j=1}^{|\mathcal{B}|} \tag{15}$$

Each mini-batch $\mathcal{B}$ consists of independently and identically distributed samples drawn uniformly from the buffer, thereby reducing the temporal correlations that can adversely affect gradient-based learning methods. Using these sampled transitions, the agent updates the Dueling NoisyNet-DQN network parameters by minimizing the expected loss function over the sampled mini-batch transitions:

$$L(\theta) = \frac{1}{|\mathcal{B}|} \sum_{j \in \mathcal{B}} \text{HuberLoss}\left(y_j - Q(s_j, a_j; \theta)\right) \tag{16}$$

where y_j is the target value calculated using the target network parameters θ^- as outlined in Eq. (8). This replay buffer mechanism not only stabilizes training but also enhances the efficiency and effectiveness of the Dueling NoisyNet-DQN by consistently focusing training updates on informative samples, thereby leading to robust policy optimization for the complex online index selection problem.

4.5 Training Algorithm

The training procedure involves iterative policy improvement based on experience replay, target network synchronization, and gradient-based optimization of the network parameters. The high-level process involves repeatedly interacting with the environment, storing transitions in a replay buffer, and periodically updating the policy network by sampling batches of transitions from this buffer. The training algorithm operates iteratively over multiple episodes, each consisting of a sequence of state-action transitions. At each timestep within an episode, the policy network uses noisy parameters to select an action, thus ensuring adaptive exploration. After executing the chosen action, the environment returns a reward and a new state. This transition is stored in a replay buffer to provide stable and uncorrelated samples for training. Periodically, a random minibatch of transitions is sampled from the replay buffer to update the network parameters by minimizing the difference between predicted Q-values and their targets computed using the target network. This target network is updated less frequently to stabilize training, as commonly practiced in deep reinforcement learning literature [11]. Below are the major components of the training procedure from Algorithm 1:

- **Replay Buffer ($\mathcal{D}$):** Stores previously experienced transitions to break correlations between consecutive samples, stabilizing network training.
- **Target Network ($Q'(s, a; \theta^{-})$):** Periodically synchronized with the primary network to compute stable targets, thus improving convergence stability.
- **Noisy Parameter Resetting:** At each action selection step, noise parameters in the NoisyNet layers are resampled, ensuring continuous adaptive exploration.
- **Gradient-based Optimization:** Utilizes Huber loss to limit the effect of extreme outlier targets, improving training stability under noisy reward conditions.

Through these carefully orchestrated mechanisms, our proposed Dueling NoisyNet-DQN algorithm efficiently explores the complex action space of online index selection, learns robust value estimations, and effectively converges to optimal indexing strategies for dynamic workloads.

5 Experimental Evaluation

5.1 Workload Setup

For all experiments, we use decision-support benchmarks from TPC-H at scale factor 1 and the Join Order Benchmark (JOB). JOB is based on real-world Internet Movie Database data featuring complex correlations and diverse distributions. We first train our agent on a static TPC-H workload and verify convergence, which we also confirm on the JOB dataset. Using the trained model on TPC-H, we evaluate performance under three workload variations–Shifting, Noisy, and Random–to assess the robustness of our indexing policy. Query costs are estimated using the 'What-if' optimizer [5]. Below, we detail each workload and its parameters.

- **Shifting Workload:** Query templates were divided into four groups, each executed for 20 rounds before shifting to a new group, resulting in 80 rounds overall.

Algorithm 1. Dueling NoisyNet-DQN

Initialize replay memory D to capacity N
Initialize primary network parameters θ, target network parameters $\theta^- \leftarrow \theta$
for episode $= 1, M$ **do**
  Reset environment state s_0
  for step $t = 1, T$ **do**
    Reset noise parameters of the NoisyNet layers
    Select action $a_t = \arg\max_a Q(s_t, a; \theta)$
    Execute action a_t, observe reward r_t, next state s_{t+1}
    Store transition (s_t, a_t, r_t, s_{t+1}) in D
    Sample random mini-batch (s_j, a_j, r_j, s_{j+1}) from D
    Set target: $y_j = r_j + \gamma Q'(s_{j+1}, \arg\max_{a'} Q(s_{j+1}, a'; \theta); \theta^-)$
    Compute loss: $L(\theta) = \frac{1}{N} \sum_j \text{HuberLoss}(Q(s_j, a_j; \theta) - y_j)$
    Perform gradient descent on $L(\theta)$, update θ
    Every C steps update target network: $\theta^- \leftarrow \theta$
    if episode ends or step limit reached **then**
      Break
    end if
  end for
end for

- **Noisy Workload:** In addition to the shifting workload, noise queries (comprising 10% of the workload) were injected during each shift, yielding 96 rounds. This setup tests the algorithm's resilience to transient workload fluctuations.
- **Random Workload:** Query instances were randomly generated from the available templates and grouped into 25 rounds, modeling highly dynamic query behavior.

5.2 Evaluation Metrics

We compare algorithm performance using the following metrics:

- **Index Recommendation Time:** Time taken to generate index configuration suggestions.
- **Index Transition Time:** Time spent creating and dropping indexes to apply configuration changes.
- **Query Execution Time:** Time required to execute queries under the current configuration.

Queries exceeding a 30-second timeout were terminated and recorded as 30 s to ensure consistent evaluation.

5.3 Training Results Analysis

We evaluate our Dueling NoisyNet–DQN agent on the TPC-H and JOB workload using a discount factor $\gamma = 0.99$ and an Adam optimizer learning rate of 1×10^{-4}.

Training runs for 5000 steps, each representing an index action. Transitions are stored in a replay buffer of 10,000 capacity, with mini-batches of 64 sampled uniformly for stable updates. The target network synchronizes every 128 steps. Exploration is driven by NoisyLinear layers injecting noise with initial scale $\sigma_{\text{init}} = 0.05$ that decays over time. The network has a shared 256-unit layer followed by separate 128-unit value and advantage streams. Gradient clipping with a maximum norm of 10 is applied during optimization to prevent exploding gradients. We track accumulated reward, batch loss, and elapsed execution time per episode, shown over 38 episodes in Figs. 2 and 3.

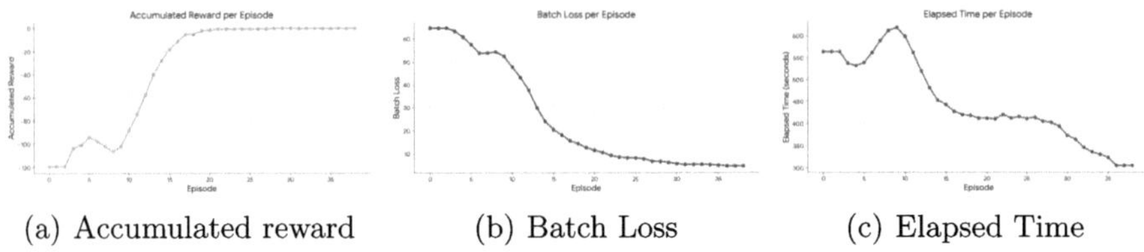

(a) Accumulated reward (b) Batch Loss (c) Elapsed Time

Fig. 2. Training performance metrics for the Dueling NoisyNet-DQN algorithm for TPC-H Benchmark. (a) Accumulated reward, (b) Batch loss, (c) Elapsed time per episode.

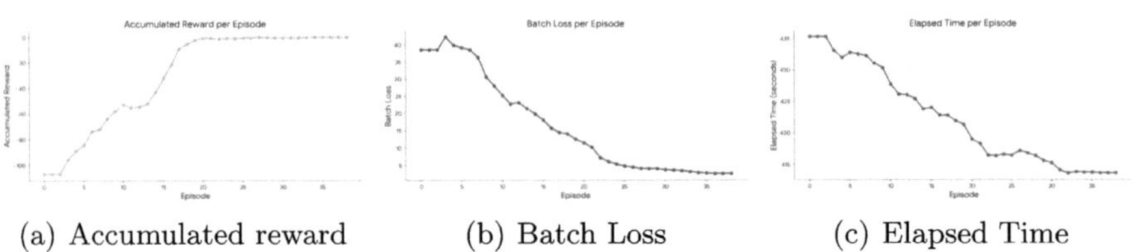

(a) Accumulated reward (b) Batch Loss (c) Elapsed Time

Fig. 3. Training performance metrics for the Dueling NoisyNet-DQN algorithm for Join Order Benchmark. (a) Accumulated reward, (b) Batch loss, (c) Elapsed time per episode.

Accumulated Reward per Episode: Initially, accumulated reward is strongly negative (around −120 in Episodes 0–2) due to poor index decisions by the untrained agent, as shown in Fig. 2A. It steadily improves to approximately −90 by Episode 5 and nears −5 by Episode 17. Temporary dips around Episodes 4, 7, and 8 occur from exploratory drops of still-useful indexes and sensitivity in the sliding-window reward. By Episode 18, the policy stabilizes, maintaining accumulated reward at zero. A similar trend is observed for the JOB workload in Fig. 3A.

Batch Loss per Episode: Batch loss, calculated using the Huber loss between predicted Q-values and TD targets (Eq. (16)), starts high near 70 in early episodes due to random initial estimates. As the replay buffer fills with diverse experiences, the loss rapidly decreases to about 20 by Episode 15 and continues falling into single digits, stabilizing around 3–5 by Episode 30, as shown in Fig. 2B for TPC-H. Spikes around Episodes 8 occur when the agent drops still-useful indexes causing large TD errors, when new informative transitions replace old ones in the replay buffer, or due to NoisyNet's exploration noise temporarily perturbing predictions. These oscillations diminish after Episode 20 as noise decays and the network converges. Figure 3B demonstrates a similar progression in batch loss for the JOB workload.

Elapsed Time per Episode: Elapsed time begins above 550 s as queries run without indexes. It decreases to 450 s by Episode 15 and stabilizes near 375 s by Episode 30 (Fig. 2C). Spikes around Episodes 5–9 result from exploratory index changes and target-network updates but vanish as noise decays and value estimates stabilize. JOB workload exhibits comparable elapsed time trends (Fig. 3C).

The combined trends in elapsed time, batch loss, and accumulated reward demonstrate rapid and stable convergence of our Dueling NoisyNet–DQN agent. Within 21 episodes, the Huber loss drops from around 70 to single digits, driven by the dueling architecture's reduced gradient variance. Accumulated reward improves from strongly negative to zero by Episode 20, indicating the agent avoids harmful index actions. Elapsed time declines from over 600 s to about 400 s by Episode 20, confirming effective index learning. Occasional spikes reflect expected exploration noise, target-network updates, and replay buffer changes, but diminish by Episode 20. Overall, our method converges quickly and robustly on both TPC-H and JOB benchmark.

5.4 Baseline Algorithms for Comparison

We evaluated our Dueling NoisyNet-DQN against the following methods:

- **Anytime** [4] Anytime is a state-of-the-art offline tuning algorithm. It is used in Database Tuning Advisor of Microsoft SQL Server.
- **SmartIX** [9]: A DRL-based index tuning algorithm. We trained their model using their publicly released implementation. Although SmartIX originally reports QphH@Size and Throughput@Size, we measured their performance in our metrics for comparability.
- **LiteSelect** [17]: Abbreviated as Lite, a recent learning-based online index selection method that employs exponential smoothing for real-time tuning.
- **C2UCB** [13]: An online tuning technique based on MAB-UCB principles that uses advanced exploration strategies in dynamic environments. We utilizes the official implementation publicly released by the original authors.

We also include a **NoIndex** baseline, which runs the workload using only the primary and foreign key indexes automatically created, to quantify the maximum possible benefit from index tuning. Due to space limitations, empirical comparisons with earlier non-learning-based algorithms are deferred to the extended version of the paper.

5.5 Performance Comparison with Baselines

To evaluate the effectiveness of our trained Dueling NoisyNet–DQN model, we conduct comparative experiments against baselines using different TPC-H workloads. Table 1 presents results for C2UCB, LiteSelect, Anytime, NoIndex, and SmartIX across Shifting, Noisy, and Random workloads. We evaluate three key metrics: query execution time, index recommendation time, and index transition time. Figure 4 visualizes the comparative performance of our method versus these baselines.

Table 1. Performance metrics across different workloads (times in seconds).

Method	Shifting			Noisy			Random		
	Exec. Time	Rec. Time	Trans. Time	Exec. Time	Rec. Time	Trans. Time	Exec. Time	Rec. Time	Trans. Time
C2UCB	1982	13.09	155.00	2235	12.00	284.86	2746	15.79	231.33
Lite	1831	8.91	16.09	2226	10.53	19.25	2452	9.21	14.54
Anytime	1885	7.57	47.49	2393	11.47	55.62	2714	32.10	22.40
NoIndex	2305	-	-	2679	-	-	3082	-	-
SmartIX	1532	1.58	18.92	2440	2.79	26.13	2200	2.31	11.78
Dueling NoisyNet–DQN	**1361**	**0.33**	**15.89**	**1651**	**0.39**	**16.33**	**1746**	**0.41**	**10.74**

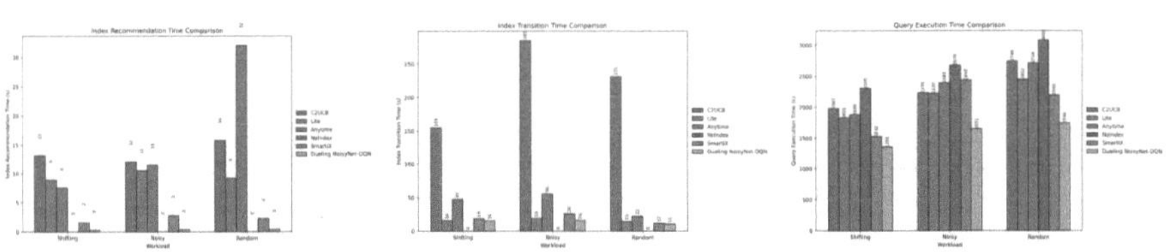

(a) Index Recommendation Time (b) Index Transition Time (c) Query Execution Time

Fig. 4. Performance metrics comparison for Dueling NoisyNet-DQN, Lite, C2UCB, SmartIX, Anytime, and NoIndex on the TPC-H shifting, noisy, and random workloads. (a) Index Recommendation Time, (b) Index Transition Time, (c) Query Execution Time.

As shown in Fig. 4A, our Dueling NoisyNet–DQN significantly outperforms all baselines in terms of index recommendation time across all workload types. Our method consistently requires less than 0.5 s for recommendation, whereas traditional methods such as C2UCB and Anytime exhibit times exceeding 7 s, reaching as high as 32 s on the Random workload. The superior efficiency of our approach stems from the NoisyNet's learnable, state-dependent exploration noise, which focuses action selection on promising indexing decisions without exhaustive search or heuristic guesswork. Baseline methods relying on heuristics or combinatorial bandits incur heavier computational overhead, especially under dynamic workloads. Figure 4B demonstrates that our method achieves the lowest index transition times, reflecting minimal overhead in physically creating or dropping indexes. This efficiency is a direct result of the agent's ability to selectively modify indexes with fewer unnecessary changes, thereby reducing the system disruption and maintenance costs common in baseline methods like C2UCB and Anytime, which often incur aggressive or redundant index updates. The combination of dueling network decomposition and NoisyNet exploration enables more precise policy refinement which minimized costly index churn. Figure 4C reports query execution times, where our Dueling NoisyNet–DQN also shows marked improvement over baselines. By learning a cost-aware, adaptive policy, our agent reduces query runtimes by up to 30% compared to the next best method (SmartIX). Methods without indexing (NoIndex) unsurprisingly have the worst execution times. Heuristic approaches like Lite and Anytime, while improving execution time, fail to match the adaptability and precision of our model, particularly in the more complex Noisy and Random workloads. The efficient and focused exploration enabled by NoisyNet allows our method to identify highly beneficial indexes faster, which translates to substantial workload runtime savings.

Overall, the metrics confirm that our Dueling NoisyNet–DQN method combines fast, accurate index recommendation with minimal index maintenance overhead, producing significantly faster query execution across diverse workload patterns. The baselines lag due to either heavy heuristic computations, excessive index transitions, and simplistic exploration policies. Our approach's learnable noise injection and dueling value-advantage separation create a more efficient and robust indexing strategy, well-suited to dynamic, real-world database workloads.

6 Conclusion

We have presented a novel approach for online index selection leveraging a Dueling Deep Q-Network architecture combined with NoisyNet exploration. Our method addresses key challenges in adaptive database tuning, including efficient exploration in large action spaces and stable convergence of value estimates. Through extensive experiments, we demonstrated that our approach achieves rapid convergence, consistently reduces query execution times, and effectively adapts to dynamic workloads. The dueling architecture's separation of state-value and advantage functions, together with the learnable noise injection of NoisyNet, provides significant improvements over traditional heuristic and standard reinforcement learning methods. Future work aim to support multidimensional and learned indexes and integrate more tightly with the query optimizer, moving toward a fully self-driving web information system.

References

1. Agrawal, S., Bruno, N., Chaudhuri, S., Narasayya, V.R.: Autoadmin: Self-tuning database systems technology. IEEE Data Eng. Bull. **29**(3), 7–15 (2006)
2. Agrawal, S., Chaudhuri, S., Narasayya, V.R.: Automated selection of materialized views and indexes in SQL databases. In: VLDB, pp. 496–505 (2000)
3. Basu, D., et al.: Regularized cost-model oblivious database tuning with reinforcement learning. Trans. Large Scale Data Knowl. Centered Syst. **28**, 96–132 (2016)
4. Chaudhuri, S., Narasayya, V.: Anytime algorithm of database tuning advisor for Microsoft SQL server (2020)
5. Chaudhuri, S., Narasayya, V.R.: Autoadmin "what-if" index analysis utility. In: SIGMOD. ACM Press (1998)
6. Fortunato, M., Azar, M.G., Blundell, C., Legg, S., et al.: Noisy networks for exploration. arXiv, abs/1706.10295 (2017)
7. Hessel, M., Modayil, J., Azar, M., Silver, D.: Rainbow: combining improvements in deep reinforcement learning. In: Proceedings of the AAAI Conference on Artificial Intelligence, vol. 32, no. 1 (2018)
8. Kossmann, J., Kastius, A., Schlosser, R.: Swirl: selection of workload-aware indexes using reinforcement learning. In: International Conference on Extending Database Technology (2022)
9. Licks, G.P., Couto, J.M.C., de Fátima Miehe, P., Meneguzzi, F.: Smartix: a database indexing agent based on reinforcement learning. Appl. Intell. **50**(8) (2020)
10. Marcus, R., Papaemmanouil, O.: Deep reinforcement learning for join order enumeration. In: Proceedings of Artificial Intelligence Techniques for Data Management, aiDM 2018 (2018)
11. Mnih, V., Kavukcuoglu, K., Silver, D., Wierstra, D., Legg, S., Hassabis, D.: Human-level control through deep reinforcement learning. Nature **518**, 529–533 (2015)
12. Pavlo, A., Angulo, G., Zhang, T.: Self-driving database management systems. In: CIDR (2017)
13. Perera, R.M., Oetomo, B., Rubinstein, B.I.P., Borovica-Gajic, R.: Hmab: self-driving hierarchy of bandits for integrated physical database design tuning. Proc. VLDB Endow. **16**(2), 216–229 (2022)
14. Sadri, Z., Gruenwald, L., Leal, E.: Online index selection using deep reinforcement learning for a cluster database. In: ICDEW 2020, pp. 158–161 (2020)
15. Sharma, A., Schuhknecht, F.M., Dittrich, J.: The case for automatic database administration using deep reinforcement learning. CoRR abs/1801.05643 (2018)
16. Wang, Z., Schaul, T., Hessel, M., Van Hasselt, H., Lanctot, M., De Freitas, N.: Dueling network architectures for deep reinforcement learning. In: ICML 2016 (2016)
17. Wu, X., Wang, S., Liu, X., Theodoratos, D., Hasan, M.R.: Liteselect: a lightweight adaptive learning algorithm for online index selection. In: DaWaK 2024 (2024)

An Advanced-PER Based Deep Reinforcement Learning Method for Adversarial Maritime Mission Planning

Mingqiang Li[1], Cong Wang[1], Yuewei Wang[1], Xiaopan Zhang[2], Xiaohui Huang[1(✉)], Binhao Li[2], Jianxin Li[3], and Yunliang Chen[1]

[1] School of Computer Science, China University of Geosciences, Wuhan, China
xhhuang@cug.edu.cn

[2] School of Computer Science and Artificial Intelligence, Wuhan University of Technology, Wuhan, China

[3] School of Business and Law, Edith Cowan University, Perth, Australia

Abstract. Maritime confrontation mission planning is a difficult task planning problem. The difficulty of planning stems from the dynamic characteristics and high complexity of the maritime environment. These factors make it extremely difficult to describe the state and refine the decision level. Traditional task planning methods based on rules or optimization algorithms suffer from limitations in dealing with these problems. They are not adaptable to dynamic environments, and the decision level is too rough. This paper proposes an Advanced-PER based Deep Reinforcement Learning Method based on double deep Q-Network (DDQN) for complex maritime confrontation task planning problems, and a new Prioritized Experience Replay method is introduced to improve the deep reinforcement learning method. The model significantly improves the learning efficiency and decision-making performance of the model by partitioning the storage experience and dynamically balancing the adoption ratio of different action experiences. Experimental results indicate the effectiveness of the proposed method.

Keywords: Adversarial maritime mission planning · Deep reinforcement learning · Experience replay

1 Introduction

Mission planning is a highly systematic process whose core lies in efficiently completing mission objectives by reasonably allocating and using existing resources. Mission planning in the field of confrontation focuses on confrontation scenarios, and studies the coordination and planning of resources, unit elements, etc., in a confrontation environment [1,2], and maritime confrontation mission planning is a common scenario in confrontation mission planning. Computer war game simulation is a standard exercise method that can simulate the real confrontation process to a certain extent and has an important reference significance [3,4]. The

I. Awan et al. (Eds.): WISE 2025, LNCS 16367, pp. 337–347, 2026.
https://doi.org/10.1007/978-981-95-7394-3_23

essence of maritime confrontation mission planning in war game simulation is to maximize the confrontation effectiveness of units such as ships and aircraft in a confrontation environment with incomplete information and a highly dynamic environment through dynamic resource allocation and multi-target coordination. In recent years, with the continuous improvement of the strategic position of the ocean, the war game confrontation scenarios in maritime scenarios have become increasingly complex, and the resulting needs have also become more complex and diverse. The coordination of multiple ships and aircraft requires coordinated path planning and combat power allocation, dynamic threat avoidance requires real-time response to sudden interference and target camouflage, and the closed-loop delay between intelligence updates and decision execution needs to be compressed to the second threshold. Faced with increasingly complex decision-making needs, building intelligent, adaptive, and scalable decision-making methods to plan tasks for maritime confrontation tasks has become an urgent need to break through the command-and-control difficulties in complex maritime scenarios.

For the problem of confrontation task planning in maritime environments, task planning methods based on established rules are efficient solutions, such as completing maritime confrontation task planning through a directed network graph structure [5], but it is difficult to analyze complex situations in real time and generate confrontation plans. Heuristic algorithms are highly applicable and have good interpretability. They are widely used in the fields of UAV swarm mission planning [6,7], island material supply planning [8], and mobile satellite imaging [9], but there are no successful application cases in maritime confrontation scenarios. In addition, the task planning method based on reinforcement learning has significant applications in the confrontation field, such as solving land confrontation tasks through the DQN algorithm [10,11], and the intelligent penetration method for missile penetration problems [12]. However, traditional task planning algorithms are difficult to cope with complex dynamic environments in maritime confrontation scenarios, and reinforcement learning methods are limited by the modeling and sample efficiency problems of complex scenarios; and further breakthroughs are still needed. In general, the practicality of maritime mission planning is still limited by two bottleneck problems. First, the mission planning problem in maritime confrontation scenarios lacks mature modeling methods due to its unique complexity. Second, the existing reinforcement learning methods have low efficiency in using samples, which aggravates the contradiction between the training data demand and feasibility and makes convergence difficult.

In response to the above problems, this paper first models the maritime confrontation scenario so that reinforcement learning can be applied to it. Then, based on the double deep Q-Network (DDQN) algorithm, the experience replay buffer partition strategy (ERBPS) is used to optimize the learning process. The main contributions of this paper are as follows:

- An advanced-PER based deep reinforcement learning method is proposed to solve the task planning problem in maritime confrontation scenarios. The proposed model refines the decision-making level to the unit level, which improves the upper limit of the model's decision-making ability.

- A new prioritized experience replay method called Experience Replay Buffer Partitioning Strategy (ERBPS), which improves the sampling process, shows a higher convergence rate, and improves the decision-making performance of the model.
- Experiments are carried out in a typical maritime confrontation scenario to prove the effectiveness of this method in solving the maritime confrontation mission planning problem.

The rest of this paper is arranged as follows. Section 2 introduces the method and elaborates on the modeling and task planning method proposed in this paper. Section 3 introduces the experiment process and analyzes the results. Section 4 concludes the paper.

2 The Proposed Method

This paper proposes an Advanced-PER based deep reinforcement learning method to solve the maritime confrontation mission planning problem and use a new prioritized experience replay method to optimize the experience replay process. The key steps include state construction, model decision-making, action implementation, reward calculation, experience sampling, etc. The overall process is shown in the Fig. 1.

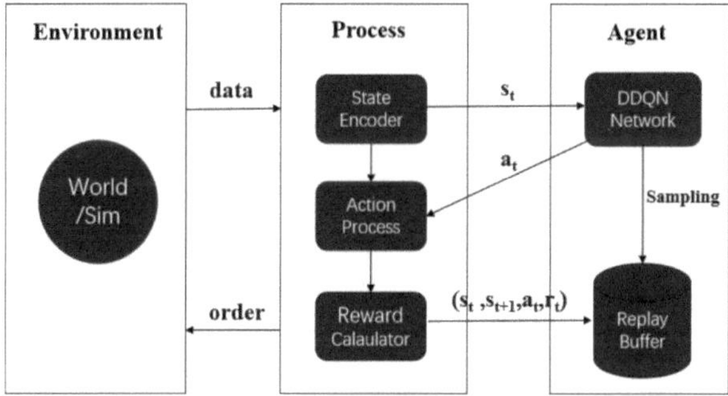

Fig. 1. The overall process of the proposed reinforcement learning method.

2.1 Modeling Based on the Markov Process

The Advanced-PER based deep reinforcement learning method is based on Markov decision process (MDP). The Markov decision process quintuple (S, A, P, R, γ), which is described as follows.

State: In the maritime confrontation environment, the information includes two parts: one's own unit information and enemy unit reconnaissance information. For each specific unit, the focus should be on the unit's confrontation, capability and endurance status. Therefore, the state s_t at each moment in this article consists of two parts: the confrontation unit state and the reconnaissance target state. The confrontation unit state describes the distribution of each confrontation unit, including unit type, quantity, weapon type, remaining fuel, and other information; the reconnaissance target state has the same structure as the confrontation unit state, but the weapon type and fuel information are set to 0, indicating their unknown state. The state information at each moment is constructed into a two-dimensional matrix, and the rows and columns are composed as follows: the rows represent the confrontation unit type and the reconnaissance unit type, and the columns contain four types of key information, namely spatial distribution, number of weapons, fuel and number of surviving units. Among them, the spatial distribution is based on the maximum activity range of the confrontation unit, and the confrontation environment is divided into 10×10 grid units. Each grid records the number of confrontation units in it, which are used to represent the spatial distribution information. To enhance the agent's ability to perceive and utilize historical information, the state s'_t used in this model is composed of the current state and the previous N states, i.e., $s'_t = (s_{t-N}, s_{t-N+1}, ..., s_{t-1}, s_t)$.

Reward: To address the issue of reward sparsity, this paper proposes a clear and effective reward feedback system that offers explicit action guidelines for intelligent agents to optimize their decision-making capabilities in complex adversarial environments.

In terms of reward calculation, this paper employs a two-tier mechanism that integrates score changes with action rewards. Specifically, the total reward is composed of a scene-fixed reward r_{env} and an additional shape reward r_{shape}, calculated by $r_t = r_{env} + r_{shape}$. r_{env} is the environment-based reward, and reflects the score change of the intelligent agent at the current and subsequent moments. This score change is determined by the difference between the score values at these two time points and is normalized according to specific application scenarios to ensure the stability of the reward signal. It is calculated by,

$$r_{env} = \frac{score_{t+1} - score_t}{dim} \tag{1}$$

where $score_t$ and $score_{t+1}$ represent the total scores at the current and next time points, respectively, and dim is the appropriate scaling dimension for normalizing score changes. The environment-based rewards are designed to incentivize intelligent agents to act in ways that enhance their scores, such as eliminating enemy units, occupying critical areas, or completing specific tasks.

The artificial shape reward r_{shape} serves as an additional incentive for the behavior of an intelligent agent, encouraging it to exhibit a desired pattern of behavior. This component of the reward is based on predefined action reward values, which provide supplementary reward signals to the intelligent agent by referencing a reward dictionary corresponding to the action name. Specifically, r_{shape} is calculated as $r_{shape} = r_{action} + r_{unit}$, where r_{action} is the reward for acting by the intelligent agent, and r_{unit} is an additional penalty for destroying certain units.

Action: To refine the decision-making process, this paper initializes the action space A for maritime confrontation as an action table comprising three core operational categories: confrontation unit deployment A_d, confrontation resource allocation A_a, and unit movement control A_m, represented as $A = (A_d, A_a, A_m)$.

This design takes into account the actual needs of the confrontation task, ensuring that the agent can make dynamic and detailed decisions based on the current confrontation environment. Specifically, confrontation unit deployment is to control the dispatch and retreat of the control unit, and the main parameter is the execution unit; confrontation resource allocation is when facing the enemy target, the agent needs to reasonably allocate the attack resources of each confrontation unit and determine the attack target. The main parameters include execution units, attack resources, and attack targets; unit movement control is used to control the movement of the unit in real time to adapt to the dynamically changing confrontation environment, and the main parameters include execution units and mobile target positions.

To clarify the types of actions, this paper further delineates the aforementioned three categories. Specifically, based on the types of execution units and the characteristics of attack targets, attack tasks are categorized into several specific enemy resource allocation operations A_{a_i}, such as air-to-air and air-to-ship mission categories, which correspond to different types of enemy units and targets, respectively. Additionally, regarding mobile control tasks, this paper further classifies these tasks into mobile control operations A_{m_i} for different types of units, based on the distinctions in control unit types and their target locations. Furthermore, in terms of deployment operations for hostile units, this paper categorizes deployment operations into various deployment tasks A_{d_i} based on the types of deployment units. Consequently, the action space can now be represented as $A = (A_{d_1}, A_{d_2}, \ldots, A_{a_1}, A_{a_2}, \ldots, A_{m_1}, A_{m_2}, \ldots)$.

2.2 Experience Replay Buffer Partitioning Strategy

This paper utilizes the Double Deep Q-Network (DDQN) algorithm as a foundational framework, employing a convolutional neural network (CNN) as the value function approximation to effectively process the states constructed in the preceding section and to extract feature representations. To ensure that the agent can discover new high-reward actions and make full use of known knowledge during the learning process, this paper adopts the $\epsilon - greedy$ strategy to dynamically balance exploration and utilization. This strategy dynamically adjusts the exploration probability ϵ to ensure that the agent can discover new high-reward actions and make use of the known best strategies during the learning process, thereby achieving efficient learning and decision-making. In addition, to make the actions legal, measures are taken for illegal actions to ensure that the decisions are legally executed.

Experience Replay Buffer is a key component in deep reinforcement learning. Its main function is to store and sample historical experience to improve the training efficiency and stability of the model. In traditional methods, uniform random sampling is usually used to obtain experience from the experience pool to train the model. However, this sampling method may be disturbed by numerous invalid actions, making it difficult for the model to capture key experience, thereby failing to effectively improve the learning effect. To solve this problem, a method that focuses on selecting high-value experiences by setting a reward threshold has been improved. However, this threshold-based method often exaggerates the proportion of certain actions and ignores other experiences, resulting in deviations in the training process and affecting the accuracy and stability of the model.

In this paper, we propose an enhancement to DDQN through an experience replay buffer partitioning strategy (ERBPS), which significantly improves the learning efficiency of reinforcement learning algorithms in complex task planning for maritime adversarial scenarios by dynamically managing the distribution of experiences across different actions. The specific design is as follows:

Multi-action Balanced Sampling: By maintaining a separate experience replay buffer for each action category, we ensure that experiences from different actions are sampled in a balanced manner. Let the total replay buffer be denoted as RB, which is denoted by,

$$RB = (RB_{A_{x_1}}, RB_{A_{x_2}}, ..., RB_{A_{x_n}}) \tag{2}$$

where $x \in \{d, a, m\}$.

Priority Sampling Mechanism: This mechanism dynamically adjusts the proportion of experiences sampled for different action categories during the sampling process. The number of prioritized action experience samples, denoted as $num_p = \alpha num_{np}$, where num_{np} represents the number of samples corresponding to non-priority actions, and $\alpha > 1$ is a hyperparameter that controls the ratio of the number of samples. The process is shown in Fig. 2:

3 Experiments

This experiment aims to provide both theoretical and practical support for addressing complex adversarial maritime mission planning problems, as well as to verify the feasibility and effectiveness of the proposed reinforcement learning framework. The experiment employs an open-source simulation platform to test specific scenarios within a maritime environment. Intelligent agents represent one party and engage in conflict against another party using the same rule-based strategy, thereby evaluating the performance and adaptability of the proposed method.

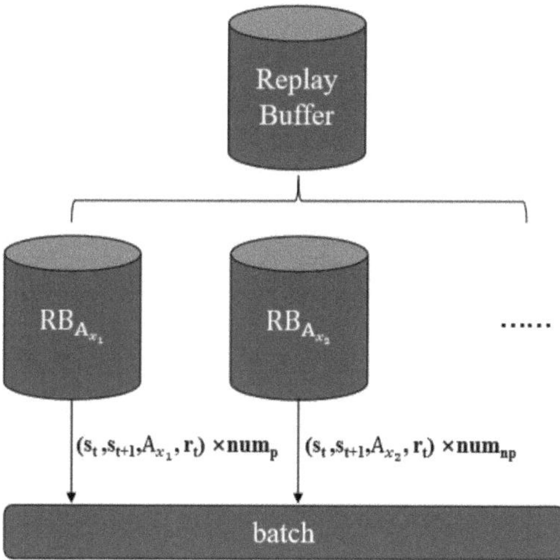

Fig. 2. The experience replay buffer partitioning strategy-based sampling process.

3.1 Settings

The experimental application scenario is based on an open-source military chess deduction simulation system, which offers a multi-domain joint confrontation simulation environment encompassing various confrontation domains on land, sea, and air. This system facilitates the rapid construction and rehearsal of confrontation scenarios, ranging from tactical to battle levels, and provides a reliable experimental platform for the verification and optimization of intelligent algorithms, including reinforcement learning.

The network structure of the model in this paper includes three convolutional layers and two fully connected layers. The first convolutional layer uses a convolution kernel of size 4×4 and stride 2 to map the input to 32 feature channels; the second convolutional layer uses a convolution kernel of size 3×3 and stride 1 to expand the number of channels to 64; the third convolutional layer uses a convolution kernel of size 2×2 and stride 1 to maintain 64 output channels. A ReLU activation function follows each convolutional layer to enhance the network's ability to express non-linearly. After flattening, the convolutional features are input to a fully connected layer with 512 neurons, further activated by ReLU, and finally mapped to the Q value in the action space through the output layer.

In the experimental setup, the positions of the two opposing units are mirrored, ensuring that they have identical models, numbers, and initial configurations to maintain fairness. During the experiment, intelligent agents employing different algorithms represent the red side, while agents using rule-based algorithms represent the blue side. Both sides control their respective units in a joint confrontation, aiming to preserve as many of their units as possible while damaging and destroying more of the enemy's units to achieve a higher overall score.

The experiment consists of a total of 400 rounds, with each round comprising 360 decision steps. The unit composition is detailed in Table 1.

Table 1. Configuration of simulated units in the adversarial environment.

Type	Unit numbers	Major weapons	Score
Major ships	1	Not equipped with weapons	130
Secondary ships	1	Anti-air missile 96 Anti-ship missile 10	80
Reconnaissance aircraft	2	Not equipped with weapons	10
Air-to-air aircraft	4	Anti-air missile 8	10
Air-to-ship aircraft	4	Anti-ship missile 4	10

The hardware environment for this experiment consists of a desktop computer equipped with an i7-10700K CPU, an NVIDIA GeForce RTX 3060 graphics card, and 64 GB of RAM.

3.2 Comparison Methods

The sampling phase employs uniform random sampling, the DDQN method with thresholded preferential sampling, and the traditional Proximal Policy Optimization (PPO) method, where the input state for the PPO model is denoted as s_t.

3.3 Results and Analysis

In the experiments, the performance differences among the algorithms are systematically revealed through multidimensional metrics. The moving average reward image is shown in Fig. 3.

The moving average reward curve depicted in the figure above indicates that the DDQN+ERBPS algorithm exhibits a significant advantage, as its moving average reward value demonstrates a steep upward trend at the beginning of the training period, surpassing the threshold of 60 within just 100 rounds, and ultimately stabilizing in the 100–120 range. In contrast, the DDQN+Random and DDQN+Threshold algorithms display suboptimal performance, with both algorithms experiencing more pronounced fluctuations during the middle phase; however, the DDQN+Threshold algorithm shows a more stable convergence trend compared to the DDQN+Random algorithm in the later stages. The PPO algorithm, on the other hand, exhibits a two-stage behavior: its reward value remains close to zero for an extended period during the first 300 rounds, before jumping to 60 in the later stages and maintaining narrow fluctuations. This behavior reveals the exploration dilemma inherent in the strategy gradient method within a discrete action space, where trust domain constraints hinder exploration efficiency in the early stages.

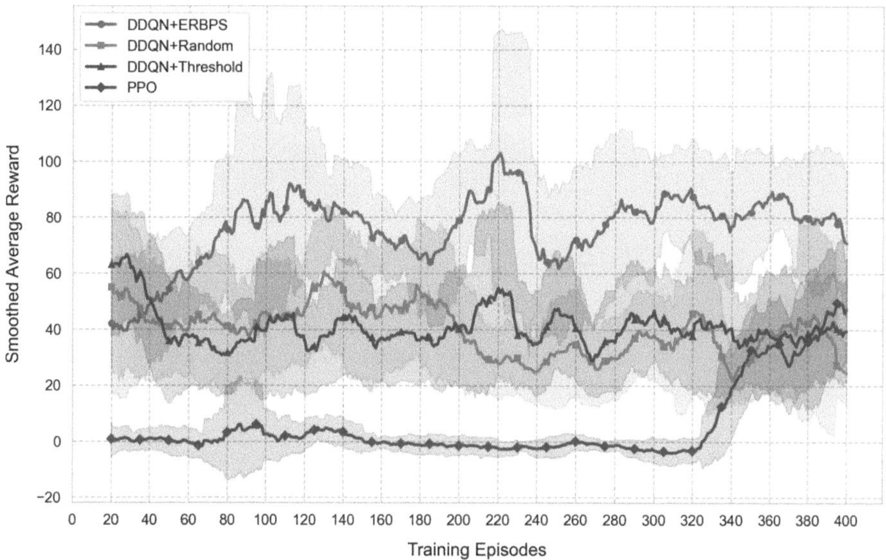

Fig. 3. The moving average reward.

In the experiments, the performance differences among the algorithms are systematically revealed through multidimensional metrics. The moving average score is shown in Fig. 4.

The moving average score metric illustrated in the graph above further highlights the distinct characteristics of the algorithms in complex tasks. The DDQN+ERBPS algorithm dominates, effectively guided by hierarchical shaping rewards. Its moving average score curve consistently breaks into the positive range early in the training period and ultimately stabilizes around 100, balancing immediate gains with long-term planning. The performance of the DDQN+Random and DDQN+Threshold algorithms is more general, exhibiting an overall trend of deteriorating strategy performance. The results from both the score and reward dimensions reveal the limitations of the PPO algorithm, whose narrow trust domain updates, while capturing reward signals, lead to a neglect of strategic goal execution, resulting in a significant loss of strategic value in the score metrics.

The winning rate and average score of the different methods are summarized in Table 2.

As can be seen from the table above, the performance of the DDQN+ERBPS method is a significant margin, and its win rate and average score far exceed those of other methods, which verifies the effectiveness of the proposed method in solving the problem of maritime confrontation mission planning. The win rates of DDQN+Random and DDQN+Threshold are less than 50% and the average

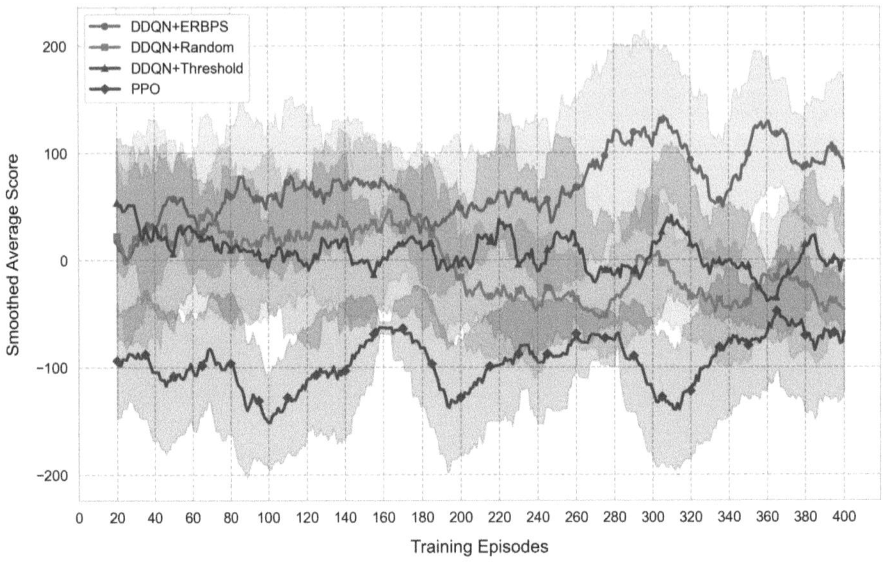

Fig. 4. The moving average score.

Table 2. Performance metrics across algorithms: winning rate and average score

Methods	Winning rate	Average score
DDQN+ERBPS	83.2%	67.9
DDQN+Random Sample	37.8%	-4.0
DDQN+Threshold Sample	46.2%	8.6
PPO	4.0%	-95.0

scores are low, highlighting the problem of weak algorithm strategy performance; the PPO algorithm performs the worst, indicating that it has adaptability defects in maritime confrontation mission planning.

4 Conclusion

In this paper, a complete framework based on reinforcement learning is innovatively designed and implemented for the complex maritime adversarial mission planning problem, which enables reinforcement learning to be successfully applied to the field of maritime adversarial mission planning for the first time. Moreover, by optimising the experience replay mechanism of reinforcement learning, this paper significantly improves the convergence efficiency and decision-making effect of the model.

Acknowledgements. This work is supported by the National Natural Science Foundation of China (No. 62076224).

References

1. Zhao, G., Luo, X.: On operation mission planning system. J. Command Control **1**(04), 391–394 (2015)
2. Ma, Y., Wu, L., Xu, X., Liu, Y.: Requirement analysis of intelligent operation task planning. Command Control Simul. **43**(04), 61–67 (2021)
3. Han, Z., Liu, S., Tang, Y., Jing, M.: Study on computer wargaming system. Comput. Simul. **28**(04), 10–13 (2011)
4. Zhu, X., Li, L., Qiu, J.: Process analysis and system construction considerations of us armed forces joint mission planning. J. Command Control **3**(04), 305–311 (2017)
5. Shen, Y., Qiu, X., Fan, Y.: Application of network planning technology in mission planning system of naval strike. J. Command Control **3**(04), 330–335 (2017)
6. Qi, X., Li, B., Fan, Y., Li, L.: A survey of mission planning on UAVs systems based on multiple constraints. CAAI Trans. Intell. Syst. **15**(02), 204–217 (2020)
7. Zhao, M., Yao, M.: Study on changeable path planning and multi-task assignment optimization design for unmanned aerial vehicles cluster. J. Univ. Electron. Sci. Technol. China **39**(04), 560–563 (2010)
8. Li, J.: Island-reef materials supply task planning based on heuristic genetic algorithm. Military Oper. Res. Assess. **35**(02), 13–17+25 (2021)
9. Gan, L., Gong, S.: Observation mission planning for maneuverable satellite constellations towards multiple targets. J. Tsinghua Univ. (Sci. Technol.) **61**(03), 240–247 (2021)
10. Tian, Z., Liu, H.: Application of intelligent algorithm in military chess antagonism deduction. Command Control Simul. **43**(01), 40–47 (2021)
11. Zhang, Y., Ni, L., Ni, W., Liu, X.: A study on combat mission planning technology based on deep reinforcement learning. Military Oper. Res. Assess. **39**(01), 60–67 (2024)
12. Cheng, K., Chen, G., Yu, X., Liu, M., Shao, T.: Knowledge traction and data-driven wargame AI design and key technologies. Syst. Eng. Electron. **43**(10), 2911–2917 (2021)

Deep Cross Networks for Intelligent Risk Prediction of Prostate Cancer

Hanshi Xu[1], Guangquan Zhang[1], Hua Lin[2], Mark Grosser[2], and Jie Lu[1](✉)

[1] Australian AI institute, University of Technology Sydney, Ultimo, Australia
Jie.Lu@uts.edu.au
[2] 23Strands, Pyrmont, Australia

Abstract. As a cutting-edge technology, deep learning has been widely applied in biomedical research, bringing revolutionary changes to biology and medicine. By integrating genomic data with deep learning, it is possible to accurately identify high-risk groups for diseases and provide recommendations for subsequent diagnosis and treatment. Prostate cancer, one of the most common malignancies affecting older males, has long posed a challenge in terms of precisely identifying individuals at high risk. However, the performance of current risk assessment models remains limited. In this study, we employed a deep learning model, the Deep and Cross Network (DCN), to assess prostate cancer risk. This model is capable of capturing potential interactions within genetic features as well as between genetic and non-genetic factors. We developed two prostate cancer risk prediction models: one based solely on genetic data and another that integrates both genetic and non-genetic factors. In both cases, the DCN model demonstrated superior predictive performance compared to traditional methods. These results suggest that there are widespread interactions both among genetic features and between genetic and environmental factors, which may provide valuable insights into the underlying mechanisms of prostate cancer.

Keywords: Deep Learning · Deep and Cross Network · Prostate Cancer Risk Prediction · Polygenic Risk Score

1 Introduction

Deep learning is a widely used and state-of-the-art technique. Due to its high efficiency and effectiveness, deep learning has been extensively applied in the biomedical field, such as disease prevention and detection [1]. However, the complexity of biological and health-related data, such as sensitivity, privacy, and bias, also poses significant challenges for deep learning. Greater collaboration and broader application between deep learning and health-related fields are urgently needed [2,3].

Globally, prostate cancer ranks fourth in incidence and eighth in mortality among all cancers [4]. Predicting the risk of prostate cancer can help reduce

I. Awan et al. (Eds.): WISE 2025, LNCS 16367, pp. 348–358, 2026.
https://doi.org/10.1007/978-981-95-7394-3_24

its incidence, avoid overtreatment, facilitate better health management planning, and ultimately improve quality of life. Prostate cancer exhibits relatively high heritability, estimated at approximately 57% [5–7], indicating that more than half of the risk can be attributed to genetic factors. In addition, several non-genetic risk factors are also associated with prostate cancer risk, including age [8], family history [9], obesity [10], smoking [11], diet [12], and other unhealthy lifestyle habits. These factors can be incorporated into risk prediction models.

Polygenic risk score (PRS) [13] is a widely used method for assessing disease risk. In general, a PRS is a weighted mean of genetic features, where each feature represents information from a specific location on the human genome, commonly referred to as a single nucleotide polymorphism (SNP). SNPs and their corresponding weights are typically selected and calculated based on case-control studies or genome-wide association studies (GWAS).

Although the PRS method is intuitive and easy to interpret, it overlooks potential interactions between feature, such as SNP–SNP interactions [14] and interactions between SNPs and non-genetic factors [15]. This limitation may result in reduced predictive power and an increased rate of false positives. Therefore, more comprehensive approaches, such as deep learning, are necessary to address these shortcomings.

This work primarily employs deep learning to build predictive models that assess the risk of prostate cancer using genetic factors alone and in combination with non-genetic factors. Our main contributions include:

- Employing a Deep and Cross Network to assess the risk of prostate cancer.
- Demonstrating that DCN model outperforms traditional PRS methods and classical machine learning approaches.

The remainder of this article is organized as follows: Sect. 2 reviews related work on disease risk prediction models using genetic data. Section 3.1 discusses data processing and method implementation. Section 4.1 presents the results. Section 5 provides the conclusion and outlines directions for future research.

2 Related Work

In this section, we introduce the deep learning applied in disease risk prediction and the current situation in prostate cancer risk prediction.

2.1 Deep Learning in Disease Risk Prediction

Wang et al. [16] developed and improved the DCN, originally designed for web-scale learning tasks such as ranking and advertising recommendation, with a focus on efficiently learning feature interactions. This capability presents promising applications in disease risk prediction. Luo et al. [17] employed a capsule network approach, leveraging PCA-reduced whole-genome data to accurately predict disease risk for amyotrophic lateral sclerosis and Parkinson's disease.

Zhou [18] applied deep learning methods to predict Alzheimer's disease risk, achieving superior performance compared to traditional PRS models, suggesting that deep learning can enhance disease risk prediction accuracy.

2.2 Prostate Cancer Risk Prediction

In 2018, a study conducted by Schumacher et al. [19] identified 62 novel SNPs associated with prostate cancer risk. Combining these with 85 previously reported SNPs, a total of 147 SNPs were used to build a PRS model for prostate cancer risk assessment. Christopher A. Haiman [20] performed a meta-analysis using data from multiple ancestry groups, discovering 86 novel SNPs associated with prostate cancer and constructing a PRS model comprising 269 SNPs. In 2023, their team [21] analyzed an even larger multi-ancestry dataset and identified 187 additional novel SNPs. Ultimately, they developed a PRS model including 451 SNPs, which demonstrated strong predictive performance across various ethnicities.

Beyond traditional PRS methods, machine learning approaches are increasingly applied to the prediction of prostate cancer and other diseases. For example, Enoma et al. [22] utilized methods such as XGBoost to build a risk model incorporating 2,798 SNPs, highlighting the importance of SNP interactions in improving predictive accuracy.

3 Methodology

This section presents a detailed overview of the DCN model, the processes of data acquisition and preprocessing, and the implementation of traditional PRS methods.

3.1 DCN Model

The architecture of the DCN is illustrated in Fig. 1.

The DCN model consists of four components: an embedding layer, a cross network layer, a deep network layer, and a final merge layer. All categorical variables, including genetic features, smoking history, and family history of prostate cancer, are first passed through the embedding layer, where they are transformed into continuous representations according to the following formula:

$$\mathbf{x}_{\text{embed},j} = \mathbf{M}_j \mathbf{G}_j$$

Here, $\mathbf{x}_{\text{embed},j}$ denotes the embedded representation of the j-th categorical feature; $\mathbf{M}_j \in \mathbb{R}^{K \times d}$ is a learnable embedding matrix; K is the number of categories for the feature; and d is the embedding dimension. Specifically, $K = 3$ is used for genetic features, while $K = 2$ is used for both smoking history and family history.

After embedding, the resulting features are concatenated with continuous variables such as age and other non-genetic traits. This combined feature vector

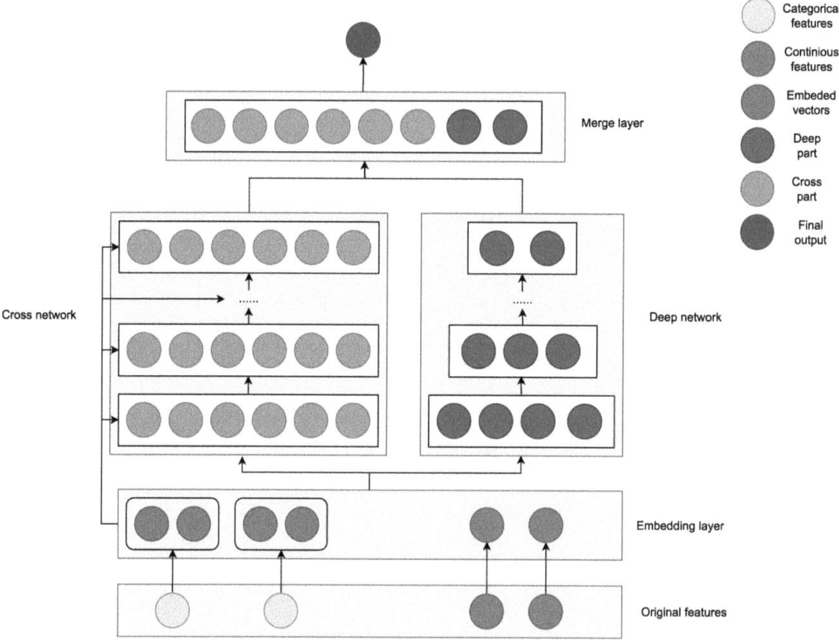

Fig. 1. DCN architecture diagram

is then fed simultaneously into both the cross network and the deep network layers.

For the deep network component, the computation at the L-th layer is defined as:

$$\mathbf{d}_L = \sigma\left(\mathbf{W}_L \mathbf{d}_{L-1} + \mathbf{b}_L\right)$$

where $\mathbf{d}_L$ and $\mathbf{d}_{L-1}$ are the outputs of the L-th and $(L-1)$-th layers, respectively; $\mathbf{W}_L$ is the weight matrix, and $\mathbf{b}_L$ is the bias vector for the L-th layer. The activation function $\sigma(\cdot)$ used in our model is the ReLU.

For the cross network component, the output of the L-th layer is computed as:

$$\mathbf{x}_L = \mathbf{x}_0 \odot \left(\mathbf{W}_{L-1} \mathbf{x}_{L-1} + \mathbf{b}_{L-1}\right)$$

where $\mathbf{x}_L$ and $\mathbf{x}_{L-1}$ are the outputs of the L-th and $(L-1)$-th layers of the cross network, respectively; $\mathbf{x}_0$ is the original input to the cross network, which is also the output of the embedding layer. Here, $\odot$ denotes element-wise (Hadamard) multiplication.

For the merge layer, the output is computed as:

$$\mathbf{O} = \mathbf{W}\mathbf{M} + \mathbf{b}$$

where $\mathbf{M}$ is the merged vector that combines the outputs from both the deep network and the cross network, $\mathbf{W}$ is the weight matrix, and $\mathbf{b}$ is the bias vector. The BCELoss function is applied in this model.

3.2 Data Acquisition

All data used in this study were obtained from the UK Biobank (UKBB), a globally leading population health database [23,24]. The UKBB has collected data from approximately 500,000 participants in the UK and continues to update its records. The dataset includes genomic information (such as whole-genome genotyping data), health status data (e.g., disease diagnoses), lifestyle information (e.g., smoking status), physical characteristics (e.g., height and weight), among many other data types. We utilized imputed whole-genome genotype data for our study.

3.3 Data Processing

To ensure data reliability, we applied the following filtering criteria to our dataset:

(1) Ambiguous bases were defined as SNPs with alleles consisting only of A and T or C and G, and a minor allele frequency (MAF) between 0.4 and 0.5. These SNPs were excluded from subsequent analyses. In this filtering step, approximately 26 million SNPs were removed, leaving around 71 million SNPs for further analysis.
(2) All individuals who self-identified as being of European descent were retained. Individuals diagnosed with prostate cancer, with no other cancer diagnoses within five years before or after their prostate cancer diagnosis, were classified as the prostate cancer cohort. Conversely, the non-prostate cancer cohort consisted of male individuals without a diagnosis of either prostate cancer or benign prostate tumors. After this filtering step, a total of 166,950 individuals remained.
(3) A gender consistency check by examining SNP heterozygosity on the sex chromosomes (X and Y) was conducted to verify that the genetically inferred sex matched the self-reported sex of each individual. Seven male individuals with discordant gender information were excluded. Additionally, since prostate cancer occurs exclusively in males, 165 female individuals were excluded regardless of concordance between genetic and reported sex.
(4) SNPs that were missing in more than 10% of individuals, as well as individuals who had more than 10% of SNPs missing, were excluded. In this filtering step, no individuals were removed; however, approximately 5 million SNPs were eliminated.
(5) SNPs with a MAF less than 1% were removed, resulting in the retention of approximately 9 million SNPs.
(6) Hardy-Weinberg equilibrium tests [25,26] was performed for each SNP. Using a significance threshold of 10^{-5}, SNPs with P-values below this threshold were considered to deviate from equilibrium and removed.

The above quality control steps were all performed using the software PLINK2 [27,28]. After completing these steps, we obtained a total of 166,778 samples, including 12,207 prostate cancer cases and 154,571 non-prostate cancer controls. Approximately 9.4 million SNPs were retained. The data processing workflow is illustrated in Fig. 2.

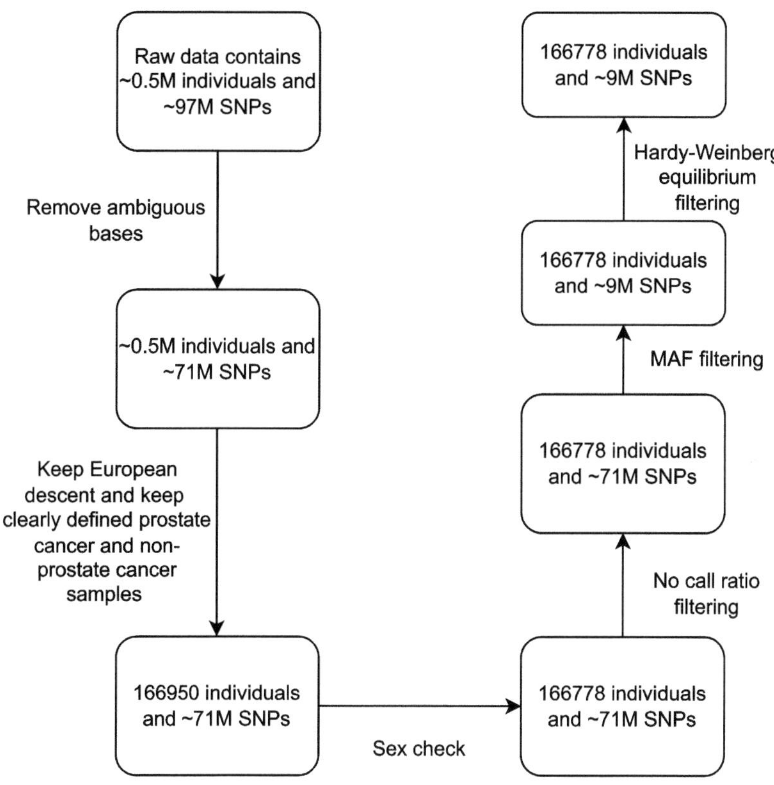

Fig. 2. Flow chat of data quality control

To address the issue of sample imbalance, we randomly removed some non-prostate cancer samples to achieve a 1:1 ratio between prostate cancer and non-prostate cancer cases. The remaining samples were then split into training and testing sets at an 8:2 ratio. The training set comprised 9,766 pairs of samples, while the testing set included 2,441 pairs.

Considering the high dimensionality of the data and that most SNPs are unlikely to be associated with prostate cancer risk, we selected a set of 451 SNPs reported in high-quality literature [21], which was previously used to build a PRS model. Among these, 412 SNPs passed our quality control and data processing steps. Consequently, the genomic features used for model training and testing consisted of these 412 SNPs.

All SNP values were encoded as 0, 1, or 2, representing the number of alternative alleles relative to a reference base. For instance, if SNP X had A as the reference base and T as the alternative base, individuals with genotype AA were assigned a value of 0, those with AT a value of 1, and those with TT a value of 2.

In addition, we incorporated non-genetic features, including body mass index (BMI), age, smoking history, tea consumption frequency, and coffee consumption frequency. Missing values in these features were imputed using the mean value calculated from all 166,788 individuals with available data.

3.4 PRS Model

Polygenic Risk Score (PRS) is calculated using the following formula:

$$\mathrm{PRS}_i = \frac{1}{N}\sum_{j=1}^{N} w_j \cdot G_{ij}$$

where PRS_i denotes the PRS for the i-th individual, N is the total number of features, w_j is the weight assigned to the j-th feature (SNP or non-genetic factor), and G_{ij} is the value of the j-th feature for the i-th individual.

The weights w_j are typically derived from logistic regression models used in genome-wide association studies (GWAS), where:

$$w_j = e^{\beta_j}$$

and the coefficient β_j is obtained from the following logistic regression equation:

$$\log\left(\frac{P(y=1)}{P(y=0)}\right) = \beta_0 + \beta_j G_j$$

Here, $P(y = 1)$ represents the probability of being diagnosed with prostate cancer, while $P(y = 0)$ represents the probability of not having prostate cancer.

4 Results

This section reports the results of prostate cancer risk prediction based on genetic features alone and on the integration of genetic and non-genetic features.

AUC and F1-score are commonly used metrics for evaluating disease risk prediction models. AUC is the most frequently used model evaluation metric. Meanwhile, risk assessment methods are not clinical diagnostic methods, but rather risk screening methods, therefore finding the optimal threshold to achieve the best F1-score, which balances precision and recall, is also commonly used in method evaluation.

4.1 Genomic Features

We first built models using only genomic features. The results are presented in Table 1. Among all models, the DCN model achieved the best performance in terms of AUC, F1-score and two other evaluation metrics. The two tree-based models, Random Forest and XGBoost, produced similar results, with XGBoost slightly outperforming Random Forest. The Artificial Neural Network (ANN) model performs slightly worse than the two tree models. The traditional PRS model performed the worst among the five models on three metrics but ranked second only to DCN in terms of recall. This suggests that the traditional PRS model tends to miss fewer true prostate cancer cases, albeit at the cost of lower precision and a higher false positive rate. Consequently, this may imply a risk of over-screening for prostate cancer when using traditional PRS models.

Table 1. Model performances using genomic features.

Module	AUC	Precision	Recall	F1-score
PRS	0.5388	0.5250	0.6419	0.5776
Random Forest	0.6016	0.6002	0.6088	0.6044
XGBoost	0.6284	0.6267	0.6354	0.6310
ANN	0.5973	0.5858	0.6239	0.6042
DCN	**0.6346**	**0.6286**	**0.6579**	**0.6429**

4.2 Genomic Features Combined with Non-Genetic Factors

We developed a new model incorporating both genomic and non-genetic features. The results are presented in Table 2. All models demonstrated improved performance, underscoring the importance of environmental factors in prostate cancer risk prediction. The DCN model achieved the highest AUC and F1-score, outperformed other models in two additional metrics, although XGBoost surpassed it in precision.

Table 2. Model performances using both genomic features and non-genetic factors.

Module	AUC	Precision	Recall	F1-score
PRS	0.6369	0.5890	0.6915	0.6361
Random Forest	0.6819	0.6528	0.7771	0.7096
XGBoost	0.7056	**0.6837**	0.7653	0.7222
ANN	0.6913	0.6512	0.5965	0.6226
DCN	**0.7083**	0.6743	**0.8058**	**0.7342**

As observed in the genomic-only results, Random Forest and XGBoost performed similarly, with XGBoost showing a slight advantage. Traditional PRS models consistently ranked lowest across all metrics, including recall, which did improve when both types of features were used.

Tree-based models are believed to capture certain interactions between features, indicating potential interplay between genomic and environmental factors. The DCN model was particularly effective in learning these interactions, leading to more substantial performance gains. In contrast, the traditional PRS model, which does not account for feature interactions, exhibited only limited improvement.

5 Conclusion and Future Work

Our study utilized genomic data alone and in combination with non-genetic factors to construct a Deep and Cross Network (DCN) for prostate cancer risk prediction. The proposed model outperformed both traditional polygenic risk score (PRS) methods and conventional machine learning approaches across multiple evaluation metrics. Although the internal workings of the DCN model resemble a "black box" and are inherently difficult to interpret, it demonstrated strong predictive capabilities, enabling accurate risk stratification and the potential for more personalized screening strategies.

Future research will focus on developing improved methods for identifying additional feature interactions that contribute to disease risk. By capturing these interactions, we aim to enhance the interpretability of the models and gain deeper insights into the underlying biological mechanisms. Moreover, recent studies [29] have suggested that traditional PRS scores may be associated with mortality risk in prostate cancer patients. Investigating whether deep learning models, such as DCN, demonstrate similar associations could offer further clinical and practical value.

Acknowledgments. This work is supported by the Australian Research Council Linkage Project: LP210100414.

Disclosure of Interests. The authors have no competing interests to declare that are relevant to the content of this article.

References

1. Swinckels, L., Bennis, F.C., et al.: The use of deep learning and machine learning on longitudinal electronic health records for the early detection and prevention of diseases: scoping review. J. Med. Internet Res. **26** (2024). https://doi.org/10.2196/48320
2. Esteva, A., Robicquet, A., et al.: A guide to deep learning in healthcare. Nat. Med. **25**(1), 24–29 (2019)
3. Lu, J., Dawson, A., et al.: AI for women's health: framework and focus areas. In: Companion Proceedings of the ACM on Web Conference 2025, pp. 845–848. ACM, New York, NY, USA (2025). https://doi.org/10.1145/3701716.3718981
4. Bray, F., Laversanne, M., et al.: Global cancer statistics 2022: globocan estimates of incidence and mortality worldwide for 36 cancers in 185 countries. CA: Cancer J. Clin. **74**, 229–263 (2024). https://doi.org/10.3322/caac.21834

5. Hjelmborg, J.B., Scheike, T., et al.: The heritability of prostate cancer in the Nordic twin study of cancer. Cancer Epidemiol. Biomark. Prev. **23**(11), 2303–2310 (2014). https://doi.org/10.1158/1055-9965.EPI-13-0568
6. Houlahan, K.E., Livingstone, J., et al.: A polygenic two-hit hypothesis for prostate cancer. JNCI: J. Natl. Cancer Inst. **115**(4), 468–472 (2023). https://doi.org/10.1093/jnci/djad001
7. Mucci, L.A., Hjelmborg, J.B., et al.: Familial risk and heritability of cancer among twins in Nordic countries. JAMA **315**(1), 68 (2016). https://doi.org/10.1001/jama.2015.17703. http://jama.jamanetwork.com/article.aspx?doi=10.1001/jama.2015.17703
8. Bergengren, O., Pekala, K.R., et al.: 2022 Update on prostate cancer epidemiology and risk factors-a systematic review. Eur. Urol. **84**(2), 191–206 (2023)
9. Brook, M.N., Ní Raghallaigh, H., et al.: Family history of prostate cancer and survival outcomes in the uk genetic prostate cancer study. Eur. Urol. **83**(3), 257–266 (2023)
10. Allott, E.H., Masko, E.M., Freedland, S.J.: Obesity and prostate cancer: weighing the evidence. Eur. Urol. **63**(5), 800–809 (2013). https://doi.org/10.1016/j.eururo.2012.11.013
11. De Nunzio, C., Andriole, G.L., Thompson, I.M., Freedland, S.J.: Smoking and prostate cancer: a systematic review. Eur. Urol. Focus **1**(1), 28–38 (2015). https://doi.org/10.1016/j.euf.2014.10.002. https://linkinghub.elsevier.com/retrieve/pii/S2405456915000036
12. Lin, P.H., Aronson, W., Freedland, S.J.: An update of research evidence on nutrition and prostate cancer. Urol. Oncol.: Seminars Original Invest. **37**(6), 387–401 (2019). https://doi.org/10.1016/j.urolonc.2017.10.006
13. Lewis, C.M., Vassos, E.: Polygenic risk scores: from research tools to clinical instruments (2020). https://doi.org/10.1186/s13073-020-00742-5
14. Franco, N.R., Massi, M.C., et al.: Development of a method for generating SNP interaction-aware polygenic risk scores for radiotherapy toxicity. Radiother. Oncol. **159**, 241–248 (2021). https://doi.org/10.1016/j.radonc.2021.03.024
15. Janssens, A.C.J.W.: Validity of polygenic risk scores: are we measuring what we think we are? Hum. Mol. Genet. **28**(R2), R143–R150 (2019). https://doi.org/10.1093/hmg/ddz205. https://academic.oup.com/hmg/article/28/R2/R143/5555564
16. Wang, R., et al.: DCN V2: improved deep & cross network and practical lessons for web-scale learning to rank systems. In: Proceedings of the Web Conference 2021, pp. 1785–1797. ACM, New York, NY, USA (2021). https://doi.org/10.1145/3442381.3450078
17. Luo, X., Kang, X., Schönhuth, A.: Predicting the prevalence of complex genetic diseases from individual genotype profiles using capsule networks. Nat. Mach. Intell. **5**(2), 114–125 (2023). https://doi.org/10.1038/s42256-022-00604-2
18. Zhou, X., Chen, Y., et al.: Deep learning-based polygenic risk analysis for Alzheimer's disease prediction. Commun. Med. **3**(1), 49 (2023). https://doi.org/10.1038/s43856-023-00269-x. https://www.nature.com/articles/s43856-023-00269-x
19. Schumacher, F.R., Al Olama, A.A., et al.: Association analyses of more than 140,000 men identify 63 new prostate cancer susceptibility loci. Nat. Genet. **50**(7), 928–936 (2018). https://doi.org/10.1038/s41588-018-0142-8. https://www.nature.com/articles/s41588-018-0142-8
20. Conti, D.V., Darst, B.F., et al.: Trans-ancestry genome-wide association meta-analysis of prostate cancer identifies new susceptibility loci and informs genetic risk prediction. Nat. Genet. **53**(1), 65–75 (2021). https://doi.org/10.1038/s41588-020-00748-0

21. Wang, A., Shen, J., et al.: Characterizing prostate cancer risk through multi-ancestry genome-wide discovery of 187 novel risk variants. Nat. Genet. **55**(12), 2065–2074 (2023). https://doi.org/10.1038/s41588-023-01534-4
22. Enoma, D., Osamor, V.C., Olubanke, O.: Extreme gradient boosting machine learning algorithm identifies genome-wide genetic variants in prostate cancer risk prediction (2023). https://doi.org/10.1101/2023.10.27.564373. http://biorxiv.org/lookup/doi/10.1101/2023.10.27.564373
23. Bycroft, C., Freeman, C., et al.: The UK Biobank resource with deep phenotyping and genomic data. Nature **562**(7726), 203–209 (2018). https://doi.org/10.1038/s41586-018-0579-z
24. Sudlow, C., Gallacher, J., et al.: UK Biobank: an open access resource for identifying the causes of a wide range of complex diseases of middle and old age. PLoS Med. **12**(3) (2015). https://doi.org/10.1371/journal.pmed.1001779
25. Graffelman, J., Weir, B.S.: Testing for Hardy-Weinberg equilibrium at biallelic genetic markers on the X chromosome. Heredity **116**(6), 558–568 (2016). https://doi.org/10.1038/hdy.2016.20
26. Wigginton, J.E., Cutler, D.J., Abecasis, G.R.: A note on exact tests of Hardy-Weinberg equilibrium. Am. J. Hum. Genet. **76**(5), 887–893 (2005). https://doi.org/10.1086/429864, papers2://publication/uuid/DCCBAB33-18E1-420D-BC50-9044CB6603EE. https://linkinghub.elsevier.com/retrieve/pii/S0002929707607356
27. Chang, C.C., Chow, C.C., et al.: Second-generation PLINK: rising to the challenge of larger and richer datasets. GigaScience **4**(1), 1–16 (2015). https://doi.org/10.1186/s13742-015-0047-8
28. Purcell, S., Neale, B., et al.: PLINK: a tool set for whole-genome association and population-based linkage analyses. Am. J. Hum. Genet. **81**(3), 559–575 (2007). https://doi.org/10.1086/519795
29. Stopsack, K.H.: Polygenic risk scores for prostate cancer. JAMA Oncol. **11**(2), 172 (2025). https://doi.org/10.1001/jamaoncol.2024.5203. https://jamanetwork.com/journals/jamaoncology/fullarticle/2827890

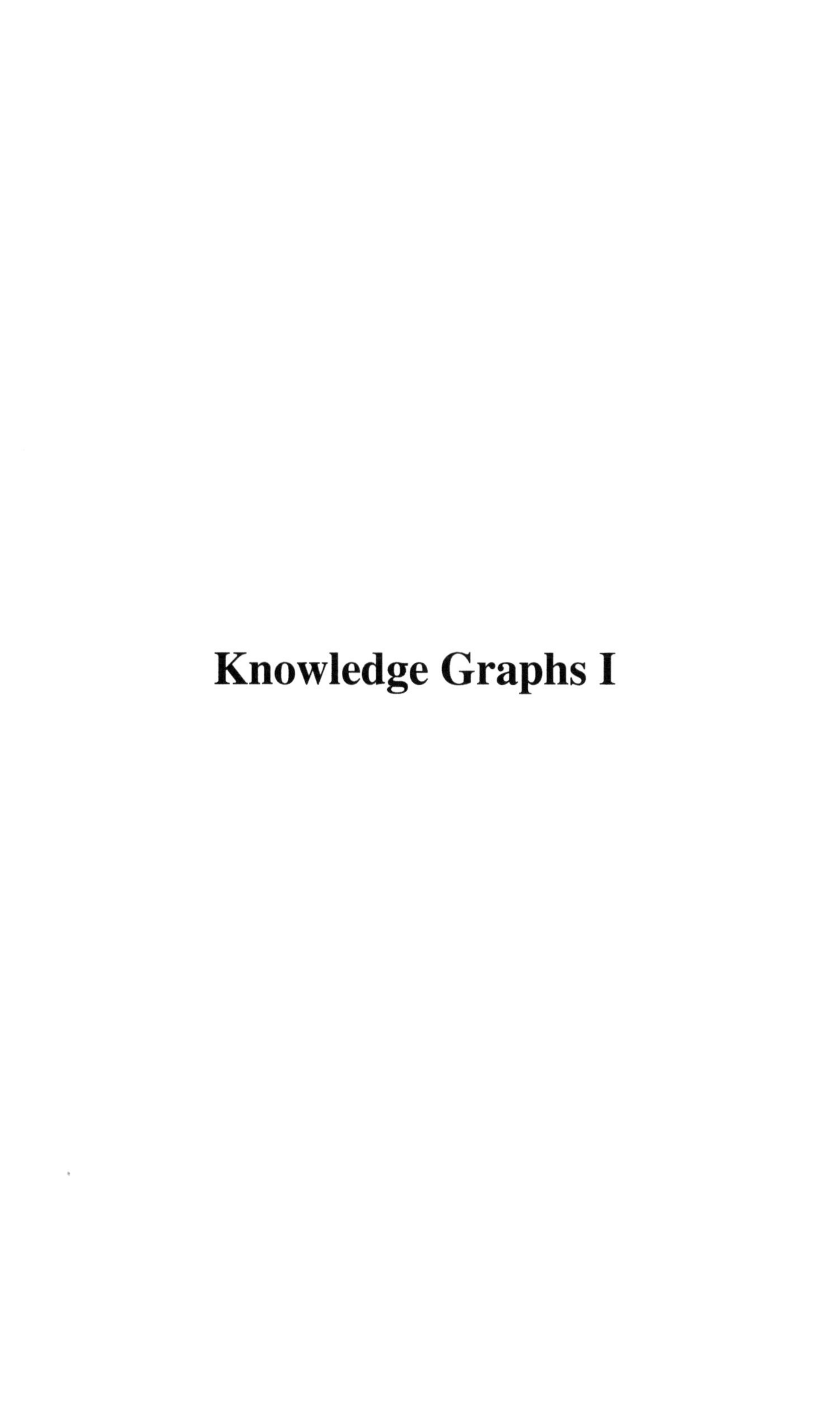

Knowledge Graphs I

Graph Reachability Queries: Empirical Evaluation and Practical Guidelines

Huangleshuai He, Zhengyi Yang(✉), Dong Wen, Wenke Yang, and John Shepherd

The University of New South Wales, Sydney, NSW, Australia
{huangleshuai.he,zhengyi.yang,dong.wen,wenke.yang, John.Shepherd}@unsw.edu.au

Abstract. Reachability queries are fundamental for analyzing connectivity in large graphs, supporting applications in domains such as finance, social networks, and program analysis. Despite the variety of proposed indexing techniques, previous evaluations are often limited to narrow graph datasets and fail to provide comprehensive comparisons or in-depth analysis. In this work, we present an extensive empirical study of representative reachability indexes across diverse graphs and query workloads. We utilize a cost-performance metric that jointly considers index size and query time, providing a unified measure of practical efficiency. Our large-scale benchmarking covers 1,400 graphs and over 38,000 query configurations, revealing how structural and query characteristics affect index performance. Furthermore, we construct a decision tree model to uncover feature-driven method preferences and provide practical guidance for index selection under varying workloads and system constraints.

Keywords: Graph Reachability · Indexing · Query Optimisation

1 Introduction

Graphs model real-world systems by capturing entities and their relationships, with numerous related studies [2,3,9,10]. Reachability queries, which determine whether a path exists between two nodes, are fundamental to graph analytics. They underpin a wide range of applications, including fraud detection in finance [14], access control in social networks [6], program analysis and vulnerability tracing [15], and efficient XML querying [20]. These examples highlight the practical significance of reachability queries in real-world scenarios.

The reachability query problem has been extensively studied in the literature [1,4,5,11–13,16–18,21–23,25,27] due to its fundamental importance. While online methods [13,16] are usually lightweight and require minimal preprocessing, they often incur high query latency on large graphs. In contrast, recent research has primarily focused on index-based methods, such as PPL [22], Ferrari [17], TOL [27], IP [21], and BFL [19], which aim to reduce query latency by precomputing auxiliary index structures that efficiently encode reachability

I. Awan et al. (Eds.): WISE 2025, LNCS 16367, pp. 361–373, 2026.
https://doi.org/10.1007/978-981-95-7394-3_25

information. Reachability indexing methods are typically classified into three main frameworks: *2-hop labeling*, *tree cover*, and *transitive closure (TC)* [26]. 2-hop labeling assigns each vertex in-labels and out-labels, and checks reachability via label intersections. Tree cover methods use interval labels from a spanning tree and augment them with non-tree edges. Transitive closure methods precompute all reachable pairs, enabling fast queries but requiring large indexes.

Motivation. While recent surveys [7,24,26] review reachability indexes, comprehensive experiments remain lacking. Prior studies use limited datasets (often low-degree graphs) and lack unified metrics for balancing query time and index size. This gap in empirical understanding can be summarized as follows:

- *Dataset:* Existing evaluations are typically conducted on graphs with low out-degrees (usually ≤ 3), which fail to capture the structural complexity of real-world networks. This motivates the need for a broader benchmark that includes graphs with diverse degree distributions.
- *Metric:* Most prior studies emphasize query latency as the primary evaluation metric, overlooking its trade-off with index size. A unified metric is needed to better capture the practical efficiency under resource constraints.
- *Analysis:* Despite the proliferation of indexing methods, there is little guidance on method selection. This motivates the need for systematic guidance to assist users in selecting appropriate methods for varying scenarios.

Contributions. In the domain of reachability indexing, existing methods can be broadly categorized into three major frameworks: **2-hop labeling based**, **tree cover based**, and **transitive closure (TC) based** [26]. To ensure a representative and comprehensive evaluation, we select one widely recognized method from each framework: **TOL** [27] for 2-hop labeling, **FERRARI** [17] for tree cover, and **BFL** [19] for transitive closure. These three methods span the spectrum of *label-only* and *label+graph* designs, and reflect distinct algorithmic philosophies in balancing index size and query efficiency. We evaluate them on 1,400 structurally diverse graphs and 38,688 varied queries to reveal their relative strengths across different graph and query characteristics. Our main contributions are summarised as follows.

- We construct a new benchmark suite with graphs that span a wide range of degree distributions, including graphs with high average and maximum degrees, which are underrepresented in past evaluations.
- We introduce the *cost-performance* metric that simultaneously considers index size and query latency, normalized against a BFS baseline, providing a fairer basis for evaluating practical trade-offs.
- We propose a feature-driven framework, validated by decision trees, to show how graph and query features impact indexing and to guide method selection that balances speed, space, and complexity.

2 Background

This paper considers simple directed graphs denoted as $G = (V, E)$, where V is the set of vertices and $E \subseteq V \times V$ is the set of directed edges. We define $n = |V|$ as the number of vertices and $m = |E|$ as the number of edges. A vertex with no incoming edges is referred to as a *source*, while a vertex with no outgoing edges is referred to as a *sink*.

Definition 1 (Reachability). *A sequence of vertices $s = v_0 \rightarrow \cdots \rightarrow v_k = t$, where $k \geq 0$, is called an s-t path if for each consecutive pair (v_i, v_{i+1}), there exists an edge $(v_i, v_{i+1}) \in E$. We write $s \rightsquigarrow t$ to indicate that there exists at least one path from s to t.*

Definition 2 (Reachability Query). *Given two vertices u and v in a graph, a reachability query determines whether $u \rightsquigarrow v$ holds. If u can reach v, then $Query(u, v) =$ `true`; otherwise, $Query(u, v) =$ `false`.*

In the graph depicted in Fig. 1, the following reachability queries hold: $Query(1, 3) =$ `true`, $Query(3, 1) =$ `false`, and $Query(1, 7) =$ `true`.

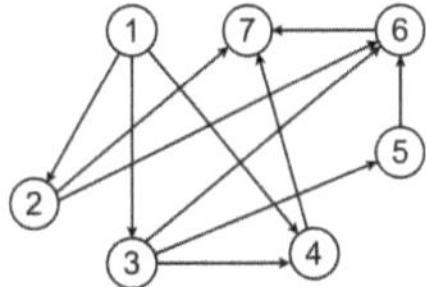

Fig. 1. An Example DAG

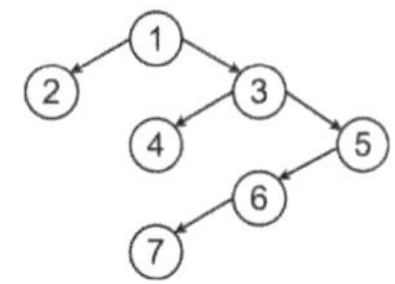

Fig. 2. Spanning Tree

Definition 3 (Directed Acyclic Graph). *A directed acyclic graph (DAG) is a directed graph that contains no cycles; that is, there exists no path that starts and ends at the same vertex while following the direction of the edges.*

In a DAG, all edges are oriented in a manner that prohibits any cyclic traversal, ensuring a strict directional flow.

Definition 4 (Spanning Tree). *A spanning tree of an undirected graph $G = (V, E)$ is a subgraph $T = (V, E_T)$ satisfying the following conditions: (1) T is a tree, i.e., it is connected and acyclic; (2) T spans G, meaning $V_T = V$; (3) $E_T \subseteq E$; and (4) T contains exactly $n - 1$ edges, where $n = |V|$.*

Definition 5 (Tree Edge and Non-Tree Edge). *Given a DAG $G = (V, E)$ and its spanning tree $T = (V, E_T)$, any edge $(u, v) \in E_T$ is referred to as a tree edge, while any edge $(u, v) \in E \setminus E_T$ is termed a non-tree edge.*

A spanning tree of the graph shown in Fig. 1 is illustrated in Fig. 2. In this example, the edge $(1, 3)$ is a tree edge, whereas the edge $(2, 7)$ is a non-tree edge.

Definition 6 (Topological Sorting [8]). *Topological sorting is a technique used to linearly order the vertices of a DAG such that for every directed edge (u, v), vertex u precedes vertex v in the ordering.*

Topological orderings are not necessarily unique; multiple valid orderings may exist for a given DAG. In the graph illustrated in Fig. 1, possible topological orderings include $[1, 2, 3, 5, 6, 7, 4]$ and $[1, 3, 4, 2, 5, 6, 7]$.

3 Method Selection

In the domain of reachability indexing, most methods can be categorized into three major frameworks: **2-hop labeling based**, **tree cover based**, and **transitive closure(TC) based** [26]. In this study, we select a representative method from each framework–**TOL** [27] for 2-hop labeling based indexing, **FERRARI** [17] for tree cover based indexing, and **BFL** [19] for transitive closure based indexing. Importantly, these methods span across two fundamental classes of indexing strategies: *label-only* and *label+graph* methods.

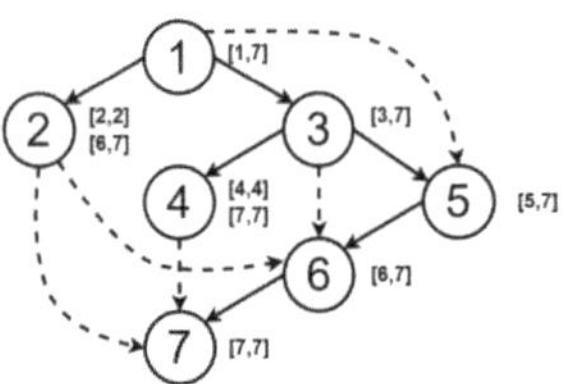

Fig. 3. An Example of Tree Cover

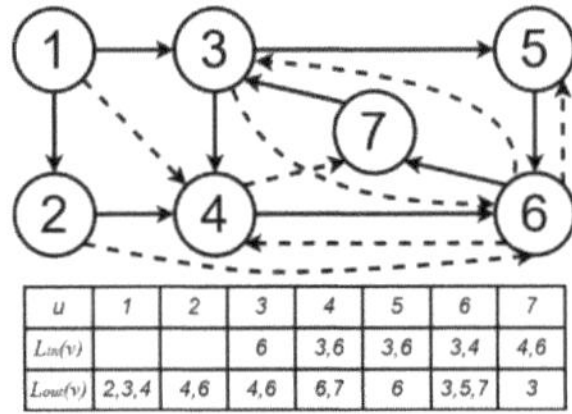

u	1	2	3	4	5	6	7
Lin(v)			6	3,6	3,6	3,4	4,6
Lout(v)	2,3,4	4,6	4,6	6,7	6	3,5,7	3

Fig. 4. An Example for 2-hop

3.1 2-Hop Labeling Framework Representative Method: TOL [27]

Overview of 2-hop Labeling [5]. 2-hop labeling is a classical method for answering reachability queries in directed graphs. For each vertex v, two sets are maintained: 1) **In-label** $\mathcal{L}_{\text{in}}(v)$: intermediate vertices from which v is reachable, 2) **Out-label** $\mathcal{L}_{\text{out}}(v)$: intermediate vertices that are reachable from v. Given a query (u, v), determine reachability by checking whether $\mathcal{L}_{\text{out}}(u) \cap \mathcal{L}_{\text{in}}(v) \neq \emptyset$. Figure 4 shows an example for 2-hop reachability labelling.

Overview of TOL [27]. TOL [27] introduces a vertex-level total order $l : V \rightarrow \{1, \ldots, |V|\}$ when constructing 2-hop labeling. Its core contributions include:

- **Label pruning**: Add u to $\mathcal{L}_{\text{in}}(v)$ only if its reachability is not already covered by other lower-level vertices, ensuring minimal and essential labels.
- **Order sensitivity**: The total order l strongly affects label size. Heuristic orders avoid redundancy and yield smaller, more efficient indexes.

- **Post-refinement**: TOL [27] reduces label size by iteratively removing and reinserting vertices to optimize label size without full reconstruction.

TOL [27] ensures minimal labels, leverages vertex order to compact labels, and supports iterative refinement without full reconstruction.

3.2 Tree Cover Framework Representative Method: FERRARI [17]

Overview of Tree Cover [1]**.** Tree-cover indexing represents reachability via a spanning tree and vertex intervals. In the tree, v is reachable from u if $\pi(v) \in I_T(u)$. For general DAGs, non-tree edges are handled by propagating intervals in reverse topological order, yielding $I(v)$ for each vertex. A query $s \rightarrow t$ is answered by checking whether $\pi(t)$ lies in $I(s)$. An example of a tree cover for Fig. 1 is illustrated in Fig. 3.

Overview of FERRARI [17]**.** FERRARI [17] builds upon the tree cover framework and introduces several key improvements to achieve scalability, compactness, and low query latency. Its core contributions include:

- **Mixed intervals:** Assigns exact intervals (no false positives) and approximate intervals (compact but with false positives), balancing size and speed.
- **Interval merging:** Uses dynamic programming to minimize approximate intervals, with a greedy heuristic for large graphs.
- **Pruning:** Improves queries with seed labels and topological filters.

FERRARI [17] bests tree-cover methods on large graphs, offering a flexible trade-off between index size and query latency for scalable reachability indexing.

3.3 Transitive Closure Framework Representative Method: BFL [19]

Overview of Transitive Closure [18]**.** Transitive closure precomputes reachability in a Boolean matrix M, enabling $O(1)$ queries but requiring $O(n^2)$ space. To reduce space, techniques like chain cover, interval labeling, and set covers have been proposed, though they incur heavy preprocessing and scale poorly.

Overview of BFL [19]**.** BFL [19] uses Bloom filters to offer low construction cost, small label size, and fast queries. Its main contributions are:

- **Containment-based pruning:** Each vertex u stores $L_{out}(u)$ and $L_{in}(u)$ by Bloom filters; Reachability is tested by subset checks.
- **Bounded false positives:** The false positive rate incurred by the Bloom filter can be analytically bounded and controlled, enabling reliable pruning.
- **Vertex merging:** Vertices with similar reachability are merged and hashes the representatives instead, to control filter size and maintain accuracy.

By combining transitive closure with the space efficiency of Bloom filters, BFL [19] provides a practical balance between index size, construction time, and query performance, making it practical for large-scale graphs.

Table 1. Complexity of Different methods

Method	Index Size	Query Time
Ferrari [17]	$O((k_f + s_f)n)$	$O(k_f)$ or $O(m+n)$
TOL [27]	$O(nm^{1/2})$	$O(\|L(s)\| + \|L(t)\|)$
BFL [19]	$(2\lceil s_{bfl}/8\rceil n)$ (Byte)	$O(s_{bfl})$ or $O(s_{bfl}n+m)$

[1] k_f is the number of intervals per vertex and s_f is the number of seed vertices. $|L(s)|$ and $|L(t)|$ are the number of elements in the labels of vertices s and t, respectively. s_{bfl} represents the size of the Bloom filter (in bits).

3.4 Performance Analysis

In this paper, we focus on two metrics: index size and query time. Table 1 shows complexities for FERRARI [17], TOL [27], and BFL [19]. The query time of the *label-only* method (e.g., TOL [27]) is fixed, while the *label+graph* method (e.g., BFL [19] and FERRARI [17]) is more uncertain but nearly linear in index size.

4 Experimental

To facilitate a comprehensive evaluation of reachability indexing methods, we construct a synthetic dataset of generated graphs and reachability queries.

Graph Generation. We generate directed acyclic graphs using two models:

- **Random DAG (RDD)**: Edges are randomly sampled from all acyclic vertex pairs (u, v) with $u < v$, ensuring the resulting graph remains a DAG.
- **Layered DAG (LDAG)**: Vertices are partitioned into layers, with edges only from earlier to later layers, forming a hierarchy.

We vary the number of vertices $n \in \{10, 15, 20, 25, 30\} \times 10^3$ and the number of edges $m \in \{3, 6, 10, 20, 30, 40, 50\} \times 10^4$, and for LDAG graphs, the number of layers $l \in \{5, 10, 20, 30, 50, 80, 100\}$. For each parameter setting, five graphs are generated to account for randomness, resulting in a total of 1400 graph instances.

Query Generation. We first compute exact reachability for all vertices via reverse topological traversal. Source vertices are then bucketed by reachability size (e.g., $[1, 10)$, $[10, 100)$, ..., $[10^k, n]$). For each bucket, we generate 100,000 positive and 100,000 negative queries. Additionally, four mixed sets are created with 20%, 40%, 60%, and 80% positive ratios. In total, 38,688 query sets are generated to support robust, fine-grained evaluation.

Parameter Semantics and Method Selection. We adopt representative configurations based on each method's design: **BFL** [19]: Bk indicates a Bloom filter size of k. The merged vertex count is fixed at 800. **FERRARI** [17]: Fk uses k

intervals per node with 32 seeds. Fn is a label-only variant with unlimited intervals and 0 seeds, treated separately from standard FERRARI. **TOL** [27]: `lower` and `upper` denote variants based on ranking strategies during label construction.

Experimental Environment. Construction and query of all methods[1] were conducted on a server equipped with 2× Intel(R) Xeon(R) Gold 6342 CPUs @ 2.80GHz (96 logical cores, 48 physical cores) and approximately 503 GB of RAM, running Ubuntu 22.04.1 LTS. All C++ programs were compiled using `g++` with the `-std=c++17` standard and the `-O2` optimization level.

Metrics Selection. In this work, we selected two traditional parameters: index size and query time. To comprehensively evaluate the trade-offs between index size and query efficiency, we introduce a new, unified cost-performance metric:

$$\text{Cost-Performance} = \frac{T_{\text{bfs}}}{S_{\text{index}} \times T_{\text{query}}}, \tag{1}$$

where T_{bfs} denotes the query time of the baseline method using breadth-first search (BFS), S_{index} represents the size of the reachability index (in MB), and T_{query} is the average query time of the tested method (in milliseconds). This metric reflects how much speed-up a method achieves over BFS per unit storage cost (in 1/MB). A higher value indicates better cost-performance.

Analysis Methods in Three Metrics. Figure 5(a) shows the average cost-performance. BFL [19] performs best, especially with small parameters, but declines as index size grows. FERRARI [17] decreases steadily due to larger indexes and moderate efficiency. Fn is a special case: as $n \to \infty$, it degenerates into a *label-only* method like TOL [27], achieving faster queries and higher cost-performance but with much larger indexes. TOL [27] also offers the fastest queries but suffers from large index size, yielding only moderate cost-performance.

Figure 5(b) shows BFL [19] and standard FERRARI [17] keep indexes nearly linear in size, while TOL [27] and Fn are often an order of magnitude larger.

Figure 5(c) shows query times: TOL [27] and Fn are fastest, followed by BFL [19], then standard FERRARI [17].

Overall, query time alone is insufficient; index size must also be considered. The cost-performance metric provides a unified measure to balance this trade-off.

Analysis Under Out-Degree Variance. Variance of out degree is the influential feature for determining the optimal indexing method. To further investigate its impact, we partition the dataset using the threshold $\theta = 12.68$.

The performance of three methods for graphs with high out-degree variance show little variation compared to all configurations. Figure 6 illustrates the results for graphs with lower out-degree variance. In this scenario, the advantage of BFL [19] diminishes, and TOL [27] shows a competitive cost-performance.

---

[1] The source code for all evaluation and subset selection is available online. **BFL** [19]: https://github.com/BoleynSu/bfl. **FERRARI** [17]: https://github.com/steps/Ferrari. **TOL** [27]: https://sourceforge.net/projects/totalorderlabeling/.

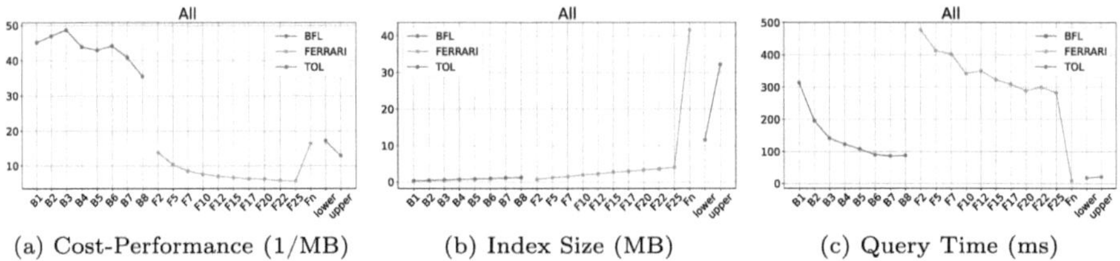

(a) Cost-Performance (1/MB) (b) Index Size (MB) (c) Query Time (ms)

Fig. 5. Performance comparison across all configurations.

This is due to its fast query time and moderately sized index. FERRARI [17] still performs worse than the other two methods.

The experiments demonstrate that **variance of out degree** plays a critical role in shaping the trade-off between index size and query speed. BFL [19] is best suited for graphs with high variance due to its compact structure and scalable query time, while TOL [27] becomes increasingly favorable on low-variance graphs where its label-only structure yields optimal latency. This suggests that simple structure-aware rules (e.g., based on degree variance) can guide the selection of indexing strategies for reachability queries.

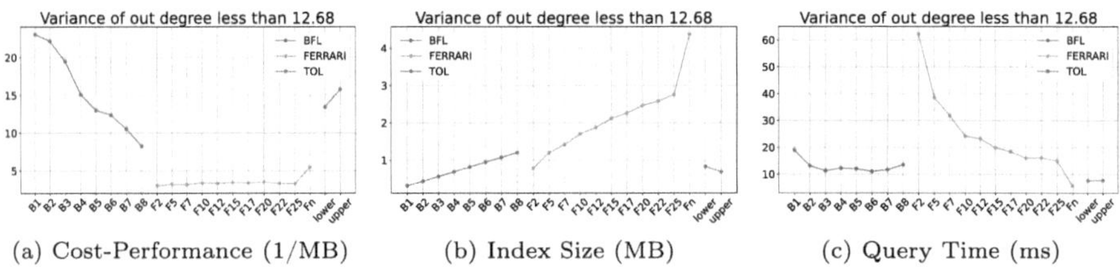

(a) Cost-Performance (1/MB) (b) Index Size (MB) (c) Query Time (ms)

Fig. 6. Performance comparison for graphs with lower variance of out degree.

Analysis Under False Ratio. False ratio is another key feature influencing the optimal method choice. To investigate its effect in isolation, we partition the dataset based on the threshold $\theta = 0.90$.

The performance of three methods for the high false-ratio subset show little variation compared to all configurations. Figure 7 illustrates the results for samples with low **false ratio**. In this case, BFL [19] still performs best, but its advantage is less pronounced. Its cost-performance gradually decreases with increasing parameter (Fig. 7a). TOL [27] and Fn start to show better cost-performance under low **false ratio** than high **false ratio**, due to its extremely low query latency (Fig. 7c) and acceptable index size (Fig. 7b). Standard FERRARI [17] continues to lag in this group, as its cost performance remains relatively low across all parameter configurations.

False ratio strongly guides method choice: with high values, BFL [19] excels via robustness and small indexes; with low values, label-only methods (e.g.,

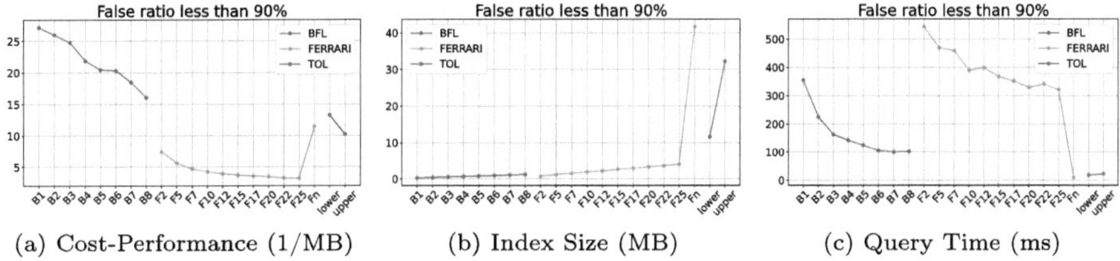

(a) Cost-Performance (1/MB) (b) Index Size (MB) (c) Query Time (ms)

Fig. 7. Performance comparison for samples with low false ratio.

TOL [27]) are preferable for fast queries. Label+graph methods lag due to costly BFS/DFS, underscoring the need for adaptive, query-aware selection.

Analysis Under Query Source Reachability. To further understand how query characteristics influence method performance, we partition queries based on the number of reachable vertices from the source vertex. Specifically, we define five bins: **from 1 to n (b0)**, **from 1 to 10 (b1)**, **from 10 to 100 (b2)**, **from 100 to 1000 (b3)** and **from 1000 to n (b4)**.

Figure 8 shows query time trends across the five bins. We find observations:

- In **b1**, As *label+graph* methods, BFL [19] and standard FERRARI [17] have similar query times. The difference is that BFL [19] slows down as the index size increases, but standard FERRARI [17] becomes faster. As *label-only* methods, Fn and TOL [27] show significant differences, with Fn performing best and TOL [27] performing worst.
- In **b2**, standard FERRARI [17] converged to BFL [19] as the scale increased.
- In **b3** and **b4**, The performance of TOL [27] is close to that of Fn, with two *label-only* methods performing best. BFL [19] starts to speed up as the index size increases, similar to standard FERRARI [17] methods, but the overall performance of BFL [19] is better than that of standard FERRARI [17].

label+graph methods slow as source reachability levels grow, while *label-only* methods are less affected. Among them, FERRARI [17] gains speed with larger indexes, but BFL [19] slows in low source reachability levels due to costly label checks on large bit arrays. This stems from different fallback strategies: BFL prunes with labels during BFS/DFS, whereas FERRARI skips labels. Thus, in low source reachability levels, BFL [19] suffers from costly label checks on large bit arrays, while in high source reachability levels, the efficient pruning enabled by large bit arrays has a more significant impact.

Since the index size remains constant across queries, cost-performance results variations are primarily driven by changes in query efficiency. We observe that in **b1**, **b2** and **b3**, BFL [19] starts strong when index size is small, but the cost performance declines rapidly with the index size increase. FERRARI [17] and TOL [27] are more stable, But none of them are as good as BFL [19].

As source reachability increases, query time dominates cost-performance: all methods improve, but the advantage of BFL [19] diminishes.

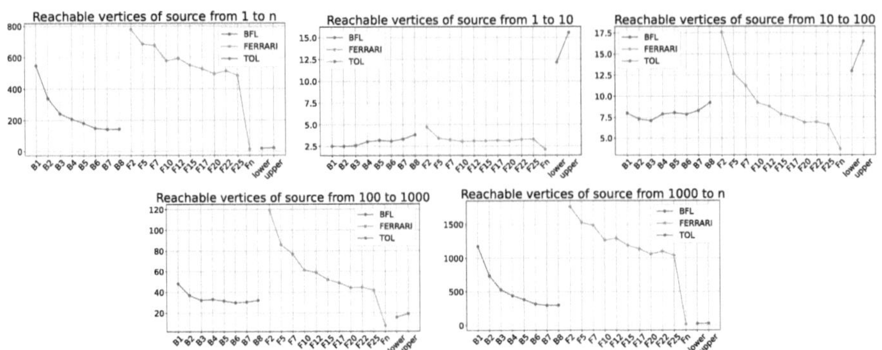

Fig. 8. Average query time (ms) as source reachability level increases.

Analysis Under Out-Degree. To explore how graph structures affect index and query, we group reachability queries based on the average out-degree of the vertices. Specifically, we analyze five intervals: *from 0 to 10 (d0)*, *from 11 to 20 (d1)*, *from 21 to 30 (d2)*, *from 31 to 40 (d3)* and *from 41 to 50 (d4)*.

For **d2**, **d3**, and **d4**, Standard FERRARI [17] shows increasing performance and eventually converges to the BFL [19] region. This implies standard FERRARI [17] benefits more from increasing out-degree. It may be because the tree cover framework has an advantage over the TC framework in this regard.

Across all intervals, Fn and TOL [27] (*label-only* methods) maintain fast query times. The *label+graph* method slows down as the degree increases, while the *label-only* method is less affected.

Index size exhibits significant growth as vertex degree increases. In **d0**, all methods are within the same scale, except for Fn, which is the largest. As degree increases, TOL [27] ultimately surpassing Fn.

The *label+graph* method shows no change in index size as the degree increases, while the *label-only* method is greatly affected. It is worth noting that the two *label-only* methods, Fn and TOL [27], reach their maximum index size at **d1** and **d2**, respectively, and then decrease as the degree increases.

Figure 9 shows cost-performance trends. We find observations:

- **d0**: BFL [19] achieves the highest Cost-Performance and drops quickly as index size increases; FERRARI [17] the lowest; TOL [27] is moderate.
- **d1**, **d2** and **d3**: FERRARI [17] and TOL [27] become closer. BFL [19] fluctuates as index size increases, but remains competitive.
- **d4**: BFL [19] still dominates Cost-Performance. The cost-performance of Fn is gradually becoming similar to that of BFL [19].

Unlike previous experiments where the index size remained constant, in this experiment, the index size of the two *label-only* methods, TOL [27] and Fn, increased with degree, reached a peak, and then decreased. This makes the Cost-Performance of Fn comparable to that of BFL [19] at **d4**. BFL [19] demonstrates stable index size and query performance, achieving better Cost-Performance in

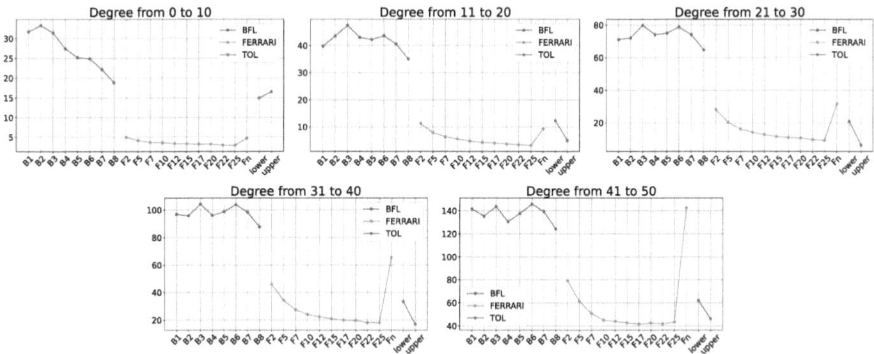

Fig. 9. Average cost-performance (1/MB) as vertex out-degree increases.

all cases. It is worth noting that, except for **d0**, the Cost-Performance of BFL [19] fluctuates with index size rather than decreasing.

Verification with Decision Trees. To verify which graph and query features influence method selection, we use decision tree models for their interpretability. Our dataset includes 38,688 graph-query configurations, each labeled with the most cost performance method. We first trained a decision tree achieving 100% training and 98.01% test accuracy. Feature importance analysis revealed three key features: 1) **variance of out degree**: Fluctuation level of all vertex out-degrees. 2) **false ratio**: Percentage of queries with negative results. 3) **average reachable ratio**: Percentage of vertices that can be reached from the source vertex in the query relative to the total number of vertices. To improve interpretability, we trained a third tree with depth limited to 3. As shown in Fig. 10, it captures key thresholds and achieves 92.85% accuracy, making it suitable for real-time method selection.

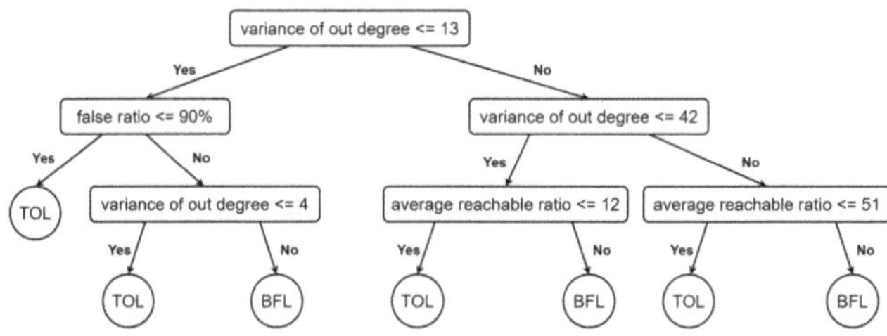

Fig. 10. Simplified decision tree using only 3 features and limited depth.

5 Method Selection and Practical Guidelines

Based on our evaluation, we summarize the use cases of the three methods:

TOL [27]: Minimal Latency, High Space Cost. TOL [27] offers minimal query latency, making it ideal for latency-critical tasks. However, its large, fixed-size index limits flexibility and suitability in space-constrained settings.

BFL [19]: Best Cost-Performance Trade-off. BFL [19] excels in most cases, especially with high false query rates or out-degree variance. Its pruning-based design makes it a reliable default for large, sparse graphs.

FERRARI [17]: Most Adaptable and Tunable. FERRARI [17] adapts between *label+graph* and *label-only* by tuning parameters, making it suitable for different environments.

6 Conclusion

This paper systematically compares TOL [27], FERRARI [17], and BFL [19] using a unified cost-performance metric. TOL offers fastest queries but high space cost; BFL achieves best efficiency; FERRARI provides adaptability. Decision tree analysis further shows simple features can guide method choice. Each method has distinct strengths, and the optimal choice depends on specific trade-offs.

References

1. Agrawal, R., Borgida, A., Jagadish, H.V.: Efficient management of transitive relationships in large data and knowledge bases. In: Proceedings of ACM SIGMOD International Conference on Management of Data, pp. 253–262 (1989)
2. Chen, Z., Chen, K., Wen, D., Yang, Z., Li, W., Zhang, Y.: Accelerating shortest path counting on road networks. In: 2025 IEEE 41st International Conference on Data Engineering (ICDE), pp. 3508–3521. IEEE (2025)
3. Chen, Z., Liang, K., Yuan, L., Zhang, W., Yang, Z.: Recent advances in efficient dynamic graph processing. Appl. Sci. **15**(11), 6003 (2025)
4. Cheng, J., Huang, S., Wu, H., Fu, A.W.C.: TF-label: a topological-folding labeling scheme for reachability querying in a large graph. In: Proceedings of the ACM SIGMOD International Conference on Management of Data (2013)
5. Cohen, E., Halperin, E., Kaplan, H., Zwick, U.: Reachability and distance queries via 2-hop labels. SIAM J. Comput. **32**(5), 1338–1355 (2003)
6. Dhia, I.B.: Access control in social networks: a reachability-based approach. In: Proceedings of the 2012 Joint EDBT/ICDT Workshops, pp. 227–232 (2012)
7. He, H., et al.: A survey on efficient graph reachability queries. In: Pacific-Asia Conference on Knowledge Discovery and Data Mining, pp. 58–77. Springer, Singapore (2025)
8. Kahn, A.B.: Topological sorting of large networks. Commun. ACM (1962)
9. Li, X., Hao, K., Yang, Z., Cao, X., Zhang, W.: Hop-constrained S-T simple path enumeration in large uncertain graphs. In: Australasian Database Conference, pp. 115–127. Springer, Cham (2022)
10. Li, X., et al.: Hop-constrained S-T simple path enumeration in billion-scale labelled graphs. In: International Conference on Web Information Systems Engineering (2022)

11. Lyu, Q., Li, Y., He, B., Gong, B.: DBL: efficient reachability queries on dynamic graphs, pp. 761–777 (2021)
12. Merz, F., Sanders, P.: Preach: a fast lightweight reachability index using pruning and contraction hierarchies. In: Proceedings of the European Symposium on Algorithms, pp. 701–712 (2014)
13. Pang, Y., Zou, L., Liu, Y.: IFCA: index-free community-aware reachability processing over large dynamic graphs. In: 2023 IEEE 39th International Conference on Data Engineering (ICDE) (2023)
14. Qiu, X., et al.: Real-time constrained cycle detection in large dynamic graphs. Proc. VLDB Endow. **11**(12), 1876–1888 (2018)
15. Scholz, B., Zhang, C., Cifuentes, C.: User-input dependence analysis via graph reachability. In: Proceedings of the 2008 8th IEEE International Working Conference on Source Code Analysis and Manipulation, pp. 25–34 (2008)
16. Sengupta, N., Bagchi, A., Ramanath, M., Bedathur, S.: ARROW: approximating reachability using random walks over web-scale graphs. In: 35th IEEE International Conference on Data Engineering, ICDE 2019, pp. 470–481. IEEE (2019)
17. Seufert, S., Anand, A., Bedathur, S.J., Weikum, G.: Ferrari: flexible and efficient reachability range assignment for graph indexing. In: Proceedings of IEEE International Conference on Data Engineering 2013, pp. 1009–1020 (2013)
18. Simon, K.: An improved algorithm for transitive closure on acyclic digraphs. Theor. Comput. Sci. **58**(1–3), 325–346 (1988)
19. Su, J., Zhu, Q., Wei, H., Yu, J.X.: Reachability querying: can it be even faster? IEEE Trans. Knowl. Data Eng. **29**, 683–697 (2017)
20. Wang, H., He, H., Yang, J., Yu, P.S., Yu, J.X.: Dual labeling: answering graph reachability queries in constant time. In: Proceedings of IEEE 29th International Conference on Data Engineering (2006)
21. Wei, H., Yu, J.X., Lu, C., Jin, R.: Reachability querying: an independent permutation labeling approach. VLDB J. **27**(1), 1–26 (2018)
22. Yano, Y., Akiba, T., Iwata, Y., Yoshida, Y.: Fast and scalable reachability queries on graphs by pruned labeling with landmarks and paths. In: 22nd CIKM 2013: San Francisco, CA, USA (2013)
23. Yildirim, H., Chaoji, V., Zaki, M.J.: Dagger: a scalable index for reachability queries in large dynamic graphs (2013)
24. Yu, J.X., Cheng, J.: Graph reachability queries: a survey. In: Managing and Mining Graph Data, Advances in Database Systems, vol. 40, pp. 181–215. Springer (2010)
25. Yıldırım, H., Chaoji, V., Zaki, M.J.: Grail: a scalable index for reachability queries in very large graphs. VLDB J. **21**(4), 509–534 (2012)
26. Zhang, C., Bonifati, A., Özsu, M.T.: An overview of reachability indexes on graphs. In: Companion of the 2023 International Conference on Management of Data, SIGMOD/PODS 2023, pp. 61–68. ACM (2023)
27. Zhu, A.D., Lin, W., Wang, S., Xiao, X.: Reachability queries on large dynamic graphs: a total order approach, pp. 1323–1334 (2014)

Context-Aware Hybrid Neuro-Symbolic Approach for Knowledge Graph Enrichment

Marwa Boulakbech(✉) and Rouaa Wannous

L3i Laboratory, University of La Rochelle, La Rochelle, France
{marwa.boulakbech,rouaa.wannous}@univ-lr.fr

Abstract. Knowledge graphs (KGs) are a powerful paradigm that produces structured representations of heterogeneous data for semantic data integration. Nevertheless, it remains a challenge to ensure rich and up-to-date KGs. Recently, large language models (LLMs) have demonstrated capabilities in understanding language, offering opportunities to automate KG construction and enrichment.

In this work, we address the problem of enriching KGs with contextual information collected from multiple sources. We propose a context-aware hybrid neuro-symbolic approach. This approach combines the capabilities of language understanding of LLMs with the formal reasoning which is provided by semantic representations. Our approach supports contextual triple generation, semantic alignment of entities and relations, constraint validation, and dynamic ontology evolution. We conduct experiments on real-world KG and compare the proposed approach to state-of-the-art methods. Moreover, it provides a transparent process by involving users in the loop and ensures a more trustworthy human–AI collaboration.

Keywords: Knowledge Graph · Neuro-Symbolic AI · Large Language Model · Hybrid reasoning

1 Introduction

Knowledge Graphs (KGs) are structured semantic representations that describe heterogeneous data through entities and their relationships in a graph format. They are built on triples (subject, predicate, object) in a machine-readable way, making them useful for a wide range of intelligent applications, such as question answering [19], knowledge discovery [2], and recommendation systems [3].

Dynamic KGs that adapt and grow with new data and changing contexts are critical for adaptive, context-sensitive AI systems. However, maintaining comprehensive, up-to-date, and semantically rich KGs are highly challenging tasks. It requires integrating data from modeling nuanced and context-dependent relationships and ensuring semantic validity throughout the enrichment process.

I. Awan et al. (Eds.): WISE 2025, LNCS 16367, pp. 374–389, 2026.
https://doi.org/10.1007/978-981-95-7394-3_26

Traditional KG enrichment approaches are based on manual curation to define the relevant entities and relationships, and populate the graph with valid facts. They are reliable but time-consuming, expensive, and difficult to scale to large and evolving domains. Neural-based approaches using deep learning techniques provide more flexibility but often struggle to handle domain-specific terminology, contextual semantics, and ontology alignment.

In recent years, large language models (LLMs) have demonstrated improvements in the KG engineering field through their contextual understanding and reasoning capabilities [8,11]. However, applying LLMs to KG still faces several challenges. LLMs may generate inconsistent or redundant facts due to the lack of an explicit, unified schema [13]. In addition, most approaches treat LLMs as generators and neglect structured validation and symbolic reasoning, both of which are crucial for maintaining the integrity of knowledge. To address these limitations, hybrid AI combines the strengths of neural models—especially LLMs—with the reasoning capability of symbolic approaches. This neuro-symbolic paradigm establishes a connection between the flexibility of natural language understanding and the formal consistency required by knowledge graphs.

In this paper, we focus on *"How to automatically extract rich, contextual knowledge, ensuring the alignment, consistency, and evolution of the underlying knowledge graph"*. For this purpose, we propose a context-aware hybrid neuro-symbolic KG enrichment approach that combines LLMs for contextual information extraction with ontology-based reasoning and validation. Specifically, we introduce the concept of generating triples using external situational data, such as temporal, spatial, environmental, or user-specific information. These triples are then mapped to the entities and relations in the knowledge graph. Finally, we facilitate dynamic ontology evolution through human-in-the-loop validation. Unlike conventional enrichment methods, we propose a novel perspective using Retrieval-Augmented Generation (RAG). RAG combines external knowledge retrieval with LLM-based generation. It is a Graph-RAG-like framework where the knowledge graph serves both as a retrieval source and an enrichment target. Our approach extends this paradigm, traditionally used for question answering, to support ontology-guided triple generation from heterogeneous context data, validation, and schema evolution, thereby enriching the KG. We propose our contributions to this paper as follows:

- A novel hybrid neuro-symbolic framework for context-aware KG enrichment, combining LLM-driven extraction with ontology-based validation and reasoning.
- An ontology evolution component for the discovery, alignment, and integration of novel classes and properties suggested by LLMs, along with a symbolic validation mechanism for entity/relation mapping with human-in-the-loop verification to ensure the trustworthiness of generated triples.
- The practical impact of our approach in a cultural heritage tourism scenario using a real-world use case implementation based on the Datatourisme KG.

The paper is organized as follows: Sect. 2 provides an overview of the state-of-the-art; Sect. 3 presents the problem definition; Sects. 4, 5 describe the proposed approach and the case study; Sect. 6 describes the implementation and the evaluation; and finally Sect. 7 concludes this paper.

2 Related Work

KG construction and enrichment approaches can be divided into four categories: (1) Traditional symbolic approaches, (2) neural-based models, (3) LLM-based methods, and (4) neuro-symbolic pipelines.

The symbolic approaches are mainly rules-based and ontology-guided methods that rely on predefined rules and pattern mining techniques to extract and validate triples [4]. These methods provide explainability and logical consistency. However, they often require manual effort by experts, limiting their scalability across domains.

The advent of deep learning offers powerful neural architectures for KG completion and enrichment. Transformer-based models, such as BERT, are increasingly used to extract, align, and generate structured knowledge from unstructured or semi-structured data with minimal feature engineering [6]. In addition, embedding-based techniques, such as translational models, tensor factorization, and graph neural networks aim to learn representations of entities and relations for link prediction. While these approaches enable more flexibility and scalability, they typically lack explainability and do not incorporate external information and schema-level constraints.

More recently, LLM have emerged as versatile tools for KG construction [13,17]. These methods leverage pre-trained language models to generate triples, entity and relation types through zero-shot prompting, few-shot learning, or fine-tuning. For instance, [7] proposes a semi-automated pipeline using open-source LLMs to assist domain experts in constructing both ontologies and instance-level KGs. [20] presents the extract-define-canonicalize pipeline for KG construction without a predefined schema. The model does not deeply integrate formal ontology constraints or symbolic reasoning components. Similarly, [1] introduces an iterative zero-shot prompting framework for constructing knowledge graphs without relying on training data. While offering a flexible and scalable alternative to supervised pipelines, it lacks structured validation and robustness across domains. [16] proposes a training-free method that enhances triple extraction from LLMs by combining entity filtering with structured prompts. However, it does not address schema alignment or ontology grounding. [18] introduces ACKG LLM, a schema-aware and LLM-embedded adaptive framework for constructing knowledge graphs across domains. However, it does not address schema alignment or ontology grounding. Some approaches focus on the enrichment problem, [9] introduces KARMA, a multi-agent framework that employs specialized LLM-based agents to automate knowledge graph Enrichment. However, it lacks symbolic validation, that limits its consistency. [12] presents GPToLODS+, which combines LLM responses with large-scale RDF repositories to facilitate knowledge enrichment for the cultural heritage domain, but the method does not support adaptive schema evolution.

Currently, studies focus on neuro-symbolic approaches which allow for the combination of the generalization ability of LLMs with symbolic reasoning and ontology alignment. [10] proposes a neuro-symbolic framework for relational discovery in cultural heritage KGs. The method focuses on relational ranking and explanation, without addressing new entity or schema integration that limits its applicability for full KG enrichment pipelines. [5] describes a neuro-symbolic pipeline to enrich graphs with real-world concepts and relationships. The approach uses heuristics and crowd-based metrics for integrity validation but lacks contextualization and ontology expansion. Few approaches involve humans in the validation process. [15] develops LXS, an intelligent assistant, to facilitate the mapping of relational databases to KG with user-driven validation. While allowing user interaction with the semantic mapping process, the method is limited to structured data.

Different from previous studies, we combine symbolic constraints with LLM-based triple generation in an integrated context-aware neuro-symbolic pipeline.

3 Problem Definition

Definition 1: Context-aware Knowledge graph enrichment. Given an existing knowledge graph $G = (E, R, T)$, where

- E: set of entities
- R: set of relations describing ontology-defined properties
- $T \subseteq E \times R \times E$: set of RDF triples representing factual knowledge.

Given a set of contextual data sources $S = \{s_1, s_2, ..., s_N\}$ where each s_i is structured, semi-structured, or unstructured input. The goal is to learn a function f_{KG}

$$f_{KG} : C \times \mathcal{O} \rightarrow 2^{T'} \tag{1}$$

that maps each contextual data source s_i into a set of new candidate triples T', where:

- $T' \subseteq E' \times R' \times E' \quad E' \supseteq E \ ; \ R' \supseteq R$
- Entities, relations, or classes may need to be added via ontology evolution

The extended graph $G' = (E', R', T \cup T')$ remains:

- Ontologically consistent with the domain schema O,
- Semantically coherent (new triples do not contradict existing facts)
  - Each triple $(s, p, o) \in T'$ must respect: domain(p)=class(s) range(p)=class(o)

- If the required class or property is missing in O, propose new ontology elements: $\mathcal{O}' = \mathcal{O} \cup \Delta\mathcal{O}$ where, $\Delta\mathcal{O}$ contains new classes or properties suggested by an ontology evolution module.

– Informatively useful, i.e., increases the graph's coverage, depth, and supports personalization capabilities.

Definition 2: LLM-based knowledge graph enrichment. The goal of LLM-based knowledge graph enrichment is to extract ontology-compliant triples from contextual data using large language models, followed by validation in order to incrementally to extend an existing knowledge graph incrementally. Formally:

$$f_{KG}(C, O) = V(f_{IE}(C, O)) \tag{2}$$

– f_{IE} extracts candidate triples. It serves as the semantic mapping submodule within the overall knowledge graph enrichment process.
– V is the validation and reasoning function (symbolic validator+userInLoop).
– The output of f_{KG} is the validated, ontology-compliant enriched triples.

4 Neuro-Symbolic KG Enrichment Approach

The proposed KG enrichment approach overview is illustrated by Fig. 1. It is structured into four main components: *Context Acquisition and Representation*, *Neuro-Symbolic Mapping*, *Ontology Evolution*, and *Validation*.

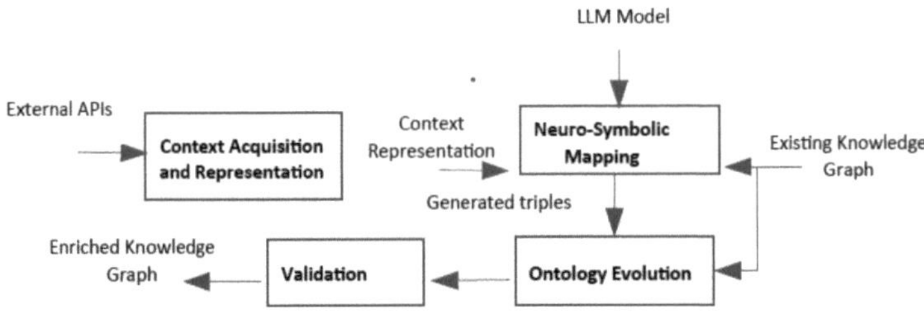

Fig. 1. Hybrid Neuro-Symbolic KG Enrichment Approach Overview.

The process starts by collecting relevant context information from external sources (e.g., Weather API, location API, ...) which typically provide semi-structured data – a mix of structured data with some fields are long-form text-Then, the neuro-symbolic information extraction and semantic mapping component aims to convert contextual data into candidate RDF triples. It combines the generative power and flexibility of large language models with the reasoning capabilities of ontological knowledge representation, leading to high-quality, context-aware knowledge graph enrichment. In cases where extracted information introduces new concepts or properties not present in the existing knowledge graph, the ontology evolution component suggests appropriate schema extensions and updates the ontology accordingly. Finally, to ensure transparency and trustworthiness, we propose human-in-the-loop validation to finalize enrichment wherein domain experts approve or reject the generated triples prior to their insertion into the knowledge graph.

4.1 Context Acquisition and Representation

This component collects, integrates, and prepare external data sources that provide situational, environmental, and user-specific context relevant to knowledge graph enrichment. It introduces dynamic and real-time contextual information into the enrichment pipeline, in order to build personalized, adaptive, and more semantically rich knowledge graph. The acquired contextual information captures multiple dimensions of real-world context, including:

- Environmental conditions (e.g., weather, temperature, climate)
- Temporal dimensions (e.g., time, date, season)
- Geospatial information (e.g., user or event location, geographic proximity)
- User characteristics or preferences (e.g., interests, profile attributes)

This heterogeneous data, gathered from diverse sources such as APIs, sensors, user profiles, or real-time event feeds, is preprocessed into intermediate representations typically modeled as a semantic JSON-like object.

For example, we can consider weather context, location context, temporal context, and user profile as shown in Listing 1.1. In addition, some sources provide semi-structured textual descriptions of events, places, or activities (e.g., "The outdoor art festival features local artists under sunny skies."), which combine structured metadata with free-text elements. This step ensures that rich contextual signals are properly captured to be effectively processed by the subsequent LLM-based information extraction and semantic mapping component.

Listing 1.1. Context data sources and representations

```
Context Type        Representation
Weather             {'weather':'Sunny','temperature':18, 'pollenLevel':'
    High'}
Location            {'latitude':46.1,'longitude':1.15, 'city':'La
    Rochelle'}
Time                {'timestamp':'2025-04-16T10:30:00'}
User Profile        {'preferredActivities':['Hiking','Art Museums','
    Festival'],
                    'healthSituation':'Asthmatic','timePreferences':['
    Afternoon'],
                    'travelMode':['bus','walking],'travelCompanion':'with
     Family'}
Event Description   'The outdoor art festival features local artists
    under sunny skies'
```

4.2 Neuro-Symbolic Information Extraction and Semantic Mapping

The neuro-symbolic mapping component is responsible of generating candidate knowledge graph triples from contextual data by combining the language understanding and semantic generalization capabilities of LLMs with the logical structure and reasoning provided by the ontology schema. Figure 2 describes the process of generating triples by the neuro-symbolic mapping component.

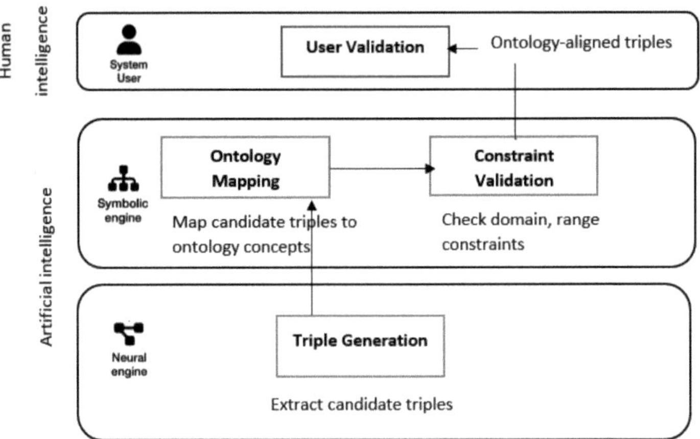

Fig. 2. Process of generating triples.

The neural engine, LLM-based information extraction module, performs contextual semantic parsing that involves extracting candidate entities, predicates, and attributes from input descriptions. This step produces a set of candidate triples T^* in RDF-like form. For example:

- (":Event573", ":hasLocation", ":La Rochelle")
- (":Event573", ":hasWeatherContext", ":Sunny")
- (":Event573", ":isPreferredBy", ":User123")

Next, the symbolic engine maps these candidate triples T^* to the ontology schema $O = (C, P)$, where C is the set of ontology classes and P is the set of properties. This process includes both entity matching and relation matching to ensure consistency with the ontology vocabulary. To filter out invalid or incoherent triples, symbolic constraints checking are applied.

It uses embedding-based semantic similarity to align extracted entities and relations with ontology concepts and properties. Each ontology concept $c \in C$ is encoded into a vector representation $\boldsymbol{v}_c$, based on a pre-trained language model such as Sentence-BERT. Similarly, each candidate entity is encoded as $\boldsymbol{v}_{cand}$. The best matching concept is selected using cosine similarity:

$$c^* = \arg\max_{c \in C} \cos\left(\boldsymbol{v}_{\text{cand}}, \boldsymbol{v}_c\right) \tag{3}$$

Table 1. Ontology Snippets

URI	Label	Description
http://example.org/Sunny	Sunny	Wather with no clouds
http://example.org/Rainy	Rainy	Wet weather condition
http://example.org/ArtExhibition	Art Exhibition	Public display of art
http://example.org/MusicConcert	Music Concert	Musical performances
http://example.org/hasLocation	has location	where something occurs
http://example.org/hasPerformer	has performer	who performers the event
http://example.org/hasDate	has date	when it occurs
.....	...	...

For instance, based on Table 1 that describes ontology snippets, given the candidate entity *"Sunny"*, the engine retrieves http://example.org/Sunny with a cosine similarity score of 0.88.

$$\arg\max_{c \in C} \cos(\boldsymbol{v}_{\text{Sunny}}, \boldsymbol{v}_c) \rightarrow http://example.org/Sunny$$

In the case of *"art festival"*, although no exact match exists, the candidate vector $\boldsymbol{v}_{\text{art festival}}$ is closer to *:ArtExhibition* than to other classes such as *:MusicConcert.* Therefore, the symbolic engine generates this result:

$$:Event573 \quad rdf:type \quad :ArtExhibition.$$

A similar process is applied for relation matching, where the goal is to align LLM- generated predicates in natural language with ontology-defined property $p \in P$. Each predicate is embedded as $\boldsymbol{v}_{\text{pred}}$, and the most semantically similar property is selected:

$$p^* = \arg\max_{p \in P} \cos(\boldsymbol{v}_{\text{pred}}, \boldsymbol{v}_p) \tag{4}$$

Based on this method, The LLM-generated predicate *"takes place in"* is mapped to the property *:hasLocation.* However, predicates such as *"suitableForWeather"* or *"isPreferredBy"*, fail to match existing properties in the ontology, which triggers the ontology evolution process to suggest or define new properties.

To ensure that mapped triples are semantically valid, the symbolic engine applies constraint validation based on ontology axioms and SHACL shape definitions. This includes checking: 1- Domain and range conformance; 2- Data type consistency; 3- Cardinality restrictions.

For example, the SHACL shape Listing 1.2 ensures that the property *:hasWeatherContext* is used only once per event and that its object is of type *:WeatherCondition.* Thus, the embedding-based semantic matching bridges the gap between the language-centric representation and the logic-grounded symbolic reasoning required for knowledge graph enrichment.

Listing 1.2. SHACL shape definition example

```
:EventShape a sh:NodeShape ;
    sh:targetClass :Event ;
    sh:property [ sh:path :hasWeatherContext ;
                  sh:class :WeatherCondition ;  sh:maxCount 1 ;
                ] .
```

4.3 Ontology Evolution

This steps ensures that the knowledge enrichment graph process remains adaptable when novel or unseen entities, or relations are encountered during LLM-driven extraction. It enables a dynamic extension of the existing ontology $O = (C, P)$ to a new version $O' = (C', P')$, where:

- $C' \supseteq C$: new classes may be added
- $P' \supseteq P$: new properties may be introduced

When the symbolic engine encounters a candidate triple $t = (s, p, o) \in T^*$ and determines that: 1- The predicate $p \notin P$, or 2- The object class type$(o) \notin C$.

The system flags for the evolution component, which is LLM-supported generation mechanism. It proposes the creation of new ontology elements by generating:

- A label and a human-readable description
- A type designation (e.g., class or property)
- Optional links to ontology elements, such as superclasses or related concepts
- For properties, suggested domain and range axioms

Once the proposal is generated, symbolic engine checks for consistency (e.g., name conflicts or inconsistencies). The validated triples are then submitted to domain experts in a human-in-the-loop validation phase, where the user can approve, refine, or reject the proposed additions before it's inserted.

For example, for the generated triples *(":Event573", ":isPreferredBy", ":User123")*, *(":Event573", ":SuitableForWeather", ":Sunny")*, if the properties *":isPreferredBy"* and *":SuitableForWeather"* are not initially in the ontology, the evolution component proposes the extention shown in Listing 1.3

Listing 1.3. Ontology Extension Example

```
:isPreferredBy a rdf:Property ; rdfs:domain :Event ;
    rdfs:range :User ; rdfs:label "is preferred by".
:SuitableForWeather a rdf:Property ; rdfs:domain :Event ;
    rdfs:range :WeatherCondition; rdfs:label "Suitable for weather".
```

This ensures that novel semantics introduced by the neural engine are formally captured, validated, and integrated into the evolving schema O', preserving both flexibility and consistency.

The steps of the proposed hybrid neuro-symbolic approach for context-aware knowledge graph enrichment are summarized in Algorithm 1. It enables the dynamic and semantically consistent enrichment of the knowledge graph by processing contextual data inputs to generate and validate candidate triples ensuring alignment with—or extension of—the existing ontology schema.

Algorithm 1: Context-Aware Neuro-Symbolic Knowledge Graph Enrichment

Input: $G = (E, R, T)$: initial knowledge graph; $\mathcal{O} = (C, P)$: ontology; $S = \{s_1, ..., s_n\}$: context data

Output: $G' = (E', R', T')$: enriched graph, $\mathcal{O}'$: evolved ontology

```
Initialize G' ← G, O' ← O;
foreach s_i ∈ S do
    T* ← LLM_ExtractTriples(s_i);
    foreach t = (s, p, o) ∈ T* do
        if p ∉ P or type(o) ∉ C then
            (p_new, meta) ← LLM_SuggestOntologyTerm(p, o);
            if ValidateOntologyAddition(p_new, meta, O) then
                O' ← O' ∪ {p_new};
        (s', p', o') ← Symbolic_Match(t, O');
        if ValidateConstraints(s', p', o', O') then
            G' ← G' ∪ {(s', p', o')};
return G', O';
```

5 Case Study

This section presents the application of our hybrid neuro-symbolic approach to enriching the Datatourisme Knowledge graph with context-aware information. Datatourisme[1] is a national French initiative aimed at semantically describing and publishing open data related to tourism activities, points of interest (POI), and cultural events across France. The ontology models various tourism-related resources using the following key concepts:

- Product: represents a tourist object that can be consumed
- Tour: represents a touristic itinerary
- EntertainmentAndEvent: represents events such as festivals, manifestations, exhibitions,...
- PlaceOfInterest: represents locations of tourist interest like cultural sites, natural sites, etc.

[1] https://info.datatourisme.fr/presentation/enjeux/.

Although it has structural richness, the Datatourisme knowledge graph remains largely static and lacks contextual semantics. It does not explicitly model dynamic, situational, or user-centric contextual information which are crucial for personalization and adaptive applications.

To demonstrate how our hybrid neuro-symbolic approach addresses these limitations, we consider an end-to-end enrichment scenario dealing with cultural sites and events in the city of La Rochelle. A simplified representation of the initial knowledge graph is illustrated in Fig. 3.

Contextual data is collected from multiple heterogeneous sources, including the OpenWeatherMap API (for real-time weather), structured event feeds, and Web metadata, as shown in Fig. 4. All contextual inputs are normalized into a structured intermediate representation that is used by hybrid AI modules.

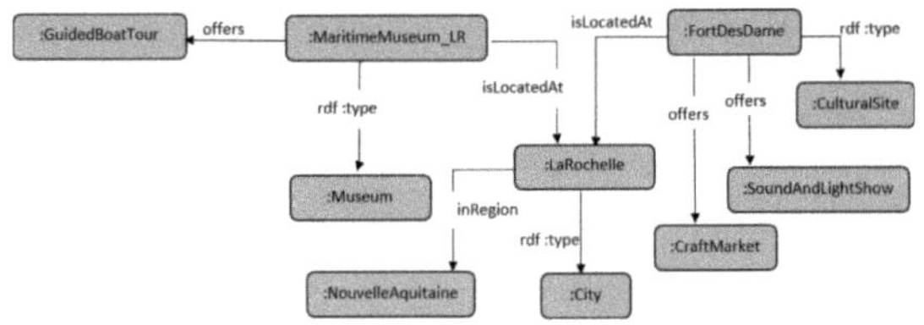

Fig. 3. Initial Knowledge Graph.

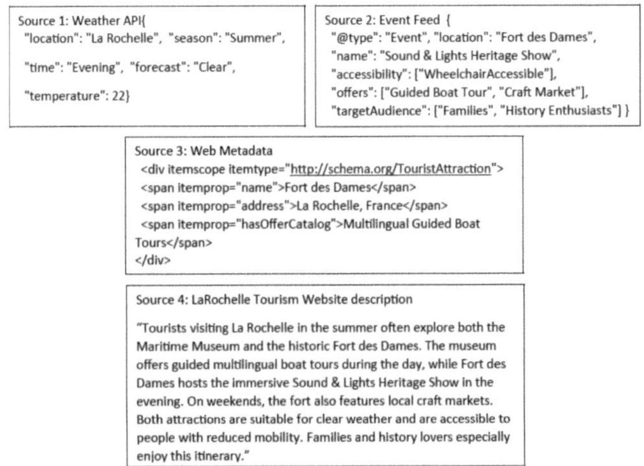

Source 1: Weather API{
"location": "La Rochelle", "season": "Summer",
"time": "Evening", "forecast": "Clear",
"temperature": 22}

Source 2: Event Feed {
"@type": "Event", "location": "Fort des Dames",
"name": "Sound & Lights Heritage Show",
"accessibility": ["WheelchairAccessible"],
"offers": ["Guided Boat Tour", "Craft Market"],
"targetAudience": ["Families", "History Enthusiasts"] }

Source 3: Web Metadata
<div itemscope itemtype="http://schema.org/TouristAttraction">
<span itemprop="name">Fort des Dames</span>
<span itemprop="address">La Rochelle, France</span>
<span itemprop="hasOfferCatalog">Multilingual Guided Boat Tours</span>
</div>

Source 4: LaRochelle Tourism Website description

"Tourists visiting La Rochelle in the summer often explore both the Maritime Museum and the historic Fort des Dames. The museum offers guided multilingual boat tours during the day, while Fort des Dames hosts the immersive Sound & Lights Heritage Show in the evening. On weekends, the fort also features local craft markets. Both attractions are suitable for clear weather and are accessible to people with reduced mobility. Families and history lovers especially enjoy this itinerary."

Fig. 4. Contextual Data Input.

Based on the contextual data, the neural component (LLM-based engine) generates a set of candidate triples, Listing 1.4, capturing information such as location, audience, temporal context, and accessibility. The symbolic component aligns these triples with the existing ontology by mapping known entities (e.g., :FortDesDames) to their canonical URIs and detecting novel concepts such as *:CulturalTour*, *:WheelchairUser* and *:SummerWeekend*, as well as new properties like *:isAccessibleTo* and *:hasTemporalContext* that are not defined in the ontology.

A human-in-the-loop validation process is then employed to approve or reject the suggested ontology extension as illustrated in Fig. 5. The resulting enriched graph, integrating the approved entities and relationships, is in Fig. 6.

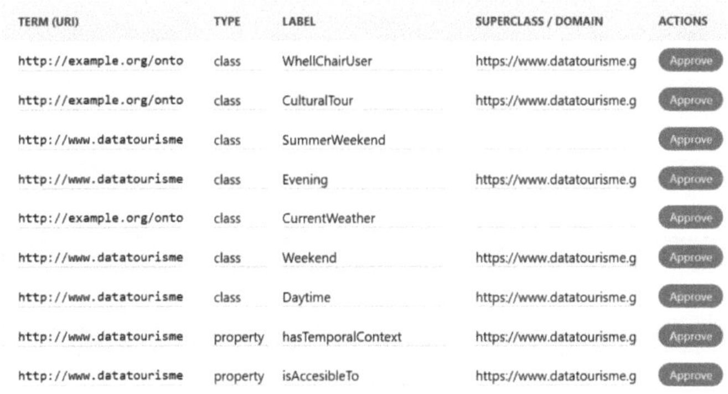

TERM (URI)	TYPE	LABEL	SUPERCLASS / DOMAIN	ACTIONS
http://example.org/onto	class	WhellChairUser	https://www.datatourisme.g	Approve
http://example.org/onto	class	CulturalTour	https://www.datatourisme.g	Approve
http://www.datatourisme	class	SummerWeekend		Approve
http://www.datatourisme	class	Evening	https://www.datatourisme.g	Approve
http://example.org/onto	class	CurrentWeather		Approve
http://www.datatourisme	class	Weekend	https://www.datatourisme.g	Approve
http://www.datatourisme	class	Daytime	https://www.datatourisme.g	Approve
http://www.datatourisme	property	hasTemporalContext	https://www.datatourisme.g	Approve
http://www.datatourisme	property	isAccesibleTo	https://www.datatourisme.g	Approve

Fig. 5. User Interface Triples Validation.

Listing 1.4. LLM-based Triple Generation

```
:Tour1 rdf:type :CulturalTour ;
        :includesPOI :MaritimeMuseum_LR , :FortDesDames ;
        :hasAudience :Families , :HistoryEnthusiasts ;
        :hasWeatherContext :Clear; :hasTemporalContext :SummerWeekend .
:MaritimeMuseum_LR rdf:type :Museum ; :offersActivity :GuidedBoatTour ;
        :isLocatedIn :LaRochelle ; :isAccessibleTo :WheelchairUser .
:GuidedBoatTour rdf:type :Tour ;
        :hasLanguage :Multilingual ; :occursDuring :Daytime .
:FortDesDames rdf:type :HistoricalMonument ;
        :offersActivity :SoundAndLightShow , :CraftMarket ;
        :isLocatedIn :LaRochelle ; :isAccessibleTo :WheelchairUser .
:SoundAndLightShow rdf:type :ImmersiveExperience ;
        :hasAudience :Families , :HistoryEnthusiasts ;
        :occursDuring :Evening ; :hasWeatherContext :Clear .
:CraftMarket rdf:type :TemporaryMarket ; :occursDuring :Weekend .
```

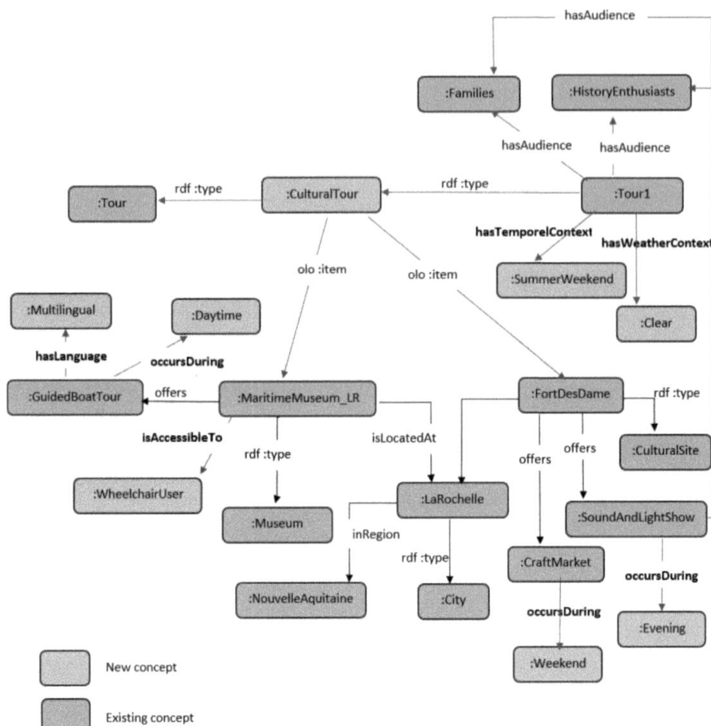

Fig. 6. Enriched Knowledge Graph.

6 Implementation and Evaluation

6.1 Experimental Setup

Table 2 describes the key statistics of the datatourisme KG including, the number of triples, properties, classes, and individual instances, as well as the number of POIs and Events that are the most frequently used entities in the dataset. The proposed hybrid neuro-symbolic knowledge graph enrichment approach was implemented using several tools such as, the OpenAI API for contextual triple extraction, RDFlib, and PySHACL to perform entity alignment, relation mapping, and ontology validation. We implement a web-based validation interface with React to enable human-in-the-loop interaction. The validated triples are persisted in an Apache Jena Fuseki RDF store. We test our approach on both LLMs: Mistral-7B and GPT-4o.

Table 2. Datatourisme KG statistics

	# triples	# properties	# classes	# entities	# event entity	# POI entity
Datatourisme KG	44 690	85	249	8938	2119	5815

6.2 Baselines and Metrics

To evaluate the effectiveness of our proposed approach, we compare it with two main categories: *symbolic methods* and *LLM-based KG construction techniques.*

- Symbolic approaches: [14] proposes a symbolic pipeline for KG construction using RML and SPARQL-based transformations.
- LLM-based approaches
  - EDC [20] uses LLMs to extract triples, define new concepts, and canonicalize outputs. Schema alignment is mostly lexical.
  - Zero-shot [1] uses GPT-style LLMs to generate triples.
  - SF-GPT [16] uses filtering and structured prompts
  - LLM-KGC [7] uses LLMs to assist users in populating KG.

We use standard information extraction metrics: Precision, Recall, and F1-score at the triple-level to evaluate the neural triple generation component. Then, we evaluate the ontology alignment module using the Ontology Match Rate (OMR), which measures the proportion of generated triples whose entities and predicates are correctly aligned with existing ontology classes and properties. We introduce Constraint Satisfaction Rate (CSR) to assess the structural validity of the enriched KG by quantifying the percentage of triples that satisfy domain-specific constraints. Finally, we define the Ontology Extension Accuracy (OEA) measuring the proportion of newly proposed ontology elements (e.g., classes, properties) that are approved by experts during the human-in-the-loop validation phase.

6.3 Results

Table 3 shows the performance of our approach compared to state-of-the-art baselines. Our hybrid neuro-symbolic approach achieves the highest performance across all metrics. It exceeds all LLM-based and symbolic baselines in terms of triple-level quality. We also note performance improvement when using GPT-4o.

Although the symbolic sparql-based approach achieves perfect OMR and CSR (100%), its low recall (0.54) drags down the F1-score to 0.66. This reflects the limitations of manual or pattern-based rules in generalizing to unseen data. Our approach shows high OMR (94%), indicating strong alignment with the existing schema and the advantage of symbolic reasoning integration with high CSR. LLM-based approaches demonstrate reasonable triple-level quality, indicating LLM's power in extracting contextual information. However, schema grounding and constraint satisfaction remain weaknesses due to the lack of ontology guidance or post-extraction validation in LLM-only approaches. Most methods do not support ontology evolution; only LLM-KGC assists in ontology design manually. Our approach demonstrates high OEA (95%) validating its ability to integrate new classes and properties with expert-in-the-loop validation.

Table 3. Performance Comparison of Different Baseline Methods

	Precision	Recall	F1-score	OMR	CSR	OEA
Symbolic Approach [14]	0.85	0.54	0.66	100%	100 %	-
LLM-based Approaches						
EDC [20]	0.9	0.76	0.82	60%	45%	-
Zero-shot [1]	0.86	0.78	0.81	68%	63%	-
SF-GPT [16]	0.93	0.71	0.80	62%	55%	-
LLM-KGC [7]	0.86	0.79	0.82	65%	58%	61%
Our approach (Mistral)	0.87	0.82	0.84	85%	89%	91%
Our approach (GPT-4o)	0.95	0.88	0.91	94%	95%	95%

7 Conclusion

In this paper, we present a context-aware hybrid neuro-symbolic KG enrichment framework that combines the contextual extraction capabilities of LLMs with the reasoning strength of symbolic ontology models: our approach supports triple generation, semantic alignment, constraint validation, and ontology evolution. Experts are involved in the KG enrichment process to validate the generated triples and new ontology terms. Experiments conducted on Datatourisme KG demonstrate superior performance compared to symbolic and LLM-based baselines, especially in Ontology Match Rate and Ontology Extension Accuracy metrics. In the future, we aim to integrate a user study and a qualitative evaluation to better understand the impact of human-AI interaction on KG quality. We also recognize the need to handle conflicting contextual inputs arising from heterogeneous sources, and plan to integrate conflict resolution mechanisms into the pipeline. In addition, we plan to enhance ontology extension using learning-based ontology evolution strategies through expert feedback and real-world usage patterns.

References

1. Carta, S., Giuliani, A., Piano, L., Podda, A.S., Pompianu, L., Tiddia, S.G.: Iterative zero-shot LLM prompting for knowledge graph construction. arXiv (2023)
2. Chandak, P., Huang, K., Zitnik, M.: Building a knowledge graph to enable precision medicine. Sci. Data **10**(1), 67 (2023)
3. Chicaiza, J., Valdiviezo-Diaz, P.: A comprehensive survey of knowledge graph-based recommender systems: technologies, development, and contributions. Information **12**(6), 232 (2021)
4. Choi, S., Jung, Y.: Knowledge graph construction: extraction, learning, and evaluation. Appl. Sci. **15**(7), 3727 (2025)
5. De Giorgis, S., Gangemi, A., Russo, A.: Neurosymbolic graph enrichment for grounded world models. Inf. Process. Manage. (4), 104127 (2025)
6. Feng, X., Wu, X., Meng, H.: Ontology-grounded automatic knowledge graph construction by LLM under wikidata schema. arXiv preprint arXiv:2412.20942 (2024)

7. Kommineni, V.K., König-Ries, B., Samuel, S.: From human experts to machines: an LLM supported approach to ontology and knowledge graph construction (2024)
8. Liu, B., Fang, Y., Xu, N., Hou, S., Li, X., Li, Q.: Large language models for knowledge graph embedding: a survey. Mathematics **13**(14), 2244 (2025)
9. Lu, Y., Wang, J.: Karma: leveraging multi-agent LLMs for automated knowledge graph enrichment. arXiv preprint arXiv:2502.06472 (2025)
10. Maree, M.: Quantifying relational exploration in cultural heritage knowledge graphs with LLMs: a neuro-symbolic approach for enhanced knowledge discovery. Data **10**(4), 52 (2025)
11. Meyer, L., et al.: LLM-assisted knowledge graph engineering: Experiments with chatgpt. In: Working Conference on Artificial Intelligence Development for a Resilient and Sustainable Tomorrow. Springer, Cham (2023)
12. Mountantonakis, M., Koumakis, M., Tzitzikas, Y.: Combining LLMs and hundreds of knowledge graphs for data enrichment, validation and integration case study: cultural heritage domain (2024)
13. Pan, S., Luo, L., Wang, Y., Chen, C., Wang, J., Wu, X.: Unifying large language models and knowledge graphs: a roadmap. IEEE Trans. Knowl. Data Eng. **36**(7), 3580–3599 (2024)
14. Stadler, C., Bühmann, L., Meyer, L.P., Martin, M.: Scaling RML and sparql-based knowledge graph construction with apache spark. In: KGCW@ ESWC (2023)
15. Stütz, J.D., Karras, O., Oelen, A., Auer, S.: A user-driven hybrid neuro-symbolic approach for knowledge graph creation from relational data. In: International Conference on Cooperative Information Systems, pp. 169–185. Springer, Cham (2024)
16. Sun, L., Zhang, P., Gao, F., An, Y., Li, Z., Zhao, Y.: SF-GPT: a training-free method to enhance capabilities for knowledge graph construction in LLMs. Neurocomputing **613**, 128726 (2025)
17. Trajanoska, M., Stojanov, R., Trajanov, D.: Enhancing knowledge graph construction using large language models. arXiv preprint arXiv:2305.04676 (2023)
18. Wang, Q., Li, C., Liu, Y., Zhu, Q., Song, J., Shen, T.: An adaptive framework embedded with LLM for knowledge graph construction. IEEE Trans. Multimed. (2025)
19. Yasunaga, M., Ren, H., Bosselut, A., Liang, P., Leskovec, J.: QA-GNN: reasoning with language models and knowledge graphs for question answering. arXiv (2021)
20. Zhang, B., Soh, H.: Extract, define, canonicalize: an LLM-based framework for knowledge graph construction. arXiv (2024)

stvd-kg: A Knowledge Graph for French Electronical Program Guides

Hoang Giang Vu(✉), Nathalie Friburger, Arnaud Soulet, and Mathieu Delalandre

LIFAT, University of Tours, Tours, France
hoanggiang.vu@etu.univ-tours.fr,
{nathalie.friburger,arnaud.soulet,mathieu.delalandre}@univ-tours.fr

Abstract. Electronic Program Guides provide detailed information on TV programs, useful for offering user services or quality datasets. Unfortunately, their exploitation is limited by the absence of standardized semantics, text descriptions that are difficult to analyze and information that is often incomplete. This paper proposes the knowledge graph stvd-kg (for the KG of large-scale TV Dataset), which enriches a year's worth of French TV EPGs by taking advantage of Wikidata and IMDb. This large KG (5.7M entities, 27.6M triples) contains 2.9M of publication events (corresponding to 1.7M television contents, 70k television collections, and 84k named entities). To achieve this, we use an ontology adapted to TV content and its broadcasting, based on the EBU Core ontology, schema.org and RDF-schema. We also propose original mechanisms for cross-enrichment of information coming from named entity recognition and entity linking systems. Experimental evaluation of the knowledge graph stvd-kg based on a ground truth shows its very high accuracy. The KG stvd-kg is made publicly available.

Keywords: Electronic Program Guides · French TV · Knowledge Graph Construction

Git repository: https://scm.univ-tours.fr/22313906t/stvd-kg
Zenodo DOI: https://doi.org/10.5281/zenodo.15368241

1 Introduction

Electronic Program Guides (EPGs) are rich and voluminous resources aimed to inform the audience about the programs being transmitted by TV stations and web TV providers. Complementary to audiovisual data, they represent an opportunity to provide advanced services to the user and to build large and high-quality datasets for computer science. First, these EPGs are useful for proposing services to the end-user, ranging from program recommendations [21,25] to navigation between different broadcast content (e.g., accessing the previous episode) or to external content (e.g., description of an actor). Secondly, the EPGs

I. Awan et al. (Eds.): WISE 2025, LNCS 16367, pp. 390–405, 2026.
https://doi.org/10.1007/978-981-95-7394-3_27

streamed daily are a strategic resource, particularly for machine learning, which requires large volumes of labelled data. For example, descriptions from EPGs could form a large corpus of Named Entities (NEs) that would be very useful for training Large Language Models (LLMs) [10,14]. At last, different works have been proposed in Computer Vision taking advantage of semantic information from EPGs. This covers the partial video copy detection [15], the fact-checking [20] and the TV video segmentation [22].

Unfortunately, the richness of EPGs cannot be directly exploited due to their lack of semantics. Indeed, even if some of the data is structured, attribute values are not based on controlled vocabularies stemming from taxonomies or ontologies (e.g., the same TV program will not always be associated with the same category, and sometimes its name changes from one broadcast to another). Secondly, the full-text search lacks semantics, which can lead to errors (e.g., the description of the movie "Le prix à payer" refers to a character named Caroline, who may be confused with the location Caroline in United States). Finally, the information contained in EPGs is sometimes very limited, and needs to be supplemented by external sources of knowledge (e.g., cast lists). For all these reasons, our work is concerned in building a knowledge graph from French EPGs for TV contents. Building a knowledge graph from French EPGs is a challenge, as French TV programs are not necessarily well covered by reference knowledge sources such as Wikidata or IMDb. In addition, the nature of the programs is heterogeneous (e.g., movies, series or news), requiring a flexible schema and construction process. Thereby, to the best of our knowledge, existing proposals for EPG enrichment suffer from significant limitations. Most often, only one type of program is treated, such as news [6] or movies [9,19]. Some approaches do not benefit from the semantic web, but from social networks [4] or their own taxonomy [21]. Most approaches focus on just a few EPGs fields (often the title), whereas we will see that the key idea behind our approach is to cross-enrich information from different fields to guarantee very high accuracy in our results.

This paper presents the knowledge graph stvd-kg, which results of the semantic enrichment of a year's worth of French TV programs. The construction of this knowledge graph has led to the following contributions:

- We propose an ontology based on the EBU Core [7] ontology and Resource Description Framework Schema [5] to model both a TV content and its broadcast event.
- We propose several advanced enrichment mechanisms to guarantee high accuracy to our KG. To improve robustness, we combine several Named Entity Recognition (NER) systems and use contextual information to guide entity linking (EL). We also cross-check information across several fields to correct NER and EL.
- We evaluate the quality of each enrichment mechanism using ground truth based on a sample day of French EPGs. Experimental results show that our resulting knowledge graph stvd-kg achieves very high accuracy.
- We analyze the main statistical characteristics of the knowledge graph stvd-kg that we make publicly available: https://scm.univ-tours.fr/22313906t/stvd-

kg. stvd-kg stands out as the largest semantically enriched collection of EPGs, and ranks among the largest corpora of named entities.

Section 2 presents the related work and an overview of our KG construction system. Section 3 details the input data used for our KG construction. Section 4 presents the proposed ontology to model the TV contents. We explain the main enriching mechanisms of our approach in Sect. 5. Section 6 provides the evaluation and Sect. 7 analyzes the main characteristics of stvd-kg. Finally, conclusions and perspectives are given in Sect. 8.

2 Preliminaries

2.1 Related Work

This related work covers all existing resources and methods dedicated to knowledge graphs and the semantic enrichment of TV programs. Indeed, this work prioritizes textual analysis, but it is important to notice that some other works deals with video content [6,19,23] or focuses only on information extraction [18]. For instance, MeMAD Knowledge Graph [11] contains textual and audiovisual information about 3,607 Radio and TV programs collections obtained mainly with machine learning approaches on video (e.g., automatic speech recognition or face recognition from the video frames). Several works have focused on broadcast event modeling, particularly for radio and television programming. The BBC Programs Ontology [3] represents radio broadcast events from BBC One London by four main factors: programs, channels, broadcast events, and the temporal annotations of each broadcast event. However, the BBC Programs Ontology does not provide a wide range of vocabulary to cover the TV content characteristics. Interestingly, the European Broadcasting Union developed the EBU Core ontology, which is often used as a standard. It mainly focuses on providing a structured way to represent and categorize information about media contents. For stvd-kg, we use the relevant structure of the EBU Core ontology to describe TV program properties, but we also use schema.org to complete it [2] due to its comprehensive vocabulary and its wide use in multimedia domain.

Interestingly, several works have proposed ontologies and enrichments for EPGs without recourse to external knowledge bases. On the one hand, OntoTV [21] defines ontologies to describe TV programs (OntoTV-Data) and user sessions (OntoTV-UserSession) for recommendation purposes. The data part of OntoTV is based on a simple taxonomy that is less complete than the Wikidata categories. On the other hand, MesoOnTV [4] exploited only social media information such as Youtube or Twitter. These semantic enrichments, while relevant for recommendation purposes, are far less semantically rich than our Wikidata-based approach. In particular, linking TV content to Wikidata gives access to a wealth of information that can be exploited by downstream applications.

Finally, several semantic annotation approaches come close to our goal, but with a much smaller scope. In [16], the authors proposed an EPG enrichment system based on news articles and DBpedia aiming to improve the poor information of Portuguese EPGs. Although the well-structured pipeline, this work

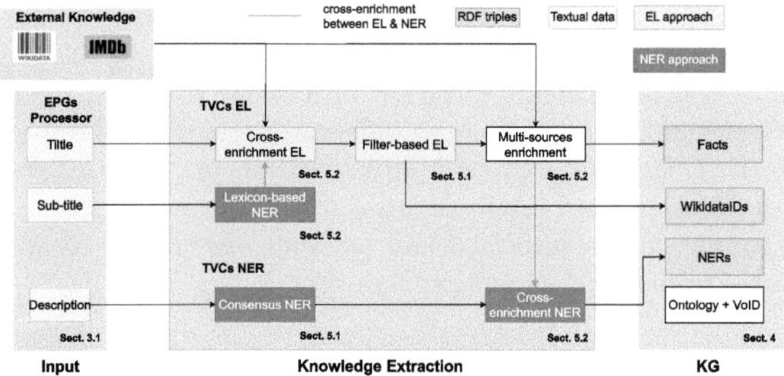

Fig. 1. stvd-kg construction pipeline

focused on soccer and TV series content only as well as a limited number of TV contents (1,697 TV contents). Moreover, the small amount of evaluation data with 36 TV contents led to the difficulties in assessing the applicability of this approach while we did the evaluation in thousands TV contents over 6 different categories. More recently, [9] proposed a general process for the semantic annotation and subsequent enrichment of EPGs using IMDb with the aim to tackle the lack of immediate availability of related information about TV contents. However, this work focused only on movies and is limited to around 3k TV contents (only movies) while our work counts more than 11k TV contents from the 'Cinema' category alone (much more considering all our TV contents).

2.2 Overview of the Method

We propose an architecture (see Fig. 1) for knowledge extraction from EPGs and its linking to Wikidata, which we take as our external reference knowledge base. We mainly focus on two tasks: 1) Named Entity Recognition (NER) from TV content descriptions and 2) Entity Linking (EL) of these named entities and TV contents themselves. It should be noted that we want to extract very high-precision information so that downstream applications do not exploit erroneous information. For this work, we consider only 3 categories of named entities: persons (PER), locations (LOC) and organizations (ORG)[1].

The extraction of knowledge and its linking to Wikidata raises difficulties both at the level of named entity recognition and at the level of entity linking. Although named entity recognition is a relatively well-mastered task, it remains difficult to extract named entities with a high degree of accuracy from French-language short descriptions of EPGs. Besides, the title of a TV content is well identified within the EPG, but linking it to Wikidata remains a challenging task, as this title can easily be confused with other entities. For example, Napoleon may refer to the movie Napoleon, the person Napoleon Bonaparte or the city

[1] There are fine-grained multilingual NEs with more categories, but leading to lower recall and precision [8].

called Napoleon in Ohio. Even with a constraint on TV titles, there are still 5 movies with the title Napoleon.

To achieve very high accuracy, the key idea of our KG construction system is to cross-reference information (i) from different systems (NER consensus, filter-based EL), (ii) from different fields (cross-enrichment) and (iii) from different sources with Wikidata and IMDb (multi-source enrichment). After introducing the inputs to our system in Sect. 3 and our ontology in Sect. 4, we present all these advanced enrichment mechanisms in Sect. 5.

3 Electronic Program Guides and Knowledge Resources

We present here the two main sources of data used to design our KG of French TV content: EPGs data and knowledge resources (e.g., Wikidata or IMDB).

3.1 Electronic Program Guides

We have constituted a dataset of EPGs. The EPGs data describe series of Publication Events (PE). They are delivered respecting the international standard XMLTV[2]. An example of a XMLTV data related to the movie "Le prix à payer" ("The Price to Pay" in English) is given in Table 1. This includes the time schedule, channel, title, description, credits and other related information.

Table 1. Example of a XMLTV data

Tag	Data
Program	start="23-11-02" "0658" stop="23-11-02" "0830" channel="Ciné+"
Title	Le prix à payer
Subtitle	Cinéma / Comédie; Durée: 1h31; Réal: A. Leclère; Sortie: 2007 ; Pays: France
Desc	Année: 2007; Résumé: Quinquagénaire ayant réussi dans les affaires, J.P. Ménard ...
Credits	Directeur : A. Leclère ; Acteur : C. Clavier
Others	icon: affiche.png url: epg/le-prix-a-payer/ rating: 5.6/10

The EPGs data can be crawled daily from different public websites and/or services to constitute the XMLTV files. We have developed a local crawler to collect daily the XMLTV files of two main French EPGs[3] during a period of one year. The Table 2 gives the details of the constituted dataset.

The XMLTV files have been processed to extract the daily contents. Some files could be missing due to the crawling errors[4]. The EPGs data are delivered for a one to two weeks interval. For recovering, the missed daily contents have been obtained from the piggybacked XMLTV data of lasted crawled files.

[2] https://wiki.xmltv.org/.

[3] https://www.telerama.fr/, https://www.programme-tv.net/.

[4] Typically, EPGs not up to date or available or local network/computer crashes.

Table 2. XMLTV dataset

EPGs	Start	Length	Files	Size	Error	Channels	Pub. events	TV col.	Desc.	Words
2	11/23	1 year	714	54 GB	2.20%	309	2.9 M	69.8 k	631.2 k	40 M

The daily contents have been parsed to extract the TV channels as well as the PE. The inconsistent PE (having a null duration or with time overlap) have been removed. A near 3M of PE have been collected across 309 channels.

The XMLTV data are captured from two EPGs in our dataset. We have used a first as an authoritative source and the second for enrichment of text descriptions. To do this, the PE have been mapped between the two sources based on the schedule, channel and title information. The supplement text descriptions, of the second source, have been then embedded for enrichment.

Then, the PE have been gathered into TV contents. A TV content is defined here as a distinct video content appearing at least in one or several PE. To do this, we have used the method [15]. It employs baseline NLP processing[5] to detect duplicate and near duplicate titles between the PE and group them into TV collections. We have detected a near amount of 69 k TV collections. We have then extracted all the descriptions and filtered out (see Footnote 5) the duplicates. We have obtained nearly 630k distinct descriptions (around 40M words).

Unfortunately, this big amount of XMLTV data is not fully consistent: the list of actors or producers could be partial, and errors in the release date, title and duration could appear. Besides, the descriptions are provided for short, and the categories tuned for the EPG access. As we aim to construct a complete KG dedicated to French TV content, we therefore must consider data from other knowledge resources.

Table 3. TV data in Wikidata and IMDb

Resource	Movies		TV contents	
	Total	French	Total	French
Wikidata	401,091	23,730	715,100	8,498
IMDb	836,263	52,975	335,079	1,214

3.2 Knowledge Resources

Wikidata [24] is a collaborative and open knowledge base where structured data about real-world entities, such as people, places, things and concepts are collected and organized. It serves as a prime example of a large-scale knowledge graph

[5] Normalization and hashing of titles/tokens resulting in $\ll 1\%$ of detection error [15].

used to power other Wikimedia projects, like Wikipedia. However, the French TV data from Wikidata have limitations in terms of data quality, completeness and semantic ambiguity. For instance, TV content named "Le Prix à payer" mentioned in Sect. 3.1 is a French movie produced in 2007. When querying this TV content, Wikidata API returned a list of promising Wikidata ID in which the first five results do not contain this TV content. As the consequence, it leads to the wrong information, as well as the ambiguous semantic. Moreover, even if we manage to find the right TV content, Wikidata provides only the actors in that movie but not the roles they played.

IMDb [1] is a popular Web dataset providing information on movies and television series. In addition, it provides different kind of services for extracting information. We made count queries to evaluate the amount of information from external knowledge. Even the large number of movies and television series information, IMDb also lacks other TV contents data such as news, television shows, and so on. Considering the same TV content "Le Prix à payer", IMDb provides the full cast and crew, as well as their roles in the movie. Besides, IMDb does not provide the identifiers of another external knowledge as Wikidata.

The combination of Wikidata and IMDb is a promising solution to overcome their disadvantages. It cannot totally solve all the issues, but it could result in significant improvements for our KG. Table 3 shows the number of movies and TV contents of these two resources (total and in French).

4 TV Content Ontology

The goal of TV content ontology is to model TV contents data coming from different sources. We need an ontology able to express the relations between TV contents, and also the contents inside them. In addition, this ontology must illustrate the relation between internal and external knowledge from EPGs and Wikidata. To this end, we rely on the EBU Core ontology and schema.org [2] due to its comprehensive vocabulary and its wide use in multimedia domain.

Figure 2 presents French TV Content's ontology. Its main components are described in the following

- **TV content:** Each TV content has a unique ID linking to its information (e.g., name, genre, episode). It can represent an unique content (e.g., a movie) or an episode in a series, with episodes connected in order by `schema:nextItem`.
- **Publication event:** Each event has a unique ID and links to a TV content via `ebucore:isPublicationOf`. It represents a broadcast session, and since a content can air multiple times on one or more channels, the relation between TV content and publication events is 1-N.
- **TV collection:** As mentioned above, each TV content is an episode of a series or a single TV content ("Le Prix à payer" is also a TV collection itself). As a result, TV contents are linked to TV collection ID by property `ebucore:partOfSeries` in order to extract present information of the whole series or the relevant information which is not included in EPGs data.

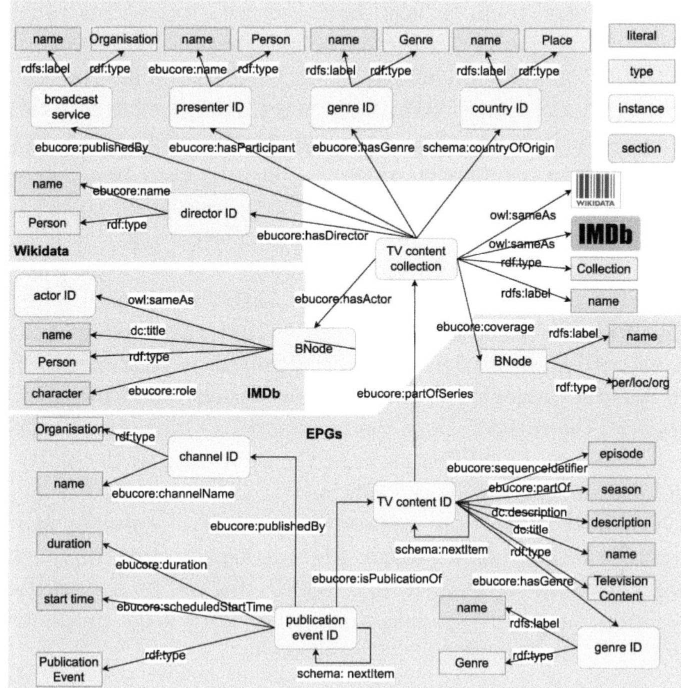

Fig. 2. TV content ontology

– **External Knowledge:** The TV collections are mapped to Wikidata IDs as well as IMDb IDs by `owl:sameAs` in order to extract information from external knowledge.

5 Advanced Enriching Methods for KG Construction

In order to guarantee a high level of accuracy in the construction of the knowledge graph, we propose three original methods for cross-referencing information from several tools and/or data sources.

5.1 Robust Enrichment

To achieve very safe and accurate results, it is important to take advantage to the information from several tools and cross them. First, we propose to use a consensus built from two NER tools for consolidating their results. Second, we consolidate the entity linking using contextual information. To illustrate our purpose, we refer to the example of Table 1: the movie "Le prix à payer".

NER Consensus for Descriptions. We want to enrich our knowledge graph with named entities (i.e., persons, locations or organizations) extracted from EPG descriptions and linked them to Wikidata. We need to create a process as precise as possible to fill the KG with reliable information. For ensuring very high accuracy of this automatic enrichment, we decided to combine two different NER systems: Spacy [12] and CasEN [17]. Spacy is a LLM system freely available, not trained for a specific domain, able to recognize basic entity types. In [13], Spacy obtains good results of coverage on a corpus relatively close to EPG descriptions. CasEN, based on rules and precise linguistic information, may get less coverage but with good accuracy without training. We therefore propose to retain only the named entities extracted by both tools assuming that the combination of their qualities (coverage for Spacy and accuracy for CasEN on French) leads to a confident agreement on the common named entities (in term of extent and category). In Sect. 6.1, we will see that this approach, denoted by NER consensus, achieves a very high accuracy, over 95%. For example, on the description of the movie "Le Prix à payer", the entities 'Jean-Pierre Ménard', 'Odile' and 'Jean-Pierre' are well detected as person by NER consensus. On the contrary, the entity 'Caroline' tagged as a location by Spacy is not retained at this stage, as it is not extracted by CasEN. The next subsection explains how the cross-enrichment mechanism finally extracts 'Caroline' as a person. More generally, this approach so called NER consensus leads to the extraction of 68,358 distinct named entities grouped by TV collection on our EPG data within the knowledge graph with 22,732 persons, 41,470 locations and 4,156 organizations.

Filter-Based EL for TV Collections. We propose to enrich our knowledge graph by linking as many named entities as possible to Wikidata. First, we use the Wikidata API search engine to identify potentially relevant entities corresponding to the searched TV collection title. Second, to increase the robustness of entity linking, we use filters to ensure that the result is consistent with contextual information. For each potential entity, we retain those that satisfy the expected contextual information using SPARQL queries. Finally, the filtered entity whose has the highest rank by Wikidata is retained. More precisely, for entity linking of TV collection, we search for potential entities based on the EPG's title as searched string. Next, we retain potential entities that are instances (property `wdt:P31`) of TV program types (e.g., `wd:Q15416` for television program or `wd:Q11424` for movie). At the end, we selected the highest ranked entity. This enhanced entity linking method leads to add 3,688 Wikidata IDs in our knowledge graph. Unfortunately, some ambiguities may remain, as several TV collections may have the same name, as it is the case for "Le Prix à payer" where there are three different movies returned by Wikidata API. The next section shows how cross-enrichment can remove these ambiguities.

5.2 Cross-Enrichment

NER and EL tasks are often performed on entities isolated in texts unrelated to external sources of information. In our case, the electronic program guide provides, in addition of the description, a coherent set of information (time schedule, channel, title, director, actors and so on) that should be considered as a whole. Indeed, some information (e.g., a director or a country) can make it easier to choose the right TV collection, despite the ambiguity of the title. We illustrate this key principle to improve both NER and EL.

Cross-Enrichment EL for TV Collection. Intuitively, having reliable information on TV collection helps to improve entity linking, especially when several TV contents have the same title. First, it is possible to retrieve very reliable named entities from the 'subtitle' tag in EPGs (see Table 1) containing information on the director, country and publication date, which are always formatted in the same way. Indeed, we use Lexicon-based NER to identify them with patterns like réalisateur <director>, pays <country>, and sortie <publication date>. Secondly, from these reliable named entities linked to Wikidata, it is then possible to query Wikidata to disambiguate a title by adding constraints on certain properties. Typically, we used the properties `wdt:P57` or `wdt:P170` for director, country of origin (`wdt:P495`) for country, and publication date (`wdt:P577`). For example, for the movie "Le prix à payer", the lexicon-based NER gives 'Alexandra Leclère' as a person and 'France' as a country. Of course, there is only one French movie involving 'Alexandra Leclère' with the title "Le prix à payer", which resolve this entity linking (see Fig. 3). We will see in Sect. 6 that this approach has 100% accuracy. In our pipeline (see Fig. 1), we decided to apply Cross-enrichment EL before Filter-based EL and we call this process CE+FB EL.

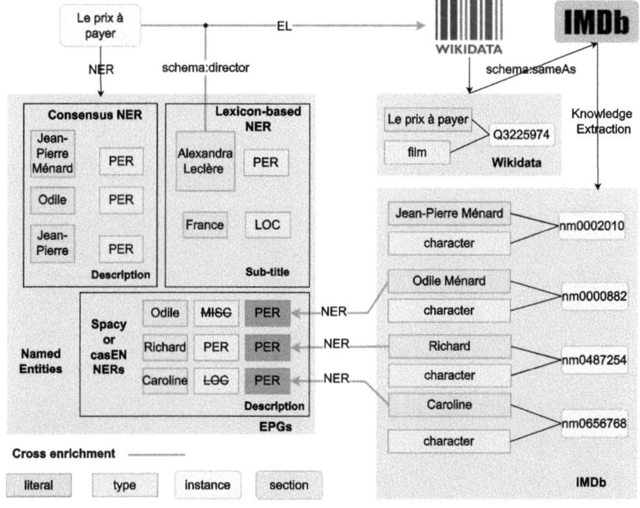

Fig. 3. Example of cross-enrichment for the movie "Le prix à payer"

Cross-Enrichment NER for Completing Descriptions. Conversely, it is possible to improve named entity recognition by taking advantage of external knowledge bases when TV collection is linked to Wikidata and also to IMDb (via the property `wdt:P345`). As a reminder, NER consensus extracts all named entities consistent between Spacy and CasEN. For the other named entities, we then search for any entities attached to the concerned TV content within Wikidata and IMDb. This allows us to recover some of the erroneous named entities or those originating from a single system. As an example, in the description of the movie "Le prix à payer", Spacy extracted several named entities with the wrong category (e.g., 'Caroline' is a character PER but was considered as a location LOC). Based on IMDb knowledge, we corrected this error and tagged 'Caroline' as PER. This Cross-enrichment NER mechanism significantly increases the total number of PER named entities extracted by 15,899 (see Sect. 6).

5.3 Multiple Sources Enrichment

As mentioned in Sect. 3.2, there is no perfect knowledge resource describing all TV collection. Wikidata has better coverage than IMDb for shows, while IMDb has better coverage for movies and TV series. Our knowledge graph reconciles these two resources to standardize information and facilitate user queries. More precisely, after EL task, we extract Wikidata statements by linked ID to enrich the knowledge of the KG. Since, we do not want to add all the information from Wikidata into our knowledge graph. We carefully chose list of properties relating to television terms to perform the queries such as presenter, actor, genre, original broadcaster, country of origin, and so on. When necessary, we perform additional data extraction from IMDb (e.g., lack of roles and actor information of TV collections from Wikidata). For example, in Fig. 3, Wikidata ID of the TV collection "Le Prix à payer" received from Cross-enrichment EL is fed into IMDb API to extract information about the TV contents such as actors, roles or crews. Similar to Wikidata, we limited the extraction in order to avoid unnecessary information (for example in IMDb, we only choose top six actors and their roles in each movie).

6 Evaluation of the KG stvd-kg

This experimental study aims to assess the reliability of the knowledge graph stvd-kg. Specifically, Sect. 6.1 measures the accuracy of our named entity recognition system applied to descriptions. Section 6.2 measures the accuracy of our entity linking system for TV contents. Note that a ground truth corpus built manually for the evaluations, all the source codes and our results are available on the Git repository: https://scm.univ-tours.fr/22313906t/stvd-kg

6.1 NER Evaluation on Descriptions

Evaluation Protocol. To evaluate the recognition of named entities on descriptions, we selected a full day of EPGs as a sample to build a ground truth set of descriptions. Specifically, we applied Spacy and CasEN to these descriptions as pre-annotation, and then, we manually checked these 13,880 pre-annotated entities. The resulting corpus is composed of 4,085 correct named entities (including 2,744 persons, 1,212 locations and 129 organizations). In the experiment, we did not remove the duplicated entities, however the named entities in the final knowledge graph are unique per collection. Table 4 provides the information of validation data. We use Spacy[6] and CasEN[7] results as baselines to ensure a fair assessment and to measure the contribution of our specific mechanisms.

Table 4. NER validation data

Date	TV contents	Description	Spacy (NEs)	CasEN (NEs)	NER consensus	NEs (ground truth)
01/11/2023	3,184	3,449	11,098	6,867	4,085	11,398

NER Consensus Evaluation. Table 5 reports the recall and precision results of Spacy, CasEN and NER consensus (see Sect. 5.1). As mentioned earlier, we can see that Spacy (better coverage) and CasEN (better precision) are complementary. More precisely, both systems have relatively similar results for persons (good precision) and organizations (bad precision and recall). Spacy has a lower precision for locations. Despite the good overall precision of CasEN around 82%, it is not possible to use it directly, as this would introduce too many errors into the knowledge graph. In contrast, we observe that NER consensus has a precision of more than 97%, which is remarkable. Our process works very well for persons and locations, but organizations remain poorly recognized by both systems. As the proportion of organizations among all the entities is low, the bad results on this type of entity do not affect the overall precision of NER consensus. An additional recent system could be used to enhance results for organizations like NLTK or Stanford [13], but the difficulty of recognizing organizations is common to all NER systems. Our choice to prefer high precision results has a strong impact on the global recall of NER consensus, which is only 35%. For this reason, we implement the NER cross-enrichment mechanism to overcome this issue.

Table 5. NER consensus evaluation for descriptions

Method	All (%)		Persons (%)		Locations (%)		Organizations (%)	
	recall	prec	recall	prec	recall	prec	recall	prec
Spacy [12]	*85.28*	64.01	*90.65*	83.54	*75.84*	39.25	*57.69*	31.56
CasEN [17]	49.74	*82.54*	43.22	*88.75*	66.85	*91.54*	56.69	*36.89*
NER consensus	35.01	**97.67**	33.87	**98.69**	42.68	**98.68**	14.38	**66.67**

[6] https://spacy.io/models/fr.

[7] https://www.ortolang.fr/market/tools/casen.

Cross-Enrichment NER. Cross-enrichment in Sect. 5.2 uses named entities from subtitles to link TV contents to external knowledge bases, which in turn enables named entities from descriptions to be corrected. First, we use a Lexicon-based NER for named entities in the EPG 'subtitle' field. As this 'subtitle' field is very regular, the patterns (e.g., réalisateur <director>) are error-free, leading to 100% precision. Second, Cross-enrichment NER reaches a 98.73% precision on named entities extracted among those only extracted by Spacy or CasEN from descriptions. Indeed, the errors of Cross-enrichment NER are due to either errors in NER process (something that is not a NE) or a confusion of two closely related entities. For example, the wrong NE is a person of the same family of the right NE (e.g., 'Commissaire Gordon' (a man) linked to 'Barbara Gordon' is daughter). Overall, Cross-enrichment NER is highly accurate and it enables the recovery of a significant number of entities. For the 5,814 named entities extracted in the one-day EPGs data by our NER approach (41.89% recall), NER consensus extracted 4,085 entities (70.26%), and Cross-enrichment NER added 1,729 entities (29.74%). Lexicon-based NER confirmed 3,111 directors, which were subsequently used by Cross-enrichment EL for entity linking.

6.2 Entity Linking Evaluation for TV Collections

We evaluate the accuracy of Cross-enrichment EL and Filter-based EL (see Sect. 5) used for linking TV collections to their corresponding entities in Wikidata. Since we used Wikidata as an external knowledge base, we consider Wikidata API as baseline to ensure a fair assessment and to measure the contribution of our specific mechanisms. We applied these entity linking methods to 26,044 TV collections to achieve 12,736 Wikidata IDs. We report separately the evaluation of the two stages and CE+FB EL corresponds to the full approach used to construct stvd-kg, which applies Cross-enrichment EL whenever possible, and Filter-based EL otherwise (Table 6).

Table 6. Entity linking evaluation for TV contents

Method	Wikidata IDs	Correct IDs	Rec. (%)	Prec. (%)
Wikidata API	8,223	6,101	23.42	74.19
Cross-enrichment EL	8,223	8,223	*31.57*	*100*
Wikidata API	4,513	3,063	11.76	67.87
Filter-based EL	4,513	3,688	*14.16*	*81.27*
Wikidata API	12,736	9,164	35.18	71.89
CE+FB EL	12,736	11,911	**45.73**	**93.52**

We observe that Cross-enrichment EL and Filter-based EL increase significantly the recall and the precision (highlighted in italic) compared to the baseline. Cross-enrichment EL achieves a very high precision of 100% justifying our use of this mechanism before Filter-based EL. Thus, this results in a final stvd-kg accuracy of 93.52% (see CE+FB EL), which is very good (+22% compared to Wikidata API). The final recall of 45.73% may seem low at first glance, but it should not be forgotten that a majority of TV collections have no corresponding entities in Wikidata (e.g., news or weather reports).

7 Analysis of the Knowledge Graph stvd-kg

The construction of the knowledge graph stvd-kg produces files in turtle format (1.47 GB). The experiments are performed on a personal computer with the processor Intel Core i9-13900H and 64GB RAM, but entity linking task relies on server-side processing of Wikidata API. In this context, the whole KG construction took 55 h for processing a full year: 2 h for processing EPGs, 46 h for advanced enrichment mechanisms, 6 h for multi-source enrichment, and 1 h for KG construction. Updating stvd-kg daily takes around 1 h due to the mapping of already existing data, and NER that requires to process all new data even duplicates.

Large Volume. To the best of our knowledge, stvd-kg is the largest dataset of EPG data. The knowledge graph stvd-kg contains 5,7M entities described by 27,6M triples divided into 21 properties. In particular, there are the 2,9M publication events for the property `ebucore:isPublicationOf`. It is ten times larger than recent datasets available in the literature (e.g., 130k PE in [18], and 192.6k PE in [11]). As we examined in Sect. 2.1, the three knowledge graphs most similar to stvd-kg [9,11,16] are much smaller. There are also the 1,860,193 triples for the property `dc:description` leading to 84,257 triples for the property `ebucore:coverage`. For the NER task, stvd-kg is competitive in term of scale with recent state-of-the-art datasets (31k NEs [10], 4M of descriptions [14]). Of course, these named entities are not uniformly distributed, and some TV contents concentrate more named entities than others. A set of queries is included in our repository to illustrate these properties, as well as the example usages of stvd-kg. Finally, 97,052 `schema:nextItem` links connect the episodes of the 4,280 series and 2,873,239 `schema:nextItem` links chronologically connect the publication events for easy navigation.

Semantic Richness. In addition to being voluminous, our enrichment process leads the knowledge graph stvd-kg to be both diverse and very rich. From the 12,458 Wikidata IDs in stvd-kg, we have for example 130 distinct countries of origin, 1,100 distinct persons, etc. Moreover, whereas the EPGs only had a coarse categorization with 6 types, Wikidata gives us 541 different kinds of TV genre, which is really very useful for certain applications like TV program recommendation (where EPG categories are really too coarse). For example, the TV collection "Le Prix à payer" is categorized as a 'comedy film' rather than the coarse category 'cinema' in EPGs. In term of IMDb, we linked 11,447 IMDb IDs, and extracted 35,730 actor IDs and 67,058 roles from these actors. These diversity in information illustrates that stvd-kg provides access to a in-depth knowledge for many TV contents and collections comparing to knowledge graphs in the literature [24,12] that focus on one or two program categories.

8 Conclusion

This paper presents the knowledge graph stvd-kg that results from the semantic enrichment of a year's worth of French EPGs. We explain several original enrichment mechanisms dedicated to named entity recognition and entity linking that enabled its construction. Our experimental study shows the very high reliability of the information contained in stvd-kg with an accuracy greater than 97% for named entities and 93% for entity linking. We highlight that combining LLM and rule-based approaches is particularly effective for French EPG data, as it not only yields higher accuracy but also better handles the multilingual content originating from different French-speaking countries. Of course, the proposed pipeline can be adapted to other combinations of NER tools. Finally, its statistical analysis also shows that it is a very large and rich resource compared with equivalent datasets. We therefore think that stvd-kg will be useful for applications requiring semantically enriched EPGs, particularly in information retrieval and recommendation [21,25]. In addition, its high reliability makes it suitable as a training dataset for LLMs [10,14]. In future work, we plan to go a step further by mapping stvd-kg to TV audiovisual data obtained from live capture for opening the way to multimodal applications such as visual language understanding, and improved media accessibility.

Acknowledgements. This work was partially supported by the university technical institute (IUT) of Blois.

References

1. IMDB. https://www.imdb.com/
2. Schema.org. https://schema.org/
3. Ali, A., et al.: Event-based ontologies: a review. IJCSNS **23**(5), 212–220 (2023)
4. Antonini, A., et al.: MeSoOnTV: ontology-based TV knowledge system. In: ACM Hypertext, pp. 208–213 (2013)
5. Brickley, D., Guha, R.: RDF schema 1.0. W3C Rec. (2004)
6. Dowman, M., et al.: TV/radio news annotation via web. In: WWW, pp. 225–234 (2005)
7. EBU: Ebucore. https://www.ebu.ch/... (2014)
8. Fetahu, B., et al.: Semeval-2023: Multilingual NER. arXiv (2023)
9. Gonzalez-Toral, S., et al.: Annotating program guides semantically. In: KGSWC, pp. 72–86 (2019)
10. Hamdi, A., et al.: Multilingual dataset for NER. In: SIGIR, pp. 2328–2334 (2021)
11. Harrando, I., Troncy, R.: Memad knowledge graph (2021). https://doi.org/10.5281/zenodo.4817403
12. Honnibal, M., Montani, I.: spaCy 2: NLU with CNNs and bloom embeddings (2017), to appear

13. Jiang, R., et al.: Evaluating NER systems. In: Named Entity Workshop, pp. 21–27 (2016)
14. Katz, U., et al.: Neretrieve: dataset for NER + retrieval. arXiv (2023)
15. Le, V., et al.: TV copy detection dataset. In: ICIAP, pp. 388–399 (2022)
16. Macedo, P., et al.: Web data for program guides. In: LiME, Crete (2014)
17. Maurel, D., et al.: Casen: French NER transducer. TAL **52**(1), 69–96 (2011)
18. Narducci, F., et al.: TV-program retrieval and classification: a comparison of approaches based on machine learning. Inf. Syst. Front. **20**, 1–15 (2018)
19. Orlandi, F., et al.: Movie analysis with knowledge graphs. In: SITIS, pp. 609–616 (2018)
20. Rayar, F., et al.: TV political content dataset. In: CBMI, pp. 181–185 (2022)
21. Redondo-García, J., et al.: OntoTV: content management for TV. Int. J. Semant. Comput. **6**(1), 111–130 (2012)
22. Souza, C., et al.: Tv video indexing and retrieval. J. AI Res. **3**, 49–61 (2014)
23. Stamou, G., et al.: Multimedia + semantic web. IEEE Multimed. **13**(1), 86–90 (2006)
24. Vrandečić, D., Krötzsch, M.: Wikidata: collaborative knowledge. Commun. ACM **57**(10), 78–85 (2014)
25. Véras, D., et al.: Tv recommender systems survey. Expert Syst. Appl. **42**(22), 9046–9076 (2015)

DO-RAG: A Domain-Specific QA Framework Using Knowledge Graph-Enhanced Retrieval-Augmented Generation

David Osei Opoku[1], Ming Sheng[2], and Yong Zhang[2](✉)

[1] Department of Computer Science and Technology, Tsinghua University, Beijing, China
daw23@mails.tsinghua.edu.cn
[2] Beijing National Research Center for Information Science and Technology, Tsinghua University, Beijing, China
{shengming,zhangyong05}@tsinghua.edu.cn

Abstract. Domain-specific question answering (QA) systems require not just generative fluency but high factual accuracy grounded in structured expert knowledge. While recent Retrieval-Augmented Generation (RAG) frameworks improve context recall, they struggle with integrating heterogeneous data and maintaining reasoning consistency. To address these challenges, we propose **DO-RAG**, a scalable and customizable hybrid QA framework that integrates multi-level knowledge graph (KG) construction with semantic vector retrieval. Our system employs a novel agentic chain-of-thought architecture to extract structured relationships from unstructured, multimodal documents, constructing dynamic knowledge graphs that enhance retrieval precision. At query time, DO-RAG fuses graph and vector retrieval results to generate context-aware responses, followed by hallucination mitigation via grounded refinement. Experimental evaluations in the database and electrical domains show near-perfect recall and over 94% answer relevancy, with DO-RAG outperforming baseline frameworks by up to 33.38%. By combining traceability, adaptability, and performance efficiency, DO-RAG offers a reliable foundation for multi-domain, high-precision QA at scale.

Keywords: Vertical Domain QA · Large Language Model · Knowledge Graph · Retrieval-Augmented Generation · Technical Knowledge Retrieval

1 Introduction

Question-Answering (QA) systems enable users to retrieve information from large corpora by posing natural-language queries. They fall into two broad categories: open-domain QA, which draws on general knowledge to answer questions, and closed-domain QA, which relies on specialized, often technical, resources

I. Awan et al. (Eds.): WISE 2025, LNCS 16367, pp. 406–421, 2026.
https://doi.org/10.1007/978-981-95-7394-3_28

to address queries. Closed-domain scenarios expose the limitations of generic models, which must be augmented with structured expert knowledge to deliver precise, reliable answers.

Recent advances in large language models (LLMs) such as DeepSeek-R1 [8], Grok 3 [27], QwQ-32B [24], and OpenAI's O3 [15] have dramatically improved fluency and contextual understanding. Yet, these models depend predominantly on parametric knowledge and can hallucinate or provide imprecise responses when confronted with domain-specific terminology or complex multi-step reasoning [29].

To address these limitations, Retrieval-Augmented Generation (RAG) has emerged as a popular approach for improving factual consistency by retrieving relevant text snippets before generation [2]. In parallel, knowledge graphs (KGs) offer a complementary solution by encoding entities and their relations in a structured form, facilitating multi-hop reasoning and precise context assembly [25].

However, existing RAG frameworks struggle to capture the intricate relationships among entities in technical manuals and multimodal resources, leading to fragmented retrieval outputs and persistent hallucinations [26,30]. When retrieval and generation components remain loosely coupled, there is no guarantee that the final answer faithfully reflects the retrieved evidence. Although knowledge graphs promise more structured context, manually constructing and maintaining high-quality, domain-specific graphs is labor-intensive, and marrying them with vector search and LLM prompting adds substantial engineering overhead. Consequently, current KG-RAG hybrids face scalability bottlenecks and require extensive manual tuning to remain robust as knowledge evolves.

In this paper, we introduce DO-RAG, a Domain-specific Retrieval-Augmented Generation framework that end-to-end automates the transformation of unstructured, multimodal documents into a dynamic, multi-level knowledge graph via an agentic chain-of-thought extraction pipeline; tightly fuses the resulting graph traversal with semantic vector search to assemble a context-rich prompt; and then grounds generation in retrieved evidence through a refinement step that detects and corrects hallucinations.

Our contributions are as follows:

- **Agentic, multi-stage KG construction.** We design and implement a hierarchical, agent-based extraction pipeline that processes text, tables, code snippets, and images to automatically build and update a knowledge graph capturing entities, relations, and attributes.
- **Hybrid retrieval fusion.** We develop a unified mechanism that merges graph-based traversal with semantic search at query time, ensuring that all relevant, structurally grounded information informs the LLM's prompt.
- **Grounded hallucination mitigation.** We introduce a post-generation refinement step that cross-verifies initial LLM outputs against the knowledge graph and iteratively corrects inconsistencies, dramatically reducing factual errors.

- **Plug-and-play modularity.** Our framework accommodates diverse LLMs and retrieval modules, enabling seamless component swapping and straightforward extension to new domains without retraining.

Evaluated on expert-curated benchmarks in the database and electrical engineering domains, DO-RAG achieves near-perfect contextual recall and over 94% answer relevancy, outperforming existing RAG platforms such as FastGPT [11], TiDB.AI [17] and Dify.AI [7] by up to 33.38%. By unifying structured and generative approaches, DO-RAG provides a scalable, high-precision solution for domain-specific QA.

The rest of this paper is organized as follows: Sect. 2 reviews existing work on domain-specific QA and RAG frameworks. Section 3 explains the design and approach of DO-RAG. Section 4 presents the experimental setup, datasets, metrics, and results, comparing DO-RAG to baselines, and ends with a discussion of limitations and future work. Section 5 summarizes the main findings and contributions.

2 Preliminary and Related Work

2.1 Preliminary

In domain-specific question-answering, a system retrieves answers from a document corpus $\mathcal{D}$ and a knowledge graph $\mathcal{G} = (V, E, W)$, where V is a set of entities, E denotes relationships, and $W : E \rightarrow [0, 1]$ assigns confidence weights. A query q is mapped to a vector:

$$Q = E(q), \quad Q \in \mathbb{R}^d, \tag{1}$$

where E is an embedding function, and d is the embedding dimension. Document chunks $c_i \in \mathcal{D}$ are similarly embedded:

$$C_i = E(c_i), \quad C_i \in \mathbb{R}^d. \tag{2}$$

The retrieval score S combines semantic and graph-based relevance:

$$S = \alpha \cdot \max_i \mathrm{sim}(Q, C_i) + (1 - \alpha) \cdot R(\mathcal{G}_Q), \tag{3}$$

where $\mathrm{sim}(Q, C_i)$ is cosine similarity, $R(\mathcal{G}_Q)$ retrieves relevant entities from $\mathcal{G}$, and $\alpha \in [0, 1]$ balances contributions. The answer is generated as:

$$A = G(Q, S, C), \tag{4}$$

where G is the generation function. The goal is to minimize factual errors:

$$\min_\theta \mathbb{E}_{(q,a^*)\sim\mathcal{D}_{\mathrm{eval}}} \mathcal{L}(G(Q, S; \theta), a^*), \tag{5}$$

with θ as model parameters, $\mathcal{D}_{\mathrm{eval}}$ as the evaluation dataset with ground-truth answers a^*, and $\mathcal{L}$ as the loss function.

2.2 Related Work

Domain-specific QA systems have evolved from rule-based approaches to advanced methods integrating structured knowledge and generative models. Early systems relied on static rules and limited knowledge bases, restricting their adaptability to complex queries [1]. Knowledge graphs address this by encoding entities and relationships, enhancing reasoning, but their manual construction is resource-intensive [33].

Large language models excel in natural language tasks but struggle in specialized domains due to hallucinations and insufficient domain knowledge [3,21]. Retrieval-augmented Generation mitigates this by grounding responses in retrieved documents [12], yet faces challenges in capturing intricate relationships in technical contexts [28,32]. Recent advances in dense passage retrieval have shown promise in improving conversational question answering through contrastive learning approaches [31] and enhanced retrieval mechanisms with exact match signals [16].

Current frameworks like KIMedQA [30] and Panda [20] are domain-specific but lack scalability and flexibility. KIMedQA achieves high medical QA accuracy but is computationally intensive, while Panda, focused on database debugging, does not support multi-domain applications. KG-RAG [22] integrates biomedical KGs with RAG but struggles with scalability. Additionally, automated feature transformation techniques [10] and multilingual approaches for aspect-based sentiment classification [9] have demonstrated the importance of domain-specific adaptations in specialized applications.

To overcome these limitations, we propose DO-RAG, a framework that automates dynamic KG construction, fuses vector retrieval with grounded generation, and enhances precision and adaptability in domain-specific QA.

3 Approach

3.1 System Overview

As illustrated in Fig. 1, DO-RAG comprises four key stages: (1) multimodal document ingestion and chunking, (2) multi-level entity-relation extraction for knowledge graph (KG) construction, (3) hybrid retrieval combining graph traversal and dense vector search, and (4) a multi-stage generation pipeline for grounded, user-aligned answers.

It begins by parsing heterogeneous domain data—such as logs, technical manuals, diagrams, and specifications—into meaningful chunk units. These chunks are stored alongside their vector embeddings in a pgvector-enabled PostgreSQL instance. Simultaneously, an agentic chain-of-thought entity extraction pipeline transforms document content into a structured multimodal knowledge graph (MMKG), capturing multi-granular relationships such as system parameters, behaviors, and dependencies.

During user interaction, the query undergoes decomposition through an intent recognition module, which segments it into one or more sub-queries representing discrete informational intents. The system first performs retrieval from

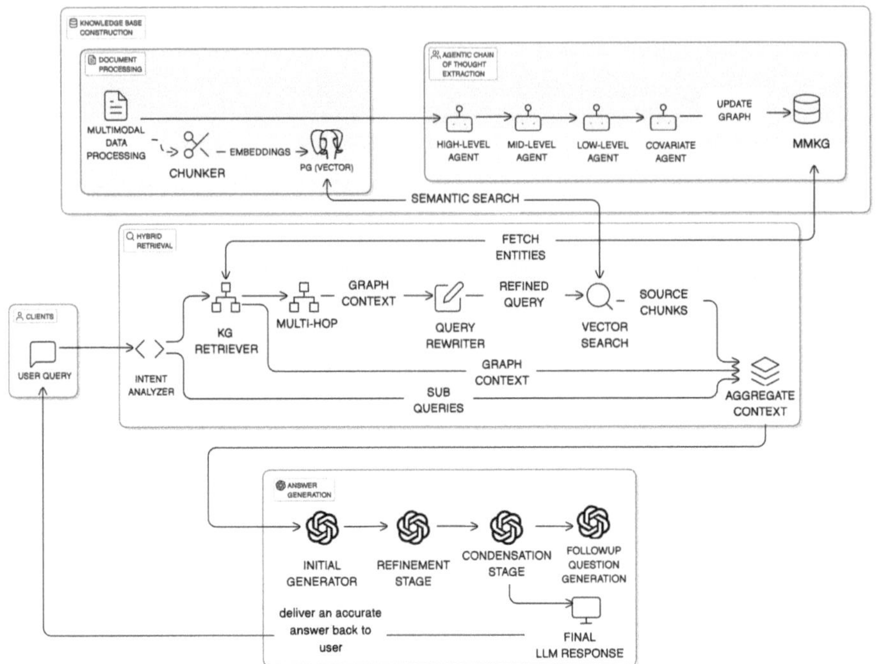

Fig. 1. High-level overview of DO-RAG methodology.

the knowledge graph by embedding the initial query and matching it to relevant entities. This is followed by a multi-hop traversal to expand the retrieval scope, yielding structured, domain-specific context grounded in entity relationships and metadata.

Subsequently, this graph-derived context is used to rewrite the original query into a more specific and disambiguated form using a graph-aware prompt template. The refined query is then encoded into a dense vector and used to retrieve top-k semantically similar chunks from the vector database.

At this point, the system consolidates all relevant information sources: the original user query, its refined version, the knowledge graph context, the retrieved text chunks, and prior user interaction history. These components are integrated into a unified prompt structure and passed into the generation pipeline.

The generation proceeds in three stages: initial answer generation, refinement for factual consistency and clarity, and condensation to ensure coherence and brevity. Finally, DO-RAG invokes a follow-up question generator, which formulates next-step queries based on the refined answer and overall conversation context, enhancing user engagement and supporting multi-turn interaction.

3.2 Knowledge Base Construction

Document processing begins with multimodal ingestion, where text, tables, and images are normalized and segmented into coherent chunks. Metadata—including source file structure, section hierarchy, and layout tags—is retained for traceability.

Document Structure Parsing Mechanisms. The document parsing system employs hierarchical decomposition to process heterogeneous content through structural element identification. Documents are tokenized and analyzed for semantic boundaries while preserving metadata including file paths, section hierarchies, and layout information. The pipeline normalizes multimodal content: text undergoes segmentation, tabular data preserves relationships, and images are processed using Vision-Language Models (VLMs) for semantic extraction.

Structural Element Identification Rules. Structural elements are identified through rule-based pattern recognition following core principles: hierarchical containment (sections→subsections→paragraphs), dependency relationships via linked edges, sequential ordering through metadata, and cross-reference resolution. Pattern matching identifies structural markers (headings, lists, formatting cues) to establish logical structure and create appropriate knowledge graph nodes.

Agent Workflow and Algorithms. The multi-agent extraction system operates through coordinated sequential processing with inter-agent communication. Algorithm 1 shows the workflow: initialize four extractors $E_{high}, E_{mid}, E_{low}, E_{cov}$, sequentially extract entities at each level, combine relationships, apply deduplication ($\tau = 0.85$, tuned via grid search on validation F1-score), and generate synopsis entities. Each agent uses DSPy signatures for consistent JSON output and structured data exchange.

Algorithm 1. Multi-Level Extraction Workflow

Require: Document text T, DSPy language model LM
Ensure: Knowledge graph $\mathcal{G} = (V, E, W)$
Initialize extractors: $E_{high}, E_{mid}, E_{low}, E_{cov}$
$entities_{high} \leftarrow E_{high}(T)$ {Extract structural entities}
$entities_{mid} \leftarrow E_{mid}(T, entities_{high})$ {Extract domain entities}
$entities_{low} \leftarrow E_{low}(T, entities_{mid})$ {Extract operational details}
$entities_{all} \leftarrow entities_{high} \cup entities_{mid} \cup entities_{low}$
$relationships_{all} \leftarrow$ Combine relationships from all levels
$covariates \leftarrow E_{cov}(T, entities_{all})$ {Extract entity attributes}
Update $entities_{all}$ with $covariates$
Apply deduplication using cosine similarity threshold $\tau = 0.85$
Generate synopsis entities for entity groups with shared topics
return $\mathcal{G}(entities_{all}, relationships_{all})$

Entity-Relation Extraction Workflows. The entity-relation extraction operates through specialized DSPy-based agents at four granularity levels: High-level extracts document structure (chapters, sections) with containment and hierarchical relationships; Mid-level targets domain entities (components, configurations, operations) with operational dependencies; Low-level captures system details (processes, memory, files, metrics) with system-level interactions; Covariate enriches entities with technical specifications, configurations, and metadata for comprehensive characterization.

The structured knowledge extraction process operates in parallel with document parsing, utilizing the multi-agent, multi-level pipeline described above. As shown in Fig. 2, this coordinated workflow ensures comprehensive knowledge capture across all abstraction levels.

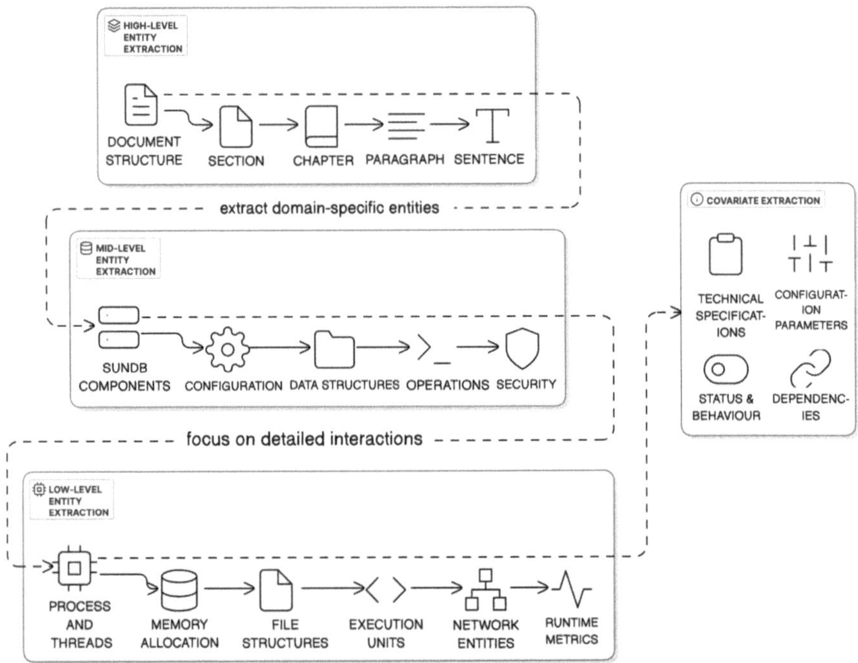

Fig. 2. Multi-level entity-relation extraction.

The output is a dynamic KG $\mathcal{G} = (V, E, W)$, where nodes V represent entities, edges E represent relationships, and weights W encode confidence scores. To avoid redundancy, deduplication is enforced using cosine similarity between new and existing entity embeddings. Additionally, synopsis nodes are synthesized to group similar entities and reduce graph complexity.

3.3 Hybrid Retrieval and Query Decomposition

As illustrated in Fig. 3, when a user submits a question, DO-RAG performs structured decomposition using an LLM-based intent analyzer. This yields sub-queries that are used to guide retrieval from both the KG and the vector store. It first retrieves relevant nodes from the KG using semantic similarity, then performs multi-hop traversal to assemble a context-rich subgraph. This graph-derived evidence is used to rewrite and disambiguate the query via a graph-aware prompt. The refined query is then vectorized and used to retrieve semantically similar chunks from the vector database. Finally, DO-RAG aggregates all sources—original and refined queries, graph context, vector-retrieved chunks, and user conversation history—into a unified prompt structure. For example, when processing the query "How does SunDB handle transaction logging?", the system embeds the query, matches against entity embeddings to identify relevant nodes (e.g., "Gserver Process", "Log Buffer"), performs K-hop expansion to discover related entities, and uses the retrieved subgraph to refine the query with structured context.

3.4 Grounded Answer Generation and Delivery

As shown in Fig. 4, the final answer is generated using a staged prompt strategy. The initial naive prompt instructs the LLM to answer based only on the retrieved evidence while explicitly avoiding unsupported content. The output is passed through a refinement prompt that restructures and validates the answer, followed by a condensation stage that aligns tone, language, and style with the original query.

To enhance user engagement and simulate expert-like guidance, DO-RAG also generates follow-up questions based on the refined answer. The final output includes (1) a polished, verifiable answer, (2) citation footnotes tracing the answer to the source, and (3) a set of targeted follow-up questions.

Hallucination Mitigation Mechanisms. DO-RAG employs multiple strategies to prevent hallucinations: (1) Evidence-grounded generation where the LLM is explicitly instructed to answer only based on retrieved evidence, (2) Confidence-based filtering using entity similarity scores and relationship weights to prioritize high-confidence information, (3) Multi-stage validation through refinement and condensation prompts that cross-check factual consistency, and (4) Explicit uncertainty handling where insufficient evidence triggers the response "Insufficient evidence available" rather than generating speculative content. For instance, if a query about "SunDB encryption algorithms" retrieves no relevant entities or chunks above the confidence threshold ($\tau = 0.7$, tuned for precision-recall balance), the system explicitly states the limitation rather than hallucinating information.

4 Experiments

To evaluate the DO-RAG framework, we selected SunDB, a distributed relational database management system developed by Client Service International,

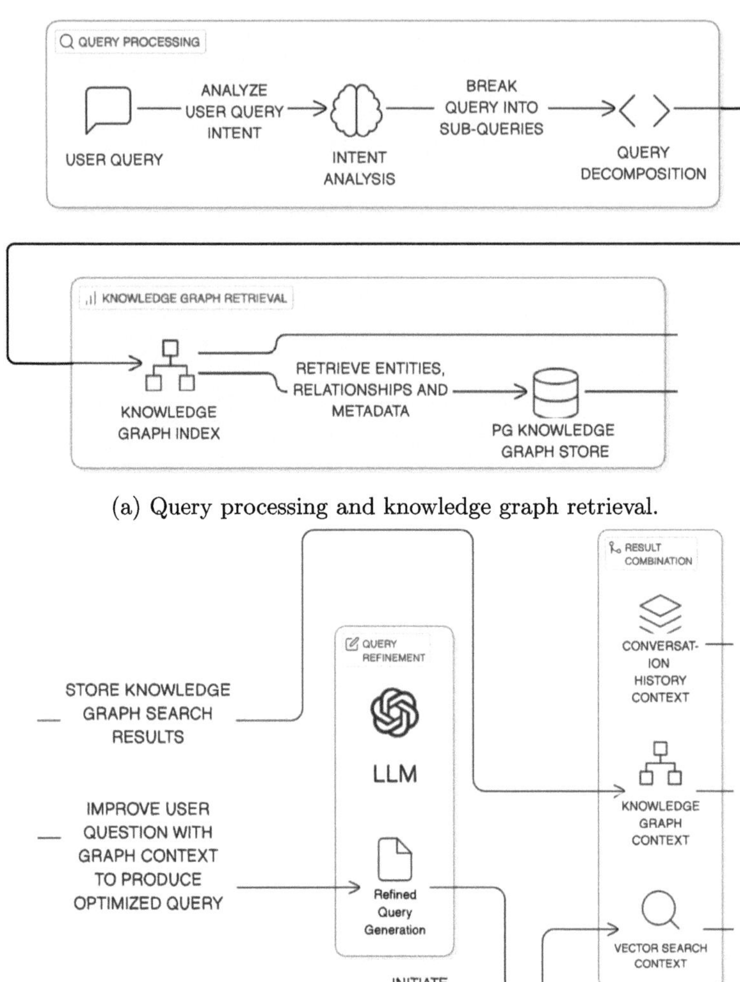

(a) Query processing and knowledge graph retrieval.

(b) Query refinement, vector Search, and result combination.

Fig. 3. Overview of the retrieval process.

Inc. (CSII), as the specialized domain. SunDB is widely used in critical industries such as banking, telecommunications, and government, offering a complex, heterogeneous dataset of technical manuals, system logs, and specifications. This

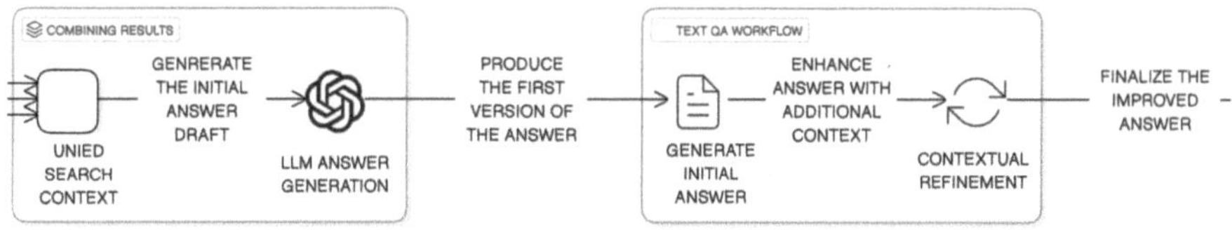

(a) Combining results and Text QA workflow.

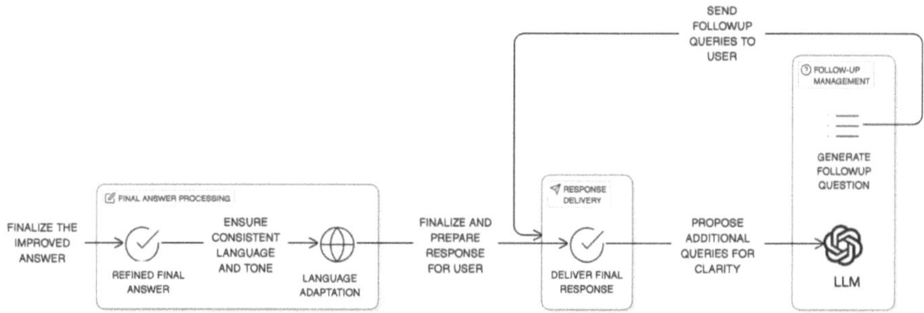

(b) Final answer processing, response delivery, and follow-up management.

Fig. 4. Overall response pipeline.

domain is ideal for testing DO-RAG's multimodal ingestion, multi-level entity-relationship extraction, hybrid retrieval, and grounded answer generation.

4.1 Experimental Setup

Hardware and Software. The evaluation was conducted on a high-performance Ubuntu workstation equipped with 64GB RAM, an NVIDIA A100 80GB GPU, and a 1TB hard disk. The experiment was implemented using locally deployed software to prioritize data security and efficiency. LangFuse (v3.29.0) [23] enabled tracing and logging of retrieval-augmented generation operations, Redis (v7.2.5) [19] managed caching, MinIO (v2025-04-22T22-12-26Z) [13] handled document storage, and ClickHouse (v25.4.3.22-stable) [4] supported high-performance analytics. PostgreSQL (v16.4) [18] served as the relational backend storage with pgvector.

Datasets. Two datasets were employed to assess cross-domain adaptability: the primary SunDB dataset, comprising technical manuals, logs, and specifications with embedded tables and code, and a secondary Electrical dataset of manuals and schematics with diagrams. Each dataset included 245 expert-curated questions with ground-truth answers, annotated with source locations (chapter, section, page) for precise validation. While the 245 questions per domain represent a focused evaluation suitable for specialized technical domains, we acknowledge this scale may limit generalizability to broader applications. This constraint reflects the challenge of obtaining expert-validated ground truth in highly technical domains, where each question requires domain expertise for accurate annotation.

Metrics and Tools. The evaluation focused on four core metrics, each with a success threshold of 0.7 (score range: 0–1), to assess retrieval and generation quality:

- **Answer Relevancy (AR)**: Measures alignment between the query and the generated answer. The framework reverse-engineers N artificial questions from the generated answer using an LLM, then computes the average cosine similarity between the original query embedding and these generated question embeddings:

$$\text{AR} = \frac{1}{N}\sum_{i=1}^{N}\cos(E_{g_i}, E_o) = \frac{1}{N}\sum_{i=1}^{N}\frac{E_{g_i}\cdot E_o}{\|E_{g_i}\|\|E_o\|},$$

  where $N = 3$ (RAGAS default for balancing computational efficiency with statistical reliability), E_{g_i} is the embedding of the i-th generated question, and E_o is the original query embedding.
- **Contextual Recall (CR)**: Evaluates whether all relevant information from the ground truth is captured in the retrieved context:

$$\text{CR} = \frac{\text{Number of Attributable Statements}}{\text{Total Number of Statements}},$$

  where *Total Statements* are all factual claims decomposed from the ground truth answer, and *Attributable Statements* are those claims that can be supported by evidence found in the retrieved context.
- **Contextual Precision (CP)**: Assesses the accuracy of retrieved context, excluding irrelevant data:

$$\text{CP@K} = \frac{\sum_{k=1}^{K}(\text{Precision@k} \times v_k)}{\text{Total number of relevant items in top } K \text{ results}},$$

  where $\text{Precision@k} = \frac{\text{true positives@k}}{\text{true positives@k+false positives@k}}$, and $v_k \in \{0, 1\}$ indicates relevance.
- **Faithfulness (F)**: Measures how accurately the answer reflects the retrieved context by decomposing the generated answer into individual statements and verifying each against the retrieved context:

$$\text{F} = \frac{\text{Number of Truthful Claims}}{\text{Total Number of Claims}},$$

  where claims are atomic factual statements extracted from the generated answer, and truthfulness is determined by LLM-based verification against the retrieved context.

These metrics were computed using RAGAS [6] for granular insights, DeepEval [23] for end-to-end analysis, and LangFuse [23] for detailed trace analysis, logging operations from query decomposition to answer generation.

Baseline. Two baseline comparisons were established. Externally, DO-RAG, implemented as SunDB.AI, was compared against FastGPT, a versatile open-source RAG framework with LLM-driven knowledge base construction; TiDB.AI, a graph-enhanced RAG framework tailored to database domain knowledge; and Dify.AI, an industrial-grade open-source RAG platform with generalized knowledge graph integration. Internally, DO-RAG with knowledge graph integration was contrasted against a variant relying solely on vector-based retrieval, isolating the knowledge graph's impact.

Evaluation Methodology. The evaluation followed a structured methodology. Identical knowledge bases were constructed for all frameworks using the SunDB and Electrical datasets. The same 245 questions were tested across frameworks and domains. Three language models—DeepSeek-R1, DeepSeek-V3 [5], and GPT-4o-mini [14]—were selected. Metrics were computed for each model, and a composite score, averaging the four core metrics, provided a balanced performance measure.

4.2 Results

External Baseline Comparison. Table 1 presents the composite scores for the external baseline comparison, evaluating SunDB.AI against FastGPT, TiDB.AI, and Dify.AI across the tested language models. SunDB.AI consistently outperformed all three baselines. Figure 5 visualizes these results, illustrating SunDB.AI's consistent superiority.

Table 1. Comparative performance of graph-enhanced RAG frameworks (External Baseline).

Model	Composite Score				Improvement over SunDB.AI		
	SunDB.AI	FastGPT	TiDB.AI	Dify.AI	vs FastGPT	vs TiDB.AI	vs Dify.AI
GPT-4o-mini	**0.741**	0.728	0.597	0.629	↑ 1.70%	↑ 24.02%	↑ 17.72%
DeepSeek-V3	**0.704**	0.623	0.704	0.601	↑ 13.10%	↑ 0.10%	↑ 17.31%
DeepSeek-R1	**0.847**	0.659	0.693	0.635	↑ 28.50%	↑ 22.21%	↑ 33.38%

Internal Baseline Comparison. Table 2 evaluates the impact of knowledge graph integration using DeepSeek-R1 and DeepSeek-V3. With the knowledge graph, both models achieved perfect Contextual Recall (1.000), with DeepSeek-V3 improving Answer Relevancy by 5.7% and Contextual Precision by 2.6%. Without the knowledge graph, recall dropped to 0.964–0.977, and Faithfulness was lower due to reliance on unstructured vector search. DeepSeek-R1 exhibited a slight Faithfulness decline (-5.6%) with the knowledge graph, likely due to creative deviations.

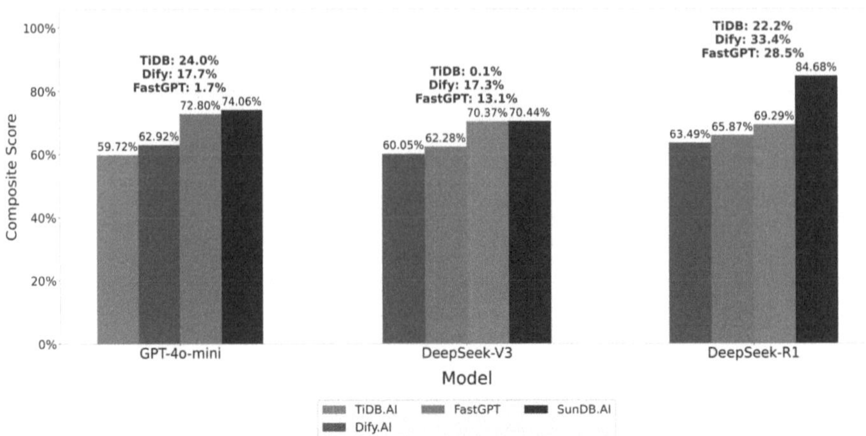

Fig. 5. Composite score comparison across frameworks and language models.

Table 2. Impact of knowledge graph integration on DeepSeek models.

Metric	DeepSeek-R1		DeepSeek-V3		KG Impact (R1)	KG Impact (V3)
	Baseline	+KG	Baseline	+KG	(Δ)	(Δ)
Answer Relevancy	0.851	0.820	0.871	**0.921**	↓ 3.6%	↑ 5.7%
Contextual Recall	0.964	**1.000**	0.977	**1.000**	↑ 3.7%	↑ 2.4%
Contextual Precision	0.907	**0.918**	0.919	**0.943**	↑ 1.2%	↑ 2.6%
Faithfulness	0.718	0.678	0.711	**0.714**	↓ 5.6%	↑ 0.4%

Domain-Specific Performance. Tables 3 and 4 display the performance metrics for each language model in the SunDB and Electrical domains, respectively. In both domains, Contextual Recall values are at or near 1.0. Variations in Answer Relevancy, Contextual Precision, and Faithfulness reveal model-specific strengths.

4.3 Discussion

Limitations. The dataset scale of 245 questions per domain may not capture the full real-world query spectrum. Creative LLMs occasionally hallucinate despite grounding mechanisms. The framework involves resource-intensive multi-level inference with multiple calls per document chunk. Graph traversal exhibits quadratic scaling with significant memory overhead for large knowledge graphs.

Future Work. We plan to optimize scalability through hierarchical graph partitioning and lazy loading mechanisms. Performance will be enhanced via adaptive extraction algorithms that balance thoroughness with computational constraints. Robustness improvements will focus on hallucination mitigation and expanded datasets for better generalizability.

Table 3. Performance comparison of LLMs in the database domain.

Model	Answer Relevancy	Contextual Recall	Contextual Precision (ragas)	Faithfulness
DeepSeek-R1	0.820407	**1.000000**	0.918463	0.677958
DeepSeek-V3	0.920967	**1.000000**	0.942694	0.714305
GPT-4o	**0.944203**	0.979167	0.950279	0.770946
GPT-4o mini	0.939535	0.977273	0.921744	**0.842160**
Grok 3	0.898365	**1.000000**	**0.953021**	0.836704

Table 4. Performance comparison of LLMs in the electrical domain.

Model	Answer Relevancy	Contextual Recall	Contextual Precision (ragas)	Faithfulness
DeepSeek-V3	0.965342	**1.000000**	0.919427	0.912089
GPT-4o	**0.975000**	**1.000000**	**0.930203**	0.870054
GPT-4o mini	0.958386	**1.000000**	0.913326	**0.943798**
O3 mini	0.949360	**1.000000**	0.888545	0.880241

5 Conclusion

This paper introduces DO-RAG, a domain-specific retrieval-augmented generation framework that addresses limitations of existing RAG systems in closed-domain QA. DO-RAG transforms unstructured, multimodal domain data into dynamic, multi-level knowledge graphs using an agentic chain-of-thought extraction pipeline. It integrates graph traversal with semantic vector search to retrieve context-rich, structurally grounded information. A post-generation refinement step cross-verifies outputs against the knowledge graph, iteratively correcting hallucinations to enhance factual accuracy. Empirical results in the database and electrical domains demonstrate near-perfect recall and answer relevancy exceeding 94%, with DO-RAG outperforming baseline frameworks by up to 33.38%. These findings demonstrate DO-RAG's effectiveness in delivering robust, high-accuracy QA across specialized domains, unifying structured knowledge representation with generative reasoning for scalable and adaptable information systems.

Acknowledgment. This work is supported by Tsinghua University - Client Service International Inc. Joint Institute for Advanced Intelligent Database, Beijing National Research Center for Information Science and Technology.

Disclosure of Interests. The authors have no competing interests to declare that are relevant to the content of this article.

References

1. Allam, A.M.N., Haggag, M.H.: Question answering in restricted domains: an overview. COLI **33**(1), 41–66 (2012). https://doi.org/10.1162/coli.2007.33.1.41
2. Bhushan, K., et al.: Systematic knowledge injection into large language models via diverse augmentation for domain-specific rag. In: NAACL (2025)
3. Chen, J., et al.: When large language models meet personalization: perspectives of challenges and opportunities. WWW **27**(42) (2024). https://doi.org/10.1007/s11280-024-01276-1
4. ClickHouse: Open source column-oriented DBMS (2025), version 25.4.3.22-stable
5. DeepSeek-AI, et al.: Deepseek-v3 technical report. CoRR abs/2412.19437 (2024)
6. Developers, R.: Ragas documentation (2023)
7. Dify: Dify.ai: Open-source LLM app development platform (2023)
8. Guo, D., et al.: Deepseek-r1 incentivizes reasoning in LLMs through reinforcement learning. Nature **645**(8012), 633–638 (2025). https://doi.org/10.1038/s41586-025-09422-z
9. Horst, S., Frasincar, F.: Multilingual, cross-lingual, and unilingual models for ABSC. In: WISE, pp. 285–299. Springer, Cham (2024)
10. Huang, S., Zhang, Z., Wen, Q., Wang, H., Sun, L.: Autotable: effective and efficient automated feature transformation. In: WISE, pp. 123–137. Springer, Cham (2024)
11. Labring: FastGPT: empower AI with your expertise (2025)
12. Lewis, P., et al.: Retrieval-augmented generation for knowledge-intensive NLP tasks. In: NIPS, vol. 33, pp. 9459–9474 (2020). https://doi.org/10.5555/3495724.3496517
13. MinIO: High performance object storage (2025), version 2025-04-22T22-12-26Z
14. OpenAI: GPT-4o mini: advancing cost-efficient intelligence (2024)
15. OpenAI: Introducing o3 and o4 mini (2024)
16. Oussaidene, S., et al.: Markeddpr: enhancing dense passage retrieval with exact match signals and synthetic data augmentation. In: WISE, pp. 42–56. Springer, Cham (2024). https://doi.org/10.1007/978-981-96-0579-8_4
17. PingCAP: Tidb.AI: an open-source graphrag knowledge base tool (2024)
18. PostgreSQL Global Development Group: Postgresql (2025), version 16.4
19. Redis: Redis (2025), version 7.2.5
20. Singh, V.Y., et al.: Panda: performance debugging for databases using LLM agents. In: CIDR (2024)
21. Singhal, K., et al.: Large language models encode clinical knowledge. Nature **620**(7972), 172–180 (2023). https://doi.org/10.1038/s41586-023-06291-2
22. Soman, K., et al.: Biomedical knowledge graph-enhanced prompt generation for large language models. CoRR abs/2311.17330 (2023)
23. Team, L.: Langfuse: observability for LLM applications (2025), version 3.29.0
24. Team, Q.: QWQ: reflect deeply on the boundaries of the unknown (2024)
25. Tu, A., et al.: Lightprof: a lightweight reasoning framework for large language model on knowledge graph. In: AAAI (2025). https://doi.org/10.1609/aaai.v39i22.34510
26. Wang, Y., et al.: Knowledge graph prompting for multi-document question answering. In: AAAI, vol. 38, no. 17, pp. 19206–19214 (2024)
27. xAI: Grok 3 beta—the age of reasoning agents (2025)
28. Yang, Y., et al.: A review on the reliability of knowledge graph: from a knowledge representation learning perspective. World Wide Web **28**(4) (2025). https://doi.org/10.1007/s11280-024-01316-w

29. Yang, Z., et al.: CuriousLLM: elevating multi-document question answering with LLM-enhanced knowledge graph reasoning. In: NAACL (2025)
30. Zafar, A., et al.: Kimedqa: towards building knowledge-enhanced medical QA models. JIIS (2024). https://doi.org/10.1007/s10844-024-00844-1
31. Zaib, M., et al.: Learning contrastive representations for dense passage retrieval in open-domain conversational question answering. In: WISE, vol. 15436, pp. 3–13. Springer, Cham (2024). https://doi.org/10.1007/978-981-96-0579-8_1
32. Zhu, X., et al.: Knowledge graph-guided retrieval augmented generation. In: NAACL, pp. 8912–8924 (2025)
33. Zhu, Y., et al.: LLMs for knowledge graph construction and reasoning: recent capabilities and future opportunities. World Wide Web **27**(58) (2024)

Security and Networking

PhishSSL: Self-supervised Contrastive Learning for Phishing Website Detection

Wenhao Li[1], Selvakumar Manickam[1(✉)], Yung-Wey Chong[2], Shankar Karuppayah[1], Priyadarsi Nanda[3], and Binyong Li[4]

[1] Cybersecurity Research Centre, Universiti Sains Malaysia, Pulau Pinang, Malaysia
wenhaoli@ieee.org, {selva,kshankar}@usm.my

[2] School of Computer Sciences, Universiti Sains Malaysia, Pulau Pinang, Malaysia
chong@usm.my

[3] Faculty of Engineering and IT, University of Technology Sydney, Sydney, Australia
priyadarsi.nanda@uts.edu.au

[4] Chengdu University of Information Technology, Chengdu, China
lby@cuit.edu.cn

Abstract. Phishing websites remain a persistent cybersecurity threat by mimicking legitimate sites to steal sensitive user information. Existing machine learning–based detection methods often rely on supervised learning with labeled data, which not only incurs substantial annotation costs but also limits adaptability to novel attack patterns. To address these challenges, we propose PhishSSL, a self-supervised contrastive learning framework that eliminates the need for labeled phishing data during training. PhishSSL combines hybrid tabular augmentation with adaptive feature attention to produce semantically consistent views and emphasize discriminative attributes. We evaluate PhishSSL on three phishing datasets with distinct feature compositions. Across all datasets, PhishSSL consistently outperforms unsupervised and self-supervised baselines, while ablation studies confirm the contribution of each component. Moreover, PhishSSL maintains robust performance despite the diversity of feature sets, highlighting its strong generalization and transferability. These results demonstrate that PhishSSL offers a promising solution for phishing website detection, particularly effective against evolving threats in dynamic Web environments.

Keywords: Anti-Phishing · Contrastive Learning · Phishing Website Detection · Social Engineering · Self-Supervised Learning

1 Introduction

Phishing websites remain one of the most pervasive and effective vectors in cyberattacks, posing significant threats to users by mimicking legitimate websites to steal sensitive information such as credentials, banking details, and personal data [1]. As phishing campaigns grow increasingly sophisticated—employing evasive techniques like domain spoofing, dynamic content generation, and semantic

I. Awan et al. (Eds.): WISE 2025, LNCS 16367, pp. 425–440, 2026.
https://doi.org/10.1007/978-981-95-7394-3_29

mimicry—developing robust and generalizable phishing detection methods has become a pressing challenge for cybersecurity researchers and practitioners [2].

Existing phishing detection methods largely rely on supervised machine learning (ML) and deep learning (DL) models. Although these approaches demonstrate strong performance in benchmark settings, their dependence on labeled data and previously observed attack patterns leads to high annotation costs and poor adaptability. As a result, they often struggle to generalize to unseen phishing tactics and exhibit limited adaptability to evolving attack strategies. In contrast, self-supervised learning (SSL) has recently demonstrated remarkable success in related security domains, such as intrusion detection and malware classification, by reducing reliance on labeled data and improving generalization to unseen patterns.

Therefore, we propose PhishSSL, a novel self-supervised contrastive learning framework that requires no labeled data during training. Instead, PhishSSL is trained entirely on unlabeled data and leverages mixed tabular augmentations to generate semantically consistent positive samples. The model learns feature-based embeddings through contrastive learning and incorporates a learnable feature attention mechanism to emphasize discriminative patterns. Our main contributions are summarized as follows:

- We design and implement PhishSSL, a self-supervised contrastive learning framework for phishing detection that operates without labeled datasets for training, integrating tabular augmentations and attention-based embedding.
- We conduct comprehensive comparisons with several unsupervised and self-supervised baselines on three phishing datasets, demonstrating the superior performance of PhishSSL.
- We perform an ablation analysis to evaluate the impact of core components such as feature attention, dropout augmentation, and traditional tabular augmentation.

The remainder of the paper is organized as follows: Sect. 2 reviews related work, Sect. 3 presents the proposed PhishSSL method, Sect. 4 describes the evaluation setup, Sect. 5 discusses the results, and Sect. 6 concludes the paper.

2 Related Work

Phishing Website Detection. Traditional phishing website detection methods predominantly leverage supervised ML and DL models trained on handcrafted features extracted from URLs, HTML content, and domain metadata [1]. Common approaches include Decision Trees, Support Vector Machines (SVMs), Convolutional Neural Networks (CNNs), Recurrent Neural Networks (RNNs), and ensemble techniques, which achieve high accuracy on benchmark datasets by modeling known phishing heuristics and statistical patterns [3,4]. More recently, graph-based models such as Graph Neural Networks (GNNs) have been introduced to capture structural and relational dependencies between Web elements [5], further enhancing detection capability. However, these models typically require large amounts of labeled data, which can be expensive and time-consuming to obtain, particularly as phishing tactics continue to evolve. Moreover, their reliance on static training data limits adaptability, as attackers frequently alter content and structure to bypass detection mechanisms [2].

Self-supervised Contrastive Learning. SSL has emerged as a compelling paradigm for representation learning without the need for manual labeling [6]. Contrastive learning, a subclass of SSL, trains models to pull semantically similar samples closer and push dissimilar ones apart in the embedding space [7], which has achieved significant success in vision and natural language processing.

Self-supervised contrastive learning has been widely applied in cybersecurity tasks. In intrusion detection, it enables the learning of robust flow- or packet-level representations from raw traffic, improving generalization across network domains [8]. In container security, contrastive learning has been used to reduce false alarms and detect runtime attacks without manual labeling [9]. In smart contract analysis, it captures semantic relationships between contracts to enhance vulnerability detection [10]. For in-vehicle networks, it supports anomaly detection in the Internet of Vehicles with high robustness under varying attack conditions [11]. In Internet of Things (IoT) malware classification, contrastive learning improves accuracy by learning discriminative representations from transformed malware samples using limited labels [12].

While ML/DL-based methods have advanced phishing detection and SSL has demonstrated effectiveness in other security domains, contrastive SSL remains largely unexplored for phishing websites. Addressing this gap offers a promising avenue to minimize reliance on labels while improving both efficacy and generalization in phishing website detection.

3 Methodology

3.1 Framework Overview

The fundamental principle underlying our approach is that legitimate and phishing websites exhibit distinct patterns in their structural, content, and external characteristics, even without explicit labels. By leveraging contrastive learning, the framework learns to distinguish between semantically similar augmented views of the same website while separating dissimilar samples in the embedding space. This approach eliminates the dependency on manual labeling while capturing intrinsic website properties that generalize across different phishing strategies.

Given an input feature vector $x_i \in \mathbb{R}^{87}$ representing comprehensive website characteristics (illustrated in Sect. 3.2), the objective is to learn an embedding function $f(\cdot) : \mathbb{R}^{87} \rightarrow \mathbb{R}^d$ that minimizes distances between semantically equivalent augmented views while maximizing distances between dissimilar samples. Formally, the learning objective can be expressed as:

$$\min_{f} \mathbb{E}_{x,x^+,x^-}[\max(0, d(f(x), f(x^+)) - d(f(x), f(x^-)) + m)] \quad (1)$$

where x^+ represents positive (augmented) views, x^- represents negative samples, $d(\cdot,\cdot)$ denotes distance metric, and m is the margin parameter.

The Fig. 1 provides an overview of proposed method. The proposed PhishSSL comprises five sequential stages that collectively enable self-supervised phishing detection: (1) feature representation construction from multi-modal website data, (2) embedding encoding with adaptive feature attention, (3) contrastive view generation through sophisticated tabular augmentation, (4) triplet margin loss optimization for discriminative learning, and (5) inference-based classification through learned representations. Algorithm 1 details the overall logic of each stage.

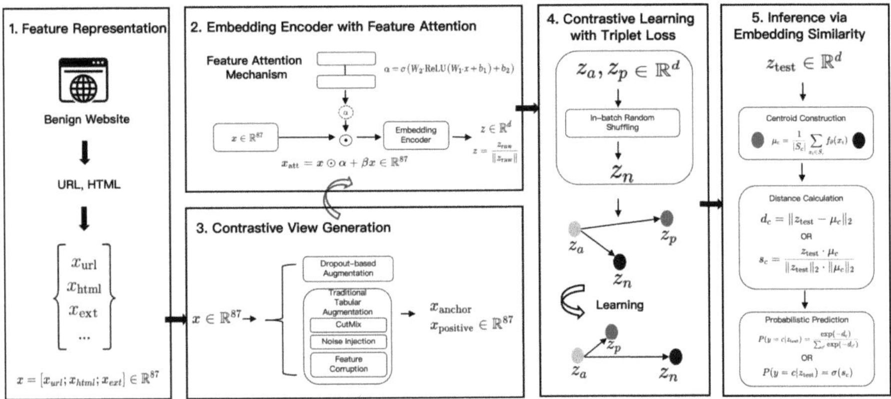

Fig. 1. Proposed PhishSSL Framework.

3.2 Feature Representation Construction

Effective phishing detection requires comprehensive understanding of website characteristics across multiple dimensions. Therefore, our framework follows a systematic extraction of 87-dimensional feature vectors as in [13], as shown in Table 1, that capture complementary aspects of website behavior and structure.

The feature construction process transforms heterogeneous website data into standardized numerical representations suitable for machine learning. The standardization enables consistent comparison and learning across diverse website types and structures. The comprehensive feature vector is mathematically formulated as: $x = [x_{\text{url}}; x_{\text{html}}; x_{\text{ext}}] \in \mathbb{R}^{87}$, where the concatenation operator $[\cdot;\cdot;\cdot]$ combines three complementary feature domains: $x_{url} \in \mathbb{R}^{56}$ captures URL structural properties, $x_{html} \in \mathbb{R}^{24}$ represents HTML content characteristics, and $x_{ext} \in \mathbb{R}^7$ encodes external service indicators.

Algorithm 1: Proposed PhishSSL Framework

Input: Raw website data $(URL, HTML, Domain)$, margin m, augmentation config $\mathcal{A}$, training epochs T
Output: Trained embedding function f, phishing classifier $\mathcal{C}$
Function PHISHSSL-TRAIN:

```
// Stage 1: Feature Representation Construction
foreach website sample w do
    x_url, x_html, x_ext ←
      FeatureConstruction(w.URL, w.HTML, w.Domain);
    x ← [x_url; x_html; x_ext] ∈ ℝ^87;
// Stage 2: Embedding Encoder with Feature Attention
θ_att ← Initialize attention parameters;
for epoch t = 1 to T do
    foreach batch B do
        // Stage 3: Contrastive View Generation via Tabular
           Augmentation
        {x_anchor, x_positive} ← AugmentationGenerator(B, A);
        // Feature Attention and Embedding
        α_weights ← FeatureAttention(x_anchor; θ_att);
        z_anchor ← EmbeddingEncoder(x_anchor ⊙ α_weights);
        z_positive ← EmbeddingEncoder(x_positive ⊙ α_weights);
        // Stage 4: Contrastive Learning with Triplet Margin Loss
        z_negative ← shuffle(z_positive);
        L ← ContrastiveLearning(z_anchor, z_positive, z_negative, m);
        Update parameters via ∇L;
// Stage 5: Inference via Embedding Similarity
// Construct class prototypes used in the evaluation phase
μ_legitimate ← 1/|S_legitimate| Σ_{x_i ∈ S_legitimate} f_θ(x_i);
μ_phishing ← 1/|S_phishing| Σ_{x_i ∈ S_phishing} f_θ(x_i);
// Setup inference classifier using centroids
C ← InferenceSetup(μ_legitimate, μ_phishing);
```

URL Structural Features capture lexical and syntactic properties that often reveal deceptive intent. These include length distributions (unusually long URLs often indicate obfuscation), character frequency patterns (excessive special characters suggest manipulation), subdomain configurations (suspicious subdomain structures), and redirection analysis (multiple redirections often hide true destinations). The ratio of digits in URLs and hostnames provides insights into automated generation patterns common in phishing attacks.

HTML Content Features quantify webpage composition and behavioral characteristics. Hyperlink density ratios reveal external dependency patterns, while resource inclusion analysis identifies suspicious external content loading. Form characteristics are particularly important as phishing sites often contain deceptive login forms. Behavioral indicators such as iframe usage, popup windows, and JavaScript-based redirection provide additional discrimination signals.

Table 1. Comprehensive Feature Taxonomy for Phishing Detection

Category	Feature Subcategory	Specific Features	Count
URL Structure Features (56)	Length Metrics	url_length, hostname_length	2
	Character Frequency	nb_dots, nb_hyphens, nb_at, nb_qm, nb_and, nb_or, nb_eq, nb_underscore, nb_tilde, nb_percent, nb_slash, nb_star, nb_colon, nb_comma, nb_semicolon, nb_dollar, nb_space, nb_www, nb_com, nb_dslash	20
	Security Indicators	ip, https_token, punycode, port	4
	Structural Properties	tld_in_path, tld_in_subdomain, abnormal_subdomain, nb_subdomains, prefix_suffix	5
	Content Analysis	http_in_path, ratio_digits_url, ratio_digits_host	3
	Redirection Patterns	nb_redirection, nb_external_redirection	2
	Lexical Properties	length_words_raw, char_repeat, shortest_words_raw, shortest_word_host, shortest_word_path, longest_words_raw, longest_word_host, longest_word_path, avg_words_raw, avg_word_host, avg_word_path, random_domain	12
	Deception Indicators	phish_hints, domain_in_brand, brand_in_subdomain, brand_in_path, shortening_service	5
	External Validation	path_extension, suspicious_tld, statistical_report	3
HTML Content Features (24)	Hyperlink Analysis	nb_hyperlinks, ratio_intHyperlinks, ratio_extHyperlinks, ratio_nullHyperlinks	4
	Resource Inclusion	nb_extCSS, external_favicon, links_in_tags, ratio_intMedia, ratio_extMedia, ratio_intRedirection	6
	Form Characteristics	login_form, submit_email, sfh	3
	Behavioral Indicators	iframe, popup_window, safe_anchor, onmouseover, right_click, empty_title, domain_in_title, domain_with_copyright, ratio_extRedirection, ratio_intErrors, ratio_extErrors	11
External Service Features (7)	Domain Registration	whois_registered_domain, domain_registration_length, domain_age	3
	Web Presence	web_traffic, dns_record, google_index	3
	Authority Metrics	page_rank	1

External Service Features leverage third-party data sources to assess domain legitimacy and reputation. WHOIS registration data reveals domain age and registration patterns, while DNS record analysis confirms proper domain configuration. Web traffic statistics and search engine indexing status provide insights into domain popularity and legitimacy that are difficult to fabricate quickly.

3.3 Embedding Encoder with Feature Attention

Traditional neural networks treat all input features equally, potentially diluting the impact of highly discriminative characteristics. In phishing detection, certain features (such as URL length, suspicious TLD usage, or external redirections) may be more indicative of malicious intent than others. Furthermore, the relative importance of features may vary across different types of websites and attack strategies.

To address these challenges, our framework incorporates a learnable feature attention mechanism that dynamically weights input features based on their discriminative power for the specific task. This adaptive approach allows the model to focus on the most relevant characteristics while maintaining the ability to leverage the full feature set when beneficial.

The feature attention mechanism employs a two-layer neural network to compute element-wise importance scores: $\alpha = \sigma(W_2 \cdot \text{ReLU}(W_1 \cdot x + b_1) + b_2)$, where $W_1 \in \mathbb{R}^{d_{att} \times 87}$ and $W_2 \in \mathbb{R}^{87 \times d_{att}}$ represent learnable transformation matrices, $b_1 \in \mathbb{R}^{d_{att}}$ and $b_2 \in \mathbb{R}^{87}$ are bias vectors, d_{att} denotes the attention hidden dimension, and $\sigma(\cdot)$ represents the sigmoid activation function. The sigmoid ensures attention weights $\alpha \in [0, 1]^{87}$, providing interpretable importance scores for each feature.

The attended feature representation combines original features with learned importance weights: $x_{\text{att}} = x \odot \alpha + \beta \cdot x$, where $\odot$ denotes element-wise multiplication, and β is a residual connection parameter that prevents complete feature suppression. This formulation ensures that even features with low attention weights retain some influence, maintaining model robustness.

The embedding encoder transforms attended features through a multi-layer architecture:

$$\begin{aligned} h_1 &= \text{ReLU}(W_{enc1} \cdot x_{att} + b_{enc1}) \\ h_2 &= \text{Dropout}(\text{ReLU}(W_{enc2} \cdot h_1 + b_{enc2})) \\ z_{raw} &= W_{enc3} \cdot h_2 + b_{enc3}, \qquad z = \frac{z_{raw}}{\|z_{raw}\|_2} \end{aligned} \tag{2}$$

where $W_{enc1} \in \mathbb{R}^{d_1 \times 87}$, $W_{enc2} \in \mathbb{R}^{d_2 \times d_1}$, and $W_{enc3} \in \mathbb{R}^{d \times d_2}$ are encoding layer weights, and $z \in \mathbb{R}^d$ represents the final L2-normalized embedding.

Layer normalization is applied after each transformation to ensure training stability: $\text{LayerNorm}(h) = \gamma \cdot \frac{h-\mu}{\sqrt{\sigma^2+\epsilon}} + \beta$, where μ and σ^2 are the mean and variance of layer activations, γ and β are learnable scale and shift parameters, and ϵ is a small constant for numerical stability.

The L2 normalization of final embeddings is crucial for contrastive learning as it ensures that distance computations focus on angular relationships rather than magnitude differences: $d(z_i, z_j) = \|z_i - z_j\|_2 = \sqrt{2 - 2\langle z_i, z_j \rangle}$.

This normalization enables the model to learn discriminative representations where legitimate and phishing websites cluster in distinct regions of the unit hypersphere.

3.4 Contrastive View Generation via Tabular Augmentation

Contrastive learning requires the generation of semantically consistent positive pairs while maintaining sufficient diversity to drive meaningful representation learning. Our framework adopts two complementary augmentation strategies designed specifically for tabular phishing data: dropout-based augmentation and traditional tabular augmentation techniques. These approaches generate positive pairs while introducing controlled perturbations essential for robust representation learning.

Dropout-Based Augmentation. This approach leverages the stochastic nature of dropout to generate different views of the same input during training. By applying distinct dropout masks to identical inputs, the model observes varied but semantically equivalent representations, encouraging learning of robust features that remain consistent across different network states. The dropout augmentation process generates positive pairs through: $z_{\text{anchor}} = f(x; \text{mask}_1)$, $z_{\text{positive}} = f(x; \text{mask}_2)$, where mask_1 and mask_2 represent independent Bernoulli random variables: $\text{mask}_i[j] \sim \text{Bernoulli}(1 - p_{\text{dropout}})$, with $p_{dropout}$ controlling augmentation intensity. Higher dropout rates increase view diversity but may compromise semantic preservation.

Traditional Tabular Augmentation. This approach combines multiple transformation techniques specifically adapted for tabular data:

1. CutMix Augmentation: Randomly mixes features between different samples to create synthetic training examples: $x_{\text{cutmix}} = \lambda \cdot x + (1 - \lambda) \cdot x_j$, where $\lambda \sim \text{Beta}(\alpha, \alpha)$ controls mixing intensity, and x_j is randomly selected from the batch. The beta distribution ensures most mixing occurs near the extremes (0 or 1), preserving semantic content.
2. Gaussian Noise Injection: Adds controlled noise to numerical features: $x_{\text{noisy}} = x + \epsilon, \quad \epsilon \sim \mathcal{N}(0, \sigma^2 I)$, where σ^2 controls noise magnitude. The noise level is carefully calibrated to avoid overwhelming feature signals while providing sufficient perturbation for contrastive learning.
3. Feature Corruption: To simulate measurement noise and enhance robustness, we randomly corrupt a subset of input features. Specifically, each feature $x[i]$ is retained with probability $1 - p_{\text{corrupt}}$, and replaced with a random value with probability p_{corrupt}, i.e., $x_{\text{corrupt}}[i] = x[i]$ with probability $1 - p_{\text{corrupt}}$, otherwise $x_{\text{corrupt}}[i] = \text{random}()$.

3.5 Contrastive Learning with Triplet Margin Loss

The core learning mechanism of our framework operates through triplet margin loss optimization, which shapes the embedding space geometry to achieve optimal separation between legitimate and phishing websites. Unlike traditional classification approaches that learn decision boundaries, contrastive learning focuses on learning meaningful distance relationships in the representation space.

The triplet formulation addresses a fundamental challenge in unsupervised learning: how to learn discriminative representations without explicit class labels. By leveraging the natural assumption that augmented views of the same website should be more similar than different websites, the framework learns to encode semantic relationships into the embedding space.

Triplet Construction and Semantics: Each training triplet consists of three components: - **Anchor** (z_a): Original sample embedding - **Positive** (z_p): Augmented view of the same sample - **Negative** (z_n): Embedding from a different sample.

The triplet margin loss enforces the constraint that positive pairs should be closer than negative pairs by at least a margin m:

$$\mathcal{L}_{triplet} = \max(0, d(z_a, z_p) - d(z_a, z_n) + m) \tag{3}$$

where $d(\cdot, \cdot)$ represents the L2 distance between normalized embeddings:

$$d(z_i, z_j) = \|z_i - z_j\|_2 = \sqrt{\sum_{k=1}^{d}(z_i^{(k)} - z_j^{(k)})^2} \tag{4}$$

Positive Sample Generation: Positive samples (z_a, z_p) are generated with the augmentation strategies described in Sect. 3.4. The key insight is that different augmented views of the same website should produce similar embeddings, regardless of the specific augmentation applied. This consistency requirement forces the model to learn invariant representations that capture essential website characteristics rather than superficial variations. Mathematically, positive pairs satisfy the semantic equivalence constraint: $\text{sem}(x) = \text{sem}(\mathcal{T}(x, \theta))$, where $\text{sem}(\cdot)$ represents semantic content and $\mathcal{T}(\cdot, \theta)$ denotes augmentation transformation.

Negative Sample Generation: Negative samples are generated through in-batch random shuffling, ensuring computational efficiency while maintaining learning effectiveness: $z_n^{(i)} = z_p^{(\pi(i))}$, where $\pi : \{1, 2, \ldots, N\} \to \{1, 2, \ldots, N\}$ represents a random permutation satisfying $\pi(i) \neq i$ for all i. This constraint prevents trivial negative pairs where a sample might be paired with itself.

Margin Parameter: The margin parameter m plays a crucial role in determining embedding space geometry. A larger margin enforces stronger separation between positive and negative pairs, potentially leading to more discriminative representations but risking overfitting. The optimal margin balances separation strength with generalization capability: $m^* = \arg\min_m \mathbb{E}[\mathcal{L}_{\text{validation}}(m)]$.

Batch-Wise Loss Computation: The complete training objective aggregates triplet losses across all samples in a batch:

$$\mathcal{L}_{batch} = \frac{1}{N}\sum_{i=1}^{N} \max(0, \|z_a^{(i)} - z_p^{(i)}\|_2 - \|z_a^{(i)} - z_n^{(i)}\|_2 + m) \tag{5}$$

where N represents batch size. This formulation enables efficient parallel computation while maintaining the semantic relationships essential for effective contrastive learning.

Embedding Space Properties: The triplet loss optimization results in an embedding space with desirable geometric properties: 1. Cluster Formation: Legitimate and phishing websites naturally cluster in distinct regions; 2. Intra-class Cohesion: Similar websites (same class) maintain small pairwise distances; 3. Inter-class Separation: Different website types exhibit large pairwise distances; 4. Metric Properties: The learned distance function satisfies triangle inequality and symmetry. These properties enable effective downstream classification through simple distance-based methods, eliminating the need for complex classifiers and improving interpretability of the learned representations.

Training Dynamics and Convergence: The contrastive learning process exhibits characteristic training dynamics where the model initially learns coarse-grained distinctions before refining fine-grained patterns. The triplet loss typically decreases rapidly in early epochs as the model learns basic clustering, then gradually refines boundaries through continued optimization.

Convergence is achieved when the embedding space reaches a stable configuration where:

$$\lim_{t\to\infty} \mathbb{E}[\mathcal{L}_{triplet}(t)] = \mathbb{E}[\max(0, d_{positive} - d_{negative} + m)] \tag{6}$$

approaches a minimum value determined by the inherent separability of the dataset and the chosen margin parameter.

3.6 Inference via Embedding Similarity

During inference, we adopt a prototype-based evaluation strategy. Each test embedding is compared against class-specific prototypes, and classification is determined by nearest-prototype similarity. Training remains fully label-free, and labels are only involved in the evaluation.

Centroid Construction and Similarity Computation: Given a class $c \in$ legitimate, phishing, its corresponding centroid $\boldsymbol{\mu}_c$ is defined as the mean of reference embeddings used in the evaluation protocol: $\boldsymbol{\mu}_c = \frac{1}{|S_c|}\sum_{\boldsymbol{x}_i \in S_c} f_\theta(\boldsymbol{x}_i)$. Here, S_c denotes the set of reference samples for class c used solely in evaluation, $f_\theta(\cdot)$ represents the trained encoder, and d_c is the Euclidean distance between the test embedding $\boldsymbol{z}_{\text{test}}$ and the prototype. Alternatively, cosine similarity captures the angular relationship between the test embedding and the centroid: $d_c = \|\boldsymbol{z}_{\text{test}} - \boldsymbol{\mu}_c\|_2$ and $s_c = \frac{\boldsymbol{z}_{\text{test}} \cdot \boldsymbol{\mu}_c}{\|\boldsymbol{z}_{\text{test}}\|_2 \|\boldsymbol{\mu}_c\|_2}$.

Probabilistic Classification and Decision Making: For Euclidean-based inference, the distance is transformed into class probabilities using a softmax-like inverse exponential function. For cosine similarity-based inference, a sigmoid activation function is employed to convert similarities into probability estimates:

$$P(y = c|\boldsymbol{z}_{\text{test}}) = \frac{\exp(-d_c)}{\sum_{c'} \exp(-d_{c'})}, \quad P(y = c|\boldsymbol{z}_{\text{test}}) = \sigma(s_c) \tag{7}$$

In both cases, the final classification decision is determined by comparing predicted class probabilities against a predefined threshold.

4 Evaluation

4.1 Dataset and Testbed

We conduct our experiments on three phishing detection datasets. The primary Benchmark dataset contains 11,430 samples with 87 extracted features, evenly split between phishing and legitimate instances [13]. To evaluate the robustness of PhishSSL, we further test it on two additional datasets: the Tan dataset [14], with 10,000 samples (5,000 phishing and 5,000 legitimate) and 48 features, and the Grega dataset [15], with 20,000 samples (10,000 phishing and 10,000 legitimate) and 111 features. The Benchmark dataset [13] provides a balanced mix of URL structural, HTML content-based, and external service features. The Tan dataset [14] emphasizes compact structural and behavioral cues while omitting most external signals. The Grega dataset [15] concentrates on fine-grained URL and protocol-level properties but includes relatively few content features. Using these datasets with diverse feature compositions allows us to examine the effectiveness of the proposed method under varying feature settings. All datasets adopt a consistent 60%/20%/20% Train/Validation/Test split. Training remains fully unsupervised, with labels used solely in the evaluation protocol to derive class prototypes and for validation and testing of model performance.

All models are trained with a batch size of 128 and a learning rate of 1e-3. PhishSSL uses a 256-dimensional encoder, a 128-dimensional projection head, and a 64-dimensional attention module. Baselines share the same settings for fair comparison. Each model is run for 20 epochs, and the best ROC AUC is reported. Experiments are conducted on an H20 NVLink GPU server with 96 GB of memory.

4.2 Baselines

To evaluate the effectiveness of the proposed PhishSSL framework, four representative unsupervised and self-supervised baseline models are employed for comparative analysis. **K-Means Clustering** partitions the feature space into distinct clusters based on Euclidean distance minimization, assuming that legitimate and phishing websites form natural clusters. Classification is performed by assigning test samples to the nearest cluster centroid. **Isolation Forest** employs an anomaly detection approach based on the isolation principle, where anomalous samples are easier to isolate than normal samples. The algorithm constructs an ensemble of random trees with anomaly scores determined by the average path length required to isolate each sample. **Autoencoder** implements a neural network-based reconstruction approach consisting of an encoder-decoder architecture that learns to compress input features into a latent representation and reconstruct the original input. Reconstruction error serves as the anomaly score. **Variational Autoencoder (VAE)** extends the standard autoencoder by introducing probabilistic encoding through variational inference. The model learns probability distributions over the latent space, incorporating Kullback-Leibler divergence regularization alongside reconstruction loss for more robust anomaly detection.

4.3 Evaluation Metrics

The performance of all models is assessed using a comprehensive set of classification metrics that provide insights into different aspects of phishing detection effectiveness. **Confusion Matrix** provides a detailed breakdown of classification results by tabulating true positives (TP), true negatives (TN), false positives (FP), and false negatives (FN), enabling a thorough analysis across both legitimate and phishing categories.

Accuracy measures the overall proportion of correctly classified samples and is defined as Accuracy $= \frac{TP+TN}{TP+TN+FP+FN}$. **Precision**, defined as Precision $= \frac{TP}{TP+FP}$, quantifies the proportion of predicted phishing websites that are actually malicious, indicating the model's ability to avoid false alarms. **Recall** measures the proportion of actual phishing websites correctly identified and is given by Recall $= \frac{TP}{TP+FN}$, reflecting the model's capability to detect malicious samples.

F1-Score provides a harmonic mean of precision and recall, defined as $\text{F1} = 2 \cdot \frac{\text{Precision} \times \text{Recall}}{\text{Precision} + \text{Recall}}$. Finally, **ROC AUC** evaluates the model's discriminative ability across all classification thresholds by plotting the true positive rate against the false positive rate, with the area under the curve ranging from 0 to 1—higher values indicate better threshold-independent performance.

5 Results

5.1 Comparative Analysis

To demonstrate the performance and robustness of the proposed PhishSSL framework, we report results across three phishing detection datasets with distinct feature sets. Table 2, Fig. 2, and Fig. 3 present a comprehensive comparison against four baseline models using standard evaluation metrics and visual diagnostics.

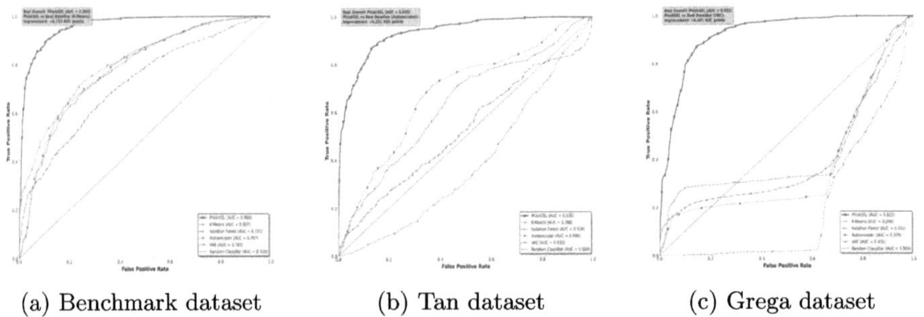

(a) Benchmark dataset (b) Tan dataset (c) Grega dataset

Fig. 2. Comparison of ROC curves across different detection models on three phishing datasets.

On the Benchmark dataset, PhishSSL achieves an ROC AUC of 0.960 and F1-score of 0.8942, outperforming the best baseline (K-Means) by a margin of +0.153 AUC points (Fig. 2a). Notably, while K-Means achieves high precision (0.9723), it suffers from extremely low recall (0.2135), suggesting it misses a

Table 2. Performance and Confusion Matrix of Models on Phishing Datasets.

Dataset/Model	TN	FP	FN	TP	Acc.	Prec.	Rec.	F1
Benchmark Dataset [13]								
K-Means	1127	7	906	246	0.6006	**0.9723**	0.2135	0.3502
Isolation Forest	1114	20	959	193	0.5717	0.9061	0.1675	0.2828
Autoencoder	998	136	579	573	0.6872	0.8082	0.4974	0.6158
VAE	1000	134	607	545	0.6759	0.8027	0.4731	0.5953
PhishSSL	1037	134	105	1010	**0.8955**	0.8829	**0.9058**	**0.8942**
Tan Dataset [14]								
K-Means	591	443	725	241	0.4160	0.3523	0.2495	0.2921
Isolation Forest	968	66	854	112	0.5400	0.6292	0.1159	0.1958
Autoencoder	821	213	562	404	0.6125	0.6548	0.4182	0.5104
VAE	790	244	581	385	0.5875	0.6121	0.3986	0.4828
PhishSSL	852	135	126	887	**0.8695**	**0.8679**	**0.8756**	**0.8717**
Grega Dataset [15]								
K-Means	760	1237	1961	42	0.2005	0.0328	0.0210	0.0256
Isolation Forest	1921	76	1697	306	0.5567	0.8010	0.1528	0.2566
Autoencoder	1677	320	1609	394	0.5178	0.5518	0.1967	0.2900
VAE	1775	222	1430	573	0.5870	0.7208	0.2861	0.4096
PhishSSL	1704	293	258	1745	**0.8622**	**0.8562**	**0.8712**	**0.8636**

large number of phishing websites. In contrast, PhishSSL maintains a balanced detection ability with a recall of 0.9058 and low false negative rate (FN = 105), demonstrating its ability to identify most phishing attempts.

On the Tan dataset, PhishSSL remains dominant with an ROC AUC of 0.935, significantly exceeding the best-performing baseline (Autoencoder, AUC = 0.684) by +0.251 AUC points (Fig. 2b). It achieves an F1-score of 0.8717, maintaining both high precision (0.8679) and recall (0.8756), while other baselines exhibit severe drops in recall, with Isolation Forest falling to 0.1159 and K-Means to 0.2495, highlighting their poor generalization on cross-dataset phishing features.

The robustness of PhishSSL is further confirmed on the Grega dataset, where it achieves an ROC AUC of 0.922 and F1-score of 0.8636. Compared to the best baseline (VAE, AUC = 0.431), this represents an improvement of +0.491 AUC points (Fig. 2c). Other models suffer from high false positives and extremely poor recall, especially K-Means (recall = 0.0210) and Autoencoder (recall = 0.1967).

The t-SNE visualizations in Fig. 3 highlight the quality of the embedding space learned by PhishSSL. On all datasets, phishing and legitimate samples form well-separated clusters, especially on the Grega and Benchmark datasets, where PhishSSL distinctly isolates phishing clusters. This confirms the effectiveness of our contrastive learning mechanism combined with adaptive attention and tabular augmentation in generating discriminative and transferable representations.

Although the three datasets differ in their feature compositions, PhishSSL consistently achieves high and stable performance across all evaluation metrics, demonstrating strong robustness and adaptability for real-world phishing detection. We also observe that both the baselines and PhishSSL obtain higher performance on the Benchmark dataset than on Tan and Grega, likely because the Benchmark dataset provides a more comprehensive combination of features, offering richer and more complementary signals.

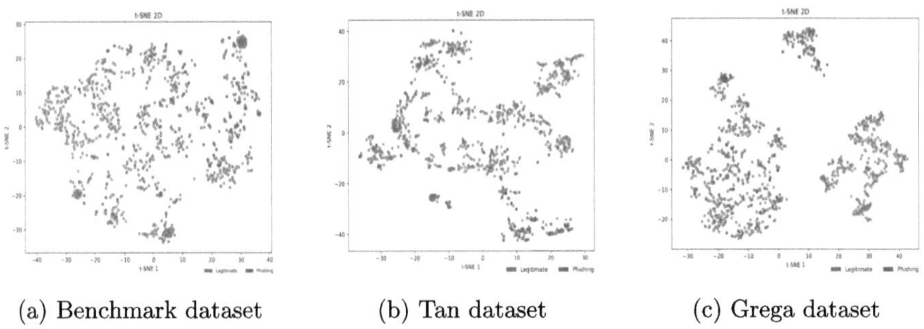

(a) Benchmark dataset (b) Tan dataset (c) Grega dataset

Fig. 3. t-SNE visualization of the learned embeddings on three phishing datasets.

5.2 Ablation Analysis

To assess the contribution of individual components within the PhishSSL framework, we conduct an ablation study by selectively removing core modules, including feature attention, traditional tabular augmentation, and dropout-based augmentation. The results are summarized in Table 3.

Table 3. Ablation Analysis of PhishSSL on Benchmark dataset.

Configuration	ROC	Accuracy	Precision	Recall	F1-Score
Baseline (All Components)	**0.9601**	**0.8955**	0.8829	**0.9058**	**0.8942**
w/o Feature Attention	0.9491	0.8920	**0.9049**	0.8700	0.8871
w/o Traditional Augmentation	0.9440	0.8780	0.8842	0.8628	0.8734
w/o Dropout Augmentation	0.9169	0.8530	0.8338	0.8726	0.8528

The full PhishSSL model achieves the best overall performance across all metrics, indicating the synergistic effect of its design components. Removing the feature attention module results in a slight drop in ROC AUC (from 0.9601 to

0.9491), accompanied by a reduction in F1-score and recall, highlighting its role in emphasizing discriminative features and improving generalization. Eliminating traditional augmentation techniques (CutMix, Gaussian noise, and feature corruption) leads to a further decrease in performance, with ROC AUC dropping to 0.9440 and F1-score to 0.8734. This underscores the importance of diverse perturbations for encouraging invariant feature learning.

The most significant degradation occurs when dropout-based augmentation is disabled. Without stochastic dropout views, ROC AUC falls to 0.9169, and F1-score declines to 0.8528. These results confirm that dropout augmentation plays a central role in generating semantically consistent views for contrastive learning and in enhancing the robustness of the learned embeddings.

Overall, the ablation analysis demonstrates that each component in PhishSSL contributes meaningfully to the final performance, and their integration yields a robust and highly discriminative phishing detection system.

6 Conclusion

This study presented PhishSSL, a self-supervised contrastive learning framework for phishing website detection that avoids reliance on labeled training data. Extensive experiments across diverse datasets confirmed its robustness, generalization, and superiority over baseline methods. Looking forward, future directions include examining the impact of different supervised classification heads, incorporating multi-modal fusion by integrating heterogeneous features through cross-modal contrastive learning, and enhancing adversarial robustness to resist evolving evasion tactics. These avenues will further strengthen the effectiveness and reliability of phishing defenses in increasingly dynamic and adversarial Web environments.

References

1. Li, W., Manickam, S., Chong, Y.W., Leng, W., Nanda, P.: A state-of-the-art review on phishing website detection techniques. IEEE Access **12**, 187976–188012 (2024)
2. Li, W., Manickam, S., Laghari, S.U.A., Chong, Y.W.: Uncovering the cloak: a systematic review of techniques used to conceal phishing websites. IEEE Access **11**, 71925–71939 (2023)
3. Almujahid, N.F., Haq, M.A., Alshehri, M.: Comparative evaluation of machine learning algorithms for phishing site detection. PeerJ Comput. Sci. **10**, e2131 (2024)
4. Kavya, S., Sumathi, D.: Staying ahead of phishers: a review of recent advances and emerging methodologies in phishing detection. Artif. Intell. Rev. **58**(2), 50 (2024)
5. Bilot, T., Geis, G., Hammi, B.: PhishGNN: a phishing website detection framework using graph neural networks. In: Proceedings of the 19th International Conference on Security and Cryptography - Volume 1: SECRYPT, pp. 428–435. SCITEPRESS - Science and Technology Publications, Lisbon, France (2022)
6. Gui, J., et al.: A survey on self-supervised learning: algorithms, applications, and future trends. IEEE Trans. Pattern Anal. Mach. Intell. **46**(12), 9052–9071 (2024)

7. Chen, T., Kornblith, S., Norouzi, M., Hinton, G.: A simple framework for contrastive learning of visual representations. In: Proceedings of the 37th International Conference on Machine Learning. Proceedings of Machine Learning Research, vol. 119, pp. 1597–1607. PMLR (2020)
8. Koukoulis, I., Syrigos, I., Korakis, T.: Self-supervised transformer-based contrastive learning for intrusion detection systems. arXiv preprint arXiv:2505.08816 (2025)
9. Tunde-Onadele, O., Lin, Y., Gu, X., He, J., Latapie, H.: Self-supervised machine learning framework for online container security attack detection. ACM Trans. Auton. Adapt. Syst. **19**(3) (2024)
10. Chen, Y., Sun, Z., Gong, Z., Hao, D.: Improving smart contract security with contrastive learning-based vulnerability detection. In: Proceedings of the IEEE/ACM 46th International Conference on Software Engineering, ICSE 2024. Association for Computing Machinery, New York, NY, USA (2024)
11. Xia, Z., Yu, Y., Tan, J., Long, K.: SSC-IDS: a robust in-vehicle intrusion detection system based on self-supervised contrastive learning. In: 2024 IEEE 23rd International Conference on Trust, Security and Privacy in Computing and Communications (TrustCom), pp. 2004–2009 (2024)
12. Wang, F., Chen, Y., Gao, H., Li, Q., Wang, C.: Self-supervised contrastive representation learning for classifying internet of things malware. Eng. Appl. Artif. Intell. **150**, 110299 (2025)
13. Hannousse, A., Yahiouche, S.: Towards benchmark datasets for machine learning based website phishing detection: an experimental study. Eng. Appl. Artif. Intell. **104**, 104347 (2021)
14. Tan, C.L.: Phishing dataset for machine learning: feature evaluation (2018). https://doi.org/10.17632/h3cgnj8hft.1, mendeley Data, V1
15. Vrbančič, G., Fister, I., Podgorelec, V.: Datasets for phishing websites detection. Data Brief **33**, 106438 (2020)

TITID: A Transformer-Based IoT Traffic Intrusion Detection Model for MQTT Networks

Li Ma[1], Sipei Wu[1], Junxian Ye[1], Bin Liu[1], Chunrong Lai[2], Fen Liu[1], and Wenyin Yang[1](✉)

[1] School of Computer Science and Artificial Intelligence, Foshan University, Foshan 528000, China
cswyyang@fosu.edu.cn

[2] Guangdong Strong Metal Technology Co., Ltd., Foshan 528000, Guangdong, China

Abstract. The Internet of Things (IoT) represents a vast global network interconnecting a wide array of smart devices. The rapid growth of the IoT has significantly expanded the number of connected endpoints, leading to new and complex challenges in network security, such as eavesdropping, weak authentication, and malicious payloads. Many IoT networks rely on lightweight protocols like MQTT, which, although efficient, are susceptible to a diverse range of cyber threats. Traditional intrusion detection methods struggle to keep pace with the evolving attack patterns due to the constrained resources of IoT devices and the dynamic nature of network traffic. This study introduces a Transformer-based IoT Traffic Intrusion Detection (TITID) model, which leverages the Transformer architecture to improve classification accuracy. By integrating feature embeddings and an Intra-Sequence Attention mechanism, the proposed model significantly enhances the detection of cyber threats within IoT networks. Experimental evaluations on the MQTT-IoT-IDS2020 dataset demonstrate the superiority of TITID over existing approaches, underscoring its potential for enhancing IoT security.

Keywords: IoT · Deep Learning · MQTT · Intrusion Detection

1 Introduction

The Internet of Things (IoT) is among the most advanced technologies that has captured the attention of both industrial researchers and practitioners. In fact, IoT has evolved into a global network, enabling the connection of smart devices across the world at any given time by assigning them a unique identity [1,2]. The operation of IoT is facilitated by the deployment of various communication protocols [3].

The IoT encompasses a wide variety of devices, including, but not limited to, IP cameras, smart cities, surveillance technologies, farming and wearable devices

I. Awan et al. (Eds.): WISE 2025, LNCS 16367, pp. 441–455, 2026.
https://doi.org/10.1007/978-981-95-7394-3_30

[4,5]. These technologies are designed to enhance convenience and improve the quality of life for users. IoT devices are expected to be continuously accessible, utilize cloud services, and operate using wireless communication protocols. The vast array of IoT standards, protocols, and devices has facilitated the development of smart cities, where numerous devices communicate across interconnected networks. However, this diversity has also introduced a range of security challenges [6]. The vast number of IoT devices, combined with their heterogeneous communication protocols and constrained computational resources, has made intrusion detection a particularly challenging task. Traditional security mechanisms often struggle to keep up with the evolving attack landscape, making effective and efficient IoT intrusion detection models a critical necessity. The proliferation of heterogeneous technologies has necessitated the development of new communication protocols for data transmission, one prominent example being the Message Queuing Telemetry Transport (MQTT) protocol [7,8].

The MQTT protocol was specifically designed to be lightweight and efficient, particularly in high-latency and unreliable network environments, making it well-suited for IoT devices [9]. It employs a publish/subscribe model, where clients receive messages by subscribing to topics, and publishers send messages to specific topics, enabling loosely coupled communication. MQTT features characteristics such as simplicity, low overhead, and persistent sessions, making it ideal for resource-constrained environments like sensors and embedded devices [10].

When the communication channel connects IoT components, it becomes vulnerable to various attacks, particularly those targeting sensitive information [11]. In this context, the frequency of cyberattacks has been rising alongside the proliferation of IoT devices [12–15]. As a result, network security has become a critical consideration in the deployment of IoT networks. To address these security concerns, Intrusion Detection Systems (IDS) are commonly employed to analyze network traffic and identify malicious activity [16–18]. In recent years, IDS models based on Machine Learning and Deep Learning have gained popularity over traditional methods, owing to their ability to process large volumes of network data, identify complex patterns, and adapt to evolving threats. They can be trained using real-time network data and enable the automated detection of cyberattacks [19,20].

As the Transformer continues to gain popularity, many Deep Learning (DL) models today utilize the transformer architecture. Although transformers were originally developed to address challenges in Natural Language Processing (NLP), their successful application has since expanded to a wide range of domains, including image classification and tabular data analysis. As such, leveraging transformers presents an innovative approach to solving the IoT intrusion detection problem. Nevertheless, existing Transformer-based models for IoT traffic classification encounter multiple challenges:

- Limitations of the attention mechanism: Conventional self-attention mechanisms may struggle to effectively capture the essential features of IoT traffic, as IoT data exhibits distinct structural patterns compared to text or images.

- Generalization challenges: Although pretraining approaches have demonstrated success, existing models frequently struggle to generalize across diverse IoT traffic scenarios, especially when handling imbalanced attack samples.
- Dataset and network applicability challenges: While several studies have applied Transformer models for IoT traffic classification, some do not employ IoT-specific datasets [21], whereas others focus on particular network types [22–24].

The main contributions of this paper can be summarized as follows:

- We introduce a Transformer-based IoT Traffic Intrusion Detection (TITID) model, built upon Transformer and an optimized attention mechanism, for the classification of IoT traffic. The overview of the proposed method workflow is shown in Fig. 1.
- The TITID model leverages the strengths of Transformers, including efficient learning through an attention mechanism, the ability to generalize across large datasets, and proficiency in sequence learning tasks, which is particularly well-suited for IoT traffic data that naturally forms sequential patterns.
- The proposed model utilizes Transformers to effectively learn contextual embeddings of both categorical and numerical features, and is capable of learning network dynamics from packet traces.
- Through extensive experiments conducted on an MQTT-based IoT traffic dataset, the proposed model demonstrates strong performance, achieving an overall accuracy of 85.99%, which is comparable to the performance of other tested classifiers, thereby highlighting the potential of the TITID model in real-world IoT intrusion detection scenarios.

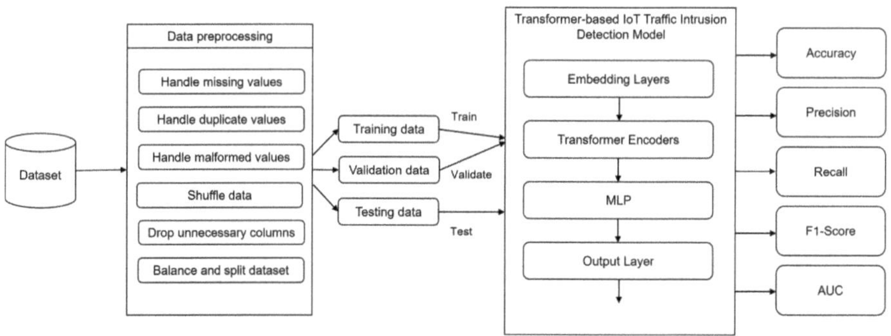

Fig. 1. The overview of the proposed workflow for intrusion detection in IoT network.

The remainder of this article is organized as follows. Section 2 provides a review of the relevant literature. Section 3 outlines the details of the proposed method. Section 4 presents the experimental results for the proposed IDS and compares them with those of other DL-based systems. Finally, Sect. 5 offers the conclusions of the study.

2 Related Works

With the rapid advancement of the Internet of Things (IoT), intrusion detection has become crucial for safeguarding IoT devices and networks against malicious attacks. In recent years, researchers have proposed a variety of methods leveraging machine learning, deep learning, and distributed computing to enhance the effectiveness and efficiency of IoT intrusion detection.

Traditional Machine learning methods previously dominated IoT traffic intrusion detection, primarily focusing on feature engineering and classification algorithms. In study [25], a Mutual Information (MI)-based approach was proposed for feature selection in Network Intrusion Detection Systems (NIDS). The study compared both linear and non-linear feature selection techniques, specifically correlation-based and MI-based methods, with the MI-based approach outperforming the correlation-based method in terms of attack detection accuracy. Subsequently, Ambusaidi et al. [26] introduced a feature selection algorithm that combined Mutual Information (MI) with a variant of the support vector machine classifier. This approach demonstrated improved accuracy and reduced model complexity compared to previous methods, on datasets such as KDD Cup 99 and NSL-KDD [27]. Disha and Waheed [28] designed a feature ranking method based on Gini Impurity using Random Forest (RF) to evaluate classification performance for NIDS, employing the latest TON-IoT dataset. However, most networking datasets are outdated and no longer suitable as benchmark datasets for evaluating classification models in NIDS for IoT security. In addition, various techniques employing heuristic optimization algorithms, such as genetic algorithms (GA), as search strategies to identify optimal feature subsets, are detailed in [29–31]. These methods demonstrated lower false alarm rates compared to baseline approaches, using datasets such as UNSW-NB15 and KDD99. Moreover, many studies have employed hybrid feature selection methods to improve the performance of attack classifiers while reducing overfitting during model training. In study [32], the authors utilized association rule mining and central attribute values, which outperformed NSL-KDD when tested on the UNSW-NB15 dataset.

DL has garnered significant attention in the field of intrusion detection systems due to its capability to handle large volumes of data and perform complex pattern recognition. DL algorithms can deliver superior accuracy and enhanced performance compared to traditional machine learning techniques by learning from and improving with more data. This has resulted in the development of several DL-based NIDS models, which have demonstrated promising results in detecting various types of intrusions, including network attacks, insider threats, and malware. Wahab [33] proposed a Dynamic Deep Neural Network (DDNN)-based IDS for IoT networks. They utilized Principal Component Analysis (PCA) to analyze the variance in intrusion data features. The DS2OS dataset was employed in their experiments to evaluate the performance of the proposed system. Mosaiyebzadeh et al. [34] proposed three DL-based IDS for predicting intrusions in MQTT-enabled networks: DNN, Long Short-Term Memory (LSTM), and a combination of Convolutional and Recurrent Neural Networks.

They evaluated these systems using the MQTT-IoT-IDS2020 dataset. In the paper [35], the authors transform packet information into images and use them as input for a metalearning model based on Convolutional Neural Networks. The authors utilized five different network traffic datasets, which were general and not necessarily specific to IoT traffic, and selected a few samples from each. A dataset called FSIDS-IoT was created specifically for few-shot models. The only evaluation metric described in the paper is the accuracy of their model, which ranged from 73.81% to 92.19%. However, this approach also faces challenges related to computational costs. Gorishniy et al. [36] proposed the FT-Transformer, a self-attention-based model for tabular data that effectively captures complex feature interactions. In IoT intrusion detection, this approach improves the representation of network traffic data and enhances detection performance. In Reference [37], the authors introduced a novel attention mechanism that performs attention across both rows and columns, enabling communication among all features from different samples. Wang et al. [24] presents a novel Transformer-based Intrusion Detection System (IDS) designed to secure smart homes using both network traffic and IoT device telemetry data. The authors introduce a self-attention mechanism to manage heterogeneous features, such as continuous and categorical data, which are commonly encountered in IoT environments. This approach effectively addresses the challenge of integrating diverse data sources, resulting in more accurate intrusion detection. When IoT telemetry data was incorporated, performance improved to 98.39% and 97.06%, respectively. The study emphasizes the effectiveness of integrating network and IoT data in intrusion detection, outperforming existing methods on the same dataset. However, this approach may not perform well in all general cases. In Reference [38], the author presents E-T-GraphSAGE, a hybrid intrusion detection system that combines Graph Neural Networks (GNNs) and Transformers. This model improves detection accuracy for both known and unknown attacks by leveraging the structural understanding of GNNs and the ability of Transformers to capture long-range dependencies. It outperforms traditional methods on datasets such as BoT-IoT, NF-BoT-IoT, and NF-ToN-IoT, achieving high accuracy (over 99%) in binary classification tasks. However, a notable limitation of this work is the model's difficulty in distinguishing between similar attack types, such as DDoS and DoS attacks, which may be due to the overlap in feature characteristics.

3 Proposed Approach

A review of existing methods reveals persistent challenges, including outdated datasets, difficulties in integrating heterogeneous data, and limited generalization across diverse IoT environments. To address these challenges and enhance intrusion detection performance, we introduce Transformer-based IoT Traffic Intrusion Detection architecture, denoted as TITID, which is a novel architecture that strategically adapts the Transformer mechanism [39] for tabular data analysis in cybersecurity contexts. Figure 2 illustrates the key components of TITID.

In summary, our model converts all features (both categorical and numerical) into embeddings and then applies a Transformer layer to these embeddings. As a result, each Transformer layer operates at the feature level of an object.

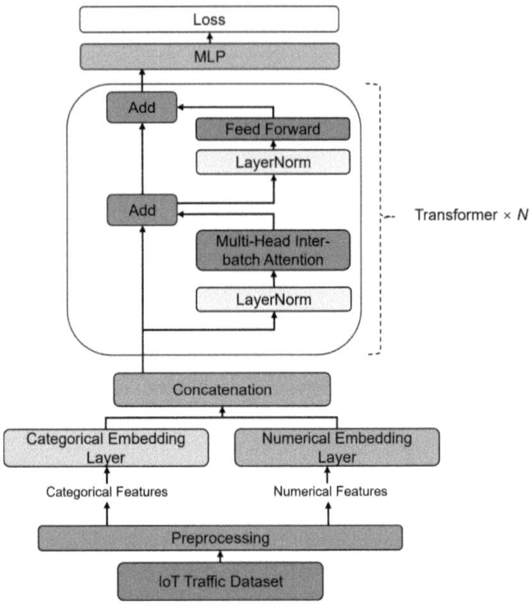

Fig. 2. Framework of the TITID Model.

3.1 IoT Traffic Data Preprocessing

In general, a dataset containing missing values may not be suitable for training a model, as it can lead to inaccurate predictions. Missing data can disrupt the learning process and hinder the model's ability to identify important patterns and relationships, which are crucial for making accurate predictions. Therefore, it is essential to handle missing data appropriately before using it in a prediction model. In this work, we adopt a mean imputation strategy, where missing values in each column are replaced with the mean of the non-missing values in that column. We chose mean imputation because it is a simple yet effective approach that preserves the statistical distribution of the data without introducing strong assumptions about temporal continuity (as in linear interpolation) or complex dependencies. This allows us to maintain data consistency while avoiding potential biases that could arise from more sophisticated imputation methods when the underlying data distribution is uncertain. Additionally, we removed features such as `timestamp`, `src_ip`, `dst_ip`, `src_port`, and `dst_port` to reduce unnecessary feature interference, thereby improving the model's generalization ability and training efficiency. While timestamps, IP addresses, and port numbers are important in network communication, they are not directly related to detecting attack patterns and may cause the model to overfit to specific network connections. By removing these columns, the dataset can focus more on features that are closely related to attack behavior, avoiding over-reliance on specific connection details, and ultimately enhancing the model's adaptability and accuracy across different environments.

3.2 Embedding

The Embedding Layers module is responsible for transforming the input feature values into learnable embeddings.

Categorical Embedding Layer is a versatile component designed to handle categorical features in machine learning tasks. It performs two primary operations: category preprocessing and embedding transformation. For each feature in the input, a `StringLookup` layer is used to map categorical values to integer indices based on the unique values in the feature. Subsequently, an `Embedding` layer is applied to these integer indices, producing dense vector representations of the categorical values.

In more detail, for each categorical feature x_i^c, the transformation is performed in two steps:

Category Preprocessing: The `StringLookup` layer maps each unique string value in the feature x_i^c to an integer index. The lookup operation is defined as:

$$\text{lookup}(x_i^c) = \text{Index of } x_i^c \text{ in the vocabulary of feature } f \tag{1}$$

Embedding Transformation: The `Embedding` layer then maps this integer index to a dense vector, which is the embedding of the feature:

$$E_i^c = \text{Embedding}(\text{lookup}(x_i^c)) \tag{2}$$

The model applies this transformation to each categorical feature and stacks the resulting embeddings to generate a combined embedding representation for the input. This approach enables the model to efficiently handle categorical data by mapping it to low-dimensional, dense representations that are suitable for downstream tasks such as classification or regression.

Numerical Embedding Layer applies a simple linear transformation to each numerical feature. Specifically, for each feature x_i^n, the transformation is defined as:

$$E_i^n = \text{ReLU}(w_i x_i^n + b_i) \tag{3}$$

where w_i is the learnable weight for the i-th feature, b_i is the learnable bias term for the i-th feature, ReLU denotes the Rectified Linear Unit activation function, which introduces non-linearity into the transformation.

In this method, the model learns a separate weight vector for each feature and applies a linear transformation, followed by a ReLU activation. This process enables the model to capture non-linear relationships between the features and the target variable.

3.3 Intra-sequence Attention

We propose Intra-Sequence Attention, an enhanced method based on the attention mechanism, designed to improve the model's representation ability by strengthening the correlation between samples. Unlike conventional self-attention mechanisms that primarily model feature-level dependencies, our approach explicitly captures interactions at the sample level, enabling each sample token to aggregate information from others within the same batch. This idea is related to the intra-batch attention proposed in IBAFormer [40], which also leverages cross-sample information within a mini-batch. However, our method differs in that it treats each entire sample as a holistic token after concatenating its features and applies standard self-attention across these sample-level tokens, whereas IBAFormer designs specialized mechanisms (MIBA/EIBA) operating at the original feature resolution without such concatenation. The key innovation of this approach is its processing of input data through the introduction of positional encoding, combined with a self-attention mechanism. An illustration of the Intra-Sequence attention process in a single head is shown in Fig. 3.

Specifically, the input is assumed to be a tensor with shape $X \in \mathbb{R}^{b \times n \times d}$, where b is the batch size, n is the number of features, and d is the embedding dimension of each feature.

Intra-Sequence Attention adds a learnable positional encoding to the input through element-wise addition. The shape of the positional encoding is $(1, n, d)$ and the input positional information, X_{pos}, is obtained by performing element-wise addition with the original input data. This process can be expressed as:

$$X_{\text{pos}} = X + PE \tag{4}$$

where PE denotes the positional encoding. The step preserves the structural order of features within each sample, ensuring that feature semantics are not lost during subsequent processing. Next, the input, after adding the positional coding, is reshaped to a tensor of shape $(1, b, n \times d)$ to be compatible with the subsequent self-attention mechanism. Here, each sample's feature representations are concatenated into a single holistic token, transforming the batch into a sequence of b sample-level tokens. This design ensures that attention is computed across samples, while the internal feature order within each token is preserved through the earlier positional encoding.

Subsequently, Intra-Sequence Attention applies the self-attention mechanism to process the reshaped input. The final output is obtained by linearly transforming the query, key, and value matrices and computing their attention weights. Specifically, it is assumed that the query, key, and value weight matrices are respectively W_q, W_k, and W_v, then the self-attention is computed as follows:

$$\text{attn} = \text{softmax}\left(\frac{QK^\top}{\sqrt{d}}\right) \tag{5}$$

where Q, K, and V denote the query, key, and value matrices, respectively, and the attention weights are computed by normalizing the dot product. Next, the weighted output is obtained:

$$\text{Output} = \text{attn} \cdot V \tag{6}$$

Finally, the output is reshaped back to (b, n, d), recovering the original batch structure with updated representations for each sample that incorporate information from the entire batch. This entire process effectively captures cross-sample correlations within a batch, thereby enhancing the model's representation ability.

As illustrated in Fig. 3, the core process of performing Intra-Sequence Attention in a single head is demonstrated. Initially, the query vectors q_1, q_2 and key vectors k_1, k_2 are used to compute attention weights $a_{1,2}$, $a_{2,2}$ through a dot product, with each weight being normalized using the softmax function. These attention weights are subsequently applied to the value vectors v_1, v_2 to produce the weighted output. This process leverages query–key relationships to aggregate information across different samples within the same batch, resulting in a weighted representation that incorporates cross-sample dependencies.

Unlike conventional self-attention, which focuses on token-level dependencies within a single sample, Intra-Sequence Attention treats each sample as a holistic token and explicitly models interactions between different samples within the same batch. Compared to IBAFormer's intra-batch attention [40], our formulation is more lightweight, as it reduces the sequence length to the batch size and preserves intra-sample order through positional encoding, while IBAFormer emphasizes tailored mechanisms for domain generalization tasks. This design enhances representation capacity, improves robustness to incomplete information, and captures meaningful dependencies across data points within the batch.

4 Experiments

To verify the effectiveness of our proposed TITID model, we conducted experiments, the details of which are presented below.

4.1 Dataset and Experimental Settings

Our experiments are based on the *MQTT Internet of Things Intrusion Detection Dataset* (MQTT-IoT-IDS2020) [41]. This dataset is specifically designed for evaluating Intrusion Detection Systems (IDS) in Internet of Things (IoT) environments, particularly those utilizing the MQTT protocol for communication. It was created by simulating a variety of attack scenarios targeting IoT devices, including normal activity, aggressive-scan attacks, UDP scan attacks,

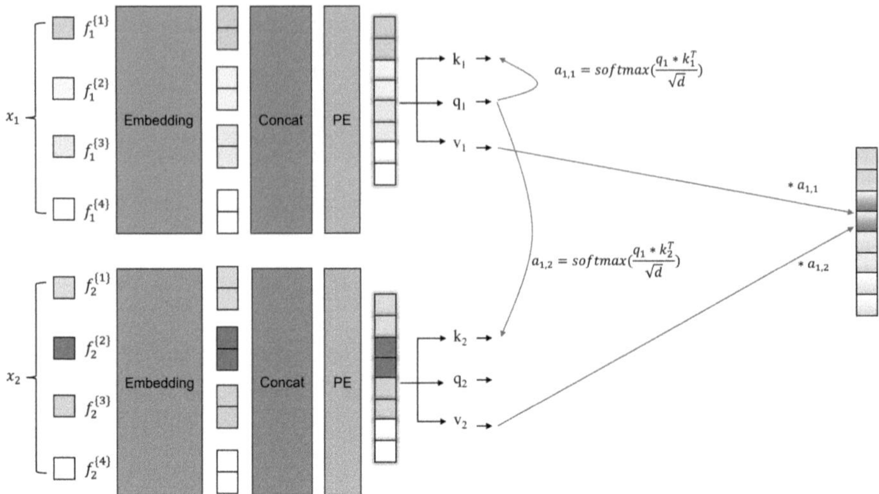

Fig. 3. Intra-Sequence Attention on a batch of 2 points. In this plot, d is the size of value vectors v_i.

Sparta SSH brute-force attacks, and MQTT brute-force attacks. The dataset was generated using 12 MQTT sensors, a broker, a simulated camera, and an attacker. The MQTT-IoT-IDS2020 dataset serves as a comprehensive resource for evaluating the effectiveness of security models in detecting and mitigating IoT-related cyber threats. We use the .csv version of the dataset, which is already in tabular format. The dataset consists of five files: four containing samples of both attacks and normal operations, and one containing only normal operation data. During the preprocessing phase, we apply a dataset balancing technique.

We allocate 80% of the samples for training, 10% for validation, and 10% for testing. Subsequently, we utilize PyTorch to construct the TITID model. We define the optimizer to be used; in this case, we employ AdamW, the most recommended choice for Transformer-based networks. Additionally, we specify the loss function as Binary Cross-Entropy, given that the task involves only two classes. After configuring the layers and parameters, the model is then compiled.

Most of the parameters remain as suggested by default, while others were adjusted to meet the specific requirements of our problem. The model is then trained using the selected dataset.

4.2 Performance Metrics

To comprehensively evaluate the model's performance, we employ a set of widely used metrics including Accuracy, Area Under the ROC Curve (AUC), Precision, Recall, and F1-score.

Accuracy measures the overall proportion of correctly classified instances, providing a general indication of predictive performance. However, in scenarios involving imbalanced datasets, accuracy may not fully reflect the model's effectiveness.

To address this, the AUC metric assesses the model's ability to distinguish between positive and negative classes by summarizing its performance across varying classification thresholds. Higher AUC values indicate better discrimination capability.

Additionally, we report Precision, Recall, and F1-score to offer a more detailed evaluation, particularly relevant for imbalanced data. Precision quantifies the accuracy of positive predictions, Recall measures the coverage of actual positive instances detected by the model, and F1-score provides the harmonic mean of Precision and Recall, balancing their trade-offs.

Together, these metrics provide a robust framework for evaluating both the overall accuracy and the class-specific predictive power of the model.

4.3 Experiment Results and Analysis

The experimental results, presented in Table 1, clearly demonstrate the superior performance of the proposed model over existing approaches, including both conventional deep learning models and recent tabular-specific Transformers. To ensure fair comparison, all models were evaluated under identical preprocessing pipelines, eliminating confounding factors related to data handling and isolating the true impact of model architecture. The deep learning models evaluated in this study include MLP (Multi-Layer Perceptron), CNN (Convolutional Neural Network), GRU (Gated Recurrent Units), and LSTM (Long Short-Term Memory), each with standard configurations of 3, 4, 2, and 2 hidden layers, respectively, and the AdamW optimizer, maintaining consistent batch sizes across experiments.

Compared to traditional deep learning baselines—MLP, CNN, GRU, and LSTM—the proposed model consistently achieves higher accuracy, precision, recall, F1-score, and AUC, reflecting comprehensive improvements across all evaluation dimensions. Notably, even against the ITCT model [42], a prior benchmark for intelligent traffic classification, our approach delivers substantial performance gains. The ITCT baseline was re-implemented based on the TabTransformer [43] architecture, utilizing categorical embeddings and column-wise Transformer layers to capture feature dependencies, with hyperparameters strictly following the published settings.

Beyond ITCT, we additionally benchmark state-of-the-art tabular-specific Transformer models, including FT-Transformer [36], which have demonstrated strong performance on structured data tasks. Despite their advantages, our model achieves the highest overall results, particularly excelling in critical metrics for imbalanced intrusion detection scenarios.

TITID achieves an accuracy of 85.99%, surpassing both ITCT (82.17%) and FT-Transformer (83.41%). More importantly, it obtains an AUC of 0.9406, the highest among all models, demonstrating exceptional capability in distinguishing between benign and malicious traffic, particularly under conditions of class imbalance. Furthermore, the proposed model delivers the best precision (0.8901),

Table 1. Comprehensive comparison of the proposed approach and existing methods.

Model	Acc (%)	Precision	Recall	F1-Score	AUC
MLP	70.23	0.7021	0.6984	0.7002	0.7256
CNN	83.17	0.8417	0.8265	0.8340	0.7593
GRU	72.08	0.7295	0.7137	0.7215	0.7426
LSTM	77.12	0.7734	0.7651	0.7692	0.7928
ITCT [42]	82.17	0.8596	0.8303	0.8149	0.8373
FT-Transformer [36]	83.41	0.8749	0.8141	0.8295	0.8857
TITID (Ours)	**85.99**	**0.8901**	**0.8574**	**0.8572**	**0.9406**

recall (0.8574), and F1-score (0.8572), ensuring not only improved detection rates but also reduced false positives and greater operational reliability.

These comprehensive results validate that our model is not merely incrementally better but represents a meaningful advancement for real-world intrusion detection, offering superior accuracy, robust performance on minority threat classes, and significantly enhanced classification stability.

In conclusion, the proposed approach establishes a new benchmark for intelligent traffic classification, outperforming both conventional deep learning methods and recent Transformer-based solutions, and demonstrating tangible benefits for practical cybersecurity deployments.

5 Conclusion

In this study, we designed the TITID model, a Transformer-based intrusion detection framework specifically designed for IoT environments. By leveraging deep learning techniques, our approach enhances the detection and mitigation of cyber threats in MQTT-enabled networks. Experimental results demonstrate that the TITID model outperforms conventional machine learning and deep learning methods, achieving an accuracy of 85.99% and an AUC score of 0.94. These results underscore the model's strong potential for practical deployment in IoT security. Additionally, the integration of feature embeddings and Intra-Sequence Attention mechanisms further enhances its capability to identify complex attack patterns.

Despite its promising performance, the TITID model has room for further improvement. Future research will focus on optimizing model efficiency, increasing dataset diversity, and incorporating real-time detection capabilities. Furthermore, investigating adversarial robustness and extending the framework to support additional IoT protocols beyond MQTT represent valuable directions for continued exploration.

Overall, this study highlights the effectiveness of Transformer-based models in IoT intrusion detection, paving the way for more advanced, adaptive, and scalable security solutions in the ever-evolving IoT landscape.

Acknowledgments. This work was supported in part by the National Natural Science Foundation of China (NSFC) under Grant 62472105, the Guangdong-Foshan Joint Fund Project of Basic and Applied Basic Research Foundation of Guangdong Province under Grants 2022A1515140096 and 2024A1515110038, and the Natural Science Foundation of Guangdong Province under Grant 2024A1515010186.

Disclosure of Interests. The authors have no competing interests to declare that are relevant to the content of this article.

References

1. Manocha, A., Bhatia, M.: IoT-inspired monitoring framework for real-time stereotypic movement analysis. IEEE Syst. J. (2021)
2. Basati, A., Faghih, M.M.: DFE: efficient IoT network intrusion detection using deep feature extraction. Neural Comput. Appl. 1–21 (2022)
3. Gupta, P.: A survey of application layer protocols for Internet of Things. In: 2021 International Conference on Communication Information and Computing Technology (ICCICT), pp. 1–6. IEEE (2021)
4. Abdel-Basset, M., Manogaran, G., Mohamed, M.: Internet of Things (IoT) and its impact on supply chain: a framework for building smart, secure and efficient systems. Futur. Gener. Comput. Syst. **86**, 614–628 (2018)
5. Hodo, E., et al.: Threat analysis of IoT networks using artificial neural network intrusion detection system. In: 2016 International Symposium on Networks, Computers and Communications (ISNCC), pp. 1–6. IEEE (2016)
6. Baig, Z., et al.: Future challenges for smart cities: cyber-security and digital forensics. Digit. Invest. **22**, 3–13 (2017)
7. Sethi, P., Sarangi, S.R.: Internet of things: architectures, protocols, and applications. J. Electr. Comput. Eng. **2017**(1), 9324035 (2017)
8. Al Enany, M.O., Harb, H.M., Attiya, G.: A comparative analysis of MQTT and IoT application protocols. In: 2021 International Conference on Electronic Engineering (ICEEM), pp. 1–6. IEEE (2021)
9. Hwang, H.C., Park, J., Shon, J.G.: Design and implementation of a reliable message transmission system based on MQTT protocol in IoT. Wirel. Pers. Commun. **91**(4), 1765–1777 (2016)
10. Hunkeler, U., Truong, H.L., Stanford-Clark, A.: MQTT-S—a publish/subscribe protocol for wireless sensor networks. In: 2008 3rd International Conference on Communication Systems Software and Middleware and Workshops, COMSWARE 2008, pp. 791–798. IEEE (2008)
11. Saharkhizan, M., Azmoodeh, A., Dehghantanha, A., Choo, K.K.R., Parizi, R.M.: An ensemble of deep recurrent neural networks for detecting IoT cyber attacks using network traffic. IEEE Internet Things J. **7**(9), 8852–8859 (2020)
12. Driss, M., Hasan, D., Boulila, W., Ahmad, J.: Microservices in IoT security: current solutions, research challenges, and future directions. Procedia Comput. Sci. **192**, 2385–2395 (2021)
13. Azrour, M., Mabrouki, J., Guezzaz, A., Kanwal, A.: Internet of things security: challenges and key issues. Secur. Commun. Netw. **2021**(1), 5533843 (2021)
14. Mazhar, T., et al.: Analysis of IoT security challenges and its solutions using artificial intelligence. Brain Sci. **13**(4), 683 (2023)

15. Ni, C., Li, S.C.: Machine learning enabled industrial IoT security: challenges, trends and solutions. J. Ind. Inf. Integr. **38**, 100549 (2024)
16. Awajan, A.: A novel deep learning-based intrusion detection system for IoT networks. Computers **12**(2), 34 (2023)
17. Fraihat, S., Makhadmeh, S., Awad, M., Al-Betar, M.A., Al-Redhaei, A.: Intrusion detection system for large-scale IoT NetFlow networks using machine learning with modified Arithmetic Optimization Algorithm. Internet Things **22**, 100819 (2023)
18. Shahin, M., Maghanaki, M., Hosseinzadeh, A., Chen, F.F.: Advancing network security in industrial IoT: a deep dive into AI-enabled intrusion detection systems. Adv. Eng. Inform. **62**, 102685 (2024)
19. Ragab, M., Sabir, M.F.S.: Outlier detection with optimal hybrid deep learning enabled intrusion detection system for ubiquitous and smart environment. Sustain. Energy Technol. Assess. **52**, 102311 (2022)
20. Heidari, A., Jamali, M.A.J.: Internet of Things intrusion detection systems: a comprehensive review and future directions. Clust. Comput. **26**(6), 3753–3780 (2023)
21. Sana, L., et al.: Securing the IoT cyber environment: enhancing intrusion anomaly detection with vision transformers. IEEE Access **12**, 82443–82468 (2024)
22. Akuthota, U.C., Bhargava, L.: Transformer based intrusion detection for IoT networks. IEEE Internet Things J. (2025)
23. Zegarra Rodriguez, D., Okey, O.D., Maidin, S.S., Umoren Udo, E., Kleinschmidt, J.H.: Attentive transformer deep learning algorithm for intrusion detection on IoT systems using automatic Xplainable feature selection. PLoS ONE **18**(10), e0286652 (2023)
24. Wang, M., Yang, N., Weng, N.: Securing a smart home with a transformer-based IoT intrusion detection system. Electronics **12**(9), 2100 (2023)
25. Amiri, F., Rezaei Yousefi, M., Lucas, C., Shakery, A., Yazdani, N.: Mutual information-based feature selection for intrusion detection systems. J. Netw. Comput. Appl. **34**(4), 1184–1199 (2011)
26. Ambusaidi, M.A., He, X., Nanda, P., Tan, Z.: Building an intrusion detection system using a filter-based feature selection algorithm. IEEE Trans. Comput. **65**(10), 2986–2998 (2016)
27. Zachos, G., Essop, I., Mantas, G., Porfyrakis, K., Ribeiro, J.C., Rodriguez, J.: Generating IoT edge network datasets based on the TON_IoT telemetry dataset. In: IEEE 26th Int. Workshop on Computer Aided Modeling and Design of Communication Links and Networks (CAMAD), Porto, pp. 1–6. IEEE (2021)
28. Disha, R.A., Waheed, S.: Performance analysis of machine learning models for intrusion detection system using Gini Impurity-based Weighted Random Forest (GIWRF) feature selection technique. Cybersecurity **5**(1), 1 (2022)
29. Khammassi, C., Krichen, S.: A GA-LR wrapper approach for feature selection in network intrusion detection. Comput. Secur. **70**, 255–277 (2017)
30. Halim, Z., et al.: An effective genetic algorithm-based feature selection method for intrusion detection systems. Comput. Secur. **110**, 102448 (2021)
31. Aslahi-Shahri, B.M., et al.: A hybrid method consisting of GA and SVM for intrusion detection system. Neural Comput. Appl. **27**(6), 1669–1676 (2016)
32. Moustafa, N., Slay, J.: A hybrid feature selection for network intrusion detection systems: central points. In: Proceedings of the 16th Australian Information Warfare Conference, pp. 5–13 (2015)
33. Wahab, O.A.: Intrusion detection in the IoT under data and concept drifts: online deep learning approach. IEEE Internet Things J. **9**(20), 19706–19716 (2022)

34. Mosaiyebzadeh, F., Rodriguez, L.G.A., Batista, D.M., Hirata, R.: A network intrusion detection system using deep learning against MQTT attacks in IoT. In: 2021 IEEE Latin-American Conference on Communications (LATINCOM), pp. 1–6. IEEE (2021)
35. Lu, C., Wang, X., Yang, A., Liu, Y., Dong, Z.: A few-shot-based model-agnostic meta-learning for intrusion detection in security of internet of things. IEEE Internet Things J. **10**(24), 21309–21321 (2023)
36. Gorishniy, Y., Rubachev, I., Khrulkov, V., Babenko, A.: Revisiting deep learning models for tabular data. In: Advances in Neural Information Processing Systems, vol. 34, pp. 18932–18943 (2021)
37. Somepalli, G., Goldblum, M., Schwarzschild, A., Bruss, C.B., Goldstein, T.: SAINT: improved neural networks for tabular data via row attention and contrastive pre-training. arXiv preprint arXiv:2106.01342 (2021)
38. Zhang, H., Cao, T.: A hybrid approach to network intrusion detection based on graph neural networks and transformer architectures. In: 2024 14th International Conference on Information Science and Technology (ICIST), pp. 1–6. IEEE (2024)
39. Vaswani, A., et al.: Attention is all you need. In: Advances in Neural Information Processing Systems, vol. 30 (2017)
40. Sun, Q., Chen, H., Zheng, M., Wu, Z., Felsberg, M., Tang, Y.: IBAFormer: intra-batch attention transformer for domain generalized semantic segmentation. arXiv preprint arXiv:2309.06282 (2023)
41. Hindy, H., Tachtatzis, C., Atkinson, R., Bayne, E., Bellekens, X.: MQTT-IoT-IDS2020: MQTT Internet of Things intrusion detection dataset. IEEE Dataport (2020)
42. Bazaluk, B., Hamdan, M., Ghaleb, M., Gismalla, M.S., da Silva, F.S.C., Batista, D.M.: Towards a transformer-based pre-trained model for IoT traffic classification. In: 2024 IEEE Network Operations and Management Symposium, NOMS 2024, pp. 1–7. IEEE (2024)
43. Huang, X., Khetan, A., Cvitkovic, M., Karnin, Z.: TabTransformer: tabular data modeling using contextual embeddings. arXiv preprint arXiv:2012.06678 (2020)

Explainable CAN Intrusion Detection via Feature Extraction

Haofan Wang, Lalith Medury, and Farah Kandah(✉)

Auburn University, Auburn, AL 36849, USA
{hzw0123,bzm0092,farah-kandah}@auburn.edu

Abstract. To combat the growing threat of car hacking, numerous detection methods have been proposed. However, many of these approaches face a critical limitation, including the lack of access to CAN Database (DBC) files, which makes it challenging to capture the complex, multidimensional distribution patterns inherent in the data. Furthermore, most machine learning and deep learning models in this context operate as black boxes, offering little transparency into their decision-making processes or the influence of data features. To address these challenges, this paper proposes an Explainable CAN Intrusion Detection via Feature Extraction (ECID-FE) framework. This approach enhances raw Controller Area Network (CAN) data through feature extraction, revealing deeper and multidimensional characteristics. It also integrates an explainability framework to visually illustrate how the extracted features contribute to the model's predictions.Experiments conducted on the CAN-MIRGU and Car-Hacking datasets demonstrate that the refined dataset achieves performance improvements across most common machine learning and deep learning models tested.

Keywords: CAN Attack · Explainability · Feature Extraction

1 Introduction

Car hacking involves exploiting vulnerabilities in a vehicle's Electronic Control Units (ECUs) and its in-vehicle network protocols, particularly the CAN bus, to perform unauthorized actions or extract sensitive data [8]. Between 2022 and 2024, the financial impact of cyberattacks on the automotive industry soared from $1.0 billion to $22.5 billion [5]. Cyberattacks surged by 225% over the past three years, with more than 60% of these incidents affecting billions of dollars in assets, including vehicles, charging stations, and applications. Large-scale attacks impacting millions of cars rose from 5% to 19% within one year [17]. In June 2024 alone, In June 2024, a ransomware attack on software for U.S. car dealerships caused three weeks of system downtime, halted sales of 56,200 new vehicles, and led to $1.02 billion [21].

The CAN bus is a message-based communication protocol in which nodes broadcast frames with unique identifiers across a shared bus, enabling all connected ECUs to receive and interpret these messages. While this broadcast

I. Awan et al. (Eds.): WISE 2025, LNCS 16367, pp. 456–467, 2026.
https://doi.org/10.1007/978-981-95-7394-3_31

nature allows for efficient and flexible communication among vehicle components, it also introduces security vulnerabilities; any compromised node can inject malicious messages that are accepted by other nodes without authentication. As a result, the CAN bus has become a critical attack surface in modern vehicles. To address these vulnerabilities and detect potential intrusions, machine learning and deep learning models have been increasingly adopted to analyze CAN message patterns and identify anomalous behavior indicative of car hacking attempts [3].

However, the DBC files, which define the mapping between the CAN message bits and their corresponding physical signals, are not publicly available for the vehicle models used in most existing datasets. This makes it challenging to interpret the specific physical quantities represented by each bit in a CAN message. Moreover, current reverse engineering techniques used to infer signal semantics often yield low accuracy [4]. Despite these limitations, one key observation is that while the bit positions representing meaningful information can differ across vehicle models, they remain consistent within a dataset collected from the same vehicle. Leveraging this property, we apply feature extraction techniques to the original dataset to uncover underlying patterns and enhance the data for downstream machine learning tasks.

Our ECID-FE framework was motivated by several challenges, including:

- The absence of DBC files, where the semantic meaning of each bit in the CAN messages is unknown, thus hindering machine learning and deep learning models from properly analyzing the original dataset.
- The black-box nature of most current detection approaches limits their effectiveness, as they obscure the underlying data distribution and provide minimal insight into how decisions are made. This lack of transparency makes it difficult to interpret model behavior or trust its outputs—particularly in safety-critical applications like car hacking detection.

To overcome these challenges, our key contributions are as follows:

- Analyze the original data patterns and perform feature extraction on the existing datasets without relying on DBC files, thereby uncovering deeper and generalizable features that help identify typical patterns of common CAN attacks.
- Develop an explainability framework that visualizes and evaluates the impact of enhanced features from multiple perspectives, providing insights into their contributions to the model's final decisions.

The rest of the article is organized as follows: We present the related work in Sect. 2. Section 3 presents the methodology and design of the ECID-FE. Our experiment and analysis are presented in Sect. 4, followed by the conclusion in Sect. 5.

2 Related Work

One of the primary challenges in CAN-based intrusion detection is the unavailability of DBC files, which prevents the translation of raw CAN messages into meaningful physical quantities. This limitation hampers both the discriminative power of machine learning models and the transparency of their decisions. Researchers have been focusing on feature extraction techniques for CAN messages in the context of car hacking detection. These methods aim to extract high-dimensional features that can better capture anomalies and enhance model performance.

For example, Marfo et al. in [18] treated CAN frames as nodes and the sequential relationships between frames as edges to construct a graph and added time-series features, specifically the mean and standard deviation over a rolling window, to each node to facilitate subsequent model learning. Kim et al. in [19] computed the time intervals between successive frames and differenced the CAN message payloads to obtain delta value sequences. Khan et al. in [20] employed a fixed-size window to calculate, within each window, the mean and standard deviation of each ID as well as the proportion of attack frames, thereby improving subsequent model performance.

While these approaches improve model input, they often emphasize only one aspect of the data, be it static, temporal, or structural, without capturing the full spectrum of feature diversity. This narrow focus limits the downstream models' ability to understand data distribution patterns and detect sophisticated attacks holistically.

In recent years, several explainability modules have been proposed for car hacking detection to enhance the transparency of model decisions and to understand the contribution of each parameter to those decisions.

Ding et al. in [12] proposed a deep learning framework integrated with an explainability module, where the Shapley Additive Explanations (SHAP) demonstrate how each feature contributes to or suppresses the prediction outcome. Compared to traditional methods, SHAP takes into account all possible combinations of subsets of features. Lee et al. in [13] proposed a vision language model that combines Local Interpretable Model-agnostic Explanations (LIME) outputs with feature importance rankings to analyze the model prediction by assessing the contribution of each feature.

Despite their value, these explainability methods each rely on a single explanation algorithm, which may introduce biases and provide only a limited perspective on model reasoning. In contrast, our proposed approach integrates multiple explainability techniques, enabling cross-validation of results and delivering more stable, comprehensive insights into feature influence and model behavior.

3 Methodology and Design

In this work, we address the challenge of unknown physical quantities in CAN messages by proposing a feature extraction method that enriches the original dataset with additional informative attributes. Furthermore, we develop an explainability framework to assess how these extracted features contribute to the model's final predictions.

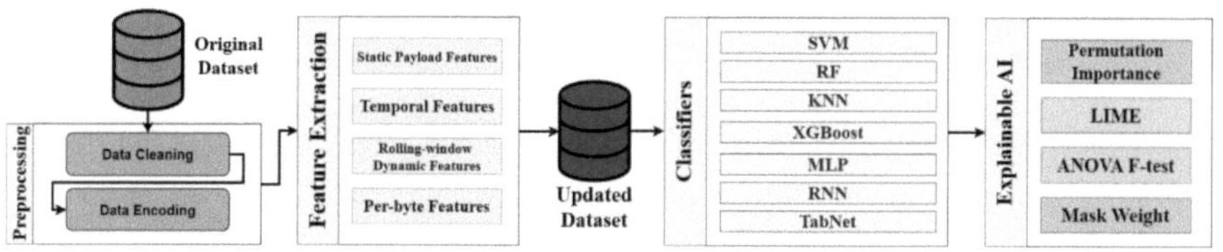

Fig. 1. Explainable CAN Intrusion Detection via Feature Extraction (ECID-FE): an overview.

An overview of the Explainable CAN Intrusion Detection via Feature Extraction (ECID-FE) framework is illustrated in Fig. 1. Our proposed framework consists of three phases: First, the data preprocessing phase transforms the original dataset into a format compatible with the subsequent pipeline and prevents outliers or dominant features from adversely affecting model training. Second, the feature extraction stage analyzes the distribution patterns of the original dataset across four dimensions, helping the downstream models uncover the data's underlying characteristics. Finally, the explainability module employs four complementary tests to explain, from multiple perspectives, how the updated features contribute to distinguishing benign and malicious CAN messages, thus enhancing the transparency of model decisions and revealing which features change most markedly under car hacking attacks.

3.1 Data Preprocessing

This phase ensures that the data is both available and compatible with the requirements of each data mining algorithm. It also addresses issues such as outliers, missing values, and inconsistent formats, preventing them from negatively impacting model analysis.

Data Cleaning: To ensure uniform processing, CAN messages with payloads shorter than 8 bytes were padded with zeros to reach the standard length. Furthermore, any incomplete or missing samples were removed from the dataset to maintain data quality and consistency.

Data Encoding: Since the original dataset contains some string-based features, label encoding techniques were applied to map them to integer values, so that they can be processed correctly by the models.

3.2 Feature Extraction

The original datasets include two main features, which are used to distinguish benign and malicious CAN messages:

Arbitration ID: The Arbitration ID is the header field that uniquely identifies a CAN frame's message type and governs bus arbitration. When multiple ECUs transmit at the same time, the frame with the lower numeric identifier value wins priority on the bus [9].

Data: The payload of the CAN frame, consisting of up to 16 hexadecimal characters, totaling 8 bytes of data.

Some other features can be reported, such as:

Timestamp, which indicates the time at which the message was received, precise to six decimal places.

Interface, which indicates the CAN bus interface on which the frame was captured. Note that, since all frames in the dataset come from 'can0', it provides no discriminative value for classification.

Flag, which represents the type of the frame.

To extract distributional patterns and structures from existing features, the model's representational capacity and classification performance must be improved when the specific physical quantities represented by CAN messages are unknown. We extract features from four dimensions: static payload features, temporal features, rolling window dynamic features, and bitwise features, thereby capturing the statistical distribution of a CAN message over time, the variation of individual bits, and the latent static and dynamic characteristics, to comprehensively help the downstream model understand both normal and anomalous behavior in the data. Additionally, since the Interface and Flag features in the original dataset were predominantly of a single category and could not be used to distinguish between benign and malicious CAN messages, they were removed from the refined dataset. The original Car-Hacking dataset includes only the aforementioned Timestamp, Arbitration ID, and Data features, so the features extracted from both datasets are identical as follows:

Static Payload Features

Data Mean: the average value of the eight payload bytes in the message.
Data Standard Deviation: the standard deviation of the eight payload bytes.
Data Max: the maximum byte value among the eight payload bytes.
Data Min: the minimum byte value among the eight payload bytes.
Entropy: the Shannon entropy of the eight payload bytes, indicating its randomness. A higher value indicates that the message is more diverse and the distribution is more uniform [10].
Hamming Weight: the total count of '1' bits across all eight payload bytes.

By combining these static features, we can fully characterize each CAN message's value range, variability, and distribution uniformity.

Temporal Features

Frequency: the reciprocal of the time interval between two consecutive messages.

ID Mean: the overall average inter-arrival time for this message's Arbitration ID.
ID Standard Deviation: the overall standard deviation of inter-arrival times for this Arbitration ID.

Because attackers often disrupt message timing by injecting extra frames, and the frequency reflects the transmission rate of messages, it can detect timing anomalies [14]. Meanwhile, the ID mean and standard deviation capture each Arbitration ID's typical inter-arrival interval and its variability, thereby capturing the anomalous timing behavior of malicious CAN messages.

Rolling Window Dynamic Features

Rolling window mean of inter-arrival times of CAN messages: computes the average time difference between consecutive CAN frames over a rolling window of recent observations.
Rolling window standard deviation of inter-arrival times of CAN messages: measures the standard deviation of those inter-arrival times within the same rolling window.
Rolling window entropy of the CAN Arbitration ID sequence: Shannon entropy of the Arbitration ID sequence across a rolling window of recent messages.

Rolling Window selects a fixed number of consecutive CAN messages at each step to compute their local features, and then shifts forward by a fixed stride to capture temporal local behavior patterns and determine whether any anomalies have occurred [11]. In this work, we set the rolling window size to 50 with a stride of 1; that is, the statistics are computed sequentially for each sample using the most recent 50 samples.

Bitwise Features

Mean of payload byte values at positions 0 to 7: the mean value of that byte for this Arbitration ID for each byte position 0 to 7.
Standard Deviation of payload byte values at positions 0 to 7: the standard deviation of that byte for this Arbitration ID for each byte position 0 to 7.

Since common injection attacks often modify only certain byte positions [16], computing these two features helps the model effectively detect specific bytes that deviate significantly from their historical means, allowing the model to focus on the most relevant byte positions and enhancing overall explainability.

The features above include frequency and interval for detecting timing anomalies, mean, variance, and entropy for identifying value anomalies, and bit-level features for capturing byte modification attacks. Together, they cover the most common attack types against the CAN bus. Moreover, the extraction of these features does not rely on DBC files, making them generalizable across different vehicle models.

3.3 Explainability Framework

To enhance the transparency of decision-making in existing detection models and to gain a deeper understanding of feature contributions and their association with model judgments, we designed a framework incorporating the following four explainability methods. This approach aims to mitigate the bias that may result from any single method and to provide complementary perspectives.

- LIME explains an individual prediction of any complex classifier in an interpretable and faithful way by learning a simple, interpretable model locally around the instance being explained [6]. However, it focuses solely on local features and struggles to capture overall statistical trends in the data.
- Permutation Importance (PI) is used to evaluate the extent to which a model's predictive performance decreases when the values of a given feature are randomly permuted [7]. However, when used in isolation, it may overlook variations at the individual-sample level by providing only a global perspective.
- ANOVA F-test scores each feature's relevance to the labels by computing the ratio of between-class variance to within-class variance (the F-value); a larger F-value indicates a greater contribution of that feature to class discrimination [15]. However, it considers only the correlation between features and class labels and cannot probe featureâĂŞclassifier interactions or the underlying decision rationale.
- Mask weight is the feature selection weight generated by its attention mechanism, representing the degree to which the model attends to each feature [22]. However, it reflects only the internal focus of the model and cannot statistically quantify feature associations, concentrating solely on the classifier itself.

By integrating the explainability modules of these methods, one can assess the features that most significantly impact model performance and contribute to its results from multiple perspectives, including both global and local viewpoints, feature associations, and interactions with the model, avoid potential biases inherent in any single explainable AI approach, calculate metrics across all samples and derive a final average rather than relying on a single instance to ensure stability, and explain how the model arrives at its final outputs, thereby enhancing transparency.

4 Experiment and Analysis

This section outlines the methodologies used for numerical analysis and model evaluation, highlighting key findings to clarify the model's effectiveness.

All experiments were conducted on an Intel i9-14900HX processor and a GeForce RTX 4070 GPU.

4.1 Datasets

To evaluate the effectiveness of our proposed method, we conducted experiments using two widely recognized CAN bus intrusion detection datasets.

CAN-MIRGU [1]: This dataset was collected from the CAN bus of a modern vehicle operating under real-world driving conditions. It contains benign samples as well as multiple realistic attack samples, making it suitable for training in-vehicle IDS.

Car-Hacking [2]: The Car-Hacking dataset contains benign samples and malicious samples, including flooding attacks, spoofing attacks, replay attacks, and fuzz testing attacks, sourced from real driving data generated by a Hyundai vehicle.

Both of these are common vehicle attack datasets with similar feature structures. For our experiments, we used a 70:30 split between training and testing sets to evaluate model performance.

4.2 Baseline Models

We evaluated the before-and-after metrics of several different machine learning and deep learning models under otherwise identical conditions to compare the impact of the original dataset versus the updated dataset on model performance. These models include Support Vector Machine (SVM), Random Forest (RF), K-Nearest Neighbors (KNN), Extreme Gradient Boosting (XGBoost), Multi-Layer Perceptron (MLP), Recurrent Neural Network (RNN), and Attentive Interpretable Tabular Learning (TabNet).

4.3 Analysis

In this work, accuracy, precision, and F1-score are applied to evaluate the performance of baseline models.

As shown in Table 1a, our updated CAN-MIRGU dataset yielded improvements in almost all metrics across all baseline models, with the RF model achieving the highest precision, accuracy, and F1-score of 91.66%, 91.85%, and 91.73%, respectively, and also demonstrating the greatest improvement. The metrics of some models have slightly declined, possibly due to increased feature dimensionality leading to gradient instability; applying dimensionality reduction to the dataset can improve the performance of these models.

As shown in Table 1b, although some of the baseline models had already achieved nearly 100% performance on the original dataset, their results still improved on the updated dataset. In addition, the subsequent explainability module provides a visual demonstration of how different parameters influence the model's ability to distinguish between labels.

As shown in Fig. 2, in the CAN-MIRGU dataset, different explainability methods consistently indicate that dynamic features (such as the standard deviation, entropy, and mean of the rolling window, as well as the standard deviation

Table 1. Comparison of baseline models on CAN-MIRGU and Car-Hacking datasets

(a) CAN-MIRGU dataset				(b) Car-Hacking dataset		
Models	Precision	Accuracy	F1-Score	Precision	Accuracy	F1-Score
	Original Dataset			Original Dataset		
SVM	72.19%	51.55%	56.77%	91.18%	83.12%	85.24%
RF	81.97%	83.97%	81.09%	99.34%	99.89%	99.61%
KNN	79.27%	81.74%	79.92%	92.56%	92.94%	92.55%
XGBoost	80.57%	82.95%	78.57%	99.94%	99.99%	99.96%
MLP	79.08%	82.23%	77.01%	83.53%	86.11%	80.43%
RNN	84.85%	81.44%	73.20%	99.16%	99.86%	99.51%
TabNet	66.19%	81.36%	72.99%	88.38%	80.88%	83.16%
	Updated Dataset			Updated Dataset		
SVM	71.14%	52.83%	58.03%	83.31%	86.02%	83.88%
RF	91.66%	91.85%	91.73%	99.88%	99.98%	99.93%
KNN	83.13%	84.64%	83.40%	93.62%	93.52%	93.57%
XGBoost	86.75%	87.56%	86.25%	99.94%	99.99%	99.96%
MLP	81.28%	82.29%	75.82%	83.36%	86.38%	82.00%
RNN	79.00%	82.20%	76.97%	99.82%	99.97%	99.89%
TabNet	77.15%	81.59%	75.20%	92.94%	91.64%	92.07%

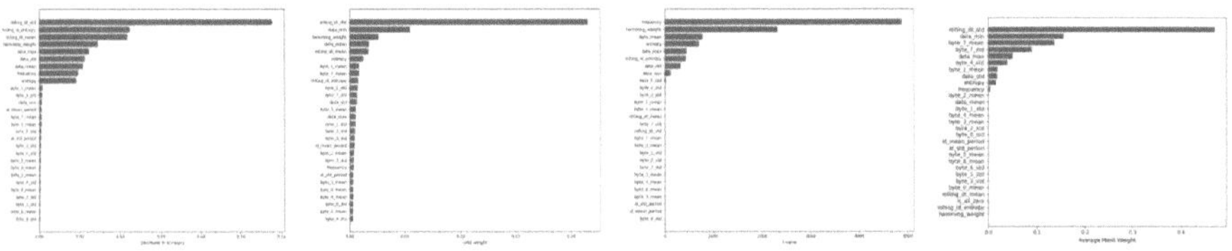

(a) PI (b) LIME (c) ANOVA F-test (d) Mask Weight

Fig. 2. Feature importance analysis for the CAN-MIRGU dataset.

of inter-message time) are most critical for model prediction and attack detection, while static features (such as Hamming weight, maximum/minimum byte values, and statistics of specific bytes) also play a supporting role; in contrast, the mean and standard deviation of individual bytes show limited discriminative power.

As shown in Fig. 3, in the Car-Hacking dataset, similarly, the model relies almost entirely on rolling window dynamic features, message frequency, and Arbitration ID-related features to distinguish between classes, while static features (such as bitwise measures, Hamming weight, and entropy) exert weaker influence, and most other features have importance values close to zero, indicating that attack detection depends primarily on temporal features and ID-related information.

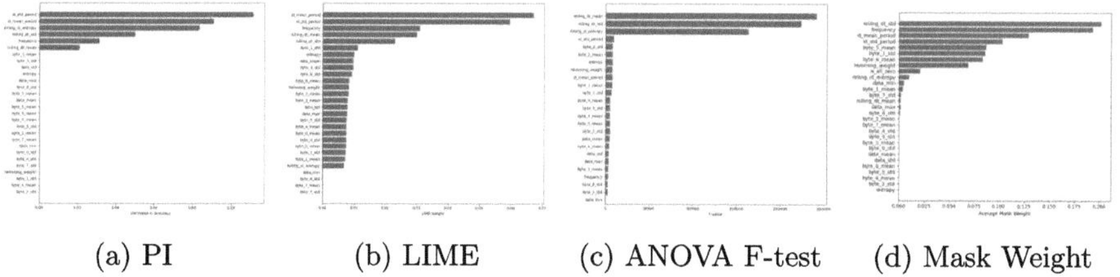

(a) PI (b) LIME (c) ANOVA F-test (d) Mask Weight

Fig. 3. Feature importance analysis for the Car-Hacking dataset.

5 Conclusion

To address the ever-increasing threat of car hacking and to improve the model's explainability and its ability to analyze latent distribution patterns in CAN message data, we propose ECID-FE in this work. ECID-FE employs a feature extraction approach to allow the model to capture the deep distributional characteristics of the data in the absence of DBC files, and incorporates an explainability framework to visualize and quantify how the updated features contribute to the model's final predictions. To validate the effectiveness of the proposed feature extraction method, we compared the performance of several common machine learning and deep learning models on both the original and updated datasets using the CAN-MIRGU and Car-Hacking datasets. The results demonstrate that our feature extraction method yields performance improvements across all models on both datasets. Moreover, explainability techniques reveal which features were instrumental in the model's decision to flag a particular frame as anomalous, with the highest contribution coming from the dynamic features based on the rolling window. In the future, when other researchers apply similar approaches to comparable datasets, they will be able to distinguish whether a model's alert was driven by genuinely relevant features for the decision or by false correlations introduced by noise and outliers.

Building on this work, we plan to apply this framework to additional datasets that encompass a wider variety of vehicle models. We will employ feature selection techniques to eliminate redundant features and reduce the risk of overfitting, and integrate further explainability methods to enhance the transparency of model decision-making.

References

1. Rajapaksha, S. Madzudzo, G., Kalutarage, H., Petrovski, A., Al-Kadri, M.O.: CAN-MIRGU: a comprehensive CAN bus attack dataset from moving vehicles for intrusion detection system evaluation. In: Network and Distributed System Security Symposium (NDSS) (2024)
2. Kang, H., Il Kwak, B., Lee, Y.H., Lee, H., Lee, H., Kim, H.K.: Car hacking: attack & defense challenge 2020 dataset. IEEE Dataport (2021). https://doi.org/10.21227/qvr7-n418

3. Lokman, S.-F., Othman, A.T., Abu-Bakar, M.H.: Intrusion detection system for automotive Controller Area Network (CAN) bus system: a review. EURASIP J. Wirel. Commun. Netw. **2019**(1), 1–17 (2019)
4. Buscemi, A., Turcanu, I., Castignani, G., Crunelle, R., Engel, T.: CANMatch: a fully automated tool for CAN bus reverse engineering based on frame matching. IEEE Trans. Veh. Technol. **70**(12), 12358–12373 (2021)
5. VicOne Inc., Shifting Gears: VicOne 2025 Automotive Cybersecurity Report, VicOne Inc. (2025). https://documents.vicone.com/reports/shifting-gears-2025-automotive-cybersecurity-report.pdf
6. Ribeiro, M.T., Singh, S., Guestrin, C.: Why should i trust you? Explaining the predictions of any classifier. In: Proceedings of the 22nd ACM SIGKDD International Conference on Knowledge Discovery and Data Mining, pp. 1135–1144 (2016)
7. Altmann, A., Toloşi, L., Sander, O., Lengauer, T.: Permutation importance: a corrected feature importance measure. Bioinformatics **26**(10), 1340–1347 (2010)
8. Payne, B.R.: Car hacking: accessing and exploiting the CAN bus protocol. J. Cybersecur. Educ. Res. Pract. **2019**(1), 5 (2019)
9. Verma, M.E., et al.: A comprehensive guide to CAN IDS data and introduction of the ROAD dataset. PLoS ONE **19**(1), e0296879 (2024)
10. Jost, L.: Entropy and diversity. Oikos **113**(2), 363–375 (2006)
11. Kulanuwat, L., et al.: Anomaly detection using a sliding window technique and data imputation with machine learning for hydrological time series. Water **13**(13), 1862 (2021)
12. Ding, W., Alrashdi, I., Hawash, H., Abdel-Basset, M.: DeepSecDrive: an explainable deep learning framework for real-time detection of cyberattack in in-vehicle networks. Inf. Sci. **658**, 120057 (2024)
13. Lee, J., Rew, J.: Vision-language model-based local interpretable model-agnostic explanations analysis for explainable in-vehicle controller area network intrusion detection. Sensors (2025)
14. Moriano, P., Bridges, R.A., Iannacone, M.D.: Detecting CAN masquerade attacks with signal clustering similarity. arXiv preprint arXiv:2201.02665 (2022)
15. Siraj, M.J., Ahmad, T., Ijtihadie, R.M.: Analyzing ANOVA F-test and sequential feature selection for intrusion detection systems. Int. J. Adv. Soft Comput. Appl. **14**(2), 1–10 (2022)
16. Demetrio, L., Coull, S.E., Biggio, B., Lagorio, G., Armando, A., Roli, F.: Adversarial exemples: a survey and experimental evaluation of practical attacks on machine learning for Windows malware detection. ACM Trans. Priv. Secur. (TOPS) **24**(4), 1–31 (2021)
17. Daniel, J.: Security report reveals alarming trends in auto cybersecurity threats. CBT News (2025). https://www.cbtnews.com/upstream-report-reveals-alarming-trends-in-auto-cybersecurity-threats
18. Marfo, W., Moriano, P., Tosh, D.K., Moore, S.V.: Detecting masquerade attacks in controller area networks using graph machine learning. arXiv preprint arXiv:2408.05427 (2024)
19. Kim, T., Kim, J., You, I.: An anomaly detection method based on multiple LSTM-autoencoder models for in-vehicle network. Electronics **12**(17), 3543 (2023)
20. Khan, J., Lim, D.-W., Kim, Y.-S.: Intrusion detection system CAN-bus in-vehicle networks based on the statistical characteristics of attacks. Sensors **23**(7), 3554 (2023)

21. Graham Hope. Cyberattacks on Auto, Mobility Industries on the Rise: Report. IoT World Today, TechTarget & Informa Tech (2025). https://www.iotworldtoday.com/security/cyberattacks-on-auto-mobility-industries-on-the-rise-report
22. Arik, S.Ö., Pfister, T.: TabNet: attentive interpretable tabular learning. In: Proceedings of the AAAI Conference on Artificial Intelligence, vol. 35, no. 8, pp. 6679–6687 (2021)

Extending Hyperbolic Temporal Graph Neural Network to Anomaly Detection for Secure Cyberspaces

Souhail Abdelmouaiz Sadat[1], Mohamed Yacine Touahria Miliani[1], and Hamida Seba[2(✉)]

[1] École Nationale Supérieure d'Informatique (ESI), LCSI, Algiers, Algeria
{js_sadat,jm_touahriamiliani}@esi.dz

[2] UCBL, CNRS, INSA Lyon, LIRIS, UMR5205, Villeurbanne, France
hamida.seba@univ-lyon1.fr

Abstract. Anomaly detection on temporal dynamic graphs enables the identification of threats in our cyberspaces. However, finding a graph representation that offers the best trade-off between execution time and accuracy remains a major challenge. To address this, we propose a novel model based on Hyperbolic Graph Neural Networks, an emerging class of learning architectures that leverages the expressive power of hyperbolic geometry to process graph-structured data. Our results show that the proposed model outperforms the state of the art, achieving over 97% accuracy across all datasets while also reducing memory consumption. Moreover, its processing time is competitive with the best-performing Euclidean models.

Keywords: Dynamic graphs · Hyperbolic embedding · Anomaly detection · Cybersecurity

1 Introduction

The web, together with the digital infrastructures and tools that we rely on, constitute our cyberspace, a dynamic and complex environment that supports nearly all modern activities. However, this cyberspace is increasingly exposed to a multitude of threats that come in many forms, each with unique methods and objectives, targeting vulnerabilities of cyberspaces. For instance, a Denial of Service (DoS) attack aims to make a network service unavailable to its legitimate users by overwhelming it with an excessive amount of traffic or requests. A Distributed Denial of Service (DDoS) attack utilizes multiple infected computers, often forming a botnet, to simultaneously flood the target with an overwhelming amount of traffic. A Botnet is a network of compromised computers, known as bots or zombies, controlled remotely by an attacker. These bots can be used to launch coordinated attacks like DDoS, send spams, or steal data. A Malware is a malicious software designed to infiltrate, damage, or gain unauthorized

I. Awan et al. (Eds.): WISE 2025, LNCS 16367, pp. 468–478, 2026.
https://doi.org/10.1007/978-981-95-7394-3_32

access to computer systems. It comes in various forms, such as viruses, worms, trojans, and ransomwares, and can cause significant harm by stealing data, disrupting operations, or taking control of a system. To deal with these threats graphs are increasingly used to represent cyberspace data to facilitate their analyzis in order to detect potential threats. A graph is a data structure composed of nodes (representing entities) and edges (representing relationships or interactions between entities). Graphs offer a natural and effective way to capture complex interconnections and dependencies within the data, making them particularly well-suited for modeling events within cyberspaces. This structural representation allows for more contextual and relational analysis, which can significantly improve the detection of sophisticated or stealthy attacks. However, an attack may unfold as a chain of discrete actions distributed over time, rather than as a set of simultaneous or immediate events. This puts dynamic graphs as more suitable than static graphs for modeling cybersecurity data, A dynamic (or temporal) graph is a time-ordered sequence of graph snapshots $G_t = (V_t, E_t)$, where each snapshot represents the state of the graph at a discrete time step t. Nodes V_t and edges E_t may vary over time to reflect the evolving structure of the system. These dynamic graphs capture the evolving nature of cyber threats as they retain historical information and reflect the graph's evolution. This contributes to enhancing the accuracy of threat detection and analysis which is crucial for early identification of attacks before they cause significant damage. This explains the growing interest in the field of graph embedding, which enables the application of machine learning techniques directly on graph-structured data. Graph embedding techniques transform nodes, edges, or entire subgraphs into low-dimensional vector representations while preserving the structural and semantic information of the original graph. These vector representations make it possible to apply a wide range of machine learning algorithms, such as classification, clustering, or anomaly detection, effectively on graph data, thus opening new possibilities for advanced threat detection in cybersecurity. This allows using intelligent anomaly detection techniques to identify potential attacks by assuming that malicious activity is dissimilar from typical user behavior. In fact, by establishing a baseline of normal behavioral in a cyberspace, we can flag any event or activity that deviates significantly from the established baseline as a potential threat. In this domain, Hyperbolic Graph neural Networks (HGNN) represent an emerging class of learning models designed to handle graph data by leveraging the representational power of hyperbolic geometry [2]. For temporal/dynamic graphs, these models aim to address two central challenges simultaneously: the evolving nature of temporal graphs, where the structure and node/edge features change over time, and the need to capture hierarchical or scale-free patterns often found in real-world networks. However, Most existing solutions are highly dependent on the downstream task. For instance, an architecture designed specifically for link prediction may not perform well on a classification task. This limitation is demonstrated in our experimental section. These architectures are also computationally intensive and cannot be used for real-time attack detection. This motivated us to develop a new architecture better suited for cyberspace security.

The remainder of this paper is organised as Follows: Sect. 2 introduces hyperbolic embedding and review the main approaches in the literature. Section 3 presents the proposed architecture and details its components. Section 4 presents the experiments we undertook to evaluate our approach and compare it with existing models. Finlay, Sect. 5 concludes the paper and gives some future work directions.

2 Background and Motivation

Traditionally, the machine learning community has primarily used Euclidean space for data representation, as it is the most familiar vector space. However, over the past decade, there has been a growing interest in exploring non-Euclidean spaces, particularly hyperbolic spaces, which are well-suited for representing data with hierarchical structures like trees and real-world graphs such as the WEB. A hyperbolic graph neural network (HGNN) is a type of neural network that learns from graph-structured data by placing the nodes in hyperbolic space. This allows to better capture the true geometry of the data, leading to improved performance on tasks like classification or link prediction. A commonly used way to represent hyperbolic space in hyperbolic graph neural networks is the Poincaré ball model. In this model, the entire infinite hyperbolic space is mapped inside a finite ball, typically a unit disk in two or more dimensions.

Several hyperbolic embedding are proposed to deal with dynamic networks that evolve over time. HTGN [14] is designed for temporal graphs, which are represented as a series of snapshots $\{G_1, ..., G_t, ..., G_T\}$ sampled from the temporal graph. Each snapshot $G_t = (V_t, A_t)$ contains the current node set V_t and its corresponding adjacency matrix A_t. HTGN operates in the Poincaré ball model with learnable curvature c and consists of three main components: (1) a hyperbolic graph neural network (HGNN), which extracts topological dependencies in hyperbolic space; (2) a Hyperbolic Temporal Attention (HTA), which aggregates historical information through an attention mechanism; and (3) a Hyperbolic Gated Recurrent Unit (HGRU), a recurrent module that captures sequential patterns. The HGNN module [3], incorporates a hyperbolic linear transformation, a hyperbolic attention-based aggregation, and a hyperbolic activation. It takes the adjacency matrix A_t and hyperbolic node features H_t as inputs and outputs $\tilde{X}_t$. The HTA component addresses the challenge of maintaining long-term temporal dependencies. The HGRU is a hyperbolic variant of GRU, where all the gate units operate in the tangent space. HGRU takes the outputs of the HGNN and HTA, denoted as $\tilde{X}_t$ and $\tilde{H}_{t-1}$, respectively, and produces the current embeddings $H_t^{\mathcal{H}}$. HTGN is optimized by minimizing the overall loss function $\mathcal{L}_t = \mathcal{L}_{t,r} + \lambda\mathcal{L}_{t,c}$, which combines two loss components. First, the HTC loss $\mathcal{L}_{t,r}$ minimizes the hyperbolic distance between node embeddings from consecutive time steps, ensuring temporal smoothness. Second, the hyperbolic homophily loss $\mathcal{L}_{t,r}$, based on cross-entropy. The hyperparameter $\lambda \in [0, 1]$ balances the contributions of these two losses. HTGN was evaluated for link prediction which predicts future edges.

Inspired by WaveNet [10] and Graph WaveNet [13], HGWaveNet [1] is a hyperbolic graph neural network framework designed for dynamic graphs. It comprises several modules: (1) a Hyperbolic Diffusion Graph Convolution (HDGC) that learns node representations from both direct and indirect neighbors in a single snapshot, (2) a Hyperbolic Dilated Causal Convolution (HDCC) module that aggregates historical information to capture temporal dependencies across past snapshots, (3) a gating mechanism, formed by two HDCCs, that computes a historical hidden state. This state, along with the current node representations (output of HDGC), is fed into an HGRU (similar to the one used in HTGN) to compute the current node embedding. Existing convolutional GNNs limit message propagation to direct neighbor nodes, which is ineffective for large graphs with long paths. To address this, HGWaveNet incorporates a diffusion process inspired by [7]. HDGC consists of two diffusion convolution layers, each performing K diffusion steps. The number of steps, K, represents the maximum path length considered in message propagation. The k-th step at layer l is given by $X_k^l = \text{HGCN}_k^l(A^k, X^{l-1})$, where X^0 is initialized to node features mapped into hyperbolic space using an exponential map, and A^k is the k-th power of the adjacency matrix A, with each entry representing the number of k-paths from node v to node u. HGCN is the method proposed by [3], and each HGCN_k^l block has a separate trainable weight matrix. The results X_k^l from all steps are aggregated using an attention mechanism, resulting in X^l, which is then passed to the next layer. The Hyperbolic Dilated Causal Convolution (HDCC) module applies convolution to past snapshot states without significantly increasing the computational cost. Unlike the attention-based historical information aggregation used in HTGN, HDCC adheres to the causality constraint, i.e., each state depends only on past and present states, not future ones. The input layer contains representations of the same node at different timestamps. At each layer, the node representation at each snapshot is updated using a fixed number S (called kernel size) of past snapshot representations, skipping inputs with a certain step d that increases exponentially. The final output captures long-range dependencies within S^D snapshots. This technique makes HDCC more appropriate for sequence problems and avoids the vanishing or exploding gradient issues that arise with Recurrent neural networks (RNNs). HGWaveNet was evaluated for link prediction.

3 A New Hyperbolic Emebedding

In this section, we introduce **Hyperbolic Variational Graph Autoencoder for Anomaly Detection (HVGAE-AD)**, a novel approach for identifying anomalies in dynamic graphs using hyperbolic embeddings. Our approach draws inspiration from HTGN [14] but deploys a completely different architecture which, as revealed in the experiments section, is better suited for anomaly detection.

3.1 Global Architecture

The overall architecture of the proposed HVGAE-AD method is depicted in Fig. 1. HVGAE-AD takes as input a dynamic graph represented by a series of snapshots $\{G_1, ..., G_t, ..., G_T\}$, where each snapshot consists of a static graph defined by its adjacency matrix A_t and its node feature matrix X_t. The objective is to generate Y_t, which represents the prediction probabilities of each node in the snapshot, classifying them as either normal or anomalous. The overall solution draws inspiration from HTGN [14] and is composed of several key components, which together enable this predictive capability.

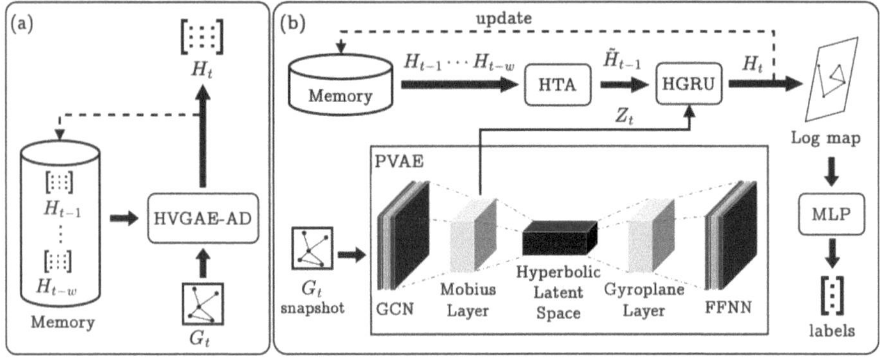

Fig. 1. Architecture of HVGAE-AD. (a) Global overview. (b) Detailed components.

- **A memory bank:** Similarly to HTGN [14], we use a memory bank to store node embeddings from previous snapshots. The memory bank has a fixed size, denoted by w, which we refer to as the *memory length*. Specifically, at time t, the memory bank holds the node embeddings from the last w snapshots, i.e., $H_{t-w}, ..., H_{t-1}$. These historical embeddings are aggregated to allow the model to capture temporal information and learn evolving dependencies and patterns over time.
- **A Poincaré Variational Autoencoder** ($\mathcal{P}$-VAE): To learn spatial patterns from each snapshot, we propose to use a variational autoencoder, $\mathcal{P}$-VAE [8] which has been shown to outperform other hyperbolic graph embedding models on static graphs [12]. $\mathcal{P}$-VAE maps each graph snapshot $\mathcal{G}_t$ into a hyperbolic latent space modeled by a wrapped Gaussian distribution on the Poincaré ball. The encoder, consisting of a Euclidean GCN followed by a Möbius layer, takes the adjacency matrix A_t and node features X_t as inputs and simultaneously produces two outputs: the Gaussian distribution parameters (Fréchet mean and standard deviation) and the hyperbolic embeddings Z_t, which follow this distribution. The $\mathcal{P}$-VAE aims to learn a distribution that captures the underlying data patterns from the adjacency and feature matrices. The embeddings Z_t are then passed to the **HGRU** module, described below.

- **A Hyperbolic Temporal Attention (HTA):** When learning temporal embeddings, preserving long-term dependencies is essential. However, recurrent models like RNNs tend to gradually lose long-term information due to their inherent monotonic nature. To overcome this limitation, we incorporate a Hyperbolic Temporal Attention (HTA) module, similarly to HTGN [14]. HTA allows the model to effectively reintroduce historical embeddings stored in the memory bank. Node embeddings $H_{t-w}, ..., H_{t-1}$ of the latest w snapshots are aggregated using an attention mechanism performed in the tangent space. The HTA module outputs a single hidden state $\tilde{H}_{t-1}$, which combines all relevant historical information from the memory bank.
- **A Hyperbolic Gated Recurrent Unit (HGRU):** To produce embeddings that capture temporal information, most graph embedding methods resort to using a recurrent unit such as RNN, GRU, and LSTM. However, only GRU has been extended to hyperbolic geometry [4,14]. Consequently, we opt to keep in our solution the Hyperbolic Gated Recurrent Unit (HGRU) module similarly HTGN [14], which is a hyperbolic variant of GRU that performs all operations in the tangent space. HGRU takes as input the embeddings Z_t of the current graph snapshot, produced by the $\mathcal{P}$-VAE encoder, along with the output of HTA, $\tilde{H}_{t-1}$, which aggregates the embeddings of the w previous graph snapshots. Finally, HGRU produces the node embeddings H_t of the current graph snapshot. The new node embeddings H_t are stored in the memory bank, while the oldest embeddings H_{t-w} are removed to keep the *memory length* invariant.

3.2 Anomaly Detection Mechanism

We choose to train our architecture in an end-to-end manner so that the HGRU can be optimized directly for anomaly detection in supervised mode. Since the architecture is based on deep neural networks, it is necessary to select a neural network-based anomaly detection model to ensure end-to-end training through back propagation. For these reasons, we opt for a multilayer perceptron (MLP) to perform the anomaly detection task. Once the node embeddings H_t of the current graph snapshot are produced, we use these vector representations in the anomaly detection model. We first map H_t into the tangent space of the origin o using the logarithmic map $\log_o$, resulting in Euclidean embeddings, which we denote as H_t^E. We feed these embeddings into a multilayer perceptron (MLP) to perform binary logistic regression. The MLP outputs a matrix Y_t, where each node i is represented by a vector concatenating the probability of each class: normal and anomalous.

3.3 Loss Function Design

While supervised embedding aims to optimize embeddings specifically for anomaly detection, unsupervised embedding focuses on learning embeddings that reflect the original structure of the graph, independent of any downstream task. Both approaches demonstrated promising performance. In our solution, we propose a hybrid of these two approaches to leverage the benefits of both supervised and unsupervised embeddings. To achieve this, we design a loss function that combines two components:

1. **Unsupervised loss:** The first component, denoted as $\mathcal{L}_{t,unsup}$, encourages the autoencoder $\mathcal{P}$**-VAE** to learn a hyperbolic latent space that follows the distribution of the original graph nodes. $\mathcal{L}_{t,unsup}$ is primarily a *reconstruction loss* aiming to minimize the difference between the distribution of the reconstructed data and the actual data.
2. **Supervised loss:** The second component, denoted as $\mathcal{L}_{t,sup}$, drives the model to accurately classify nodes into normal or abnormal categories. $\mathcal{L}t, sup$ is a *classification loss* based on the Negative Log-Likelihood (NLL) loss, which penalizes incorrect classifications as follows:

$$\mathcal{L}_{t,sup} = \frac{1}{N}\sum_{i=0}^{N} log(y_i),$$

where N is the size of the graph and y_i represents the predicted probability assigned to the correct class for node i.

To jointly learn embeddings in both a supervised and unsupervised manner, we define the overall loss function as a linear combination of the two component:

$$\mathcal{L}_t = \mathcal{L}_{t,sup} + \lambda \mathcal{L}_{t,unsup},$$

where $\lambda \in [0, 1]$ is a hyperparameter that balances the contributions and controls the impact of each loss component. The backpropagation process affects only the MLP, HGRU, and the $\mathcal{P}$-VAE encoder, whereas the decoder remains fully unsupervised. This setup enables us to perform training in a single phase rather than two, ensuring that the MLP and HGRU account for classification loss while the $\mathcal{P}$-VAE encoder considers reconstruction loss.

4 Experiments

In this section, we detail the experiments we undertook to evaluate the proposed model. The aim is to provide a clear understanding of the environment under which the experiments were conducted, ensuring the reproducibility of the results and facilitating an accurate assessment of the approaches' effectiveness. All experiments are achieved on a Linux powred machine with 32 GB RAM, NVIDIA GeForce RTX 3060 12 GB GPU and an AMD Ryzen 5 5600 6-Core, 12-Thread @ 3.5 GHz base speed CPU.

4.1 Datasets

To ensure comprehensive, rigorous experimentation and derive generalizable results, we selected the following datasets from cybersecurity domain:

- Darknet2020 [5]: was created to help in developing algorithms for the classification and detection of traffic originating from the darknet, which refers to the unused address space of the internet associated with illegitimate hosts and anonymous services such as the dark web. The dataset aims to facilitate research on countering illegal activities before they emerge in cyberspace. It includes both benign and darknet traffic across various activities, namely browsing, chat, email, file transfer, streaming, etc.
- TON_IoT [9]: It is a dataset incorporating both network-based and host-based data. It covers nine types of cyber-attacks, including scanning, DoS, DDoS, ransomware, backdoors, cross-site scripting (XSS), data injection, password cracking, and man-in-the-middle (MITM). Each row is labeled as either normal or attack, with a type feature indicating the specific attack sub-class, allowing for multi-class classification.

4.2 From Network Flows to Dynamic Graphs

We model a dynamic graph G as a series of snapshots $G_1, ..., G_t, ..., G_T$, where each snapshot $G_t = (A_t, X_t)$ contains a fixed number of flows. This allows for control over the size of each snapshot, ensuring that the memory footprint remains manageable. Additionally, we introduce a mechanism where each snapshot shares $r\%$ of flows with its predecessor, with $r\%$ representing the *percentage of overlap*. This overlap facilitates the analysis of temporal transitions between consecutive snapshots by capturing trends and changes over time. We refer to this method as a *sliding window mechanism* where each window of flows is transformed into a graph snapshot.

4.3 Class Balancing in Snapshots

The datasets used in this work are constructed by simulating both benign and malicious network traffic in distinct scenarios, causing the rows to follow a specific pattern. For example, normal traffic may appear at the start, followed by flows representing a particular type of attack, and then another set of flows corresponding to a different attack. However, this ordering leads to graph snapshots that might represent only one class of data at a time, which can destabilize the learning process. To address this, we leverage the independence between different categories (benign and attack, or different attack types) and the dependence within the same category (normal or same type of attack). In other terms, the flows that belong to the normal class or the same attack type must maintain their chronological order within the graph snapshots, whereas the order of flows from different class types is not critical. This insight allows us to *reorganize* the dataset, ensuring that flows from different classes are mixed in a way that better reflects real-world conditions. The *reorganization* process starts by dividing the dataset into two subsets: one containing benign flows and the other malicious flows, both sorted chronologically. To ensure a balance between the two classes and across various attack types, we alternate between selecting rows from the normal and attack subsets. Once reorganized, a sliding window mechanism is applied to generate graph snapshots from the dataset.

4.4 Evaluation Metrics

To comprehensively evaluate the performance of the proposed model, we have chosen the following metrics as key indicators:

- **Classification performance:** Anomaly detection is approached as a classification problem where the goal is to distinguish between normal and abnormal patterns. In this context, correctly identifying these patterns is vital to ensuring robust security measures, and the effectiveness of this detection relies heavily on classification metrics. So, we evaluate the models' classification performance using the usual accuracy, precision, recall, F1 score, and AUC metrics.
- **Training time (TT):** This metric represents the duration in *seconds* needed for the model to learn from the training dataset, including the optimization of parameters for both the graph embedding and the anomaly detection model. We apply this metric exclusively to static models trained in a transductive setting, where the arrival of new instances requires retraining the model. Thus, training time is crucial for evaluating the efficiency of static models.
- **Processing time (PT):** This refers to the time, in *milliseconds*, a pre-trained model takes to classify new inputs as normal or abnormal. We use this metric to assess the inference speed of dynamic models, which are designed to operate in real time.
- **Occupied memory (OM):** This metric measures the amount of memory, in *megabytes*, the model consumes during inference. It is specifically used to evaluate our dynamic solution, focusing on memory efficiency when storing historical hidden states in the memory bank.

4.5 Results

Table 1 compares our model, using the three datasets introduced earlier, with other temporal graph embedding models. These include hyperbolic models, specifically HTGN and HGWaveNet (discussed in Sect. 2), as well as Euclidean models, EvolveGCN and VGRNN, which are summarized below:

- **EvoloveGCN** [11]: A GNN-based method for dynamic graphs, EvolveGCN uses a GCN to generate node embeddings and an RNN to dynamically update the GCN's parameters over time.
- **VGRNN** [6]: The Variational Graph Recurrent Neural Network (VGRNN) is designed for dynamic graph embedding, combining RNNs with a Variational Graph Autoencoder (VGAE) to encode both structural and temporal information in a latent space.

Table 1. Comparison of HVGAE-AD with other state-of-the-art methods.

Dataset	Method	Accuracy	F1-score	Recall	Precision	AUC	OM	PT
Darknet2020	EvolveGCN	94,41	95,77	91,8	99,91	95,87	493,47	11,12
	VGRNN	49,44	65,1	96,47	49,17	50,45	893,72	**4,93**
	HTGN	67,26	50,69	**100,0**	50,69	50,0	2213,61	43,39
	HGWaveNet	67,2	50,69	**100,0**	50,69	50,0	1886,39	742,82
	HVGAE-AD	**99,96**	**99,96**	99,99	**99,93**	**99,96**	**82,48**	29,19
TON_IoT	EvolveGCN	88,5	86,13	92,38	84,08	84,93	1602,28	9,94
	VGRNN	51,4	67,9	**100,0**	51,4	50,0	6777,64	**5,12**
	HTGN	94,72	94,9	93,56	96,74	94,41	52,41	23,56
	HGWaveNet	94,38	94,2	93,08	96,14	94,2	565,96	821,44
	HVGAE-AD	**97,39**	**97,37**	95,52	**99,4**	**97,4**	**47,49**	19,34

In Darknet2020, our model achieved a perfect score and outperformed existing dynamic hyperbolic models in the literature by 33%, which is a significant improvement. It also surpassed EvolveGCN, which performed excellently (near 95%). VGRNN struggled to exceed 50% accuracy. Once again, our solution had the best memory usage, being five times more efficient. Although the Euclidean models remain the fastest, HVGAE-AD is still the best hyperbolic model in terms of processing time for a single snapshot.

In TON_IoT, all hyperbolic models outperformed the Euclidean models in classification metrics and memory usage, though they were still slower. Our model remained the best, with VGRNN scoring around 51% accuracy.

5 Conclusion

In this paper, we proposed a new HGNN architecure adapted for anomaly detection in dynamic graphs representing events and data in cyberspaces. The proposed approach consistently outperformed the Euclidean counterparts as well as other hyperbolic models from the state of the art, across various dimensions and metrics, achieving higher accuracy, better memory efficiency, and competitive processing times. The proposed approach has set new state-of-the-art results in embedding graph nodes in hyperbolic space and anomaly detection in cybersecurity. Our model is capable of detecting complex attacks in real time due to its neural network architecture, autoencoder design, inductive training approach, and graph-based nature, which emphasizes the relationships between attack traffic. Our approach focused on node-level anomalies, specifically malicious flows represented as nodes. Future studies should investigate anomalies at other levels, including edges, subgraphs, and entire graphs, allowing for the detection of more sophisticated attacks, such as coordinated attacks, botnets, and large-scale DDoS.

Acknowledgments. This study was funded by Agence Nationale de la Recherche under grant number ANR-20-CE23-0002 and ANR-20-CE39-0008.

References

1. Bai, Q., Nie, C., Zhang, H., Zhao, D., Yuan, X.: Hgwavenet: a hyperbolic graph neural network for temporal link prediction. In: Proceedings of the ACM Web Conference 2023, pp. 523–532 (2023)
2. Chami, I., Abu-El-Haija, S., Perozzi, B., Ré, C., Murphy, K.: Machine learning on graphs: a model and comprehensive taxonomy. J. Mach. Learn. Res. **23**(1), 3840–3903 (2022)
3. Chami, I., Ying, Z., Ré, C., Leskovec, J.: Hyperbolic graph convolutional neural networks. Adv. Neural Inf. Process. Syst. **32** (2019)
4. Ganea, O., Bécigneul, G., Hofmann, T.: Hyperbolic neural networks. Adv. Neural Inf. Process. Syst. **31** (2018)
5. Habibi Lashkari, A., Kaur, G., Rahali, A.: Didarknet: a contemporary approach to detect and characterize the darknet traffic using deep image learning. In: Proceedings of 10th International Conference on Communication and Network Security, ICCNS '20, pp. 1–13. ACM, New York (2021). https://doi.org/10.1145/3442520.3442521
6. Hajiramezanali, E., Hasanzadeh, A., Narayanan, K., Duffield, N., Zhou, M., Qian, X.: Variational graph recurrent neural networks. Adv. Neural Inf. Process. Syst. **32** (2019)
7. Li, Y., Yu, R., Shahabi, C., Liu, Y.: Diffusion convolutional recurrent neural network: data-driven traffic forecasting. arXiv preprint arXiv:1707.01926 (2017)
8. Mathieu, E., Le Lan, C., Maddison, C.J., Tomioka, R., Teh, Y.W.: Continuous hierarchical representations with poincaré variational auto-encoders. Adv. Neural Inf. Process. Syst. **32** (2019)
9. Moustafa, N.: A new distributed architecture for evaluating ai-based security systems at the edge: network ton_iot datasets. Sustain. Cities Soc. **72**, 102994 (2021). https://doi.org/10.1016/j.scs.2021.102994
10. Oord, A.V.D., et al.: Wavenet: a generative model for raw audio. arXiv preprint arXiv:1609.03499 (2016)
11. Pareja, A., et al.: Evolvegcn: evolving graph convolutional networks for dynamic graphs. In: Proceedings of the AAAI Conference on Artificial Intelligence, vol. 34, pp. 5363–5370 (2020)
12. Touahria Miliani, M.Y., Sadat, S.A., Haddad, M., Seba, H., Amrouche, K.: Comparing hyperbolic graph embedding models on anomaly detection for cybersecurity. In: Proceedings of the 19th International Conference on Availability, Reliability and Security, ARES '24. Association for Computing Machinery, New York (2024). https://doi.org/10.1145/3664476.3670445
13. Wu, Z., Pan, S., Long, G., Jiang, J., Zhang, C.: Graph wavenet for deep spatial-temporal graph modeling. arXiv preprint arXiv:1906.00121 (2019)
14. Yang, M., Zhou, M., Kalander, M., Huang, Z., King, I.: Discrete-time temporal network embedding via implicit hierarchical learning in hyperbolic space. In: Proceedings of the 27th ACM SIGKDD Conference on Knowledge Discovery & Data Mining, pp. 1975–1985 (2021)

Security and Trust

Building Trust on User Attributes for Identity Assurance Frameworks

Salameh Abu Rmeileh[1], Esther Palomar[2(✉)], Asma Patel[3], and Hanifa Shah[1]

[1] School of Architecture, Built Environment, Computing and Engineering, Birmingham City University, 15 Bartholomew Row, Birmingham B5 5JU, UK
{salameh.aburmeileh,hanifa.shah}@bcu.ac.uk

[2] Higher Technical School of Computer Engineering, Institute of Technologies for Sustainability, University Rey Juan Carlos, Mostoles, 28933 Madrid, Spain
esther.palomar@urjc.es

[3] College of Business and Social Sciences, Aston Business School, 295 Aston Express Way, Birmingham B4 7UP, UK
a.patel122@aston.ac.uk

https://www.bcu.ac.uk/computing-engineering-and-the-built-environment/steamhouse, https://www.itps-urjc.es/en/, https://www.aston.ac.uk/bss/aston-business-school

Abstract. Identity management serves as a critical enabler of digital ecosystems, extending across mobile applications, IoT, and emerging platforms like the Metaverse. While identity assurance frameworks offer structured approaches to trust across domains, they often lack mechanisms for dynamic, context-aware, and fine-grained trust evaluation. This paper addresses this gap by implementing the Attribute Level Of Confidence (ALOC) metric, which assesses trust at the level of individual attributes using indicators such as timestamp, revision number, and validity period. The ALOC metric is deployed as a Chrome Extension and tested in a controlled scenario to evaluate its effectiveness in enhancing user control and trust transparency. Results show a 15% improvement in performance, accessibility, and privacy over existing OpenAM-based frameworks. The implementation demonstrates how fine-grained attribute assurance can support selective disclosure and strengthen identity trustworthiness, offering a practical pathway toward more user-centric and privacy-preserving identity management systems.

Keywords: Attribute assurance · Level of Assurance (LoA) · Attribute Level of Confidence · User-centered identity management · SAML Assertions · Decentralised Trust

1 Introduction

Attribute-Based Credentials (ABCs) are increasingly central to modern identity and access management systems, offering fine-grained, context-aware authorization based on user attributes such as roles, location, device type, and group

I. Awan et al. (Eds.): WISE 2025, LNCS 16367, pp. 481–491, 2026.
https://doi.org/10.1007/978-981-95-7394-3_33

memberships rather than static identifiers like usernames or passwords [2]. This shift supports privacy-preserving and decentralized models, aligning with principles like minimal disclosure and user consent [5]. ABCs associate an entity's identity with verifiable attributes that may vary across contexts and domains, resulting in dynamic and overlapping identities [11].

As digital services such as e-payment, e-voting, and crowdsourcing grow, so does the need for secure, user-controlled identity mechanisms. Frameworks like OpenAM offer robust identity and access management capabilities and can be extended to support ABCs. When integrated with blockchain technologies, they enable decentralized and verifiable credential management, allowing users to retain control over their attributes and selectively disclose them based on context [7]. This supports self-sovereign identity (SSI) models, but also introduces challenges in integrating these technologies into existing systems. To address these challenges, identity assurance frameworks have emerged to coordinate trust across domains by defining standards for validating digital identities. These frameworks assess factors such as registration processes, credential types, and delivery methods [4]. Attribute assurance frameworks extend this by focusing on the validation of individual attributes, which is critical for trust in decentralized environments. In addition, regulatory bodies and standardization agencies have defined levels of assurance (LoA) to guide secure identification practices, including eIDAS Regulation EU No 910/2014, ISO/IEC 29115:2013, and NIST SP 800-63-3 [3]. Identity Providers (IdPs) assign LoA values to attributes based on authentication strength and identity proofing methods. Relying Parties (RPs) then use these values to enforce risk-based access control policies tailored to the sensitivity of specific transactions [4].

Based on a user-centered approach to attribute assurance, our proposal aims to enhance the quality, integrity, and accessibility of the identity lifecycle from creation and registration, where users play an active role in attribute evidence collection and proofing, to maintenance and revocation. Our work[1] focuses on establishing trust in user attributes during the creation process, ensuring the authenticity of evidence even when attributes are self-asserted. It aligns with ongoing efforts in attribute aggregation [5], which seek to integrate Levels of Assurance (LoA) and identity metadata in decentralized identity systems. Additionally, reputation systems have been explored to measure confidence among entities in such ecosystems [8]. However, current solutions often fall short in managing trust at the attribute level, particularly for self-asserted data. Our motivating scenario shares the vision of [12], which extends identity meta-representation using SAML, but emphasizes the user as the primary manager and issuer of their credentials. The main contributions of our work are threefold:

1. We present the ALOC (Attribute Level Of Confidence) framework, a user-centric attribute assurance model that empowers users, i.e., attribute holders, to create, manage, and maintain their attributes and credentials. The

[1] Preliminary work compiling conceptual ALOC model and metric was presented in a Summer School and published in [9].

attribute structure is extended with a new metric, ALOC, which aggregates assertions and endorsements.
2. We implement the ALOC framework as a Chrome Extension on the client side and a web service on the provider side. Users can create, modify, and delete attributes and associated privacy policies, while ALOC-enabled service providers (SPs) simulate acceptance of user requests. A cloud-based ALOC Provider (ALOCP) intermediates between users and SPs for performance and trust computation.
3. We evaluate the ALOC framework's efficiency, scalability, and security, and assess its privacy-preserving capabilities. Usability and accessibility are also analyzed from the perspective of different stakeholders.

The rest of the article is structured as follows. In Sect. 2, we describe model, design and implementation decisions for the ALOC framework. Empirical results of framework validation through simulations are described in Sect. 3. Finally, Sect. 4 compiles findings and their implications for future research and development.

2 The ALOC Framework: Design and Implementation

2.1 Key Roles and Example Scenario

The ALOC framework for attribute assurance involves four key stakeholders: the User, the ALOC Provider (ALOCP), the Service Provider (SP), and the Endorser. Figure 1-(left) illustrates the interaction flow among these entities:

1. The User manages her attributes via the ALOC client (a web browser extension), including creation, modification, deletion, and endorsement requests. She also defines disclosure policies. Both SPs and Users may act as Endorsers.
2. The User attempts to access an ALOC-enabled SP that enforces an access policy requiring specific attributes.
3. The SP queries the ALOCP for attribute assertions in accordance with its access policy.
4. Acting as a gateway, the ALOCP facilitates attribute assurance during both authentication and authorization phases. It evaluates the SP's access control policy and the User's disclosure policy before computing the ALOC token.
5. Based on the received ALOC token, the SP either grants or denies access.
6. The SP may issue an endorsement (approval or denial) on the User's attributes, contributing to their trustworthiness.

In decentralized identity systems, self-asserted attributes lack cryptographic endorsements from trusted issuers, necessitating alternative trust mechanisms to preserve system integrity. These include reputation systems, social attestations, and contextual risk scoring, which estimate credibility based on indirect or behavioral evidence. Unlike deterministic cryptographic proofs, these mechanisms are probabilistic, relying on patterns, endorsements, or historical behavior. For instance, a self-asserted claim may gain credibility through multiple peer endorsements in a web-of-trust model or a strong reputation score from prior interactions. To address this, and because user attributes are inherently dynamic—evolving over time, context-dependent, and often requiring real-time validation, the ALOCP integrates an ALOC engine that computes the Level of Assurance (LoA) for user attributes considering factors such as trust in Endorsers, authentication mechanisms and attribute change frequency. The ALOC framework captures this fluidity by incorporating the following factors into its LoA computation:

F1 **Trustworthiness**: Is the attribute cryptographically verifiable, and is the issuer recognized within the governance framework?
F2 **Mutability**: How likely is the attribute to have changed since issuance, and how often should it be revalidated?
F3 **Timeliness**: How recent is the attribute, and is it still valid at the time of verification?
F4 **Reputation**: How consistently reliable has the issuer or subject been across previous attestations?

These factors ([F1-F4]) are embedded into the framework's data structures and processes, supporting a user-centric approach to identity management.

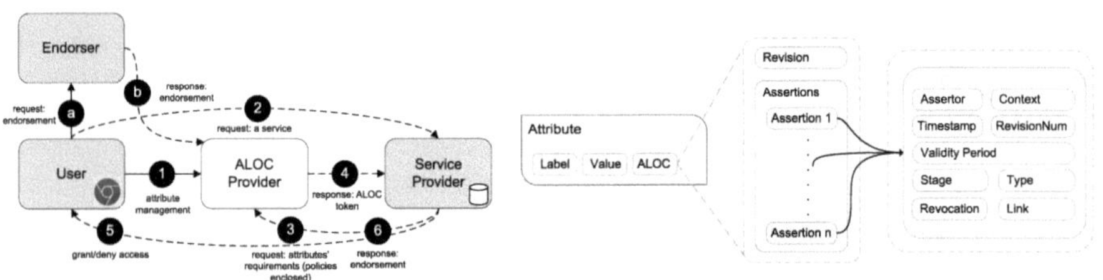

Fig. 1. (Left) The main entities in the ALOC framework and the relations among them. (Right) Extended Attribute Structure: The ALOC element.

Definition 1. We define a new element—ALOC—within the attribute data structure: $\langle l, v, ALOC \rangle$ where l and v represent the label and value of the attribute, respectively. The ALOC element encapsulates the dynamic trust factors by: i) Aggregating assertions to assess the reliability of the attribute value.

ii) Introducing a novel metric for relying parties to quantify the LoA of the attribute at a given point in time.

The `ALOC` element consists of (see Fig. 1-right):

- *Revision* [F2]: An integer representing the number of times the attribute's v has changed.

- *Assertions* [F1, F3, F4]: A list of *Assertions* enclosing the following information:
  - *Assertor* [F1, F4]: The assertion issuer's *unique identifier*, his/her correspondent *publickey* and a *signature* on the whole assertion.
  - *Context* [F1]: Methods used by the assertor to identify and authenticate the user (further details below).
  - *Timestamp* [F3]: Assertion's creation date and time.
  - *RevisionNum*: The attribute's revision number at the time of the assertion.
  - *Validity Period* [F2, F3]: The assertion's starting and expiration date/time.
  - *Stage* [F1]: The stage at which the assertion has been issued, i.e., Creation, Registration, Authentication or Authorisation (details below in this section).
  - *Type* [F1, F4]: Type of the assertion between *Approval* or *Denial.*
  - *Revocation* [F1, F3]: Date of revocation, if exists, and *signature.*
  - *Link* [F1]: Hash-based linked list to maintain the integrity of the assertions list.

SPs and other Users can aggregate attribute assertions into the *Assertions* list either upon user request or authentication operations. We have identified four non-exclusive stages for the Stage field to capture the issuance of assertions during the identity lifecycle, as follows:

Creation assertion is issued at the creation time of the attribute. A User can create new attributes by signing self-issued assertions, and/or requesting a creation assertion to an IdP/SP, e.g., the attribute containing her driving license number to the Driver and Vehicle Licensing Agency. Type of such assertions is always *Approval.*

Registration assertion is aggregated by the SP once the User registers the attribute for that SP service. Both assertion types apply depending on the result of the registration process.

Authentication assertion can be issued by IdP/SPs and other users upon authentication operations. Basically, IdP/SPs can aggregate authentication assertions to certify or not the authenticity of the attribute value at a certain time. Users can also ask IdP/SPs and other users, e.g., Amazon.com for asserting the authenticity of her current address. Both assertion types apply depending on the result of the authentication process.

Authorisation assertion is issued by the SP and aggregated to the list of the user attribute once the authorisation process is completed; both assertion types apply depending on the result of the authorisation process.

Our model adopts the SAML authentication context classes [6] to define the methods applied to user identification (e.g., face-to-face, online, shared secret) and authentication (e.g., username/password, digital certificate). The assertion context allows SPs to assess the LoA that they can place in each assertion, i.e. by computing the `ALOC` with finer granularity according to those methods and depending on their own risk management. Note that, although the validity period and the revocation fields are different, the `ALOC` metric will treat revoked assertions and expired assertions the same way. The model does not consider a revoked assertion as a denial assertion for two reasons. First, denial assertions can be revoked; and secondly, considering that an assertor might issue an assertion, either approval or denial, by mistake, he/she can revoke it afterwards.

2.2 ALOC Computation

The ALOC metric utilises multi-trust dynamic weighted sum for trust formation and is influenced by the number of assertions, assertions' contexts, assertions' stages, assertions' types and assertions' decay over time (which foregrounds new assertions' relevance over old ones). First, assessing the trustworthiness of an attribute relies on the trustworthiness of its issuers or `Assertors` and their contexts, particularly at the time of the attribute creation. Hence, RPs/SPs computing the `ALOC` of an attribute need to assign a quantitative estimate of trust in other entities to supply trusted attributes. We denote such a value as the level of trust (LoT), i.e., $T_c \in \{0 \dots 1\}$, for the attribute assertor of assertion c, where 0 represents no trust on the assertor and 1 full trust. We have identified four main factors $g_{\{1-4\}}$ that affect trust amongst parties as to quantify LoT from an RP's viewpoint: i) trust relationship, that is usually classified into direct trust and transitive or indirect trust, ii) dependency, iii) reliability, and iv) consequences, in case the trusted party does not perform as expected. A local trust model [10] is then built allocating weights according to the RP's own criteria.

Similarly, RPs/SPs need to establish LoT for the different identification $I_c \in \{0 \dots 1\}$ and authentication $U_c \in \{0 \dots 1\}$ methods, namely Method's Level of Confidence (MLoC); e.g., an assertion c upon a physical verification of the attribute value could yield higher trust than an online verification at the identification stage[2]. Thus, the trustworthiness of a creation assertion c can be obtained from

$$\Upsilon(c) = \beta_1 T_c + (1 - \beta_1) I_c U_c = Q_c \tag{1}$$

where the RP/SP considers its own trust model in the computation of LoT for the assertor (T), the identification method (I) and the authentication method (U), all weighted by the factor $\beta_1 \in \{0 \dots 1\}$ comprising own priorities and policies.

Secondly, the `ALOC` computation takes account of all the approval assertions in A, excluding c, with the same attribute's revision, i.e., assertions in A with an up-to-date attribute's value, and quantifies their LoT based on the time decay factor as follows:

$$A := A \setminus \{K, c\}, \qquad \Upsilon(A) = \frac{\sum_{i=1}^{|A|} \delta_i Q_i}{|A|} \qquad \forall i \in A : r_i = r_c \tag{2}$$

[2] A comparative study of the different authentication solutions can be found in [1].

where $\delta_i = \lambda(t_i) \in [0 \ldots 1] \;\; \forall i \in A$ is the time decay factor[3] of the assertion i's reputation value according to the RP/SP's level of trust given to the attribute's type of information and the age t_i of the attribute's value, i.e., time difference between the approval assertion's time and the time of computing Υ. Note that, the lower δ the more impact of the decay occurs on the computation Υ; $\delta = 1$ represents a RP/SP unconcerned about the decay of trust over time. The same process applies to the set of denial assertions in D.

Finally, we formulate the *aloc* metric for the extended attribute x by assigning the set of weights $\beta_{1\ldots3}$ to the factors below such that

$$aloc(x) = \begin{cases} \beta_1\Upsilon(c) + \beta_2\Upsilon(A) + \beta_3(1 - \Upsilon(D)), & \text{if } r_x \leq R \\ 0.0, & \text{otherwise} \end{cases} \tag{3}$$

where $\sum_{i=1}^{3} \beta_i = 1$ and given the threshold R for the revision change frequency accepted by the SP/RP. Value of R is computed at the SP's side such as

$$\Upsilon(R) = \frac{1 + e^{-1}}{1 + e^{-\frac{r}{rt}}} \tag{4}$$

The *aloc* metric in Eq. (3) produces a positive real number between 0.0 and 1.0 representing the RP/SP's confidence in the attribute information; so it will be checked against her local access control policies before granting User access.

2.3 Personal Information Disclosure and Access Control Policies

In the ALOC model, a policy is an unordered list of policy alternatives that contains a set of constraints. Basically, a constraint describes the requirement/s needed to fulfill a security goal and also specifies the information about what needs to be secured and how. On the SP's side, the user attribute's ALOC element along with the local trust variables are informing access control decisions. These variables are as follows:

- **Decay factor** (δ): SPs/RPs may require that fresher assertions have higher weights affecting the ALOC than old ones (e.g., address), or lower impact (e.g., skills and experience). This variable allows the SP to increase/decrease the significance of assertions over time.
- **Revision factor** (R): It presents the maximum number of attribute revisions over a period of time as computed in Eq. (4). For example, a SP that defines $0.0833r/month$ for attributes of type $address$ will not accept assertions which have been changed more than once a year. SPs will assign a revision factor of 0 when changes do not matter.
- **Weights** (β_n): The *aloc* formula in Eq. (3) comprises three parts (Source, Approval assertions, and Denial assertions). SPs can dictate the significance of each of those parts and how they affect the final *aloc* computation with the corresponding weight.

[3] The time decay factor results out of isolating λ from the equation $w_{attr} = 1 - \lambda e^{-\lambda t_i}$ where w_{att} is the trust level, at the SP's side, set to that attribute's type of data.

Policy-consistency proofs will be presented as part of the empirical evaluation of our framework prototype.

3 Implementation and Results

The ALOC framework implementation consists of three main modules: the ALOC library, the ALOCP and the ALOC-enabled SP. The ALOC library is implemented as a dynamic link library (DLL) integrated into the ALOCP for interoperability. The ALOCP is deployed as a Windows Communication Foundation (WCF) service with a REST interface backed with a MongoDB database for storage. The SP is developed as a conventional service provider using ASP.Net and is extended with an ALOC module. All interactions in the framework use customised JSON HTTPS POST messages. We also install[4] ForgeRock Access Management System (OpenAM) 14.7 configured as an IdP in pure SAML 2.0 mode and Identity Gateway (OpenIG) as a baseline against which we demonstrate incremental gains during our performance and communication evaluation. The user interface design is shown in Fig. 2.

Fig. 2. UX at the ALOC client side for Users.

Experimental Methodology. Our testbed's workload generator compiles an Apache JMeter 5.6 (thread-group mode), a custom Java Sampler that simulates ALOC-specific types of requests and interactions and signatures, and base-64-encoded `samlp:AuthnRequest` for safe transmission over HTTP. Our evaluation requires WireShark 4.2 capture filters to timestamp each TCP-level request/response pair, a Net System.Diagnostics.Stopwatch wrapper around the ALOC computation routine, and Visual Studio Diagnostic Tools (sampling profiler) for memory deltas. A dataset comprising 5000 synthetic records is generated

[4] Prototype of the ALOCP and the SP has been deployed on two HP DL380 Gen9 servers, with 128 GB of RAM, Dual Xeon CPUs, and 600 GB SAS 15K HDD. Both servers are Windows 2016 Server with Microsoft IIS and MongoDB community server; servers are connected over a 1 GB Ethernet local area network.

with Mockaroo: 7 attributes for each user, i.e., Firstname, Lastname, Gender, NiN, Address, DoB, and Phone. The synthetic data is injected into, both, ForgeRock OpenAM using Curl and the ALOCP MongoDb database after a JSON conversion. Moreover, five SP instances (ExampleSP1-5) assert randomly selected subsets of those attributes.The ALOC framework is evaluated considering three key areas: performance, security, and usability.

Table 1. Latency and Throughput Comparison between ALOCP and OPENAM

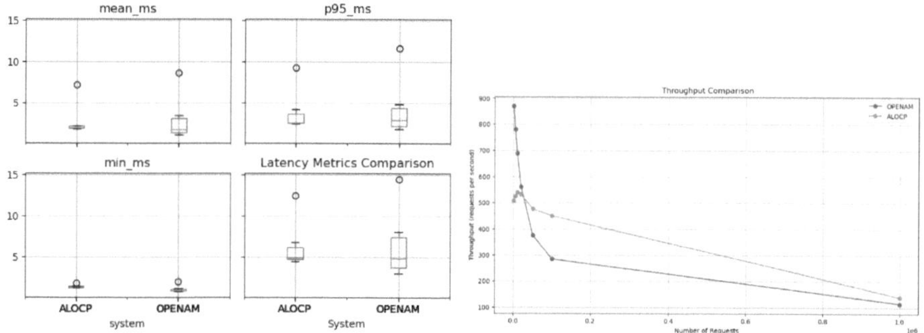

Performance. Experiments evaluate the latency taken by the prototype to process and validate SAML assertions under various conditions, including different assertion sizes and attribute complexities, varying LoA, simulated network and system loads. Synthetic SAML requests are generated and injected to ALOC-enabled authentication, ForgeRock/OpenAM. Results show an average gap of 0.9 ms due to the additional trust computations in ALOC's extended SAML 2.0 messages, the larger wire payload (3.04 KB vs. 2.52 KB request; 5.93 KB vs. 2.45 KB response) and a single extra HMAC verification step. A comparative performance evaluation between the ALOCP and OpenAM frameworks as shown in Table 1 reveals distinct trends in latency and throughput across varying request volumes. The mean latency plot demonstrates that OpenAM consistently outperforms the ALOCP in terms of lower average response times for smaller workloads (1,000 to 20,000 requests). However, as the request volume increases beyond 50,000, ALOCP begins to exhibit more stable latency characteristics, with a notably lower mean latency at 100,000 and 1,000,000 requests compared to OpenAM. Similarly, the 95th percentile latency–a critical metric for assessing worst-case performance–follows a comparable pattern. While OpenAM maintains a slight advantage at lower volumes, the ALOCP demonstrates more predictable and bounded latency under high-load conditions, suggesting better tail-end performance scalability.

Informal Security Analysis. Each type of assertion introduces distinct threat vectors, necessitating tailored countermeasures to ensure integrity, authenticity, and trustworthiness. The threat model identifies three primary categories: i) false identity attribute registration, ii) assertion manipulation, and

iii) replay attacks. On i), self-issued assertions are susceptible to attribute forgery, where individuals may assert false or exaggerated claims about themselves. The absence of a trusted issuer complicates provenance verification. Regarding ii), when assertions are issued/endorsed by third parties, the primary threats include impersonation, assertion tampering, and reliance on untrusted issuers. A malicious third party could issue assertions on behalf of another user or alter assertion contents during transmission. Dealing with iii), the registration phase is vulnerable to misrepresentation, where the SP may submit incorrect or unauthorized data, and to replay attacks involving the reuse of old assertions. The ALOC metric inherently mitigates all these risks by assigning low trust levels to unverifiable assertors, utilising reputation weighting, and implementing time-based assertion decay to prevent fraudulent endorsements. Also, digital signatures can be employed to bind the assertion to the subject's identity. Additionally, RPs maintain a whitelist of trusted issuers/endorsers that inform the evaluation of multi-signed assertions and federation metadata. Finally, common SAML and OpenID vulnerabilities such as XML signature tampering, unauthorized payload access, and lack of mutual authentication are addressed through TLS encryption, digital signatures, and nonce-based request validation. ALOC enforces privacy by design, ensuring user control over personal information and User consent mechanisms and policies. Users determine which attributes are disclosed, and data remains encrypted in transit and at rest. The ALOCP does not share data with third parties or engage in user tracking across SPs.

In addition, ALOC streamlines authentication by serving as an intermediary that enforces user-defined privacy policies. However, its reliance on explicit integration by service providers limits broader compatibility. Additionally, users must manually configure disclosure settings, highlighting the need for improved UI/UX design to enhance usability and accessibility.

4 Conclusions

In this paper, we introduced the ALOC framework, a comprehensive and effective tool for managing digital identities and credentials at the attribute level required for accessing web services. The framework enhances attribute assurance by extending the traditional SAML structure with a novel third component: the Attribute Level of Confidence (ALOC). This metric provides a quantitative assessment of the claimed attribute value, empowering users to define and enforce their own data usage, sharing rules, and privacy policies via a user-friendly Google Chrome extension. The ALOC library, implemented as a dynamic link library (DLL), facilitates metric computation and policy enforcement, aligning client-side rules with service provider authorization policies. Performance evaluations show that ALOC outperforms existing OpenAM-based frameworks, delivering a 20% speed improvement, 15% lower memory usage, and 25% higher robustness. However, a 10% performance trade-off was observed in specific scenarios due to the preliminary centralized implementation. Future work will focus on decentralizing the ALOC computation and data storage by eliminating the intermediary gateway. This shift to a client-side architecture aims to enhance scalability, reduce latency, and further strengthen user autonomy and privacy. Additionally, we plan to explore integration with emerging decentralized identity standards and investigate the applicability of ALOC in cross-domain trust negotiation and federated identity systems.

References

1. Alizadeh, M., Abolfazli, S., Zamani, M., Baharun, S., Sakurai, K.: Authentication in mobile cloud computing: a survey. J. Netw. Comput. Appl. **61**, 59–80 (2016)
2. Camenisch, J., et al.: Concepts and languages for privacy-preserving attribute-based authentication. J. Inf. Secur. Appl. **19**(1), 25–44 (2014)
3. Dumortier, J.: Regulation (EU) no 910/2014 on electronic identification and trust services for electronic transactions in the internal market (eIDAS regulation). In: EU Regulation of E-Commerce, pp. 247–280. Edward Elgar Publishing (2022)
4. Grüner, A., Mühle, A., Gayvoronskaya, T., Meinel, C.: A comparative analysis of trust requirements in decentralized identity management. In: Proceedings of the 33rd International Conference on Advanced Information Networking and Applications (AINA-2019), vol. 33. pp. 200–213. Springer, Heidelberg (2020)
5. Grüner, A., Mühle, A., Meinel, C.: Atib: design and evaluation of an architecture for brokered self-sovereign identity integration and trust-enhancing attribute aggregation for service provider. IEEE Access **9**, 138553–138570 (2021)
6. Kemp, J., Cantor, S., Philpott, R., Security, R.S.A., Hughes, J., Origin, A.E.A.: Authentication Context for the OASIS Security Assertion Markup Language, pp. 1–70 (2005)
7. Liu, Y., He, D., Obaidat, M.S., Kumar, N., Khan, M.K., Choo, K.K.R.: Blockchain-based identity management systems: a review. J. Netw. Comput. Appl. **166**, 102731 (2020)
8. Mosteiro-Sanchez, A., Barcelo, M., Astorga, J., Urbieta, A.: "Are you what you claim to be?" Attribute validation with iota for multi authority CP-ABE. In: International Congress on Blockchain and Applications, pp. 279–288. Springer, Heidelberg (2022)
9. Rmeileh, S.A., Palomar, E., Shah, H.: Aloc: attribute level of confidence for a user-centric attribute assurance. In: IFIP International Summer School on Privacy and Identity Management, pp. 239–252. Springer, Heidelberg (2015)
10. Supriya, M., Sangeeta, K., Patra, G.: Trustworthy cloud service provider selection using multi criteria decision making methods. Eng. Lett. **24**(1) (2016)
11. Wang, F., De Filippi, P.: Self-sovereign identity in a globalized world: credentials-based identity systems as a driver for economic inclusion. Front. Blockchain **2**, 28 (2020)
12. Yildiz, H., Ritter, C., Nguyen, L.T.E.A.: Connecting self-sovereign identity with federated and user-centric identities via SAML integration. In: 2021 IEEE Symposium on Computers and Communications (ISCC), pp. 1–7. IEEE (2021)

GCN-InjectionDetect: Injection Attack Detection Method Based on Graph Convolutional Networks

Wei Wan[1,2], Huiyuan Pei[1,2], Yuhai Lu[1,2], Jing Zhao[1,2], Guanyao Du[1,2], Jinxia Wei[1,2], and Chun Long[1,2(✉)]

[1] Computer Network Information Center of the Chinese Academy of Sciences, No. 2 Dongsheng South Road, Haidian District, Beijing, China
anquanip@cnic.cn

[2] University of Chinese Academy of Sciences, Beijing, China

Abstract. Cross-site scripting (XSS) attacks, SQL injection attacks, and command injection attacks are among the most prevalent types of web attacks, accounting for 58.3% of all web attacks according to statistical findings. Numerous detection methods have been developed to address these injection attacks, primarily focusing on analyzing the URL portion of HTTP requests to determine if they constitute an attack. Our analysis of injection attack alerts generated by an IDS system deployed in a real network reveals that only 4.26% of the attack payloads are located within the URL segment. This indicates that current detection methods, when applied to real-world networks, may result in a significant number of false negatives. Furthermore, existing methods fail to analyze the relationships between different fields of HTTP messages to uncover deeper latent features of attack payloads. To address these limitations, we propose an injection attack detection method called GCN-InjectionDetect, which is based on graph convolutional neural networks (GCNs). GCN-InjectionDetect constructs an entire HTTP message into a graph and utilizes GCNs models to classify graph nodes, thereby achieving comprehensive injection attack detection. Experimental results demonstrate that GCN-InjectionDetect achieves a maximum detection accuracy of 99.2%, representing an improvement of up to 8.65% compared to similar methods.

Keywords: Attack Detecting · Graph Convolutional Network · Injection Attack

1 Introduction

With the continuous and rapid development of information technology, Web applications have been integrated into all aspects of daily life. However, alongside the rapid expansion of web applications, cyber attacks targeting them have persistently continued. Web attacks are still one of the main threats to the Internet, posing serious security risks to both individuals and organizations.

Web attacks come in various forms. Among them, injection attacks [1] refer to an attack method in which attackers inject malicious payloads (such as malicious scripts,

I. Awan et al. (Eds.): WISE 2025, LNCS 16367, pp. 492–506, 2026.
https://doi.org/10.1007/978-981-95-7394-3_34

commands, etc.) into HTTP request packets to carry out their assaults, including cross-site scripting attacks [2], SQL injection attacks [3], command injection attacks [4], etc. Due to their relatively low execution cost, injection attacks continue to be one of the most common types of web attacks. According to cybersecurity company statistics on the 2023 distribution of web attack types [5], injection attacks accounted for 58.3% of all incidents.

To date, numerous research endeavors have been dedicated to addressing injection attack detection problems, including static analysis-based detection, rule-based matching detection, and model-based detection. A review of the existing research efforts reveals the following persistent deficiencies:

(1) Existing research efforts primarily detect injection attacks by analyzing only the request line (URL) of HTTP request packets [6], while neglecting inspection of request headers and request body. We conducted a statistical analysis on the 1925 entries of injection attack alerts generated by the IDS devices deployed in the backbone network. The results are shown in Table 1. Among them, the attack payload injection in the URL only accounts for 4.26%.

Table 1. Distribution of payload in HTTP messages

Location	Ratio
Request line (URL)	4.26%
Request header	30.0%
Request body	65.8%

(2) Model-based detection methods have emerged as a prominent research focus in injection attack detection in recent years. However, existing model-based detection methods mainly capture the characteristics of attack payloads at the textual level, yet they fall short in capturing the deeper potential characteristics of attack payloads and the relationship between different fields within HTTP packets.

To address these limitations, this paper proposes GCN-InjectionDetect, a novel graph convolutional network-based [7] detection method for injection attacks. Our main contributions are summarized as follows:

1. We propose a method for detecting injection attacks on the entire HTTP packet, not just the URL. First, we construct the entire HTTP packet into a graph by using the relationship between the attack payload, words, and HTTP packet, and define two types of weight information as edges to represent the potential relationship between nodes. Then, we classify the graph nodes to achieve attack detection.
2. We designed a novel injection attack detection method that uses the GCNs model to analyze the graph structure to mine potential features of nodes and transfer information between nodes, ultimately achieving node classification.
3. We propose an automatic HTTP packet segmentation method. The word segmentation method used in this paper does not require any prior knowledge, but uses five parameters: segment length lower limit, segment length upper limit, minimum word

frequency, minimum cohesion, and left and right entropy to achieve automatic word segmentation of HTTP messages.

2 Related Work

In recent years, many researchers have proposed various detection methods aimed at identifying injection attacks. These methods can be categorized into three types based on their characteristics: static analysis-based detection methods, rule-based matching detection methods, and machine learning-based detection methods.

2.1 Static Analysis-Based Methods

This method detects inject attacks with the combination of the source code, standards of web pages to analyses the payload or the source code. By analyzing the position of the data in the code in detail to seek whether the code implementation is secure.

C. Luo et al. in literature [8] proposed a model named TChecker, modeling the PHP object as well as related object oriented programming features and analyzing the data flow iteratively to identify the stored-XSS. H. Su proposed the first static analysis framework [9] which uses the data access layer to identify the reading/writing process of database. After locating the contaminated data trace, the framework will shut down the contaminated paths and concat in static to get the full infection transmission pathway of the stored-XSS.

Static analysis-based methods are generally insufficient with the development of the dev tools iteratively. The analysis-based detection may face the expired and introducing the extra vulnerabilities.

2.2 Rule-Based Matching Methods

Rule-based matching methods work which identify data that may contain injection attempts by analyzing and examining input data. By using known attack patterns and benign input patterns as templates, new inputs are matched to detect injection attacks.

Regular expressions are most commonly used in this area, B. Soewito et al. [10] analyzed SQL injection payload and its patterns, using regular expressions and string escaping to prevent SQL injection. O.C. Abikoye et al. also adopted the classic way of detecting attacks [11]. Their team proposed to match the input data with existing malicious patterns with using the KMP algorithm.

This kind of way is exhausting and expensive to maintain a pattern corpus. Meanwhile, with the newer patterns included, the overhead of processing will also experience an explosive increase.

2.3 Machine Learning-Based Methods

Learning the representations of malicious payload by training the machine learning model or deep learning model, this solution is considered the most appropriate answer to injection attacks detection.

F.M.M. Mokbal et al. [12] proposed a XSS detection scheme combining multi-layer perceptron and dynamic feature extractor based on artificial neural network which achieved high performance on a large-scale real dataset. Furthermore, Mokbal released an XSS dataset which contains 130 thousand XSS samples [13], but which of them are composed of statistic features. S.O. Uwagbole et al. [11] proposed a method that extract datasets from known malicious patterns and generate classifiers to detect SQL injections attacks, meanwhile, this method alleviates the lack of availability of readymade robust corpus or dataset. Since T.N Kipf and Max Welling [7] finally improved the graph convolutional network, a plethora of non-Euclid data obtained a new way of processing. Many studies have been conducted in this area [14, 15] and implementation [16, 17] as well with different convolutional functions [18–20]. Z. Liu et al. [21] firstly detect XSS with graph convolutional neural network as well as the pioneer to convert URLs to graph. It's a rather preliminary work, the weight of the graph are set to be Boolean, Q. Wang et al. ameliorated it with Pointwise Mutual Information (PMI) [22]. They are using PMI as the weight to replace the default, enhanced the ability of classifying. H. Pan et al. [23] classified the XSS attacks by few-shot learning, but I think it is inappropriate to classify the XSS attacks as well as the other injection attacks.

This detection method is mainly used currently, but most of which only focus on URLs, whereas the other parts of HTTP message carry the malicious payload as well.

Existing research efforts primarily detect injection attacks by analyzing only the request line (URL) of the HTTP request packets, while neglecting inspection of request headers and request body. Existing model-based detection methods mainly capture the characteristics of attack payloads at the textual level, but are unable to capture the deeper potential characteristics of attack payloads and the relationship between different fields within HTTP packets.

3 Framework of GCN-InjectionDetect

In this section, we provide a comprehensive demonstration of the proposed method and its theory. An overview of the system architecture is illustrated in Fig. 1.

3.1 Overview

To address the limitations of existing detection methods, such as insufficient mining of deep latent features in attack payloads and the underreporting of attacks caused by solely inspecting URLs, the GCN-InjectionDetect proposed in this paper performs comprehensive detection on the entire HTTP message (including URL, request header, and request body) by converting HTTP messages into graph structures. It then leverages graph convolutional network to identify malicious nodes within the graph, enabling effective detection of injection attacks. The overall framework of GCN-InjectionDetect is illustrated in Fig. 1.

3.2 Data Preprocessing

The data processing workflow, as depicted in Fig. 2, comprises three sequential stages: decoding, generalization, and tokenization.

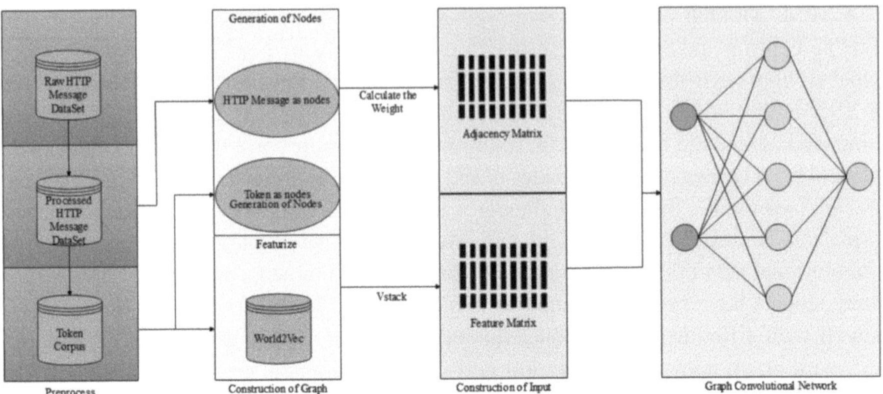

Fig. 1. Framework overview

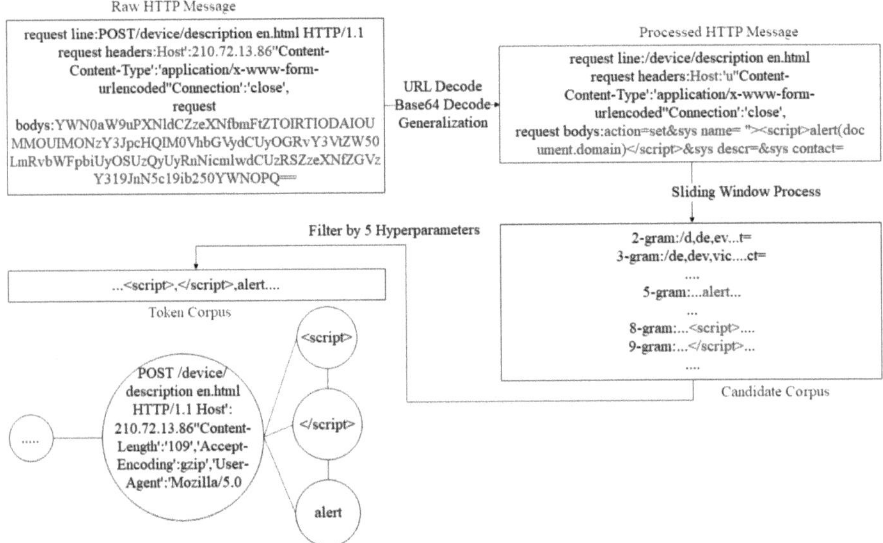

Fig. 2. Data processing flow

Decode and Generalization. Attackers generally encode (including HTML encoding, URL encoding, and Base64 encoding) the injected payloads to bypass security defense mechanisms. Therefore, it is necessary to decode the original HTTP messages to obtain the plaintext data. Specific decoding methods are shown in the Table 2.

The original HTTP messages contain redundant data unrelated to attack payload features, which may interfere with the proposed model's ability to learn attack payload features. Therefore, it is necessary to generalize this part of the data and abstract them into a simpler representation. Through analysis of injection attack packets, we primarily generalize the domain name of the URL and replace it with 'HTTP://u', as shown in Table 3.

Table 2. Decoding examples

Type	Example	Decoded
HTML decode	<script></script>	<script> </script>
URL decode	%3Cscript%3Ealert%28%29%3C/script%3E9	<script>alert()</script>
Base64 decode	PHNjcmlwdD5hbGVydCgxKTwvc2NyaXB0Pg==	<script>alert(1)</script>

Table 3. Generalization examples

Before generalization	After generalization
'Host': 'www.lt.cas.cn'…	'Host': 'u'...
'Referer': 'http://www.hrzyyy.cn:80/yygk-show.asp? <script>ijv = 360</script>'...	'Referer': 'http://u:80/yygk-show.asp? <script>ijv = 360</script>'...

Tokenization. The tokenization process involves segmenting an HTTP message into multiple tokens. Currently, various tokenization methods have been proposed [21, 22, 24], which generally rely on specific prior knowledge. For injection attack messages, tokenization may require prior knowledge such as HTML tags, JavaScript functions, calling functions, URL structures, and attack payload structures. The acquisition of prior knowledge typically depends on manual expert experience, and insufficient or incorrect prior knowledge may lead to tokenization errors, such as splitting a single token into two parts or misidentifying unrelated character combinations as a single token. Through the study of various tokenization methods, this paper ultimately adopts an automated tokenization method [25]. It achieves automated tokenization by controlling five parameters: minimum token length, maximum token length, token frequency, cohesion degree, and left-right entropy. The tokenization process of the automation method primarily consists of two steps.

Generating the Candidate Tokens. HTTP messages are processed sequentially by using a sliding window (as shown in Fig. 3) to generate candidate tokens, which consists of tokens with different lengths. The size of the sliding window is set based on two configured parameters: minimum token length and maximum token length.

Filtering the Candidate Tokens. We use three parameters of token frequency, cohesion degree, and left-right entropy to filter the candidate tokens. Those tokens below the word frequency threshold, below the cohesion degree threshold, or the left-right entropy threshold are removed from the candidate tokens. The remaining tokens constitute the final tokenization results for HTTP messages. Token frequency refers to the number of times a candidate token appears in the candidate corpus. Cohesion degree measures the binding strength between internal components of the candidate word, a higher value indicates a greater likelihood that the candidate is a standalone token. Left-right entropy

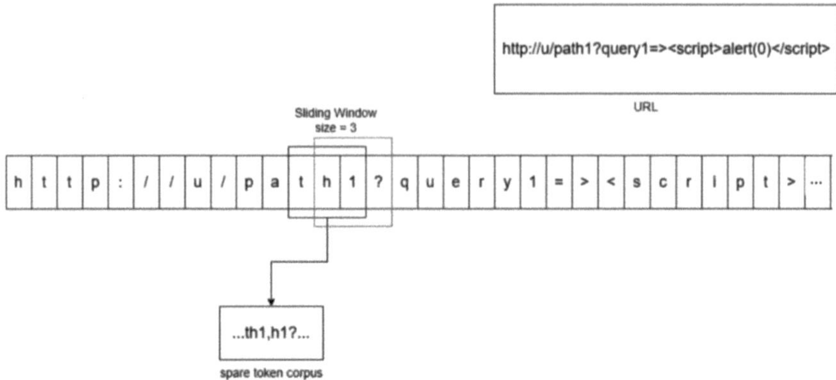

Fig. 3. Sliding window with size equals three

represents the information entropy of all left-context characters and right-context characters adjacent to the candidate token, a higher value indicates a greater likelihood that the candidate is a standalone token.

3.3 Constructing Graph Structure

In order to use the GCN model to detect HTTP messages, it is necessary to convert HTTP messages into a graph named the HTTP graph. The HTTP graph contains two types of nodes, HTTP message nodes and token nodes; and two types of edges, HTTP message-to-token edges and token-to-token edges.

HTTP Message-to-Token Edges: This type of edge reflects the relationship between HTTP messages and tokens. If a token is part of an HTTP message, an edge is added between the node representing that HTTP message and the node representing the token. PathSim [26] is commonly utilized to measure the similarity between two nodes in a graph. In this paper, we employ PathSim as the basis for calculating the weight of such edges. The calculation formula for PathSim is as follows:

$$PathSim\left(http_i, http_j\right) = \frac{2 * \overrightarrow{http_i} * \overrightarrow{http_j}}{\overrightarrow{http_i}^2 + \overrightarrow{http_j}^2} \tag{1}$$

In the context where $http_i$ and $http_j$ denote the ith and j^{th} HTTP message nodes respectively, the vector $http_i$ has dimensions equivalent to the size of the vocabulary. The values within this vector represent the frequency of occurrence of each token within the corresponding HTTP message. As illustrated in Table 4, given a vocabulary size of 5, if $Token_1$, $Token_2$, $Token_3$, $Token_4$ and $Token_5$ appear 3 times, 3 times,1 time, 2 times and 0 time respectively within the message $http_i$, then $http_i = \overrightarrow{(3, 3, 1, 2, 0)}$. Assuming that a token node $token_k$ simultaneously belongs to m HTTP messages (including message $http_1$, the formula for calculating the weight of the edge between $http_1$ and $token_k$ is as follows:

$$Weight(http_1, token_k) = \frac{\left(\sum_{i=2}^{m-1} PathSim(http_1, http_i)\right)}{m-1} \quad \forall token_k \in http_i \tag{2}$$

Token-to-Token Edges: This type of edge represents the relationships between tokens. If two tokens belong to the same HTTP message, an edge is added between their corresponding token nodes, and the weight of this edge is determined using PMI, as introduced in [22, 24]. PMI is a measure that quantifies the degree of mutual dependence between two token nodes. The formula for calculating PMI is given below:

$$PMI(token_i, token_j) = \frac{P(token_i, token_j)}{P(token_i) * P(token_j)} \tag{3}$$

In this context, $P(token_i, token_j)$ represents the probability that $token_i$ and $token_j$ co-occur, which can also be interpreted as the ratio of edges connecting $token_i$ and $token_j$ to the total number of edges in the graph. Similarly, $P(token_i)$ represents the frequency of $token_i$ relative to the total number of tokens in the dataset.

Table 4. Examples of HTTP messages

Http Messages	Token1	Token2	Token3	Token4	Token5
$HTTP_1$	3	3	1	2	0
$HTTP_2$	4	0	1	3	5
$HTTP_3$	2	1	3	0	4
$HTTP_4$	0	1	1	2	3

3.4 GCNs-Based Detection Model

Embedding. In this paper, we employ the Word2Vec neural network model [27] to process all tokens, converting each token into a 256-dimensional feature vector representation, then perform a weighted sum on the feature vectors of tokens to obtain the feature vector of the HTTP request. Assuming an HTTP request contains n tokens, the formula for calculating the feature vector of the HTTP request is as follows:

$$FeatureVector(HTTP) = \sum_{i=1}^{n} FeatureVector(token_i) * weight(token_i) \tag{4}$$

Here, $FeatureVector(token_i)$ represents the feature vector of $token_i$ which is calculated using Word2Vec. $weight(token_i)$ indicates the weight of $token_i$, which is determined based on its term frequency in the token set and normalized accordingly.

Matrix Representation. For the graph structure of HTTP messages introduced previously, we ultimately need to convert this graph structure into a feature matrix and an adjacency matrix to serve as inputs for the GCNs model. The feature matrix is a $(N + M) \times 256$ matrix, where each row represents the feature vector of an HTTP message or a token obtained after embedding processing. Here, N denotes the number of HTTP messages, and M represents the total number of tokens. The adjacency matrix is a $(N + M) \times (N + M)$ matrix, with element values being the weights of the edges, specifically PathSim, PMI, or 0 if no edge exists between two nodes.

Selection and Design of GCNs Model. Considering the variable length characteristic of HTTP messages, we analyzed several convolution functions suitable for heterogeneous graphs, including GATConv [15], ResGatedGraphConv [28], and GCNConv [7]. We have opted for GCNConv [7] as the convolution function for our model in this paper.

We conducted an evaluation of several machine learning models for the purpose of injection attack detection and recognition. It was observed that Transformer-based architectures, such as BERT [29, 30], are primarily designed for natural language processing (NLP) tasks, where they excel in capturing textual and semantic information. Besides, we are aiming to leverage the connections between tokens and HTTP messages, which means building graphs is our top priority. Consequently, these models were deemed unsuitable for our specific application domain and were excluded from further consideration.

From the perspective of feature representation, prior studies [12, 13] have commonly employed statistical characteristics of input data as feature vectors. However, given the structural and sequential nature of HTTP packet data, we determined that such statistical features may not adequately capture the underlying patterns relevant for injection attack recognition. Therefore, these models are excluded as well. Thus, we adopted a tokenization-based representation method, wherein each HTTP packet is decomposed into multiple tokens. These tokens are then embedded into a continuous vector space using the Word2Vec model, generating meaningful feature representations.

The resulting non-Euclidean structure of the learned feature space suggests that graph-based modeling approaches are particularly appropriate for this task. Accordingly, Graph Convolutional Neural Networks (GCNs) are adopted to effectively model the complex relationships among tokens within HTTP packets.

Our GCN-InjectionDetect model consists of a three-layer graph convolutional network. We employed the negative log-likelihood function as the loss function and utilized the Adam optimizer with a learning rate of 0.01. The feature matrix and adjacency matrix, established in the preceding sections, serve as inputs to this network.

4 Experiment and Evaluation

4.1 Experimental Setup

The software and hardware specifications used in our experiments are as follows: The CPU is an Intel i7-11700, the GPU is an NVIDIA T400, and the operating system is Windows 11 (64-bit). The algorithm was implemented in Python, with the specific software packages and their corresponding version numbers detailed in Table 5. And the framework of this neural network is a 3-layer GCN model, with negative log likelihood loss as loss function, and the numbers of convolutions are 64,108,3 respectively.

Table 5. Python libraries

Packages	Version
python	3.10.14
jupyter	1.1.1
numpy	1.26.4
torch	2.5.0dev20240715 + cu124
tqdm	4.66.5
scipy	1.13.1
scikit-learn	1.15.1

The attack sample data utilized in the experiments comprises injection attack (XSS attack) URLs collected from XSSed.com [31], consisting of 43934 payloads from all over the world, including attacks for education facility and government department and so on. The experimental HTTP messages dataset employed in this study was obtained from the Intrusion Detection System (IDS) of the China Science and Technology Network (CSTNET) during August 2024. The resulting dataset consists of 20,000 verified XSS samples, 20,000 SQLi samples, and 20,000 CI samples, each containing active attack payloads. In compliance with institutional policies and cybersecurity regulations governing CSTNET operations, the raw network traffic and complete payload contents are not publicly accessible. These alerts encompass entire HTTP messages; after preprocessing, they were used as attack sample data. And the benign datasets are composed of two parts, the URL part was from the dataset named Benign and Malicious URLs from Kaggle, and the HTTP messages part was from the dataset named CIC_IDS2017. Due to the sufficient benign data, we maintain the balanced dataset while the whole experiment with the ratio 1:1. During the experiments, the dataset was divided into a test set and a validation set. We employed 10-fold cross-validation to evaluate the experimental results, ensuring robust and reliable performance assessment of the model.

Currently, representative injection attack detection methods based on graph convolutional neural networks include GraphXSS [21], GCNXSS [24], and IGXSS [22]. Therefore, we compared our proposed method, GCN-InjectionDetect, with these three methods.

4.2 Detection Effectiveness

GraphXSS, GCNXSS, and IGXSS are all designed for detecting XSS attacks and focus solely on the URL portion of HTTP messages. Therefore, we conducted a comparative analysis of the detection effectiveness between our proposed method, GCN-InjectionDetect, and these baseline methods using the XSSed.com dataset. The experimental results are shown in Fig. 4 and Table 6. As illustrated in Fig. 4, our proposed

Table 6. Evaluation of our method and benchmark

Name	Accuracy	Precision	Recall	F1 Score
Our Method	**0.992**	**0.999**	**0.987**	**0.995**
GraphXSS	0.929	0.944	0.912	0.927
GCNXSS	0.9055	0.920	0.884	0.896
IGXSS	0.918	0.926	0.908	0.916

method achieves the highest accuracy (99.2%), with improvements of 6.3%, 8.65%, and 7.4% over the baseline methods, respectively. Additionally, it demonstrates the fastest convergence rate, reaching a stable state in approximately 30 epochs, whereas the other three methods require around 100 epochs to converge. Furthermore, as indicated in Table 6, our method outperforms the others across various evaluation metrics, including Accuracy (ACC), Recall, F1 Score, and Precision.

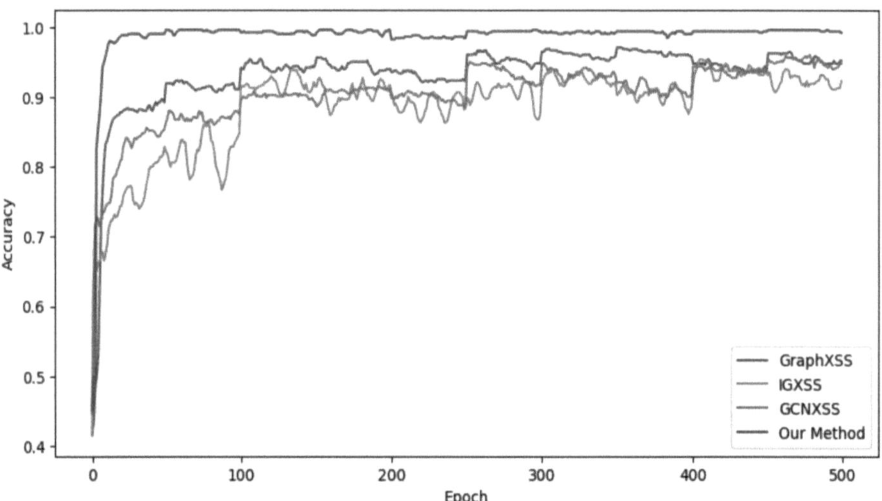

Fig. 4. The accuracy of our method and benchmark

Table 7. Evaluation about detecting three kinds of attacks

Attacks	Accuracy	Precision	Recall	F1 Score
XSS	0.9865	0.9959	0.978	0.978
Command Injection	0.954	0.9912	0.906	0.946
SQL Injection	0.951	0.975	0.926	0.947

We evaluated the detection effectiveness of our proposed method on three types of injection attacks (XSS attacks, SQL injection attacks, and command injection attacks) using alert data generated by an IDS system deployed on a backbone network. We filtered the relevant alerts for these three types of injection attacks from the raw alert data and further removed irrelevant fields to construct labeled HTTP attack messages. The experimental results are presented in Fig. 5 and Table 7. Specifically, the detection accuracy for XSS attacks is 98.65%, for command injection attacks it is 95.4%, and for SQL injection attacks, it is 95.1%. Among these, the detection accuracy for XSS attacks is the highest. The primary reason for this higher accuracy is that XSS attacks are the most common type; thus, the training samples include a more comprehensive set of XSS attack features, which aids the model in learning more precise XSS attack characteristics. Along with the other reason is as follows: the length of XSS attack is longer than the other two kinds of injection attacks, which means HTTP messages contains more featured tokens than the rest of injection attacks.

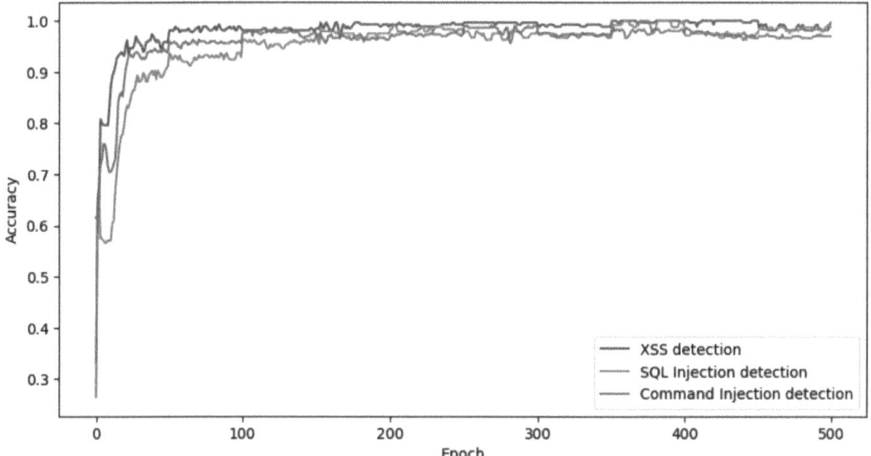

Fig. 5. The accuracy of detection of three kinds of attacks

4.3 Parameters Analysis

As previously mentioned, this study employs an automated tokenization method controlled by five hyperparameters. Different parameter settings can influence the tokenization outcomes and, consequently, the detection performance of the model. Therefore, we conducted experiments to analyze the detection efficiency of the model under various parameter values.

Considering that the minimum word length, maximum word length, and word frequency have relatively minor impacts on the tokenization results and model detection performance, these parameters were empirically set to 4, 12, and 100, respectively, in our parameter analysis experiments. We then focused on adjusting the values of cohesion and left-right entropy to observe changes in the model's detection performance.

In the experiments, the cohesion value was increased from 10 to 50 with a step size of 5, while the left-right entropy value was increased from 0.2 to 1.0 with a step size of 0.2. The experimental results, as shown in Table 8, indicate that the best detection performance is achieved when cohesion is set to 20 and left-right entropy is set to 0.4, resulting in an accuracy rate of 98.97%. When evaluating the detection performance of our proposed model, we set cohesion and left-right entropy to 20 and 0.4, respectively. In practical applications of our proposed model for detecting injection attacks, users can also experiment to determine the optimal parameter combination to achieve the best detection performance.

Table 8. The performance of different combinations (accuracy)

CohesionEntropy	0.2	0.4	0.6	0.8	1.0
10	0.9875	0.9701	0.9675	0.9518	0.9572
15	0.9852	0.9895	0.9879	0.9582	0.9647
20	0.9740	**0.9897**	0.9805	0.9436	0.9425
25	0.9627	0.9412	0.9385	0.9151	0.9286
30	0.9087	0.8931	0.9065	0.7587	0.9174
35	0.9142	0.9140	0.9312	0.9235	0.9072
40	0.9214	0.9261	0.9242	0.9165	0.9158
45	0.9158	0.9290	0.8702	0.9281	0.9289
50	0.9264	0.9205	0.8869	0.9032	0.8637

To prove that the minimum word length, maximum word length have relatively minor impacts on the tokenization results and model detection performance, we also did a parameter analysis about the length of the word. The results as shown in Table 9..

Table 9. The performance of different lengths (accuracy)

minimummaximum	10	11	12	13	14	15
3	0.9748	0.9760	0.9822	0.9781	0.9813	0.9791
4	0.9865	0.9799	**0.9897**	0.9701	0.9524	0.9784
5	0.9862	0.9895	0.9874	0.9870	0.9868	0.9847

5 Conclusion

Our method excels in detecting various forms of injection attacks, such as SQL Injection, Cross-Site Scripting (XSS), and Command Injection, by analyzing the entire structure of HTTP messages rather than focusing solely on specific components like URLs. This comprehensive analysis allows our model to identify malicious payloads embedded in different parts of the message, enhancing its detection capabilities.

About the auto tokenizer algorithm, we have a conclusion that we know the traditional tokenizer way is using the regular expressions to quantify the malicious payload or the code fragments. But the auto algorithm lists all the possible fragments in a brute-force way. This requires high overhead, but we can change the hyperparameters to avoid this situation.

Acknowledgements. This work was supported by the following funding programs: the National Key Research and Development Program of China (Grant No. 2023YFC3304704), the Youth Innovation Promotion Association of the Chinese Academy of Sciences (Grant No. 2022170), and the Cybersecurity and Informatization Special Project of Chinese Academy of Sciences (Grant No. CAS-WX2022GC-04).

References

1. OWASP TOP 10 2021, https://owasp.org/www-project-top-ten/,last Accessed 31 Dec 2024
2. Nagarjun, P.M.D.: Cross-site scripting research: a review. Int. J. Adv. Comput. Sci. Appl. **11**(4), 626–632 (2020)
3. Abdullayev, V.: SQL injection attack: quick view. Mesopotamian J. Cybersecurity. **2023**, 30–34 (2023)
4. Shantanu, C.: Detection of malicious command injection attacks on phase shifter control in power systems. IEEE Trans. Power Syst. **36**(1), 271–280 (2021)
5. 2023 Network Security Vulnerability Situation Report, https://www.h3c.com/cn/d_202402/2056604_30003_0.htm, last Accessed 31 Dec 2024
6. HTTP RFC, https://tools.ietf.org/html/rfc7230,last Accessed 15 Feb 2025
7. Thomas N.K.: Semi supervised classification with graph convolutional networks, arXiv preprint arXiv:1609.02907 (2016).
8. Luo, C.: Tchecker: precise static inter-procedural analysis for detecting taint-style vulnerabilities in php applications. In: Proceedings of the 2022 ACM SIGSAC Conference on Computer and Communications Security, pp. 2175–2188. Association for Computing Machinery, Los Angeles (2022)
9. Su, H.: Splendor: static detection of stored xss in modern web applications. In: Proceedings of the 32nd ACM SIGSOFT International Symposium on Software Testing and Analysis, pp. 1043–1054. Association for Computing Machinery, Seattle (2023)
10. Soewito, B.: Prevention structured query language injection using regular expression and escape string. Procedia Comput. Sci. **135**, 678–687 (2018)
11. Abikoye, O.C.: A novel technique to prevent SQL injection and cross-site scripting attacks using Knuth-Morris-Pratt string match algorithm. EURASIP J. Inf. Secur. **2020**, 1–14 (2020)
12. Mokbal, F.M.M.: MLPXSS: an integrated XSS-based attack detection scheme in web applications using multilayer perceptron technique. IEEE Access. **7**, 100567–100580 (2019)
13. Fawaz, F.M.M.: XGBXSS: an extreme gradient boosting detection framework for cross-site scripting attacks based on hybrid feature selection approach and parameters optimization. J. Inf. Secur. Appl. **58**, 102813 (2021)
14. Zhang C.: Heterogeneous graph neural network, In: Proceedings of the 25th ACM SIGKDD International Conference on Knowledge Discovery & Data Mining, pp. 793–803, Association for Computing Machinery, Anchorage (2019)
15. Veličković P.: Graph attention networks, arXiv preprint arXiv:1710.10903 (2017).
16. Zhao, J.: Cyber threat intelligence modeling based on heterogeneous graph convolutional network. In: 23rd International Symposium on Research in Attacks Intrusions and Defenses, pp. 241–256. Association for Computing Machinery, Donostia (2020)

17. Gao, X.: Graph condensation for inductive node representation learning. In: In: 2024 IEEE 40th International Conference on Data Engineering IEEE, pp. 3056–3069. Institute of Electrical and Electronics Engineers, Utrecht (2024)
18. Hamilton, W.: Inductive representation learning on large graphs. In: Advances in Neural Information Processing Systems 30, pp. 1025–1035. Curran Associates Inc., California (2017)
19. Morris, C.: Weisfeiler and leman go neural: higher-order graph neural networks. In: Proceedings of the AAAI Conference on Artificial Intelligence, pp. 4602–4609. AAAI Press, Hawaii (2019)
20. Shi Y.: Masked label prediction: Unified message passing model for semi-supervised classification", arXiv preprint arXiv:2009.03509 (2020)
21. Liu, Z.: GraphXSS: an efficient XSS payload detection approach based on graph convolutional network. Comput. Secur. **114**, 102597 (2022)
22. Wang, Q.: IGXSS: XSS payload detection model based on inductive GCN. Int. J. Netw. Manag. **34**, e2264 (2024)
23. Pan, H.: Few-shot graph classification on cross-site scripting attacks detection. Comput. Secur. **140**, 103749 (2024)
24. Pan, H.: GCNXSS: an attack detection approach for cross-site scripting based on graph convolutional networks. KSII Trans. Internet Inf. Syst. (TIIS). **16**(12), 4008–4023 (2022)
25. Matrix64 Homepage, https://www.matrix67.com/blog/archives/5044, last accessed 12 Jan 2025
26. Sun, Y.: PathSim: meta path based top-K similarity search in heterogeneous information networks. VLDB Endow. **4**(11), 992–1003 (2011)
27. Mikolov T.: Efficient estimation of word representations in vector space, arXiv preprint arXiv:1301.3781 (2013).
28. Bresson X.: Residual gated graph convnets, arXiv preprint arXiv:1711.07553 (2017).
29. Vaswani, A., et al.: Attention Is all you Need. *Advances in neural information processing systems.* **30** (2017)
30. Devlin, J., Chang, M.W., Lee, K., Toutanova, K.: Bert: pre-training of deep bidirectional transformers for language understanding. In: Proceedings of the 2019 Conference of the North American Chapter of the Association for Computational Linguistics: Human Language Technologies, Volume 1 (Long and Short Papers), pp. 4171–4186 (2019, June)
31. XSSed.com, https://www.xssed.com/, last Accessed 15 Nov 2024

Improving Trust in AI-Driven Diabetes Prediction: Explainability Through SHAP and Counterfactual Analysis

Razan Malluhi[1(✉)], Mahmoud Barhamgi[1], Saeed Salem[1], Ahmad Qadeib Alban[2], and Ahmed Badawy[1]

[1] Department of Computer Science and Engineering, Qatar University, Doha, Qatar
{razan.malluhi,mbarhamgi,saeed.salem,badawy}@qu.edu.qa

[2] Paris DauphinePSL University, Paris, France
ahmad.qadeib-alban@dauphine.eu

Abstract. The rising prevalence of Type 2 diabetes presents a significant global health challenge that requires early detection and effective management. While machine learning models offer strong predictive capabilities for diabetes risk assessment, their lack of interpretability limits trust and clinical adoption. This paper proposes an explainability-driven prediction framework that integrates two complementary techniques: (1) SHAP-based feature attribution, enhanced through percentage-based normalization for better accessibility, and (2) personalized counterfactual explanations that generate actionable "what-if" scenarios tailored to individual user profiles. Unlike prior work that focuses solely on feature importance or abstract visualizations, our framework delivers both justification ("why" a prediction was made) and guidance ("how" risk can be reduced) through natural language insights and medically aligned recommendations. The framework is evaluated on a public dataset, achieving 96.7% accuracy. A user study involving general users and healthcare professionals demonstrates high satisfaction with the clarity, usefulness, and actionability of the explanations. Results show that integrating SHAP and counterfactual reasoning provides both justification and guidance, advancing explainable AI adoption in healthcare.

Keywords: Explainable AI · SHAP · Counterfactual explanations · Diabetes prediction · Trust in AI · Health Informatics

1 Introduction

The prevalence of Type 2 diabetes has been steadily increasing, posing a significant public health challenge worldwide [1]. As a chronic disease, diabetes can lead to serious complications such as cardiovascular disease, kidney failure, and vision loss, imposing substantial health and economic burdens [18]. According to the Atlas of the International Diabetes Federation, the global number of people living with diabetes is projected to increase from 537 million in 2021 to 643

I. Awan et al. (Eds.): WISE 2025, LNCS 16367, pp. 507–521, 2026.
https://doi.org/10.1007/978-981-95-7394-3_35

million in 2030 and 783 million by 2045 [1]. This alarming trend underscores the urgent need for early detection and effective management strategies to prevent complications and improve patient outcomes.

Advancements in healthcare technology have made Machine Learning (ML) models instrumental in predictive diagnostics, particularly in identifying individuals at risk of developing diabetes [15]. By analyzing complex clinical and demographic data, such as blood glucose levels, body mass index (BMI), age, and family history, ML algorithms have shown remarkable precision in predicting diabetes, offering a pathway to personalized treatment plans and proactive care [13]. However, despite their predictive capabilities, these models often function as black boxes, producing results without providing clear explanations of how decisions are made. In healthcare, where decisions significantly impact patient outcomes, the inability to understand the predictions undermines trust, limits adoption, and potentially compromises the delivery of care [19].

This lack of explainability creates challenges not only for clinicians but also for patients, who may struggle to interpret and act on opaque predictions. Explainability, the ability to provide clear and user-friendly justifications for AI-driven decisions, is essential to bridge this gap [3]. Existing Explainable AI (XAI) tools, such as SHapley Additive exPlanations (SHAP) and Local Interpretable Model-agnostic Explanations (LIME), have attempted to improve interpretability by assigning importance scores to features [10,17]. However, their outputs, which often rely on complex graphs and charts, are primarily designed for technical audiences and fail to resonate with patients. Research has shown that people prefer clear, actionable, and contextually relevant explanations, but current XAI implementations often fall short of making insights accessible to a broad audience [5]. Furthermore, SHAP does not explain how patients could modify their risk. As a result, SHAP-based explanations remain abstract and do not provide actionable insights to end users, particularly those without technical expertise.

To address these limitations, this paper proposes an explainability-focused diabetes prediction framework that extends traditional feature importance rankings. In addition to user-friendly SHAP explanations, the framework integrates counterfactual reasoning to provide actionable "what-if" scenarios. These explanations illustrate how specific changes in health-related factors, such as lowering blood glucose levels, could alter the risk of diabetes. Unlike conventional methods that only explain why a prediction was made, counterfactuals offer concrete guidance on how users can modify key factors to achieve a different outcome.

By integrating explainability techniques with personalized counterfactual reasoning, this work aims to enhance patient and clinician understanding of AI-driven predictions, enabling informed decision-making. The contributions of this paper are as follows:

- We build on existing efforts by proposing a structured explainability framework that combines SHAP-based feature attribution with personalized counterfactual explanations, offering both justification ('why') and actionable guidance ('how') for individual diabetes risk predictions.

- We enhance the interpretability of SHAP values by converting raw attributions into percentage-based contributions, making feature importance more understandable for non-technical users.
- Develop a user-friendly explanation system that translates complex model outputs into intuitive, natural language insights, aiming to make AI predictions understandable and useful for both technical and non-technical users.
- We evaluate the clarity and perceived usefulness of the framework's explanations through a small-scale user study involving both non-expert users and healthcare professionals, focusing on trust, interpretability, and actionable insights.

The remainder of the paper is organized as follows: Sect. 2 reviews related work on diabetes prediction and XAI. Section 3 details the proposed methodology. Section 4 presents experimental results and user feedback. Section 5 discusses the results. Section 6 proposes directions for future work. Finally, Sect. 7 presents the conclusion.

2 Related Work

The development of ML models for diabetes prediction and the advancement of XAI techniques have been active research areas. Traditional ML approaches focus on improving accuracy in disease prediction, while more recent efforts aim to enhance transparency and interpretability to make AI-driven decisions more trustworthy and actionable. This section reviews prior work in three key domains: accuracy-focused models, XAI techniques for model interpretability, and counterfactual explanation methods.

2.1 Accuracy-Focused Models in Diabetes Prediction

ML research has focused on improving classification performance through a combination of various modeling techniques and preprocessing methods.

Latest research employed ensemble learning techniques, including the use of Random Forest, AdaBoost, and XGBoost algorithms on the Pima Indian Diabetes (PID) dataset. This resulted in an impressive Area Under the Curve (AUC) score of 0.95, highlighting the effectiveness of ensemble methods in enhancing prediction accuracy for diabetes diagnosis [8].

Other studies, such as [15] and [7], have explored a variety of model combinations, from single algorithms to hybrid models, to further refine diabetes prediction accuracy. Despite these advancements in accuracy, they do not provide transparent explanations of how decisions are made. This lack of interpretability creates challenges, particularly for non-expert users such as patients or healthcare providers who may need to understand and trust the predictions to make informed decisions.

While these works focus on maximizing accuracy, our approach shifts the emphasis toward explainability, ensuring that users not only receive accurate predictions but also understand why and how a prediction was made. The next section discusses recent literature on XAI.

2.2 Explainable Models

XAI has become important in addressing the black-box nature of many ML models, especially in critical domains like healthcare. It has been acknowledged due to the need for models to provide actionable insights that stakeholders can trust and understand [9].

A study on ML interpretability emphasizes the societal and ethical necessity of explainable models, particularly in high-stakes applications such as healthcare and criminal justice. Explainability is often presented using technical tools such as SHAP and LIME, which usually produce visual representations of feature importance. Although effective for experts, these tools are primarily designed for technical audiences and may not provide user-friendly explanations for non-expert users [5].

Chen and Hernández proposed a sensitivity analysis that is integrated with Random Forest classifiers to identify key biomarkers for sepsis detection. Their method focused on generating feature importance metrics and providing detailed technical insights. Although highly effective for clinicians, the explanations required domain knowledge for complete comprehension and were not designed for greater accessibility [6].

In contrast, Balasubramaniam et al. highlighted the importance of user-centered explainability. Their research proposed a model for defining explainability requirements, emphasizing the use of templates to align explanations with stakeholder needs. They advocated for combining graphs with structured plain-language explanations, tailored to diverse user groups such as patients, clinicians, and policymakers. This approach focused on improving accessibility and usability for non-technical stakeholders [4].

To address these limitations, researchers have emphasized human-centric approaches to explainability. Interactive explanation interfaces and participatory design methods have been proposed to align explanations with the needs and preferences of end-users [9]. Such approaches ensure that explanations are not only accurate but also comprehensible and actionable for diverse audiences [4]. Ethical guidelines from multiple organizations also advocate for AI systems that provide clear, actionable, and contextually relevant explanations, underscoring the connection between explainability and transparency [16].

Despite these advances, most existing methods focus on explaining why a prediction was made but do not address how users can modify key factors to achieve a different outcome. The next section explores recent literature on counterfactual reasoning.

2.3 Counterfactual Explanations in XAI

Counterfactual explanations illustrate how small, targeted changes in input features can alter the model's prediction. Recent literature has explored this concept.

One such study, [12], introduced a GAN-based approach to generate counterfactual explanations for medical images. Instead of numerical or categorical feature adjustments, this framework modified X-ray images to visually depict how a patient's scan might look if they did not have a specific condition (e.g., pneumonia). This approach enhances explainability for non-experts by offering a direct, image-based comparison of different health states. However, while this method is useful for visual interpretability, it does not translate well to structured medical data, such as diabetes risk factors. Additionally, it lacks explicit recommendations for how patients can alter their health parameters to lower their risk.

Another study [2] proposed an enhanced version of SHAP that integrates counterfactual information into the background dataset used for computing Shapley values. This modification improves the actionability of SHAP-based explanations by making feature attributions more tailored to individual cases. While this approach enhances SHAP's interpretability, it primarily focuses on adjusting the importance scores rather than generating explicit counterfactual scenarios for users. Furthermore, it does not provide clear recommendations on how users should modify their behaviors to achieve a more favorable outcome.

The authors of [20] examined how counterfactual explanations can be leveraged to explore alternative medical scenarios for research purposes. The authors emphasized the potential of counterfactuals to model different treatment strategies, allowing researchers to assess hypothetical interventions. While this approach is valuable for scientific exploration, it does not offer direct, patient-specific recommendations.

Despite these advancements, existing studies focus on either adjusting feature importance rankings, but few frameworks provide a unified approach that integrates prediction, feature attribution, counterfactual reasoning, and actionable recommendations. Additionally, prior work often lacks an emphasis on patient usability, making it difficult for non-experts to translate counterfactual insights into concrete health interventions.

Our proposed framework builds on these existing efforts by integrating a dual explainability approach with SHAP-based feature importance and counterfactual reasoning in a structured diabetes prediction model. Our approach first uses SHAP to explain the current prediction and then generates counterfactual explanations suggesting how specific input feature changes can reduce diabetes risk. Furthermore, we provide actionable recommendations for users. This combination of explainability and actionability enhances user trust and ensures that AI-driven insights translate into meaningful health decisions. The next section details the methodology of the proposed explainability framework.

3 Methodology

This section outlines the methodology for developing the explainable diabetes prediction framework. Starting off with data pre-processing and model development, followed by the detailed XAI framework.

3.1 Data Processing and Model Development

Our experimental setup begins with a preprocessing and normalization pipeline, followed by the model prediction stage. The dataset used for this study is the Diabetes Prediction Dataset, sourced from Kaggle [14]. It contains 100,000 samples and 9 features, including clinical and demographic data such as age, gender, BMI, blood glucose level, and hypertension status. The target variable is binary: whether a patient has diabetes or not.

To ensure data quality and consistency, many preprocessing steps were applied. This included handling missing values, removing duplicated rows, and feature encoding where categorical variables were transformed using one-hot encoding to ensure compatibility with ML algorithms. Lastly, feature standardization was done, where continuous variables were standardized using a StandardScaler for improved numerical stability.

To maintain interpretability while reducing model complexity, the RandomForestClassifier was used to rank features by importance. The features above a significance threshold were selected for model training.

A feedforward neural network was selected as the predictive model due to its suitability for this task [11]. The following steps were used for model development. Firstly, the dataset was split into training (80%), validation (6%), and testing (14%) sets using stratified sampling. Secondly, a single hidden-layer neural network was implemented. The number of hidden units and the learning rate were optimized through validation. Thirdly, the model was trained using the Adam optimizer and binary cross-entropy loss. Then performance was assessed. Since model optimization and accuracy were not the primary objectives, hyperparameter tuning was kept minimal, focusing instead on interpretability.

3.2 Explainable AI Framework

This section corresponds to the steps shown in Fig. 1, which provides post-prediction explanations using SHAP, counterfactual reasoning, and recommendation generation. The main components of this framework are described below.

SHAP-Based Feature Contribution Analysis: As seen in the first explainability component in Fig. 1, SHAP values were used to quantify the contribution of each feature to the model's prediction. The KernelExplainer from the SHAP library was employed to compute these values for each input instance, providing model-agnostic explanations by comparing the predicted outcome to a baseline derived from the training data. To enhance interpretability for non-technical users, the raw SHAP values were normalized and converted into percentage-based contributions. To calculate the percentage contributions, we first took the absolute SHAP value of each feature for a given instance, then normalized them by dividing each value by the sum of absolute SHAP values across all features. This ensured that the total contribution summed to 100%, enabling a clear comparison of each feature's relative importance in the prediction.

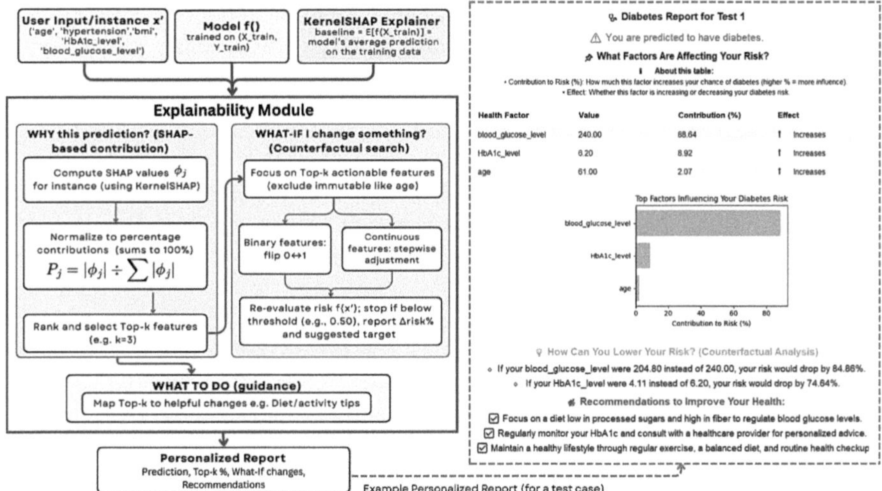

Fig. 1. Workflow of the proposed explainability framework. The module integrates SHAP-based attribution (to answer why a prediction was made), counterfactual analysis (to explore what-if scenarios), and guidance generation (to suggest what to do). The outputs are combined into a personalized report tailored to each patient.

For each prediction, features were ranked based on these percentage-based contributions, and the top three contributors were highlighted in the explanation. This ranking ensured that the most influential factors were communicated clearly. The framework generates personalized, human-readable explanations for each prediction, including the model's classification output (diabetes or no diabetes), the top three contributing features, their values, their SHAP scores, and their corresponding percentage contributions to the prediction, and whether the feature influences the prediction negatively or positively.

Recommendation Generation. In addition to explaining predictions, the framework provides actionable health recommendations based on the key contributing features. These recommendations are aligned with established medical guidelines, such as those found in the World Health Organization, and focus on modifiable factors. Examples include: For high BMI: "Aim for a balanced diet and regular exercise to maintain a healthy BMI." The inclusion of these recommendations enhances the utility of the model by not only explaining the predictions of the model but also offering guidance for improved health outcomes for the patients.

Counterfactual Explanation Generation. While SHAP explains why a prediction was made, it does not offer actionable advice on how users can alter their diabetes risk. To bridge this gap, the proposed framework incorporates counterfactual explanations as seen in Fig. 1 that provide "what-if" scenarios to illustrate how modifying specific features can change the model's prediction. For each instance, counterfactual explanations were generated using the following process:

1. **Obtain Initial Prediction:** The model's predicted probability of diabetes was computed for the input instance.
2. **Identify Features:** The top three features contributing to the predictions were considered. Features such as age were not considered since they can't be altered through lifestyle changes or medical interventions.
3. **Determine Adjustment Steps:**
   - **For continuous features** (e.g., blood glucose, HbA1c): A stepwise adjustment method was used, where the feature value was incrementally decreased (or increased) within the range observed in the dataset until the predicted probability of diabetes fell below a threshold (e.g., 50%).
   - **For binary features** (e.g., hypertension): The framework tested whether flipping the feature's value (e.g., from "Yes" to "No") significantly reduced diabetes risk.
4. **Generate Counterfactual Explanation:** If modifying a feature resulted in a lower diabetes risk, the framework produced a statement in natural language to explain it. For example, it would specify: 'If your blood glucose level were reduced to X, your diabetes risk would decrease by Y%.

Integrating Counterfactuals with SHAP Explanations. By combining SHAP-based importance rankings and recommendations with counterfactuals, users not only receive an explanation of why they are at risk but also guidance on how exactly they can lower their risk. This is the personalized report, as seen in Fig. 1, an example test case of one of the test cases of a final report that combines everything together in a user-friendly way is presented. The diabetes report presents all the calculated values using different methods like bullet points, tables, and graphs to make everything clear. This dual-explanation approach enhances the interpretability and actionability of AI-driven predictions.

3.3 User Feedback Survey Design

To evaluate the interpretability and user satisfaction of the proposed explainability framework, a structured user feedback survey was developed and distributed. The goal was to assess how end-users perceive the clarity, trustworthiness, and usefulness of the explanations generated by the system. The survey was created using Google Forms and was designed to accommodate diverse user groups. It included the following components:

- **Audience-specific Sections:** Two distinct sections were included within the form: A section targeting patients or individuals (non-experts), evaluating ease of understanding and perceived usefulness of the AI explanations and recommendations. Another section targeting healthcare professionals, focusing on technical clarity, actionability, and trust in the AI system.

- **Question Types:** The questionnaire consisted of a combination of scale questions, multiple-choice items, and optional open-ended fields. Key themes covered include: clarity and understandability of the explanation, trust in the AI's prediction, usefulness and actionability of the counterfactuals and recommendations, Preferred components, and suggestions for improvement
- **Distribution Strategy:** The survey was distributed online via social media platforms and emails. Efforts were made to ensure the inclusion of both technical and nontechnical participants.

This survey structure allowed the collection of both quantitative and qualitative feedback across different user demographics, providing a comprehensive understanding of how the framework communicates AI-generated predictions in a real-world context. The results of this survey are analyzed and discussed in the results section.

4 Results

This section presents the results of the proposed diabetes prediction framework, with a focus on its explainability through SHAP-based feature importance and counterfactual reasoning. The evaluation includes model performance, explainability analysis, and user feedback.

4.1 Model Performance

The model's performance was evaluated on the testing dataset using standard metrics such as accuracy, precision, recall, and F1-score. Table 1 summarizes the results achieved by the best-performing neural network configuration.

Table 1. Model Performance Metrics

Metric	Training Set	Validation Set	Testing Set
Accuracy (%)	*96.8*	*96.5*	*96.7*
Precision (%)	*96.2*	*95.8*	*95.6*
Recall (%)	*69.5*	*67.5*	*68.9*
F1-Score (%)	*80.7*	*79.2*	*80.1*

The results demonstrate that the proposed neural network is able to generalize well to unseen data. The hyperparameter optimization process significantly contributed to these results, with the best configuration utilizing 16 hidden units and a learning rate of 0.01.

4.2 Explainability Results

The XAI framework was evaluated using SHAP values and counterfactual explanations to provide individual-level explanations for the model's predictions. The survey was used to assess the applicability to the real world.

SHAP-Based Feature Contribution Analysis: Two instances from the test set were analyzed to showcase the interpretability of both positive and negative predictions.

Negative Prediction Case (No Diabetes): For the first instance, the model predicted no diabetes. Figure 2 shows the SHAP force plot for this instance, where the base value corresponds to the average model prediction. Features such as HbA1c level, blood glucose level, and age had the most significant influence in reducing the prediction value below the decision threshold. Specifically, HbA1c level had the largest negative contribution, driving the prediction towards a lower probability of diabetes.

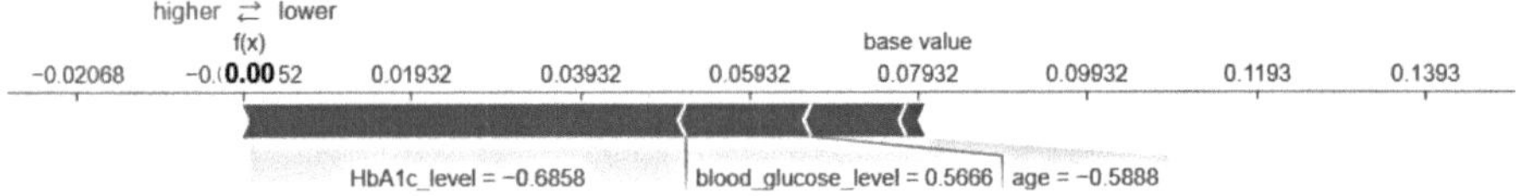

Fig. 2. SHAP Force Plot for Negative Prediction (No Diabetes).

Positive Prediction Case (Diabetes): For the second instance, the model predicted diabetes. As shown in Fig. 3, the SHAP force plot highlights the most influential features that increased the prediction above the threshold. Key observations included that HbA1c level was the most dominant feature, positively contributing to the prediction. Hypertension, on the other hand, exerted a small negative influence, slightly lowering the prediction.

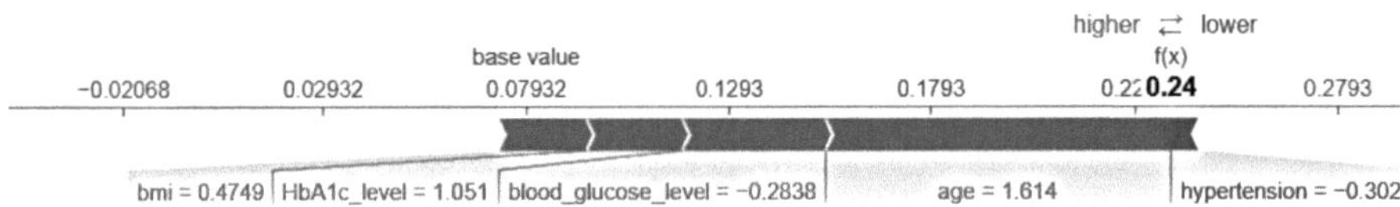

Fig. 3. SHAP Force Plot for Positive Prediction (Diabetes).

These SHAP force plots clearly illustrate how individual features interact to influence the model's decision. While SHAP values effectively illustrate why a decision was made, they do not provide actionable advice on how an individual could alter their health factors to reduce risk. This limitation is addressed through counterfactual explanations and recommendations.

Counterfactual Explanations and Recommendations: To complement SHAP feature importance, counterfactual reasoning was applied to generate personalized what-if scenarios that explain how modifying certain health parameters would alter the model's prediction.

For a patient where the model predicted diabetes, counterfactual explanations provided insights on how small changes to their high contributing features (as determined by SHAP) could lower their risk. The threshold at which the model predicts no diabetes is calculated for each feature using the user data. Below is an example:

> *"If your blood glucose level were 209.20 mg/dL instead of 240.00 mg/dL, your risk of diabetes would drop by 50.83%."*

This provides a direct and actionable interpretation of how a patient could reduce their diabetes risk by making specific lifestyle or medical adjustments. Beyond SHAP and counterfactuals, the system also generates health recommendations based on the most influential features identified in the prediction. These recommendations align with medical guidelines and are tailored to each user's high-risk contributing factors.

4.3 User Feedback

A total of 20 responses were collected through the mini-survey, comprising responses from general users and healthcare professionals. Notably, 2 out of the 20 participants reported having diabetes.

General Users (Non-Experts). A total of 12 general users participated in this evaluation. Participants were asked to evaluate the understandability of the AI explanations, the usefulness of counterfactual reasoning, and the clarity of the personalized recommendations.

- 10 out of 12 participants found the AI's explanations either *clear* or *very clear*, indicating effective communication of model output.
- 10 out of 12 reported that the AI's explanations increased their trust in the prediction compared to seeing the prediction alone; the remainder reported no difference.
- All 12 of the participants found the counterfactual explanations useful in understanding how to reduce their diabetes risk.
- When asked which component they found most useful, 5 selected the visual bar chart showing the top contributing features, followed by 4 for the counterfactual explanations, and 2 for the SHAP breakdown.

Participants were also asked how the explanations and recommendations could be improved. This was a multiple-choice question allowing multiple selections. The most common suggestions included:

- 9 respondents recommended improving the visual representation (e.g., graphs, tables, or layout clarity).
- 7 participants suggested simplifying the explanations further.
- 6 respondents wanted more personalized recommendations based on individual lifestyle.
- 5 participants requested the ability to see the impact of multiple changes together, rather than one at a time.

Healthcare Professionals. A total of 8 healthcare professionals participated in the evaluation. They assessed the system from both clinical and technical perspectives, focusing on the clarity, actionability, and alignment with medical practice.

- All 8 participants found the SHAP-based explanations either useful or somewhat useful in interpreting the prediction.
- 6 out of 8 rated the counterfactual explanations as *very useful*, while the remaining 25% considered them useful.
- 5 out of 8 felt the generated report was clear and understandable; the remaining participants expressed that it was not sufficiently clear.

Healthcare professionals were also asked how the AI report could be improved to better support patient understanding and trust. Their responses revealed strong consensus on several areas:

- All of the respondents suggested simplifying explanations further for non-expert users.
- 5 out of 8 recommended, including more detailed medical references for key risk factors.
- 4 respondents proposed enhancing counterfactual analysis to show how multiple factors changing simultaneously would affect outcomes.

The following section provides a detailed interpretation of these findings.

5 Discussion

The results presented in this study highlight the effectiveness of the proposed diabetes prediction framework in terms of model performance, explainability, and user feedback. This section discusses the key findings, their implications, and potential areas for improvement.

5.1 Model Performance Analysis

While the performance metrics demonstrate that the proposed model achieves competitive accuracy in train, validation, and test sets, it is important to note that the primary focus of this work is on interpretability and transparency. The explainability results, discussed later, highlight how the framework effectively bridges the gap between complex model outputs and user understanding. The model was able to achieve an accuracy of 96.7% on the testing set. Notably, the precision remained consistently high for training, validation, and test sets, indicating the model's ability to minimize false positives. However, the recall was relatively lower for all sets, reaching a minimum of 67.5% on the validation set, suggesting that the model occasionally struggles to correctly identify all positive cases of diabetes. This trade-off between precision and recall reflects the model's conservative behavior, which prioritizes minimizing incorrect diabetes diagnoses over capturing all positive cases. The F1-Score (e.g., test set 80.1%) further highlights the balance between precision and recall, demonstrating that the model performs reasonably well for imbalanced data. Despite the lower recall, the overall results indicate that the model generalizes effectively to unseen data, achieving consistent performance across evaluation sets.

5.2 Interpretation of User Feedback

The feedback from both groups highlights several key strengths of the proposed framework, as well as areas for further improvement.

- **Clarity and Understandability.** 10 out of the 12 general users found the SHAP-based and visual explanations clear and easy to interpret. Similarly, 5 of the 8 healthcare professionals rated the report as understandable, indicating the system's ability to communicate complex AI outputs in an accessible way. The bar chart summarizing key contributing features was well received, showing the importance of visual aids in enhancing user comprehension.
- **Trust in Model Predictions.** 10 out of the 12 general users reported increased trust in the prediction after viewing the explanations. This suggests that transparency plays a significant role in user confidence. For healthcare professionals, the alignment of SHAP rankings with clinical intuition further validated the model's reliability from a medical perspective.
- **Actionability and Counterfactual Explanations.** Both groups valued the counterfactual explanations, with all 12 of the general users and all 8 professionals rating them as useful or very useful. These "what-if" scenarios helped users understand how specific lifestyle or health adjustments could reduce their diabetes risk. The ability to link predictions with potential interventions reinforces the framework's strength in patient education.
- **Suggestions for Improvement.** Despite positive feedback, several improvement areas were consistently highlighted. Both groups requested simpler, more concise explanations, especially for non-experts. Users expressed a need for enhanced visuals, like the use of more graphs and tables. In addition, there was a clear desire for multi-factor counterfactual analysis to reflect the combined effect of multiple changes. These suggestions point to a need for iterative design focused on clarity.

Overall, the discussion highlights that the proposed framework not only delivers strong predictive performance but also addresses the crucial need for transparency and user engagement in AI-driven healthcare.

6 Conclusion

This paper presents a novel explainability-driven framework for diabetes prediction that integrates SHAP-based feature importance and counterfactual reasoning to enhance user understanding and trust. While achieving a high predictive accuracy, the framework goes beyond traditional black-box models by offering intuitive and actionable explanations for individual predictions. SHAP visualizations help users understand the key factors contributing to their risk, while counterfactuals provide clear guidance on how specific health changes could reduce that risk. The user study involving both general users and healthcare professionals confirmed the value of this approach. Participants reported high clarity, increased trust, and strong appreciation for the actionable outputs. The feedback also revealed key areas for improvement, including simplifying explanations, enhancing visual design, and supporting multi-factor interventions.

Looking forward, counterfactual explanations could be improved through systematic approaches such as DiCE or optimization-based methods, enabling the generation of diverse, minimal, and more realistic suggestions. Beyond SHAP, incorporating alternative XAI methods (e.g., LIME, Integrated Gradients) would allow a richer comparative analysis of interpretability techniques. In addition, expanding the user interface into an interactive, user-friendly platform and conducting rigorous usability testing will be essential for translating this framework into real-world practice. Finally, while our empirical evaluation demonstrated strong performance on the Diabetes Prediction Dataset, future work will extend the empirical study to additional datasets and settings to further validate generalizability.

By bridging the gap between accuracy and interpretability, this work contributes a practical and user-centered solution to AI-powered healthcare. The proposed framework promotes transparency, facilitates informed decision-making, and supports equitable adoption of AI in clinical contexts.

Acknowledgments. This research was supported by the IRCC-2024-499 International Research Collaboration Co-Fund between Qatar University, Paris-Dauphine and Madrid Universities.

This work was also made possible by the Graduate Sponsorship Research Award (GSRA11-L-2-0518-24044) from Qatar Research, Development and Innovation Council "QRDI", (a member of The Qatar Foundation). The contents herein are solely the responsibility of the authors.

This research is also funded by Qatar University Collaborative Grants Program QUCG-CENG-25/26-687. The research findings are the responsibility of the investigators.

References

1. Diabetes around the world in 2021. https://diabetesatlas.org/
2. Albini, E., Long, J., Dervovic, D., Magazzeni, D.: Counterfactual shapley additive explanations. In: ACM International Conference Proceeding Series, vol. 17 (2022)
3. Ali, S., Abuhmed, T., et al.: Explainable artificial intelligence (xai): what we know and what is left to attain trustworthy artificial intelligence. Inf. Fusion **99** (2023)
4. Balasubramaniam, N., Kauppinen, M., Rannisto, A., Hiekkanen, K., Kujala, S.: Transparency and explainability of ai systems: from ethical guidelines to requirements. Inf. Softw. Technol. **159** (2023)

5. Carvalho, D.V., Pereira, E.M., Cardoso, J.S.: Machine learning interpretability: a survey on methods and metrics. Electronics **8** (2019)
6. Chen, M., Hernández, A.: Towards an explainable model for sepsis detection based on sensitivity analysis. IRBM **43** (2022)
7. Febrian, M.E., Ferdinan, F.X., Sendani, G.P., Suryanigrum, K.M., Yunanda, R.: Diabetes prediction using supervised machine learning. Procedia Comput. Sci. **216** (2023)
8. Hasan, M.K., Alam, M.A., Das, D., Hossain, E., Hasan, M.: Diabetes prediction using ensembling of different machine learning classifiers. IEEE Access **8** (2020)
9. Hassija, V., et al.: Interpreting black-box models: a review on explainable artificial intelligence. Cogn. Comput. **16** (2024)
10. Lundberg, S.M., Lee, S.I.: A unified approach to interpreting model predictions. Adv. Neural Inf. Process. Syst. (2017)
11. Malathy, S., Santhiya, M., Vanitha, C.N., Karthiga, R.R.: Diabetes disease prediction using artificial neural network with machine learning approaches. In: Proceedings of the 5th International Conference on Electronics, Communication and Aerospace Technology, ICECA 2021 (2021)
12. Mertes, S., Huber, T., Weitz, K., Heimerl, A., André, E.: Ganterfactual–counterfactual explanations for medical non-experts using generative adversarial learning. Front. Artif. Intell. **5** (2022)
13. Miotto, R., Wang, F., Wang, S., Jiang, X., Dudley, J.T.: Deep learning for healthcare: review, opportunities and challenges. Brief. Bioinf. **19** (2018)
14. Mustafa, M.: Diabetes prediction dataset (2022). https://www.kaggle.com/datasets/iammustafatz/diabetes-prediction-dataset
15. Parimala, G., Kayalvizhi, R., Nithiya, S.: Diabetes prediction using machine learning. In: International Conference on Computer Communication and Informatics (2023)
16. Praveenraj, D.D.W., et al.: Exploring explainable artificial intelligence for transparent decision making. In: E3S Web of Conferences, vol. 399. EDP Sciences (2023)
17. Ribeiro, M.T., Singh, S., Guestrin, C.: "why should i trust you?": explaining the predictions of any classifier. In: KDD Conference (2016)
18. Swamy, S., Noor, S.M., Mathew, R.O.: Cardiovascular disease in diabetes and chronic kidney disease. J. Clin. Med. **12** (2023)
19. Tanim, S.A., Aurnob, A.R., Shrestha, T.E., Emon, M.R.I., Mridha, M.F., Miah, M.S.U.: Explainable deep learning for diabetes diagnosis with deepnetx2. Biomed. Signal Process. Control **99** (2025)
20. Tanyel, T., Ayvaz, S., Keserci, B.: Beyond known reality: exploiting counterfactual explanations for medical research (2023)

SLF-DF: A Framework for Fraud Detection in Airdrop Business Processes

Oumaima Rjab(✉), Layth Sliman, and Souheib Yousfi

Efrei Paris Pantheon-Assas University, Villejuif, France
{oumaima.rjab,layth.sliman,souheib.yousfi}@efrei.fr

Abstract. Airdrops are widely used to promote projects, encourage community engagement, and foster the adoption of blockchain-based financial products, also known as Decentralized Finance (DeFi). Airdrops operate as structured processes, automating token distribution to the customers. However, their open and transparent nature also exposes them to fraudulent behaviours that aim to maximize attackers' rewards. One of the most known fraudulent patterns is combining Sybil and Front-running attacks to manipulate transaction order execution in a way to increase the attacker's financial benefit. As a result, fairness, efficiency, and trust in cryptocurrency markets can be compromised. In this paper, we propose the Sybil-Linked Front-running Detection Framework (SLF-DF), a novel framework designed to detect fraudulent behaviours in airdrop workflows. The framework uses Machine Learning to systematically identify Front-running transactions originating from Sybil-blacklisted addresses, thereby mitigating risks posed by malicious actors in decentralized financial systems. Unlike existing approaches that treat Sybil and Front-running attacks separately, SLF-DF introduces a unified detection framework that captures their combined impact within airdrop workflows. To validate our framework, we construct a structured dataset from Uniswap transaction records, linking Front-running attempts to corresponding victim interactions and including normal transactions to support accurate classification. The result of the experimentation shows the efficiency of the framework, namely its high discriminative capability, with an AUC of 0.98 for Front-running transactions and 0.92 for both victim and normal transactions, along with 94.86% accuracy in detecting fraudulent transactions.

Keywords: Airdrops · Sybil Attacks · Front-Running · Blockchain · Anomaly Detection

1 Introduction

Economic incentives play a fundamental role in shaping user participation and fostering the adoption of blockchain-based financial products. Across various domains, businesses implement incentive-driven mechanisms to attract users and sustain engagement in their ecosystems. In traditional finance, banks employ

I. Awan et al. (Eds.): WISE 2025, LNCS 16367, pp. 522–537, 2026.
https://doi.org/10.1007/978-981-95-7394-3_36

referral programs to encourage customer acquisition, offering financial rewards to existing clients who bring in new users [14]. Similarly, in Decentralized Finance (DeFi), airdrops serve as an incentive mechanism to distribute tokens, enhance liquidity, and encourage community engagement [15]. Airdrops automate token distribution based on predefined eligibility criteria, such as wallet activity, participation in governance, or interaction with Decentralized Applications (DApps). Airdrops are not merely marketing tools but structured business workflows that encompass eligibility verification, transaction execution, fraud prevention, and compliance with economic incentive structures [13]. Their reliance on smart contracts ensures process automation and transparency [16]. However, this transparency also introduces vulnerabilities, exposing airdrops to fraudulent exploitation that disrupts their intended fairness and efficiency. Among the most severe fraudulent patterns in blockchain-based incentive mechanisms are Sybil attacks and Front-running exploits. While these threats are often studied separately, they become particularly dangerous when combined within airdrop workflows, amplifying their disruptive impact.

1. **Sybil attacks** occur when malicious actors generate multiple fake identities (wallet addresses) to artificially inflate their eligibility for an airdrop, accumulating more tokens than intended by the distribution rules [1,17].
2. **Front-running** attacks involve attackers monitoring the blockchain mempool[1] and reordering transactions to gain an unfair financial advantage [8]. This often occurs after an airdrop, when recipients attempt to trade tokens on Decentralized EXchanges (DEXs) like Uniswap[2], making them prime targets.

These two attacks present a unique threat to blockchain-based business processes. Malicious actors not only manipulate token allocation through Sybil schemes but also amplify their profits by Front-running unsuspecting traders immediately after receiving their fraudulent airdrop tokens. This exploit distorts market conditions, reduces liquidity fairness, and undermines trust in decentralized incentive mechanisms. To address these challenges, this paper introduces the Sybil-Linked Front-running Detection Framework (SLF-DF), a novel framework designed to identify and mitigate fraudulent behaviours within airdrop-driven business processes. Our approach systematically links Sybil attacks and Front-running strategies, leveraging a combination of business process intelligence and fraud detection. The core components of SLF-DF include:

- Systematic analysis of front-running transactions on Uniswap linked to Sybil-blacklisted addresses, enabling the detection of fraudulent trading behaviours.
- A structured dataset, constructed from Uniswap transaction records, associating Front-running attempts with victim interactions and normal transactions to enable robust anomaly detection.
- Machine learning-based classification, applied to the labelled dataset, to automate fraud detection and enhance the identification of Front-running patterns within airdrop workflows.

[1] https://mempool.space.
[2] https://app.uniswap.org/.

Unlike existing approaches that treat Sybil and Front-running attacks independently, SLF-DF offers a unified detection framework capable of capturing their combined impact within airdrop workflows. This approach integrates real-time transaction analysis into structured business process monitoring. By leveraging Blocknative[3], the system monitors transaction activity within the mempool, enabling early detection of Front-running patterns and their correlation with Sybil-generated wallets. The remainder of this paper is structured as follows:

- Section 2 presents airdrops as structured business processes in decentralized finance, examining their vulnerabilities to Sybil attacks and Front-running, and their impact on token distribution workflows.
- Section 3 provides an overview of Sybil attacks and Front-running behaviours within airdrop processes, discussing their impact and the limitations of existing mitigation strategies.
- Section 4 introduces SLF-DF, detailing its fraud detection mechanism, dataset construction, and Machine Learning-based classification model for identifying malicious activities.
- Section 5 concludes the paper by summarizing key findings and outlining directions for future research.

2 Background

Blockchain-based incentive mechanisms, such as airdrops, have emerged as popular tools to promote the adoption of DApps, enhance token liquidity, and foster user engagement [13,17,18]. Airdrops automate token distribution based on predefined eligibility criteria, making them scalable and transparent. However, this transparency and openness also expose airdrop mechanisms to significant vulnerabilities. Among the most critical threats are Sybil attacks, which involve the creation of multiple fake identities to claim excessive rewards [19], and Front-running attacks, where adversaries manipulate transaction order to gain a financial advantage [8]. Combined, these two attack vectors can seriously compromise the fairness and security of token distribution processes in DeFi ecosystems.

To illustrate these vulnerabilities and the necessity of robust fraud detection mechanisms, we present below a motivating example comparing two contrasting airdrop scenarios: a legitimate airdrop distribution, and one exploited by a Sybil-based Front-running strategy. This example highlights the importance of integrating real-time fraud detection into airdrop workflows.

2.1 Motivating Example: Legitimate vs. Fraudulent Airdrop Execution

We consider two scenarios involving a token airdrop campaign conducted by a DeFi project.

[3] https://www.blocknative.com/.

Scenario A Legitimate Airdrop Execution. A DeFi platform distributes 1000 tokens to users who have not interacted previously with the smart contract, in order to attract new participants. Alice, a newly onboarded user, qualifies under this criterion and receives her 1000 tokens. Shortly afterwards, she sells her tokens on a DEX (Uniswap) at a market rate of 0.5 USDC[4] per token, expecting to receive 500 USDC. The transaction is executed normally, and Alice receives the expected amount, demonstrating a fair and efficient token distribution mechanism.

Scenario B Airdrop Exploited by Sybil and Front-Running Attacks. An attacker, Eve, exploits the absence of identity verification by creating 100 Sybil addresses that have never interacted with the smart contract, making them eligible under the same rules. Each address receives 1000 tokens, totalling 100,000 tokens fraudulently claimed. Immediately after the airdrop, Eve monitors the Ethereum mempool using a bot. Upon detecting Alice's sell order, Eve promptly coordinates sell orders from her Sybil wallets, submitting them with higher gas fees to ensure priority execution through Front-running

As Eve's transactions execute first, the token price on Uniswap drops from 0.5 to 0.3 USDC. When Alice's transaction is finally executed, she only receives 300 USDC instead of 500, incurring a loss of 200 USDC due to slippage caused by the attacker's aggressive token dumping.

Observed Consequences.

- **Price Manipulation:** Eve's Front-running actions distort token pricing on the exchange.
- **Increased Slippage:** Honest users like Alice receive less value due to liquidity depletion.
- **Unfair Profit:** The attacker, like Eve, extracts value through both Sybil-based eligibility abuse and transaction reordering.
- **Loss of Trust:** Such attacks undermine user confidence in airdrop mechanisms and DeFi platforms.
- **Reduced Participation:** Perceived unfairness may discourage future engagement.

This scenario is far from hypothetical. Airdrops have historically been prime targets for Sybil exploitation. For instance, the 2020 Uniswap airdrop faced criticism for an unbalanced token distribution that favoured a small number of addresses [12]. In DeFi ecosystems like Uniswap, Sybil nodes often operate across multiple accounts using coordinated transactions to manipulate liquidity and token prices [11]. These fraudulent behaviours underscore the need for enhanced detection mechanisms to preserve the integrity of token distribution processes.

These real-world incidents highlight the growing threat posed by fraudulent activity in airdrop-based incentives. Two particularly damaging strategies, Sybil

[4] https://www.coinhouse.com/usdc.

attacks and Front-running, undermine the fundamental fairness and security principles of decentralized financial systems.

To gain a deeper understanding of these vulnerabilities and simulate fraudulent behaviour programmatically, we provide below a formalized version of the airdrop process. The following pseudocode models both legitimate participants and adversarial actors exploiting Sybil identities and transaction-ordering attacks.

Process Abstraction of the Airdrop Scenarios. To better understand the internal dynamics of both scenarios and model the interactions between legitimate users and Sybil attackers, we present a simplified algorithm that captures the essential process logic. The goal is to abstract the eligibility verification, token distribu-

Algorithm . Airdrop Execution Under Legitimate and Fraudulent Conditions

```
Input: User list 𝒰, Token amount T, Gas threshold ε, Blacklisted attacker
  addresses 𝒜, Pending swap transactions 𝒫
Output: Labeled transaction set 𝒯_exec (each labeled as front_run, victim, or
  normal)
//Initialize the output set of executed transactions
𝒯_exec ← ∅
// Step 1: Token Distribution Phase
for all u ∈ 𝒰 do
    //Eligibility: only users with no prior contract interaction
    if u.activity = 0 then
        u.balance ← u.balance + T
    end if
end for
// Step 2: Swap Execution and Front-running Labelling
for all tx ∈ 𝒫 do
    //Attacker transaction detected via gas bidding
    if tx.sender ∈ 𝒜 and tx.gas > VictimTx.gas + ε then
        //Token price decreases due to front-run execution
        Price ← Price − Impact(tx.amount)
        tx.label ← "front_run"
        VictimTx.label ← "victim"
        ExecuteTransaction(tx)
        ExecuteTransaction(VictimTx)
        //Both transactions are executed with updated prices
        𝒯_exec ← 𝒯_exec ∪ {tx, VictimTx}
    else
        //No front-running detected, normal execution
        tx.label ← "normal"
        ExecuteTransaction(tx)
        𝒯_exec ← 𝒯_exec ∪ {tx}
    end if
end for
return 𝒯_exec
```

tion, and swap transaction prioritization phases, especially in the presence of gas-based Front-running tactics.

Explanation. This algorithm simulates the behaviour of an airdrop distribution system under both normal and adversarial conditions. It begins by allocating tokens only to users who have no prior interaction history, following the eligibility criterion described in Scenario A. Each user meeting this condition receives a predefined token amount T.

After distribution, the algorithm processes pending swap transactions. If a transaction originates from a known attacker address and includes a gas fee significantly higher than a corresponding victim transaction (`VictimTx`), it is labelled as `front_run`, and the corresponding victim's transaction is labelled as `victim`. The attacker's transaction is executed first, affecting the token price through slippage before the victim's transaction is processed. This reflects the dynamics observed in Scenario B.

All other transactions that do not meet these conditions are labelled as `normal` and are executed without interference. The final output, $\mathcal{T}_{\text{exec}}$, is a labelled set of executed transactions that captures the effect of Sybil-driven front-running on token trading behaviour.

Due to the high volatility of airdrop-related transactions, these scenarios are particularly vulnerable to Front-running attacks. This highlights the need for effective detection strategies, which we examine in Sect. 3.

3 Related Works

In recent years, extensive research has been conducted to address security and efficiency challenges within blockchain networks, focusing on mitigating Sybil attacks and Front-running behaviours. Among these threats, Sybil attacks pose a serious risk to the security and decentralization of blockchain systems. Originally discussed by [2], a Sybil attack involves creating multiple fake identities controlled by a single malicious entity. This strategy allows an adversary to gain disproportionate influence within the network, undermining its consensus mechanisms by manipulating transaction validation processes. Bonneau et al. [3] provides a comprehensive analysis of cryptocurrency vulnerabilities, specifically focusing on Sybil attacks and illustrating how they can damage blockchain governance by compromising decision-making within consensus protocols. Through the use of multiple nodes, attackers can threaten network integrity, destabilizing the decentralized nature of blockchain environments. Conti et al. [4] further investigate security risks within blockchain ecosystems, examining the broader implications of Sybil attacks in Bitcoin and other cryptocurrencies. Their research shows that Sybil nodes can manipulate transactions and enable attacks, notably the 51% attack, where one entity controls most of the network's hash power. An innovative approach to countering Sybil attacks is presented in [1], where the authors propose a decentralized method for monitoring miner behaviour to prevent Sybil activity. This approach highlights how adversaries could deploy Sybil nodes to disrupt block propagation and reduce network efficiency. Sybil attacks are also prominent in cryptocurrency airdrops, where attackers exploit multiple fake accounts to claim a disproportionate share of tokens. To address this challenge, recent research like [11] has explored advanced detection techniques. For instance, graph analysis methods have been proposed to analyze user interactions and identify suspicious patterns. One such method, as tested on the Hop protocol, leverages algorithms like DBSCAN to group accounts exhibiting Sybil-like behaviour. While this approach has proven effective, it remains reliant on existing data. Future improvements, such as integrating external data sources, are suggested to enhance the reliability and fairness of airdrops. These efforts underline the growing importance of securing airdrop mechanisms as a critical part of blockchain ecosystems [11]. Closely associated with Sybil attacks, Front-running is a form of arbitrage in which attackers anticipate transactions before their confirmation, capitalizing on privileged information. This issue is particularly prevalent in public blockchains like Ethereum, where transaction transparency enables actors to manipulate pricing structures for financial gain. In the context of DeFi, [5] discusses how DeFi is changing financial ecosystems by eliminating intermediaries. However, despite its benefits, DeFi introduces security concerns, as Front-running attacks may lead to considerable financial losses and compromise ecosystem stability. In their examination of Front-running, Daian et al. [6] introduce the concept of Maximum Extractable Value (MEV), defined as the maximum profit a miner can extract by re-ordering transactions within a block. This practice has become a disrupting factor in decentralized networks, as it encourages miners who have early access to transactional information. Zhang et al. [7] also address Front-running within smart contracts, where adversaries anticipate transactions by monitoring contract interactions. Their research proposes an attack model that analyzes historical transactions to identify large-scale vulnerabilities, resulting in a benchmark of 513 attacks and 235 vulnerable contracts. Their findings highlight significant limitations in existing detection tools, which currently achieve a low recall rate of at most 6.04%. This work underscores the need for improved security measures, potentially by limiting transaction transparency or delaying visibility until confirmation. Recent research has increasingly focused on employing machine learning techniques to detect Sybil attacks and Front-running practices in blockchain networks. Eskandari et al. [8] propose real-time detection strategies for Front-running in public blockchains, analyzing pending transactions to identify malicious behaviours and enabling rapid intervention. Similarly, [9,10] leverage machine learning models, such as MultiLayer Perceptrons (MLP), to classify suspicious transactions in real-time, achieving accuracy rates of 84.59% and 85%, respectively. These methods incorporate specific transaction features to create feature vectors that facilitate the identification of malicious transactions, and some utilize models like Long Short-Term Memory (LSTM) networks to predict gas prices. However, these methods do not yet address interactions between Sybil addresses and arbitrage strategies, such as Front-running, leaving a gap for future exploration.

Research Scope:

While Sybil attacks and Front-running are widely studied as independent threats to blockchain security, their combined impact within business process workflows, particularly in cryptocurrency airdrops, remains largely unexplored. Sybil nodes not only manipulate token allocation but also engage in Front-running strategies to maximize financial gains from token swaps. This interplay creates workflow anomalies that compromise efficiency, compliance, and trust in DeFi. The convergence of these fraudulent behaviours introduces systemic inefficiencies, highlighting the need for real-time fraud detection mechanisms. Traditional security models fail to account for the dynamic interactions between Sybil-generated wallets and transaction sequencing anomalies, leaving decentralized workflows vulnerable to manipulation. To address these challenges, Sect. 4 presents SLF-DF, a hybrid fraud detection framework that systematically analyzes Sybil-blacklisted addresses, monitors Front-running behaviours, and strengthens security in decentralized business processes.

4 Proposed Approach

To counter Sybil-based Front-running in airdrops, we introduce SLF-DF, a fraud detection framework combining blockchain data analysis and machine learning. It systematically identifies Sybil addresses, tracks their trading patterns, and detects Front-running attempts through three layers: Blockchain Data Layer (data collection), Data Analysis Layer (behavioural insights), and Machine Learning Layer (fraud classification).

The three-layered architecture operates sequentially, where the Blockchain Data Layer extracts raw transaction data and Sybil-labelled addresses. This data is passed to the Analysis Layer, which applies heuristics to identify behavioural features such as gas anomalies and transaction ordering. Finally, the Machine Learning Layer consumes the structured and labelled dataset to perform binary classification for Front-running detection.

4.1 Architecture of the Proposed Approach: SLF-DF

To address Sybil-based Front-running behaviours, we introduce in Fig. 1 a structured detection framework integrating blockchain data collection, transaction analysis, and machine learning techniques. This approach systematically identifies Sybil-generated addresses, tracks their transactional behaviours, and detects Front-running attempts. The framework is organized into three main layers: the Blockchain Data Layer, the Data Analysis Layer, and the Machine Learning Layer.

Blockchain Data Layer. This layer is responsible for constructing a structured dataset of DEX swap transactions, enabling the identification of high-risk Front-running activities. We analyze a pool of blacklisted Sybil addresses and track

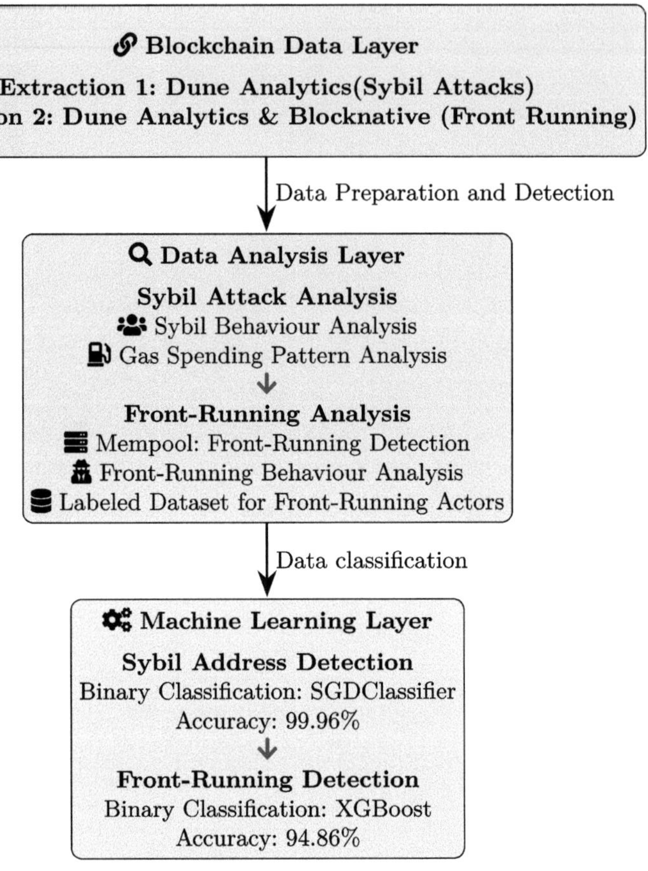

Fig. 1. SLF-DF Approach

their swap transactions on platforms like Uniswap. The data is extracted from two main sources:

- **Dune Analytics**[5] provides structured SQL-based blockchain queries to retrieve:
  - A list of blacklisted Sybil addresses.
  - Transaction data from DEXs.
  - High-activity periods of targeted addresses in trading environments.

- **Blocknative** is a platform that provides real-time and historical transaction data from the Ethereum mempool. It plays a crucial role in analyzing transaction sequencing and detecting anomalies in blockchain-based trading activities. Blocknative enables:

[5] https://dune.com.

- Tracking transaction arrival times in the mempool to analyze execution priority.
- Monitoring gas fees to identify cost manipulation strategies.
- Analyzing transaction propagation and validation order to detect front-running attempts.

Extraction 1: Sybil Detection Dataset We utilized an open-source dataset published on GitHub[6], derived from Dune Analytics queries. This dataset identified 2,663 Sybil addresses from an initial pool of over 300,000 wallets. These addresses were flagged based on behavioural indicators relevant to Sybil detection.

Gas Spending Patterns in Sybil Attacks. One of the most distinctive characteristics of Sybil wallets is their gas spending behaviour. Our analysis reveals a significant discrepancy in gas expenditures between Sybil and non-Sybil addresses, as illustrated by the results below:

- Sybil addresses spend an average of 0.133882 ETH on gas.
- Non-Sybil addresses spend significantly less, averaging 0.008072 ETH.
- Sybil transactions exhibit gas expenditures that are 16.6 times higher than non-Sybil transactions, indicating a deliberate strategy to prioritize execution and gain an unfair advantage.

This leads us to formulate a key hypothesis in our research: *"The high gas expenditure of Sybil addresses suggests a direct link to Front-running activities"*.

Since Front-running actors prioritize transaction execution by bidding higher gas fees, Sybil nodes may leverage this tactic to gain priority in transaction sequencing, maximizing their arbitrage opportunities. However, detecting Front-running behaviours among Sybil addresses presents multiple challenges, particularly due to the lack of structured datasets specifically capturing Sybil-based Front-running transactions.

Extraction 2: Front-Running Detection Dataset. To investigate Front-running activities, we expanded the scope of blacklisted addresses, incorporating additional flagged wallets engaged in suspicious trading behaviours. Unlike Extraction 1, which focused solely on Sybil address identification, this step aims to identify Front-running transactions by analyzing a broader set of blacklisted addresses involved in manipulative trading strategies.

Following a Dune Analytics query[7] targeting Sybil-blacklisted addresses, we focused our analysis on three peak activity dates: January 15, 2024, which recorded the highest volume of Sybil-driven fraudulent trading; January 18, 2024, which marked the second-highest peak; and January 13, 2024, which represented an earlier surge used for comparative purposes. By including multiple high-activity periods in our dataset, we aimed to capture a broader spectrum

[6] https://github.com/LimaRods/Sybil-Detection--.git.
[7] https://dune.com/queries/5188948/8538918.

of fraudulent trading behaviours, emphasising Sybil-linked Front-running activities.

- **Mempool Analysis for Front-Running Detection:** To further analyze execution patterns, we leveraged Blocknative to examine mempool activity for transactions extracted via Dune Analytics. This approach enabled us to:
  - Track transaction propagation within specific timeframes.
  - Analyze transaction sequencing, focusing on arrival times, gas fees, and execution orders in the mempool.
  - Identify Front-running indicators, validating our hypothesis that fraudulent wallets leverage gas bidding strategies to execute Front-running attacks.

Combining on-chain transaction data from Dune Analytics with mempool-level analysis from Blocknative, we constructed a dataset capable of capturing both Sybil-driven and non-Sybil Front-running behaviours. This structured dataset serves as the foundation for detecting coordinated fraudulent trading activities within DeFi ecosystems, providing deeper insights into how blacklisted addresses manipulate token swaps through Front-running strategies.

Data Analysis Layer. The Data Analysis Layer processes extracted transactions to detect Sybil activities and Front-running behaviours.

- **Sybil Behavior Analysis** Gas spending anomalies serve as a key indicator of fraudulent Sybil activities. Sybil addresses consistently exhibit significantly higher gas expenditures than legitimate users, reinforcing their involvement in aggressive Front-running strategies.
- **Front-Running Behavior Analysis** This phase detects Front-running patterns within swap transactions. To identify a Front-running event, we apply four key detection criteria:
  - **Confirmation Timing** The Front-running transaction is confirmed before the victim's but within 300 s[8].
  - **Token Quantity Discrepancy** The attacker buys a higher quantity than the victim (slippage manipulation).
  - **Token Consistency** Both transactions involve the same token pair.
  - **Mempool Order Manipulation** The attacker's transaction arrives first in the mempool, ensuring priority execution.
- **Final Dataset Labeled by Front-Running Actors** After applying these filters, our final labelled dataset contains 42990 transactions, including:
  - 40641 normal transactions.
  - 1417 confirmed Front-running transactions.
  - 932 victim transactions.

[8] Cryptomus: Secure Crypto Payments and Transactions.

This dataset provides the basis for fraud detection in decentralized token distribution workflows. By combining domain-specific transaction filtering, heuristic-based anomaly detection, and structured data validation, the proposed framework improves detection accuracy while maintaining system integrity. Machine learning is incorporated as an enhancement layer to strengthen fraud identification and generalization. This hybrid approach offers a scalable and adaptive solution for mitigating risks in DeFi ecosystems by embedding detection logic directly into the transaction analysis pipeline.

Machine Learning Layer. To detect fraudulent transactions, we apply binary classification models, ensuring high precision and recall in identifying Sybil addresses and Front-running transactions.

Sybil Address Detection Performance. We utilized an SGDClassifier to classify Sybil vs non-Sybil addresses. The model achieved:

- Accuracy: 99.96% → Reliable Sybil detection with minimal errors.
- F1-score: 98% → Strong balance between precision and recall, ensuring high detection of Sybil addresses while minimizing false positives and false negatives.

Front-Running Detection Performance. We employed an XGBoost[9] binary classifier trained on our structured dataset to classify Front-running transactions. The model achieved strong predictive performance across all transaction classes.

As shown in Fig. 2a, the ROC[10] curves demonstrate high discriminative capability, with an AUC[11] of 0.98 for Front-running transactions and 0.92 for both

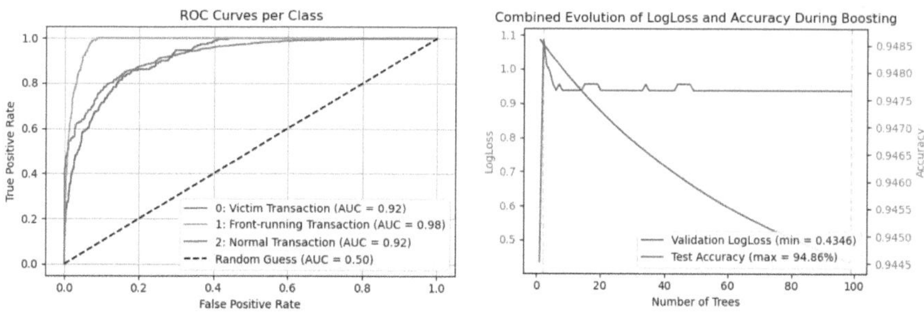

(a) ROC curves for each transaction class. (b) XGBoost training performance (LogLoss and Test Accuracy).

Fig. 2. XGBoost performance: ROC curves (Subfig. (a)) and training convergence (Subfig. (b)).

9 https://xgboost.ai/.

10 Receiver Operating Characteristic.

11 Area Under the Curve.

victim and normal transactions. The diagonal line corresponds to a random classifier (AUC = 0.5) and serves as a baseline, emphasizing the model's superior predictive performance. Additionally, Fig. 2b illustrates the learning behaviour of the model over boosting iterations, showing stable convergence with decreasing log-loss and steadily increasing accuracy. The model reaches its highest test accuracy of 94.86% as early as the fourth iteration, confirming fast and effective learning dynamics while maintaining strong generalization capability.

XGBoost proves effective in detecting front-running behaviors with strong generalization to unseen data. Its reliability is reinforced by consistent performance across transaction types, though normal transactions remain easier to identify due to stable gas usage and timing. Detecting minority classes may benefit from the future use of oversampling or ensemble methods.

Front-Running Execution Speed Analysis: A Case Study on 1222 Transactions from January 15, 2024 .

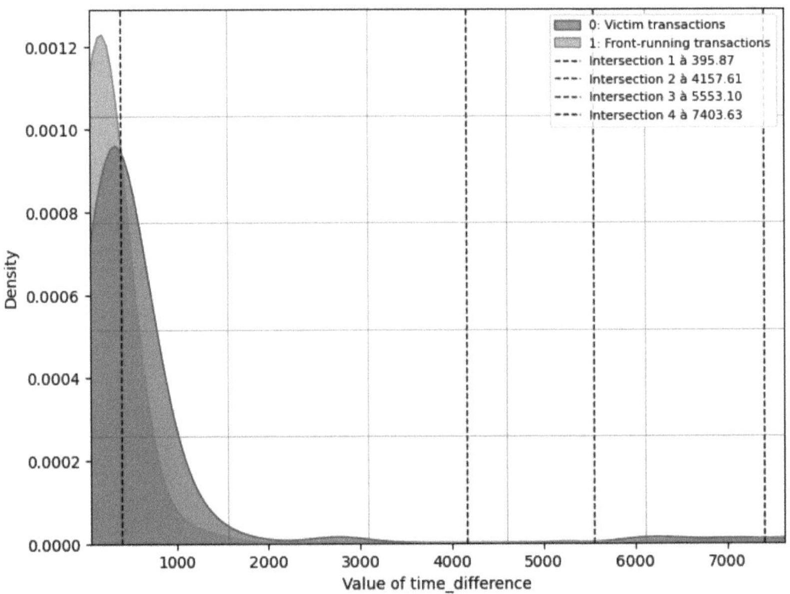

Fig. 3. Distribution of Transaction Execution Times for Front-Running Detection.

Figure 3 and Table 1 illustrate the time difference between:

- Front-running transactions (Group 1): Executed quickly after submission.
- Victim transactions (Group 0): Show a longer, more variable execution time.

Table 1. Descriptive Statistics of the Dataset

Index	Count	Mean	Std Dev	Min	25%	50%	75%	Max
0	416	3503.8197	10161.7658	15.0	80.0	205.5	537.25	42165.0
1	806	173.5558	1545.7112	0.0	6.0	10.0	24.0	27114.0

Key Observations

- Front-runners optimize execution timing, minimizing delays.
- Victim transactions take longer, making them vulnerable to reordering.

This pattern confirms that Front-running is characterized by rapid execution, allowing attackers to exploit token price changes.

4.2 Discussion and Insights

The results confirm the feasibility of combining Sybil detection with Front-running classification to improve fraud prevention in decentralized finance. Our approach demonstrates:

- Higher detection accuracy, leveraging structured process analysis for identifying Sybil-based Front-running.
- Better generalization, ensuring reliable fraud detection across different trading conditions.
- Scalability, as transaction behaviours evolve, our machine learning framework can be adapted to identify new fraud patterns.

These insights highlight the importance of integrating business process monitoring with machine learning-based fraud detection, offering a novel approach to securing airdrop workflows in DeFi.

5 Conclusion

Airdrops are an economic incentive mechanism designed to promote cryptocurrency adoption and encourage user participation in DeFi ecosystems. However, the lack of robust identity verification makes them vulnerable to fraudulent exploitation. One of the most prevalent fraudulent behaviours involves the combined use of Sybil and Front-running attacks, disrupting fair token distribution. To address these challenges, we introduced SLF-DF, a fraud detection framework that integrates airdrop business process analysis with blockchain monitoring to systematically identify Sybil-linked Front-running transactions. By leveraging structured datasets and Machine Learning, SLF-DF improves fraud detection accuracy while maintaining process integrity. From a business process perspective, strengthening anomaly detection mechanisms can enhance fraud mitigation in airdrop workflows.

Future work will focus on enhancing behavioural fraud detection through intent-based analysis, enabling the identification of strategic manipulation patterns in decentralized incentive systems.

References

1. Swathi, P., Modi, C., Patel, D.: Preventing Sybil attack in blockchain using distributed behavior monitoring of miners. In: 10th International Conference on Computing, Communication and Networking Technologies (ICCCNT), pp. 1-6. IEEE (2019)
2. Douceur, J.R.: The Sybil attack. In: International Workshop on Peer-to-Peer Systems, pp. 251–260. Springer (2002)
3. Bonneau, J., Miller, A., Clark, J., Narayanan, A., Kroll, J.A., Felten, E.W.: SoK: research perspectives and challenges for Bitcoin and cryptocurrencies. In: IEEE Symposium on Security Privacy, pp. 104–121. IEEE (2015)
4. Conti, M., Kumar, E.S., Lal, C., Ruj, S.: A survey on security and privacy issues of Bitcoin. IEEE Commun. Surv. Tutor. **20**(4), 3416–3452 (2018)
5. Alam, T., Ali, M.A., Rahman, M.H., et al.: Front-running attack in decentralized finance in the metaverse: a systematic review. Int. J. Sci. Res. Arch. **11**(1), 2315–2324 (2024)
6. Daian, P., et al.: Flash boys 2.0: front-running, transaction reordering, and consensus instability in decentralized exchanges. arXiv preprint arXiv:1904.05234 (2019)
7. Zhang, W., et al.: Combatting front-running in smart contracts: attack mining, benchmark construction, and vulnerability detector evaluation. IEEE Trans. Softw. Eng. **49**(6), 3630–3646 (2023)
8. Eskandari, S., Moosavi, S., Clark, J.: SoK: transparent dishonesty: front-running attacks on blockchain. In: Financial Cryptography and Data Security: FC 2019 International Workshops, pp. 170–189. Springer (2020)
9. Maddipati, V., Palanisamy, B., Sural, S.: Mitigating front-running attacks in Ethereum. In: Proceedings of the 4th ACM International Symposium on Blockchain and Secure Critical Infrastructure, pp. 115–124 (2022)
10. Zhang, Y., et al.: FRAD: front-running attacks detection on Ethereum using a ternary classification model. In: International Conference on Ubiquitous Security, pp. 63–75. Springer (2023)
11. Liu, Z., Zhu, H.: Fighting Sybils in airdrops. arXiv preprint arXiv:2209.04603 (2022)
12. Allen, D.: Crypto airdrops: an evolutionary approach. J. Evol. Econ. 1–24 (2024)
13. Allen, D., Berg, C., Lane, A.: Why airdrop cryptocurrency tokens? J. Bus. Res. **163**, 113945 (2023)
14. Yan, Z., Liang, X., Yang, L.: How can incentive mechanisms and blockchain benefit each other? A survey. ACM Comput. Surv. **55**(6), 1–35 (2022). https://doi.org/10.1145/3539604
15. Smajgl, A., Schweik, C.: Advancing sustainability with blockchain-based incentives and institutions. Front. Blockchain **5**, 963766 (2022)
16. Chikov, I., Koliadenko, S., Supryhan, V., Tabenska, O., Nitsenko, V., Holinko, O.: Smart contracts and business process automation: the technical aspect. Naukovyi Visnyk Natsionalnoho Hirnychoho Universytetu **2023**(5), 186–192 (2023). https://doi.org/10.33271/nvngu/2023-5/186
17. Messias, J., Yaish, A., Livshits, B.: Airdrops: giving money away is harder than it seems. arXiv preprint arXiv:2312.02752 (2023)

18. Yaish, A., Livshits, B.: TierDrop: harnessing airdrop farmers for user growth. arXiv preprint arXiv:2407.01176 (2024)
19. Siddarth, D., Ivliev, S., Siri, S., Berman, P.: Who watches the watchmen? A review of subjective approaches for Sybil-resistance in proof-of-personhood protocols. arXiv preprint arXiv:2401.03267 (2008)

Sentiment Analysis and Classification

EmoCIE: Emotion-Cause Identification with Intensity Estimation

Joseph Schmidt[1], Anthony Romano[1], Ademola Adesokan[2], and Sanjay Madria[1(✉)]

[1] Missouri University of Science and Technology, Rolla, MO 65401, USA
{jpshkt,adrgpz,madrias}@mst.edu
[2] University of Central Arkansas, Conway, AR 72035, USA
aadesokan@uca.edu

Abstract. Understanding emotions in text is crucial for applications in various domains, including mental health, microeconomics, social media analysis, and human-computer interaction. However, most systems focus only on classifying emotions, overlooking their underlying causes and the intensity with which they are felt. We introduce EmoCIE, a 3-step framework that performs emotion classification, cause extraction, and intensity estimation. The model extends a transformer-based architecture with optimized thresholds and integrates sentence embeddings for semantic reasoning, as well as a psychological lexicon (VAD) for modeling emotion strength. Across three benchmark baselines, including GoEmotions, HatEmoTweet, and NeuEmot, our approach outperforms state-of-the-art models in both high-resource and low-resource emotion categories. Our findings reveal that combining cause and intensity signals enhances accuracy and interpretability. Additional analysis shows alignment between emotion strength and model confidence. This work provides (1) a comprehensive model linking emotional labels to their causes and strength, (2) a psychologically informed method for estimating emotional intensity, (3) a novel interpretability framework that connects confidence with emotional reasoning, and (4) empirical results validating the model's improved performance and transparency over prior approaches. Our code is publicly available at https://github.com/ademola1802/EmoCIE.

Keywords: Social Media · Emotion Classification · Cause Extraction · Emotion Intensity Estimation · Interpretability · Transformer Models · Affective Computing

1 Introduction

In today's digital landscape, users are increasingly expressing emotions across various platforms, including social media, online forums, and mental health applications. Understanding these emotions and their underlying causes is pivotal for numerous applications, including mental health support, sentiment-aware recommendation systems, and social behavior modeling [1,2]. While significant progress has been made in emotion detection using transformer-based

I. Awan et al. (Eds.): WISE 2025, LNCS 16367, pp. 541–566, 2026.
https://doi.org/10.1007/978-981-95-7394-3_37

models [3,4], existing frameworks often treat emotion as a categorical output, neglecting the intensity or explanation behind such expressions.

Emotion-Cause Pair Extraction (ECPE) has emerged as a solution to link emotions with their causes; however, many ECPE models operate under rigid constraints, lack generalizability to informal text [5], or focus solely on classification without providing context [6]. Furthermore, most frameworks do not model the strength of emotions or provide interpretable justifications for predictions, an issue critical for real-world, high-stakes domains.

Modeling emotional intensity enables systems to distinguish between subtle sentiments and urgent psychological states (e.g., sadness vs. despair), which is crucial for early intervention in mental health settings or prioritizing the moderation of toxic content [7]. Equally important is interpretability, especially in domains such as mental health or legal analytics, where transparency is essential for trust and accountability [8]. Current approaches fall short by offering black-box predictions without insight into why specific emotional labels are assigned or whether the causes align semantically and psychologically.

Domains such as mental health diagnostics [9], COVID-related public health communication [10], and hate speech detection [11] benefit mostly from a holistic model that can detect multiple emotions, their causes, and their intensities, especially in noisy and user-generated contexts.

This research introduces **EmoCIE**, a 3-step, end-to-end framework designed to perform multilabel emotion classification, contextual cause span extraction, and emotion intensity estimation from user-generated texts. Unlike prior approaches, EmoCIE integrates psychologically informed metrics via the Valence–Arousal–Dominance (VAD) lexicon [12] to model emotional intensity and leverages semantic similarity techniques (Sentence-BERT and KeyBERT) to enhance cause identification.

To promote model transparency and trust, EmoCIE also incorporates novel interpretability metrics–comprehensiveness (how much the presence of a cause affects emotion prediction) and sufficiency (how predictive the cause alone is). These metrics enable a deeper examination of model behavior and the alignment between predicted emotions and underlying causes.

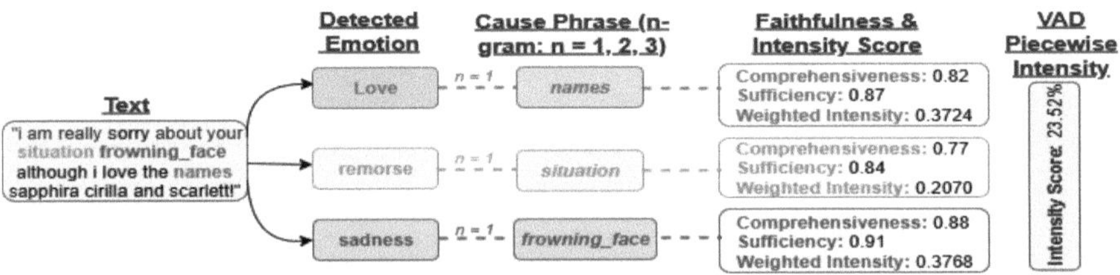

Fig. 1. Overview of EmoCIE, which links multilabel emotions to cause phrases and calculates interpretability metrics and VAD-based intensity

To illustrate, consider Fig. 1 above. It shows EmoCIE analyzing the sample sentence: *"i am really sorry about your situation frowning_face although i love the names sapphira cirilla and scarlett!"* The model detects three co-occurring multilabel emotions–*love*, *remorse*, and *sadness*–and links each to a distinct cause phrase using n-gram phrase extraction and semantic similarity modeling. For *love*, the model identifies *names* as the emotional trigger, reflecting direct linguistic positivity. This pairing yields a comprehensiveness score of 0.82 and a sufficiency score of 0.87, indicating the phrase is both essential and sufficient for accurate emotion prediction. For *remorse*, the phrase *"situation"* is contextualized by the apology *"sorry"*, serving as the underlying cause. The model assigns it a comprehensiveness score of 0.77 and a sufficiency score of 0.84, reflecting strong contextual alignment with reflective sorrow. Most notably, *sadness* is linked to the *frowning_face*, a paralinguistic cue that intensifies emotional negativity. This cause yields the highest interpretability scores with a comprehensiveness of 0.88, sufficiency of 0.91, and a VAD-based intensity score of 23.52%, demonstrating EmoCIE's ability to correlate symbolic cues with psychological affect strength. On average, the cause phrases achieve a comprehensiveness score of 0.82 and a sufficiency score of 0.87, indicating that identified causes are both informative and predictive across emotions.

This example highlights the need for systems like EmoCIE, which combine multilabel emotion detection, cause reasoning, and psychologically grounded intensity modeling within a combined, interpretable framework.

The key contributions of our work are as follows:

- We introduce **EmoCIE**, a 3-step NLP-based framework that performs multi-label emotion classification, cause span extraction, and emotion intensity estimation within a scalable architecture.
- The model integrates psychologically grounded emotion modeling using VAD dimensions [12], alongside semantic-based intensity scoring via Sentence-BERT [25], enabling the robust detection of emotional strength across various contexts.
- A novel interpretability framework is proposed, leveraging n-gram-based faithfulness metrics (comprehensiveness and sufficiency) and a quadrant-based alignment of model confidence and emotional salience to assess the transparency of reasoning.
- Extensive experiments on the GoEmotions [3], HatEmoTweet [11], and NeuEmot [4] benchmarks demonstrate that **EmoCIE** consistently outperforms prior methods in both high-resource and low-resource emotion categories, with up to 27–55% absolute F1 gain in sparse-label classes such as *grief*, *pride*, and *remorse*, and achieving state-of-the-art macro-F1 scores under both neutral-included and neutral-removed conditions.
- Our findings illustrate that removing the neutral class and incorporating cause-aware prediction significantly improves model recall, coverage, and performance on ambiguous emotional categories, affirming the framework's practical utility for affective computing tasks.

2 Related Work

Recent research in affective computing has made strides in recognizing emotions and linking them to their causes. Emotion-cause analysis has seen substantial innovation in recent years. However, most existing methods are either narrowly focused, limited to emotion classification and/or cause detection, or constrained by domain specificity, weak interpretability, or lack of intensity modeling. Table 1 summarizes different existing key approaches and introduces how EmoCIE bridges many of these gaps by offering an explainable, and psychologically grounded framework for multi-label emotion detection, cause identification, and emotion intensity estimation.

Table 1. Comparative Summary of Emotion-Cause Models

Model	Emotion Detection Method	Cause Extraction Approach	Interpretability Features	Key Limitation
RSTIAG [5]	Discourse-based rhetorical analysis	Inference-aware graph networks	Symbolic reasoning	Requires structured rhetorical data
DeCoDE [9]	Multimodal (BERT + audio/visual)	Contextual Fourier Transformers	Cross-modal attention	Needs future dialogue, which limits real-time use
EMOCOV [10]	Multi-headed BiLSTM	Phrase extraction via RoBERTa-QA	COVID-specific visual dashboard	Domain-limited to COVID-19 tweets and phrases might not equate to causes
ECPE [6]	BiLSTM-based multi-task	Emotion-cause pair filtering	None	Error propagation in a two-step process
CENTER [13]	Graph neural network	Center-event detection and reasoning	Event-focused graph modeling	Requires annotated conversational structures
GoEmotions [3]	BERT with 27-class labeling	None	Emotion taxonomy	No causal inference or intensity modeling
HatEmoTweet [11]	RoBERTa + topic modeling	None	Spatio-temporal trend analysis	No emotion-cause linking
N2NCause [14]	Hierarchical Transformer	Contrastive learning	Mental health dataset augmentation	Lacks intensity and explainability
CauERC [15]	2D Window Transformer	Bidirectional reasoning	Causal entailment	Limited generalization to unstructured text
NeuEmot [4]	RoBERTa (neutral reclassification)	None	Neutral sentiment filtering	No causal detection or interpretability techniques
LAED [16]	LSTM-based encoder-decoder	OCC emotion model	Temporal emotional shift tracking	Depends on handcrafted lexicons
ECCTE [17]	Span-based tagging + classifiers	Triplet extraction	Fine-grained triplets	Relies on category-specific cues
EmoCIE (Our Approach)	RoBERTa-based multi-label model	SBERT + KeyBERT + VAD metrics	Comprehensiveness, sufficiency, and intensity (VAD)	A simple causal extraction and explainable metrics (faithfulness assessment) with domain-generalizable

For example, RSTIAG [5] employs rhetorical structure theory and symbolic inference for emotion-cause pair extraction; however, it is constrained by its dependency on structured discourse, which does not generalize to informal texts, such as social media. Similarly, DeCoDE [9] adopts a robust multimodal approach that incorporates text, audio, and visual cues, but it depends heavily on future dialogue context, making it unsuitable for real-time applications.

EMOCOV [10] utilizes BiLSTM and RoBERTa for fine-grained emotion analysis of COVID-19 tweets, but its domain-specific design limits its applicability. ECPE [6] and ECCTE [17] offer multi-task and span-level triplet extraction, respectively. However, their multi-step and category-dependent mechanisms introduce errors and hinder generalizability.

In conversational AI, CENTER [13] and CauERC [15] utilize graph reasoning and causal entailment for emotion-cause linking; nevertheless, neither incorporates emotion intensity or broader semantic grounding. Classification-focused resources, such as GoEmotions [3], and transformer models, like NeuEmot [4], offer broad emotion coverage but lack causal explanations and interpretability.

Other specialized models, such as HatEmoTweet [11] and N2NCause [14], explore hate speech analysis and mental health causality, respectively, but fall short in modeling emotional intensity or providing psychologically grounded metrics. Similarly, LAED [16] focuses on emotional volatility in Weibo posts but relies on handcrafted lexicons, which limits its adaptability.

By contrast, EmoCIE unifies emotion classification (via RoBERTa), cause extraction (using Sentence-BERT and KeyBERT), and intensity modeling (with VAD lexicon scores), while integrating interpretability measures such as comprehensiveness, sufficiency, and semantic intensity alignment. This enables scalable applications across varied text sources, including clinical dialogues, social media, and user-generated content, making EmoCIE a versatile and impactful advancement in the field.

3 Our Approach

EmoCIE operates through a three-step pipeline: (1) multi-label emotion classification, (2) contextual cause span extraction, and (3) emotion intensity estimation. Each component is modular yet synergistic, allowing the model to analyze user-generated content holistically.

3.1 Emotion Classification

The emotion classification module of EmoCIE, as shown in Fig. 2, is designed to detect co-occurring emotional states in short-form, user-generated text such as social media posts. Recognizing that emotional expression is inherently subjective and often multi-faceted, this module adopts a multi-label classification paradigm, allowing multiple emotions to be assigned to a single instance. The model leverages the GoEmotions taxonomy [3], which comprises 27 fine-grained emotion categories and one neutral class. Unlike single-label or binary emotion models, this configuration enables the model to capture complex and concurrent emotional cues prevalent in noisy and informal online text.

At its core, the module employs a fine-tuned RoBERTa-based transformer [18], which encodes an input sequence $x = \{w_1, w_2, \ldots, w_n\}$ into a contextualized embedding $\mathbf{h} \in \mathbb{R}^d$, where d is the hidden size of the model (typically 768). A classification head maps this representation to a real-valued output vector

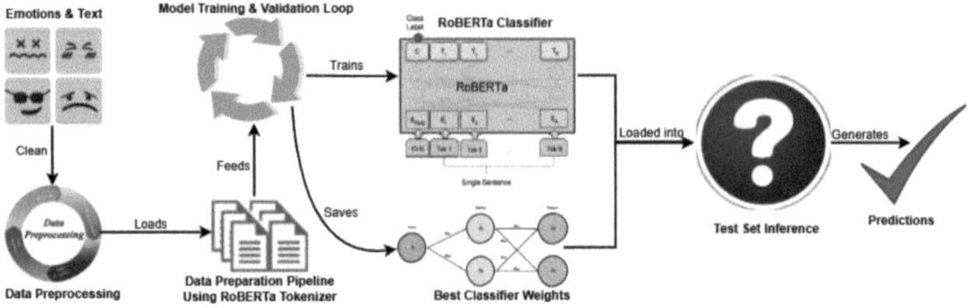

Fig. 2. EmoCIE multilabel emotions classifier

$\hat{\mathbf{y}} \in [0, 1]^K$, where $K = 28$ denotes the number of emotion classes. To support multi-label classification, a sigmoid activation is used instead of softmax:

$$\hat{y}_k = \sigma(z_k) = \frac{1}{1 + \exp(-z_k)}, \quad \text{for } k = 1, \ldots, \text{K}$$

where z_k is the logit for the k-th emotion class.

The model is trained using Binary Cross-Entropy (BCE) loss, which independently evaluates each label's prediction:

$$\mathcal{L}_{\text{BCE}} = -\frac{1}{K} \sum_{k=1}^{K} [y_k \log(\hat{y}_k) + (1 - y_k) \log(1 - \hat{y}_k)]$$

To address class imbalance and better focus on hard-to-classify examples, the BCE loss is replaced with Focal Loss [20], which adds a modulating factor to down-weight well-classified samples:

$$\mathcal{L}_{\text{Focal}} = -\frac{1}{K} \sum_{k=1}^{K} \alpha_k (1 - \hat{y}_k)^\gamma y_k \log(\hat{y}_k) + \alpha_k \hat{y}_k^\gamma (1 - y_k) \log(1 - \hat{y}_k)$$

where α_k balances class importance and γ (focusing parameter) controls the rate at which easy examples are down-weighted.

The architecture includes dropout for regularization and a linear output layer initialized with a truncated normal distribution to stabilize the training process. Tokenization is handled using `RobertaTokenizerFast`, which ensures efficient subword segmentation. To reduce memory overhead and accelerate computation, intermediate hidden states are disabled.

Before training, we preprocess the dataset, which includes pre-split and pre-cleaned training, validation, and test sets containing both raw text and corresponding one-hot encoded emotion labels. Given the informal, non-standard language prevalent on platforms such as Twitter, Reddit, and YouTube, our preprocessing pipeline plays a crucial role in enhancing model performance. The strategy includes inserting spaces between punctuation and adjacent words to support proper tokenization and converting emojis into their textual representations using Emojinet [19] *(e.g., ": 'D" or "XD" → ":face_with_tears_of_joy")* to retain semantic affective cues. We also expand contractions *(e.g., "can't" → "cannot")* using the contractions library and normalize all text to lowercase to reduce vocabulary sparsity.

Furthermore, we implement a series of handcrafted regular expressions to standardize internet slang and emotionally expressive shorthand *(e.g., "ikr" → "i know right", "idk" → "i do not know")*, aligning user-generated language with the more formal language distributions expected by pretrained transformer models. Emotionally exaggerated spellings such as *"yaaaaay"* or *"gooooal"* are normalized to canonical forms like *"yay"* and *"goal"*, preserving emotional intensity while reducing token variability. Visual emoticons are also replaced with descriptive textual equivalents *(e.g., ":)" → "smiling_face")* to ensure emotional information is preserved in text form. Additional steps include collapsing stylized spacing *(e.g., "h a m b e r d e r s" → "hamberders")*, standardizing interjections, reducing repeated punctuation to placeholders, removing non-alphabetic noise, and trimming extra whitespace, yielding semantically clean and compact inputs ready for encoding.

Processed texts are converted into tokenized tensors containing `input_ids`, `attention_mask`, and `labels`, and are wrapped into PyTorch `Dataset` and `DataLoader` objects to enable efficient batching and shuffling. The training process uses discriminative learning rates–a lower rate for the pretrained transformer layers η_{base}, and a higher rate η_{head} for the classification head:

$$\eta_{\text{head}} > \eta_{\text{base}}$$

The AdamW optimizer is used, with weight decay for regularization and a linear scheduler with warm-up to stabilize training dynamics.

Training is conducted using a mixed-precision loop to minimize memory consumption and enhance computation efficiency on GPUs. At each epoch, the model is evaluated using the macro-averaged F1 Score, and early stopping is applied based on the validation performance. The best-performing model weights are preserved and restored at the end of training to ensure generalization:

$$F1_{\text{macro}} = \frac{1}{K}\sum_{k=1}^{K} F1_k$$

To convert emotion probabilities $\hat{y}_k$ into binary predictions, a per-class thresholding strategy is applied. For each emotion class k, the threshold τ_k is selected from a range $[0.1, 0.99]$ based on which value maximizes the validation F1-score:

$$\tau_k = \arg \max_{\tau \in [0.1, 0.99]} F1_k(\tau)$$

This approach provides finer control over the trade-off between false positives and false negatives compared to applying a static threshold across all classes. It is particularly beneficial when distinguishing between frequent emotions (e.g., joy, love) and rare ones (e.g., remorse, grief). Prior studies, such as HatemoTweet [11] and NeuEmot [4], applied a fixed threshold (usually 0.5) across all labels, which often yields suboptimal results in imbalanced datasets. In contrast, our per-class tuning enhances both interpretability and classification balance, particularly in high-stakes applications such as mental health monitoring or social robotics.

For inference, the model supports batch prediction on new input texts through a dedicated prediction function, which applies the tuned thresholds and outputs the corresponding emotion labels. Additionally, for downstream interpretability and standardization, we include a mapping function that projects fine-grained GoEmotions predictions onto the broader Ekman emotion categories [21]. This enables high-level analysis or alignment with other psychological models of emotion. In cases where no emotion exceeds its threshold, the system implements a fallback mechanism, assigning the most probable emotion or defaulting to the "neutral" label to ensure complete and interpretable output.

3.2 Causal Extraction

Our causal extraction technique, as illustrated in Fig. 3, is inspired by the work of KeyMinES [22], which we designed to identify the most semantically relevant cause phrase for a given emotion expressed in raw user-generated text. This is achieved through a hybrid approach that combines unsupervised keyword extraction with semantic alignment using transformer-based models. The method operates in a zero-shot setting, i.e., it does not require annotated cause spans during training, making it suitable for domain-agnostic affective computing applications.

Following preprocessing, if the resulting input string is empty, we immediately return an empty cause string as a safeguard. Next, candidate cause phrases are extracted from the normalized text using KeyBERT. This keyword extraction method leverages BERT embeddings to score candidate phrases based on their similarity to the original input [23]. For this study, we utilize unigrams, bigrams, and trigrams (i.e., n-gram range of (1, 3)), and retrieve the top 10 most relevant and diverse keyword candidates. To ensure diversity, the Maximal Marginal Relevance (MMR) algorithm is employed, which balances relevance with diversity by penalizing redundancy among the selected phrases [24]. Formally, MMR is computed as:

$$\text{MMR} = \arg \max_{D_i \in R \setminus S} \left[\lambda \cdot \text{sim}(D_i, Q) - (1 - \lambda) \cdot \max_{D_j \in S} \text{sim}(D_i, D_j) \right]$$

where Q is the query (original text), D_i is a candidate keyword, S is the set of already selected candidates, R is the full candidate pool, and $\lambda \in [0, 1]$ (set to 0.3 in our case) is a tunable parameter that governs the relevance-diversity trade-off.

If no candidates are extracted, the function returns early. Otherwise, it retrieves the emotion prototype embedding, which represents the semantic definition of an emotion (e.g., sadness: emotional pain). These prototypes are embedded using Sentence-BERT (SBERT) [25] and stored in a lookup table for effi-

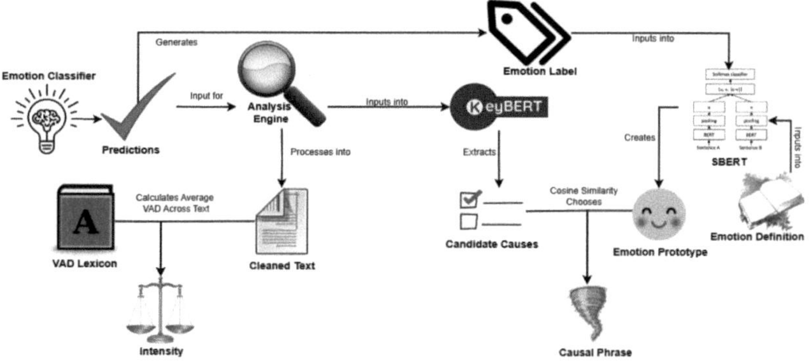

Fig. 3. EmoCIE causal and intensity model.

cient retrieval. If no prototype is found for a given emotion, an empty result is returned.

Each candidate phrase p_i is encoded using SBERT into a dense vector $\mathbf{v}_i \in \mathbb{R}^d$, where $d = 768$ is the embedding dimension. The semantic alignment between the candidate phrase and the target emotion prototype $\mathbf{v}_e$ is quantified using cosine similarity, calculated as:

$$\text{sim}(\mathbf{v}_i, \mathbf{v}_e) = \frac{\mathbf{v}_i \cdot \mathbf{v}_e}{\|\mathbf{v}_i\| \cdot \|\mathbf{v}_e\|}$$

The candidate phrase with the highest similarity score is selected as the most probable cause for the given emotion. This selection process ensures that the extracted phrase is both contextually salient (via KeyBERT) and semantically consistent with the emotional construct (via SBERT).

The resulting cause phrase is returned and typically used in a loop over the predicted emotions for a given input. This ensures that each detected emotion is aligned with a corresponding semantically plausible cause from the exact text, without the need for supervised cause-span annotations.

From a research perspective, this method offers an appealing trade-off between interpretability, scalability, and domain generalizability. By treating emotional definitions as semantic anchors and employing unsupervised keyword extraction, the system can infer plausible causes across diverse contexts. This is particularly useful in real-world applications such as mental health monitoring or social media surveillance, where gold-standard cause annotations are rarely available. Furthermore, because the system operates in embedding space, it integrates well with interpretability metrics such as comprehensiveness and sufficiency [26], which quantitatively assess the alignment between cause phrases and emotional predictions.

3.3 Intensity Estimation

The intensity estimation process is a crucial component of affective computing pipelines that aim to quantify not just the presence of emotions but their strength of expression. In this framework in Fig. 3, emotional intensity is inferred by incorporating textual content into psychological norms using the Valence-Arousal-Dominance (VAD) model [12].

To control the influence of each VAD dimension–valence (v), arousal (a), and dominance (d)–the system introduces tunable weights: w_{val}, w_{ar}, and w_{dom}. These weights can be either manually set or optimized using hyperparameter tuning frameworks, such as Optuna [27]. The default configuration uses empirically derived values (e.g., $w_{\text{val}} = 4.458$, $w_{\text{ar}} = 4.751$, and $w_{\text{dom}} = 3.362$). However, they may be adjusted based on downstream performance metrics or domain-specific needs.

Following the setup, tokenization is applied to normalize the data, and we then apply the preprocessing step explained earlier in Sect. 3.1. Each cleaned sample is then transformed into a set of tokens $T = \{t_1, t_2, ..., t_n\}$, which is primarily used for intensity scoring operations.

For intensity estimation, the system retrieves VAD values for each token $t \in T$ from the lexicon, such that each token is associated with a VAD triplet:

$$\text{VAD}(t) = (v_t, a_t, d_t)$$

The emotion intensity of a sample is computed as a weighted Euclidean distance from the neutral point $(0, 0, 0)$ in the VAD space:

$$I_{\text{raw}} = \sqrt{(w_{\text{val}} \cdot v_t)^2 + (w_{\text{ar}} \cdot a_t)^2 + (w_{\text{dom}} \cdot d_t)^2}$$

This calculation is applied to all tokens with valid VAD entries, and the final raw intensity per sample is the mean across all valid tokens:

$$I_{\text{sample}} = \frac{1}{|T'|} \sum_{t \in T'} I_{\text{raw}}(t), \quad \text{where } T' \subseteq T \text{ and VAD}(t) \text{ exists}$$

To make these raw scores interpretable across datasets, they are linearly normalized into the $[0, 100]\%$ range:

$$I_{\text{norm}} = \frac{I_{\text{sample}} - I_{\text{min}}}{I_{\text{max}} - I_{\text{min}}} \cdot 100$$

where I_{min} and I_{max} are the minimum and maximum raw intensity values in the dataset.

To further improve interpretability and distributional balance, the normalized scores undergo a piecewise-linear transformation based on intensity quartiles. This transformation aligns specific quantiles, the 25th percentile (Q_1), the median (Q_2), and the 75th percentile (Q_3) to fixed anchors (25%, 50%, 75%). The piecewise function is defined as:

$$I_{\text{piecewise}}(x) = \begin{cases} 25 \cdot \frac{x - \min}{Q_1 - \min}, & x \leq Q_1 \\ 25 + 25 \cdot \frac{x - Q_1}{Q_2 - Q_1}, & Q_1 < x \leq Q_2 \\ 50 + 25 \cdot \frac{x - Q_2}{Q_3 - Q_2}, & Q_2 < x \leq Q_3 \\ 75 + 25 \cdot \frac{x - Q_3}{\max - Q_3}, & x > Q_3 \end{cases}$$

This transformation ensures that intensities are evenly distributed while preserving ordinal semantics.

To statistically assess normality, the system employs both the D'Agostino–Pearson and Shapiro–Wilk tests [28]. In the observed output, both tests yielded very small p-values (e.g., $p < 10^{-8}$), indicating strong evidence against the null hypothesis of normality. This non-Gaussian nature is critical for downstream modeling decisions, suggesting the need for non-parametric tests or transformation strategies.

4 Experimental Setup

To evaluate the performance of the EmoCIE framework, we conducted a series of experiments without additional fine-tuning or training-specific data splits beyond those defined by existing benchmarks. All components utilized the base weights of pretrained transformer models (e.g., RoBERTa and Sentence-BERT), thereby allowing for reproducibility and setting a strong zero-shot baseline.

All experiments were conducted on a high-performance computing environment comprising a single NVIDIA Tesla A100 GPU and an Intel Xeon CPU. This setup ensured sufficient computational throughput for processing large-scale, short-form user-generated text and executing multiple inference modules in real-time. Table 2 outlines the hyperparameters employed across all components of the EmoCIE pipeline.

Table 2. Emotion Classification and Causal/Intensity Module Hyperparameters

Emotion Classification			Causal and Intensity		
Hyperparameter	Value	Description	Hyperparameter	Value	Description
MODEL_NAME	*roberta-base*	Pretrained transformer model used for emotion classification	W_VAL	*4.458*	Weight for valence in VAD-based intensity scoring
MAX_LENGTH	*256*	Maximum token length for input sequences	W_AR	*4.751*	Weight for arousal in VAD-based intensity scoring
BATCH_SIZE	*16*	Batch size for processing texts	W_DOM	*3.362*	Weight for dominance in VAD-based intensity scoring
DROPOUT_PROB	*0.3*	Dropout probability in the classification head	SBERT_MODEL	*all-MiniLM-L6-v2*	Sentence-BERT model used for semantic similarity and cause extraction

4.1 Datasets

For emotion classification and downstream tasks, we used the GoEmotions dataset [3], which contains over 58,000 user comments annotated with 27 fine-grained emotional labels (excluding neutral). These emotion labels were further mapped onto Ekman's six primary emotions–happiness, sadness, anger, fear, disgust, and surprise–to enable coarse-grained evaluation and facilitate alignment with psychological emotion theories [21].

The dataset was partitioned following the standard practice adopted in previous works, such as GoEmotions, HatEmoTweet [11], and NeuEmot [4], using an 80-10-10 split for training, development (validation), and testing, respectively.

4.2 Evaluation Metrics

Each component of the EmoCIE pipeline was evaluated using a tailored set of metrics appropriate to its function.

(a) Emotion Classification performance was measured using Precision, Recall, and F1-score at the individual label level. Additionally, macro-averaged scores were reported across sentiment groupings–positive, negative, and ambiguous–to account for the class imbalance commonly observed in emotion datasets.

(b) Cause Extraction was evaluated using interpretability-oriented metrics adapted from the faithfulness literature. These include:

- *Comprehensiveness*, which quantifies the drop in model confidence when the predicted cause phrase is removed. Mathematically, if $f(x)$ is the model's prediction on input x, and $f(x \setminus c)$ is the prediction without the cause span c, then:
$$\text{Comprehensiveness} = f(x)_e - f(x \setminus c)_e$$
- *Sufficiency*, which tests whether the cause phrase alone is enough to trigger the correct prediction. If $f(c)$ is the model output using only the cause phrase, then:
$$\text{Sufficiency} = f(c)_e$$
where e is the target emotion class.

(c) Intensity Estimation was assessed using both lexicon-based and semantic similarity methods. The VAD Intensity Score was computed by retrieving normalized Valence–Arousal–Dominance (VAD) scores $\mathbf{v}_t = (v_t, a_t, d_t)$ for each token $t \in T$ and applying a weighted Euclidean formula. The final score for a sample was the mean intensity across all valid tokens:

$$I_{\text{sample}} = \frac{1}{|T'|} \sum_{t \in T'} I_{\text{raw}}(t)$$

To complement this psychological grounding, *Semantic Intensity* was evaluated by computing the cosine similarity between Sentence-BERT embeddings of the emotion prototype vector $\mathbf{v}_e$, the extracted cause $\mathbf{v}_c$, and the overall sentence context $\mathbf{v}_x$.

4.3 Baselines for Comparison

To contextualize the performance of EmoCIE, we benchmarked its three modules against a series of competitive baselines:

- **Multi-label Emotion Classification:** We compared our results against state-of-the-art transformer models trained on GoEmotions [3], including HatEmoTweet [11] and NeuEmot [4], which employ uniform thresholding and fixed architectures.
- **Causal Extraction:** Baselines included comparisons with other deep transformer models trained to predict emotion-cause pairs without semantic alignment or interpretability constraints, often relying on n-gram keyword matching alone.
- **Intensity Modeling:** For comparison, we implemented traditional lexicon-based sentiment scoring models and semantic similarity methods (e.g., SBERT-only), which lack psychological structure or VAD-based calibration.

5 Experimental Results and Findings

In this section, we present the results of our three-step approach, which includes emotion classification, causal span extraction, and emotion intensity estimation. First, we evaluate the effectiveness of our EmoCIE framework in both fine-grained and core emotion taxonomies, demonstrating superior performance and robustness across high-and-low-resource categories. Next, we assess the quality of extracted emotion causes using alignment and overlap metrics, highlighting EmoCIE's ability to identify meaningful causal spans. Finally, we examine emotional intensity through both semantic and lexicon-based estimates, using quadrant-based analyses to explore the relationship between intensity and model confidence. These results validate the accuracy, interpretability, and emotional granularity of our proposed approach.

5.1 Emotion Classification

We evaluated EmoCIE on two benchmarks, namely, GoEmotions and Ekman, to assess its performance in multi-label emotion classification. Across both datasets, the model outperformed baselines, showing strong results in high-density emotions and notable gains in sparse or ambiguous categories. Removing the neutral label further improved recall and interpretability, confirming the model's robustness across fine-grained and core emotional classes.

5.1.1 GoEmotions Classification (with and Without Neutral)

To rigorously assess the effectiveness of the proposed EmoCIE framework, we conducted a comprehensive evaluation against several established baselines, including GoEmotions [3], HatEmoTweet [11], and NeuEmot [4]. The task was

Table 3. GoEmotion Classification for 27 + Neutral Label

Emotion	GoEmotions [3]			HatEmoTweet [11]			NeuEmot [4]			EmoCIE		
	Prec	Rec	F1	Prec	Rec	F1	Prec	Rec	F1	Prec	Rec	F1
Admiration	0.53	0.83	0.65	0.70	0.52	0.60	0.78	0.51	0.62	0.68	0.73	0.71
Amusement	0.70	0.94	0.80	0.77	0.86	0.81	0.75	0.90	0.82	0.77	0.89	0.83
Anger	0.36	0.66	0.47	0.43	0.52	0.47	0.39	0.56	0.46	0.49	0.54	0.52
Annoyance	0.24	0.63	0.34	0.40	0.17	0.24	0.31	0.21	0.25	0.32	0.49	0.39
Approval	0.26	0.57	0.36	0.47	0.25	0.33	0.81	0.15	0.26	0.52	0.37	0.43
Caring	0.30	0.56	0.39	0.35	0.37	0.36	0.35	0.56	0.43	0.52	0.41	0.46
Confusion	0.24	0.76	0.37	0.35	0.46	0.40	0.31	0.58	0.41	0.38	0.52	0.44
Curiosity	0.40	0.84	0.54	0.46	0.65	0.54	0.46	0.71	0.56	0.44	0.79	0.56
Desire	0.43	0.59	0.49	0.31	0.72	0.44	0.40	0.65	0.50	0.50	0.61	0.55
Disappointment	0.19	0.52	0.28	0.29	0.23	0.26	0.31	0.27	0.29	0.39	0.36	0.37
Disapproval	0.29	0.61	0.39	0.33	0.45	0.38	0.49	0.26	0.34	0.36	0.55	0.44
Disgust	0.34	0.66	0.45	0.32	0.60	0.42	0.30	0.69	0.42	0.44	0.63	0.52
Embarrassment	0.39	0.49	0.43	0.26	0.54	0.35	0.18	0.59	0.28	0.57	0.46	0.51
Excitement	0.26	0.52	0.34	0.26	0.59	0.36	0.27	0.57	0.37	0.51	0.42	0.46
Fear	0.46	0.85	0.60	0.44	0.83	0.57	0.39	0.86	0.53	0.75	0.69	0.72
Gratitude	0.79	0.95	0.86	0.88	0.91	0.90	0.94	0.89	0.91	0.95	0.89	0.92
Grief	0.00	0.00	0.00	0.25	0.50	0.33	0.11	0.67	0.19	0.67	0.33	0.44
Joy	0.39	0.73	0.51	0.36	0.73	0.48	0.49	0.64	0.55	0.59	0.67	0.63
Love	0.68	0.92	0.78	0.69	0.88	0.77	0.71	0.88	0.78	0.78	0.84	0.81
Nervousness	0.28	0.48	0.35	0.19	0.48	0.27	0.17	0.74	0.28	0.56	0.43	0.49
Neutral	0.56	0.84	0.68	0.65	0.49	0.56	0.62	0.59	0.60	0.63	0.78	0.69
Optimism	0.41	0.69	0.51	0.54	0.55	0.55	0.56	0.45	0.50	0.56	0.60	0.58
Pride	0.67	0.25	0.36	0.14	0.50	0.22	0.28	0.44	0.34	0.86	0.38	0.52
Realization	0.16	0.29	0.21	0.27	0.28	0.27	0.33	0.18	0.23	0.23	0.34	0.28
Relief	0.50	0.09	0.15	0.07	0.73	0.13	0.17	0.82	0.28	0.45	0.45	0.45
Remorse	0.53	0.88	0.66	0.54	0.86	0.66	0.53	0.89	0.67	0.56	0.88	0.69
Sadness	0.38	0.71	0.49	0.53	0.52	0.53	0.40	0.64	0.50	0.63	0.52	0.57
Surprise	0.40	0.66	0.50	0.44	0.65	0.53	0.40	0.63	0.49	0.56	0.60	0.58
Macro-Avg	0.40	**0.63**	0.46	0.42	0.57	0.45	0.44	0.59	0.46	**0.56**	0.58	**0.56**

framed as a multi-label emotion classification problem, utilizing an extended version of the GoEmotions dataset, which comprises 27 fine-grained emotion categories, along with a neutral label. For each model, we computed per-class precision, recall, and F1-score, as well as macro-averaged metrics, which serve as a class-agnostic indicator of overall performance, essential in imbalanced datasets.

As presented in Table 3, the performance of each model is strongly influenced by the distribution of emotion labels in the dataset. Emotions with abundant training samples, such as admiration, approval, gratitude, and amusement (each with over 10,000 examples), tend to yield higher F1-scores across all models. In these high-density and high-agreement categories, EmoCIE achieves consistently strong performance, with F1-scores of 83% for amusement, 92% for gratitude, and 71% for admiration, highlighting its ability to effectively leverage semantically rich and densely annotated data.

Importantly, EmoCIE also demonstrates clear advantages in low-resource and ambiguous categories, such as grief, pride, and remorse, each of which has fewer than 2,000 annotated examples. Unlike prior models that often collapse in these settings, EmoCIE achieves a 44% F1 for grief–a significant improvement from the 0% score in GoEmotions–and raises pride from 36% to 52% in F1. These gains underscore the value of EmoCIE's causal reasoning and intensity-aware classification in enhancing model robustness in sparse-label regimes. Overall, the macro-F1 score for EmoCIE surpasses those of all baselines, indicating that it generalizes better across the full spectrum of emotions.

In addition to the 28-label evaluation that includes the neutral class, we conducted a secondary experiment on the same dataset, this time excluding the neutral label to reduce label noise and improve interpretive clarity. The motivation stems from the observation that many instances originally labeled as neutral in the GoEmotions dataset contained subtle emotional cues detectable through contextual or linguistic signals. Therefore, to avoid emotional dilution and ensure finer granularity, we removed the neutral class and replaced the default neutral fallback mechanism with a highest-probability fallback strategy. In this configuration, when no label exceeds the classification threshold, the label with the highest predicted probability is selected, preserving emotional salience even in ambiguous cases.

To further validate our framework, we benchmarked the modified EmoCIE (referred to as EmoCIE-B and EmoCIE-R, based on BERT and RoBERTa backbones, respectively) against four competitive baselines: HatE-B, HatE-R, NeuEmot-B, and NeuEmot-R. As reported in Table 4, EmoCIE-R demonstrated superior performance across the board, achieving a macro-F1 of 60%, surpassing HatE-R by 10%, HatE-B by 8%, and NeuEmot-R by 7%. The performance gain is especially notable in sparse categories, including grief, remorse, embarrassment, and pride, reflecting EmoCIE's ability to exploit contextual cues and causal associations even in low-signal conditions. For example, grief attains an F1-score of 55% in EmoCIE-R, up from 24% in HatE-R and 27% in NeuEmot-R, underscoring the value of neutral removal and cause extraction in disambiguating subtle emotions.

Moreover, in high-density categories with well-aligned annotations such as gratitude, amusement, and love, EmoCIE-R continues to excel, achieving F1-scores of 93%, 86%, and 82%, respectively. These gains further reinforce that the model not only benefits from contextually rich and semantically coherent labels but also maintains robustness across a range of emotional intensity levels and label distributions. The dataset's high interrater agreement for such cate-

Table 4. GoEmotion Classification for 27 Labels without the Neutral Label

Label	HatE-B [11]			HatE-R [11]			NeuEmot-B [4]			NeuEmot-R [4]			EmoCIE-B			EmoCIE-R		
	P	R	F1	P	R	F1	P	R	F1	P	R	F1	P	R	F1	P	R	F1
Admir	0.77	0.59	0.66	0.82	0.51	0.63	0.80	0.56	0.66	0.75	0.71	0.73	0.69	0.79	0.74	0.72	0.77	0.74
Amuse	0.78	0.88	0.83	0.80	0.84	0.82	0.82	0.81	0.81	0.81	0.88	0.85	0.83	0.88	0.85	0.83	0.90	0.86
Anger	0.50	0.58	0.54	0.53	0.51	0.52	0.55	0.57	0.56	0.48	0.59	0.53	0.54	0.57	0.55	0.55	0.58	0.57
Annoy	0.52	0.32	0.40	0.59	0.13	0.21	0.46	0.36	0.41	0.52	0.33	0.41	0.40	0.51	0.45	0.36	0.66	0.47
Appro	0.57	0.41	0.48	0.65	0.44	0.53	0.50	0.43	0.47	0.51	0.50	0.51	0.44	0.61	0.51	0.55	0.54	0.55
Carin	0.48	0.55	0.51	0.44	0.59	0.50	0.46	0.53	0.49	0.51	0.54	0.52	0.58	0.51	0.55	0.55	0.53	0.54
Confu	0.32	0.69	0.44	0.47	0.57	0.51	0.45	0.56	0.50	0.42	0.67	0.51	0.45	0.68	0.54	0.45	0.63	0.53
Curio	0.62	0.80	0.70	0.64	0.73	0.68	0.67	0.71	0.69	0.63	0.75	0.68	0.62	0.79	0.70	0.62	0.82	0.71
Desir	0.51	0.60	0.55	0.53	0.55	0.54	0.72	0.51	0.60	0.49	0.59	0.54	0.64	0.58	0.61	0.62	0.60	0.61
Disap	0.44	0.34	0.39	0.51	0.24	0.32	0.46	0.25	0.32	0.42	0.30	0.35	0.37	0.35	0.36	0.40	0.46	0.43
Dispr	0.56	0.51	0.54	0.53	0.49	0.51	0.54	0.46	0.50	0.54	0.54	0.54	0.53	0.54	0.53	0.54	0.57	0.56
Disgu	0.33	0.71	0.45	0.42	0.67	0.52	0.49	0.57	0.52	0.39	0.68	0.49	0.70	0.50	0.58	0.51	0.59	0.55
Embar	0.25	0.54	0.34	0.22	0.51	0.31	0.62	0.43	0.51	0.22	0.54	0.31	0.59	0.46	0.52	0.82	0.38	0.52
Excit	0.27	0.65	0.39	0.38	0.49	0.43	0.41	0.50	0.45	0.34	0.54	0.42	0.53	0.44	0.48	0.58	0.45	0.51
Fear	0.47	0.86	0.60	0.50	0.76	0.60	0.55	0.71	0.62	0.54	0.82	0.65	0.67	0.79	0.73	0.86	0.64	0.74
Grati	0.94	0.88	0.91	0.93	0.89	0.91	0.91	0.90	0.91	0.92	0.93	0.92	0.94	0.92	0.93	0.98	0.88	0.93
Grief	0.11	0.50	0.18	0.14	1.00	0.24	0.29	0.67	0.40	0.17	0.67	0.27	0.50	0.50	0.50	0.60	0.50	0.55
Joy	0.47	0.71	0.57	0.53	0.60	0.56	0.63	0.61	0.62	0.47	0.71	0.57	0.72	0.56	0.63	0.63	0.64	0.63
Love	0.75	0.88	0.81	0.70	0.90	0.79	0.75	0.82	0.78	0.73	0.93	0.82	0.76	0.88	0.82	0.79	0.86	0.82
Nervo	0.24	0.52	0.33	0.27	0.61	0.38	0.43	0.43	0.43	0.29	0.61	0.39	0.48	0.48	0.48	0.62	0.43	0.51
Optim	0.54	0.53	0.53	0.65	0.53	0.59	0.59	0.59	0.59	0.58	0.59	0.58	0.62	0.58	0.60	0.62	0.59	0.60
Pride	0.24	0.50	0.32	0.20	0.50	0.29	0.26	0.44	0.33	0.18	0.44	0.25	0.62	0.50	0.55	0.70	0.44	0.54
Reali	0.33	0.36	0.35	0.35	0.35	0.35	0.29	0.26	0.27	0.36	0.29	0.32	0.44	0.29	0.35	0.29	0.50	0.37
Relie	0.29	0.64	0.40	0.10	0.73	0.17	0.45	0.45	0.45	0.13	0.73	0.22	0.58	0.64	0.61	0.50	0.45	0.48
Remor	0.57	0.89	0.70	0.55	0.80	0.65	0.54	0.77	0.63	0.56	0.88	0.69	0.67	0.80	0.73	0.62	0.93	0.74
Sadne	0.57	0.58	0.57	0.56	0.45	0.50	0.63	0.59	0.61	0.63	0.56	0.60	0.70	0.55	0.62	0.65	0.65	0.65
Surpr	0.45	0.70	0.55	0.48	0.69	0.56	0.59	0.56	0.58	0.48	0.63	0.54	0.61	0.63	0.62	0.60	0.57	0.58
Macro	0.48	0.62	0.52	0.50	0.60	0.50	0.55	0.56	0.54	0.48	**0.63**	0.53	0.60	0.60	0.60	**0.61**	0.61	**0.60**

gories likely supports these improvements, consistent with findings by Demszky et al. [3].

When applied to complex or affectively ambiguous classes such as confusion, nervousness, and disappointment, EmoCIE-R again outperforms baselines, leveraging its dual approach of contextual understanding and psychologically grounded emotion intensity modeling. Notably, the F1-score for confusion increases to 53%, compared to 44% in HatE-B and 50% in NeuEmot-B. These improvements indicate EmoCIE's capacity to capture subtle affective distinctions that are often overlooked by standard classifiers.

It is worth noting that the removal of the neutral class contributes not only to improved precision but also to a boost in macro-recall. With fewer samples defaulting to the non-informative neutral label, the model is effectively "forced" to assign emotionally meaningful labels, leading to improved class coverage. In this configuration, EmoCIE-R achieves the highest macro-recall at 61%, outperforming all other model variants and confirming that its predictions span a broader emotional spectrum.

The integration of per-class thresholding within a fine-tuned transformer architecture enables EmoCIE to deliver more accurate, semantically consistent, and interpretable multi-label emotion classification. The consistent macro-level improvements across all 27 emotion labels, and particularly in low-resource, high-ambiguity, or affective edge cases, affirm the effectiveness of removing the neutral class and incorporating causal inference as key mechanisms for achieving nuanced emotional understanding.

5.1.2 Ekman Emotion Classification *(with and Without Neutral)*

To evaluate the efficacy of various models in detecting core emotional categories, we conducted experiments on Ekman's primary emotion set: anger, disgust, fear, joy, sadness, surprise, and neutral. This evaluation was carried out using several competitive baselines, including GoEmotions (GoEmo), HatE-BERT (HatE-B), NeuEmot-BERT (NeuEm-B), and our proposed EmoCIE-R model. Importantly, we assessed model performance under two distinct configurations: one that included the neutral class and another that excluded it. The results are reported in Tables 5 and 6, using standard classification metrics such as precision (P), recall (R), and F1-score, for each emotion, followed by macro-averaged scores to capture overall performance across categories.

In the first configuration, which includes the neutral label (Table 5), the GoEmo model [3] serves as a foundational baseline. It achieved its highest F1-score for joy–82%, followed by fear–68% and surprise–61%. However, its performance was comparatively weaker for disgust–53% and sadness–59%, suggesting limitations in handling negative or ambiguous emotions. HatE-BERT (HatE-B) slightly improved on joy–80% and surprise–59%, though it underperformed on disgust–42%, revealing inconsistencies in cross-category generalization. NeuEm-BERT (NeuEm-B), which incorporates neutral-sensitive embeddings to enhance contextual understanding, yielded incremental gains across most categories, culminating in a macro-F1 of 58%.

In contrast, EmoCIE-R, our proposed model, consistently outperformed all baseline models across most metrics in the neutral-included setting. It demonstrated superior performance in detecting fear, with both precision and recall reaching 71%. It also matched GoEmo's top F1 score in joy–82% while delivering significant gains in the neutral class–69%, highlighting its capacity to effectively disambiguate emotionally flat expressions. This is a notable strength, as the neutral category often serves as a catch-all for subtle or mixed signals in emotion classification. Comprehensive, EmoCIE-R attained a macro-F1 of 65%, the highest among all models, validating the impact of its emotion-cause-aware architecture when handling Ekman's taxonomy with neutral presence.

Table 5. Ekman Emotion with Neutral

Emo	GoEmo [3]			HatE-B [11]			NeuEm-B [4]			EmoCIE-R		
	P	R	F1	P	R	F1	P	R	F1	P	R	F1
Ange	0.50	0.65	0.57	0.54	0.47	0.50	0.61	0.39	0.47	0.50	0.67	0.57
Disg	0.52	0.53	0.53	0.32	0.60	0.42	0.30	0.69	0.42	0.54	0.51	0.53
Fear	0.61	0.76	0.68	0.48	0.79	0.60	0.46	0.83	0.59	0.71	0.71	0.71
Joy	0.77	0.88	0.82	0.78	0.82	0.80	0.83	0.78	0.80	0.80	0.84	0.82
Neut	0.66	0.67	0.66	0.65	0.49	0.56	0.62	0.59	0.60	0.61	0.80	0.69
Sadn	0.56	0.62	0.59	0.58	0.56	0.57	0.52	0.62	0.57	0.63	0.59	0.61
Surp	0.53	0.70	0.61	0.54	0.66	0.59	0.55	0.65	0.60	0.55	0.68	0.61
Avg	0.59	0.69	0.64	0.55	0.63	0.58	0.56	0.65	0.58	0.62	0.69	0.65

Table 6. Ekman Emotion w/o Neutral

Emo	HatE-R [11]			NeuEm-R [4]			EmoCIE-R		
	P	R	F1	P	R	F1	P	R	F1
Ange	0.77	0.52	0.62	0.75	0.63	0.68	0.65	0.77	0.70
Disg	0.42	0.67	0.52	0.39	0.68	0.49	0.51	0.59	0.54
Fear	0.56	0.76	0.65	0.60	0.80	0.68	0.80	0.69	0.74
Joy	0.91	0.86	0.88	0.89	0.89	0.89	0.90	0.91	0.91
Sadn	0.63	0.56	0.59	0.61	0.61	0.61	0.64	0.69	0.67
Surp	0.67	0.73	0.70	0.67	0.73	0.70	0.63	0.76	0.69
Avg	0.66	0.68	0.66	0.65	0.72	0.68	0.69	0.74	0.71

To further analyze the model's robustness in emotion-only contexts, we repeated the evaluation by removing the neutral label and reassigning its samples. This approach was based on empirical observations indicating that many neutral-tagged samples in the dataset exhibited latent emotional cues that could be reclassified with greater accuracy. The results, summarized in Table 6, offer a clearer lens into emotion discrimination capabilities, free from the confounding influence of a dominant neutral class.

In this neutral-excluded configuration, HatE-R achieved a macro-F1 score of 66%, with its highest score in joy–88%, indicating a bias toward high-salience emotions. NeuEm-R offered marginal improvements over HatE-R, particularly in fear–68% and disgust–49%, and achieved a total macro-F1 of 68%. However, EmoCIE-R once again outperformed all baselines, achieving a macro-F1 of 71%. Its performance was especially noteworthy in joy–91%, anger–70%, and fear–74%, demonstrating that the model maintains high precision and recall even when deprived of a neutral fallback. Additionally, it delivered stable F1 performance across sadness–67% and surprise–69%, reflecting its robustness across the full emotional spectrum, including both positive and negative affective states.

These findings underscore the superior generalization and discriminative power of EmoCIE-R in both neutral-included and neutral-excluded environments. Ultimately, the model's success in handling both ambiguous and polar emotional categories affirms its potential for real-world affective computing applications.

5.2 Causality and Intensity

To evaluate the interpretability and intensity estimation capabilities of emotion classification models, we employed a two-pronged approach. First, we conducted a faithfulness analysis using comprehensiveness and sufficiency metrics derived from n-gram masking techniques. This allowed us to assess the degree to which specific input tokens or phrases influenced the model's predictions. Second, we examined emotion intensity alignment through a quadrant-based framework that cross-analyzes semantic and lexicon-based emotion scores with model confidence, thereby offering a deeper understanding of how emotional salience relates to predictive certainty.

5.2.1 Faithfulness Analysis Using N-Gram-Based

Faithfulness refers to the extent to which the input is necessary and sufficient to support a model's emotion classification. We measured this using two standard interpretability metrics: comprehensiveness, which assesses the decline in model confidence when key input tokens are masked, and sufficiency, which gauges the extent to which only the highlighted (most salient) tokens can preserve the original prediction. These metrics were computed across multiple n-gram windows, such as unigram, bigram, and trigram, for four transformer-based models: BERT, DistilBERT, BERTweet, and RoBERTa.

As reported in Table 7, DistilBERT achieved the highest comprehensiveness score in the unigram setting, reaching 38.33%. This suggests that masking single words had the greatest impact on DistilBERT's prediction confidence, implying a firm reliance on individual token contributions. It also led marginally in sufficiency with a score of 40.83%, indicating that key individual tokens were sufficient to retain predictive power more effectively than in the other models. As the analysis window expanded to bigrams, DistilBERT maintained its lead, achieving 45.32% in comprehensiveness and 42.93% in sufficiency. This performance highlights its heightened sensitivity to emotionally informative short phrases.

The trend became even more pronounced in the trigram analysis. Here, DistilBERT's comprehensiveness soared to 58.24%, underscoring its ability to leverage contextual triplets as reliable emotional cues. While sufficiency scores across models remained relatively stable, DistilBERT consistently demonstrated superior interpretability, particularly when emotion reasoning depended on multi-token constructs. This outcome is significant, as it reinforces the notion that emotional meaning is often embedded in phrases rather than isolated words, making trigram-based reasoning especially valuable. In short, the improved comprehensiveness at the trigram level highlights DistilBERT's capacity to better identify and rely on semantically rich, multi-token emotional expressions.

5.2.2 Emotion Intensity Estimation: *S-BERT vs. VAD Framework*

To further probe the interpretability of emotion models, we turned to the task of intensity estimation, comparing two frameworks: (i) a semantic vector-based method using Sentence-BERT (S-BERT) [25], and (ii) a psychologically grounded approach employing Valence–Arousal–Dominance (VAD) lexicon scores. We utilized a quadrant-based analysis to align intensity scores with model confidence, thereby capturing the relationship between affective strength and predictive trust. This schema partitions predictions into four categories based on thresholded intensity and confidence values: (a) High-Intensity High-Confidence (High-I High-C), (b) High-Intensity Low-Confidence (High-I Low-C), (c) Low-Intensity High-Confidence (Low-I High-C), and (d) Low-Intensity Low-Confidence (Low-I Low-C). Each quadrant reflects distinct model behavior in responding to emotionally charged content.

Table 7. Faithfulness Scores (N-gram)

Models	Unigram		Bigram		Trigram	
	Comp	Suff	Comp	Suff	Comp	Suff
BERT	0.3561	0.4075	0.4198	0.4252	0.4094	0.3901
DistilBERT	0.3833	0.4083	0.4532	0.4293	0.5824	0.3939
BERTweet	0.3378	0.3944	0.4052	0.4245	0.4002	0.3931
RoBERTa	0.3286	0.3764	0.3888	0.4090	0.3861	0.3815

Table 8. S-BERT vs. VAD Intensity Scores

Quadrants	S-BERT Intensity			VAD Intensity		
	Score	Conf	%	Score	Conf	%
High-I High-C	0.3935	0.9130	8.72	0.7929	0.9353	7.03
High-I Low-C	0.3837	0.6575	16.28	0.7858	0.7252	17.99
Low-I High-C	0.1648	0.9168	16.28	0.4107	0.9327	17.99
Low-I Low-C	0.1819	0.6128	58.72	0.3972	0.7077	57.00

For the S-BERT framework, we defined high emotional intensity as weighted scores equal to or above the 75th percentile ($\geq 32\%$) and high confidence as predictions with confidence $\geq 73\%$. The quadrant analysis (Table 8) revealed that S-BERT's High-I High-C quadrant captured 8.72% of the samples, with an average intensity of 39.35% and confidence of 91.30%. This intersection signifies instances where the model was both specific and attuned to strong emotional signals. Conversely, 16.28% of samples fell into the High-I Low-C quadrant, cases where high emotional salience was detected but the model exhibited lower confidence, possibly due to ambiguities in expression. Notably, Low-I High-C cases showed 91.68% confidence despite weak emotional signals, reflecting emotionally neutral but semantically clear statements. The largest portion belonged to the Low-I Low-C quadrant, characterized by both low intensity and low confidence, suggestive of texts with subtle or ambiguous emotional cues.

A similar thresholding strategy was applied to the VAD-based analysis, where high intensity was defined as $\geq 75\%$ and high confidence as $\geq 78\%$. VAD demonstrated stronger intensity estimates in the High-I High-C quadrant than S-BERT, albeit covering a slightly smaller subset of the data. In the High-I Low-C quadrant, VAD maintained high intensity but showed reduced confidence, indicating challenges in classifying emotionally potent yet semantically uncertain texts. The Low-I High-C category mirrored the pattern found in S-BERT, maintaining high confidence despite lower affective strength. The Low-I Low-C segment also emerged as the dominant category for VAD, though with slightly elevated intensity and reduced confidence compared to its S-BERT counterpart.

These methods yield two key insights. First, both S-BERT and VAD exhibit the expected but non-universal alignment between emotional intensity and prediction confidence, where high-intensity inputs are more likely to generate confident predictions; however, ambiguity remains a complicating factor. Second, VAD systematically assigns higher intensity scores across all quadrants, consistent with its psychological foundations, while S-BERT adopts a more conservative and semantically grounded estimation strategy. These complementary analyses validate EmoCIE's ability to provide nuanced emotional reasoning, coupling fine-grained intensity detection with reliable confidence metrics. This dual-layered interpretability offers a richer understanding of affective behavior in neural models and supports more trustworthy applications in emotionally sensitive domains.

6 Discussion

The EmoCIE framework offers a multi-faceted approach to emotion understanding by jointly modeling emotion classification, cause identification, and intensity estimation. Our evaluation reveals that this integrated approach yields improvements not only in classification accuracy but also in the interpretability and explainability of model predictions.

To illustrate these capabilities, in Table 4, we present randomly selected qualitative examples that demonstrate how emotion classification aligns with the extracted causes and corresponding faithfulness metrics, namely, comprehensiveness and sufficiency. For instance, in the unigram-level analysis, the sentence "thank you for asking questions and recognizing that there may be things that you do not know or understand about police tactics, seriously thank you" was correctly classified as expressing gratitude, with "things" identified as the underlying cause. However, both its comprehensiveness (0.0018) and sufficiency (0.0464) scores were relatively low, suggesting that single-token masking may not fully

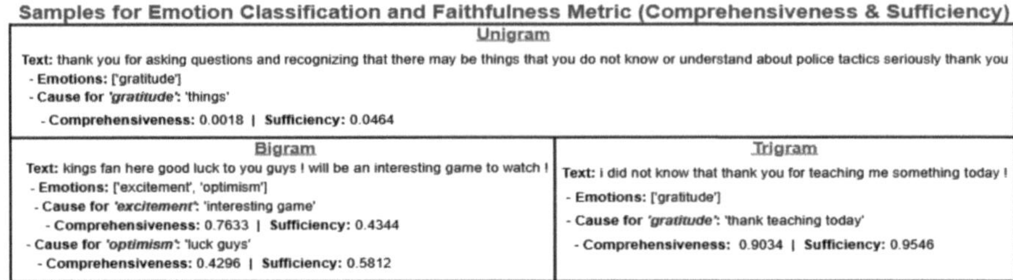

Fig. 4. Samples for Classification and Causal

capture the underlying reasoning in such diffuse statements. In contrast, bigram analysis yielded stronger interpretability. For example, the sentence "kings fan here good luck to you guys! will be an interesting game to watch!" expressed both excitement and optimism. The cause for excitement–"interesting game"–had a comprehensiveness score of 0.76, indicating that masking this phrase led to a significant confidence drop, while its sufficiency score (0.43) suggested it was moderately self-sufficient. For optimism, the phrase "luck guys" had sufficiency as high as 0.58, demonstrating that short multi-word phrases often carry stronger emotional cues. At the trigram level, performance continued to improve. The example "I did not know that, thank you for teaching me something today!" was again labeled as gratitude, with the cause "thank teaching today" showing high comprehensiveness (0.90) and sufficiency (0.95). This supports our finding that trigram-level interpretability better captures contextual cues critical for emotional reasoning.

Samples for Each VAD Quadrant with respective their Intensity and Confidence Score Category

Low Intensity - Low Confidence	Low Intensity - High Confidence
Text: it is still interesting to watch though from far away with no personal involvement whatsoever - VAD Intensity: 47.33% - Confidence Score: 57%	Text: thanks for sharing you could definitely post some of your other tales - VAD Intensity: 24.12% - Confidence Score: 94%
High Intensity - Low Confidence	**High Intensity - High Confidence**
Text: she can take her boring drunk husband with her he is not interesting at all - VAD Intensity: 75.40% - Confidence Score: 61%	Text: just read your list sounds great !! you have some creatures even i did not think about thumbs_up !! - VAD Intensity: 76.75% - Confidence Score: 83%

Fig. 5. Samples for Intensity

Beyond interpretability, we analyzed the model's emotional grounding in Table 5 through VAD-based intensity scores and model confidence, organizing the data into four quadrants: Low-Intensity/Low-Confidence (Low-I Low-C), Low-Intensity/High-Confidence (Low-I High-C), High-Intensity/Low-Confidence (High-I Low-C), and High-Intensity/High-Confidence (High-I High-C). In the Low-I Low-C quadrant, a sample like "it is still interesting to watch though from far away with no personal involvement whatsoever" had a VAD intensity of 47.33% and confidence of 0.57, suggesting affective ambiguity and limited emotional salience. In contrast, the Low-I High-C quadrant included emotionally restrained but semantically clear expressions such as "thanks for sharing, you could definitely post some of your other tales", where the model showed high confidence (0.94) despite low emotional intensity (24.12%). The High-I Low-C quadrant comprised emotionally strong but ambiguous statements, such as "she can take her boring drunk husband with her, he is not interesting at all", which had a high VAD score of 75.40% but lower confidence (0.61), highlighting cases where affect is present but difficult to disambiguate. Finally, in the High-I High-C quadrant, clear and vivid emotional expressions such as "just read your list sounds great!! you have some creatures even I did not think about!" scored both high in intensity (76.75%) and model confidence (0.83), indicating successful alignment between human-perceived affect and model predictions.

Collectively, these results validate the three-step modeling strategy of EmoCIE, which synergistically enhances classification accuracy, interpretability, and emotional granularity. However, these gains are not without trade-offs. Incorporating interpretable metrics, such as comprehensiveness and sufficiency, introduces a slight computational overhead. Additionally, while emotion-cause pairs improve semantic transparency, they may sacrifice marginal performance in favor of model interpretability–a deliberate trade-off favoring explainability in sensitive domains such as healthcare, education, and crisis monitoring.

Compared to prior Emotion-Cause Pair Extraction (ECPE) models, EmoCIE exhibits significant strengths. Traditional ECPE frameworks often require separate pipelines for classification and extraction, whereas our architecture fuses these steps, reducing error propagation and improving joint reasoning. Moreover, the integration of psychologically grounded VAD scores enables the estimation of emotion intensity–a dimension often overlooked in conventional emotion models.

The practical applicability of this framework spans several domains, such as social media relevancy/urgency identification [29], fact-checking information [30], event detection [31], and public health [32]. In public and mental health, the ability to detect emotion causes and intensities can assist in monitoring affective shifts and triggering timely interventions. In educational settings, modeling student emotions with causal context can enhance feedback loops and engagement strategies. Similarly, in social media analytics, the system can discern public sentiment more accurately during crises by not only labeling emotions but also extracting their causes and intensities.

EmoCIE advances the state of emotion understanding by fusing classification, causality, and affective strength in a combined, interpretable model. The accompanying interpretability and quadrant-based analyses further highlight its potential for real-world deployment in emotionally sensitive applications.

7 Conclusion and Future Works

In this work, we introduced EmoCIE, a 3-step framework that integrates emotion classification, cause extraction, and emotion intensity estimation into a combined NLP-based architecture. By combining contextual modeling with psychologically grounded VAD-based scoring, EmoCIE enhances the interpretability and accuracy of emotion predictions, particularly in low-resource and affectively ambiguous scenarios. Our experimental results across multiple benchmarks demonstrate that the model significantly outperforms existing baselines in both overall performance and interpretability metrics, particularly when handling subtle or sparse emotional cues.

In future, our work will explore extending EmoCIE to multimodal datasets, incorporating visual and audio signals alongside text to capture richer affective contexts. Additionally, we plan to integrate personalized emotion modeling, which accounts for user traits and contextual history, to improve predictions in real-world applications such as mental health monitoring, conversational agents, and social media analytics. We aim to enhance our approach by integrating multicause extraction techniques, allowing us to identify and differentiate various causes associated with multiple labels. Finally, further human-centered evaluations will be conducted to assess the practical utility and transparency of the model's predictions in diverse domains.

References

1. Picard, R.W.: Affective computing: challenges. Intl J. HC Stud. **59**(1–2), 55–64 (2003)
2. Calvo, R.A., D'Mello, S.: Affect detection: an interdisciplinary review of models, methods, and their applications. IEEE Trans. Affect. Comput. **1**(1), 18–37 (2010)
3. Demszky, D., Movshovitz-Attias, D., Ko, J., Cowen, A., Nemade, G., Ravi, S.: GoEmotions: A dataset of fine-grained emotions. In: Proceedings of the 58th ACL, pp. 4040–4054 (2020)
4. Adesokan, A., Madria, S.: NeuEmot: mitigating neutral label and reclassifying false neutrals in the 2022 FIFA world cup via low-level emotion. In: 2023 IEEE BigData, pp. 578–587 (2023)
5. Zhang, Q., Wang, B., Zhu, P., Zhao, J., Liu, K.: A rhetorical structure theory and inference-aware graph network for emotion-cause pair extraction. Complex Intell. Syst. **11**(338) (2025)
6. Xia, R., Ding, Z.: Emotion-cause pair extraction: a new task to emotion analysis in texts. In: Proceedings of the 57th Annual Meeting of the ACL, pp. 1003–1012 (2019)
7. Mohammad, S.: Obtaining reliable human ratings of valence, arousal, and dominance for 20,000 English words. In: Proceedings of the 56th ACL (Volume 1: Long Papers), pp. 174–184 (2018)
8. Doshi-Velez, F., Kim, B.: Towards a rigorous science of interpretable machine learning. Stat **1050**, 2 (2017)
9. Singh, G.V., Ghosh, S., Ekbal, A., Bhattacharyya, P.: DeCoDE: detection of cognitive distortion and emotion cause extraction in clinical conversations. In: Proceedings of the 45th ECIR 2023. Lecture Notes in Computer Science, vol. 13981, pp. 156–171. Springer (2023)
10. Kabir, M.Y., Madria, S.: EMOCOV: machine learning for emotion detection, analysis and visualization using COVID-19 tweets. OSNEM **23**, 100135 (2021)
11. Adesokan, A., Madria, S., Nguyen, L.: HatEmoTweet: low-level emotion classifications and spatiotemporal trends of hate and offensive COVID-19 tweets. SNAM **13**(1), 136 (2023)

12. Warriner, A.B., Kuperman, V., Brysbaert, M.: Norms of valence, arousal, and dominance for 13,915 English lemmas. Behav. Res. Methods **45**(4), 1191–1207 (2013)
13. Wang, B., Tang, K., Zhu, P.: Enhancing emotion-cause pair extraction in conversations via center event detection and reasoning. In: Finding of the ACL: EMNLP 2024, pp. 10773–10783 (2024)
14. Liang, Y., Liu, L., Ji, Y., Huangfu, L., Zeng, D.D.: Identifying emotional causes of mental disorders from social media for effective intervention. Inf. Process. Manage. **60**(4), 103407 (2023)
15. Liu, H., Wei, R., Tu, G., Lin, J., Jiang, D., Cambria, E.: Knowing what and why: causal emotion entailment for emotion recognition in conversations. Expert Syst. Appl. **274**, 126924 (2025)
16. Jiang, S., Zhang, H., Qi, J., Fang, B., Xu, T.: Perceiving social-emotional volatility and triggered causes of COVID-19. Intl J. Environ. Res. Public Health **18**(9), 4591 (2021)
17. Li, X., Yang, D., Zhu, X., Huang, F., Zhang, P., Zhao, Z.: Span-level emotion-cause-category triplet extraction with instruction tuning LLMs and data augmentation. arXiv preprint arXiv:2504.12331 (2025)
18. Liu, Y., et al.: RoBERTa: a robustly optimized bert pretraining approach. arXiv preprint arXiv:1907.11692 (2019)
19. Wijeratne, S., Balasuriya, L., Sheth, A., Doran, D.: EmojiNet: building a machine readable sense inventory for emoji. In: International Conference on Social Informatics, pp. 527–541. Springer, Cham (2016)
20. Lin, T.Y., Goyal, P., Girshick, R., He, K., Dollár, P.: Focal loss for dense object detection. In: Proceedings of the IEEE International Conference on Computer Vision, pp. 2980–2988 (2017)
21. Ekman, P.: An argument for basic emotions. Cogn. Emot. **6**(3–4), 169–200 (1992)
22. Adesokan, A., Madria, S.: Keymines: extracting minimal keyphrases for sub-events in disaster situations. In: Proceedings of the 2024 IEEE Intl Conf on BigData, pp. 1–10 (2024)
23. Grootendorst, M.: KeyBERT: minimal keyword extraction with BERT (Version 0.3.0) [Software]. Zenodo (2020). https://doi.org/10.5281/zenodo.4461265
24. Carbonell, J., Goldstein, J.: The use of MMR, diversity-based reranking for reordering documents and producing summaries. In: Proceedings of the 21st Annual Intl. ACM SIGIR Conference on Research & Development in Information Retrieval, pp. 335–336 (1998). https://doi.org/10.1145/290941.291025
25. Reimers, N., Gurevych, I.: Sentence-BERT: sentence embeddings using siamese BERT-networks. In: Proceedings of the 2019 Conference on EMNLP & the 9th IJCNLP, pp. 3982–3992 (2019)
26. DeYoung, J., et al.: ERASER: a benchmark to evaluate rationalized NLP models. In: Proceedings of the 58th Annual Meeting of the ACL, pp. 4443–4458 (2020). https://doi.org/10.18653/v1/2020.acl-main.408
27. Akiba, T., Sano, S., Yanase, T., Ohta, T., Koyama, M.: Optuna: a next-generation hyperparameter optimization framework. In: Proceedings of the 25th ACM SIGKDD, pp. 2623–2631 (2019)
28. Saculinggan, M., Balase, E.A.: Empirical power comparison of goodness of fit tests for normality in the presence of outliers. J. Phys.: Conf. Series **435**(1), 012041 (2013)
29. Adesokan, A., Madria, S.: CURD: context-aware relevance and urgency determination. In: Proceedings of the 36th International Conference on Scientific and Statistical Database Management, pp. 1–12 (2024)

30. Adesokan, A., Hu, H., Madria, S.: DisFact: fact-checking disaster claims. In: International Conference on Web Information Systems Engineering, pp. 421–437. Springer, Singapore (2024)
31. Adesokan, A., Madria, S., Nguyen, L.: DisTGranD: granular event/sub-event classification for disaster response. Online Soc. Netw. Media **45**, 100297 (2025)
32. Adesokan, A.A.: Covid-19 control: face mask detection using deep learning for balanced and unbalanced dataset. Int. J. Intell. Syst. Appl. **14**(6), 50–62 (2022)

Knowledge Injection in a Neural Model for Aspect-Based Sentiment Classification

Stijn Coremans, Bram Wisse, Arthur van Klei, Sameeksha Aggarwal, Lakshita Bhatti, and Flavius Fransincar(✉)

Erasmus University Rotterdam,PO Box 1738, 3000 DR Rotterdam, The Netherlands
{581362sc,619807bw,577410ak,560575sa,575717lb}@student.eur.nl, frasincar@ese.eur.nl

Abstract. Text-based reviews are extremely valuable for companies and institutions, but also hard to process if there are many. Aspect-Based Sentiment Classification (ABSC) requires techniques for classifying sentiments in reviews towards different aspects. Neural network models turn out to be of great use in this domain. In this paper, we further explore the possibilities of knowledge injection into these models. Our research focuses on knowledge injection in the state-of-the-art LCR-Rot-hop-ont++ model. We explore the possibilities of injecting knowledge at training time, test time, and training and test times using various SemEval datasets. Based on statistically significant results, we conclude that knowledge injection during both the training and testing phases significantly enhances performance across the restaurant and laptop domains for larger datasets, surpassing the LCR-Rot-hop++ model. Additionally, our results demonstrate that injecting knowledge at the testing phase in the case of the laptop domain improves model performance even further.

Keywords: ABSC · Knowledge injection · Domain ontology

1 Introduction

In today's society, where Web data collection is becoming increasingly popular and usage of this data to derive relevant insights is common practice, decision-making processes are undergoing a fundamental transformation toward data-driven approaches. Major improvements in computational resources are facilitating this fundamental change, allowing academics and industry professionals to experiment with new and improved methods for effectively using vast quantities of data. Customer reviews are an example of an especially valuable data source, containing an extensive amount of information about consumer attitudes toward products and services. Businesses that use this huge quantity of feedback can help them identify areas of improvement, enhance processes by prioritising operational changes, and, ultimately, increase overall client satisfaction. Insights into the sentiments expressed in textual data are thus of great importance for

I. Awan et al. (Eds.): WISE 2025, LNCS 16367, pp. 567–578, 2026.
https://doi.org/10.1007/978-981-95-7394-3_38

businesses across a wide range of sectors, emphasising the need for sentiment analysis in today's data-driven environment.

Aspect-Based Sentiment Analysis (ABSA) is a sub-field of sentiment analysis that allows for a better understanding of opinions expressed in textual data by focusing on specific subjects in a text which are referred as aspects [7]. Unlike sentiment analysis of documents or sentences, which can be difficult due to the presence of multiple subjects, ABSA limits its scope to single aspects, making sentiment classification more useful.

The ABSA process generally consists of two main steps: aspect detection and sentiment classification [7]. Aspect detection involves finding the specific aspects being addressed in the text [9]. Once the aspects have been identified, sentiment classification can be used to assign a polarity score to each aspect based on the context in which the aspect is mentioned [1].

This research primarily focuses on sentiment classification within ABSA, also known as Aspect-Based Sentiment Classification (ABSC). However, it is important to note that aspect detection requires distinguishing between explicit and implicit aspects [9]. For the purpose of this study, the classification of explicit aspects is the main focus, as these aspects provide a clear and identifiable target for sentiment classification. [1] provides a comprehensive overview of the current state of ABSC, including valuable insights into the techniques, difficulties, and advancements in this field. Due to data sparsity, training and testing neural models are difficult, which can potentially be solved by developing new hybrid models [1]. Hybrid models use a combination of knowledge bases and machine-learning models to improve their predictive performance and have already been shown to outperform non-hybrid alternatives.

This paper combines a hybrid model with knowledge injection to explore if a better neural model can be developed. Knowledge injection is the process of incorporating domain-specific or external knowledge to make the models more robust or increase interpretability. [1] highlights the advantages of knowledge injection, especially for knowledge-driven specific-domain tasks. Knowledge injection is explored in various ways in this paper through input knowledge injection. As not a lot of research is done on knowledge injection, this paper delves to find which method gives better results, hence the main research question of this research is: *How to inject knowledge from a domain sentiment ontology in a neural model for ABSC?*

The main contribution of this paper is as follows. We analyse knowledge injection in a state-of-the-art ABSC model at training, testing and training and testing times. We perform these computations on datasets of various sizes and from different domains. In addition, we use statistical tests to determine which knowledge injection regime works best. The Python source code of our model has been made publicly available at: https://github.com/StijnCoremans/LCR-Rot-hop-ont.

The rest of the paper is organised in the following manner. Section 2 presents the used data for experiments and Sect. 3 provides a detailed description of the proposed methods. Section 4 shows the results of our experiments and lastly, Sect. 5 gives an overview of our conclusions and suggestions for further research.

2 Data

In this research, to train and evaluate the performance of our model we have used the SemEval 2014 Task 4 [6], the SemEval 2015 Task 12 [5], and the SemEval 2016 Task 5 [4]. The SemEval 2015 and SemEval 2016 restaurant datasets have been widely used for research in ABSC, therefore making these datasets a good option for comparing our model with other models in ABSC. The datasets contain restaurant reviews consisting of one or multiple sentences. Additionally, we use two SemEval 2014 datasets which are less used for other models in ABSC. Using these datasets we aim for a more extensive evaluation. One of the SemEval 2014 datasets also contains restaurant reviews, we call this dataset the SemEval 2014 (Restaurant) dataset. The second SemEval 2014 dataset contains laptop reviews, we call this dataset the SemEval 2014 (Laptop) dataset. Similarly to the restaurant reviews, the laptop reviews consist of one or more sentences.

In the restaurant and laptop reviews, each sentence expresses one or more opinions about specific aspects. These aspects can have a target associated with them. The aspects get a polarity assigned to them. The polarity can be classified as positive, neutral, or negative.

In Table 1 the frequencies of the polarities and the respective sizes of the datasets of the different datasets are shown. These are the frequencies and the sizes of the processed data. Our model only operates on reviews containing explicit aspects, as explicit aspects are the most common type of aspects and make up the vast majority of the aspects in our data. So, before using the datasets we pre-process the data by deleting all reviews with implicit aspects from the datasets. We delete the implicit aspects from the dataset by iterating through all sentences and deleting the opinions that have *null* as their target.

Table 1. Polarity frequencies of the SemEval 2014(Laptop), SemEval 2014 (Restaurant), SemEval 2015, and SemEval 2016 datasets.

	Training data				Test data			
	Positive	Neutral	Negative	Total	Positive	Neutral	Negative	Total
SemEval 2014 (Restaurant)	60.0%	17.6%	22.4%	3608	65.0%	17.5%	17.5%	1120
SemEval 2014 (Laptop)	42.7%	19.9%	37.4%	2313	53.4%	26.5%	20.1%	638
SemEval 2015	75.3%	2.8%	21.9%	1279	59.1%	6.1%	34.8%	597
SemEval 2016	70.2%	3.8%	26.0%	1880	74.3%	4.9%	20.8%	650

We inject knowledge into our model using two domain sentiment ontologies. For the SemEval 2014 (Restaurant), SemEval 2015, and 2016 datasets, we use a restaurant ontology [8]. Similarly, for the SemEval 2014 (Laptop) dataset, we use a laptop ontology [11].

Lastly, we use the pre-trained word embeddings from the uncased BERT base model [2]. This model has 12 transformer layers, a hidden size of 768, and 12 self-attention layers.

3 Methodology

In this section, we present our methodology. In Subsect. 3.1 we describe the proposed approaches for knowledge injection in the used neural model. Then in Subsect. 3.2 we explain how to determine the statistical significance of our results.

3.1 Knowledge Injection

We inject knowledge in the state-of-the-art ABSC neural model, LRC-Rot-hop++ [10], from a domain ontology. We use a restaurant domain ontology and a laptop domain ontology. The knowledge is injected during the training time, test time, or both at the same time by using input knowledge injection inspired by the K-BERT model [3]. To extract lexical representations we define a k-hop as the process of navigating k classes through the ontology from the current concept on, for $k = 0, ..., N - 1$, where N is the number of classes. For example, a 0-hop will lead to only injecting synonyms of the concept as there will be no navigation through the ontology.

Input Knowledge Injection. The input knowledge injection inspired by the K-BERT model consists of four modules the knowledge layer, embedding layer, visibility layer, and mask-transformer layer. The knowledge layer first injects knowledge from the ontology into the sentence, creating a knowledge-rich sentence tree. All these extra added words disrupt the order of the words, that is why we use soft-positioning. All the words in the branches get the same soft-position as the word that these words are related to. The sentence tree then goes into the embedding layer and the visibility layer. After that, it becomes a token-level embedding representation and a visibility matrix.

The knowledge from the ontology is injected with the following series of steps. First K-Query, we get all the lexical representations for each k-hop. We define $w_{i,k}$ as the word i in the sentence for which lexical representations were obtained from ontology O by navigating k-hops. The words corresponding to the concepts are thereafter added to the sentence. The selection of these words is given in Eqs. 1 and 2.

$$E = \text{K-Query}(s, O, k) \tag{1}$$

The collection of words of a k-hop is:

$$E = \cup_{w_i \in s}[(w_i \cup \{w_{i,0}\} \cup ...\{w_{i,k}\})] \tag{2}$$

where $\{w_{i,n}\}$ is the set of words obtained from word i in the sentence using n hops.

Second, K-Inject injects the knowledge from E into the sentence s by placing the words in their corresponding positions and generating a sentence tree. Soft branches are added to the sentence tree for synonyms. The other words obtained by k-hops of the concepts get inserted via hard branches. An example of a sentence tree is shown in Fig 1. The dashed line shows a soft branch and the full black lines show the hard branches. The blue numbers beneath the words represent the hard-positions, and the red numbers above the words represent the soft-positions.

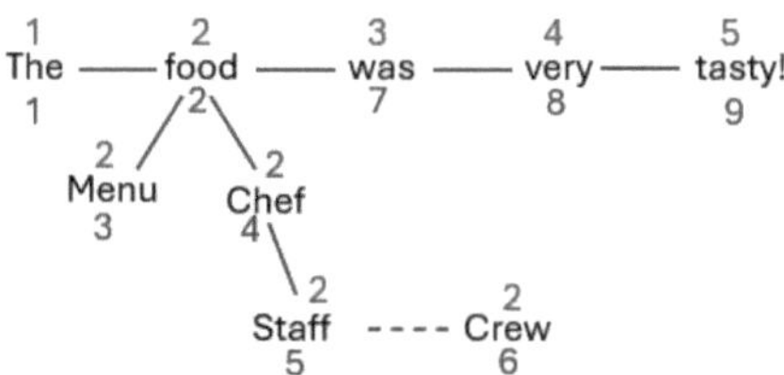

Fig. 1. An example of a sentence tree.

In the embedding layer, these sentence trees are converted into embedding representations that can be fed to the mask-transformer layer. The biggest difference between BERT and K-BERT is in the visibility layer. The visibility layer gets a sentence tree as input instead of just a sentence in the K-BERT model. To prevent that the meaning of the altered sentence diverges from its original meaning because of all the parallel branches, a matrix M is introduced. This matrix has values 0 or $-\infty$ depending on whether words are in the same branch (original sentence words can all view each other). An example of a visibility matrix related to the sentence tree shown in Fig. 1 is shown in Fig. 2.

	1	2	3	4	5	6	7	8	9
1	0	0	-∞	-∞	-∞	-∞	0	0	0
2	0	0	0	0	-∞	-∞	0	0	0
3	-∞	0	0	-∞	-∞	-∞	-∞	-∞	-∞
4	-∞	0	-∞	0	0	-∞	-∞	-∞	-∞
5	-∞	-∞	-∞	0	0	0	-∞	-∞	-∞
6	-∞	-∞	-∞	-∞	0	0	-∞	-∞	-∞
7	0	0	-∞	-∞	-∞	-∞	0	0	0
8	0	0	-∞	-∞	-∞	-∞	0	0	0
9	0	0	-∞	-∞	-∞	-∞	0	0	0

Fig. 2. An example of a visibility matrix.

The last layer is the mask-transformer, we cannot use the same transformer as the one in the BERT model because this cannot receive M. In the same way as in BERT, we go through L encoder layers. The mask-self-attention blocks are given by Eqs. 3, 4, and 5. The formula for the attention scores includes the matrix M to ensure that only words within the same branch can affect each other. For the first layer, we provide the input $h_0 = sum(E_t, E_s, E_{seg})$ holding the embeddings of the tokens, soft-positions, and segments, respectively.

$$Q^{i+1}, K^{i+1}, V^{i+1} = h^i W_q, h^i W_k, h^i W_v \tag{3}$$

$$S^{i+1} = \text{softmax}\left(\frac{Q^{i+1}{K^{i+1}}^{\top} + M}{\sqrt{d_k}}\right) \tag{4}$$

$$h^{i+1} = S^{i+1} V^{i+1} \tag{5}$$

where Q, K, V, and S are matrices with queries, keys, values, and self-attention scores, respectively. The W matrices are trainable parameters, and d_k is a scaling parameter given by the dimension of the current head k. The output h denotes the hidden states between the layers. As shown in Eq. 4, the attention score becomes zero if M has a value equal to $-\infty$ (i.e., words are in different branches).

Hop Weights. Injecting knowledge into our model from the ontology using multiple hops may change the original meaning of the sentence. As we use increasing amounts of knowledge with each hop, knowledge may become less relevant to the original meaning. Therefore, we apply a hop-weighting mechanism to the token embeddings. We assign weights according to how deep the words are into a branch. Each step into a branch away from the original sentence we call a hop. We use a weight inversely proportional to the number of hops in the ontology. This way, knowledge obtained further into the ontology will get a lower weight. We define a hop weight as:

$$hw_i = \begin{cases} 1, & \text{if } t_i \text{ in original sentence} \\ e^{-(n_{hops}+\gamma)}, & \text{otherwise} \end{cases} \tag{6}$$

where n_{hops} is the number of hops in the ontology to reach token t_i, and γ is a hyperparameter.

3.2 Statistical Significance

In this section, we briefly explain how we determine whether our results are statistically significant. We first explain how we use the bootstrapping mechanism and then how we compute the *p-values*.

The bootstrapping method is used in our work to provide us with more data samples. The concept of bootstrapping is creating samples by randomly taking data points from a sample with the possibility of choosing the same data points multiple times. The motivation behind using this approach is the lack of a sufficient amount of data samples available for this research. Thus, with this mechanism, we create a large set of dependent data samples which we use to see if we can prove the statistical significance of our results.

To prove statistical significance we use the Wilcoxon-test. This rank test can be used to determine statistical significance when the assumption of normally distributed samples is not made. The null hypothesis states that the results of the different approaches are the same, and the alternative hypothesis states that there is indeed a difference in the results. We report the corresponding p-values of the tests. For small p-values we reject the null hypothesis and deem the results to be statistically significant.

4 Results

In this section, we present the results that we have gained in our research. There were two concepts we wanted to test in the domain of input knowledge injection. The first concept was injecting the knowledge of *0*-hops into the ontology at different phases during the process, and the second concept was the statistical significance of the results. Additionally, differences between the restaurant and laptop domains are also analysed.

Injection in Different Phases. As explained in the methodology section we injected the knowledge into the input at training time, testing time, and both times. The results of different injections can be seen in Table 2. In Table 3 the average accuracy for each model is shown for the employed datasets. We mention average accuracy because we performed bootstrapping on the datasets to create more samples. We have used 100 bootstraps for the test data of the datasets.

As it becomes clear from Table 3, the accuracy of the models without input knowledge injection is higher than the ones with input knowledge injection, for the SemEval 2015, and SemEval 2016 datasets. On the other hand, the models with injecting knowledge during both training and testing as well as only testing perform better for the SemEval 2014 (Laptop) and SemEval 2014 (Restaurant) datasets. SemEval 2014 (Restaurant) is the largest dataset followed by SemEval 2014 (Laptop), SemEval 2016, and SemEval 2015. For larger datasets, we can thus conclude that injecting knowledge either at testing or at both training and testing boosts the performance of the model. We believe a possible reason for this phenomenon is that large datasets have more training data, and therefore the extra knowledge added can be used more frequently increasing the information used during training compared to smaller datasets. The results for the SemEval 2014 (Laptop) dataset are inconsistent with the SemEval 2014 (Restaurant) dataset results, as injecting knowledge at testing works best for the laptop domain, while both training and testing is better for the restaurant domain. For both domains, however, it holds that knowledge injection can boost the model's performance.

When comparing the differences in injecting knowledge in different phases of the process from Table 3, we see based on the percentages displayed that there is no unambiguous answer across domains. In the SemEval 2014 (Restaurant), SemEval 2015, and SemEval 2016 datasets, the model with injecting knowledge in both phases performs the best when compared to only injecting knowledge at training or testing, however in the SemEval 2014 (Laptop) case this does not hold. Injecting knowledge only in the testing phase is the best case for the SemEval 2014 (Laptop) dataset. From Table 3 it can be inferred that injecting

Table 2. Accuracy of LCR-Rot-hop++ for the SemEval 2014 (Laptop), SemEval 2014 (Restaurant), SemEval 2015, and SemEval 2016 datasets.

Model	SemEval 2014 (Laptop)	SemEval 2014 (Restaurant)	SemEval 2015	SemEval 2016
LCR-Rot-hop++	76.33%	81.70%	80.07%	86.92%
LCR-Rot-hop-ont++ (training)	76.65%	80.36%	74.04%	84.62%
LCR-Rot-hop-ont++ (testing)	77.59%	82.05%	78.56%	85.38%
LCR-Rot-hop-ont++ (both)	77.43%	82.32%	78.39%	85.54%

Table 3. Average accuracy of LCR-Rot-hop++ and LCR-Rot-hop-ont++ for the SemEval 2014 (Laptop), SemEval 2014 (Restaurant), SemEval 2015, and SemEval 2016 datasets.

Model	SemEval 2014 (Laptop)	SemEval 2014 (Restaurant)	SemEval 2015	SemEval 2016
LCR-Rot-hop++	76.55%	81.76%	80.41%	86.90%
LCR-Rot-hop-ont++ (training)	76.80%	80.24%	73.96%	84.77%
LCR-Rot-hop-ont++ (testing)	77.85%	82.02%	78.61%	85.36%
LCR-Rot-hop-ont++ (both)	77.35%	82.20%	78.81%	85.71%

knowledge in the training phase is always outperformed by injecting knowledge at both the training and testing phase or solely at the testing phase. For the SemEval 2014 (Laptop) dataset, the difference between injecting knowledge at training and at both training and testing is not statistically significant, as seen in Table 4. The model with injecting knowledge at both phases does, however, significantly outperform the model without knowledge injection, while the model with knowledge injection at training does not. We furthermore conclude that the difference between injecting knowledge in the test phase and injecting knowledge in both phases is not large, and not always statistically significant. In the case of SemEval 2014 (Laptop), only injecting the knowledge in the testing phase provides the best results, and this is statistically significant, as seen in Table 4. In the SemEval 2014 (Restaurant), SemEval 2015, and SemEval 2016 datasets injecting knowledge in both the training and the testing phase yields better results. Still, these results are not statistically significant compared to injecting knowledge at testing, which can be inferred from Tables 5, 6, and 7. We can thus only conclude that injecting knowledge in the training phase is outperformed by the other cases. A possible explanation for this is that injecting knowledge in the training phase creates too much knowledge noise to improve the accuracy of the model.

Table 4. Wilcoxon signed-rank test p-values for the SemEval 2014 (Laptop) dataset.

Model	LCR-Rot-hop++	LCR-Rot-hop-ont++ (training)	LCR-Rot-hop-ont++ (testing)	LCR-Rot-hop-ont++ (both)
LCR-Rot-hop++	–	–	–	–
LCR-Rot-hop-ont++ (training)	0.279	–	–	–
LCR-Rot-hop-ont++ (testing)	0.000	0.000	–	–
LCR-Rot-hop-ont++ (both)	0.000	0.060	0.013	–

Table 5. Wilcoxon signed-rank test p-values for the SemEval 2014 (Restaurant) dataset.

Model	LCR-Rot-hop++	LCR-Rot-hop-ont++ (training)	LCR-Rot-hop-ont++ (testing)	LCR-Rot-hop-ont++ (both)
LCR-Rot-hop++	–	–	–	–
LCR-Rot-hop-ont++ (training)	0.000	–	–	–
LCR-Rot-hop-ont++ (testing)	0.090	0.000	–	–
LCR-Rot-hop-ont++ (both)	0.005	0.000	0.321	–

Statistical Significance. We repeatedly test for statistical significance of our models using the respective bootstraps. For each dataset, we made a separate Table displaying the statistical significance based on a Wilcoxon signed-rank test. The results for SemEval 2014 (Laptop), SemEval 2014 (Restaurant), SemEval 2015, and Semeval 2016 are visible in Tables 4, 5, 6, and 7, respectively. The values visible in these tables represent the p-values of testing the null hypothesis that the models yield the same results.

Almost all the p-values that are shown in the tables refer to a statistically significant result at a 5% significance level. This means that for each test the difference in performance between the two models is statistically significant. There are six exceptions, two in the SemEval 2014 (Laptop) dataset in Table 4, two in

Table 6. Wilcoxon signed-rank test p-values for the SemEval 2015 dataset.

Model	LCR-Rot-hop++	LCR-Rot-hop-ont++ (training)	LCR-Rot-hop-ont++ (testing)	LCR-Rot-hop-ont++ (both)
LCR-Rot-hop++	–	–	–	–
LCR-Rot-hop-ont++ (training)	0.000	–	–	–
LCR-Rot-hop-ont++ (testing)	0.000	0.000	–	–
LCR-Rot-hop-ont++ (both)	0.000	0.000	0.254	–

Table 7. Wilcoxon signed-rank test p-values for the SemEval 2016 dataset.

Model	LCR-Rot-hop++	LCR-Rot-hop-ont++ (training)	LCR-Rot-hop-ont++ (testing)	LCR-Rot-hop-ont++ (both)
LCR-Rot-hop++	–	–	–	–
LCR-Rot-hop-ont++ (training)	0.000	–	–	–
LCR-Rot-hop-ont++ (testing)	0.000	0.003	–	–
LCR-Rot-hop-ont++ (both)	0.000	0.000	0.064	–

the SemEval 2014 (Restaurant) dataset in Table 5, one in the SemEval 2015 in Table 6, and one in the SemEval 2016 dataset in Table 7. The p-value of 0.279 in the SemEval 2014 (Laptop) dataset in Table 4 is a large p-value comparing the performance of LCR-Rot-hop++ against LCR-Rot-hop-ont++ (training). Therefore, we can not conclude that the two methods perform significantly differently in the context of the SemEval 2014 (Laptop) dataset. Furthermore, the SemEval 2014 (Laptop) models with injecting knowledge at training and at both training and testing are not significantly different. As previously discussed, for the SemEval 2014 (Restaurant), SemEval 2015, and SemEval 2016 datasets the models with injecting knowledge at testing and at both training and testing are not statistically significantly different. Additionally, in the case of SemEval 2014 (Restaurant), the model with injecting knowledge at testing does not significantly outperform the model without injecting knowledge. We can thus conclude that injecting knowledge at both training and testing increases the performance of the model compared to the model without knowledge injection for both domains for larger datasets. Furthermore, for the laptop domain, the model with injecting knowledge at testing can improve the performance even further.

5 Conclusion

In our research, we inject knowledge from a domain sentiment ontology into the LCR-Rot-hop++ model. We inject knowledge into the model using K-BERT in three different ways. Knowledge is injected during the training phase, testing phase, and in both. Furthermore, we test the statistical significance of all our models using the bootstrapping method. To obtain knowledge from the ontology we take hops in the ontology. To improve the relevance of the knowledge injection we use a hop-weighting mechanism using a weight that is inversely proportional to the number of hops in the ontology. We apply the widely used SemEval 2015 dataset and SemEval 2016 dataset containing restaurant reviews, and as an extension, we apply two less-used SemEval 2014 datasets one also containing restaurant reviews and one from a different domain which contains laptop reviews. All the results are repeated for *0*-hops.

Our results show that for the 2015 and 2016 datasets, the benchmark model without knowledge injection performs best and is statistically significant in both cases. However, for the SemEval 2014 (Restaurant) and SemEval 2014 (Laptop) datasets, the models with knowledge injection at testing and at both training and testing outperform the LCR-Rot-hop++ model. For the SemEval 2014 (Laptop) dataset, the model with knowledge injection at testing time performs the best and is statistically significant compared to all other models. For the SemEval 2014 (Restaurant), the model with knowledge injection at both training and testing has the highest accuracy but is not statistically significant compared to the model with knowledge injection at testing. Since the SemEval 2014 (Restaurant) and SemEval 2014 (Laptop) datasets are the largest datasets, we can conclude that injecting knowledge at both training and testing boosts the performance of the model. We believe one of the reasons for this is that large datasets have more training data, and therefore extra knowledge can be used more frequently increasing the information used during the training compared to smaller datasets.

References

1. Brauwers, G., Frasincar, F.: A survey on aspect-based sentiment classification. ACM Comput. Surv. **55**(4), 65:1–65:37 (2023)
2. Devlin, J., Chang, M., Lee, K., Toutanova, K.: BERT: pre-training of deep bidirectional transformers for language understanding. In: 17th Conference of the North American Chapter of the Association of Computational Linguistics: Human Language Technologies (NAACL-HLT 2019), pp. 4171–4186. ACL (2019)
3. Liu, W., et al.: K-BERT: enabling language representation with knowledge graph. In: 34th AAAI Conference on Artificial Intelligence (AAAI 2020), vol. 34, pp. 2901–2908. AAAI (2020)
4. Pontiki, M., et al: SemEval-2016 task 5: aspect based sentiment analysis. In: 10th International Workshop on Semantic Evaluation, (SemEval 2016), pp. 19–30. ACL (2016)

5. Pontiki, M., Galanis, D., Papageorgiou, H., Manandhar, S., Androutsopoulos, I.: SemEval-2015 task 12: aspect based sentiment analysis. In: 9th International Workshop on Semantic Evaluation, (SemEval 2015), pp. 486–495. ACL (2015)
6. Pontiki, M., Galanis, D., Pavlopoulos, J., Papageorgiou, H., Androutsopoulos, I., Manandhar, S.: SemEval-2014 task 4: aspect based sentiment analysis. In: 8th International Workshop on Semantic Evaluation, (SemEval 2014), pp. 27–35. ACL (2014)
7. Schouten, K., Frasincar, F.: Survey on aspect-level sentiment analysis. IEEE Trans. Knowl. Data Eng. **28**(3), 813–830 (2016)
8. Schouten, K., Frasincar, F., de Jong, F.: Ontology-enhanced aspect-based sentiment analysis. In: 17th International Conference on Web Engineering (ICWE 2017). LNCS, vol. 10360, pp. 302–320. Springer (2017)
9. Trusca, M.M., Frasincar, F.: Survey on aspect detection for aspect-based sentiment analysis. Artif. Intell. Rev. **56**(5), 3797–3846 (2023)
10. Trusca, M.M., Wassenberg, D., Frasincar, F., Dekker, R.: A hybrid approach for aspect-based sentiment analysis using deep contextual word embeddings and hierarchical attention. In: 20th International Conference on Web Engineering (ICWE 2020). LNCS, vol. 12128, pp. 365–380. Springer (2020)
11. Zhuang, L., Schouten, K., Frasincar, F.: SOBA: semi-automated ontology builder for aspect-based sentiment analysis. J. Web Semant. **60**, 100544 (2019)

Model Knowledge Injection for Aspect-Based Sentiment Classification

Danique Thaens and Flavius Frasincar(✉)

Erasmus University Rotterdam, PO Box 1738, 3000 DR Rotterdam, The Netherlands
571216dt@student.eur.nl, frasincar@ese.eur.nl

Abstract. The number of online reviews has increased exponentially with the growing use of the Web and social media platforms. To handle the large amount of reviews, machine learning methods are needed to analyze these opinions properly. Aspect-Based Sentiment Classification (ABSC) attempts to determine the sentiment of each aspect within a text, to give a more in-depth overview of the opinion. In this work, a new model called LCR-Rot-hop-Kfont++ is introduced. This model injects knowledge into the state-of-the-art LCR-Rot-hop++ model inspired by previous work on Kformer. We evaluate the model using the SemEval-2015 and SemEval-2016 datasets, for which knowledge is injected during training, testing, and both training and testing using a domain-specific ontology. We show that injecting knowledge improves the accuracy of ABSC. For smaller datasets, it is advised to inject knowledge at training time, while for larger datasets it is advised to inject knowledge at testing time.

Keywords: ABSC · Knowledge injection · Ontology · Hybrid method

1 Introduction

In the last few decades, the Web has become an imperative part of daily life. New, easy ways have been created to search for information, view media, and share your opinion. This provides a rich source of information for companies to find improvements in their business. For smaller companies, going through each review manually is still possible. However, for larger businesses and organisations these opinions often come in high quantities. Hence, novel ways are needed to deduce their meaning. This field is called sentiment analysis [11].

It is most common that sentiment analysis is conducted on a document or sentence level, hence labelling the whole document or sentence as having one sentiment [25]. However, for companies or organisations, aiming to enhance their business, it is important to gain detailed information to identify high-quality parts of the company and those features which need improvement. Consequently, in recent years, Aspect-Based Sentiment Analysis (ABSA), which is responsible for detecting aspects and their related sentiment, has become more popular [25].

I. Awan et al. (Eds.): WISE 2025, LNCS 16367, pp. 579–594, 2026.
https://doi.org/10.1007/978-981-95-7394-3_39

ABSA consists of two sub-tasks: Aspect Detection (AD) [20] and Aspect-Based Sentiment Classification (ABSC) [2], where the first is concerned with identifying and extracting all the aspects from a text and the latter focuses on classifying the sentiment towards these extracted targets [16]. This sentiment is often represented as polarity and usually has three categories: positive, negative, and neutral. This work takes the aspects as given and focuses solely on ABSC.

Many methods to classify sentiments have been created in the past. These methods can be divided into three categories: knowledge-based methods, machine learning methods, and hybrid methods, which combine the previous two methods [16]. [17] has demonstrated that knowledge-based methods and machine learning methods can complement each other, leading to improved performance. The hybrid models come in two forms, either the two types of methods are combined in one step or they are sequentially applied in two steps.

Many of the hybrid methods apply a two-step approach. The first step of these methods often uses a knowledge-based approach based on a domain-specific ontology. A domain-specific ontology represents here the concepts, their relationships, and the corresponding sentiments within a specific domain. If the first step is unable to classify, a machine learning method is deployed. One of the methods that provides the best results is the HAABSA++ model [21]. This approach combines a domain-specific ontology in the first step with the state-of-the-art LCR-Rot-hop++ neural network in the second step.

The other type of hybrid method is a one-step method, where knowledge is injected into a machine learning model. This means knowledge from an external source is added to the method to give the model more information. Often, such a method focuses on injecting knowledge into the input sentence before the neural network is utilized or training the neural network on extra data [3]. A newer area of research is on injecting knowledge directly into the neural network. One of these methods is called Kformer and focuses on the feed-forward layers of transformers for knowledge injection [24]. [24] showed that this method outperforms other tested methods that only inject knowledge during input for two knowledge-intensive tasks different from ABSC.

This work contributes to existing research by creating a new model that combines two state-of-the-art approaches applied to ABSC. The new model called LCR-Rot-hop-Kfont++ combines the LCR-Rot-hop++ neural network with the promising knowledge injection method Kformer. Kformer has not been tested on an ABSC task yet, nor has it been combined with another neural network like LCR-Rot-hop++. Moreover, in Kformer, textbooks are used as external knowledge, while in our work a domain-specific ontology is used for knowledge injection. This means that not only the concepts but also their relationships and sentiments are included. The embeddings from the ontology are initialized through OWL2Vec* [4]. This means that for each lexicalization in the ontology, OWL2Vec* creates a vector, that reflects the content and positioning of the lexicalization within the ontology. The Python code is made freely available at https://github.com/DaniqueT/LCR-Rot-hop-Kfont_plus_plus.

The remaining work is organised in the following way. Section 2 discusses relevant previous research. Section 3 briefly describes the data used. Section 4 provides the details of the proposed method. Section 5 analyses its performance, while Sect. 6 provides our conclusions and discusses suggestions for future work.

2 Related Works

In the related works we concentrate on the one-step hybrid approaches, as these are the focus of our research. For these methods knowledge can be injected at the input, model, or output level.

Input Knowledge Injection. Injecting knowledge at the input level means enhancing the original text. This is done by adding knowledge from an external resource before the sentence is processed by the neural network. The most simple method is to transform all important concepts from a knowledge graph into a string. This string is then concatenated with the initial text [3]. [3] showed that adding this information before using BERT outperforms regular BERT.

[12] designed a more intricate way of injecting knowledge into the input sequence, which is called Knowledge-enabled BERT (K-BERT). This model injects triplets of a knowledge graph into the original text by using soft-positioning and a visibility matrix. These are needed to limit the amount and effect of knowledge injected into the model. Too much knowledge can lead to knowledge noise, which indicates that the meaning of the original input is changed [12]. Both [3,12] find that K-BERT significantly outperforms BERT on a variety of NLP tasks. Especially on smaller datasets, K-BERT seems to perform well [3].

One promising avenue is first using a transformer with knowledge injection at the input level for sentence embedding and afterwards an additional neural network for classification. For example, [6] created the LCR-Rot-hop-ont++ model, which uses K-BERT in combination with the LCR-Rot-hop++ model [21]. Moreover, for the knowledge injection, [6] uses a domain-specific ontology instead of a knowledge graph in an attempt to fit the model even better to the domain data. The authors conclude that their model always outperforms the LCR-Rot-hop++ model without knowledge injection and outperforms the two-step HAABSA++ approach [21] for smaller datasets. This again demonstrates the usefulness of knowledge injection, especially for limited data.

Model Knowledge Injection. Another approach, rather than altering the input text, is to incorporate the knowledge into one of the neural network layers during the analysis. One of the methods exploring this is Kformer [24]. In this method, the authors make use of knowledge neurons found in the Feed Forward Network (FFN) of the transformer, which store implicit knowledge [5]. [24] aims to combine this stored model knowledge with external information by injecting knowledge into the FFN layers of the transformer. [24] finds that injecting knowledge directly into the FFN layers outperforms other approaches that inject knowledge at the input. This indicates that the neural network is now able to make use of both knowledge stored in the model and external knowledge.

However, the layer in which the knowledge is injected can influence the results. On both tasks tested by [24] the model is enhanced through knowledge injection in the bottom three or the top three layers, while injecting into intermediate layers is beneficial in one case and detrimental in the other. In general, the authors conclude that the top three layers are best able to capture semantic information.

Output Knowledge Injection. A last option is to process the external knowledge in parallel to a transformer model [3]. [13] embeds the text to classify using BERT and concatenate that output with additional features from outside knowledge. This concatenated output is then combined in a MultiLayer Perceptron (MLP) after which it goes to the final output layer. This model outperforms the BERT baseline significantly [13] and even outperforms K-BERT on larger datasets [3]. Hence, this method seems promising but only appears to obtain better results than other knowledge injection models on larger datasets. As our dataset is limited in size, we will not explore this approach further.

3 Data

To evaluate the performance of the model, two different datasets from the SemEval workshop series are used. Specifically, the model is evaluated for the SemEval-2015 Task 12 [15] and the SemEval-2016 Task 5 Subtask 1 [14] datasets. These were specially designed to test the performance of ABSC models. The datasets contain restaurant reviews where each review has a variable number of sentences with one or more aspects within each sentence. Each sentiment towards these aspects is classified as either positive, negative, or neutral.

Each sentence contains one or multiple aspects which can be categorized. For each of these aspects, a polarity is determined. Moreover, the target in these sentences can be implicit. The sentiments associated to implicit targets are more difficult to classify and will not be the focus of this work. Hence, they will be removed from the dataset and left for further research.

The frequency distribution of the two datasets with respect to their polarities, after removing the implicit targets, is shown in Table 1. The SemEval-2015 and SemEval-2016 datasets are quite similar, in both the positive polarity is most frequent, followed by the negative polarity and then by the neutral polarity. SemEval-2016 is the bigger data set containing about 47% more training data and 9% more testing data compared to SemEval-2015. In SemEval-2016, the training and testing data are relatively similar in their frequency distribution. In SemEval-2015 training and test data differ slightly more with less positive and more negative sentiments in the test data compared to the training data.

For the knowledge injection, a domain-specific ontology is used, created for the restaurant domain [18]. This ontology contains concepts belonging to the

Table 1. Distribution of the sentiment polarities in the SemEval-2015 and SemEval-2016 datasets.

	Training Data				Test Data			
	Positive	Neutral	Negative	Total	Positive	Neutral	Negative	Total
SemEval 2015	75.3%	2.8%	21.9%	1279	59.1%	6.1%	34.8%	597
SemEval 2016	70.2%	3.8%	26.0%	1880	74.3%	4.9%	20.8%	650

restaurant domain and the relations between these concepts. In this work, the focus is exclusively only on 0-hops in the ontology. This means that for each word in a sentence that also appears in the ontology, synonyms of that specific word are used.

Lastly, the pre-trained BERT base model [7] is used to obtain embeddings for the data. This model contains 12 transformer layers, 768 hidden dimensions, and 12 self-attention heads. Moreover, a feedforward size of 3072 is used, which is exactly 4 times larger than the hidden size. For consistency, the dimension size of the knowledge representations is set to 100 and is expanded to 400 before concatenating it with the transformer representations.

4 Methodology

In this paper, we propose a methodology that combines Kformer and LCR-Rot-hop++ called LCR-Rot-hop-Kfont++. Kformer performs very well as a knowledge injection model [24], but has not been tested for ABSC yet. Furthermore, LCR-Rot-Hop++ is a state-of-the-art method for ABSC and could possibly even perform better with this added knowledge. We inject knowledge using Kformer methodology into BERT to create sentence embeddings, which are then classified by the LCR-Rot-hop++ model. In Fig. 1 the entire model is shown. In Sect. 4.1 the Kformer method combined with BERT is explained and in Sect. 4.2 the details of the LCR-Rot-hop++ network are provided.

4.1 Kformer

For the knowledge injection into the model, the Kformer method [24] is used together with the BERT model [7]. This approach builds the contextual word embeddings as output which afterwards can be used in the LCR-Rot-hop++ model. BERT is a multi-layer bidirectional transformer encoder [22]. This transformer encoder has two main layers in each of its L transformer layers: a Multi-Head Attention layer followed by an FFN layer. The FFN layer consists of two linear transformations together with a GELU activation function [10]. In this layer, the knowledge is injected. For this knowledge injection, a domain-specific ontology is used displaying the most relevant concepts and their connections. The full FFN layer with knowledge injection can be seen in Fig. 2.

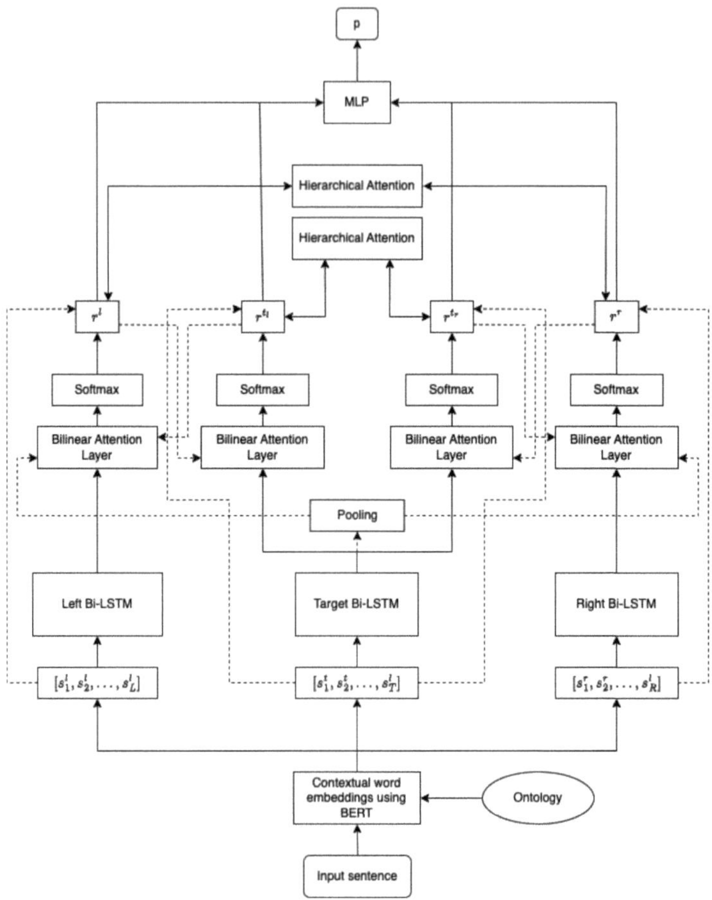

Fig. 1. The complete LCR-Rot-hop-Kfont++ model.

The final output of the two linear layers in the FFN is:

$$\text{FFN}(\underset{n\times d}{H^l}) = f(\underset{n\times d}{H^l} \times \underset{d\times d_m}{U^l}) \times \underset{d_m\times d}{V^l}, \tag{4.1}$$

where the final attention output of the layer l is $H^l \in R^{n\times d}$ with n representing the size of the input, and d is the size of the hidden states. $U^l \in R^{d\times d_m}$ and $V^l \in R^{d_m\times d}$ are parameter matrices of the first and second linear layers, respectively, where d_m represents the intermediate size of the transformer within the FFN layer and d is the size of the hidden states and the size of the word embeddings. f is the non-linear GELU function [10].

However, the output of the FFN layer will change because of the knowledge injection. For the knowledge injection, the top N-related concepts are used, this N can be varied to obtain better performance. In this case, we use a domain-specific ontology [18] to obtain the related concepts. The closeness of these concepts to

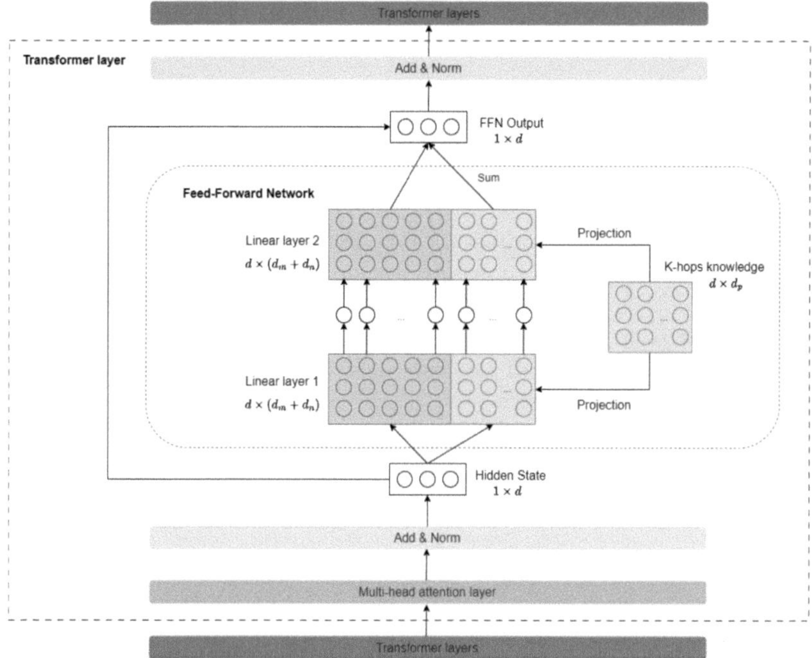

Fig. 2. The FFN layer with knowledge injection.

the original word is defined by their k-hop, where each hop means traversing the ontology one more class, with the ontology containing M classes in total. Hence, $hop = 0$ represents only injecting synonyms, since no traversing is done.

Differently than [24], each knowledge concept k has its lexical representations tokenized into n tokens that are later embedded into $k_1, k_2, ..., k_n$. The embeddings are initialized using OWL2Vec* [4]. Moreover, these embeddings are updated and learned during the training phase, if this is where knowledge is injected. If knowledge is only injected during testing, random vector embeddings are utilized. To finally represent the external knowledge, the weighted average of these token embeddings is taken. For the 0-hop case, the simple average is used:

$$\underset{d_p \times 1}{k} = \text{Avg}(\underset{d_p \times 1}{k_1}, \underset{d_p \times 1}{k_2}, ..., \underset{d_p \times 1}{k_n}). \tag{4.2}$$

where d_p represents the size of the knowledge token embeddings ($d_p = 100$ in our case).

When k-hops are used the weight of the knowledge concept will decrease the more hops are taken, since this external concept is less closely related to the original. This leads to the following equation:

$$\underset{d_p \times 1}{k} = \sum_{i \in hops} \underset{1 \times 1}{w_i} \sum_{j \in syn(i)} \underset{d_p \times 1}{k_{ij}}, \tag{4.3}$$

where i represents the hops from the original concept, j represents the synonyms used in the layer of hop i, and $k \in R^{d_p}$. The weight can be defined in the following way:

$$w_i = \begin{cases} 1 & \text{if } i = 0 \\ e^{-(n_{hops}+\gamma)} & \text{otherwise,} \end{cases} \tag{4.4}$$

where n_{hops} represents the number of hops in the ontology and γ is a hyperparameter. In this work, only 0-hops are explored, hence solely direct synonyms are used.

This knowledge first needs to be mapped to the vector spaces of the layer l in which it is injected. Both of the two linear layers within the FFN layer are used to project the knowledge:

$$\underset{d_n \times d}{\phi_u^l} = \mathrm{Pr}_u \underset{d_p \times 1}{k} = \underset{d_n \times d_p}{W_u^l} \times \underset{d_p \times d}{[k]_d} \tag{4.5}$$

$$\underset{d_n \times d}{\phi_v^l} = \mathrm{Pr}_v \underset{d_p \times 1}{k} = \underset{d_n \times d_p}{W_v^l} \times \underset{d_p \times d}{[k]_d} \tag{4.6}$$

where Pr represents the knowledge projection, $[k]_d$ represents the repetitiom d times of the vector k, W_u^l, $W_v^l \in R^{d_n \times d_p}$ are the weights of the two linear layers with u representing the first layer and v the second layer. These matrices are randomly initialized and updated during fine-tuning ($d = 768$ in our case). After this projection, the projected knowledge is concatenated to the end of the linear layer and the expanded $U_E^l \in R^{d \times (d_m + d_n)}$ and $V_E^l \in R^{(d_m+d_n) \times d}$ are obtained ($d_n = 400$ and $d_m = 3072$ in our case). This leads to the final output of the FFN layer with knowledge injection:

$$\begin{aligned} \mathrm{FFN}(\underset{n \times d}{H^l}) &= f(\underset{n \times d}{H^l} \times \underset{d \times (d_m+d_n)}{U_E^l}) \times \underset{(d_m+d_n) \times d}{V_E^l} \\ &= f(\underset{n \times d}{H^l} \times [\underset{d \times d_m}{U^l} : \underset{d \times d_n}{\phi_u^{l'}}]) \times [\underset{d_m \times d}{V^l} : \underset{d_n \times d}{\phi_v^l}] \end{aligned} \tag{4.7}$$

where : represents the concatenation operator.

This injection can be done in any of the L layers in the transformer. The information will be processed and aggregated by the following transformer layers. In this work, the knowledge is injected into the top three layers of the model since [24] achieved good performance with this. We use the pre-trained BERT Base model which has 12 layers, 12 attention heads in each of its multi-head attention layers, and 768 hidden states which is also the size of the word embeddings ($L = 12, A = 12, H = 768$). As suggested by [7], the final representation of the words is computed by summing the word embeddings of the final four layers. This means that for word i the final output would be:

$$\underset{d\times 1}{\text{BERT}_i} = \sum_{l=9}^{12} \underset{d\times 1}{H_i^l}. \tag{4.8}$$

4.2 LCR-Rot-Hop++

The LCR-Rot-hop++ network is deployed after the embeddings with BERT and Kformer are completed and this model gives the final classification. For the LCR-Rot-hop++ network, the same methodology is used as described by [21,23]. The first step is to split the N words of the sentence embeddings S $= [s_1, s_2, ..., s_N]$ into three parts of length L, T, and R which are the left context $[s_1^l, s_2^l, ..., s_L^l]$, target phrase $[s_1^t, s_2^t, ..., s_T^t]$, and right context $[s_1^r, s_2^r, ..., s_R^r]$, respectively. These parts are used as input for three bi-directional Long Short-Term memory modules (bi-LSTMs), namely a left-, centre-, and right-bi-LSTM that model the left context, target phrase, and right context separately. The output of these bi-LSTMs are the hidden states $[h_1^l, h_2^l, ..., h_L^l]$ for the left context, $[h_1^t, h_2^t, ..., h_T^t]$ for the target phrase, and $[h_1^r, h_2^r, ..., h_R^r]$ for the right context.

Then, a two-step rotary attention mechanism is applied over these three parts to capture the surrounding context and highlight the most important words in the target and context. This rotary attention mechanism is applied iteratively three times since [23] found this to be the optimal number. This results in four representations of the input: left context, right context, left-aware target representation, and right-aware target representation. Next, each step of the model will be explained in more detail.

Step 1: Target2Context Attention Mechanism. The first step focuses on finding the most important words from both the left and right contexts. In the first iteration, a representation of the target phrase is needed. The r^{t_p} target vector is calculated using average pooling:

$$\underset{2d\times 1}{r^{t_p}} = \text{pooling}([\underset{2d\times 1}{h_1^t}, \underset{2d\times 1}{h_2^t}, ..., \underset{2d\times 1}{h_T^t}]), \tag{4.9}$$

where d is the size of the word embeddings. During the following iterations, based on the context considered, r^{t_p} is replaced by either r^{t_l} or r^{t_r}, representing the left- or right-aware target representation, respectively.

Next, a representation of the left and right contexts is obtained through a score function f. This is achieved by utilizing the representation of the target phrase (in iteration one, the average target pooling r^{t_p}) and the hidden states of all the context words. For example, for the left context, the score function is:

$$\underset{1\times 1}{f(h_i^l, r^{t_p})} = \tanh(\underset{1\times 2d}{h_i^{l'}} \times \underset{2d\times 2d}{W_c^l} \times \underset{2d\times 1}{r^{t_p}} + \underset{1\times 1}{b_c^l}), \tag{4.10}$$

where h_i^l are the hidden states, for $i = 1, ..., L$, W_c^l is a weight matrix, and b_c^l a bias term. Then, a softmax function is used with f as input that normalises the scores. The attention normalised scores α_i^l for the left context are calculated as follows:

$$\alpha_i^l = \frac{\exp(f(h_i^l, r^{r_p}))}{\sum_{j=1}^{L} \exp(f(h_j^l, r^{r_p}))}. \tag{4.11}$$

Lastly, the hidden states weighted by the normalised attention scores are used to compute the context representation. For example, for the left context:

$$\underset{2d\times 1}{r^l} = \sum_{i=1}^{L} \underset{1\times 1}{\alpha_i^l} \times \underset{2d\times 1}{h_i^l}. \tag{4.12}$$

The right context representation r^r can be computed similarly as in Eqs. 4.10, 4.11, and 4.12, by replacing h_i^l by h_i^r.

Step 2: Context2Target Attention Mechanism. In the second step of the rotary attention mechanism, context-aware target representations are obtained using the previously calculated context representations from step 1. The approach is quite similar to step 1. As before, the score function f is calculated. Now, instead of using the target representation, the context representations are used. Hence, for the left context, the formula becomes:

$$\underset{1\times 1}{f(h_i^t, r^l)} = \tanh(\underset{1\times 2d}{h_i^{t'}} \times \underset{2d\times 2d}{W_t^l} \times \underset{2d\times 1}{r^l} + \underset{1\times 1}{b_t^l}), \tag{4.13}$$

where h_i^t are the hidden states for the words in the target phrase for $i = 1, ..., T$, W_t^l is a weight matrix, and b_t^l is a bias term. Then the normalized attention scores $\alpha_i^{t_l}$ are computed using a softmax function:

$$\alpha_i^{t_l} = \frac{\exp(f(h_i^t, r^l))}{\sum_{j=1}^{T} \exp(f(h_j^t, r^l))}. \tag{4.14}$$

Lastly, the left-aware target representation can be computed by multiplying the hidden states of the context with their respective attention scores:

$$\underset{2d\times 1}{r^{t_l}} = \sum_{i=1}^{T} \underset{1\times 1}{\alpha_i^{t_l}} \times \underset{2d\times 1}{h_i^t}. \tag{4.15}$$

To obtain the right-aware target representation, Eqs. 4.13, 4.14, and 4.15 are repeated with r^l replaced by r^r.

Hierarchical Attention. The rotary attention mechanism creates an output of four vector representations: left context, right context, left-aware target, and right-aware target. However, these are computed using only local information from the sentence. We provide a higher level of representation by including the information on the sentence level as well. This layer is called hierarchical attention, in which each vector of the previous two steps is updated. This hierarchical attention is applied separately in each of the iterations of the rotary attention mechanism. It is used on the intermediate context and target vector pairs. Firstly, an attention function f is used for each of these vectors:

$$\underset{1\times 1}{f(\,v^i\,)} = \tanh(\underset{1\times 2d}{v^{i'}} \times \underset{2d\times 1}{W} + \underset{1\times 1}{b}), \tag{4.16}$$

where $v^i \in \{r^r, r^l, r^{t_r}, r^{t_l}\}$, for $i = 1, 2, 3, 4$, is the representation i of the input sentence, W is a weight matrix, and b is the added bias. Next, new attention scores are computed for each v^i in a context and target pair using f:

$$\alpha^i = \frac{exp(f(v^i)}{\sum_{j=1}^{2} exp(f(v^j))}. \tag{4.17}$$

Now the new representation of each of the old context and target representations $(r^r, r^l, r^{t_r}, r^{t_l})$ can be computed:

$$\underset{2d\times 1}{v^i_{new}} = \underset{2d\times 1}{v^i_{old}} \times \underset{1\times 1}{\alpha^i}. \tag{4.18}$$

Classification and Training. To obtain the final representation of the full sentence, the left context representation r^l, right context representation r^r, left-aware target representation r^{t_l}, and the right-aware target representation r^{t_r} are concatenated:

$$\underset{8d\times 1}{v} = [\underset{2d\times 1}{r^l}\,;\,\underset{2d\times 1}{r^{t_l}}\,;\,\underset{2d\times 1}{r^{t_r}}\,;\,\underset{2d\times 1}{r^r}]. \tag{4.19}$$

A linear layer then transforms this representation into a vector of length $|C|$ depicting the sentiment prediction vector p, where C represents the sentiment classes. Lastly, a softmax layer predicts the final sentiment polarity of the target phrase:

$$\underset{|C|\times 1}{p} = \text{softmax}(\underset{|C|\times 8d}{W_c} \times \underset{8d\times 1}{v} + \underset{|C|\times 1}{b_c}), \tag{4.20}$$

where p is the conditional probability distribution, W_c is a weight matrix, and b_c is a bias term.

The model is trained using the back-propagation algorithm that minimizes the cross-entropy loss function with $L2$ regularization:

$$\underset{1\times 1}{L} = -\sum_j \underset{|C|\times 1}{y_j} \times \log(\underset{|C|\times 1}{p_j}) + \lambda||\Theta||^2, \tag{4.21}$$

where y_j is the vector of the true sentiment classification, p_j is the vector containing the predicted sentiment classifications, both for the j-th observation. The weight of the $L2$ regularization term is depicted by λ, and Θ is a parameter set which contains the LSTM parameters, the LCR-Rot-hop++ parameters $\{W_c^l, W_c^r, W_t^l, W_t^r, b_c^l, b_c^r, b_t^l, b_t^r\}$, and the Kformer parameters $\{W_u^l, W_v^l\}$.

A uniform distribution is used to initialize all the weight matrices and biases and updated through the use of stochastic gradient descent with a momentum term. Moreover, the hyperparameters of the model are tuned, specifically the learning rate, dropout rate, L2 regularization term λ, and the momentum term. Of the training data, 80% of the data is used for tuning and the rest for validation. To speed up the hyperparameter tuning, a Tree-structured Parzen Estimator (TPE) algorithm is used [1].

Lastly, the training of the LCR-Rot-hop++ model has changed slightly compared to the method used in HAABSA++ [21]. Previously, the embeddings were created by BERT before the model was trained. Now, to ensure the weights of the knowledge injection matrices can also be learned and tuned, creating the embeddings using BERT is added to the model and these embeddings are also included in the back-propagation. Moreover, the knowledge from the domain ontology is initialized using OWL2Vec* [4]. When knowledge is injected during training times these vectors are updated. However, when knowledge injection is only done during testing, random vector embeddings are used.

5 Results

In this section, we present the results of our LCR-Rot-hop-Kfont++ model. The model is evaluated on the SemEval-2015 and SemEval-2016 datasets using three different variants: with knowledge injection during training, with knowledge injection during testing, and with knowledge injection during both training and testing. These were compared to the benchmark model LCR-Rot-hop++.

First, the hyperparameters of the models are tuned, after which the models are trained using 100 epochs. Moreover, an early stopping rule was implemented. This means that when for 20 epochs the validation loss did not decrease, the training was stopped to prevent overfitting. The knowledge injection takes place in the top three layers of the transformer: layers 10 through 12. This has been chosen because [24] concluded in their research that these layers are usually the best performing and are best able to capture semantic information.

The testing accuracy of the benchmark and our knowledge injection models are displayed in Table 2. Starting with the SemEval-2015 dataset, it can be seen that knowledge injection does improve accuracy. Both knowledge injection during training and knowledge injection in training and testing outperform the LCR-Rot-hop++ benchmark. Knowledge injection only during training is superior and achieved a 0.84% points higher accuracy than the model without knowledge injection. However, only injecting knowledge during testing should not be done for SemEval-2015. This results in a 2.17% points lower out-of-sample accuracy compared to LCR-Rot-hop++.

In the larger dataset of SemEval-2016, the results differ. Now, knowledge injection during testing outperforms the other models with a higher accuracy of 1.39% points compared to the second-best. In this case, injecting knowledge during training leads to the lowest accuracy.

These differences between the models could be explained by how the knowledge is injected and by the size of the datasets. For the smaller dataset SemEval-2015, injecting knowledge only during testing decreases its performance. An explanation for this is that many words injected by the domain ontology, have not appeared in the training data before. Hence, words that the model has not yet learned are injected, possibly changing the meaning of the sentence which makes it more difficult for the model to classify.

In larger datasets like SemEval-2016, the above problem is not present, since there is a bigger chance that words from the sentiment ontology are already included in the training data and hence the model recognizes these. Moreover, when knowledge is only injected during testing, the vector embeddings of the domain ontology knowledge are not updated, instead random vector embeddings are used. [19] have demonstrated that random embeddings can actually outperform trained and updated embeddings. This effect is especially present for larger datasets [19], hence explaining why these random vectors perform better for the SemEval-2016 dataset than for the SemEval-2015 dataset.

For larger datasets, when only injecting knowledge in training, the problem is the other way around. As the results for SemEval-2016 demonstrate, injecting knowledge during training for larger datasets decreases the accuracy. This is due to knowledge noise, which causes the model to incorrectly learn input semantics. The effect of such an incorrect meaning is less big for injecting knowledge during testing. This is a local knowledge noise since the model only predicts the wrong sentiment for that specific sentence but does not train the model using this incorrect meaning. However, when this happens in training, the model uses this input to train the model and it could impact all further predictions. It is more likely that such knowledge noise happens with larger datasets since more sentences are used for training. This could explain why injecting knowledge during training works well for SemEval-2015 but decreases the models' performance for SemEval-2016.

Table 2. Out-of-sample accuracy of LCR-Rot-hop++ and LCR-Rot-hop-Kfont++ for the SemEval-2015 and SemEval-2016 datasets.

	SemEval-2015	SemEval-2016
LCR-Rot-hop++	79.56%	85.69%
LCR-Rot-hop-Kfont++ (train)	**80.40%**	85.54%
LCR-Rot-hop-Kfont++ (test)	77.39%	**87.08%**
LCR-Rot-hop-Kfont++ (train + test)	80.07%	85.69%

6 Conclusion

In this work, we have proposed a new ABSC model: LCR-Rot-hop-Kfont++. We inject knowledge from a domain ontology into the state-of-the-art LCR-Rot-hop++ model for ABSC inspired by previous work on Kformer. When only considering accuracy, knowledge injection generally leads to improved performance. However, the dataset size affects when knowledge injection is most effective. In smaller datasets, knowledge injection should only be done during training so the model can learn a larger amount of words. These extra knowledge can be utilized during testing to classify more sentiments correctly. For larger datasets, on the other hand, it is better to inject knowledge only during testing since this prevents training on knowledge noise. Moreover, having a larger training dataset increases the chance that injected knowledge during testing was already seen during training and thus boosts the performance of the model.

In this research, only synonyms of the words in the sentence are added, also called 0-hop knowledge injection. Hence for further research, we want to test if 1-hop, 2-hops, or even more hops could give more context to the sentence and would be able to improve the model's accuracy. Moreover, only knowledge was injected into the top layers of the transformer: layers 10 through 12. Exploring the injection of knowledge in other layers would be an intriguing area for further work. Lastly, we would like to explore knowledge injection in sentiment mining models that use argumentation theory [8] or cross-domain similarities [9].

References

1. Bergstra, J., Bardenet, R., Bengio, Y., Kégl, B.: Algorithms for hyper-parameter optimization. In: 25th Annual Conference on Neural Information Processing Systems (NIPS 2011), pp. 2546–2554. Curran Associates, Inc. (2011)
2. Brauwers, G., Frasincar, F.: A survey on aspect-based sentiment classification. ACM Comput. Sur. **55**(4), 65:1–65:37 (2023)
3. Cadeddu, A., et al.: A comparative analysis of knowledge injection strategies for large language models in the scholarly domain. Eng. Appl. Artif. Intell. **133**, 108166 (2024)
4. Chen, J., Hu, P., Jimenez-Ruiz, E., Holter, O.M., Antonyrajah, D., Horrocks, I.: OWL2Vec*: embedding of OWL ontologies. Mach. Learn. **110**(7), 1813–1845 (2021)
5. Dai, D., Dong, L., Hao, Y., Sui, Z., Chang, B., Wei, F.: Knowledge neurons in pretrained transformers. In: 60th Annual Meeting of the Association for Computational Linguistics (ACL 2022), pp. 8493–8502. ACL (2022)
6. Dekker, R., Gielisse, D., Jaggan, C., Meijers, S., Frasincar, F.: Knowledge injection for aspect-based sentiment classification. In: trauss, C., Amagasa, T., Kotsis, G., Tjoa, A.M., Khalil, I. (eds.) 34th International Conference on Database and Expert Systems Applications, (DEXA 2023). LNCS, vol. 14147, pp. 173–187. Springer, Cham (2023). https://doi.org/10.1007/978-3-031-39821-6_14
7. Devlin, J., Chang, M.W., Lee, K., Toutanova, K.: BERT: Pre-training of deep bidirectional transformers for language understanding. In: 2019 Conference of the North American Chapter of the Association for Computational Linguistics: Human Language Technologies (NAACL-HLT 2019), pp. 4171–4186. ACL (2019)

8. Dragoni, M., da Costa Pereira, C., Tettamanzi, A.G., Villata, S.: SMACk: An argumentation framework for opinion mining. In: 25th International Joint Conference on Artificial Intelligence (IJCAI 2016), pp. 4242–4243. AAAI Press (2016)
9. Dragoni, M., Petrucci, G.: A fuzzy-based strategy for multi-domain sentiment analysis. Int. J. Approximate Reasoning **93**, 59–73 (2018)
10. Hendrycks, D., Gimpel, K.: Bridging nonlinearities and stochastic regularizers with Gaussian error linear units. arXiv preprint arXiv:1606.08415 (2016)
11. Liu, B.: Sentiment analysis: mining opinions, sentiments, and emotions. Cambridge University Press, second edn. (2020)
12. Liu, W., Zhou, P., Zhao, Z., Wang, Z., Ju, Q., Deng, H., Wang, P.: K-BERT: enabling language representation with knowledge graph. In: 34th AAAI Conference on Artificial Intelligence (AAAI 2020), pp. 2901–2908. AAAI Press (2020)
13. Ostendorff, M., Bourgonje, P., Berger, M., Moreno-Schneider, J., Rehm, G., Gipp, B.: Enriching BERT with knowledge graph embeddings for document classification. In: 15th Conference on Natural Language Processing (KONVENS 2019), pp. 307–314. University of Erlingen-Nuremberg (2019)
14. Pontiki, M., et al.: SemEval-2016 task 5: aspect based sentiment analysis. In: 10th International Workshop on Semantic Evaluation (SemEval 2016). pp. 19–30. ACL (2016)
15. Pontiki, M., Galanis, D., Papageorgiou, H., Manandhar, S., Androutsopoulos, I.: SemEval-2015 task 12: aspect based sentiment analysis. In: 9th International Workshop on Semantic Evaluation (SemEval 2015), pp. 486–495. ACL (2015)
16. Schouten, K., Frasincar, F.: Survey on aspect-level sentiment analysis. IEEE Trans. Knowl. Data Eng. **28**(3), 813–830 (2016)
17. Schouten, K., Frasincar, F.: Ontology-driven sentiment analysis of product and service aspects. In: Gangemi, A., et al. (eds.) 15th International Semantic Web Conference (ESWC 2018), LNCS, vol. 10843, pp. 608–623. Springer, Cham (2018). https://doi.org/10.1007/978-3-319-93417-4_39
18. Schouten, K., Frasincar, F., de Jong, F.: Ontology-enhanced aspect-based sentiment analysis. In: Cabot, J., De Virgilio, R., Torlone, R. (eds.) 17th International Conference on Web Engineering (ICWE 2017). LNCS, vol. 10360, pp. 302–320. Springer (2017). https://doi.org/10.1007/978-3-319-60131-1_17
19. Tokarchuk, E., Niculae, V.: The unreasonable effectiveness of random target embeddings for continuous-output neural machine translation. In: 2024 Conference of the North American Chapter of the Association for Computational Linguistics: Human Language Technologies (NAACL-HLT 2024), pp. 653–662. ACL (2024)
20. Truşcă, M.M., Frasincar, F.: Survey on aspect detection for aspect-based sentiment analysis. Artif. Intelli. Rev. **56**(5), 3797–3846 (2022)
21. Truşcă, M.M., Wassenberg, D., Frasincar, F., Dekker, R.: A hybrid approach for aspect-based sentiment analysis using deep contextual word embeddings and hierarchical attention. In: 20th Conference on Web Engineering (ICWE 2020), LNCS, vol. 12128, pp. 365–380. Springer, Cham (2020). https://doi.org/10.1007/978-3-030-50578-3_25
22. Vaswani, A., et al.: Attention is all you need. In: 31st International Conference on Neural Information Processing Systems (NIPS 2017), pp. 6000–6010. Curran Associates, Inc. (2017)
23. Wallaart, O., Frasincar, F.: A hybrid approach for aspect-based sentiment analysis using a lexicalized domain ontology and attentional neural models. In: Hitzler, P., et al. (eds.) 16th Extended Semantic Web Conference (ESWC 2019), LNCS, vol. 11503, pp. 363–378. Springer, Cham (2019). https://doi.org/10.1007/978-3-030-21348-0_24

24. Yao, Y., Huang, S., Dong, L., Wei, F., Chen, H., Zhang, N.: Kformer: knowledge injection in transformer feed-forward layers. In: Lu, W., Huang, S., Hong, Y., Zhou, X. (eds.) 11th International Conference on Natural Language Processing and Chinese Computing (NLPCC 2022), LNCS, vol. 13551, pp. 131–143. Springer, Cham (2022). https://doi.org/10.1007/978-3-031-17120-8_11
25. Zhang, W., Li, X., Deng, Y., Bing, L., Lam, W.: A survey on aspect-based sentiment analysis: tasks, methods, and challenges. IEEE Trans. Knowl. Data Eng. **35**(11), 11019–11038 (2023)

Happiness Maximization Queries with Two-Sided Fairness

Jie Dong[1] and Jiping Zheng[1,2](✉)

[1] College of Computer Science and Technology, Nanjing University of Aeronautics and Astronautics, Nanjing, China
{djnuaa,jzh}@nuaa.edu.cn

[2] State Key Laboratory for Novel Software Technology, Nanjing University, Nanjing, China

Abstract. The happiness maximization query which overcomes the inherent drawbacks of the top-k and skyline queries has been an important tool for multi-criteria decision making in the last decades. To ensure decisions made by these queries to capture users' diverse needs and preferences, and to be more applicable against data discrimination and bias, fairness from the data-side and user-side needs to be considered simultaneously. In this paper, we consider the problem of answering the happiness maximization query with two-sided fairness which has never been investigated before. By truncating the happiness ratio function of the query, we transform our problem to a submodular function maximization problem with constraints, and the data-side fairness is modeled similar to the matroid constraint while the user-side fairness along with the happiness maximization query is treated as a multi-objective optimization problem. Further, we provide the GREEDY2F algorithm by incorporating the elaborate techniques of above two areas. Extensive experiments on both real-world and synthetic datasets illustrate the effectiveness and efficiency of our proposed algorithm.

Keywords: Happiness Maximization Query · Two-sided Fairness · Submodular Maximization · Multi-objective Optimization

1 Introduction

Extracting a small representative subset based on a combination of multiple criteria from a large dataset is an important functionality of modern database systems [1,27,29]. In the community, the most widely used tools to fulfill this task are the top-k query [10,16], the skyline query [2] and the happiness maximization query [23,40,44,48] (a.k.a. the regret minimization query [45,47]). The happiness maximization query, which overcomes the drawbacks of the top-k query needing to specify an exact utility function and the skyline query outputting uncontrollable size of the results, has received great attention in the last decades. For the happiness maximization query, the notion of happiness ratio is used to quantify how happy a user is if she/he obtains the best point in the selected subset instead of the best point in the whole dataset with regard to a utility function. Moreover, a utility space is given and the minimum of happiness ratios among the utility functions in the space is expected to be maximized. However, the decisions

I. Awan et al. (Eds.): WISE 2025, LNCS 16367, pp. 595–610, 2026.
https://doi.org/10.1007/978-981-95-7394-3_40

or the results of the query usually neglect users' diverse needs and preferences, *i.e.*, fairness from the user-side [25,50]. In addition, data discrimination and bias, *i.e.*, fairness from the data-side are also not fully taken into account [4,18,31,34,42].

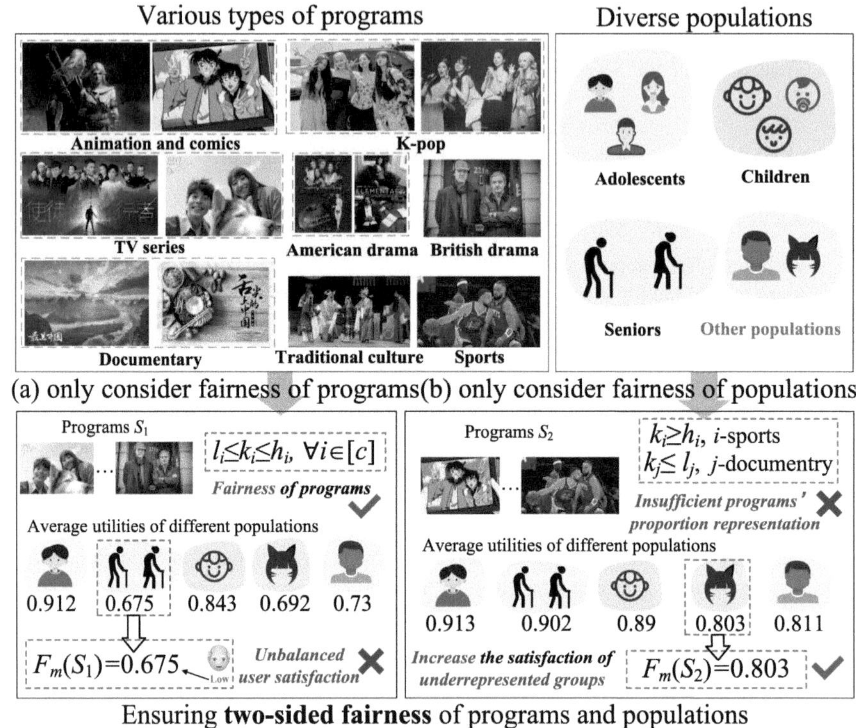

Fig. 1. Illustration of the two-sided fairness between TV programs and diverse populations of users. In this example, we observe that considering fairness only on the program's side or the user's side leads to unfairness on the other side.

Since the returned extracted subset of the happiness maximization query is determined by both user utilities and the dataset, only considering fairness from one-side is not reasonable in real applications. Following we provide an example of recommending TV programs for users composed of diverse populations as illustrated in Fig. 1. For the fairness from TV program-side, we expect the returned subset to satisfy the popular group fairness constraints [4,18,31,42] (a.k.a. statistical parity [7], equal acceptance rate [52]). That is, the number of TV programs of each type k_i is limited to a range $[l_i, h_i]$ [9]. For the fairness from user-side, we denote the satisfaction by the average utility of each population and we expect the minimum value of the satisfaction denoted by F_m among the diverse populations to be maximized, *i.e.*, no population of users is overlooked. In Fig. 1(a), enforcing fairness only on TV program-side may achieve balanced exposure among various types of TV programs, but the results are unfair to the population of seniors who gets the minimum value of the satisfaction, *i.e.*, $F_m = 0.675$. As a contrast, Fig. 1(b) shows that only focusing on fairness from user-side may increase the satisfactions of diverse populations, *i.e.*, $F_m = 0.803$, but violating the group fairness where the results may be biased to some types of programs, *e.g.*, the number of sports programs k_i exceeds the upper bound h_i while the number of documentary programs k_j falls below the lower bound l_j. Therefore, to make the results really reflect the distributions of data and the preferences of users, it's vital to simultaneously ensure fairness from both user-side and data-side.

In the literature, since the returned results for querying or subset selecting tasks are heavily affected by discriminatory and biased data, most of the researches consider fairness across many applications only from data-side [6,22,24,28,43]. There are some works considering fairness from data providers/curators/items, *i.e.*, data-side, and users/consumers, *i.e.*, user-side, in search and recommendation [5,15,37–39] and market analysis [17,33] areas. For the happiness maximization query, only a few works [48,51] consider fairness when processing. However, from the example and analysis above, a practical and reasonable extracted subset returned by the happiness maximization query should consider fairness from the two sides and the existing two-sided methods from the areas of search, recommendation and market analysis cannot be directly applied to the happiness maximization query since they have distinct definitions leading to completely different techniques.

In this paper, we first investigate the problem of answering the happiness maximization query with two-sided fairness. After transforming the happiness ratio function of the happiness maximization query to a monotone non-decreasing submodular function by the truncation technique, we formulate our problem to a submodular maximization problem with constraints. Since the data-sided fairness is similar to the matroid constraint for submodular maximization, we utilize the greedy process of maximizing a submodular function under matroid constraints to satisfy the fairness from this side. To the user-sided fairness, we need to maximize the satisfaction among the populations along with the happiness ratio of the users, we treat the task as a multi-objective optimization problem. Further, to satisfy the two-sided fairness for the happiness maximization query, we propose the GREEDY2F algorithm by incorporating the elaborate techniques of *submodular maximization* and *multi-objective optimization* areas. Extensive experiments on both real-world and synthetic datasets illustrate the effectiveness and efficiency of our proposed GREEDY2F algorithm.

In summary, our main contributions are listed as follows:

- We investigate the problem of the happiness maximization query with two-sided fairness and construct the fairness models from the user-side and data-side respectively.
- We propose an efficient and effective algorithm, called GREEDY2F by exploiting the submodularity maximization and multi-objective optimization techniques.
- Extensive experiments on both real-world and synthetic datasets illustrate the effectiveness and efficiency of our proposed GREEDY2F algorithm.

The rest of this paper is organized as follows. In Sect. 2, we propose related concepts and formally define the problem of happiness maximization query with two-sided fairness, then illustrate the properties of happiness ratio function. We propose the

GREEDY2F algorithm in Sect. 3. In Sect. 4, we conduct the experiments and analyze the results. Finally, we conclude our work in Sect. 5.

2 Preliminaries

In this section, we first introduce some basic concepts, then formulate the fairness models from two sides and finally define our problem of *the happiness maximization query with two-sided fairness* followed by the concepts of the minimum happiness ratio function, group fairness and minimum fairness models.

2.1 Basic Concepts

Let D be a set of n d-dimensional points with positive real values. For each point $p = \langle p[1], p[2], ..., p[d]\rangle \in D$, the value on the i-th dimension is denoted by $p[i]$. Without loss of generality, we assume that each numeric attribute is normalized to range [0, 1].

Linear Utility Function and User Preferences of Populations. User preferences tend to be modeled as the class of non-negative linear functions, where a utility vector $u = \langle u[1], u[2], ..., u[d]\rangle$ represents a user's preference over d attributes. Given a utility function u, the utility of a data point p is denoted as the inner product of u and p, *i.e.*, $u(p) = \sum_{i=1}^{d} u[i] \cdot p[i]$. Accounting for the scale invariance of happiness ratio [23,48], we assume that the utility vector is re-scaled to be a unit vector based on the l_1-norm, *i.e.*, $\sum_{i=1}^{d} u[i] = 1$. All user preferences of diverse populations can be defined as a set of linear utility functions $U = \{U_1, U_2, ..., U_t\}$, where U_i reflects the preferences of a specific population.

Definition 1. ***Happiness ratio.*** *Given a dataset D, a subset $S \subseteq D$ and a utility function u, the happiness ratio of S, represented as $hr_{u,D}(S)$, is defined as*

$$hr_{u,D}(S) = \frac{\max_{p \in S} u(p)}{\max_{p \in D} u(p)}. \tag{1}$$

Obviously, hr ranges from 0 to 1. The user with utility function u will be happier if hr approaches 1.

Definition 2. ***Minimum happiness ratio*** [23,48]. *Given a dataset D, a subset $S \subseteq D$ and a class of utility functions U, the minimum happiness ratio of S,* i.e., $mhr_{U,D}(S)$ *is defined as*

$$mhr_{U,D}(S) = \min_{u \in U} \frac{\max_{p \in S} u(p)}{\max_{p \in D} u(p)}. \tag{2}$$

2.2 Fairness Model

In this section, we formulate the *group fairness* model from data-side and the *minimum fairness* model from user-side. Follwing the Fig. 1, we present the normalized statistics of 10 TV programs with three numeric attributes in Table 1 and the preference of twelve diverse user populations in Table 2 as an example.

Definition 3. ***Group fairness*** [4,18,31,34]. *Given a dataset D divided into c disjoint groups $\{D_1, D_2, \ldots, D_c\}$ through sensitive attributes, the lower bounds set $L = \{l_1, l_2, \ldots, l_c\}$ and upper bounds set $H = \{h_1, h_2, \ldots, h_c\}$ where l_i and h_i, $i \in [c]$, are positive integers, the group fairness constraints are defined by restricting that the number of points k_i selected from each group D_i is between a lower bound l_i and an upper bound h_i,* i.e., $l_i \leq k_i \leq h_i$.

Based on Table 1, the recommendation system aims to select a size-4 subset from the total 10 TV programs. If we utilize the happiness maximization query to address this issue, the subset $\{p_1, p_3, p_4, p_5\}$ is returned. However, it is abnormal that no program from TV series is included which has the largest group size, obviously violating the group fairness constraints. Instead, one of the reasonable subset may be $\{p_1, p_3, p_4, p_6\}$.

Table 1. An Example of Various TV Programs.

TV program	Group	Score	Click rate	Collection
p_1	Sports	0.97	0.75	0.86
p_2	Sports	0.30	0.73	0.51
p_3	Documentary	0.66	0.87	0.71
p_4	Documentary	0.89	0.63	0.60
p_5	Documentary	0.83	0.68	0.61
p_6	TV series	0.61	0.57	0.37
p_7	TV series	0.25	0.27	0.48
p_8	TV series	0.28	0.27	0.56
p_9	TV series	0.51	0.71	0.76
p_{10}	TV series	0.44	0.11	0.50

Definition 4. ***Minimum fairness*** [13,15,35]. *Given a dataset D, a subset $S \subseteq D$, partitioning the users set U into t disjoint populations where $\bigcup_{i=1}^{t} U_i = U$, $U_i \cap U_j = \emptyset$ for $\forall i, j \in [t], i \neq j$ and $|U_i| = m_i$. The user-sided fairness presented by the minimum average utility F_m among the populations is defined as*

$$F_m(S) = \min_{i \in [t]} \frac{1}{m_i} \sum_{u \in U_i} hr_{u,D}(S). \tag{3}$$

We provide a simple example to illustrate this concept by considering two result sets $S_1 = \{p_1, p_3, p_4, p_5\}$ and $S_2 = \{p_2, p_5, p_7, p_{10}\}$. Obviously, $F_m(S_1) = \min\{\frac{1}{1} \times 1, \frac{1}{5} \times (1+1+1+1+0.1047), \frac{1}{2} \times (1+1), \frac{1}{4} \times (0.8684+1+0.3231+0.2133)\} = \min\{1, 0.82094, 1, 0.6012\} = 0.6012$, $F_m(S_2) = \min\{\frac{1}{1} \times 1, \frac{1}{5} \times (1+1+1+1+1), \frac{1}{2} \times (1+1), \frac{1}{4} \times (1+1+1+1)\} = \min\{1,1,1,1\} = 1$. Notably, $F_m(S_1) = 0.6012$ is relatively low, indicating an uneven distribution of utility across different user groups, particularly with one group having significantly lower average utility value. In contrast, S_2 achieves the optimal value of F_m for the user-sided fairness with $F_m(S_2) = 1$ in the example, demonstrating the effectiveness of minimum fairness model.

Table 2. The Preference of Diverse User Populations

User	Population	Preference	User	Population	Preference
u_1	Adolescents	$\{0.97, 0.02, 0.01\}$	u_7	Seniors	$\{0.20, 0.53, 0.27\}$
u_2	Children	$\{0.71, 0.16, 0.13\}$	u_8	Seniors	$\{0.17, 0.44, 0.39\}$
u_3	Children	$\{0.03, 0.61, 0.36\}$	u_9	Adults	$\{0.29, 0.33, 0.38\}$
u_4	Children	$\{0.07, 0.48, 0.45\}$	u_{10}	Adults	$\{0.36, 0.46, 0.18\}$
u_5	Children	$\{0.05, 0.73, 0.12\}$	u_{11}	Adults	$\{0.14, 0.21, 0.65\}$
u_6	Children	$\{0.09, 0.05, 0.86\}$	u_{12}	Adults	$\{0.09, 0.16, 0.75\}$

2.3 Problem Definition

Next, we formally define our problem of *the happiness maximization query with two-sided fairness* based on above notions.

Given a dataset D with c disjoint groups $\{D_1, D_2, \dots, D_c\}$, a positive integer $k \in \mathbb{Z}^+$, a set of $2c$ positive integers $l_1, l_2, \dots, l_c$ and $h_1, h_2, \dots, h_c$, partitioning the users set U into t disjoint user populations $\{U_1, U_2, \dots, U_t\}$, the goal is to select a subset of k data points $S \subseteq D$ that ensuring two-sided fairness while maximizing *mhr* simultaneously. Formally, we extract a subset

$$S = \underset{S \subseteq D:|S|=k}{\arg\max}\ mhr(S)\ s.t.\ \max F_m(S), l_i \leq |S \cap D_i| \leq h_i, \forall i \in [c]. \tag{4}$$

Based on the existing results from [23], the problem is NP-hard for any $d \geq 3$, demonstrating it cannot be solved optimally in polynomial time unless $P = NP$.

2.4 Properties

Given a database D, a set function $f : 2^D \rightarrow \mathbb{R}_+$, a subset $S \subseteq D$ and a point $p \in D \backslash S$, let $f(p|S) = f(S \cup \{p\}) - f(S)$ be the marginal gain of adding point p to the set S. We define *submodularity* and *monotonicity* of function f.

Definition 5. ***Submodularity.*** *A set function f is submodular iff for any $S_1 \subseteq S_2 \subseteq D$ and $p \in D \setminus S_2$, it holds that $f(p|S_1) \geq f(p|S_2)$, which can be equivalently defined as satisfying the inequality $f(S_1) + f(S_2) \geq f(S_1 \cup S_2) + f(S_1 \cap S_2)$.*

Definition 6. ***Monotonicity.*** *A set function f is monotone non-decreasing iff for any $S \subseteq D$ and $p \in D \backslash S$, it holds that $f(p|S) \geq 0$.*

Note that the happiness ratio function hr is submodular and monotone as indicated in Lemma 1.

Lemma 1. *The happiness ratio function $hr_{u,D}(S)$ is submodular and monotone for any vector $u \in \mathbb{R}_+^d$ [26, 46, 48].*

A notion closely related to the above-defined *group fairness constraints* is *matroid* [19]. Specifically, a matroid M is defined on a finite ground set D and a family $\mathcal{I}$ of subsets of D called *independent sets*.

Definition 7. ***Matroid*** [8,9]. *A matroid* $M = (D, \mathcal{I})$ *based on the group fairness constraints, where the family of independent sets is*

$$\mathcal{I} = \left\{ S \subseteq D : \sum_{c=1}^{C} \max\{|S \cap D_c|, l_c\} \leq k \wedge |S \cap D_c| \leq h_c, \forall c \in [C] \right\}.$$

All feasible size-k subsets of D under the group fairness constraints are in $\mathcal{I}$ [9]. Hence, the group fairness constraints will be treated as a special case of matroid constraints in our proposed algorithms.

3 Algorithm

In this section, we present our GREEDY2F algorithm to answer the happiness maximization query with two-sided fairness.

3.1 The GREEDY2F Algorithm

According to the definition, our problem can be divided into two sub-problems, *i.e.*, computing a size-k solution S that maximizes $mhr(S)$ for all users and satisfying the *group fairness* from the data-side while simultaneously maximizing F_m from the user-side.

From the perspective of grouped data according to sensitive attributes, we attempt to consider the group fairness constraints with upper and lower bounds. For user populations with heterogeneous preferences, emphasis is put on the population with F_m when selecting data points. By Lemma 1, since the monotonicity and submodularity properties of hr, the linear combination $\frac{1}{m_i}\sum_{u \in U_i} hr_{u,D}(S)$ of hr is also monotone and submodulor. The truncated form of $\min\{\tau \cdot OPT_0, \frac{1}{m_i}\sum_{u \in U_i} hr_{u,D}(S)\}$ utiliting a capped value $\tau \cdot OPT_0$ and aiming to minimize the monotone submodular function along with the capped value, has been proved to be monotone and submodulor [14]. Therefore, we transform F_m into a monotone submodular function $\overline{F_m}(S) = \frac{1}{t}\sum_{i \in [t]} \min\{\tau \cdot OPT_0, \frac{1}{m_i}\sum_{u \in U_i} hr_{u,D}(S)\}$ via the *truncation technique* [14,21,48,49] which has been widely used in submodular applications. Then this constraint is represented as *the multi-objective optimization problem* [11,12,30,32,35,36] expressed as $\overline{F_m} \geq \tau \cdot OPT_0$ by a threshold parameter $\tau \in (0, 1)$ because its goal is to bridge the gap between the optimal values with and without the fairness in each loop thus achieving the all user groups' fairness. Similarly, mhr is converted into a monotone submodular function in the same way as F_m's, *i.e.*, $\overline{mhr}(S) = \min\{OPT_0, mhr_{U,D}(S)\}$, and we further exploit the *greedy selection strategy* for submodular maximization under matroid constraints for our problem.

As shown in Algorithm 1, the GREEDY2F algorithm begins by applying the SATURATE algorithm as shown in Algorithm 2 on F_m to obtain an initial solution S_0 along with its optimal value OPT_0 (Line 3). Based on these results, we define a new truncated function $\overline{F_m}(S)$ by the computed results through SATURATE (Line 4). Next, the algorithm proceeds in three stages. In the first stage (Lines 5–13), the algorithm generally adopts a *greedy selection strategy* based on the function's submodularity property by

Algorithm 1: The GREEDY2F algorithm

Input: A dataset D with c disjoint groups $\{D_1, D_2, \dots, D_c\}$, t user populations $U = \{U_1, U_2, \dots, U_t\}$ and the number of users among each population $m_i = |U_i|$, the integer $k \in \mathbb{Z}^+$, balance factor $\tau \in (0, 1)$, bounds set collection $\mathcal{L} = \{\{l_1, h_1\}, \dots, \{l_c, h_c\}\}$.

Output: A feasible solution $S \subseteq D$ s.t. $|S| = k$.

1 Initialize $S \leftarrow \emptyset$;
2 $F_m(S) \leftarrow \min_{i\in[t]} \frac{1}{m_i} \sum_{u\in U_i} hr_{u,D}(S)$;
3 $S_0, OPT_0 \leftarrow$ SATURATE(F_m) ;
4 $\overline{F_m}(S) \leftarrow \frac{1}{t} \sum_{i\in[t]} \min\{\tau \cdot OPT_0, \frac{1}{m_i} \sum_{u\in U_i} hr_{u,D}(S)\}$;
5 **while** $|S| < k$ **do**
6   **foreach** $i \in [c]$ *where* $|S \cap D_i| < l_i$ **do**
7         $p^* \leftarrow \arg\max_{p\in D_i\setminus S} \{\overline{F_m}(S \cup \{p\}) - \overline{F_m}(S)\}$;
8         $S \leftarrow S \cup \{p^*\}$;
9   **if** $\overline{F_m}(S) < \tau \cdot OPT_0$ **then**
10   **foreach** $i \in [c]$ *where* $l_i \leq |S \cap D_i| < h_i$ **do**
11             $p^* \leftarrow \arg\max_{p\in D_i\setminus S} \{\overline{F_m}(S \cup \{p\}) - \overline{F_m}(S)\}$;
12             $S \leftarrow S \cup \{p^*\}$;
13   **else break**
14 $\overline{mhr}(S) \leftarrow \min\{OPT_0, mhr_{U,D}(S)\}$;
15 **if** $|S| = k$ *and* $\overline{F_m}(S) < \tau \cdot OPT_0$ **then**
16     $S \leftarrow S_0$;
17 **else if** $|S| < k$ **then**
18   **foreach** $i \in [c]$ *where* $l_i \leq |S \cap D_i| < h_i$ **do**
19         $p^* \leftarrow \arg\max_{p\in D_i\setminus S} \{\overline{mhr}(S \cup \{p\}) - \overline{mhr}(S)\}$;
20         $S \leftarrow S \cup \{p^*\}$;
21   **if** $|S| = k$ **then break**
22 **return** S ;

adding the points that provide the maximum marginal gain on $\overline{F_m}$ to S at each iteration. Specifically, priorities are first given to groups that have not yet met the lower bounds. The process is similar to the greedy process of maximizing a submodular function with matroid constraints [3,8,20]. Once all the lower bounds are satisfied but $\overline{F_m}(S) < \tau \cdot OPT_0$, the algorithm continues selecting data points from groups without violating the fairness constraints to further improve the value of $\overline{F_m}$. In the second stage (Lines 15–16), if the current solution S reaches the size k but $\overline{F_m}(S) < \tau \cdot OPT_0$, S_0 is returned by the SATURATE algorithm to ensure quality guarantees. The third stage (Lines 17–21) is invoked when the cardinality constraint k is not reached. To make the function value as large as possible, the algorithm selects the data point that maximizes the gain of $\overline{mhr}(S)$ while still satisfying the group fairness constraints, until the size of the solution S is k.

3.2 The SATURATE Algorithm

In this section, we explain the SATURATE algorithm in detail. Algorithm 2 presents the process of a truncated function $\overline{F}(S)$ to realize the optimal approximation solution. The main idea of SATURATE is to probe different values of θ in the range $[\theta_{\min}, \theta_{\max}]$ for the problem and find the optimal θ value. To achieve this, we exploit the binary search to asymptotically approach θ with an error parameter ε and use a greedy strategy to construct a size-k subset that approximately maximizes the truncated function $\overline{F}(S) = \min\{\theta, F_{mi}(S)\}$.

Specifically, the algorithm begins by initializing the lower bound $\theta_{\min}$ at 0 and the upper bound $\theta_{\max}$ at 1 for the binary search since the function value in our algorithm must be in the interval [0,1] (Line 1). When entering the binary search loop, it continues as long as $\theta_{\min} < (1-\varepsilon) \cdot \theta_{\max}$: In each iteration process, the current value of the truncated function $\overline{F}(S)$ is computed (Line 4). While the current solution set does not satisfy the cardinality constraint k, the algorithm selects the point p^* from the dataset D that maximizes the marginal gain of $\overline{F}(S)$ and adds it to the current solution set S (Lines 5–7). If $\overline{F}(S)$ reaches or exceeds the current threshold θ, $\theta_{\min}$ is updated to θ and the current solution is recorded as the optimal solution; Otherwise, the $\theta_{\max}$ is adjusted to θ (Lines 8–11).

Algorithm 2: The SATURATE algorithm

Input: A dataset D, t user populations $U = \{U_1, U_2, \ldots, U_t\}$ and the number of users among each population $m_i = |U_i|$, the integer $k \in \mathbb{Z}^+$, an error $\varepsilon \in (0,1)$.
Output: A feasible solution S^* and the $\overline{F}(S^*)$ value.

1 Initialize $\theta_{min} \leftarrow 0$, $\theta_{max} \leftarrow 1$, $S^* \leftarrow \emptyset$;
2 **while** $\theta_{min} < (1-\varepsilon) \cdot \theta_{max}$ **do**
3     $S \leftarrow \emptyset$, $\theta \leftarrow \frac{\theta_{min}+\theta_{max}}{2}$;
4     $\overline{F}(S) \leftarrow \frac{1}{t}\sum_{i\in[t]} \min\{\theta, F_{mi}(S)\}$;
5   **while** $|S| < k$ **do**
6         $p^* \leftarrow \arg\max_{p\in D\setminus S} \{\overline{F}(S \cup \{p\}) - \overline{F}(S)\}$;
7         $S \leftarrow S \cup \{p^*\}$;
8   **if** $\overline{F}(S) \geq \theta$ **then**
9         $\theta_{min} \leftarrow \theta$, $S^* \leftarrow S$;
10   **else**
11         $\theta_{max} \leftarrow \theta$;
12 **return** S^* and $\overline{F}(S^*)$;

Time Complexity Analysis. Let $m' = \max_{i\in[t]} |U_i|$, $m = |U|$. The SATURATE Algorithm runs in $O(km'nt \cdot \log \frac{1}{\varepsilon})$ time. The time complexity of greedy process for maximizing $\overline{F_m}$ and the supplementary data point operation to maximize mhr are $O(ckm'nt)$ and $O(cnk)$ respectively. Thus, the time complexity of algorithm 1 is $O(km'nt \cdot (\log \frac{1}{\varepsilon} + c))$.

4 Experiments

In this section, we evaluate the performance of our proposed algorithms on synthetic and real-world datasets. We first introduce the experimental setup in Sect. 4.1. The experimental results are reported in Sect. 4.2.

4.1 Setup

All algorithms are implemented in C++, and all experiments are conducted on a PC running Ubuntu 20.04 LTS with a 3.00GHz processor and 32GB memory.

Datasets. We run the experiments on four real-world datasets and synthetic datasets created by the generator [2], as shown in Table 3.

Table 3. Statistics of datasets in the experiments.

Dataset	Group	d	n	c
AntiCor [2]	-	2–6	10^2-10^7	2–5
Adult[a]	Gender, Race, G+R	5	32,561	2, 5, 10
Compas[b]	Gender, isRecid, G+iR	9	4,743	2, 2, 4
Lawschs[c]	Gender, Race, G+R	2	65,494	2, 5
YouTube[d]	City	4	9010	10

[a] https://archive.ics.uci.edu/ml/datasets/adult
[b] https://github.com/propublica/compas-analysis
[c] http://www.seaphe.org/databases.php
[d] https://opendatalab.org.cn/OpenDataLab/YouTube-8M

Baselines. We compare GREEDY2F with three baselines as follows, which differ in how they satisfy constraints.

- SATURATE [21] is a bicriteria approximation algorithm for *robust submodular maximization*, which is used as a subroutine to maximize F_m in our algorithm.
- BIGREEDY [48] is a bicriteria approximation algorithm for the happiness maximization query while achieving the group fairness.
- SPHERE [41] is a *state-of-the-art* algorithm for the happiness maximization query without fairness guarantees.

Metrics. The algorithms are evaluated with four metrics: *MHR*, F_m *value*, *err* for solution quality, and *Runtime* for efficiency. *err* represents the number of group fairness violations [9], *i.e.*, for a given S, $err(S) = \sum_{i\in[c]} \max\{|S \cap D_i| - h_i, l_i - |S \cap D_i|, 0\}$. $err(S) = 0$ means that S satisfies the group fairness constraints. Note that the larger values are better for *MHR* and F_m *value*, and the smaller value is better as to *err*.

We set the number of user populations to $d+1$ in the experiments, for the first d user populations are each assigned a distinct preference distribution on each dimension, while the $(d+1)$-th user population is designed to exhibit balanced preferences across all the d dimensions. Moreover, we set $\tau = 0.9$ in our experiments on experience.

4.2 Experimental Results

In Fig. 2, we present the performance of all the algorithms under the four metrics as the size constraint k varies where $k \in \{10, 20, 30, 40, 50\}$. Note that for the Adult, Lawschs and Compas datasets, we only present the results using their third sensitive attributes while for the AntiCor datasets only present the case $d = 3, n = 10000$ due to space limitations.

Performance on Multi-Dimensional Datasets. We observe that the *MHR* of almost each algorithm's solution exhibits an increasing trend with respect to k in the majority of cases, where SPHERE always outperforms all of the others as expected. However, it violates group fairness constraints all the time while its F_m values fluctuate unstably and with the worst quality in Fig. 2(b). This is because it only concentrates on optimizing the overall solution quality expressed by *MHR* but disregards disparities among user populations. BIGREEDY's *MHR* is notably unstable in Fig. 2(c), due to the higher dimensionality of the Compas dataset, which affects the accuracy of *MHR* estimation relied on an approximate utility space technique.

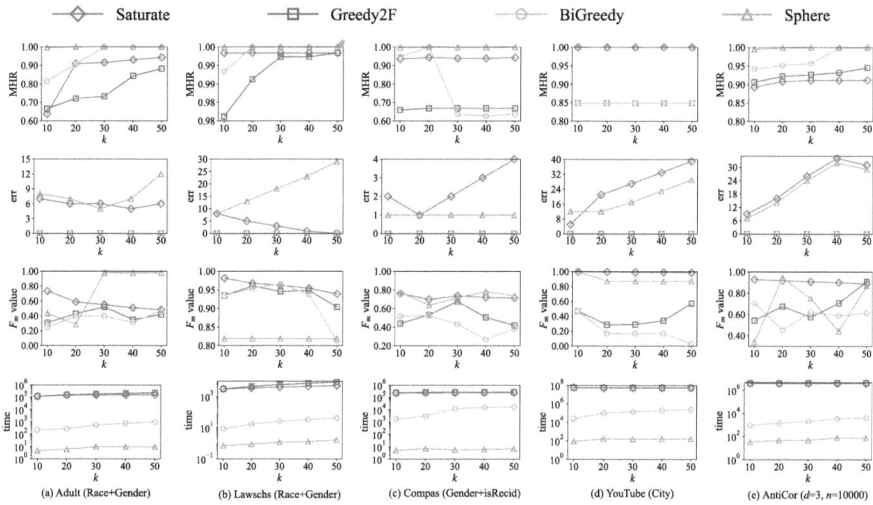

Fig. 2. Comparisons between GREEDY2F and SATURATE, BIGREEDY, SPHERE by varying solution size k on the Adult, Lawschs, Compas, YouTube and AntiCor datasets.

The cost of the two-sided fairness constraints for GREEDY2F leads to a slight decline in *MHR*. Meanwhile, our algorithm satisfies the two-sided fairness constraints all the time in the experiments. Specifically, it maintains $err(S) = 0$ and F_m values are relatively high in comparison to the baselines since we set the balance parameter $\tau = 0.9$. All the baseline algorithms fail to satisfy the two-sided fairness constraints simultaneously. Notably, SATURATE and BIGREEDY, designed for single fairness constraint respectively, demonstrate completely different behaviors. SATURATE consistently achieves good performance in terms of *MHR* by prioritizing the maximization of F_m values. Whereas, the strict group fairness constraints imposed in BIGREEDY result in unstable trends in both *MHR* and F_m value.

In terms of time efficiency, BIGREEDY and SPHERE obtain high efficiency by avoiding many computations to satisfy the minimum fairness constraints while SATURATE and GREEDY2F run slowly to satisfy the fairness due to a large number of submodular function evaluations.

Scalability w.r.t. Dataset Size n and Dimensionality d. To evaluate the scalability of all algorithms in terms of dataset size n and dimensionality d, we conduct experiments on the AntiCor datasets with varying n from 10^2 to 10^6 ($d = 3$ and $k = 3$) and d from 3 to 7 ($n = 10^4$ and $k = 3$) in Fig. 3.

In Fig. 3(a), we observe that GREEDY2F achieves higher *MHR* solution quality and always satisfies the two-sided fairness constraints with $err = 0$ and F_m values having a steady increase. As the dataset size n increases, the running time of each algorithm increases greatly. The SPHERE algorithm runs the fastest, but the quality of the solution set drops significantly, which is reflected in the increase of err and the F_m value's instability.

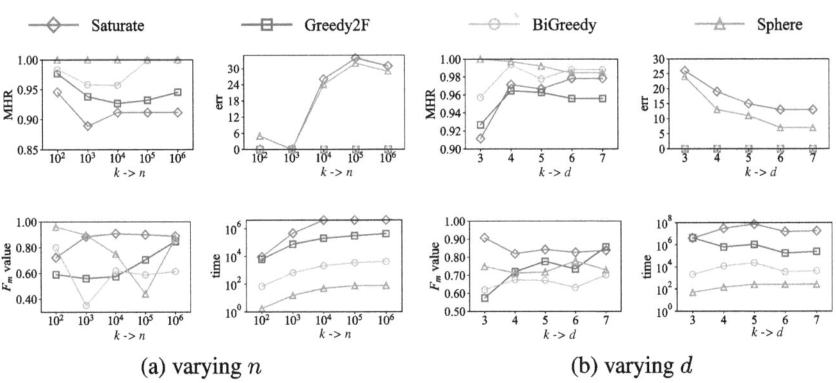

Fig. 3. Performance between GREEDY2F and SATURATE, BIGREEDY, SPHERE by varying dataset size n and dimensionality d on the AntiCor datasets.

Figure 3(b) shows that the results of different algorithms on the AntiCor datasets by varying the dimensionality $d \in \{3, 4, 5, 6, 7\}$. Our GREEDY2F algorithm's performance is slightly inferior to that of SATURATE in other aspects, but it always ensures fairness constraints. SPHERE runs the fastest, but is with the worst quality for all d's. Both scalability experiments show that the user-side fairness guarantee of the BIGREEDY algorithm is not reliable enough.

In summary, compared with the three baseline algorithms, the GREEDY2F algorithm has better scalability, higher solution quality in terms of minimum happiness ratios, and higher efficiency.

5 Conclusion

In this paper, we investigate the problem of the happiness maximization query with two-sided fairness. After showing monotonicity and submodularity of the truncated form of the happiness ratio function, we refer to elaborate techniques from submodular maximization and multi-objective optimization areas and propose the GREEDY2F algorithm to solve our problem. Extensive experiments verify its effectiveness and efficiency. In future work, we would like to explore additional fairness constraints for application in more complex real-world scenarios and improve the algorithm's adaptability.

Acknowledgments. This work is partially supported by the Natural Science Foundation of Jiangsu Province of China under grant No. BK20252032, the Fundamental Research Funds for the Central Universities of China under grant No. NS2024056 and the Postgraduate Research & Practice Innovation Program of NUAA of China under grant No. XCXJH20241601.

References

1. Alonso, O., Baeza-Yates, R. (eds.): Information Retrieval: Advanced Topics and Techniques. Association for Computing Machinery (2024)
2. Borzsony, S., Kossmann, D., Stocker, K.: The skyline operator. In: Proceedings of the 17th International Conference on Data Engineering (ICDE), pp. 421–430 (2001)
3. Calinescu, G., Chekuri, C., Pál, M., Vondrák, J.: Maximizing a monotone submodular function subject to a matroid constraint. SIAM J. Comput. (SICOMP) **40**(6), 1740–1766 (2011)
4. Celis, E., Keswani, V., Straszak, D., Deshpande, A., Kathuria, T., Vishnoi, N.: Fair and diverse dpp-based data summarization. In: Proceedings of the International Conference on Machine Learning (ICML), pp. 716–725 (2018)
5. Do, V., Corbett-Davies, S., Atif, J., Usunier, N.: Two-sided fairness in rankings via lorenz dominance. In: Proceedings of the Advances in Neural Information Processing Systems (NeurIPS), pp. 8596–8608 (2021)
6. Dong, Y., Ma, J., Wang, S., Chen, C., Li, J.: Fairness in graph mining: a survey. IEEE Trans. Knowl. Data Eng. (TKDE) **35**(10), 10583–10602 (2023)
7. Dwork, C., Hardt, M., Pitassi, T., Reingold, O., Zemel, R.: Fairness through awareness. In: Proceedings of the 3rd Innovations in Theoretical Computer Science Conference (ITCS), pp. 214–226 (2012)
8. El Halabi, M., Fusco, F., Norouzi-Fard, A., Tardos, J., Tarnawski, J.: Fairness in streaming submodular maximization over a matroid constraint. In: Proceedings of the International Conference on Machine Learning (ICML), pp. 9150–9171 (2023)
9. El Halabi, M., Mitrović, S., Norouzi-Fard, A., Tardos, J., Tarnawski, J.M.: Fairness in streaming submodular maximization: Algorithms and hardness. In: Proceedings of the Advances in Neural Information Processing Systems (NeurIPS), pp. 13609–13622 (2020)
10. Fagin, R.: Combining fuzzy information from multiple systems. In: Proceedings of the 15th ACM SIGACT-SIGMOD-SIGART Symposium on Principles of Database Systems (PODS), pp. 216–226 (1996)
11. Fazzone, A., Wang, Y., Bonchi, F.: Fair representation in submodular subset selection: A pareto optimization approach. Trans. Mach. Learn. Res. (TMLR) 1–26 (2024)
12. Feng, C., Qian, C.: Multi-objective submodular maximization by regret ratio minimization with theoretical guarantee. In: Proceedings of the AAAI Conference on Artificial Intelligence (AAAI), pp. 12302–12310 (2021)

13. Fu, X., Bhatt, R.R., Basu, S., Pavan, A.: Multi-objective submodular optimization with approximate oracles and influence maximization. In: Proceedings of the 2021 IEEE International Conference on Big Data (Big Data), pp. 328–334 (2021)
14. Fujito, T.: Approximation algorithms for submodular set cover with applications. IEICE Trans. Inf. Syst. **83**(3), 480–487 (2000)
15. García-Soriano, D., Bonchi, F.: Maxmin-fair ranking: individual fairness under group-fairness constraints. In: Proceedings of the 27th ACM SIGKDD Conference on Knowledge Discovery and Data Mining (SIGKDD), pp. 436–446 (2021)
16. Ilyas, I.F., Beskales, G., Soliman, M.A.: A survey of top-k query processing techniques in relational database systems. ACM Comput. Sur. (CSUR) **40**(4), 1–58 (2008)
17. Jain, P., Jha, P., Solanki, S.: Fairness and efficiency in two-sided matching markets. arXiv preprint arXiv:2504.10232 (2025)
18. Kleindessner, M., Awasthi, P., Morgenstern, J.: Fair k-center clustering for data summarization. In: Proceedings of the International Conference on Machine Learning (ICML), pp. 3448–3457 (2019)
19. Korte, B., Vygen, J.: Combinatorial optimization: theory and algorithms. Springer (2008)
20. Krause, A., Golovin, D.: Submodular function maximization. Tractability **3**, 71–104 (2014)
21. Krause, A., McMahan, H.B., Guestrin, C., Gupta, A.: Robust submodular observation selection. J. Mach. Learn. Res. (JMLR) **9**(12), 2761–2801 (2008)
22. Mehrabi, N., Morstatter, F., Saxena, N., Lerman, K., Galstyan, A.: A survey on bias and fairness in machine learning. ACM Comput. Surv. (CSUR) **54**(6), 1–35 (2021)
23. Nanongkai, D., Sarma, A.D., Lall, A., Lipton, R.J., Xu, J.: Regret-minimizing representative databases. In: Proceedings of the VLDB Endowment (PVLDB), pp. 1114–1124 (2010)
24. Pessach, D., Shmueli, E.: A review on fairness in machine learning. ACM Comput. Sur. (CSUR) **55**(3), 1–44 (2022)
25. Pradhan, R., Zhu, J., Glavic, B., Salimi, B.: Interpretable data-based explanations for fairness debugging. In: Proceedings of the 2022 International Conference on Management of Data (SIGMOD), pp. 247–261 (2022)
26. Qiu, X., Zheng, J., Dong, Q., Huang, X.: Speed-up algorithms for happiness-maximizing representative databases. In: Proceedings of the APWeb-WAIM 2018 International Workshops: MWDA, BAH, KGMA, DMMOOC, DS (APWebWAIM DS Workshop), pp. 321–335 (2018)
27. Qu, M., Ren, X., Han, J.: Automatic synonym discovery with knowledge bases. In: Proceedings of the 23rd ACM SIGKDD International Conference on Knowledge Discovery and Data Mining (SIGKDD), pp. 997–1005 (2017)
28. Raj, A., Ekstrand, M.D.: Measuring fairness in ranked results: An analytical and empirical comparison. In: Proceedings of the 45th International ACM SIGIR Conference on Research and Development in Information Retrieval (SIGIR), pp. 726–736 (2022)
29. Serbos, D., Qi, S., Mamoulis, N., Pitoura, E., Tsaparas, P.: Fairness in package-to-group recommendations. In: Proceedings of the 26th International Conference on World Wide Web (WWW), pp. 371–379 (2017)
30. Soma, T., Yoshida, Y.: Regret ratio minimization in multi-objective submodular function maximization. In: Proceedings of the AAAI Conference on Artificial Intelligence (AAAI), pp. 905–911 (2017)
31. Stoyanovich, J., Yang, K., Jagadish, H.: Online set selection with fairness and diversity constraints. In: Proceedings of the 21st International Conference on Extending Database Technology (EDBT), pp. 241–252 (2018)
32. Udwani, R.: Multi-objective maximization of monotone submodular functions with cardinality constraint. In: Proceedings of the Advances in Neural Information Processing Systems (NeurIPS), pp. 9513–9524 (2018)

33. Wang, L., Joachims, T.: User fairness, item fairness, and diversity for rankings in two-sided markets. In: Proceedings of the ACM SIGIR International Conference on Theory of Information Retrieval (ICTIR), pp. 23–41 (2021)
34. Wang, Y., Fabbri, F., Mathioudakis, M.: Fair and representative subset selection from data streams. In: Proceedings of the Web Conference 2021 (WWW), pp. 1340–1350 (2021)
35. Wang, Y., Li, Y., Bonchi, F., Wang, Y.: Balancing utility and fairness in submodular maximization. In: Proceedings of the 27th International Conference on Extending Database Technology (EDBT), pp. 1–14 (2024)
36. Wang, Y., Zheng, J., Meng, F.: Improved algorithm for regret ratio minimization in multi-objective submodular maximization. In: Proceedings of the AAAI Conference on Artificial Intelligence (AAAI), pp. 12500–12508 (2023)
37. Wang, Y., Sun, P., Ma, W., Zhang, M., Zhang, Y., Jiang, P., Ma, S.: Intersectional two-sided fairness in recommendation. In: Proceedings of the ACM Web Conference 2024 (WWW), pp. 3609–3620 (2024)
38. Wu, H., Ma, C., Mitra, B., Diaz, F., Liu, X.: A multi-objective optimization framework for multi-stakeholder fairness-aware recommendation. ACM Trans. Inf. Syst. (TOIS) **41**(2), 1–47 (2023)
39. Wu, Y., Cao, J., Xu, G., Tan, Y.: Tfrom: A two-sided fairness-aware recommendation model for both customers and providers. In: Proceedings of the 44th International ACM SIGIR Conference on Research and Development in Information Retrieval (SIGIR), pp. 1013–1022 (2021)
40. Xie, M., Wong, R.C.W., Lall, A.: An experimental survey of regret minimization query and variants: bridging the best worlds between top-k query and skyline query. VLDB J. **29**(1), 147–175 (2020)
41. Xie, M., Wong, R.C.W., Li, J., Long, C., Lall, A.: Efficient k-regret query algorithm with restriction-free bound for any dimensionality. In: Proceedings of the 2018 International Conference on Management of Data (SIGMOD), pp. 959–974 (2018)
42. Yuan, J., Tang, S.: Group fairness in non-monotone submodular maximization. J. Comb. Optim. **45**(88), 1–15 (2023)
43. Zehlike, M., Yang, K., Stoyanovich, J.: Fairness in ranking, part i: Score-based ranking. ACM Comput. Sur. (CSUR) **55**(6), 1–36 (2022)
44. Zheng, J., Chen, C.: Sorting-based interactive regret minimization. In: Proceedings of the 4th Asia Pacific Web (APWeb) and Web-Age Information Management (WAIM) Joint International Conference on Web and Big Data (APWeb-WAIM), pp. 473–490 (2020)
45. Zheng, J., Dong, Q., Qiu, X., Huang, X.: Accelerated algorithms for maximizing average happiness ratio in databases. Front. Comput. Sci. (FCS) **15**(6), 156618 (2021)
46. Zheng, J., Dong, Q., Wang, X., Zhang, Y., Ma, W., Ma, Y.: Efficient processing of k-regret minimization queries with theoretical guarantees. Inf. Sci. **586**, 99–118 (2022)
47. Zheng, J., Ma, W., Wang, Y., Wang, X.: Continuous k-regret minimization queries: a dynamic coreset approach. IEEE Trans. Knowl. Data Eng. (TKDE) **35**(6), 5680–5694 (2023)
48. Zheng, J., Ma, Y., Ma, W., Wang, Y., Wang, X.: Happiness maximizing sets under group fairness constraints. In: Proceedings of the VLDB Endowment (PVLDB), pp. 291–303 (2022)
49. Zheng, J., et al.: Hybrid regret minimization: a submodular approach. IEEE Trans. Knowl. Data Eng. (TKDE) **36**(7), 3151–3165 (2024)
50. Zhu, J., Pradhan, R., Glavic, B., Salimi, B.: Generating interpretable data-based explanations for fairness debugging using gopher. In: Proceedings of the 2022 International Conference on Management of Data (SIGMOD), pp. 2433–2436 (2022)

51. Zhu, K., Zheng, J., Yang, Z., Dong, J.: Identifying rank-happiness maximizing sets under group fairness constraints. In: Proceedings of the 8th Asia-Pacific Web and Web-Age Information Management Joint International Conference on Web and Big Data (APWeb-WAIM), pp. 325–341 (2024)
52. Zliobaite, I.: On the relation between accuracy and fairness in binary classification. In: Proceedings of the 2nd workshop on Fairness, Accountability, and Transparency in Machine Learning (FATML) at ICML'15, pp. 1–5 (2015)

Correction to: Web Information Systems Engineering – WISE 2025

Irfan Awan, Muhammad Younas, Yanchun Zhang, Mahmoud Barhamgi, and Hua Wang

Correction to:
I. Awan et al. (Eds.): *Web Information Systems Engineering – WISE 2025*, LNCS 16367, https://doi.org/10.1007/978-981-95-7394-3

The book was published with a typo in the book title, in this book. The title of the book as "Web Information Systems Engineering - WISE 2025 PhD Symposium, Demos and Workshops", whereas it should read "Web Information Systems Engineering – WISE 2025" both in the cover and on the Title page of the front-matter correctly. This has been corrected in the book accordingly.

The updated version of this book can be found at
https://doi.org/10.1007/978-981-95-7394-3

I. Awan et al. (Eds.): WISE 2025, LNCS 16367, p. C1, 2026.
https://doi.org/10.1007/978-981-95-7394-3_41

Author Index

I. Awan et al. (Eds.): WISE 2025, LNCS 16367, pp. 611–613, 2026.
https://doi.org/10.1007/978-981-95-7394-3

MIX
Papier aus verantwortungsvollen Quellen
Paper from responsible sources
FSC® C105338

If you have any concerns about our products,
you can contact us on
ProductSafety@springernature.com

In case Publisher is established outside the EU,
the EU authorized representative is:
Springer Nature Customer Service Center GmbH
Europaplatz 3, 69115 Heidelberg, Germany

Printed by Libri Plureos GmbH
in Hamburg, Germany